CRITICAL SURVEY
OF
LONG FICTION

CRITICAL SURVEY

OF

LONG FICTION

Second Revised Edition

Volume 5

Thomas McGuane - J. B. Priestley

Editor, Second Revised Edition
Carl Rollyson
Baruch College, City University of New York

Editor, First Edition, English and Foreign Language Series
Frank N. Magill

SALEM PRESS, INC.
Pasadena, California   Hackensack, New Jersey

CRITICAL SURVEY
OF
LONG FICTION

Thomas McGuane

Born: Wyandotte, Michigan; December 11, 1939

PRINCIPAL LONG FICTION

The Sporting Club, 1969
The Bushwhacked Piano, 1971
Ninety-two in the Shade, 1973
Panama, 1978
Nobody's Angel, 1982
Something to Be Desired, 1984
Keep the Change, 1989
Nothing but Blue Skies, 1992

OTHER LITERARY FORMS

In addition to writing novels, Thomas McGuane produced work for motion pictures and for popular magazines. He wrote the screenplay and directed the film version of *Ninety-two in the Shade* (1975), wrote the scripts for *Rancho DeLuxe* (1973) and *The Missouri Breaks* (1975), and shared credit with Bud Shrake for *Tom Horn* (1980) and with Jim Harrison for *Cold Feet* (1989). *An Outside Chance: Essays on Sport* (1980) contains many of his magazine pieces, and *To Skin a Cat* (1986) is a collection of short fiction.

ACHIEVEMENTS

Early in his career, McGuane was heralded as one of the most promising writers of his generation, one with a good chance to become a major American writer. He appeared on the cover of *The New York Times Book Review* and was compared favorably with Ernest Hemingway, William Faulkner, and Saul Bellow. *The Bushwhacked Piano* won the Rosenthal Award, and *Ninety-two in the Shade* was nominated for a National Book Award. In the mid-1970's, however, when he began to devote the majority of his energies to writing for films, McGuane was dismissed as a sellout. In the late 1970's, his film career seemingly over, McGuane returned to publishing novels. Although Hollywood would continue to option screenplays written in the 1970's, McGuane maintained that novels were his true calling and that his

goal was to be "a true man of literature, . . . a professional." *Something to Be Desired* and *Keep the Change* reaffirmed his position as a contender for inclusion in the American canon. In 1989, Thomas McGuane received the Montana Centennial Award for Literature.

BIOGRAPHY

Thomas McGuane was born in Wyandotte, Michigan, on December 11, 1939. He was graduated with honors from Michigan State University in 1962, took an M.F.A. from the Yale Drama School in 1965, and spent 1966-1967 at Stanford on a Wallace Stegner Fellowship. His parents were New England Irish who migrated to the Midwest, where his father became an auto-parts tycoon. McGuane once stated that he inherited his storytelling impulse from his mother's family, who loved verbal sparring and yarn spinning. Newspaper and magazine articles on McGuane often comment on the manic behavior, heavy drinking, and

(Marion Ettlinger)

NOBODY'S ANGEL

Nobody's Angel is McGuane's first novel to be set entirely in the West, a West which McGuane characterizes as "wrecked." In Deadrock, Montana, farmers abuse the land, cowboys are lazy, and American Indians are nowhere to be found. Returning to this damaged world is thirty-six-year-old Patrick Fitzpatrick. Patrick is as unconventional as earlier McGuane protagonists. As a whiskey addict and a professional soldier, he has been a tank captain in the army for all of his adult life, most recently in Europe, and the only place he feels secure is inside his womblike tank. Suffering from "sadness for no reason," he has returned to the family ranch, which he will someday own. He feels stranded on the ranch because becoming a property owner is not a meaningful achievement for him. Patrick appears to be in the worst shape of any McGuane protagonist. He is not only without goals but also without any sense of himself, conventional or unconventional.

The effect of the wrecked West is seen in the character of Patrick's grandfather. The old man has been a cowboy all of his life, has known real gunfighters, and has run the ranch like an old-time outfit. The West has changed, however, and everything from sonic booms to valleys cluttered with yard lights has got the old man down. The only things he feels good about are Australia, which he has heard is open country like Montana once was, and Western films. His one fit of excitement comes when he signs on to be an extra in a Western about to be filmed locally. Even that, however, is accompanied by overtones of sadness and ends in disappointment. The film is *Hondo's Last Move*, evocative of a legendary but nonexistent West popularized by actor John Wayne and writer Louis L'Amour. Even then, the "last move" refers to the dying of the West and perhaps Hondo himself. To make matters worse, the project folds when the distributor forsakes Westerns for science fiction. In the end, the old man moves into town and takes an apartment from which he can see the local film theater, which plays old Westerns, and a little bar in which hangs the head of the best elk he ever shot. The open West has been reduced to one-bedroom apartments, yesterday's films, and mounted animals, which serve only to remind him of a glorious past.

In *Nobody's Angel*, McGuane continued to work the theme of unfulfilled love. Patrick hopes to bring purpose into his life by means of a love affair with Claire Burnett. Claire and her husband, Tio, are second-generation nouveau-riche Oklahomans summering in Montana. Not a genuine stockman like Patrick's grandfather, Tio is mainly interested in oil, cattle futures, row crops, and running horses. Since Tio's main hobby is pretending to be a good old boy, Patrick sees him as a personification of the substanceless modern West.

Patrick believes that "Claire could change it all" and wishes theirs could be a sentimental love story, the kind found in romantic books. Claire, however, will not become a part of Patrick's dream. Her commitment to Tio goes beyond Patrick's understanding. Her family provided the money to support their lifestyle. Tio's people are poor Okies, and this discrepancy in their backgrounds has driven him to incurable delusions of grandeur, to the point that Claire has promised that she will not abandon him. Even though she tells Patrick that she loves him, she never stops loving Tio, and Patrick's dream of a storybook romance crumbles. Even when Tio dies, Claire will not marry Patrick. She makes love to him one last time, explaining that love is "nothing you can do anything with." Patrick is not able to cope with Claire's pragmatic attitude about love and their relationship. She gives him a picture of herself, but he does not keep it with him, because it reminds him of the frustrations of his romantic hopes.

In the end, Patrick survives, but not in the West. When he was a teenager, Patrick invented an imaginary girlfriend named Marion Easterly. Even though he was eventually discovered, the fantasy has remained a part of his consciousness. He had hoped that Claire would replace Marion, but a living woman will never become the woman of a man's imagination, and when Claire dismisses him, Patrick rejoins the army and finds fulfillment in his fantasy. Word filters back that he is now a blackout drinker in Madrid and that he is living with a woman named Marion Easterly. Patrick Fitzpatrick remains "at large"—in the sense that his heavy drinking and fantasy lover keep him outside the normal boundaries of life—but without the hope and energy of Nicholas Payne. The McGuane protagonist seemingly must find a way to accommodate himself, at least partially, to the concerns of conventional life.

SOMETHING TO BE DESIRED

In *Something to Be Desired*, the McGuane protagonist combines both unconventional and conventional goals. Lucien Taylor grows tired of normality and destroys his perfectly fine marriage with self-absorbed erratic behavior. Once his single life becomes empty, he, like Chet, tries to put it back together again by reuniting with his former wife, Suzanne, and their son, James. Lucien's plight is not entirely the result of his disenchantment with conformity; he is victimized by his capricious lust.

Lucien's sense of sexual discipline was broken in college by Emily, who slept with him on their first meeting. Emily was engaged to a medical student and continued to sleep with both young men at the same time. Ultimately, she is abused by her surgeon husband and becomes totally self-absorbed and manipulating. Emily is a woman as selfish as Claire, and she continues her self-absorbed actions throughout the novel, exploiting everyone, including Lucien. Lucien, however, married Suzanne, who "took the position that this was a decent world for an honest player." This basic decency is what Lucien eventually comes to value, but when he hears that Emily is free of her marriage, he thinks nothing of destroying his own and returning to Montana in quest of her. Lucien is troubled by the lack of romance in his life, an element that Suzanne and James cannot provide. Suzanne sums up Emily by calling her the queen of the whores, an assertion which is borne out when, on her penultimate appearance in the novel, she is seen sleeping naked next to her purse.

Such a portrayal of women who do not measure up to male ideals or fantasies is not rare in McGuane's fiction: Ann (*The Bushwhacked Piano*) and Claire (*Nobody's Angel*) are two other disappointing women. Lucien has dreamed of Emily since their first encounter. Not until he finally decides that he wants nothing more to do with her does she tell

him that she regards his concern for her an infantile gesture, a thing she holds in contempt. Indeed, she does not even think enough of him to shoot him, which she has done to her husband and, by this time, another lover. Lucien, however, like Nicholas Payne in *The Bushwhacked Piano*, does not lose momentum. He pulls off a crackpot piece of venture capitalism. Through a series of exchanges, he comes to own Emily's ranch and develops its sulfur spring into a thriving health spa. In short, he becomes rich. In this way Lucien remains unconventional, at the same time—new for a McGuane protagonist—gaining that which is admired by conventional society. Even though McGuane still maneuvers his protagonist through some outlandish paces because of his peripatetic penis, McGuane at the same time imbues Lucien with a sense of purpose higher than sport or making the world tense. Lucien, once his new wealth requires him to bring a semblance of order into his life, begins to want to think of himself as a working man with a family to support.

When Suzanne and James come for a visit, Lucien first attempts to reach James from the security of his own masculine interests. He takes him out to band some hawks. He baits the trap with a live pigeon. When the hawk strikes the pigeon, James screams and crawls off. As Lucien bands the hawk, James shakes. While Lucien admires the hawk, James's natural inclination is to cradle the dead pigeon; he manifests a sense of compassion that his father lacks. The violent world of nature is awful to him. Lucien actually finds himself liking the fact that his son is timid and made of more delicate and sensitive stuff than his father. Still, McGuane is not becoming sentimental. Later, when he understands how nature works, James explains that killing pigeons is how hawks have to live, but the fact remains that James was terrified by the killing. His explanation is not so much an emulation of his father's more hard-boiled ways as it is an acceptance of them as his father's ways. James is actually reaching toward a relationship with his father.

What is important here is that Lucien is attempting to reestablish his family because such a reestablishment would be better for all of them, not only for him alone. Lucien's is one of the few nonselfish acts committed by a McGuane protagonist. He would like not to see the child become a "hostage to oblivion." He wonders how he could leave him unguarded. His reward is that James begins not to fear his father.

Winning back Suzanne, however, is not as easy. She is too skeptical to welcome the sadder-but-wiser protagonist back into her arms. She tells him the truth about himself: He is self-absorbed, insensitive to those who love him, and not worth the effort of reconciliation. Lucien is going to have to recognize her as an independent and worthy person. Before the novel's end, she works through her sense of him as a totally selfish person, but even though she admits to loving Lucien, she is not sure if she is ready to trust him. As she and James drive away from the ranch, she does not look back. She is charting her own course, which may or may not include Lucien.

What is important here is that the McGuane protagonist has progressed through the state of self-absorption with adventure and sport. He has begun to understand that what matters about life is not being "at large" to commit glorious exploits, but being a part of a larger whole that includes the other people in the world. The full life is not lived in furious battle with the forces of conventionality, but in achieving deep and lasting relationships with human beings.

KEEP THE CHANGE

In *Keep the Change*, Joe Starling, Jr., an artist of limited talent, must come to understand this same truth. Chained by the ghost of his father, an overachiever who ultimately dies a failure, the young Starling's life is empty for no reason. He is not satisfied with his various successes as an artist, craftsperson, cowboy, or lover, because everything pales in comparison with his expectations for himself. He ricochets among Montana, Florida, and New York City without fully realizing that individual human meaning is something created rather than found.

Two of McGuane's most fully realized female characters offer Starling the possibility of a fully actualized life, but he is too full of himself to seize the opportunity. Ellen Overstreet, a rancher's daughter as wholesome as the new frontier, presents him with the vulnerability of awkward young love. The dynamic Cuban Astrid, whom Starling loves for her outland-

ishness, sticks by him until he is hopelessly lost in pointlessness. After she leaves him, Starling seems to be beginning to understand that sharing the routine concerns of daily life with Astrid may be the source of true meaning.

Keep the Change signals a new development in McGuane's perception of male competition. Games are no longer seen as means to make sport of conventionality. Joe Starling's rival here is Billy Kelton, an honest and simple, if luckless, cowboy, who marries Ellen Overstreet. Kelton is Starling's physical superior and twice humiliates him with beatings. Violence here is real, not comic, and because it is real, it is bewildering and confusing. Kelton understands that his physical prowess is dehumanizing, and, in facing the struggles of life with his wife and daughter, he shows Starling the importance of a deeper, if simpler, emotional life.

The key to the novel is found in a painting of Montana mountains, the white hills, which hangs in a decaying mansion that once belonged to the most powerful man in the territory. The work itself is indistinguishable: "It had seemed an unblemished canvas until the perplexity of shadows across its surface was seen to be part of the painting." Ultimately, Starling discovers that the shadows are in fact its only real feature. There is no painting; there never has been a painting. Yet "somewhere in the abyss something shone." That "something" is the meaning Starling seeks. He is the one who determined meaning in the painting and, by extension, in the hills themselves. He must then act to create a life for himself; he must determine his own meaning.

NOTHING BUT BLUE SKIES

Nothing but Blue Skies, McGuane's eighth novel, continues the progression from self-absorption to maturity begun in *Something to Be Desired* and *Keep the Change*. Perhaps his most expansive work, it follows the breakdown and recovery of Frank Copenhaver after his separation from his wife, Gracie. An ex-hippie turned real estate speculator and cattle trader, Frank gradually loses control of his minor empire of rental properties, turning his scattered attention instead to awkward sexual encounters with the local travel agent and episodes of drunken self-destructiveness. Only a visit by his college-age daughter, Holly, can keep him momentarily in balance. Her brief stay includes an idyllic afternoon of fishing that buoys Frank's spirits, only to intensify the sense of loneliness and loss when she leaves again.

It is Holly who manages to suspend Frank's downward spin by creating a family crisis. She summons her estranged parents to Missoula to meet her new "boyfriend," Lane Lawlor, a gray-haired arch-conservative campaigning to "impound" the streams and rivers in Montana in order to retain the water that flows out of the state. Frank and Gracie meet to discuss the situation, but at each of the meetings Frank makes a fool of himself by failing to control his temper. The couple is finally brought together at a political rally where Lane Lawlor is the speaker and Holly his piano-playing assistant. The rally ends when Gracie, like Frank, secretly in attendance, attacks Lane and Frank joins the melee. In the aftermath they realize that Holly has engineered their reunion by pretending to fall for Lane. Frank also understands that Gracie has "nearly ruined" him in an attempt to break down his self-involvement and force him to see her and himself in a new way.

Nothing but Blue Skies is clearly McGuane's most optimistic and fully developed novel. In Frank Copenhaver, McGuane gives his typical protagonist a complexity and vulnerability that many of his earlier versions lack. Perhaps more notable, the novel's women show a richness of characterization often missing from earlier works. Gracie, Holly, and Lucy Dyer, the travel agent, all transcend easy generalities and stand firmly as independent, fully formed characters.

The core of *Nothing but Blue Skies* is Frank's bewilderment in the face of losing Gracie and his rehabilitation through public humiliation. McGuane's strength in creating such a character lies in his understanding of how life can be renewed through the comic downfall of the protagonist, his fall into public degradation a necessary starting point for rebuilding the life he has sold away through the soul-shrinking manipulations of business. Stripped of all attainments and pride, Frank Copenhaver can only start

over. After all, as Gracie tells him, "There's nothing crazier than picking up exactly where you left off."

In Thomas McGuane's contemporary West, life is what you make it, nothing more, nothing less. His protagonists must work to fulfill hopes not by going against the grain of the conventional life, but by partaking of its normal flow and by building useful foundations on its undramatic but real joys.

Dexter Westrum, updated by Clark Davis

OᴛʜᴇR MAJOR WORKS

SHORT FICTION: *To Skin a Cat*, 1986.

SCREENPLAYS: *Rancho DeLuxe*, 1973; *Ninety-two in the Shade*, 1975; *The Missouri Breaks*, 1975; *Tom Horn*, 1980 (with Bud Shrake).

NONFICTION: *An Outside Chance: Essays on Sport*, 1980; *The Longest Silence: A Life in Fishing*, 1999; *Some Horses*, 1999.

BIBLIOGRAPHY

Carter, Albert Howard, III. "Thomas McGuane's First Three Novels: Games, Fun, Nemesis." *Critique* 17 (August, 1975): 91-104. Although McGuane's use of the pathos and humor inherent in competition has become decidedly more sophisticated as he has matured, this article is essential for understanding the early novels.

Grant, Kerry. "On and Off the Main Line: The Failure of Compromise in the Fiction of Thomas McGuane." *Mid-American Review* 3 (Spring, 1983): 167-184. This article is a very good explanation of the McGuane protagonists' failure to compromise with reality without first attempting to change the world through the maintenance of a unique self.

Klinkowitz, Jerome. *The New American Novel of Manners: The Fiction of Richard Yates, Dan Wakefield, Thomas McGuane*. Athens: University of Georgia Press, 1986. Examines the twentieth century novel of manners and customs. Includes index.

McCaffery, Larry. "On Turning Nothing into Something." *Fiction International* 4-5 (Fall/Winter, 1975): 123-129. This accurate introduction to early McGuane argues that his protagonists are transcendent beings because they maintain their ideals—

education for former slaves and their offspring and for poor immigrants from Portugal than was possible in Rio de Janeiro itself. Humble by today's standards, the Assises' condition seems to have been good for the times. They were artisans, including Maria Leopoldina, who probably had black help for her heavy household chores; moreover, they were relatively literate and on their way up the social scale. Undoubtedly, they enjoyed a degree of intimacy, if not equality, with the proprietress's family. Machado de Assis's formal schooling, if any, was slight; however, in addition to what he was taught at home, he may well have been tutored by a loving godmother until her death (of measles, three months after that of Machado de Assis's sister) and thereafter by priests attached to the estate or to churches where the youngster served, perhaps as an altar boy, perhaps as a sacristan. There can be no question that Machado de Assis was largely self-taught, but without the basic learning acquired in the extended family situation, he could never have succeeded in his heroic task.

Machado de Assis's youth, from the time he left home at about fifteen until he married at thirty, was relatively normal in some respects, most extraordinary in others. In order to earn his living, never better than a precarious one, he tried a number of occupations, all of them connected in some way with the printed word. At first probably a clerk in a book or stationery shop, he became a typesetter, a proofreader, and eventually an editor and a staff writer. He entered the field of journalism enthusiastically, expecting to be able to live, more or less well, by his pen; he soon discovered how poorly remunerated this profession was. Not until 1867 would Machado de Assis achieve some measure of economic security in the bureaucracy of government service, where he worked first on the *Diário oficial* and, from 1874, as a functionary in the Ministry of Agriculture.

Machado de Assis was an astonishingly prolific writer. Although much of his work was published in periodicals and newspapers and was far from lucrative, he continued his frenetic production of such work even during the years in which he was producing his great and successful novels, at the same time

that he was all but submerged in the bureaucratic paperwork of government service. Apart from his literary work, Machado de Assis participated in numerous other artistic and social endeavors. His considerable interest in and contribution to opera and theater in Rio de Janeiro and São Paulo, both in original works and in translations or adaptations, are evidenced by his work for the Conservatório Dramático Brasileiro, where for some years he served as censor, passing judgment on the moral and political propriety of manuscripts submitted to the conservatory and giving his literary opinions as well. During this period, Machado de Assis was assiduous in his attendance at the theater and at musical events in Rio de Janeiro, becoming personally or professionally acquainted with many artists and contributing numerous reviews to the periodicals of that city at the time. As though all of this activity were not enough, Machado de Assis held various positions in a number of literary societies and often contributed and even recited poems, his own or others'—despite his supposed timidity and severe stammering—and created short plays for special meetings and benefits. Machado de Assis's significant participation in the cultural life of Rio de Janeiro was recognized in 1867, when he was decorated with the Order of the Rose by Emperor Dom Pedro II.

Among Machado de Assis's many acquaintances before 1869 was a Portuguese poet, Faustino Xavier de Novaes, who, like others of his family, went to Brazil to seek his fortune. Beset by financial and marital problems, Faustino eventually suffered a severe nervous breakdown with serious physical manifestations. After his parents' death in Oporto, his youngest sister, Carolina, was sent to assist in caring for Faustino. Almost five years older than Machado de Assis, Carolina was intelligent, sensitive, and affectionate, and she and Machado de Assis fell in love. Her suffering, which Machado de Assis mentions as one of the reasons for his love, may have been caused by an earlier love affair and possibly influenced her departure for Portugal. Very little is known of the courtship of Machado de Assis and Carolina except for one letter and a substantial fragment of a second, written to "Carola" by her "Machadinho" during the de Novaeses' stay in Petrópolis, in which there is evidence of their great concern and love for each other.

She chided him for not confiding in her. In response, Machado de Assis told her briefly of his earlier loves. The first was Corinna, who did not requite his love, and consequently there is nothing more to say (although in the tradition of such matters, Machado de Assis had published some 385 verses to Corinna). The second, who remains nameless but was possibly an actress and married, loved him in return and was the greater love. The situation was a painful one, however, and Machado de Assis was persuaded to break off the affair. Carolina was the one true love of his life. Despite a probable infidelity on the part of her husband—an "infidelity of the senses"—she was to be so always.

Against the wishes of some of her family, they were married November 12, 1869, a short time after the death of Faustino. In spite of some sorrow, it would seem that their marriage was a very happy one. In the style of the day, Carolina remained in the shadow of her husband, who was himself reserved and, in spite of fame, did not seek public acclaim. As has been mentioned, except for rare references to her in his correspondence, mostly very conventional in nature, Machado de Assis never wrote directly of his wife. Some of the feminine characters in the author's novels may well have Carolina's qualities, and a few of his poems were inspired by her, especially one sonnet, "A Carolina," published after her death. Her literary influence on him, grossly exaggerated by some critics, was at best very slight.

Once Machado de Assis was established as comptroller in the Ministry of Agriculture—later the Ministry of Transportation, as promotions and the evolution of ministries led him into related positions—and he and Carolina were settled in a chalet-style house on the Rua Cosme Velho in the city, they had no serious financial worries. Their great sorrow was to be childless. In addition, there were problems of health, first those of Machado de Assis, who for a time had an extremely serious eye ailment and later suffered from increasingly frequent and grave attacks of epilepsy, then Carolina's growing fragility and a tumor

that eventually caused her death. Nothing, however, kept Machado de Assis from his literary production, which, if it did not bring him wealth, was a source of many satisfactions and gave him fame.

Machado de Assis was motivated in his activities by love for those who were close to him (especially promising young writers in need of encouragement), by deep interest in humanity and culture, and certainly by a desire to leave something lasting of himself, his thought, and his art. Posterity perhaps assumed greater importance for him than for other artists, because he had no children. Further, his works were not fully understood or appreciated in his day, often bringing him no more than a *succès d'estime*, and so posterity was probably all the more important to him.

Everything that Machado de Assis represents is embodied in the Brazilian Academy of Letters. When at last in 1905 its membership honored him, he was presented with the oak branch from the tree growing over Torquato Tasso's tomb that Joaquim Nabuco, the famous statesman and man of letters who was a friend of Machado de Assis and a member of the Academy, had sent from Italy for such a symbolic ceremony. Machado de Assis treasured the branch and other mementos, leaving them to be housed in the Academy after his death, brought about by a variety of as yet poorly defined causes on September 29, 1908.

ANALYSIS

The first four novels by Joaquim Maria Machado de Assis constitute his apprenticeship as a novelist, during which he refined the vision and the skills that came to focus in *The Posthumous Memoirs of Brás Cubas* and the powerful novels that followed. In his famous criticism (1878) of Eça de Queiroz's *O Primo Basílio* (1878; *Cousin Bazílio*, 1953; also as *Dragon's Teeth*, 1889), Machado de Assis states that the aim of the novel should be to describe action derived from the passions and ideas of its characters. He refers to William Shakespeare's *Othello* (1604), in which the natures of Othello, Iago, and Desdemona are the chief ingredients of the action, not the handkerchief. Thus, Machado de Assis favors the tenets of realism and opposes naturalism as too often superficial and therefore artificial, not to mention tasteless.

Machado de Assis's persistent concern with character—his references to *Othello* and his creation of the figure of Felix in *Resurreicão*—leads one to think that he was interested above all in tragedy. Felix, torn between a sincere desire for love and cynical doubt regarding his and others' sincerity, is a tragic figure surrounded by characters drawn too much either from life or from less noble forms of literature. The whole, therefore, falls short of being tragic. In *The Hand and the Glove*, there is a clash between two strong-willed characters, developed in a structure of Romantic comedy. Some significant details are reminiscent of Shakespeare's *All's Well That Ends Well* (1602-1603), as well as the triumph rather than the defeat of love in the conclusion.

Helena, which also contains reminiscences of *All's Well That Ends Well*, is not a Romantic comedy; its main characters are fully developed. Unfortunately, their passions and consequent frustrations stem from a case of Rio de Janeiro etiquette largely regarding the status of women. The substance is so slight as to lack any claim to the universality required for genuine tragedy. The reader experiences both comic and tragic emotions, but at times he or she is incredulous and even impatient with what proves to be a melodramatic situation and conclusion. In *Yayá Garcia*, Machado de Assis uses classical allusions and symbolism to a high degree and elaborates on the class, family, and personal pride of women as never before. Above all, there is the theme of love thwarted by society, whose interference is caused by the evils of self-love. Ultimately it is love that triumphs in *Yayá Garcia*, both in the main plot and principal characters and in the figure of the ex-slave, Raymundo, a symbol of Brazilian civilization as opposed to that of Europe. In future novels, Machado de Assis was to stress the passions of individuals in their struggle to be true to themselves, which, for the author, meant to love. Social problems would reappear only whenever love became subordinate to vanity.

THE POSTHUMOUS MEMOIRS OF BRÁS CUBAS

In *The Posthumous Memoirs of Brás Cubas*, for the first time in Machado de Assis's works, the main character is a man. Never again was a woman to be his principal subject. Self-love is the theme, and with it the several forms of evil and death to which vanity gives rise. Brás Cubas, the narrator of these memoirs, is dead, not only at the time of publication but also at the time of composition. Brás Cubas writes to pass time in eternity, still preoccupied with his fellows and in a detached mood much like the one that was his throughout life. Despite its seemingly misanthropic theme and its deep pessimism, the novel can be interpreted as profoundly comic.

There are many literary allusions and influences in *The Posthumous Memoirs of Brás Cubas*. Very early in the novel, the reader is made aware of the importance of the picaresque genre, especially Charles Dickens's *Pickwick Papers* (1836-1837), Laurence Sterne's *The Life and Opinions of Tristram Shandy, Gent.* (1759-1767), and Alain-René Lesage's *The History of Gil Blas of Santillane* (1715-1735). The picaresque novel is comic in its parody, satire, and irony; at the same time, it may be very serious in its portrayal of manners, with philosophical implications, as is Miguel de Cervantes' *Don Quixote de la Mancha* (1605, 1615).

The traditional picaresque novel has one main character, usually male, who, whatever the circumstances of his birth, finds himself in the criminal or low class of society, rising after many adventures of all sorts to marry and settle down to lead a respectable if somewhat parasitic life. The life of the picaro is customarily traced in minute detail, from his origins through his childhood, adolescence, and early maturity and into middle age. Machado de Assis parodies his predecessors by having Brás Cubas begin his narrative after death and move backward through a series of regressions to his funeral and last illness. Contrary to the practice of his predecessors, however, Machado de Assis's is most economical and dramatic. Brás sees Virgília, his former mistress, when he is on his deathbed, not as she is, but as she was when they were lovers, and in his delirium he is taken back in time to his birth.

Brás has the proper genealogy for a picaro. The Cubas family is well-to-do—their wealth is based on the efforts of the founder of the family in Brazil, who was originally a mender of *cubas* (vats or barrels)— and Brás's father named his son after a famous early Brazilian patriot in the hope of associating his relatively humble family with the more distinguished one. The name of Brás further suggests Brazil, and there are numerous references and overtones to suggest that Brás may be taken as a kind of epic figure for Brazilians. Brás's upbringing is typical for the son of such a family in the Rio de Janeiro of the early nineteenth century. Spoiled by his parents and debauched by one uncle, he is little influenced by the ineffectual religious education of his other uncle. When Brás takes up with Marcella, a high-priced girl who promptly sets about depleting the Cubas fortune, his father has him abducted and sent off to the University of Coimbra. Typically, Brás forgets Marcella even before the ship reaches Portugal.

Although he claims to be inclined to melancholy, Brás never experiences serious emotion for very long. Like Jacques in Shakespeare's *As You Like It* (1599-1600), he leads a frivolous, empty life. Awareness of his apathy gives Brás the overtones of a tragic figure, but he does not struggle in the manner of an epic or tragic hero. Rather, he uses his great intelligence to observe, analyze, and write of his defects, which are also those of his fellows. He is thus primarily the comic author of a kind of comedy, human if not divine. The reader is occasionally led to expect more emotion of Brás, to no avail. During his long affair with Virgília, for example, she conceives a child by him but soon miscarries. He does not have time to feel emotion for mother or child. When Virgília at last passes out of his life, Brás, then in his forties, decides that it is time to marry. Alas, the lovely young Eulália dies of yellow fever before the wedding. Again there is no opportunity for very serious involvement.

Whether as the hero of a serious genre or of the picaresque, Brás must consider himself a failure. He lists his many defeats, including his one bid for fame, the invention of his medicinal plaster, which, instead of curing his melancholy, caused his death. When finally he balances the good against the evil in his life, Brás finds the only credit to be that, having had no child, he has bequeathed the legacy of human wretchedness to no one.

Despite the apparent pessimism of this last remark, often applied to Machado de Assis himself, Brás has the spirit if not the luck of a true picaro, both in his tour of life and in his tomb. Although he stresses pessimism and death, Brás is a most carefree corpse, and his tomb seems cozy enough. *The Posthumous Memoirs of Brás Cubas* is a comedy of human vanity, of which almost all the characters are guilty, to the virtual exclusion of any other flaw. Vanity gives rise to ambition, which is the source of much that is good as well as evil. The point is that good, generous actions have the same source as vicious ones. Indeed, the latter are merely exaggerations of the former; as such, vice and virtue are one and the same.

"Humanitism"—the mad philosophy of Quincas (a nickname for Joaquim, Machado de Assis's given name) Borba, a secondary character in this novel—is a complete expression of egotism. In the elaboration of humanitism, Machado de Assis was no doubt satirizing many "isms" (and perhaps even himself as something of a philosopher). As he had previously criticized the determinism of naturalism in literature, Machado de Assis was now criticizing above all the positivism of Auguste Comte that had taken root as a religion in Brazil. Although Brás Cubas is sane and Quincas Borba insane, there is considerable similarity between their philosophies. Brás's determinism, expressed in his theory of "rolling balls," when projected in the action of the novel suggests that a combination of human will and chance governs life. The "pessimism" of Machado de Assis's work is thus relieved by a certain moral tone. Like much comedy, it has a moral purpose. Moreover, its author and its hero are not to be confused. If at times they bear some resemblance to each other—as posterity and the critics (to whom the novelist alluded as "worms") have not always understood—it must be understood that Machado de Assis often poked fun at himself, as he causes Brás to poke fun at himself and life in all of its aspects. Brás's true cure for melancholy is not his medicinal plaster but his book.

DOM CASMURRO

Machado de Assis's seventh novel, *Dom Casmurro*, both incorporates elements of its predecessors and is a more nearly perfect work of art than any of them. Especially impressive is Machado de Assis's progress in the use of symbolism. The narrator and chief character, Bento Santiago, explains early his nickname and the title of the work, but only partially. *Dom*, an honorary term applied only to the highest nobility and clergy, was given to him to ridicule his aristocratic pretensions. *Casmurro* meant "stubborn" in Machado de Assis's day, but was added to the *Dom* by an angry neighbor to signify "morose and withdrawn." This meaning has since found its way into Portuguese dictionaries; however, both meanings of the word characterize Santiago, his obstinacy making him morose and withdrawn.

Like other of Machado de Assis's characters, Santiago is two men in one. In his case, the combination comprises Othello and Iago, creating an almost purely tragic figure and one to bring about tragedy for others. Santiago is born into a family of wealth and rank, and he is handsome, well educated, and quite intelligent. Moreover, the narrator creates a semidivine aura for himself by telling the reader that his safe birth was considered miraculous by his mother and the family priest, and that in thanksgiving he was named Bento (blessed) and destined for the seminary. Santiago tells the reader directly that he is an Othello with a guilty Desdemona. Indirectly, because he likes to confide in his reader, he reveals that he is Iago as well, innately evil and determined to find an object for his jealousy.

Machado de Assis intrudes not at all. The reader must therefore be attentive to discover the real Santiago as, often with considerable wit, he narrates his life, describes the members of his family and his acquaintances, and above all paints a wonderful portrait of his lovely Capitu as a girl, young woman, and wife. Bento and Capitu conspire to persuade his mother to break her vow to make a priest of him, a vow that she does not wish to keep in any case. It is easy to see how Capitu captivates Bento, especially as he cleverly includes details that encourage the careless reader to accept the eventual adultery of which he accuses her. The real culprit, one learns, is Santiago, a man who refused to love and to be loved.

Again, the action in *Dom Casmurro* stems from the characters' passions, from a clash of opposing wills. Both are found in the principal character, the will to love and the will to deny that love. He is not without feelings of guilt, however, and must project that guilt onto others, especially Capitu. Again, the theme is self-love, evil, and death (albeit a living death) versus love, good, and life. Santiago suggests that it is Capitu and Escobar, her supposed lover, who murdered his love; even if they were guilty of adultery, however, the tragic jealousy was in him even before his wife and best friend met. At the end, Santiago, made to love, faces a terrible life without love. Any victory on the part of Capitu or the other characters pales before the tragedy of the dominant figure of the narrator.

COUNSELOR AYRES' MEMORIAL

Counselor Ayres' Memorial is a sequel to *Esau and Jacob*, an allegorical work the characters of which are largely abstractions. Ayres, the narrator of both novels, becomes a real human being in the sequel at the same time that he embodies Machado de Assis's customary theme. His heart desires love, and in order to attain it he must undergo the emotional evolution that others of the author's protagonists have failed to accomplish. An intimate diary aptly replaces the somewhat self-conscious narrative of *Esaú and Jacob*.

The action of *Counselor Ayres' Memorial* takes place during 1888 and 1889, although the characters are so universal as to be of any period. Old Ayres and his sister, the faithful widow Rita, are the only characters taken from *Esau and Jacob*, but they are very different emotionally if not physically. In addition, there is the loving middle-aged couple Aguiar and Carmo—he a self-made banker but an honest and kindly man, she a homebody who, though childless, is a motherly type. These and other atypical characters reflect changing times in Brazil as well as a mellower attitude on the part of Machado de Assis favoring social and economic progress. Political change had been initiated under the Empire, was continued through the period of emancipation, and brought about Dom Pedro II's abdication. A new nationalism prevailed during the Republic, and Brazilians loved their country as never before.

With most of Brazilian society, Ayres has been under foreign influence, particularly English. As the name suggests, he has been much like the stereotype of the cold, dry, rational, and detached Englishman. Not only has he preferred foreign authors and foreign women, but he has also traveled in Europe and, as a diplomat, has lived most of his life abroad. In early 1888, however, Ayres is glad to come home to Brazil. Among the first entries in his diary, Ayres reports a visit paid by him and his sister Rita to the cemetery, a symbol of nonexistent or dead love, where he notices a beautiful young woman in black.

As Rita tells him of the romantic and tragic love of Fidélia and Eduardo, Ayres compares them to Romeo and Juliet. Their story is similar to a point, but the outcome is quite different, for they are not English, but Portuguese. With Portuguese stubbornness on all sides, they were permitted to marry but were disowned by their fathers. After less than a year of happiness, Eduardo died, and Fidélia has been faithfully tending his grave for more than two years. Ayres is still cynical enough to remark that she may remarry, with which Rita, of course, disagrees, but says that, as her brother is a very well preserved sixty-two, he can try to woo Fidélia.

Ayres persists in his fondness for English literature, so that, when he meets Fidélia at the home of Aguiar and Carmo, he recalls the first line of a love sonnet by Percy Bysshe Shelley that he has been unable to translate into Portuguese with the passionate conclusion of the original. Now begins a new kind of odyssey, during the course of which Ayres composes his poem with the desired conclusion, as Bento Santiago could not. Unlike the latter, Ayres is successful in conquering coldness and achieving resurrection through love. He learns to love not only from Shelley but also from the happily married Aguiar and Carmo; behind them are Machado de Assis and his Carolina.

Unlike Rita, who gives her love for her dead husband to everyone around her, Ayres has never loved. He married for convenience and, when his wife died, buried her in Europe and forgot about her. None of the women with whom he has had affairs abroad means anything to him. He has never been a father and has no regrets in this matter. Yet in Europe he ex-perienced nostalgia for home and for the warmth of Rio de Janeiro and his native language. His heart, it seems, was not entirely dead. When Ayres comes to know Fidélia, he first experiences sexual attraction, then appreciation of her beauty, later admiration for her intellectual and spiritual qualities, and finally a disinterested love for her happiness that includes everyone who made or could make her happy.

Much of the transformation in Ayres and similar ones in other characters are brought about by Aguiar and Carmo, not only in love with each other for twenty-five years but also full of love for all people and animals around them. Under Carmo's maternal love, Fidélia's heart comes alive again, at first symbolically when she resumes playing the piano, then more concretely when she falls in love with Tristão. Another of Carmo and Aguiar's foster children, Tristão has a cold heart, too, when he arrives from Portugal on an English ship. He, like most of the other characters, has fallen under Aguiar's spell, however, and comes to replace Eduardo for Fidélia.

The several resurrections developed in *Counselor Ayres' Memorial* are mutually influential, but the one that affects Ayres most is Fidélia's. Her return to love is his as well. The old habits die hard, however, and the cynical old diplomat is intermittently beset by doubts regarding the other's sincerity. It is only his own sincere love for Fidélia that makes him recognize that she loves Tristão just as sincerely. Eduardo continues to be remembered and loved, but life has its rights, the same as death. Fidélia's love for Tristão must therefore be understood as a continuation of her love for Eduardo. Ayres understands many seemingly contradictory things that escaped him as a skeptic. His new faith gives him a father's love for Fidélia, Tristão, and all children. Indeed, under the influence of love he has become like a child himself. With his attainment of the ideal of love, Ayres completes his sonnet and his odyssey.

Richard A. Mazzara, updated by Stephen Hart

OTHER MAJOR WORKS

SHORT FICTION: *Contos fluminenses*, 1870; *Histórias da meia-noite*, 1873; *Papéis avulsos*, 1882; *Histórias sem data*, 1884; *Várias histórias*, 1896; *Histó-*

rias románticas, 1937; *The Psychiatrist and Other Stories*, 1963; *What Went on at the Baroness'*, 1963.

PLAYS: *Desencantos*, pb. 1861; *Quase ministro*, pb. 1864; *Os deuses de casaca*, pb. 1866; *Tu só, tu, puro amor*, pb. 1880; *Teatro*, pb. 1910.

POETRY: *Crisálidas*, 1864; *Falenas*, 1870; *Americanas*, 1875; *Poesias completas*, 1901.

NONFICTION: *Páginas recolhidas (contos ensaios, crônicas)*, 1899; *Relíquias de Casa Velha (contos crônicas, comêdias)*, 1906; *Critica*, 1910; *A semana*, 1910; *Crítica por Machado de Assis*, 1924; *Crítica literária*, 1937; *Crítica teatral*, 1937; *Correspondência*, 1938.

MISCELLANEOUS: *Outras relíquias*, 1908; *Obra completa*, 1959.

BIBLIOGRAPHY

Caldwell, Helen. *The Brazilian Othello of Machado de Assis: A Study of "Dom Casmurro."* Berkeley: University of California Press, 1960. Chapters on Santiago's love story, his Desdemona, the disease of jealousy, why Santiago publishes his narrative, and Machado de Assis's use of symbols. Includes an appendix with a biography of Machado de Assis and detailed notes.

_____. *Machado de Assis: The Brazilian Master and His Novels.* Berkeley: University of California Press, 1970. The introduction describes Machado de Assis's life before he began writing novels; the next section discusses his first four novels; then there are separate chapters on *The Posthumous Memoirs of Brás Cubas* and *Dom Casmurro*, followed by a section on the last two novels, with an epilogue about the relationship between autobiography and biography in Machado de Assis's writing. Includes detailed notes.

Dixon, Paul B. *Myth and Modernity.* West Lafayette, Ind.: Purdue University Press, 1989. Contains a perceptive discussion of *Dom Casmurro*.

Fitz, Earl E. *Machado de Assis.* Boston: Twayne, 1989. Part of Twayne's World Authors series, this study is a standard introduction to the life and times of Machado de Assis.

Graham, Richard, ed. *Machado de Assis: Reflections on a Brazilian Master Writer.* Austin: University of Texas Press, 1999. Part of the Critical Reflections on Latin America series, this volume has essays by John Gledson, Daphne Patai, and Sidney Chalhoub.

Neto, Jose Raimundo Maia. *Machado de Assis, the Brazilian Pyrrhonian.* West Lafayette, Ind.: Purdue University Press, 1994. Part 1 explores Machado de Assis's first phase (1861-1878)—from writing essays to stories to his first novels. Part 2 concentrates on his second phase (1879-1908), with separate chapters on *The Posthumous Memoirs of Brás Cubas*, *Dom Casmurro*, and later fiction. Includes detailed notes and bibliography.

Nunes, Maria Luisa. *The Craft of an Absolute Winner: Characterizations and Narratology in the Novels of Machado de Assis.* Westport, Conn.: Greenwood Press, 1983. The introduction describes previous criticism of the novelist, and subsequent chapters deal with his early career, his handling of plot and character, point of view in his later work, and his treatment of time.

HUGH MacLENNAN

Born: Glace Bay, Nova Scotia, Canada; March 20, 1907

Died: Montreal, Canada; November 7, 1990

PRINCIPAL LONG FICTION

Barometer Rising, 1941

Two Solitudes, 1945

The Precipice, 1948

Each Man's Son, 1951

The Watch That Ends the Night, 1959

Return of the Sphinx, 1967

Voices in Time, 1980

OTHER LITERARY FORMS

Throughout his career, Hugh MacLennan was a prolific writer of nonfiction. Following his youthful attempts at poetry and the publication of his dissertation on a Roman colonial settlement in Egypt, *Oxy-*

(AP/Wide World Photos)

rhynchus: An Economic and Social Study (1935, 1968), MacLennan began writing articles, reviews, autobiographical pieces, travel notes, and essays, publishing in a variety of magazines, including *The Montrealer, Maclean's*, and *Holiday*. Journalism sometimes served as a necessary supplement to his income and occasionally was used to try out material later incorporated into his novels. It has been claimed that his talent finds truer expression in his essays than in his novels; while this may be a questionable judgment, there is no denying the excellence of much of his nonfiction. Selections from the more than four hundred essays that he wrote have been collected in four books, the first two of which won Canada's Governor-General's Award: *Cross-Country* (1948), *Thirty and Three* (1954), *Scotchman's Return and Other Essays* (1960), and *The Other Side of Hugh MacLennan: Selected Essays Old and New* (1978, Elspeth Cameron, editor). Additionally, his concern for Canada's history and geography has found expression in his *Seven Rivers of Canada* (1961, revised as *Rivers of Canada*, 1974) and *The Colour of Canada* (1967). *Rivers of Canada*, in which MacLennan provided the text to accompany the beautiful photography of John DeVisser, contains some of his best writing.

Achievements

MacLennan, as his biographer, Elspeth Cameron, has observed, "set out to be a writer, not a 'Canadian' writer," yet it was as a Canadian "nationalist" that he was first recognized, and in spite of his intermittent attempts to renounce this label, it was as a distinctively Canadian writer that his career and his reputation developed. He held a solid place as something like the dean of Canadian letters; for many years he was a public figure in Canada, appearing on radio and television, frequently being asked to comment not only on Canadian writing but also on culture generally, and politics. He made continual attempts to tap the American market (with some success, especially with *The Watch That Ends the Night*); his works have been translated into many languages; his last novel, *Voices in Time*, is international in setting, yet MacLennan was thought of both in his own country and elsewhere as a, perhaps *the*, Canadian novelist.

Having written two unpublished novels with international settings, MacLennan turned to his own Halifax, Nova Scotia, when writing *Barometer Rising*. This first published novel was immediately successful and was praised for its Canadian nationalism. His next novel, *Two Solitudes*, treated the divisions between the English and French cultures in Quebec; the book's title, taken from Rainer Maria Rilke, entered popular usage as a convenient phrase to sum up this cultural schism. MacLennan continued to be hailed for his contributions to defining a Canadian identity. When his third novel, *The Precipice*, attempted to develop an international theme, presenting the love between a Canadian woman and an American man, he met with less critical acceptance. He returned to writing about Nova Scotia in *Each Man's Son* and followed this with a novel set primarily in Montreal, *The Watch That Ends the Night*. This work was both a critical success and a best-seller, not only in Canada, but also throughout the English-speaking world; it also sold well in translation. MacLennan's reputation as a major novelist was assured; it was bolstered by

sonal experience, for he drew less upon "pure" invention than do many novelists. His method, in both his essays and his novels, was to use personal experience to support general and philosophical concepts.

This means that, fundamentally, MacLennan wrote novels of ideas; it does not mean, however, that his ideas were necessarily free from self-contradiction or that they remained entirely consistent throughout his career. His ideology, complex but ultimately growing from a sense of the fundamental importance of geography, is most explicit in his first three published novels, in which he worked toward a definition of Canadian identity by first contrasting Canada to England (*Barometer Rising*), then dealing with the potentials of Canadian unity (*Two Solitudes*), and finally differentiating Canada from the United States (*The Precipice*). The next novel, *Each Man's Son*, is transitional in that it conveys a strong sense of the land, Cape Breton in this case, while anticipating the greater interest in psychology that characterized his subsequent novels. Even in these later novels, however, history as geography remains a basic concept. While psychological concepts became more important to MacLennan, he employed topographical images to express this interest.

Character, then, in a MacLennan novel is closely related to theme, as is plot, and the theme is tied to setting. While he created a fairly wide range of characters, including some minor figures that are presented with Dickensian humor, the central focus in his characterization was either on the "love interest" or on a conflict of generations. Both of these recurring motifs are normally subservient to theme in that the characters, whether they come together in love, as, for example, Paul and Heather in *Two Solitudes*, or stand apart in years, as do Alan Ainslie and his son in *Return of the Sphinx*, represent different value systems or cultures. Their psychology, which motivates their interactions, is seen in terms of their conditioning by history and, ultimately, by geography.

Admittedly, this emphasis is modified, especially in the later novels, by MacLennan's concern with various ideological factors, such as Calvinism in *Each Man's Son*, and by his interest in psychological theories, especially Freudianism, particularly notable

in *Return of the Sphinx*. Nevertheless, similar imagery and recurring motifs, reflecting a sense of historical causation, run through both his earlier and later works. One finds, for example, the antithesis between the city and the country; the retreat into the woods; the theme of the wanderer, exiled from his or her roots; frequent references to weather; and imagery of trees, gardens, and water, in all of his novels.

MacLennan's novelistic techniques did change, however, as he developed his craft, as can be seen in his plotting, use of point of view, and style. In plotting, as in many aspects of his craft, MacLennan was old-fashioned; he kept the reader interested in how the story will come out. MacLennan was by nature given to relatively happy endings, but after the upbeat conclusions characterizing his first three novels, his optimism became tempered, appearing more as a coda following climactic elements of tragedy in *Each Man's Son, The Watch That Ends the Night*, and *Return of the Sphinx*. *Voices in Time* has a series of climaxes occurring at different points in the novel and producing different effects on the reader. That MacLennan was able to unify the various narratives included in this, the most complex of his works in its plotting, is an indication of the development of his craftsmanship.

His ability to manipulate increasingly complex narrative patterns is closely related to his mastery of point of view. Although none of MacLennan's novels approaches a Jamesian concern for this aspect of the art of fiction, with *The Watch That Ends the Night*, as he moved away from straightforward chronological sequences, he slipped skillfully between first- and third-person narration. *Return of the Sphinx* uses third-person narration but with a shifting between the viewpoints of different characters. This novel, however, lacks what Henry James called "a fine central intelligence." Alan Ainslie does not provide this unifying quality as effectively as does John Wellfleet in *Voices in Time*; Wellfleet's perspective gives coherence to the novel's varied narrative strands.

As MacLennan's ability to structure his novels developed, slowly and within a fairly conventional framework, yet with increasing skill in his craft, so did his style mature. His earlier novels exhibited some tendency toward overwriting. *Barometer Rising* has "set-pieces" that skirt the borders of sentimentality; *Two Solitudes* is sometimes verbose; *The Precipice* is not free from clichéd expression. In *Each Man's Son*, the style, reflecting the dramatic structure, is tightened. *The Watch That Ends the Night* contains superior passages of description, although the dialogue (never one of MacLennan's strengths) occasionally shows some of the stilted qualities of the earlier novels. *Return of the Sphinx* is notable for its economy of style and in this respect prepares for *Voices in Time*, in which MacLennan's style is the most fully unselfconscious and "organic."

MacLennan, then, is a novelist who may be read for the pleasure to be found in an interesting story well told, but he remains a writer less likely to be remembered as a storyteller or fictional craftsperson than as a man of ideas, a dramatizer of history.

BAROMETER RISING

When, following his wife's advice to write of that which he knew best, MacLennan turned to his hometown, Halifax, he used it not only as the novel's setting but also as its subject. In *Barometer Rising*, he was also writing of Canada; Halifax, with its colonial attitudes overlaying social and ideological divisions, is a microcosm of a new Canada. The book's title is in large part explained in a subsequent essay, in which MacLennan describes Halifax as a barometer for the whole country.

Yet what goes up must have been down; if the barometer rises, if, by implication, Canada faces a halcyon future, it does so only after a great storm and a particularly violent stroke of lightning. The action of *Barometer Rising* is centered on an actual historical event, the blast that occurred when a munitions ship exploded in Halifax harbor on December 6, 1917. The largest single human-made explosion before Hiroshima, it destroyed a major portion of the town and killed some two thousand people.

A result of Halifax's role in World War I, the explosion is also symbolically related to Canada's involvement in that bloody conflict. While the concurrent destruction of life, property, and outworn colonial beliefs—the old world dying with a monstrous bang—constitutes the core of the book, a number of

other motifs are woven into its thematic patterns. The conflict of generations, the return of the wanderer and the Odysseus theme, the psychological aspects of technological change—these are all important elements of the novel that continued to reverberate in MacLennan's subsequent work. Underlying all the thematic strands is the author's view of historical process, a view that puts a strong emphasis upon the conditioning significance of physical geography.

It is Halifax's geographical situation that underlies the book's basic contrast, that between old and new Canada, colony and country. The harbor gives the town its meaning; facing away from the rest of Canada, Halifax looks toward Britain and the Continent, both in a literal and a figurative sense. From the topographical facts, carefully elaborated at the beginning of the novel, derive the prevailing attitudes of the Haligonians: it is the preservation of England that motivates all of what happens in Halifax; the colonial mentality prevails. Had the geography been different, the town's development and activity would have been different, and, consequently, its people would have been different.

Yet if geography is destiny, there is no rigid determinism in MacLennan's view of that destiny. Halifax, although pointed toward Britain physically and thus psychologically as well, is part of the New World and has, therefore, the potential for a different orientation. This reorientation follows from the book's central event, the explosion, an event which, while the result of accident, is influenced by topography in both cause and effect. The explosion is a result of the collision, in Halifax harbor, of a munitions ship with a Norwegian freighter; the crash occurs because the physical nature of the harbor limits visibility. As a result of the destruction, new values arise from the rubble of the old; Halifax is no longer dominated by the rigid ideas of its old colonial aristocracy.

While the story has this allegorical quality, with a message made explicit in a concluding passage on what might be termed Canada's "manifest destiny," its allegory is fleshed out with particular, three-dimensional characters, conditioned by geography and history, but living out their private lives within the interstices of that conditioning framework.

Neil Macrae, the book's hero, is, like Odysseus, a soldier returned from the war, bearing an assumed identity acquired after he was falsely accused of disobeying an order during an attack in which he was thought to have been killed. His accuser is the novel's villain, Colonel Wain, representative of the old order, and father of Penelope—whose Homeric name is intentional—the heroine with whom Neil is in love. The cast is completed by a number of skillfully drawn secondary characters derived from MacLennan's memories, including Penny's younger brother Roddie, modeled on MacLennan himself, and Angus Murray, also in love with Penny, the first in a series of heroic doctors who appear in MacLennan's novels.

Following the explosion and the vindication of Neil's conduct during the attack in France (the outcome of the battle depending, just as does the collision in the harbor, on terrain), Neil and Penelope are finally united; the storm is over, and the future is bright. While the novel is marred by this rather facile happy ending and by its general didacticism, the basic interest in both action and character, reinforced with symbolism, makes *Barometer Rising* artistically satisfying. Although MacLennan was to write more subtly in future novels, *Barometer Rising*, representing clearly his basic approach, fiction as dramatized history, remains one of his best achievements.

Two Solitudes and The Precipice

MacLennan's next two novels also used a love story to express theme and continued to demonstrate his interest in the impact of geography upon the character of a people. *Two Solitudes*, centered upon the romance between Paul Tallard and Heather Methuen, begins with a description of the landscape of Quebec; throughout, the symbolism of the river, the forest, and the town reinforces the theme of the relationship of the English and French in Quebec. *The Precipice*, with its love affair between a Canadian woman and an American man, contrasts Canada and the United States by relating the character of the peoples to their respective terrains. Set primarily in Ontario, the novel uses Lake Ontario as a dominant symbol, reinforced by references to weather, gardens, the city, and other prevalent MacLennan imagery.

Each Man's Son

Similar imagery informs *Each Man's Son*; thematic conflicts are drawn between two sides of the Scottish Highland character, between religion as a sense of sin and religion as inspiration, and between science and superstition, particularly focused through the contrast between the mines and the sea of Cape Breton. A major turning point in the plot occurs when Dr. Ainslie (whose name is taken from a Cape Breton place-name) gives his to-be-adopted son, Alan, a lesson in history, followed by one in geography.

The Watch That Ends the Night

Arguably MacLennan's best novel, *The Watch That Ends the Night* demonstrates a significant advance in his technique. The didactic quality of his earlier novels is reduced; the imagery becomes more involved, as does the handling of time; characters take on more interest, not as symbols, but in their own right. Concurrently, the sense of the formative power of geography upon character is moved more to the background, as though Canada, having been conditioned by geography, is able to go beyond this conditioning. Nevertheless, in this, as in all his novels, MacLennan writes from essentially the same perspective on history and employs many of the same patterns in fictional construction.

Again, just as in the earlier novels, the book is based on a strong sense of place, in this case Montreal, described in memorable, often loving detail. Again, the plot centers upon a love interest, a triangle involving George Stewart, who has autobiographical connections with MacLennan; Jerome Martell, a doctor with mythic qualities; and Catherine Carey, a remarkable woman (who takes on, for Canada, some of the symbolism Kathleen ni Houlihan did for Ireland) whose portrait owes something to MacLennan's wife Dorothy. George loves Catherine, but she marries Martell. After Martell is thought to have been killed by the Nazis, Catherine and George eventually marry, but, much later, Martell reappears. (The story begins at this point, and is told primarily through flashbacks.) Although Catherine stays with George, suffering a heart condition, she has little time left to live.

Within this framework, MacLennan presents a rich picture, with numerous well-realized minor characters, of Montreal during the Depression and during the time of the Korean War. For all his interest in psychology in this work, it is, as are all his novels, less a "novel of character" than a working out, through characters, of ideas, and a dramatization of social-historical processes. While the plot (except in the New Brunswick section) does not hinge on terrain, the imagery does. Images derived from nature control much of the book's tone, with references to rivers and oceans particularly important. In *The Watch That Ends the Night*, MacLennan moved beyond any mechanistic application of historical theory to the novel; he did not, however, change his fundamental view of the forces underlying human events.

RETURN OF THE SPHINX

His next novel, *Return of the Sphinx*, reintroduced Alan, from *Each Man's Son*, now a grown man with his own son. Dealing, on the surface, with events of the Quebec liberation movement in the 1960's, it is set mainly in Montreal and Ottawa but contains a "retreat to the woods" section and begins with an explicit statement of the impact of geography and weather upon culture; it ends with images of the land. Beneath the political action lies a deeper psychological theme, in essence that of the Oedipus complex, as MacLennan extends in this novel his interest in psychological theory, begun in *Each Man's Son* and continued in *The Watch That Ends the Night*; he also extends his use of imagery derived from nature and geography to express psychological states.

VOICES IN TIME

In MacLennan's final novel, *Voices in Time*, his lifelong interest in the perspective provided by history is obvious and central to the book's structure. Indeed, the direct, albeit complicated manner in which this interest informs the novel may be a key to its success. MacLennan's focus on history was always essentially pragmatic—to use the past to understand the present and anticipate the future; this is what *Voices in Time* undertakes.

The book intertwines the story of three men from three different generations: Conrad Dehmel, born in Germany in 1910, a concentration-camp survivor; Timothy Wellfleet, a Canadian born in 1938 who be-

comes a television interviewer; and John Wellfleet, another Canadian, born in 1964. John Wellfleet is the central narrator. He is one of the few humans who has lived through the "destructions" of atomic explosions, and when the novel opens in 2039, he is approached by the young André Gervais, who has found materials related to Wellfleet's family and wants the old man to use them to reconstruct the past that has, in effect, been destroyed for Gervais and his friends. Wellfleet works out Dehmel's story, involving opposition to Hitler and love for a Jewish woman, and finds it subsequently connecting to Dehmel's stepson Timothy, who interviews Dehmel on television in 1970. As a result of the interview, during which Timothy accuses Dehmel of having been a Nazi, Dehmel is assassinated.

Obviously, the presentation of this material, these voices from different times, calls for a complicated structure: Timothy's story is told by John Wellfleet; Dehmel's by both Wellfleet and, through diaries, by himself; and Wellfleet's own story is concluded by Gervais. The time scheme moves from 2039, to the late 1960's, to 1909, to 1918-1919, to 1932-1945, to a climax in 1970, and finally to 2044.

Like the time scheme, MacLennan's view of causation which underlies this historical presentation is intricate, especially as compared to *Barometer Rising* and his earlier novels. Nevertheless, his belief in the significance of geography, nature, and landscape in motivating character can still be seen, even though the landscape has become primarily urban, and character may be formed, or deformed, by *separation* from fundamental geography. Nature continues to provide MacLennan with a thematic contrast to the urban, technological environment and to be a source of much of his imagery. Timothy is cut off, in his technological world, from natural geography; at nineteen thousand feet, he flies over the woods his father's generation had known intimately. Dehmel finds a temporary salvation, in both the world wars, in Germany's Black Forest. John Wellfleet lives on the outskirts of what was once Montreal, with trees, flowers, and birds. Drawing upon Walt Whitman, MacLennan uses lilacs and a star to make a contrast with urban technology and its sense of time; he has Wellfleet think of the "time-clocks" of plants and birds. In one key passage, civilization is compared to a garden. Most significantly, perhaps, when compared to the thoughts about civilization, its rise and fall, and time, which MacLennan presents in *Rivers of Canada*, is the mentioning of rivers, as when, for example, the cautious optimism that tempers the tragic events narrated in *Voices in Time* is symbolized by the return of salmon to the St. Lawrence River.

Voices in Time was MacLennan's final novel and was a fitting climax to a successful career. It indicated that although he assuredly has a major position in the history of Canadian letters, he was one of those novelists who, although solidly rooted in time and place, transcended both. His ability to dramatize his geographical sense of history suggests that MacLennan is a writer who will continue to speak to future generations, to be, himself, a voice not stilled by time.

William B. Stone

OTHER MAJOR WORKS

NONFICTION: *Oxyrhynchus: An Economic and Social Study*, 1935, 1968; *Cross-Country*, 1948; *Thirty and Three*, 1954; *Scotchman's Return and Other Essays*, 1960; *Seven Rivers of Canada*, 1961 (revised as *Rivers of Canada*, 1974); *The Colour of Canada*, 1967; *The Other Side of Hugh MacLennan: Selected Essays Old and New*, 1978 (Elspeth Cameron, editor); *On Being a Maritime Writer*, 1984.

EDITED TEXT: *McGill: The Story of a University*, 1960.

BIBLIOGRAPHY

Buitenhuis, Peter. *Hugh MacLennan*. Edited by William French. Toronto: Forum House, 1969. Contains a biography of MacLennan, critical analyses of his six novels and his nonfiction, and a bibliography. In general, Buitenhuis supports MacLennan's preoccupation with Canadian nationhood. The assessment of MacLennan's strengths and weaknesses as a writer is even-handed but somewhat too academic.

Hochbruck, Wolfgang, and James O. Taylor, eds. *Down East: Critical Essays on Contemporary Maritime Canadian Literature*. Trier, Germany: Wissenschaftlicher, 1996. Contains Susanne Bach's useful study "The Geography of Perception in Hugh MacLennan's Maritime Novels."

Leith, Linda. *Introducing Hugh MacLennan's "Two Solitudes": A Reader's Guide*. Toronto: ECW Press, 1990. An excellent source for students of the novel. Includes bibliographical references and an index.

Lucas, Alec. *Hugh MacLennan*. Canadian Writers 8. Toronto: McClelland and Stewart, 1970. Each chapter addresses a different component of MacLennan's vision in general and social morality in particular. The introduction, conclusion, and a bibliography comprise the rest of this clear assessment of MacLennan's fiction and essays.

Tierney, Frank M., ed. *Hugh MacLennan*. Ottawa, Ont.: University of Ottawa Press, 1994. A good critical study of MacLennan. Provides bibliographical references.

Twigg, Alan. "Hugh MacLennan." In *Strong Voices: Conversations with Fifty Canadian Authors*. Madeira Park, British Columbia: Harbour, 1988. This absorbing 1979 interview focuses mainly on MacLennan's lifelong interest in Canadian nationhood and the influence of that interest on his writing.

Woodcock, George. *Introducing Hugh MacLennan's "Barometer Rising": A Reader's Guide*. Toronto: ECW Press, 1989. This careful, instructive methodology for reading the novel also includes a chronology of MacLennan's life and publications, biographical details, an assessment of MacLennan's place in Canadian literature, and a partially annotated "Works Cited."

_____. "Surrogate Fathers and Orphan Sons: The Novels of Hugh MacLennan." In *Northern Spring: The Flowering of Canadian Literature*. Vancouver, British Columbia: Douglas & McIntyre, 1987. In this essay from his two-part book on Canadian prose writers and poets, Woodcock examines what he perceives in MacLennan's writing as a central metaphor for the definition of "Canadian" nation: a generational theme. Also discusses the strongly didactic element that pervades MacLennan's works.

LARRY MCMURTRY

Born: Wichita Falls, Texas; June 3, 1936

PRINCIPAL LONG FICTION

Horseman, Pass By, 1961
Leaving Cheyenne, 1963
The Last Picture Show, 1966
Moving On, 1970
All My Friends Are Going to Be Strangers, 1972
Terms of Endearment, 1975
Somebody's Darling, 1978
Cadillac Jack, 1982
The Desert Rose, 1983
Lonesome Dove, 1985
Texasville, 1987
Anything for Billy, 1988
Some Can Whistle, 1989
Buffalo Girls, 1990
The Evening Star, 1992
Streets of Laredo, 1993
Pretty Boy Floyd, 1994 (with Diana Ossana)
The Late Child, 1995
Dead Man's Walk, 1995
Zeke and Ned, 1997 (with Ossana)
Comanche Moon, 1997
Duane's Depressed, 1999

OTHER LITERARY FORMS

In a Narrow Grave (1968) is a collection of nine essays Larry McMurtry wrote for various periodicals, mostly concerning Texas. He collaborated on the script for the 1971 motion-picture adaptation of his novel *The Last Picture Show* and wrote other scripts. In 1975-1976 he wrote monthly articles for *American Film* magazine, some of which were collected in *Film Flam: Essays on Hollywood* (1987). *Crazy Horse* (1999) was McMurtry's first foray into biography.

ACHIEVEMENTS

McMurtry's early reputation was based on his depiction of hard modern times in North Texas. *Horseman, Pass By*, *Leaving Cheyenne*, and *The Last Pic-* *ture Show* are all located in that area, where the frontier and the old ranching way of life were disappearing while McMurtry was growing up. The second group of three novels, *Moving On*, *All My Friends Are Going to Be Strangers*, and *Terms of Endearment*, concerns an interrelated group of characters in the Houston area and focuses primarily on failed marriages. McMurtry's Pulitzer Prize and his greatest public success, however, came with his first venture into the traditional Western, his novel of the frontier past, *Lonesome Dove*, considered by many critics to be his finest achievement and the finest novel ever written in that form.

BIOGRAPHY

Larry Jeff McMurtry was born in Wichita Falls, Texas, in 1936, grandson of a pioneer cattleman in North Texas and one of four children of a ranching family. McMurtry grew up on the ranch, was graduated from high school in Archer City, Texas, the locale of much of his early fiction, in 1954, and after one semester at Rice University attended North Texas

(Lee Marmon)

State University, from which he was graduated in 1958. He was married to Josephine Ballard in 1959; the marriage, which produced one son, ended in divorce in 1966.

McMurtry went back to Rice as a graduate student in English in 1958, beginning work on his first two novels. *Horseman, Pass By* was accepted for publication while he was at Rice and was published while he was a writing student at Stanford University in 1961. Between 1961 and 1969 he taught off and on at Texas Christian University and at Rice, while two more novels were published and he worked on his first long novel, *Moving On*. He had worked occasionally as a book scout for California bookstores while at Stanford, and in 1969 McMurtry left Houston and moved to Washington, D.C., where he became a partner in a bookstore. Thereafter, he divided his time between the store and his writing.

Many of McMurtry's books have been made into motion pictures, most notably *Hud* (1963; the screen name of *Horseman, Pass By*), *The Last Picture Show*, which was filmed by Peter Bogdanovich in Archer City, and *Terms of Endearment* (1983). Actors in all these films (Patricia Neal, Cloris Leachman, Shirley MacLaine, and Jack Nicholson) won Oscars for their performances. *Lonesome Dove* was made into a miniseries for television, with Robert Duvall and Tommy Lee Jones in the major roles. A film version of *Texasville* was released in 1990. McMurtry chose to lead a quiet life, devoted mostly to his two professions, and avoided talk shows and gossip columns.

Analysis

Larry McMurtry's best fiction has used the Southwest as its location and the characters typical of that area for its subjects. In the early years of his career, he dealt with life in the dying towns and decaying ranches of North and West Texas, often using boys on the brink of manhood to provide perspective on a way of life that had reached a stage of corruption and betrayal. His trilogy, following these early novels, dealt with the tangled relationships among somewhat older characters and reflected McMurtry's own move from Archer City to Houston. Later, he invested the Western novel with new vigor in two novels, his clas-

sic *Lonesome Dove* and the satiric *Anything for Billy*, which holds the legend of Billy the Kid up to ridicule.

McMurtry has shown the ability to change his locales and his subject matter when he feels the need for novelty, and he has been willing to revive characters from earlier novels to suit new purposes. He has been most successful in exploring the past and present of his native Texas, a state and a state of mind that provide seemingly inexhaustible material for his special blend of satire, romance, and tragedy.

McMurtry has used a variety of styles, from the elegiac to the rapid narrative, from the hilarious to the mournful. He has shown an unusual ability to depict interesting and sometimes outrageous characters, especially women. While his fictional locales moved away from Texas for a time, in his later works he has gone back to the settings and sometimes the characters of his earlier works. A regional writer, he has transcended the usual limitations of regional writers and attracted a broad audience.

Horseman, Pass By

McMurtry himself eventually said that *Horseman, Pass By*, published when he was only twenty-two, was an immature work. This first novel, a story of ranch life, narrated by a seventeen-year-old boy whose grandfather's livelihood and life are ended when his herd of cattle must be destroyed, sets many of McMurtry's themes: the ease with which people learn to betray others, in this case the old man's betrayal by Hud, his stepson; the mental and physical wear inflicted by the harsh Texas land; and the importance of the affection an older woman (in this case the Bannon family's black cook, Halmea) can give to a young man. This novel and McMurtry's next, *Leaving Cheyenne*, are clearly preparations for the success of *The Last Picture Show*.

The Last Picture Show

McMurtry's third novel is set in the small, dying North Texas town of Thalia (there is a town with that name in Texas, but its geography does not fit the fictional town, which is clearly modeled on Archer City). Its central characters are Sonny Crawford and Duane Moore, two boys in their last year of high school. Neither is in fact an orphan, but neither lives with his surviving parent; they rent rooms in the town's rooming house, support themselves working in the oil fields, and hang out at the town's pool hall, run by their aging friend and mentor Sam the Lion. In the course of about six months, Duane and Sonny learn hard lessons about life and love.

Sonny is the more sensitive of the two. He falls into a passionate affair with Ruth Popper, the frustrated and lonely wife of the high school athletic coach—a stock figure whose latent homosexuality is masked by an aggressive masculinity in the presence of his athletes. Ruth begins the affair in desperation and is startled by the depth of her feeling for Sonny, while the boy is surprised and gratified by the experience. Both realize that the affair cannot last, but Ruth is devastated when Sonny leaves her at the invitation of the town's reigning beauty, Jacy Farrow.

Jacy has been Duane's girlfriend, a monster of selfishness who plays games with both Sonny and Duane, almost destroying their friendship. She keeps putting off Duane's demands that she marry him and insists on seeing another young man and going with him to wild parties in Wichita Falls. When Duane leaves town to work in the oil fields, Jacy decides to take Sonny away from Ruth Popper. Duane finds out, fights with Sonny, and blinds his friend in one eye by hitting him with a beer bottle. Jacy convinces Sonny to elope with her as an adventure, arranging matters so that her father will stop them before they are actually married. Jacy's wise and experienced mother, Lois, offers Sonny brief consolation and shows him that he must make peace with Ruth Popper.

The boys' adventures have been made possible by the wise counsel and care of Sam the Lion. He has taught them about life, given them parental refuge, and shown them the limits of behavior by closing them out when they are involved in the mistreatment of his retarded ward, Billy. The safety of their world is shattered when Sam dies suddenly, leaving his pool hall and restaurant in the care of Sonny. The young man is forced to face the cruelty of the world when Billy, sweeping the streets of Thalia in his customary way, is hit and killed by a passing truck. The boys are reconciled when Duane leaves to join the army and fight in Korea.

The Last Picture Show, named for the film theater that is forced to close, symbolizing the decay of Thalia, is a compound of nostalgia, harsh realism, and tragedy. It deals with the inevitable loss of innocence of its central characters and with the hard realities of injury, loss, and death. It is frank about sex (Australian authorities banned the novel at one time), but it makes clear the price Sonny and Ruth Popper pay for their affair. At the same time, its depiction of adolescence is often amusing and colorful; the boys take off on a wild adventure south through Texas and into Mexico, they enjoy playing bad basketball for an increasingly frustrated Coach Popper, they enjoy earning their own livings. With the exception of the incident involving the joke played on Billy, they do harm only to themselves.

The Last Picture Show shows the meanness of the people in a small town: Ruth Popper is scorned for loving a boy much younger than herself; the sheriff and other observers are callously indifferent when Billy is killed; Sam the Lion has had to live without the love of his life, Lois Farrow, because of the mores of the town; the coach, despite his poor teams and his general ignorance and stupidity, is looked up to and admired by most of the town. Duane, the more conventional of the two central figures, is sometimes a bully and sometimes a fool.

There is a kind of soft quality to the novel, nevertheless. Most of those the boys encounter are sympathetic to them, including the waitress in Sam's café, the woman who is forced to close the theater, Ruth Popper, and Sam himself. They have no parents, but there are plenty of surrogates to guide and care for them, and they seem always to be forgiven by those they have hurt. Billy carries no grudge against either of them, Sam eventually shows that Sonny has done his penance, and even Ruth forgives Sonny for leaving her. Duane is hard enough not to need forgiveness.

TEXASVILLE

McMurtry revived Thalia, Sonny, and Duane in *Texasville*, a comic look at Thalia after it has experienced the boom of high oil prices and then been hit by the oil depression of the early 1980's. In *Texasville* Sonny recedes into the background, a forgetful and lonely middle-aged man who seems to suffer from something like premature Alzheimer's disease. The focus is on Duane, whose oil business has gone to pot, whose marriage to Karla (a new character) is in deep trouble, and whose love life and civic responsibilities provide material for comedy. His life is further complicated by the return to Thalia of Jacy, thrice-married film starlet, mother of three children, saddened and made more human by the death of her young son. *Texasville* is longer, more comic, and more complicated than *The Last Picture Show*, but it is less affecting. Only the episode in which Sonny wanders off and is found sitting in the wreckage of the old theater recalls the tone of the earlier novel.

The Last Picture Show was McMurtry's sometimes bitter, sometimes nostalgic farewell to the North Texas setting of his early work. The next stage in his career focused on young people in the Houston area, beginning with *Moving On*, a long depiction of the damage wrought by a marriage that is falling apart, and a sad picture of university life and the lives of traveling rodeo performers. This second phase of McMurtry's career ended with *Terms of Endearment*, the story of a lively widow and her troubled daughter, who eventually dies of cancer.

All My Friends Are Going to Be Strangers

Typifying this second stage is *All My Friends Are Going to Be Strangers*, a novel held together only by the central character and narrator, Danny Deck, who was introduced in *Moving On*. Danny's experience is to some extent based on that of his creator. Early in the book, while he is a graduate student at Rice, Danny's first novel is accepted for publication. In the euphoric mood that follows, he leaves Rice and marries Sally, a beautiful and sexy young woman who holds no other interest for Danny and who proves to be a monster. Her former lover accompanies them part of the way to California, leaving after they survive a flash flood in West Texas. Once the couple has moved to San Francisco and Sally has become pregnant, she relieves her boredom by engaging in an affair with a blind musician and pushes Danny out of her life. Danny goes downhill, lives in a rundown hotel, and finds himself unable to do satisfactory work on his second novel.

Jill, a brilliant film cartoonist he meets on a brief excursion to Hollywood, pulls Danny out of his slump and lives with him for a while, setting his life in order. Temporarily he thinks that he has found the love of his life, and his writing is stimulated by an idea she has provided. Jill, however, has lost interest in sex (which seems to be Danny's chief interest), and their relationship deteriorates until she leaves him to return to Hollywood and Danny sets out for Texas.

The episodic nature of *All My Friends Are Going to Be Strangers* continues when Danny returns to Texas. He pays a visit to his Uncle L, providing a satiric picture of an old-time cowboy gone eccentric; he returns to Houston and makes love to various women, including Emma, the wife of his best friend, and Jenny, who had been his landlady; he goes through a nightmarish experience signing copies of his book at a bookstore; he has a horrible, violent encounter with Sally's parents, who prevent him from seeing his newborn daughter; he is harassed and cruelly beaten by two Texas Rangers who take a dislike to his long hair. He goes for several days without any real sleep. In the end he walks into the Rio Grande, pushing the manuscript pages of his new novel under the water and possibly intending to commit suicide by drowning; that is never clear.

Danny's experiences are intended to show the dislocating effects of early success on a young man who has cut himself off from his roots and has become unable to establish real connections with any other human beings. He falls in love easily enough, but neither Sally nor Jill can return his love in the way he needs, and he has no way to extend his brief affair with Jenny. His encounter with Emma can lead only to guilty feelings for both of them.

Danny is just as much at sea in the other kinds of life he experiences. The editor of his publishing house takes him briefly into a world of authors and sophisticates in which he feels himself to be totally out of place. His brief experience in Hollywood exposes him to people who mystify and amaze him, but for whom he has no respect. He twice pays brief visits to the Stanford campus where McMurtry spent two years, but what he gets from those experiences is the knowledge that he enjoys taking drugs and that he is no scholar. Uncle L shows him that there is nothing for him in ranching life, and the professor from whom he took Sally in the beginning makes it clear that the professorial life is dull and unrewarding.

All My Friends Are Going to Be Strangers is a depressing book. Danny Deck is neither admirable nor particularly amusing. The book is saved by two things. One is McMurtry's undoubted skill as a writer, which enables him to describe scenes as disparate as the flash flood, Uncle L's encounter with his wife, and a literary party in a posh San Francisco suburb vividly and entertainingly. The other is the presence of several interesting minor characters, from Wu, the exiled Chinese writer who admires Danny's work and plays table tennis with him, to Mr. Stay, the former-Communist bookstore owner and sonnet writer who hosts the book-signing party. Several of the women, including Jill, Emma, and Jenny, are memorable and distinctive. The novel suggests, however, that McMurtry's Houston years did not provide the material or the inspiration for his best fiction.

Some Can Whistle

In a much later work, Danny Deck proves not to have killed himself: McMurtry brings him back in *Some Can Whistle* as a successful middle-aged writer who has chosen to live in relative isolation. He finds the daughter he has never known, T. R., and brings her and her two children to live with him. She is lively, engaging, and interesting; for a while she seems to be able to revive Danny's wish to be in closer touch with other human beings, but in the end, when T. R. is suddenly killed, the habits of his lifetime are too strong. He has not changed enough from his earlier self.

McMurtry, in the group of novels which followed *All My Friends Are Going to Be Strangers*, seemed to be trying to demonstrate that he could write successful novels that had nothing to do with Texas or with the life of a writer. The brief satiric glimpse of Hollywood given in *All My Friends Are Going to Be Strangers* was expanded in *Somebody's Darling*, whose central character is a film director trying to cope with her early success and the demands of two

men she loves. The world McMurtry entered as a bookstore owner is reflected obliquely in *Cadillac Jack*, whose protagonist is an itinerant antique dealer and whose chief setting is Washington, D.C. The entertainment industry comes under further examination in *The Desert Rose*, which has as its heroine an aging topless dancer in Las Vegas. Each of these novels is entertaining and well written, but none did much to enhance McMurtry's reputation.

Lonesome Dove

That enhancement had to wait until McMurtry decided to write a novel in one of the oldest and most persistently popular of American fictional traditions, the Western. With rare exceptions, Western novels have not been treated by critics as serious literature, since they have tended to follow hackneyed patterns of characterization and action. Patterns established by such writers as Ned Buntline and Doc Holliday in the nineteenth century were passed on almost intact to more recent writers such as Zane Grey and Louis L'Amour. What McMurtry did in *Lonesome Dove* was to reinvent the Western novel by taking its basic elements and elevating them to the level of epic. *Lonesome Dove* has attained the status of a classic of Western fiction.

The characters in *Lonesome Dove* are familiar to readers of Western fiction, here given new names: the silent hero, Woodrow Call, who cares more for horses than for women and who leads other men by example and by courage; the other hero, Gus McCrae, talkative and easygoing, always ready for emergencies; the prostitute with a heart of gold, Lorena (Lorie) Wood; the evil renegade half-breed, Blue Duck; the naïve but courageous boy, Newt; the strong almost-widow, Clara Allen; the handsome but weak gambler, destined to come to a bad end eventually, Jake Spoon; the unimaginative but dependable sheriff, July Johnson; the comic deputy, July's aide Roscoe; and a cast of thousands.

McMurtry's achievement in *Lonesome Dove* is twofold. First, he puts his huge cast of characters into motion. Beginning with a run-down livery stable and cattle-trading business in a tiny Texas town south of San Antonio called Lonesome Dove, the former Texas Rangers Call and Gus put together a herd by

on the isolated ranch in Montana. Clara and Lorie remain on the ranch outside Ogallala, with July hoping to marry Clara and Dish hopelessly in love with Lorie. Call has no idea where to go after the trip back to Lonesome Dove is ended.

ANYTHING FOR BILLY

The tone of McMurtry's next novel about the frontier, *Anything for Billy*, is very different. This book is a satiric retelling of the story of Billy the Kid, seen from the perspective of an asterner who has been addicted to dime novels of the West. The combination of humor and violent action that marked *Lonesome Dove* is present in the later novel but without the tragic undertone that gives *Lonesome Dove* its special power.

STREETS OF LAREDO, DEAD MAN'S WALK, and COMANCHE MOON

McMurtry's besetting weakness has clearly been his penchant for reviving characters and using them in sequels to novels that seem to have been sufficient in themselves. Most of his novels can be classified as parts of trilogies, sometimes widely separated in their dates of publication. For example, *Duane's Depressed*, published in 1999, returns to the setting and characters introduced in *The Last Picture Show* and updated in *Texasville*. The pattern is stretched even further in the Lonesome Dove cycle. That very long novel, which fittingly concludes in tragedy and pathos, has since become the basis for a virtual library of sequels and prequels. In *Streets of Laredo*, *Dead Man's Walk*, and *Comanche Moon*, the leading *Lonesome Dove* characters of Augustus McCrae and Woodrow Call, as well as lesser figures, are revived.

Adding to the confusion, the order of publication of the three later novels in the cycle does not follow the chronological stages in the characters' lives. *Streets of Laredo* is a true sequel, following the career of Woodrow Call after he has returned Augustus McCrae's body to the nearly deserted village of Lonesome Dove. It ends with a crippled Call, minus an arm and a leg, dependent on Pea Eye and his wife Lorena and their many children. *Dead Man's Walk* jumps back in time to the years between the Mexican War and the Civil War when McCrae and Call are about twenty years old and are new recruits to the

Texas Rangers. It takes its title from the Spanish phrase (*jornada del muerto*) describing a barren stretch of land in what is now central New Mexico, where much of the action of the novel takes place. *Comanche Moon* takes the heroes through the years of the Civil War to their decision to leave the Rangers and settle in the village of Lonesome Dove.

As is the case with the earlier cycles, the first book in the series is the most successful. One reason for this is that most of the salient facts are known. It is clear from *Lonesome Dove* that Gus never marries Clara Allen. The manner of his and Deets's deaths is presented in the earlier book, as are many other references to events earlier in time. Inevitably, this causes an absence of suspense. More important, however, there is in the later books of the series a sense of strain and a feeling that the author is adding incidents and plot lines simply to provide excitement. This is especially true of *Comanche Moon*, in which there is no clear, dominant plot line. Instead there are several plots interwoven in brief chapters, and much of the information is superfluous. It is enough to know that Blue Duck is a brutal savage, for example; the details of his early life add very little to the character.

The strain is more evident in the invention of two major new characters, Inish Scull and his wife Inez. Scull is a Boston millionaire and Harvard graduate who is the captain of the company of Texas Rangers in which McCrae and Call are enrolled. His relentless search for adventure leads him to enter Mexico on foot with only a Kickapoo scout for company. He finds his enemy, Ahumado, known as the Black Vaquero, but is taken prisoner. Subjected to a variety of tortures, climaxing with the removal of his eyelids, he manages to survive, although he temporarily goes crazy. Inez, while Inish is so engaged, is indulging her proclivities for young men and for spending Inish's and her own money. Their role in the story ends in farce, back in Boston. Inez continues to beat her husband with a bullwhip, and Inish turns down an invitation from Generals Sherman and Sheridan to take command of the Western regiments that are crushing any remaining American Indian resistance. These exaggerated characters do not fit well into a realistic novel.

DUANE'S DEPRESSED

After McMurtry's relative lack of success with the five historical novels which followed *Lonesome Dove*, he returned to a contemporary setting in *Duane's Depressed*, which completes the trilogy begun with *The Last Picture Show* and continued in *Texasville*. Duane Moore, now on the brink of old age, is the mayor of Thalia. To the astonishment of the rest of the town, he abandons his pickup truck one day and begins to walk wherever he needs to go. His marriage in trouble again, he also breaks with convention by going for help to a young woman psychiatrist. *Duane's Depressed* is not McMurtry's finest novel, but it is fresher and less strained than the books that preceded it and is a clear improvement over its predecessor, *Texasville*.

John M. Muste

OTHER MAJOR WORKS

NONFICTION: *In a Narrow Grave: Essays on Texas*, 1968; *It's Always We Rambled: An Essay on Rodeo*, 1974; *Film Flam: Essays on Hollywood*, 1987; *Crazy Horse*, 1999; *Walter Benjamin at the Dairy Queen: Reflections at Sixty and Beyond*, 1999.

BIBLIOGRAPHY

Busby, Mark. *Larry McMurtry and the West: An Ambivalent Relationship*. Denton: University of North Texas Press, 1995. Examines McMurtry's treatment of the West in his works. Includes bibliographical references and an index.

Jones, Malcolm. "The Poet Lariat." *Newsweek*, January 11, 1999, 62-63. This review of *Duane's Depressed* contains a great deal of useful factual information about McMurtry's life and career.

Jones, Roger Walton. *Larry McMurtry and the Victorian Novel*. College Station: Texas A&M University Press, 1994. A brief study of one of McMurtry's models, the long and complex novel with easily recognizable heroes and villains.

Neinstein, Raymond L. Afterword to *All My Friends Are Going to Be Strangers*, by Larry McMurtry. Albuquerque: University of New Mexico Press, 1982. Neinstein's brief book and the essay are sensitive and intelligent introductions to the first half dozen of McMurtry's novels.

Nelson, Jane. "Larry McMurtry." In *A Literary History of the American West*, edited by Max Westbrook and James H. Maguire. Fort Worth: Texas Christian University Press, 1987. A brief study placing McMurtry in the context of the modern Western novel and showing some of the ways in which he has reinvented the form and given it more tragic shadings.

Reynolds, Clay. "Back Trailing to Glory: *Lonesome Dove* and the Novels of Larry McMurtry." *The Texas Review* 8 (Fall/Winter, 1987): 22-29. This essay discusses the ways in which McMurtry's earlier novels about Texas, especially *Horseman, Pass By* and *Leaving Cheyenne*, prepared the way for the reviving of the more traditional Western novel in *Lonesome Dove*.

_____, ed. *Taking Stock: A Larry McMurtry Casebook*. Dallas, Tex.: Southern Methodist University Press, 1989. A valuable collection of essays, containing a bibliography edited by Charles Williams and important essays by Louise Erdrich and Ernestine P. Sewell.

Woodward, David. "Larry McMurtry's *Texasville*: A Comic Pastoral of the Oil Patch." *Huntington Library Quarterly*, Spring, 1993, 167-180. A study of the author's use of an old traditional form in a contemporary setting.

DAVID MADDEN

Born: Knoxville, Tennessee; July 25, 1933

PRINCIPAL LONG FICTION
The Beautiful Greed, 1961
Cassandra Singing, 1969
Brothers in Confidence, 1972
Bijou, 1974
The Suicide's Wife, 1978
Pleasure-Dome, 1979
On the Big Wind, 1980
Sharpshooter: A Novel of the Civil War, 1996

OTHER LITERARY FORMS

David Madden is a prolific writer who has worked in almost every literary genre. Besides his novels, he has published numerous essays, short stories, and poems in a range of journals and magazines; short-story collections, *The Shadow Knows* (1970) and *The New Orleans of Possibilities* (1982); several plays, including both one-act and three-act versions of *Cassandra Singing* (1955); a number of book-length critical studies; as well as a film script for the television film of *The Suicide's Wife*. Additionally, Madden has edited more than ten volumes on such diverse subjects as the proletarian and tough-guy writers of the 1930's, James Agee, Nathanael West, the short story, film and the commedia dell'arte, and the popular culture explosion.

ACHIEVEMENTS

Madden's work has been unevenly recognized throughout his career. His early novels—*The Beautiful Greed*, an M.A. thesis project, and "Hair of the Dog," initially published in *Adam* but never reprinted as a book—received virtually no attention at the time of their publication. Although Harry T. Moore praised *Cassandra Singing*, *Brothers in Confidence*, and *Bijou* as "significant contributions to contemporary American fiction," other critics have not viewed Madden's work so favorably. While writer Walker Percy found *Bijou* "a triumphant, brutal story of growing up," some reviewers faulted it for lack of unity and excessive nostalgia. Mixed responses also greeted *Pleasure-Dome*. One critic praised it as a "lyrical, quite wonderful novel"; another found it too "demanding and sometimes a bore."

Madden's short stories, however, have received more consistent recognition. Two appeared in *Best American Short Stories*, for 1969 and 1971, respectively, and *The Shadow Knows*, Madden's first collection of short fiction, was the National Arts Council selection for 1970. In 1969, Madden was also the recipient of a Rockefeller grant for fiction.

Madden's achievement in the novel form rests in his exploration of the oral storytelling tradition and his evocation of east Tennessee and Kentucky landscapes and experiences, especially those of his youth. He often reworks autobiographical material— the major exception is *The Suicide's Wife*—much of it found in earlier novels or stories. Characters and situations recur; earlier stories reappear as segments of a later novel. Though redundant and at times tedious for the reader engaged in surveying all of Madden's novels, the retelling of this material in different forms allows the novelist to experiment with narrative voice and to explore in depth the relationship between the storyteller and the listener, a subject that has fascinated Madden since his youth.

BIOGRAPHY

Jerry David Madden was born July 25, 1933, in Knoxville, Tennessee, to James Helvy and Emile Merrit, models for the parents of Lucius Hutchfield in *Bijou* and *Pleasure-Dome*. Madden's two brothers both figure in his fiction. As a child, Madden worked as a newsboy and a theater usher, two jobs also held by the autobiographical Lucius. Madden was also an avid storyteller, a trait inherited from his grandmother. "Telling stories as a child," he comments in *The Poetic Image in Six Genres* (1969), "acting out all the parts, doing all the voices, I was an actor on a stage, my spectators within reach. When I wasn't telling stories, I was day-dreaming them." Like the characters in his novels—Lucius, Hollis Weaver in *Brothers in Confidence*, Big Bob Travis in *On the Big Wind*—Madden "wanted to be able to affect people" with his stories: his "two brothers, curled under quilts . . . neighborhood kids, huddled on our high front steps, and later . . . classmates during recess in grammar school." Inspired by the motion pictures he saw as an usher at the Bijou, Madden wrote his first story at age ten and thus discovered "the private, lonely thrill of affecting individual, absent readers— a relationship remote from the public, communal transaction of movies." With writers Thomas Wolfe as his "romantic," "nonliterary" model and Ernest Hemingway as the literary one, Madden launched himself in high school on a writing career that included sharing with Wolfe a nostalgic response to hometown and family and acquiring the same literary agent as detective novelist Raymond Chandler.

During high school, Madden worked as a radio

announcer—an experience that figures in the Big Bob stories and *On the Big Wind*. He also wrote, acted in, and directed a number of radio plays, feeding his interest in narrative voice and the teller-listener relationship. "Radio drama," after all, as Madden has acknowledged, "demands that listeners see through their ears" and grants thereby enormous evocative power and control to the actors.

By the time he graduated from Knox High School in 1951, Madden had already won a state play contest that included having the award-winning play produced at the University of Tennessee. Madden enrolled for a time at the University of Tennessee, but he interrupted his education for the sake of adventure: travel, work in New York, and a stint as a messman on a United States merchant marine ship, an experience that provided the basis for *The Beautiful Greed*. From 1955 to 1956, Madden also served in the Army in Alaska. He reenrolled in college in 1956, first at Iowa State Teachers College, then once again at the University of Tennessee, where he received a B.S. degree in 1957. In 1956, he married Roberta Margaret Young, whom he had met while working at a radio station in Iowa. During this period Madden continued to write, working on and off again on *Cassandra Singing* as a radio drama, a stage play, and a novel—a fourteen-year project. Indeed, the first one-act version of *Cassandra Singing* won third place in a contest at the University of Tennessee as early as 1954, and the planning of the novel was already under way in 1955 while Madden was stationed in Alaska.

In the fall of 1957, following completion of his undergraduate work at the University of Tennessee, Madden enrolled at San Francisco State College, where he continued to work on *Cassandra Singing* and completed the M.A. in creative writing. He then taught at Appalachian State Teachers College in Boone, North Carolina, for one year. From 1959 to 1960, he attended the Yale Drama School as a John Golden Fellow in playwriting. After 1960, Madden taught in colleges and universities throughout the central, eastern, and southern United States: from 1960 to 1962 at Centre College in Danville, Kentucky; from 1962 to 1964 at the University of Louisville; from 1964 to 1966 at Kenyon College in Gam-

bier, Ohio, where he was also assistant editor of the *Kenyon Review*; in 1966 at Ohio University in Athens; and in 1967 at the University of North Carolina at Chapel Hill. In 1968, Madden became writer-in-residence at Louisiana State University. He was named distinguished visiting professor of English at the University of Delaware in the spring of 1980. In 1988 he held the Chair of Excellence at Austin Peay State University in Tennessee. Beginning in 1992 he served as Director of the U.S. Civil War Center at Louisiana State University, and he was awarded a Certificate of Commendation from the American Association for State and Local History for his work at the center. From 1992 to 1994 he also served as the school's creative-writing program director.

ANALYSIS

In *The Poetic Imagic in Six Genres*, David Madden acknowledges two principal influences on his work, both explored in the autobiographical novel *Bijou*: his grandmother's storytelling and Hollywood films. He considers both to be "extremes." Nevertheless, from his grandmother he learned the impact of the storyteller on his or her listeners and from motion pictures he learned the techniques for making his own "stories more vivid, the action more immediate." These two extremes or opposite forces—the oral storytelling tradition in the South and the visual realm of popular-culture films—combine in Madden's novels to produce an abiding fascination with the role of the narrator-performer and the contrast between the life of action, that of the speaker or storyteller, and the life of the imagination, that of the listener or audience. To some extent, most of Madden's novels explore this duality while also drawing on a nostalgia for old films and film heroes.

Because he comes out of the southern oral storytelling tradition, Madden, like William Faulkner, relies heavily on a fairly fixed source of raw material that he reworks in various forms. Thus, characters from one novel may reappear, sometimes under different names; situations may recur as well, in stories retold from a different point of view or stitched into a novel. All of *Brothers in Confidence*, for example, reappears as part of *Pleasure-Dome*, a much later work, with changes in the principal characters' names. Most notably, Hollis Weaver, the narrator in *Brothers in Confidence*, is replaced by Lucius Hutchfield, who narrates both *Pleasure-Dome* and the earlier work, *Bijou*. Retelling the material from *Brothers in Confidence* allows Madden to reshape this material into a sequel for *Bijou*. *On the Big Wind*, which appeared in 1980, combines stories appearing in magazines as early as 1966, including "The Singer," a variation on the *Cassandra Singing* material which Madden reworked for fourteen years. Madden's justification for this reworking of material rests in his interest in the storytelling tradition, where repetition of a favorite story only enhances the storyteller-listener relationship, and in his interest in experimenting with point of view. "In this shifting from one perspective to another on the same material," he comments in *The Poetic Image in Six Genres*, "I have learned more about . . . my own interests, and about the teller-listener relationship."

One corollary of this fascination with the teller-listener relationship is Madden's concept of the artist-storyteller as "con man," an idea the novelist claims to have borrowed from Thomas Mann. In his 1980 essay, "Let Me Tell You the Story," Madden speaks of this metaphor as one way of focusing his interest. "The relationship between the storyteller and the listener," he adds,

> is like that between the con man and his mark, who charge each other through phantom circuits of the imagination; the storyteller uses many of the same techniques for capturing attention, holding it, and projecting the reader into a totally different world from the one he is living in.

Such creation Madden calls the "pleasure-dome," the concept explored in his sixth novel. Not surprisingly, most of Madden's novels involve some form of storytelling by central characters with listeners swayed or held captive by the magical words of the speakers. Often it is the con man, such as Travern Weaver in *Brothers in Confidence* or Lucius Hutchfield's corrupt older brother, Earl, who weaves these tales; often it is the artist-hero himself, Lucius in *Pleasure-Dome* or Hollis Weaver in *Brothers in Confidence*.

Even a minor work such as "Hair of the Dog," a detective story showing the influence of the "tough-guy" writers of the 1930's on Madden's fiction, involves a story told in prison, as do *Brothers in Confidence* and *Pleasure-Dome*.

The two novels which do not explicitly explore this teller-listener relationship are *The Beautiful Greed* and *The Suicide's Wife*. Although both employ storytelling in at least one episode as a means of revealing character, even to some extent altering a relationship between the speaker and the listener, in neither novel is storytelling the focus of the book. Alvin Henderlight in *The Beautiful Greed* has shared a cabin for months with the mysterious Franco before Franco tells his story; in *The Suicide's Wife*, Ann Harrington's lack of inhibition in bed with her husband's colleague serves as a device for altering her life, not that of the listener.

Of these two novels, only *The Suicide's Wife* is not autobiographical. While it grew from a dramatic monologue concerning a suicide that happened on "the periphery" of Madden's life, it does not concern the writer or a writer-hero, the autobiographical hero in most of Madden's novels. Incidents from *The Beautiful Greed*, perhaps because they are largely autobiographical, do appear elsewhere, notably in Lucius's artist-con man scheme in *Pleasure-Dome*. Only *The Suicide's Wife* remains outside of this storytelling context, unique also in its treatment of the duality of passivity and action within one central character, Ann Harrington, the suicide's wife.

THE BEAUTIFUL GREED

Madden's first novel, *The Beautiful Greed*, was published by Random House in 1961 as part of the publisher's First Novel series. The book was Madden's M.A. thesis project at San Francisco State College and drew heavily on his stint as a crewman aboard a United States merchant marine ship scheduled for Brazil but, in the novel at least, destined for Taltal, Chile, on a mercy mission to aid Chilean earthquake victims. The novel's protagonist, Alvin Henderlight, is clearly autobiographical. Besides sharing with the novelist his merchant marine experience, Alvin is also from Knoxville, has motion-picture ideas about going to sea, reads voraciously (particularly Joseph Conrad and Herman Melville), and bears a physical resemblance to the novelist with his short stature and balding head. He also has a family much like Madden's own and that of other autobiographical heroes in Madden's novels: a father who drinks, a mother who works, most often as a maid or in a factory, and two vagabond brothers.

The Beautiful Greed is also a very conscious literary work strongly influenced by Joseph Conrad's sea fiction. The title comes from a passage from *Lord Jim* (1900) referring to the insatiable hunger of the seaman for experience and adventure, a passage that serves as the epigraph for Madden's book. Like Conrad's novel, *The Beautiful Greed* takes illusion and reality as its central theme, particularly Alvin's gradual disillusionment. As the novel progresses, so does Alvin's awakening to the brute reality of life. His spiritual and psychological journey parallels the ship's slow progress south, through the Panama Canal and eventually on to Chile and, for Alvin, to true knowledge and experience.

The ship is another conscious literary device, a microcosm of the world's society. Young, old, bestial, intelligent, all different nationalities and human types are represented on board. Using these varieties of human beings, Madden explores the conflict between intellect—Alvin is dubbed the "professor" for his reading habits—and brute, insensitive action. Alvin and his cabin mate—the mysterious, remote Franco—are pitted against a crew of men whose brutal jokes include pitilessly trapping a sea bird and mercilessly using Franco as a scapegoat. For the most part, the novel follows the pattern of the *Bildungsroman*, but its message is clearly existential. When the enigmatic, falsely dignified Franco reveals the truth about himself in a compelling story, he also leaves Alvin to face the consequences of his choices and actions aboard ship. Once committed to staying on board the *Polestar*, Alvin must face the brutish men whom Franco escapes by returning to his home in Taltal. Alvin has passed the opportunity to leave with Franco; his change of mind comes too late to alter the implied course of events with which the novel ends: Alvin's own torture at the hands of the brutish crew. While relying excessively on conscious literary devices and on the author's own experiences, *The Beautiful Greed* is nevertheless noteworthy as a first novel for the author's attempt to deal with important issues about people's relationship with themselves and others and the meaning of their actions.

CASSANDRA SINGING

In *Cassandra Singing*, Madden turned away from predominantly autobiographical material to work with a story originating in a conversation with a messman aboard the novelist's merchant marine ship—a tale of a girl who joined a motorcycle gang after "her brother was killed in a smashup." Analogies exist in several forms, including various play versions and at least two short stories, "The Singer" and "Lone Riding." Madden acknowledges being obsessed with the story for more than fourteen years.

Set in eastern Kentucky rather than the Knoxville of the novelist's childhood, the story revolves around what Madden has described in *The Poetic Image in Six Genres* as "the strange relationship between a motorcyclist named Lone and his invalid sister Cassie. . . ." Besides this nearly incestuous relationship, Madden also attempts to capture the life of the mountain people and the threat to their folk existence posed by progress represented in the novel by the steady encroachment of bulldozers that will raze Lone and Cassie's home. His efforts are successful, for he is able to depict in detail the violence and deceptive simplicity of the mountain people, particularly through their dialect and mannerisms.

Perhaps because the story existed in dramatic form first, the novel relies heavily on dialogue, making immediate the conflict between Lone, who represents action, and his sister Cassie, who represents imagination. Through Lone's vivid retelling of his motorcycle adventures with his companion Boyd, Cassie, bedridden for years with rheumatic fever, is able to envision the life of action she has longed for but never had. Thus, she becomes one of the earliest of Madden's characters enchanted by the storyteller's art and imaginatively transported into a "pleasure-dome" of his own making. Lone likewise becomes one of the first of Madden's storytellers to dramatize the oral storytelling tradition prevalent among mountain and southern people.

Despite its successes, *Cassandra Singing* moves too slowly at times. It represents a testament to Madden's love of words, an essential trait in any writer, and his skill in capturing the speech of mountain people, yet the conversations become too repetitive, the action too prolonged. Like *The Beautiful Greed*, moreover, the novel draws heavily on other literary works and motifs. Cassie and Lone's relationship, as Madden has acknowledged in *The Poetic Image in Six Genres*, is "partly inspired" by the "brother-sister relationship in the *Oresteia* [458 B.C.E.], O'Neill's *Mourning Becomes Electra* [1931], Sartre's *The Flies* [1943], and Cocteau's *Les Enfants terribles* [1929]," and Cassie herself by Frankie in Carson McCullers's *The Member of the Wedding* (1950) and Cassandra, "the Greek prophetess of doom, who was condemned never to be believed." Coupled with the biblical allusions that accompany Boyd's attempted crucifixion and threatened castration of Lone near the end of the novel, these powerful literary antecedents overtake the meaning of Madden's tale, leaving it wanting for power and impact.

BROTHERS IN CONFIDENCE

Brothers in Confidence, which appeared in part in the *Southern Review* four years before its publication as an Avon paperback—the book has not been published in a hardbound edition—returns to largely autobiographical material. It is also one of the most playful and humorous of Madden's novels and the first to explore in depth the concept of the artist as con man. The first-person narrator, Hollis Weaver, is that artist. His goal is to save his younger brother, Cody, from serving a sentence on a chain gang for forgery. Like his brothers—Cody and the older Travern, also a criminal and forger—Hollis, though a writer and teacher by profession, must act the con man to persuade several good citizens of east Tennessee to accept a token payment as promise that Cody will make retribution and to agree to drop all charges against him. To do this, Hollis must travel the countryside weaving tales of Cody's neglected childhood—his parents resemble Lone and Cassie's as well as Lucius Hutchfield's—and ensnaring his audience with his storytelling art. His success depends on his skill in playacting, manipulating his audience,

and vividly dramatizing Cody's life in order to win pity—all talents which the oral storyteller must possess. Only Travern's pose as a fancy lawyer, Mr. French, outshines Hollis's art. Travern, a genuine rogue since his youth and a thief who steals from his own family, goes directly to the judge and, by using a soapy story about holding the judge's only son as he dies in combat, convinces the old man to release Cody and accept several bogus checks as payment for court costs and ready cash so the Weaver brothers can leave town.

Brothers in Confidence is a lively, quick-paced, humorous portrait of three witty con artists caught in the act of writing bad checks and weaving outrageous tales. Like Madden, they delight in holding their audiences, both listeners and readers, with the magic of their stories. Episodic in structure, the novel follows the exploits of the narrator-hero as he travels the countryside, attempting to stay out of jail while trying also to free his brother. In these two respects, *Brothers in Confidence* is a picaresque novel, though sexual adventures are noticeably absent, having been saved for abundant use in *Bijou*. Also noteworthy is Madden's reliance on Hollis's storytelling to handle exposition and family history—a dramatic device from oral storytelling—and his use of motion pictures as a means of enhancing action and character. Hollis, like the later Madden hero Lucius Hutchfield and the novelist himself, has worked as an usher in a film theater and served in the merchant marines. He envisions himself a romantic hero, an Alan Ladd figure acting out various roles assigned to him. Like Madden, he also has two brothers who have served time in prison.

BIJOU

In 1969, Madden received a Rockefeller grant in fiction to work on his fourth novel, *Bijou*. He wrote part of the novel in Yugoslavia, part in Venice—an "ideal place," he told Ruth Laney in an interview for the *Southern Review*. "When I got the grant," Madden continued, "I thought the best place to go to begin the book would be to a city that paralleled the exotic quality of the Bijou, both in the movies and in real life." In effect, through its focus on the aging theater at which its hero works, the novel duplicates the author's own nostalgia for the past. Its purpose is to capture the "seediness" of that theater, once a site for legitimate stage productions, now a place where pornographic films are shown.

Set in Cherokee, Tennessee, *Bijou* is another largely autobiographical *Bildungsroman*, tracing the life and adventures of thirteen-year-old Lucius Hutchfield during one turbulent and painful year. The period is immediately after World War II, and the romantic Lucius is infatuated with film stars and the memorable and not so memorable motion pictures of Hollywood's golden era. Like Madden, Lucius grows as an artist through two principal sources, both dramatized in the novel: his grandmother's storytelling and films.

Because the novel has little plot other than Lucius's growth over one year and his emergence as a young writer, it is highly episodic. *Bijou*, one critic complained, is "so long" (five hundred pages), "so unresponsive, and even irresponsible about itself" that the reader becomes bored and repulsed. Madden records virtually every intimate detail and every event, including bowel movements, every day of Lucius's life for a year. Some of the details are successful in capturing the formative factors in Lucius's growth; others are not. There is humor but also vulgarity and tedium.

Defending the novel, Madden told Ruth Laney that he had wanted "a concentration of effect, a sort of captivity in the Bijou" paralleling the enchantment the storyteller weaves through words and movements, here created by a place. The problem is that the book lacks the "unity of place [which] would have enabled [the author] to shorten the novel and to realize [his] original purpose." To accomplish his task, Madden dramatizes his own adolescence and growth as a writer, filtering every detail through Lucius's consciousness, yet Lucius is incapable of distinguishing the valuable from the useless in his experience.

Madden also experiments with several narrative patterns. Some work, others do not. Film sequences and bits of motion-picture dialogue blend with Lucius's thoughts and imaginings, successfully dramatizing the creative process and the impact of what Madden calls the "charged image" on the creative

consciousness. Segments of night reveries in which Lucius nostalgically reviews his life, sections of the hero's diary, letters between him and his girlfriend Raine—including one borrowed from a Joseph Cotton film—even whole stories written by the young Lucius appear as sections of narrative. Many of these bog down, particularly Lucius's and Raine's letters, which are often adolescent professions of love. The stories, though demonstrating the hero's early attempts at fiction-writing, mirror the artist's growth only part of the time. Finally, *Bijou* is not a successful novel; Madden's long autobiographical piece testifies, as does *Cassandra Singing*, to his love of literature, but it is also an instance of the novelist's having been caught in his own storytelling trance and nostalgia for the past.

THE SUICIDE'S WIFE

The Suicide's Wife, which was made into a television film for which Madden wrote the script, is in many ways the novelist's most unusual—some might say successful and original—novel. It is unusual among his novels in focusing solely on a female character—*Cassandra Singing* does so only partially. Aside from a dramatic monologue by the wife, the novel has no predecessors in Madden's oeuvre, an unusual feature. It is also, in Madden's own words, "a very short novel inspired by something that happened" not in his own life, but "on the periphery, a suicide." The novel is also unique in that it does not dramatize the oral storytelling tradition, as do Madden's other works, and is crisp and Hemingwayesque in style. Filtered through the intelligence of the suicide's wife, Ann Harrington, the wife of an English teacher at a West Virginia university, the novel studies the struggle of "the wife" to acquire an identity of her own following her husband's apparent suicide. Her lack of knowledge about her husband and about herself is her source of motivation after her husband's death thrusts her into a world she is unprepared to confront. Set against the backdrop of the student riots and Civil Rights movement of the late 1960's, Ann's story becomes a parable for the women's movement, a tale of progression from passivity and emptiness toward action and self-fulfillment.

At the outset of the novel, Ann defines herself almost solely in terms of her vagina, an emptiness to be filled by her husband. Madden skillfully does not give his heroine a name in this opening section. Her identity is not yet established, either with the reader, or, more important, with herself. As the book progresses, however, Ann's painful growth is recorded increasingly in terms of herself, with the narrative moving in and out of her thoughts, at times allowing Ann to think in first person as she develops some identity through action. The wife who is "still a wife" at the beginning of the novel "even though she doesn't have a husband" eventually realizes that the man to whom she felt inferior for years was in fact a nobody, as vague as she, as passive and purposeless and lost.

PLEASURE-DOME

With *Pleasure-Dome*, Madden returned to the comic tone and first-person narrative voice he used in *Brothers in Confidence*, part of which is reworked here with Travern, Hollis, and Cody becoming Lucius Hutchfield of *Bijou* and his two brothers, Earl and Bucky. Like that earlier work, the novel is autobiographical and retells stories found in other forms and books. *Pleasure-Dome* is also a sequel to *Bijou*, with Lucius seven years older and experienced through travel and the merchant marines. At twenty, Lucius is also seeking more than his own past, though he must deal with his troublesome family members who are frequently in trouble with the law.

Pleasure-Dome is an interesting novel for what James Park Sloan in *The New York Times Book Review* cited as its combination of "profligate storytelling with reflections on the storytelling process. . . ." The narrator's consciousness—seen to a lesser degree but very evident nevertheless in *Brothers in Confidence*—emerges on the first page when he invites the reader into his tale with the traditional storyteller's line, "Did I ever tell you about the time. . . ?" In this first half of the novel, Lucius adopts what he calls his Mark Twain persona, retelling, as he must to save Bucky, sad stories about his childhood in Tennessee, while at the same time he is reporting to the reader-listener the chronicle of his adventures in conning those citizens pressing charges against Bucky.

Pleasure-Dome also moves beyond *Brothers in Confidence* and *Bijou* by adding a segment on Lucius's quest for a past other than his own, that of the legendary Jesse and Frank James. His search involves the attempt to learn the tale of Zara Ransom, an old woman who reportedly had a brief romance with Jesse James when she was a girl. To get her story, Lucius must once again successfully con his audience, here by using Zara herself; one of the fascinating complications is that it is Zara who enchants Lucius by telling her own story. *Pleasure-Dome* then contains two or more stories: the autobiographical one concerning the Hutchfields, and another, a second tale, of Zara Ransom and her relationship with a figure from America's legendary past. Both stories concern the past; both are narrated by oral storytellers. Both create a pleasure-dome for the reader-listener.

Pleasure-Dome is clearly a more sophisticated work than Madden's earlier novels which experimented with point of view and narrative art. By adding Zara Ransom's story and having her tell that story as Lucius writes it, Madden captures the storytelling process and the transmission of a dying art to the writer. As in *Cassandra Singing*, progress in the form of razing bulldozers is threatening the folkways of which the oral storytelling tradition is a part. Without Lucius's written record of Zara's story, handled with what he calls his Henry James persona, and his interpretation of the ending, the tale would be lost. Zara may or may not have been Jesse James's lover, but she is a legend that reminds people, Lucius thinks, "that those who do not remember the past are doomed never to relive it in the imagination." Significantly, at the end of the novel, Zara is destroyed, and Lucius is moved to guilt and deep feelings of "something . . . for the first time besides nostalgia."

ON THE BIG WIND

With *Pleasure-Dome*, *On the Big Wind* dramatizes more successfully than any other Madden novel what the writer has described in *The Poetic Image in Six Genres* as "the teller's compulsion to tell a story," "the oral tradition" and the process by which it depicts, renders, and stimulates the art of oral storytelling. The book consists of seven episodes, most of which were originally published as short stories in a variety of magazines. The tone is clearly comic, as the subtitle indicates: "Seven Comic Episodes in the Fitful Life of Big Bob Travis." What is especially fascinating here is that each episode explores a different dramatic relationship between the storyteller and his audience. Thus, Madden's major theme of the power of storytelling gains power itself through the variety of ways in which the narrative voice of radio announcer Big Bob manipulates his audience. As the novel's epigraph, taken from Charlotte Brontë's *Jane Eyre* (1847), observes: "The eagerness of a listener quickens the tongue of a narrator."

In the opening episode, Big Bob is a night-owl country music disc jockey in Nashville given to having affairs with the women who call him. The "magic" in his voice enthralls countless women, but Big Bob, married to a meek housewife, is honest enough to have only one affair at a time. Problems occur when his wife, Laura, masks her voice and calls and seduces him as the deep-throated Morina. When Bob cannot resist a rendezvous with the mythical Morina, the result of the confrontation is divorce.

In later episodes, Big Bob's status in the radio business declines, then rises again. In each episode he plays a different role, sometimes with a different professional name, including a Jewish one. As David Epstein, he becomes a spokesperson for environmental and social causes. As a rock-music disc jockey, he must fend off the attack of a menacing motorcycle gang by telling a story that mesmerizes the group. In another episode, he draws a huge crowd of people to a sleazy mobile-home sales park by narrating the activities of a van of hippies. In that scene, Big Bob, in the tradition of the oral storyteller, both creates and "narrates the news."

As in his other novels, Madden's concern in *On the Big Wind* is with narrative techniques more than with originality in character creation or invention in plot. Like the oral storyteller who draws on a seldomly changed repertoire, Madden is content to repeat a story if the retelling draws another member of the audience into his pleasure-dome.

SHARPSHOOTER

Madden's storyteller-listener theme and allegiance to the southern oral tradition extend to his novel *Sharpshooter*, a fictional memoir of a Civil War soldier, Willis Carr, who, at the age of thirteen, leaves his Tennessee home to accompany his father and brothers on a Union raid into Confederate territory. Captured, he agrees to join the rebel army rather than face execution. Soon, he becomes a sharpshooter while serving under General Longstreet during several major battles against Union forces. Eventually he deserts but is recaptured by Confederate troops and ends up as a guard at the infamous Andersonville prison, where he is taught by a slave to read and write.

In recounting the experiences of the war through the eyes of the young Willis, Madden concentrates on a recurring theme: What is fact and what is fiction? Buffeted throughout the war by events he does not entirely understand, Willis comes to realize that his personal recollections are clouded, leaving him to contemplate at war's end not only the disconcerting effects of battle but also the meaning of his own participation. Troubled by his memories and the belief he may have missed something, he decides to put his experiences in writing. In so doing, he chooses to revisit the battlefields, examine photographs and memoirs, and listen to other veterans, as well as civilians, as they relate their experiences. However, he finds he is not alone in his difficulty in recalling events. Only a moment of intense personal recollection that brings everything into focus allows him to connect with what is essential to his imaginative and intellectual welfare.

In retracing his steps, Willis demonstrates another of Madden's favorite themes, that of a central character separated from the past, either mentally or physically, who as a consequence suffers from a loss of identity. It is only when Willis sees the war through the emotions, intellects, and imaginations of others that he is able to view it with a sense of completion. Yet, as he observes, the truth is never complete. He points to the legend-making inclinations of people to select actual incidents from the past and color them with imagined constructions. The retelling of tales by participants carries risks, because accounts can conflict, having been subjected to a variety of historical processes, some more reliable than others. While Willis's vantage point as a sharpshooter permitted him to see more than the infantryman, his mission was also single-minded, and no event played out on the battlefields, he concludes, could be solitary. There are other vantage points and other views that may or may not conflict but nevertheless must be considered if the past is to be interconnected. By connecting one experience with the other, especially the opposites, the participant integrates the pieces into a recognition and finally into a comprehension of the past. At this stage Madden's storyteller operates in the realm of the impersonal with an omniscience that is able to accommodate simultaneous events, both real and imagined.

Unlike *Bijou*, Madden's *Sharpshooter* does not get bogged down in repetitive detail or gratuitous sentiments. Instead, it maintains an undercurrent of subdued thought and emotion that steadily steers the reader to the story's final moments of revelation. It is thus not surprising that, highly acclaimed by critics, the novel was nominated for a Pulitzer Prize.

Stella A. Nesanovich, updated by William Hoffman

OTHER MAJOR WORKS

SHORT FICTION: *The Shadow Knows*, 1970; *The New Orleans of Possibilities*, 1982.

PLAYS: *Cassandra Singing*, pr. 1955; *From Rome to Damascus*, pr. 1959; *Casina*, pr. 1960; *Fugitive Masks*, pr. 1966; *The Day the Flowers Came*, pr. 1975; *Three Mean Fairy Tales*, pr. 1979.

NONFICTION: *Wright Morris*, 1964; *The Poetic Image in Six Genres*, 1969; *James M. Cain*, 1970; *Harlequin's Stick, Charlie's Cane*, 1975; *A Primer of the Novel: For Readers and Writers*, 1980; *Writer's Revisions*, 1980 (with Richard Powers); *Cain's Craft*, 1985; *The Works of Carson McCullers*, 1988; *Revising Fiction: A Handbook for Writers*, 1988; *The Fiction Tutor*, 1991.

EDITED TEXTS: *Tough Guy Writers of the Thirties*, 1968; *Proletarian Writers of the Thirties*, 1968; *American Dreams, American Nightmares*, 1970; *Rediscoveries: Informal Essays in Which Well-Known Novelists Rediscover Neglected Works of Fiction by One of Their Favorite Authors*, 1971; *The Popular Cultural Explosion: Experiencing Mass Media*, 1972 (with Ray B. Browne); *Nathanael West: The Cheaters and the Cheated*, 1973; *Remembering James Agee*, 1974; *Creative Choices: A Spectrum of Quality and Technique in Fiction*, 1975; *Studies in the Short Story*, 1975 (with Virgil Scott); *Rediscoveries II*, 1988 (with Peggy Bach); *Classics of Civil War Fiction*, 1988 (with Bach); *Eight Classic American Novels*, 1989; *The World of Fiction*, 1989; *A Pocketful of Prose: Contemporary Short Fiction*, 1991; *A Pocketful of Prose: Vintage Short Fiction*, 1992; *Critical Essays on Thomas Berger*, 1995; *A Pocketful of Poems: Vintage Verse*, 1996; *A Pocketful of Plays: Vintage Drama*, 1996; *Remembering James Agee*, 1997 (with Jeffrey J. Folks).

BIBLIOGRAPHY

Bach, Peggy. "The Theatrical Image." *The Southern Quarterly* 33 (Winter/Spring, 1995): 215-226. In this article, Madden offers his views on the adaptation of works of southern novelists to the stage and screen.

Madden, David. Interview by Ruth Laney. *Southern Review* 11 (Winter, 1975): 167-180. This lengthy discussion with Madden during the second decade of his literary career explains much about his sources of inspiration, particularly his debt to folk tradition and popular culture.

_____. "Let Me Tell You the Story: Transforming Oral Tradition." *Appalachian Journal* 7 (1980): 210-229. Madden describes the influence of the southern tradition of storytelling on his own developing imagination during his childhood years and explains how oral anecdotes develop into the written works of a conscious artist.

_____. "True Believers, Atheists, and Agnostics." Introduction to *American Dreams, American Nightmares*, edited by David Madden. Carbondale: Southern Illinois University Press, 1970. Madden explains his analysis of American literature, which like American life he sees as strongly influenced by the ideal called the "American Dream." In addition to those who embrace the dream and those who bitterly reject it, there are some who are preoccupied with the ironic difference beween the ideal and the reality. The ideas expressed in this critical work are evident in Madden's own fiction.

Morrow, Mark. "David Madden." In *Images of the Southern Writer*. Athens: University of Georgia Press, 1985. Morrow's one-page report of his visit with Madden at his Baton Rouge home includes Madden's own comments on the influences which shaped his work, both events in his life and his historical and literary heroes. Opposite the interview is a full-page portrait of Madden in his library.

Pinsker, Sanford. "The Mixed Chords of David Madden's *Cassandra Singing*." *Critique* 15 (1973): 15-26. In this interesting essay, Pinsker deals with the common perception of Madden as a brilliant writer who is, however, too undisciplined to produce the effects of which he is capable. Pinsker points out the ironic meanings which have been deliberately achieved in *Cassandra Singing*.

Richards, Jeffrey. "David Madden." In *Contemporary Poets, Dramatists, Essayists, and Novelists of the South*. Westport, Conn.: Greenwood Press, 1994. In this profile of Madden, Richards examines the recurring themes of the author and notes that his diversity has not always served him well in being accepted as a serious writer of fiction.

Schott, Webster. "Stories Within Stories." *The Washington Post Book World* (January 6, 1980): 9. Schott finds that Madden's novel *Pleasure-Dome* suffers from his preoccupation with the subject of his own craft, which causes him to digress, seemingly to admire his own art. Despite the defects in plotting, Schott finds the work intellectually stimulating.

NAGUIB MAHFOUZ

Born: Cairo, Egypt; December 11, 1911

PRINCIPAL LONG FICTION

'Abath al-Aqdār, 1939
Khān al-Khalīli, 1945
Zuqāq al-Midaqq, 1947 (*Midaq Alley*, 1966, revised 1975)
Bidāya wa-nihāya, 1949 (*The Beginning and the End*, 1951)

Bayn al-qaṣrayn, 1956 (*Palace Walk*, 1990)
Qaṣr al-shawq, 1957 (*Palace of Desire*, 1991)
Al-Sukkariya, 1957 (*Sugar Street*, 1992; previous 3 titles collectively known as *Al-Thulāthiya* [*The Trilogy*])
Awlād Ḥāratinā, 1959 serial, 1967 book (*Children of Gebelawi*, 1981, also known as *Children of the Alley*, 1996)
Al-Liṣ wa-al-kilāb, 1961 (*The Thief and the Dogs*, 1984)
Al-Summān wa-al-kharīf, 1962 (*Autumn Quail*, 1985)
Al-Ṭarīq, 1964 (*The Search*, 1987)
Al-Shaḥḥādh, 1965 (*The Beggar*, 1986)
Tharthara fawq al-Nīl, 1966 (*Adrift on the Nile*, 1993)
Mirāmār, 1967 (*Miramar*, 1978)
Al-Marāya, 1972 (*Mirrors*, 1977)
Al-Karnak, 1974 (*Karnak*, 1979)
Ḥikāyāt Ḥāratinā, 1975 (*The Fountain and the Tomb*, 1988)
Ḥaḍrat al-muḥtaram, 1975 (*Respected Sir*, 1986)
Malḥamat al-ḥarāfīsh, 1977 (*The Harafish*, 1994)
Afrāḥ al-qubbah, 1981 (*Wedding Song*, 1984)
Layāṣī alf Laylah, 1982 (*Arabian Nights and Days*, 1995)
Yawm Qutila al-Zaʿīm, 1985 (*The Day the Leader Was Killed*, 1989)

OTHER LITERARY FORMS

Naguib Mahfouz is primarily known for his long fiction, although he wrote many short stories and some one-act plays, five of which he published with collections of his short stories in *Taḥt al-maẓalla* (1967). His first publication was a translation into Arabic from English, *Miṣr al-Qadīmah* (1931), of James Baikie's *Ancient Egypt* (1912). Mahfouz also published numerous pieces of popular journalism and his memoirs, including *Echoes of an Autobiography* in 1997.

ACHIEVEMENTS

In 1988 Mahfouz received the Nobel Prize in Literature, and he was cited by the Swedish Academy for works that are richly realistic. In 1989 he received

Qadri murders his brother Humam, Adham is forgiven in a dream by Gabalawi. In the second tale, Gabal (a Moses-like figure) kills a henchman of Overseer, his foster father, and flees into the desert, where a snake charmer gives Gabal his daughter in marriage. Gabal returns home, and Gabalawi commands Gabal to oppose injustice. Gabal charms snakes away and becomes a lawgiver.

The Jesus-like Rifaa disappears into the desert to avoid marriage and returns, after a conversation with Gabalawi, preaching mercy. He protects a prostitute from a mob and then marries her. He acquires a reputation as a healer, but he is clubbed to death by gangsters and buried in the desert. There are rumors of his resurrection. The hero of the fourth tale is Qassem, who resembles the Prophet Muhammad. He is visited by a servant of Gabalawi, telling Qassem to bring justice to his people. He organizes athletic clubs to attract young men from the outcast tribe of Desert Rats, who train for combat; then he leads his men to overcome Overseer and establish peace. Arafa, a magician-scientist, and his brother Hanash arrive in the alley to avenge the death of their mother. Arafa steals into the house of Gabalawi and accidentally kills a servant, causing Gabalawi to die of shock. Arafa searches for magic to bring Gabalawi back to life. Arafa is summoned by Overseer, who forces him to share a bottle of explosive powder that Arafa has invented, but Arafa is kidnapped and buried alive in the desert, while his brother tries to protect the formula for the magic powder.

THE THIEF AND THE DOGS

The Thief and the Dogs alternates between interior monologues of the obsessed thief, Said Mahran, and objective descriptions of events in the days of his life after he is released from prison. Seeking revenge against his former friend and his former wife, he goes to the Sufi Sheikh Ali al-Junaydi, who gives him aid and religious advice. Then Said searches for an old political comrade, journalist Rauf Ilwan, who tells Said to find a job. Said attempts to rob Rauf's home, but he is caught and thrown into the night. He obtains a gun and meets Nur, a prostitute and old friend, who takes him into her home. Said kills a stranger whom he mistakes for the husband of his ex-wife. He

tries to kill Rauf, but again he kills the wrong man. The full fury of the police and public are launched, through Rauf's newspaper, to find and punish Said. He flees into a cemetery, and there, among the tombs, he is pursued by men and dogs; he opens fire and is cut down in a hail of bullets, raving at the dogs who have found him at last.

ARABIAN NIGHTS AND DAYS

Arabian Nights and Days is a retelling of the famous Arabic stories *The Arabian Nights' Entertainments* (fifteenth century). Sultan Shahriyar announces he will no longer kill virgins. Gamasa al-Bulti, the chief of police, captures a genie, Singam, while fishing, then watches himself being beheaded because the genie has put a double in his place. The real Gamasa has assumed the form of Abdullah the porter. He begins a holy war, murdering people in the government. Abdullah confesses his murders, is ordered to a lunatic asylum, and disappears. Sakhrabout and Zarmabaha, drunken genies, scheme against people for fun. Foolish people are saved by Abdullah the madman, and the sultan becomes more righteous as he stalks the night streets to learn truth.

Aladdin is falsely arrested, then executed unjustly. The sultan is tricked, through a mock trial, into recognizing this injustice. Genies give a magic cap of invisibility to Fadil Sanaan, who can do anything except what his conscience dictates; yet he must not commit evil. He promptly violates these conditions, enjoying his powers and harassing people throughout the city, before he returns the cap, confesses his sins, and boldly meets his death. After the cobbler, Marouf, learns the limits of powers from genies, the sultan appoints him governor, and Marouf appoints the madman as police chief. Sindbad the Sailor teaches the sultan moral lessons, and in the final tale the sultan abandons his throne and family and finds a great rock, which opens to admit him to a beautiful eternal bride. However, he cannot resist opening a door which says, Everything is clear except for this door. The door takes him back outside the rock, and he cannot return. In despair, he hears Abdullah the madman saying there is no path to truth, and so it cannot be attained, but it cannot be escaped.

Richard D. McGhee

OTHER MAJOR WORKS

SHORT FICTION: *Hams al-junūn*, c. 1948; *Dunyā Allāh*, 1963 (partial trans. *God's World*, 1973); *Bayt sayyi' al-sumᶜa*, 1965; *Khammārat al-qiṭṭ al-aswad*, 1968 (*The Tavern of the Black Cat*, 1976); *Hikaya bila bidaya wala nihaya*, 1971; *Al-Jarima*, 1973; *Al-Ḥubb fawqa haḍabat al-haram*, 1979; *Al-Shaytan Yaᶜiz*, 1979; *Ra'aytu ftmā yarā al-nā'im*, 1982; *Al-Tanẓīm al-sirri*, 1984; *Al-Fajr al-kādhib*, 1989; *The Time and the Place and Other Stories*, 1991.

PLAY: *One-Act Plays*, pb. 1989.

NONFICTION: *Asda' al-sirah al-dhatiyah*, 1995 (*Echoes of an Autobiography*, 1997).

TRANSLATION: *Miṣr al-Qadīmah*, 1931 (of James Baikie's *Ancient Egypt*).

MISCELLANEOUS: *Taḥta al-miẓallah*, 1967.

BIBLIOGRAPHY

Enani, M. M., ed. *Egyptian Perspectives on Naguib Mahfouz: A Collection of Critical Essays*. Cairo, Egypt: General Egyptian Book Organization, 1989. Local opinions of the author, translated from articles in Arabic which were published during the years of Mahfouz's early career.

el-Enany, Rasheed. *Naguib Mahfouz: The Pursuit of Meaning*. London: Routledge, 1993. Groups Mahfouz's novels according to their treatment of history, idealism, and episodic structural designs, with a detailed analysis of *Respected Sir* and one chapter dealing with short stories and plays.

Gordon, Haim. *Naguib Mahfouz's Egypt: Existential Themes in His Writings*. New York: Greenwood Press, 1990. Examines the impressionistic view of Egyptian society in the writings of Mahfouz.

Jad, Ali B. *Form and Technique in the Egyptian Novel, 1912-1971*. London: Ithaca Press, 1983. A comprehensive survey of the fiction of the period, with a brief study of Mahfouz in that context.

Mattityahu, Peled. *Religion My Own: The Literary Works of Najib Mahfuz*. New Brunswick, N.J.: Transaction Books, 1983. Analysis of the early historical novels and the context of Islamic beliefs.

Milson, Menahem. *Najib Mahfuz: The Novelist-Philosopher of Cairo*. New York: St. Martin's Press, 1998. Good for the beginning student of Mahfouz, this study offers insight into the works and life.

Somekh, Sasson. *The Changing Rhythm: A Study of Najib Mahfuz's Novels*. Leiden, The Netherlands: E. J. Brill, 1973. Provides a brief survey of Egyptian fiction as a basis for reading Mahfouz's novels. Several detailed analyses of the novels through the 1960's.

NORMAN MAILER

Born: Long Branch, New Jersey; January 31, 1923

PRINCIPAL LONG FICTION

The Naked and the Dead, 1948
Barbary Shore, 1951
The Deer Park, 1955
An American Dream, 1965
Why Are We in Vietnam?, 1967
The Armies of the Night: History as a Novel, the Novel as History, 1968
Marilyn, 1973
The Executioner's Song, 1979
Of Women and Their Elegance, 1980
Ancient Evenings, 1983
Tough Guys Don't Dance, 1984
Harlot's Ghost, 1991
Oswald's Tale: An American Mystery, 1995
The Gospel According to the Son, 1997

OTHER LITERARY FORMS

Beginning with *The Armies of the Night*, Norman Mailer published several works that cross the conventional boundaries of fiction and nonfiction: a "novel biography," *Marilyn*; a "true life novel," *The Executioner's Song*; and an "imaginary memoir," *Of Women and Their Elegance*. Because of his sophisticated handling of style, structure, point of view, and characterization, much of Mailer's journalism and reportage approaches the novel's complexity of language and form: *Miami and the Siege of Chicago: An Informal History of the Republican and Democratic*

(Library of Congress)

Conventions of 1968 (1969), *Of a Fire on the Moon* (1970), *The Prisoner of Sex* (1971), *St. George and the Godfather* (1972), and *The Fight* (1975). His essays, interviews, short stories, and poems have been collected in *Advertisements for Myself* (1959), *Deaths for the Ladies and Other Disasters* (1962), *The Presidential Papers* (1963), *Cannibals and Christians* (1966), *The Short Fiction of Norman Mailer* (1967), *The Idol and the Octopus: Political Writings on the Kennedy and Johnson Administrations* (1968), *Existential Errands* (1972), and *Pieces and Pontifications* (1982). His work in drama and literary criticism appears in *The Deer Park: A Play* (1967) and *Genius and Lust: A Journey Through the Major Writings of Henry Miller* (1976).

ACHIEVEMENTS

With the appearance of *The Naked and the Dead* in 1948, Mailer was hailed by many critics as one of the most promising writers of the postwar generation. Since his early acclaim, Mailer's reputation has risen and fallen repeatedly—in part because of the unevenness of his writing and in part because of his intense participation in the causes and quarrels of his age.

More important, however, his work has often been misunderstood because of its remarkably changing character and its innovative procedures, for Mailer relentlessly searches for the style and structure that can most effectively express his ambition to make "a revolution in the consciousness of our time."

By whatever standard Mailer is judged, it is clear that several of his books have a secure place not only in postwar literary history, but also in the canon of significant American literary achievements. *The Naked and the Dead* and *The Armies of the Night* continue to receive attention as masterpieces, and his other novels have begun to benefit from the serious exploration accorded to the finest works of fiction. *The Executioner's Song*—very favorably reviewed when it first appeared—may eventually rank with Mailer's greatest writing because it contains a complexity of point of view and characterization rivaled only by *The Naked and the Dead, An American Dream*, and *Why Are We in Vietnam?*

In addition to receiving several literary honors and distinctions—including the National Book Award, the Pulitzer Prize, and election to the National Institute of Arts and Letters—Mailer has been the subject of more than a dozen book-length studies and hundreds of articles. His work is an essential part of college syllabi in contemporary literature, not only because he has addressed crucial events, concerns, and institutions such as World War II, the Cold War, Hollywood, Vietnam, the Pentagon, and capital punishment, but also because he has treated all of his important themes in the light of a deeply imaginative conception of literary form. As Robert Merrill notes, far too many critics have treated Mailer's writing as simply a record of his opinions. They have taken his musings for assertions, and they have failed to see that he aims at conveying the "meaning" of characters and events with the fluidity of metaphor. What Mailer *imagines* rather than what he *believes* is important in assessing all of his prose—and what he imagines consists of entertaining several possible selves, and several sides of issues and events, simultaneously. In other words, he rejects fixity of thought in favor of the play of prose, which in turn parallels the complex play of characters and events.

BIOGRAPHY

Norman Mailer grew up in Brooklyn, New York, and attended Harvard University (1939-1943), where he studied aeronautical engineering and became interested in writing. After he was graduated from Harvard, he married Beatrice Silverman and was inducted into the U.S. Army, serving with the 112th Cavalry out of San Antonio, Texas. He was overseas for eighteen months in Leyte, Luzon, and with occupation forces in Japan. His varied experience as a Field Artillery surveyor, clerk, interpreter of aerial photographs, rifleman, and cook undoubtedly contributed to the comprehensive portrayal of the military in *The Naked and the Dead*.

After his discharge from the army in May, 1946, Mailer immediately began work on *The Naked and the Dead* and completed it within fifteen months. In the next two years (1948-1950), he traveled in Europe, studied at the Sorbonne, wrote articles and delivered speeches, campaigned for the election of Henry Wallace, worked briefly as a screenwriter in Hollywood, and finished his second novel, *Barbary Shore*, which was poorly received—in part because of his sympathetic engagement with Marxist ideas and his aggressive exploration of shifting political attitudes in the postwar years.

For the next ten years, Mailer was beset by various personal and professional traumas. He divorced his first wife—they had one daughter—in 1952. He married Adele Morales in 1954; he stabbed her with a penknife on November 19, 1960, after a party organized to launch his New York City mayoral campaign. The couple was divorced in 1962. During this period, Mailer had difficulty getting his third novel, *The Deer Park*, published, while he simultaneously struggled to complete another novel. After the births of his second and third daughters, Mailer married Lady Jeanne Campbell, who gave birth to his fourth daughter in 1962. With the publication of *Advertisements for Myself*, he began to find a way of rescuing the fragments and dead ends of his career, and with his essay "Superman Comes to the Supermarket" (1960), he evolved a supple way of dramatizing and musing on social and political issues that freed him from the constraints of his not entirely successful first-person narrators in *Barbary Shore* and *The Deer Park*.

In many ways, the 1960's were Mailer's most productive years. Not only did he publish his two most sophisticated novels, *An American Dream* and *Why Are We in Vietnam?*, and adapt *The Deer Park* for the stage, but also he directed and acted in three films—*Wild 90* (January, 1968), *Beyond the Law* (October, 1968), and *Maidstone* (1971)—which provoked him to write important essays on the nature of film and prepared him for his innovative "novel biography," *Marilyn*. He was an active journalist during this period, covering political conventions and the moon shot, and out of his reportage he created a book, *The Armies of the Night*, that transcends the immediate occasion of its conception—a protest march on the Pentagon—in order to probe the shaping processes of history and fiction and their mutuality as human constructs. In 1963, Mailer divorced Lady Jeanne Campbell and married the actress Beverly Bentley, with whom he had two sons. He campaigned unsuccessfully for mayor of New York City in 1969 and fathered a fifth daughter by Carol Stevens in 1971. He subsequently married and divorced her, taking Norris Church as his sixth wife.

In the 1970's and 1980's, Mailer continued to write nonfiction while working on his Egyptian novel, *Ancient Evenings*. Although he began in the mid-1970's to withdraw from public attention, his appearance in the film *Ragtime* (1981) and his defense of Jack Abbott, a writer-convict who committed a murder shortly after his release from prison, revived the image of a controversial, embattled author. As several reviewers pointed out, both *Ancient Evenings* and *Tough Guys Don't Dance* have first-person narrators who bear considerable resemblance to Mailer. His controversial tenure as president of the U.S. chapter of PEN (Association of Poets, Playwrights, Editors, Essayists, and Novelists), along with the film of *Tough Guys Don't Dance*, which Mailer wrote and directed, once again focused public attention on him.

In the 1990's, Mailer produced three very different books, none of which seemed to enhance his reputation. *Harlot's Ghost*, a very long novel, is a comto be so familiar, so easily apprehended, is elusive, strange, and terrifying.

THE DEER PARK

It is not difficult to regard Mailer's third novel, *The Deer Park*, as a mature rewriting of *Barbary Shore*. Once again, there is a first-person narrator, Sergius O'Shaugnessy, who, like Lovett, is a writer. Although Sergius knows his past, he is an orphan who shares Lovett's sense of uncertainty: "I was never sure of myself. I never felt as if I came from any particular place, or that I was like other people." His feeling of being like a "spy or a fake" recalls Lovett's adamant refusal to become a spy for Guinevere. Sergius, however, is more self-aware, more active as a writer in this novel than Lovett is in *Barbary Shore*, where his writing is a given but is not really explored. *The Deer Park*, on the other hand, is the product of Sergius's imagination; it represents his coming to terms with himself and the world. Although his friendship with Charles Eitel, a blacklisted Hollywood scriptwriter and director, is reminiscent of Lovett's friendship with McLeod, Eitel's story is framed in Sergius's words; Sergius contrasts Eitel's defeat with his victory.

Cold War politics play just as important a part in *The Deer Park* as in *Barbary Shore*, but the former eschews the strained allegorical rhetoric of the latter. Some of *The Deer Park*'s finest passages are the dialogues of Hollywood studio executives and politicians, in which the exploitative aspects of capitalist culture and government become apparent in the language, even in the physical gestures and tones of voice the characters employ, so that Mailer avoids merely talking *about* political issues by demonstrating how they arise in careers such as Eitel's. He has been a Communist sympathizer, a fellow traveler, whose presence embarrasses his motion-picture bosses. He then alienates them by refusing to cooperate with a congressional committee investigating subversives. Eitel turns from Hollywood with the hope that he can recover his talent honestly as an artist but finds that the great film he had always dreamed of creating has been corrupted by his absorption of the cheap techniques of commercial filmmaking. Eventually, he capitulates by agreeing to testify about his Communist past and to construct his film according to Hollywood conventions.

At the same time, Sergius's own life story—from orphan to war hero—draws Hollywood interest, and he is sorely tempted to sell his biography—sell himself, in effect—to the studio, where he may also become a film star. What prevents him from doing so is Eitel's example, or rather Sergius's interpretation of Eitel's biography, for at the end of the novel it is Sergius who has made some meaning out of Eitel's career:

> "For you see," [Eitel] confessed in his mind, "I have lost the final desire of the artist, the desire which tells us that when all else is lost, when love is lost and adventure, pride of self, and pity, there still remains that world we may create, more real to us, more real to others, then the mummery of what happens, passes, and is gone."

Sergius goes on to imagine that Eitel equates the creative act with Sergius's rebellion, with "the small trumpet of your defiance."

Sergius invents an Eitel from whom he can learn, and his lessons are facilitated by his relationships with many of Eitel's friends and lovers. Lulu Meyers, for example, has been married to Eitel but now is free to engage in an affair with Sergius, which eventually terminates, much to his despair. Sergius, however, avoids the extremes of self-pity and self-aggrandizement by reconstructing the affair between Elena Esposito and Eitel that is taking place during his pursuit of Lulu. Eitel's coldness, arrogance, and self-deceptiveness come through in Sergius's version of the affair, but, like McLeod, Eitel is essentially a sympathetic figure and more believably so than McLeod, since Eitel's tragic realization of his limitations is not muffled by the slightest self-justification at the end of the novel.

If the novel's Hollywood milieu is like Louis XV's Deer Park, that gorge in which innocents like Sergius are engulfed, Sergius barely escapes the gorge by imagining for himself the lives of its victims, of its pimps and prostitutes, of its sultans and sycophants. If *Barbary Shore* begins to put the first-person narrator, the writer as actor, in a paramount position, then *The Deer Park* examines the drama of that position, which Mailer directly comments on in *Advertisements for Myself*, where he acknowledges the increasingly autobiographical nature of his narrators. Not that Sergius is in any simple way Mailer— in fact, he is far less self-conscious about his style than Mailer usually is—but Sergius's quest as a writer who needs to find his words, his style, through direct involvement that tests him against his characters' actions, provided Mailer with the conception of himself and the process of literary creation that has become central to nearly all of his work. Indeed, the process of literary creation itself becomes his theme. In other words, the writer himself becomes his subject.

AN AMERICAN DREAM

An American Dream, by its very title, points to Mailer's fascination with the notion that America is a complex fiction, a drama of reality that is captured in the dynamic language of its narrator, Steven Rojack, Mailer's hipster hero *par excellence*, a war hero, a college chum of John Kennedy, a congressman, college professor, psychologist, television personality, and actor resembling the Sergius O'Shaugnessy who was supposed to be the major figure in Mailer's uncompleted novel, delivered in the form of "Advertisement for Myself on the Way Out" at the conclusion of *Advertisements for Myself.*

Rojack is also the first Mailer narrator to have an intellect, a vocabulary, and a multiplicity of roles that are commensurate with his author's own activities as soldier, writer, politician, film director, actor, and television personality. As a result, Rojack, like Mailer, registers and revalues his experience. Like his creator, he is never content with a single formulation of reality; on the contrary, he is a complex of shifting moods in response to the modulations of his environment. As Jennifer Bailey phrases it, in Mailer's mature work "identity is always a fiction insofar as it depends upon a constantly changing milieu for its definition."

All of Rojack's actions have to be viewed within the existential requirements of reality in the novel rather than within rigid moral codes applied by readers who want to keep "concepts firmly in category." For some readers, the novel's sense of absolute rela-

tivity, of moral fluidity, is repugnant, and *An American Dream* has been rejected out of hand as Mailer's most disturbing work, since Rojack as hipster does not merely live close to violence: He purges and cleanses himself through murdering his wife, Deborah.

In conventional fiction, Rojack's murder might be taken as the surest sign that he has lost control of himself. Yet, quite the contrary is true in Mailer's daring fiction, for Rojack regains possession of himself in committing his crime. In some of his most sharply driven, economical prose, Mailer has Rojack explain in the first chapter that he doubts his perception of the world in terms of a rational paradigm. He notes that "the real difference between the President and myself may be that I ended with too large an appreciation of the moon, for I looked down the abyss of the first night I killed: four men, four very separate Germans, dead under a full moon—whereas Jack, for all I know, never saw the abyss." In other words, Rojack senses the occult nature of reality, of forces that terrorize him until he has the courage to act in harmony with them.

Until he reached a point of self-identification, Rojack "remained an actor. My personality was built upon a void." He quit politics "before I was separated from myself forever by the distance between my public appearance which had become vital on television, indeed nearly robust, and my secret frightened romance with the phases of the moon." Virtually the entire novel is written in a style that dramatizes Rojack's search for a new basis on which to live. After considering suicide, after literally expelling from his system the rotting, half-digested food and drink that signify a life he cannot ingest, he confronts his estranged wife, "an artist with the needle," a woman from an influential family who has represented his "leverage" on life. Doing away with Deborah means confronting his case by himself, and he has never had "the strength to stand alone."

Rojack begins to stand alone by following the hipster's course set out in *The White Negro* (1957). He recognizes, in the words of that essay, that "one must grow or else pay more for remaining the same (pay in sickness, or depression, or anguish for the lost opportunity), but pay or grow. . . . What he must do . . .

ing, Mailer had finally become a Harvard dean and could be addressed by the appropriate limb. "I'm delighted because I liked *your* speech so much."

By using circular dialogue, the search for an agreeable exchange between very different personalities—Lowell, "at once virile and patrician," and Mailer, "the younger, presumptive, and self-elected prince"—they have made a story of their relationship which they can share and repeat. The fictive quality of real events—one of Mailer's major points—is ably demonstrated by his own style. As Mailer says before this dialogue, "the clue to discovery was not in the substance of one's idea, but in what was learned from the style of one's attack."

The book shuttles from such intimate dialogue and precise character delineation to panoramic sweeps of the crowds of the Pentagon march. Book 1, "History as a Novel," portrays Mailer as actor in order to show that history is understood only through a deep appreciation of the intersection of very personal feelings and public affairs. No episode, no idea, no impression remains unqualified by the circumstances out of which it arises, and chapter titles constantly emphasize the way in which the literary imagination shapes historical experience.

Book 2, "The Novel as History," goes even further than book 1 in suggesting that history as a whole can make sense only when the interpreter employs all the "instincts of the novelist," for the record of the march is contradictory, fragmentary, and skewed by various viewpoints. Only an act of profound imagination, a reading of the significance of the event itself, can possibly make its constituent parts coalesce, and Mailer convincingly shows that he has studied the record and found it wanting. History is essentially interior and intuitive, he avers. He then proceeds to elaborate a complex recreation of events that concretely exposes the factitiousness of newspaper accounts.

Beyond the immediate causes and consequences of the march on the Pentagon, Mailer sees the event as a rite of passage for the young marchers, especially the ones who refuse to flee when their fellows are brutally beaten into submission in one of the most riveting and frightening pages in all of Mailer's writ-

ing. The coming of knowledge, of a historical fatalism, creeps into both Mailer's prose and his characters' weary postures as he recites events from America's past which reveal that it was founded on a rite of passage. It is as if these young people are suddenly imbued with historical consciousness, although Mailer's ruminations and their agony are kept separate on the page. Nevertheless, in his coda he suggests that if the march's end took place in the "isolation in which these last pacifists suffered naked in freezing cells, and gave up prayers for penance, then who was to say they were not saints? And who to say that the sins of America were not by their witness a tithe remitted?" His final words balance an earlier passage where he describes the marchers' opponents, "the gang of Marshals" who in their "collective spirit" emit "little which was good," and one of whom "paid tithe to ten parallel deep lines rising in ridges above his eye brows." Mailer achieves a harmony of form and an equilibrium of language that make the novel's ending seem as complex as the history it imagines, and as moving in its depiction of ignorance and confusion as the Matthew Arnold poem, "Dover Beach," from which Mailer's title is taken.

MARILYN

While they are satisfactory in sections, *Of a Fire on the Moon*, *The Fight*, and Mailer's other writings from the late 1960's to the mid-1970's do not equal *Marilyn*, his follow-up study of the ambiguities of fiction and history so magnificently explored in *The Armies of the Night*. *Marilyn* has a twofold purpose: to measure faithfully and evaluate the obstacles that bar the biographer's way to a full understanding of his subject's life, and to suggest tentatively a biographical method which will aim at re-creating the whole person even though conceding that the search for wholeness is elusive and problematical.

Furthermore, Monroe ranks with Mailer's other major characters, such as General Cummings. Just as Cummings works to make himself an instrument of his own policy, so Monroe paints herself into the camera lens as an instrument of her own will. She is Napoleonic and yet divided against herself, a Dreiserian character who traverses the continent in quest of her true self in much the same way as Lovett,

O'Shaugnessy, and Rojack do, detecting voids in themselves and voyaging to find their genuine identities. Much of Mailer's work in film, and his discussions of film in "Some Dirt in the Talk" and "A Course in Film-Making" (both collected in *Existential Errands*), lead directly to his perception of Monroe's disrupted sense of self. Although his later "imaginary memoir," *Of Women and Their Elegance*, in which Monroe recalls her last years, seems less substantial than *Marilyn*, he carries his concern with "twin personalities" a step further by integrating his narrative with Milton Greene's provocative photographs, which are studies in the doubling of personality in a divided world.

THE EXECUTIONER'S SONG

Set against the background of his reflexive writing of the 1960's and 1970's, *The Executioner's Song*, Mailer's next major work of fiction, is a startling book. Its sentences are simple and clear, with an occasionally striking but not elaborate metaphor. Absent from the narrative is Mailer's characteristic sentence or paragraph, which is long and comprehensive—an encyclopedic attempt to gather all of reality in one magnificent statement. There is no intrusive voice to sum up the life of Gary Gilmore, a convicted and executed murderer, and the age in which Gilmore grows to kill. Mailer does not explicitly explore a theory of biography and does not comment, except in his afterword, on his interaction with the life he has written. His book seems keyed to a new aesthetic.

In spite of its 1,056 pages, *The Executioner's Song* is not a garrulous work; it is a quiet book punctuated by myriad silences. There is a double space following nearly every paragraph of the book, indicating the gap between events, the momentary pause that intervenes even in events that seemingly follow one another swiftly and smoothly. Reality is defined by these frequent intervals of silence, periods of stillness that intimate how much is left unsaid and how many characters fail to connect with one another. Gilmore is the most solitary character of all, cut off in large part from humanity and therefore able to murder.

A great deal of the book is dialogue or paraphrase of dialogue, which enhances the dramatic clash of details and conflicting points of view. Even the long descriptive passages and the evocations of characters' thoughts consist only of the results of the reporter who has interviewed these characters for their thoughts and who conveys what he has heard and observed. Hence, there is no privileged retrospective narrator to unify the book's disparate materials.

Mailer has called *The Executioner's Song* a "true life novel." By "novel" he seems to mean something somewhat different from his use of the term in *The Armies of the Night* and *Marilyn*, in which he employs a novelistic narrator to probe the unspoken motivations of his characters and to organize reality in creative metaphors. Of his unusual departure from past practice he remarks in *The New York Times Magazine* (September 9, 1979):

> I was convinced from the start that the materials were exceptional; it had the structure of a novel. Whenever I needed a character for esthetic balance—a new character of imposing dimensions—one just appeared out of nowhere. If I had conceived *The Executioner's Song* as a novel entirely drawn from my own imagination, I doubt I could have improved on those characters.

Mailer conceives of the characters as revealing themselves to him, so that he does not have to serve as a mediating voice. Instead, he orchestrates their disclosures by surrounding them with a quiet space and spare style that preserves their individual integrity.

Reading such sparely created scenes, one is tempted to comb through the details over and over again in order to search for the pertinent clue that will point to the meaning of Gilmore's story, but as Joan Didion points out in her review in *The New York Times Book Review* (October 7, 1979), "the very subject of *The Executioner's Song* is that vast emptiness at the center of the Western experience, a nihilism antithetical not only to literature but to most other forms of human endeavor, a dread so close to zero that human voices fade out, trail off, like skywriting." Mailer has chosen, this time, to make a literature that is articulately mute, almost muzzled in its restrained revelations of actions which remain voiceless, dumb, and frighteningly uncommunicative:

> "Why'd you do it, Gary?" Nielsen asked again quietly.
> "I don't know," Gary said.

"Are you sure?"

"I'm not going to talk about that," Gilmore said. He shook his head delicately, and looked at Nielsen, and said, "I can't keep up with life."

For Mailer, *The Executioner's Song* is biography in a new key, since he attends to the integrity of individual lives without quickly elevating those lives into symbolic significance. At the same time, the continuity of his concerns is apparent in his ambitious desire to show that true life must be mediated through the imaginative power of a singular intelligence. He understood that *The Executioner's Song* required a voice, flexible and comprehensive, in order to embody the myriad voices that make up reality. There are patterns that can be perceived on rereading the book, yet no single pattern is definitive. Gilmore seems to reach some genuine self-understanding and consistency, but his behavior is still sometimes contradictory and enigmatic. He approaches his execution wanting to die, and yet he searches for every possible means of escape. *The Executioner's Song* remains faithful to the elusiveness of self, to both the revelation and the inscrutability of identity.

ANCIENT EVENINGS

Beginning with the opening sentence—"Crude thoughts and fierce forces are my state"—*Ancient Evenings* embarks on a style that is new to Mailer and to his readers who have been accustomed to an active voice transforming everything it articulates. Something very strange is happening to the passive voice of the novel's first narrator-protagonist, the ka (spiritual emanation) of Menenhetet II, who is undergoing the process of rebirth. The first book of the novel is awesome and quite wonderful in its depiction of a consciousness trying to differentiate itself from all that surrounds it.

After the first book, much of the novel is narrated by Menenhetet I, the great-grandfather of Menenhetet II. Menenhetet I is the great ancestor who has been able to live four lives (1290-1100 B.C.E.) by learning how to ejaculate into a woman at the very moment of his death, thereby conceiving himself anew in a lover who becomes his mother. Menenhetet I aspires in his first life to supplant his Pharaoh as ruler of Egypt and dies in the act of sexual intercourse with the Pharaoh's queen. Menenhetet I carries Mailer's conception of himself and of the hero in his fiction to the farthest extreme: He is a man of many ages, the self-invented avatar of Menenhetet II's quest for distinction. Menenhetet I has been a warrior and high priest, a scholar and man of action, a great lover of queens and yet a farmer of peasant origin. In his fourth life, Menenhetet I would like to be the vizier of Ramses IX (Ptahnem-hotep). In the very act of telling his four life histories to Ramses IX, however, Menenhetet I reveals an overweening ambition and fatal attraction to magical practices (including the repulsive eating of bat dung) that disqualify him for the role of Pharaonic confidant.

Ancient Evenings is embedded in the lush details of ancient Egypt, in the rhythms of an alien time. Even sympathetic readers have noted a numbing sameness in the prose that suggests that the author has striven too hard for unity, for the merging of the opposites that create so much exciting tension in *The Naked and the Dead, The Armies of the Night,* and *The Executioner's Song. Ancient Evenings* is Norman Mailer at his neatest, with the loose ends of his philosophy and his prose knit together rather impressively. Nevertheless, it seems static and too thoroughly thought-out; absent from it is the rough-edged stimulation of a writer on the make, who is best when he is suggestive rather than explicit, when he is promising to complete the circle and join the halves without ever quite doing so.

TOUGH GUYS DON'T DANCE

Like Mikey Lovett in *Barbary Shore,* Tim Madden in *Tough Guys Don't Dance* is an amnesiac: He cannot remember what happened the night before, and he cannot account for the large amount of blood on his car seat. He is clearly kin to Stephen Rojack. More or less kept by his prized wife, the wealthy Patty Lareine, Madden, a writer, finds that he cannot work when she deserts him.

As her name suggests, Lareine has been Madden's imperious queen, and he seems at a loss when he is not in the service of his "medieval lady." At the same time, he has clearly chafed under her rule, for he regrets having broken his code of male self-sufficiency.

As a result, the couple's marriage has been turbulent, and in its later stages, husband and wife seem most alike in their murderous inclinations. The novel begins with Madden wondering whether the severed head he discovers in his marijuana hideaway is the result of a drunken evening's debauchery with another woman, which turned violent when Patty Lareine returned home.

The characters in *Tough Guys Don't Dance* relate to one another as in an Arthurian romance. Madden discovers that his wife has had another lover, the Deputy Police Chief, Alvin Luther Regency, a powerfully built, maniacal rival, who is part of the plot to set up Madden (who has already served a short term for possession of cocaine). Complicating matters further for Madden is the lurking presence of his envious former schoolmate, Meeks Wardly Hilby III, who was once married to Patty Lareine and from whom Madden stole her. If Madden can make sense of the two murders, he can also begin to put his life back together—including his failed relationship with Madeleine Falco, his witty, tough counterpart, who left him when he took up with Patty Lareine and who now finds herself mired in a bad marriage to the dangerous Regency.

Readers who prefer murder mysteries with taut, spare plots and prose may bristle at the complications of Mailer's syntax and philosophizing. The heads and bodies buried in different locations are indicative of the splits in the human psyche that Mailer has pursued in much of his writing. Usually Mailer is able to finesse the shifts between the novel's ideas and events, and his delineation of characters through clipped dialogue is convincing. At a few points, his narrative flags, perhaps because he has tried to do too much, to integrate characters, ideas, and plot simultaneously in a single narrative voice.

HARLOT'S GHOST

Harlot's Ghost is a mammoth and intermittently gripping novel of the CIA, charting the career of Harry Hubbard, protégé of the legendary Hugh Tremont Montague ("Harlot"), and a key participant in CIA operations in Berlin, Uruguay, Washington, D.C., Miami, and Cuba. The novel is based on a close reading of nearly one hundred books about the organization and on Mailer's vivid imagination, which often calls upon themes and characters he has rehearsed in several works of fiction and nonfiction, including speculations on the murder of Marilyn Monroe, Ernest Hemingway's suicide, and the nature of Cuban leader Fidel Castro's heroism.

Mailer's thesis is that a CIA operative is by definition a deceiver, a person who is always playing more than one role, an actor whose sense of reality is constantly shifting, making it difficult to maintain loyalties and friendships, never sure of his or her own ground. Harry Hubbard, the son of a fabled CIA agent, worries that he is not "tough enough" and takes on risky ventures such as the Bay of Pigs fiasco. As a matter of survival within the agency, he finds himself acting as a double agent—at one point reporting to both his mentor, Harlot, and to his father, Cal.

Through Harry's letters, diaries, and first-person narrative, Mailer manages to cover most of the dramatic events involving the CIA from 1955 to 1963. This very long novel (near thirteen hundred pages) is burdened with too much learning and too little plot—no detail is too trivial to include as long as it impinges on Harry's consciousness. There are some wonderfully realized characters (E. Howard Hunt and William King Harvey), but they do not quite redeem Mailer's turgid prose.

THE GOSPEL ACCORDING TO THE SON

By contrast, *The Gospel According to the Son* is a restrained retelling of the Christ story from Christ's point of view. Mailer successfully finds a voice quite different from his own for the first-person narrator. Christ is portrayed as very much of a man—driven by his divine mission but also doubting his ability to carry it out. Christ often compares himself to Moses, another reluctant prophet who feared he was not worthy of the Lord's trust.

Mailer's Christ gently but firmly takes issue with certain aspects of the gospels. He is a miracle worker, yet he notes how often accounts of his powers have been exaggerated—the projections of those who fervently believe in him. Mailer ingeniously accounts for many of Christ's most famous sayings, such as "Render unto Caesar the things that are Caesar's."

placed and alienated as the Jewish ones. He received numerous awards for his fiction, including two National Book Awards and a Pulitzer Prize.

Biography

Bernard Malamud was born in Brooklyn to Russian immigrant parents. His father, like Morris Bober in *The Assistant*, was a small grocer, and the family moved around Brooklyn as business dictated. When Malamud was nine years old, he had pneumonia and began a period of intensive reading. Later, encouraged by his teachers, he also began writing short stories.

From 1932 to 1936, Malamud was a student at the City College of New York. He later began work on an M.A. at Columbia University, and, while teaching night school at Erasmus Hall, his own alma mater, he started writing in earnest. He married Ann de Chiara in 1945, and four years later, he and his family moved to Corvallis, Oregon, where for twelve years Malamud taught English at Oregon State. A son was born before he left for Corvallis, a daughter after he arrived. While there, he published his first three books; after leaving, he wrote his satire of academic life in an English department, *A New Life*. Returning to the East in 1961, Malamud taught for many years at Bennington College in Vermont. He died in New York on March 18, 1986.

Analysis

In *The Natural*, Iris Lemon tells the protagonist that all people have two lives, "the life we learn with and the life we live with after that. Suffering is what brings us toward happiness." Although her statement requires qualification, it is a suggestive summary of the major theme of Bernard Malamud's work: the journey toward a new life, a journey marked by suffering, which may or may not be redemptive. In fact, however, Malamud's characters usually have three lives: one from which they have not learned and which they are attempting to leave behind, a life the reader sees in flashbacks and confessions as well as in brief opening scenes; a middle life, the learning life, which is the substance of the books; and the new life promised to successful characters at the end. Malamud's novels, then, are in the tradition of the

Bildungsroman, but they have older protagonists than do most American novels of education. What Malamud depicts in each of his novels is a renewed attempt to find new life and to convert suffering to meaning, a second journey toward knowledge.

Of the old life, Malamud usually shows his readers little. *The Natural* opens with a brief pregame sketch that quickly shows Roy Hobbs's past. In *The Assistant*, the reader sees the robbery for which Frankie Alpine will try to atone, and in *The Fixer*, there is a short portrait of Yakov Bok's past in his village. Malamud's characters are trying to forget the past, so even when it enters their minds, they try to shove it away. Moreover, Malamud's novels usually begin with a journey away from a past life. Whether European Jews coming to America or moving from their *shtetl* to Kiev, or whether American Jews traveling from New York to Oregon or baseball players leaving the country for the big city, Malamud's protagonists are always travelers, uneasy with their past, uncertain of their future. In fact, they often try to conceal their past: Alpine and Hobbs work conscientiously to obliterate the stories of their earlier lives. Yakov Bok drops his prayer things, a reminder of his old life and its ways, into a river. One of Malamud's most frequent devices is to have characters change their names in an attempt to escape their past identity. Bok, trying to pass as a Gentile, becomes Yakov Ivanovitch Dologushev, his initials ironically spelling "yid."

What all of Malamud's characters must learn, however, is that they have to accept responsibility for their past actions. Paradoxically, while the evil that his characters have done remains with them and so must be acknowledged, the good can be erased. At the end of *The Natural*, Roy Hobbs, a failure in his quest for a new life, discovers that for his part in throwing the league playoffs, all of his baseball records will be expunged from the record books.

The journey is always a quest, as the mythological base of *The Natural*, Malamud's first and prototypal novel, makes clear. The public part of the quest takes place in the world of men, and its lesson is that of law, of the inner check, of renunciation. Hobbs is a natural hitter, but he lacks good judgment, both on the field and off. Frankie Alpine in *The Assistant* continually steals from Morris Bober. Saving Bober's daughter Helen from being raped, he is unable to control his own sexual appetite and rapes her himself. "Why do Jews suffer so much?" he asks Morris Bober, and after replying that to live is to suffer, Morris adds, "I think if a Jew don't suffer for the Law, he will suffer for nothing." Although Alpine is not yet a Jew, he does suffer for nothing.

Acceptance of the law, curbing one's appetite, is the first lesson. As Levin thinks in *A New Life*, "Renunciation was what he was now engaged in. It was a beginning that created a beginning." Yet law alone is not enough, and Malamud's questers must pass a second test as well for their journeys to be successful: the test of love, of dream, of acceptance of life in its fullness and ambiguity. Helen Bober could marry Nat Pearl, studying to be a lawyer but lacking dreams, or she could choose Louis Karp, pure appetite, lacking law. She chooses neither, and at the novel's conclusion a chance remains for Frankie Alpine, who is learning what W. H. Auden calls a "law like love." In *A New Life*, Levin first picks up Henry James's *The American* (1876-1877), a book that makes a case for renunciation, but Pauline Gilley, another man's wife whom Levin first renounces but later accepts, moves the discussion to William Dean Howells, who, like Malamud, prefers the economy of pain.

Another qualification to Iris Lemon's statement is necessary: Suffering is what *may* bring one toward happiness. The quest is not successful for all of Malamud's characters. Many of them, already displaced from their European homelands, refuse to undertake another journey. Others learn the wrong lesson from their old life. "*Rachmones*, we say in Hebrew," says Yakov Bok. "Mercy, one oughtn't to forget it." Many, particularly women (there are no Jewish mothers in Malamud), do forget it and harden their hearts. Still others, having undertaken the journey, are, like Roy Hobbs, too selfish ever to move beyond themselves.

Not only do Malamud's novels tell and retell the same story, but they do so with similar casts and with the same images. The protagonist is typically without a close family, sometimes orphaned. He is often a *schlemiel* or a *schlemazl*, always wanting to escape his past, but unlucky and clumsy in the attempt. He is likely to be self-deceived. Early in *The Assistant*, while still stealing, Alpine tells himself that he is "an honest guy." Later he says, "Even when I am bad I am good," inaccurately viewing himself as a man of stern morality.

Especially in the early novels and short stories, there is a father figure, and the learning relationship is dramatized in terms of an apprenticeship. These figures become less important in the later novels. By *A New Life*, a transitional book, both would-be father figures, the inane Fairchild and the more scholarly but weak Fabrikant, are failures. After *A New Life*, the questers are orphaned even in this middle life.

Malamud also makes frequent use of the double, figures both actual and dreamed. Roy and Bump Baily, the player he replaces, are identified with each other: They share the same girl and the same fault. Frankie Alpine enacts in his dreams the crimes Ward Minogue, his darker opposite, actually commits. In *The Tenants*, Harry Lesser and Willie Spearmint (born Bill Spear—blacks also change names in Malamud) act out the common racial stereotypes, reverse them, and then destroy each other's work and life. An image from William Shakespeare's *King Lear* (1605-1606), each as the other's shadow, dominates the book.

Women in Malamud's work are of two types: the dark ladies (Memo Paris, who betrays Roy Hobbs, and Harriet Bird, who shoots him; Avis Fliss, who spies on Levin; and Zenaida, who gives false testimony against Bok) and the potentially redemptive ladies of the lake (Iris Lemon, Helen Bober, Pauline Gilley, Fanny Bick in *Dubin's Lives*). The function of the good women is in part to hear the hero's confession, enabling him to acknowledge his past, but the women confess too, and, as in Nathaniel Hawthorne, an earlier fabulist, the protagonists have the obligation to accept the women's ambiguous moral nature, a test they often fail. Roy, for example, who wants Iris's sympathy, is disquieted when she tells him that at thirty-three she is a grandmother.

Malamud is also consistent in his metaphors. The journey is often from a prison to freedom. Stores are identified as prisons; Alpine feels both imprisoned and entombed in Bober's grocery. Bok exchanges a

she has learned from her suffering, has transformed it into meaning. Roy is thirty-four, but something about Iris's confession repels him. They make love, and Iris becomes pregnant—she is the only fruitful woman in the novel—but Roy finally rejects her. In the last game of the playoffs, he sees her in the stands, but he is intent on trying to hit a dwarf who habitually heckles him from the bleachers. The ball instead hits Iris, who has stood to cheer for Roy. In the final scene between them, Iris tells Roy that she is pregnant, that he has created a new life for another at least, and she asks Roy to hit one for their child. It is too late, and Roy strikes out. He thinks of all the wrong choices he has made and wants to undo them, but he cannot.

In addition to the myth of the wasteland and the quest for new life, a central image of the novel occurs in a dream Roy frequently has. It involves Roy and his dog in a forest, a secluded place where he can follow his innermost thoughts without shame. Driving once with Memo, Roy thinks he sees a boy and a dog emerging from a woods, a boy whom Memo seems to hit. Whether she has or not, Memo speeds on—leaving behind her destruction of Roy's innocence and his illusions. In the forest he thinks he will lose his directions in order to find himself, lose his life in order to save it, but for Roy, whose middle life is marked with nothing but wrong choices, there is no salvation, no learning. The boy and his dog have vanished along with Roy's innocence, and he has rejected Iris, who could have saved him.

THE ASSISTANT

In Malamud's second novel, *The Assistant*, the surface of the myth is quite different. The pastoral world of baseball gives way to an urban business setting. The rustic king gives way to the petty thief, and the myth of heroic action on which the fate of many depends is replaced by the legend of a saint. Spaciousness is superseded by narrowness, movement by confinement. *The Natural* is often humorous and always marked by energy; even evil is active. In *The Assistant*, gloom and lethargy hand over every scene, and the despair is oppressive. The mythic parallels in *The Natural* are elaborate and schematic; in *The Assistant*, implicit and suggestive.

These differences sketched, however, *The Assistant* remains another telling of Malamud's basic myth. For most critics, it is his most successful; the fusion of romance and realism, of surface accuracy with poetic evocation, is seamless and compelling. Like Roy Hobbs, Frankie Alpine, the protagonist of *The Assistant*, is without parents. Both find older men from whom to learn, and both are partially responsible for their deaths. When the lessons they encounter involve renunciation, a check on their passions, they refuse to heed the wisdom. Both learn the wrong lessons from their suffering, at least for a time, and both cheat for financial gain. The two novels are stories of their protagonists' education, and they both open with a glimpse of the old life: Frankie Alpine and a friend rob Morris Bober, the Jewish shopkeeper to whom Alpine apprentices himself. That old life indicated, Malamud settles into the central concern of his books: the middle life, the learning life, where suffering may promise the characters a new and better future.

Frankie returns to the scene of his robbery and begins to help Morris Bober in the grocery store. The relationship between the two is one of father and son, typically cast as master-assistant, an educational apprenticeship. There are three pairs of natural fathers and sons in the novel, and they contrast with Frankie and Morris in their inadequacy. The most promising of these is that of Nat Pearl, one of Frankie's rivals for Helen Bober's affection, with his father. Nat becomes a lawyer, but although he rises financially, he is shallow compared to Alpine, and his treatment of Helen is unkind. Less successful is the relationship of the loutish Louis Karp with his father, who is trying to arrange a marriage between Louis and Helen. The worst is that between Detective Minogue, who investigates the burglary, and his son Ward, who, with Frankie, has perpetrated it.

What Frankie must learn from his surrogate father is stated in a crucial scene in which Frankie asks Morris why Jews suffer so much. Morris first answers that suffering is a part of human existence: "If you live, you suffer." He goes on, though, to indicate that suffering can be meaningful if one suffers not only *from*, but also *for*: "I think if a Jew don't suffer for the Law, he will suffer for nothing." Frankie's question is ironically self-directed, for it is Alpine himself, the non-Jew, who is suffering more than he has to: He is suffering not only the existential guilt that comes with living but also the contingent guilt that comes from his own stealing. Like Roy Hobbs, Alpine cannot check his appetite, and he continues to steal from Morris even while trying to atone for the earlier robbery. Though he steals only small amounts, though he promises himself he will repay Bober, and though he assures himself that he is really a good man, Alpine continues to violate the law, and he suffers unnecessarily for this violation. At the end of the novel, Alpine becomes a Jew and replaces Bober in the store. This action is not, as some critics have suggested, the pessimistic acceptance of a Jew's suffering or a masochistic embracing of Morris's despair; it is rather an acknowledgment of guilt for the suffering Alpine has imposed on others and on himself and the resolve to be like a Jew in suffering *for* something, in making suffering meaningful.

Alpine must learn more than just law, however, for human needs are more complex than that. When Helen Bober meets Nat Pearl on the subway, he is carrying a thick law book; her own book seems to her protection, and when he asks what it is, she replies, Miguel de Cervantes' *Don Quixote de la Mancha* (1605, 1616). Like Quixote, she is a dreamer, unsatisfied with her life as it is, and it is this quality that she will share with Frankie and that draws them together. The dialectic that informs Malamud's work is represented here: the law book, from a discipline that recognizes human limitations and demands attention to the responsibilities of this world, and *Don Quixote*, the book that allows one to look beyond these limits and provides a model for noble action. Helen rejects Nat Pearl because the law is insufficient by itself. Her action is not, of course, a rejection of the law, for she rejects Alpine too, when he lives in a world of dreams, unbound by law, for his dreams lead him into actions the law forbids. The generative force is a synthesis of the two.

Helen is, then, the other person from whom Frankie will learn. That he has the capacity for knowledge and for gentle action—as well as for the law-

lessness that has marked his life—is shown by his constant identification with St. Francis. He is from San Francisco, and his name resembles that of the saint. He looks at pictures of and dreams about St. Francis, striving for his quality of goodness. With Helen, too, though, Frankie must learn to moderate his passions; with her, too, he violates the law. A voyeur, like so many Malamud characters, he climbs an airshaft to watch her showering. The mirror having been replaced by a glass, the glass remains itself a partition, separating the dreamer from the object of his desires. More serious is his rape of Helen in the park. It is the low point of the novel: Morris fires Frankie; his business is failing, and Morris tries to commit suicide. Frankie looks at himself in the mirror, finds himself trapped inside a prisonlike circle, and hates himself for always having done the wrong thing. He returns to the store and resolves to bring it back to life for the hospitalized Morris. Although Helen and her mother do not like Frankie's return, they have little choice but to accept him, and although Frankie occasionally backslides, he makes firmer progress at controlling his passions.

Helen never fully accepts Frankie in the course of the novel, but she does reject her other suitors, and in a series of dreams, the reader discovers a tentative acceptance of Frankie: In his dreams, Frankie, like St. Francis, performs a miracle, turning a wooden rose he has carved and given to Helen into a real flower. In life, she has thrown the present away, but in the dream she accepts it. Helen, too, dreams of Frankie, out in the snow, making "a wife out of snowy moonlight."

Unlike *The Natural*, with its unambiguously pessimistic ending, *The Assistant* ends on a note of hope. Morris has died and Frankie has taken his place, and there is a suggestion that Frankie may be entrapped by the small grocery and the poverty of the Bobers' life, but there is also, in his conversion to Judaism and in his gradual winning of Helen's trust, a more powerful suggestion that he has learned the lessons of love and law, of dream and check, and that this middle life, for all its suffering, may indeed bring him toward happiness and offer him the promise of new life.

The Fixer

The Fixer is Malamud's most ambitious novel, both because the reality he creates to embody his myth—the historical trial of a Russian Jew accused of murdering a Christian boy—is the most distant from his own experience and because the purposes of the tale, its philosophic underpinnings, are the most explicit and have the most scope.

As usual the novel opens with a journey. The main character, Yakov Bok, sees his travels, the leaving of his *shtetl* for a new life in Kiev, as an escape from his past. Bok attempts to strip away his Jewishness: He shaves his beard and cuts his earlocks. On the ferry across the river to his new hell, he drops his prayer things into the water. Like many of Malamud's characters, Bok is first adopted by an older man as an employee/foster son. This father figure, whom Yakov finds lying drunk in the snow, is without wisdom; indeed, he is a member of a militantly anti-Semitic organization. His daughter is the first woman with whom Bok becomes involved, but she also turns against Bok, accusing him of raping her. Because, however, she has written him letters avowing her love, even those who want to cannot believe her.

There are other dark women. On leaving the village, Bok is given a ride by a Jew-cursing Christian; he dreams of Lilith. The most powerful of these women is a member of a gang; she has killed her own son and accuses Bok of the deed and of a sexual assault on the boy. In this version of Malamud's story, not only does the father figure fail but there is also no redemptive counterpart of these betraying women to offer Bok hope or love.

Most of the novel takes place after the discovery of the murdered child's body and the imprisonment of Bok. The prison is a consistent metaphor in Malamud for the confined lives of his characters; Bok has left a figurative prison for a literal one. Malamud allows Bok escape through the agency of his mind, especially in his dreams. Like those of most of Malamud's characters, however, Yakov's dreams are full of bitterness and terror. If they provide him with a vision and a remembrance of life beyond the prison, they also remind him of the limits of his existence.

A second relief for Bok is that one of the Russian prosecutors, Bibikov, knows of Bok's innocence, and they share a philosophical discussion, its base in Baruch Spinoza, throughout the novel. Bok emphasizes that Spinoza, although he is a philosopher who asserts humanity's freedom, recognizes that people are limited; his name for that restrictive force is Necessity. The accumulated suffering in *The Fixer* is a powerful documentation of Necessity, and forces outside human control play a more significant role in this novel than in any other of Malamud's works.

If Necessity is so powerful, asks Bibikov, where does freedom enter? Bok replies that freedom lies within the mind: One rises to God when one can think oneself into nature. Bok also learns from one sympathetic guard, who quotes to him from the Bible that those who endure to the end will be saved. Yakov learns to endure, and he does so through the freedom his mind creates. He learns also that thoughtful endurance is not enough, for neither Bibikov nor that guard, Kogin, is allowed even to survive: Bibikov takes his own life, and Kogin is murdered.

Bibikov has explained to Bok that there is in Spinoza something Bok has missed, another kind of freedom, more limited but nonetheless real: "a certain freedom of political choice, similar to the freedom of electing to think." It is this freedom that Bok finally affirms. He has undergone the extreme suffering that Necessity entails. For most of the novel there is hope that in his mind he is at least free and can create new worlds, and there is hope that he will endure. The novel ends with a more political hope. Bok, at least in his dreams, elects to shoot the czar. He has created political freedom by electing to think of himself as free. Again he cites Spinoza that if "the state acts in ways that are abhorrent to human nature, it's the lesser evil to destroy it."

Much of *The Fixer* is a moving dramatization of these ideas, and much of it as well conforms to the basic pattern of Malamud's myth, which he has developed so often and so well. Yet *The Fixer* is marred, and its faults suggest those that damage many of Malamud's later works. The philosophy seems too often grafted onto a rather static tale, the story itself an excuse for the ideas rather than the ideas a product of the story. The historical events have been distorted to fit the ideas. There is no reason Malamud should be bound by fidelity to historical truth, but all of his revisions seem to be in the direction of simplicity—not the simplicity that allows the novelist focus, but a simplicity that reduces moral complexity to schematism. All the intellectual weight of *The Fixer* is given to one set of people who hold one set of values; it is not simply that the novel presents good versus evil, but that it presents eloquent and intelligent good versus inarticulate and stupid evil.

In the novels that followed *The Fixer*, Malamud's problems with form and with integrating form and meaning became more noticeable. *The Tenants* suffers from inadequately worked-out ideas. *Dubin's Lives* is marred by structural redundancy and by a facile ending, although it features an articulate and convincing hero, a failed artist's search to find himself. Dubin's own life is finally one of promise, and that is the story Malamud knew to tell.

GOD'S GRACE

God's Grace is the story of Calvin Cohn, the only surviving human after humankind has destroyed itself in a nuclear war. The novel opens with Cohn aboard a ship, where he discovers another survivor, a chimpanzee. Most of the book is set on an island where they discover other chimps, a reclusive gorilla, and some baboons. Unlike *Dubin's Lives, God's Grace* returns to the playfully fantastic style of Malamud's early stories, but like all of his work, it is another accounting of the middle life. For Cohn, the old life is completely dead; this is his new chance to recreate a life for himself—and for all the world. In part resembling Robinson Crusoe and his story of survival, *God's Grace* is more centrally a fable about Cohn's attempt to maintain his faith in a God who has allowed this destruction and his faith that humankind can develop order among the creatures that remain. He plays a record of his father singing, "They that sow in tears shall reap in joy," and that becomes Cohn's rationalistic credo.

When the chimpanzees begin talking, Cohn has a chance to verbalize his thoughts, but though this development would seem promising, Cohn's thoughts are insistently didactic. He is intent on teaching the animals to act morally, but his attempt fails: The tone darkens and the animals begin destroying each other and finally Cohn himself. His faith in the efficacy of reason to tame nature's cruelty is naïve, and just as he underestimates the darker passions, he omits love entirely from his list of virtues. In an ending reminiscent of the close of "The Magic Barrel," another story about the relationship of law and love, the gorilla George, who has remained outside the group, attracted only when Cohn is playing records of his cantor father's chanting, begins a Kaddish for the dead Cohn and his vanished dreams. Malamud asks perhaps too much of this work: The realism of survivorship does not always blend with the fantasy of animal speech; the playful beginning gives way too abruptly to the brutal ending, yet much that is sustained recalls Malamud's work at its best.

THE PEOPLE

At the time of his death, Malamud was working on a novel entitled *The People*, having completed the first draft of sixteen of a projected twenty-one chapters. This unfinished work, published posthumously, is the story of a Jewish refugee who, like Levin in *A New Life*, is an anomalous figure set down in the American West. In *The People*, however, the time frame is the late nineteenth century, not the 1950's, and Malamud's protagonist is captured by a group of Native Americans whose chief and advocate he eventually becomes. Like *God's Grace, The People* is a fable, a darkly comic tale marked by the bleakness faintly laced with hope that characterizes Malamud's last works.

Howard Faulkner

OTHER MAJOR WORKS

SHORT FICTION: *The Magic Barrel*, 1958; *Idiots First*, 1963; *Pictures of Fidelman: An Exhibition*, 1969; *Rembrandt's Hat*, 1973; *The Stories of Bernard Malamud*, 1983; *The People and Uncollected Stories*, 1989.

BIBLIOGRAPHY

Abramson, Edward A. *Bernard Malamud Revisited.* New York: Twayne, 1993. A good study of Malamud that updates earlier books. Includes bibliographical references and an index.

and the English language, which would be significant in his subsequent literary development. Law studies begun at the University of Buenos Aires were abandoned after three years in favor of a literary career, perhaps as the result of Mallea's association with a group of young writers around 1922 who were planning to launch a magazine. This periodical, *Revista de América*, provided some of his apprenticeship editorial and writing experience and, although his contributions were limited, offered a forum for an exchange of literary views. Several short stories appeared in prestigious journals during the 1920's, and about 1927, Mallea commenced his association with the daily *La nación*, which would last until the mid-1950's and bring him considerable power among literary groups.

Mallea's first assignment for *La nación* was to cover the Olympic Games in Amsterdam in 1928, the same year he began to collaborate with Jorge Luis Borges in translating works of James Joyce. His rise to editorship of the literary supplement of *La nación* came in 1931. From the 1940's onward, he received many prestigious literary prizes, including the Primer Premio Nacional de Letras (1945), the Gran Premio de Honor de la Sociedad Argentina de Escritores (1946), the Forti Glori Prize (1968), and the Gran Premio Nacional de las Artes (1970). In 1944, he married Helena Muñóz Larreta, and in 1955 he resigned his editorial position to represent Argentina before UNESCO in Paris and in India the following year. His trip to India undoubtedly played a role in the inspiration of his novel *Triste piel del universo* (sad skin of the universe). Mallea died in Buenos Aires in 1982.

ANALYSIS

Critics are not in accord as to whether Eduardo Mallea's *Nocturno europeo* (European nocturne) ought to be termed a novel; it consists largely of impressions of the writer's travels, the most important of which are derived from a lecture tour of France and Italy taken the previous year. It might be classed a fictionalized travel book, with meditative and philosophical tendencies that impart an essaylike character.

NOCTURNO EUROPEO

The main character—and in fact, the only one—Adrian, something of a globetrotter, has spent much of his life in travel (a symbolic voyage through this world), reaching old age without encountering the ontological objective of his search. On an individual plane, he seeks himself, his identity; on a more universal level, he seeks the meaning of life. Having abandoned his own country because he found no meaning there, he belongs spiritually to the "lost generation" (no gratuitous association, since Mallea quotes Gertrude Stein's comment to Ernest Hemingway: "You are the lost generation"). The search for identity frequently takes the form of comparisons and contrasts between Argentina and Europe and, given the protagonist's interest in art, includes much analysis of works in galleries that are explicitly or implicitly juxtaposed to his own heritage.

Lacking a plot in the traditional sense, the novel is saved from becoming a travelogue by virtue of the subthemes injected by Mallea, which add a valuable dimension of intellectual substance. Not only are contrasts established in the areas of art and the protagonist's heritage, but also the sociopolitical situation of Europe during the 1930's provides material for comparisons with the Argentine background, much as occasional human encounters inspire a comparative view of mores and morality. The liberated females the protagonist finds in Paris prove much too threatening and his puritanical upbringing much too rigid to allow him to risk libidinal release: His alienation is thus even more pronounced. Adrian spends his evenings surrounded by the wealthy and their sycophants, silently watching the human comedy around him, unable to communicate, empty and bored. The novel's most important dimension is constituted by Adrian's constant self-analysis and search for identity, his efforts to transcend his confining middle-class origins and his own limited state.

FIESTA IN NOVEMBER

Mallea's novel *Fiesta in November* is the work of an independent and contemplative intellectual, little indebted to the literary fashions of the day. During the 1930's, the vogue in Spanish America was the *criollista* novel, in which man appears as the victim of the mindless, overpowering forces of nature. *Fiesta in November*, in both a formal and a thematic departure, offered two juxtaposed yet seemingly unrelated story lines linked by problems of existential authenticity and the motif of art, artistic creation, and its meaning and value. Some critics have suggested that part of the novel was inspired by the murder of Spanish poet and playwright Federico García Lorca at the outbreak of the Spanish Civil War in July of 1936 (an event that might well have coincided with the novel's genesis, for it appeared in 1938). Inasmuch as one of the two narratives relates the kidnapping and murder of a young poet, this interpretation acquires credence. Events in this story line—set against the background of civil strife in an unnamed European country—are intercalated between episodes of the other narrative, producing not a contrapuntal effect but an opportunity for the reader to observe the ironic contrast and to reflect upon what is "real" and important in life and what is not.

Fiesta in November is a title with different levels of meaning. First, it refers to the frivolous party on which the novel's second story line is centered; second, it refers to a celebration or rite and in Spain is used to denote the bullfight, so that its associations with violence and death are appropriate to the contrasting narrative. The party that is the title's primary referent is an elegant soiree given by the very wealthy Mrs. de Rague, to which the cream of *porteño* (Buenos Aires) society has been invited: ambassadors, financiers, judges, politicians, artists, and the landed gentry. Its atmosphere could hardly be more inane, with shallowness the norm among the guests and pseudoartistic conversations the order of the evening, thanks to the de Ragues' collections of paintings. Lintas, the male protagonist, is an existential hero who has been to Europe and aspires to transcendence via his art. The de Ragues talk of the monetary rather than intrinsic artistic worth of their acquisitions, causing Lintas to commit the *faux pas* of telling the hostess that the prices of some paintings were inflated, with the result that he is forced to leave the party. Marta, daughter of the family, accompanies Lintas to his studio, where they engage in typical existentialist dialogues questioning the class structure, their place in life, and how to reach fulfillment.

In the novel's other story line, the poet, about to add a line to a poem in progress and holding a piece of bread in one hand, has his human and creative activity interrupted by the intrusion of his country's internal strife into his private domain. Soldiers invade the home of the nameless writer, taking him to the outskirts of the town, where he is executed. On the way, his sensations, his thoughts about dying, and the reflection that his white shirt will be covered with blood, together with his final perceptions, are detailed by an omniscient narrator. The tragic reality of this episode becomes even more stark in juxtaposition to the banality of the de Ragues' party, their meaningless existence and bourgeois decadence in contrast with humanity's need for physical and intellectual nourishment, as symbolized by the bread and poetry.

THE BAY OF SILENCE

Mallea's next novel, *The Bay of Silence*, established him as one of Argentina's most important writers. Probably one of his most autobiographical works, it reflects the novelist's constant struggle to convince his people of the need to espouse certain social ideals. The protagonist's suffering as he contemplates a misguided Argentina and perceives the reactions of an uncaring and impersonal public is the novel's most important and obsessive theme. Mallea's attempt to encompass and portray a far more vast setting in time and space than in his previous novels, together with the work's complexity, has caused some critics to view it as too rambling and amorphous. The novel is divided into three parts, "Los jóvenes" ("The Young Men"), "Las islas" ("The Islands"), and "Los derrotados" ("The Defeated"), spanning the period between 1926 and 1939. Set both in Argentina and in Europe, it shares with *Nocturno europeo* a contrast between the two cultures, a search for identity, and political themes reflecting the crises of the 1930's. The novel is narrated in diary form by Martín Tregua, a former law student attempting to become a famous novelist (and thus a probable mask of Mallea). The coeditor of a magazine who is surrounded by intellectuals, he is working on a long

SIR THOMAS MALORY

Born: Warwickshire (?), England; early fifteenth century
Died: London (?), England; March 14, 1471

PRINCIPAL LONG FICTION

Le Morte d'Arthur, 1485

OTHER LITERARY FORMS

Le Morte d'Arthur is the only work attributed to Sir Thomas Malory. It was published in 1485 by William Caxton, England's first printer. The 1485 edition, for centuries the only source of Malory's tale, is a continuous narrative of twenty-one "books," though at the end of some books that clearly complete a larger grouping or "tale," Caxton included "explicits" (concluding comments) by the author. These explicits indicate that Malory may have intended the work to be organized in a fashion somewhat different from that of the published version. A manuscript of *Le Morte d'Arthur* discovered in 1934 at Winchester Cathedral indicates that Malory did not write it as a single long work, but rather as a series of eight separate tales, each of which deals with some aspect or character of the Arthurian legend.

ACHIEVEMENTS

Any assessment of Malory's achievement as a literary artist is inevitably bound up with a judgment of the form of *Le Morte d'Arthur:* Is it a single story or eight separate tales? As critic Stephen Knight points out, this question of form is central to critical inquiry, for "if we are not clear whether we have before us one book or eight, or something in between, then our attitude towards the work or works must be obscure and tentative." That Malory's *Le Morte d'Arthur* should be considered a series of separate "works" is argued forcefully by Eugène Vinaver, editor of the modern standard edition, conspicuously entitled *The Works of Sir Thomas Malory* (1947, 3 volumes). Vinaver argues in the introduction to his edition that the unity that scholars have found in *Le Morte d'Arthur* was imposed by Caxton, not intended by Malory, and his edited text, based on the Winchester manuscript, restores many passages excised by Caxton in the 1485 edition. Vinaver's opinion has been challenged by several critics, most notably by R. M. Lumiansky, who has argued that even in the Winchester manuscript one can see a unity of design and a progression from early to late tales, suggesting that Malory himself conceived of his eight tales as forming a single "work."

Unfortunately, although this issue has been debated at length, it has not been settled with any real certainty, and any final judgment of Malory's talents as an original artist may remain in abeyance for some time. Yet, whether one considers the Caxton edition of *Le Morte d'Arthur*, where a stronger sense of unity is prevalent, or the Winchester manuscript, from which the argument for eight separate tales can be made more forcefully, one can see an unmistakable unity imparted by the ordering of the tales. Malory's story moves progressively from the birth of Arthur to his assumption of kingship and defeat of all opposition, through the numerous stories depicting the adventures of knights in service to him, to his death at the hands of his traitorous, illegitimate son, Mordred. This kind of chronological progress is noticeably absent in the romances which Malory used as sources for his work. In the romances, especially that amorphous collection known as the French Vulgate Cycle, from which Malory borrowed much of his materials, there is often little sense of direction or completeness to the knights' adventures. From the modern reader's point of view, Malory deserves special credit for unifying these disparate tales and arranging them in an order that lends motivation to certain characters' actions and—perhaps more important—gives the reader a sense of the cause-and-effect relationship between certain incidents that is lacking in the "French books" from which Malory says he has "drawn out" his tales.

Malory's achievement in condensing and organizing his sources has also been a matter of debate. Nineteenth century scholars, possessed of newly discovered Arthurian manuscripts of the twelfth through fifteenth centuries, were divided on the issue. Several noted medievalists branded Malory as a mere "compiler"; others, equally respected, praised him for his originality. Perhaps the most laudatory comment was offered by George Saintsbury, who claimed that in *Le Morte d'Arthur*, Malory made a significant advance over the romance tradition by developing a firm sense of narrative purpose, akin to that of the modern novelist. Saintsbury sees Malory exhibiting "the sense of *grasp*, the power to put his finger, and to keep it, on the central pulse and nerve of the story." Saintsbury and others, notably W. P. Ker, also praised Malory for his strong, original prose style. T. S. Eliot has called Malory "a kind of crude Northern Homer," a fine prose stylist.

Regardless of the criticisms leveled at Malory's tale as an artistic achievement in its own right, there can be little question about the importance of *Le Morte d'Arthur* in literary history. Since its publication, it has stood as the preeminent English-language document to which readers of succeeding centuries have turned to learn of the Arthurian legend. Caxton's edition was followed by two others early in the sixteenth century, attesting to Malory's immediate popularity. Intellectuals during the Renaissance may have agreed with Roger Ascham, who commented in *The Scholemaster* (1570) that the chief pleasure of *Le Morte d'Arthur* lay in two points, "open manslaughter and bold bawdy." Nevertheless, the appearance of still more editions of the work and the numerous references to the Arthurian legend in the literature of the period offers further proof of the influence of Malory's work long after its publication. When English society developed a renewed interest in chivalric materials and especially in the Arthurian legend, *Le Morte d'Arthur* was the work to which writers from Sir Walter Scott to Alfred, Lord Tennyson turned as the *locus classicus* of the legend. It was by comparison to Malory that Tennyson's *Idylls of the King* (1859-1885) and the Arthurian poems of A. C. Swinburne, William Morris, and Matthew Arnold were judged by their contemporaries, and all openly acknowledged their debt to the author of *Le Morte d'Arthur.*

In part, *Le Morte d'Arthur*'s influence as a source for Arthurian adventure and chivalric virtue may be attributed to the good fortune of its having been printed, while hundreds or even thousands of Arthurian tales existed only in manuscript until the late nineteenth or even the twentieth century. Nevertheless, even after scholarly and popular bookshelves began to be filled with other versions, Malory's work continued to be regarded as the premier English rendition of the Arthurian story. In the twentieth century, T. H. White, who had at his disposal both medieval and modern accounts of the legend numbering in the hundreds, turned to Malory for inspiration in writing what is no doubt the most important twentieth century Arthurian tale, *The Once and Future King.* John Steinbeck, whose accomplishments as a novelist earned him the Nobel Prize, began a modern adaptation of Malory because he wanted to bring to "impatient" modern readers the "wonder and magic" of *Le Morte d'Arthur.* While the literary purist may question the value of modernizing Malory, one cannot quarrel too much with Steinbeck's motive, for he speaks truly when he observes that these stories "are alive even in those of us who have not read them." To write a work that becomes a part of the cultural heritage of one's country, and a classic of one's language and literature, is an achievement few writers accomplish; Malory is one of the exceptions.

BIOGRAPHY

Though it is clear that "Sir Thomas Malory, knight prisoner," wrote *Le Morte d'Arthur,* there is serious debate about which Thomas Malory actually authored the work. Records of fifteenth century England contain references to more than a dozen Thomas Malorys. Most modern scholars believe that the author of *Le Morte d'Arthur* was Sir Thomas Malory of Newbold Revell, Warwickshire, in southern England, but there are other candidates, most notably Thomas Malory of Hutton and Studley, Yorkshire, in the north.

That Thomas Malory of Newbold Revell was the author of *Le Morte d'Arthur* was first proposed in 1894 by George L. Kittredge, who examined both the Caxton text and historical records and deduced that the Newbold Revell knight met all the necessary criteria for authorship. From the explicit at the end of book 21 of *Le Morte d'Arthur,* Kittredge concluded that Thomas Malory was a knight, that he was in prison (he prays for "good delyveraunce"), and that the book was concluded in the ninth year of the reign of Edward IV, that is, March, 1469, to March, 1470. Extant records indicated that the Malory from Newbold Revell was the son of a gentleman and therefore probably received the education requisite to produce the work. He had been exposed to knightly virtues while in service to Richard Beauchamp, earl of Warwick, who was said to have embodied the knightly ideals of the age. He is reported to have died on March 14, 1471, after the *terminus ad quem* of the book's composition.

Kittredge's identification of Malory was reinforced when, in the early 1920's, Edward Cobb found an indictment consisting of eight charges against the Newbold Revell knight. Although it is not clear that Malory was ever found guilty on any of the charges, it is certain that he spent time in jail; in fact, it appears that between 1460 and 1471, the Newbold Revell knight spent most of his time at Newgate prison. His presence there would explain his having access to the books upon which he based *Le Morte d'Arthur*, because Newgate was situated near a monastery with an excellent library. Malory may well have bribed his keepers to allow him to borrow the books.

The Winchester manuscript, discovered in 1934, contains several new explicits that provide additional information about the author. For example, at the end of the "Tale of Sir Gareth," Malory petitions his readers to pray that God will send him "good delyveraunce sone [soon] and hastely." Even more clear is the explicit at the end of the "Tale of King Arthur," in which the author says that "this was drawyn by a knyght presoner sir Thomas Malleorre." On this evidence, the knight from Newbold Revell has emerged as the leading candidate for the authorship of *Le Morte d'Arthur*.

The primary arguments discrediting the Newbold Revell knight have been made by William Matthews in *The Ill-Framed Knight* (1965). According to Matthews, no evidence suggests that this Malory had any familiarity with northern poetry, yet the dialect of *Le Morte d'Arthur* and its English sources (especially the alliterative *Morte Arthure*) are clearly northern.

Further, none of the references to real places (many are mentioned in the text) are to locations near Warwickshire. Matthews contends, too, that it is doubtful that a criminal would have had access under any circumstances to the library near Newgate, and that there is no evidence that the monastery's library had the books upon which *Le Morte d'Arthur* is based. At the time the work was completed, Thomas Malory of Newbold Revell could have been seventy-five years old, much too old to have completed such an arduous task. Finally, the Newbold Revell knight's political alliances were Yorkist, and *Le Morte d'Arthur* is distinctly Lancastrian in outlook. Kittredge had also cited two documents to support his claim, but this documentary evidence is discounted by Matthews. Matthews says that Kittredge's Malory was too old to have participated in a 1462 winter siege in which a Malory is recorded to have taken part. Similarly, the Newbold Revell knight could not have been the one named in the pardon made by Edward IV in 1468, since the pardon applied to political prisoners, and the Warwickshire man was a common criminal.

Matthews has proposed a second candidate, Thomas Malory of Hutton and Studley in Yorkshire. This Malory was a member of an eminent northern family; it is realistic to assume that he could read French, had access to the necessary source documents, was familiar with northern poetry and places, and spoke the northern dialect prominent in *Le Morte d'Arthur*. In addition, he supported the Lancastrian cause. The objections to his candidacy for authorship are that he is not described in family genealogies as a knight or chevalier, and there is no record of his ever being a prisoner. Matthews argues, however, that these are not serious discrepancies. Many men who could do so did not claim the title of knight. That there is no record of the Yorkshire Malory being a prisoner is also explainable. Although records abound detailing the imprisonment of criminals, it was not a fifteenth century custom to keep records of prisoners of war. These prisoners often had some measure of freedom and several wrote books while in captivity. It seems more likely that a work the scope of *Le Morte d'Arthur* would be written under these conditions than under those imposed on criminals.

Further, the expression "knight-prisoner," used by Malory to refer to himself in the explicits, is applied in *Le Morte d'Arthur* to Lionel, Lancelot, and Tristram when they become prisoners of war. Similarly, "good deliverance" is used when Malory speaks of Tristram's trials in prison. Thus, the term "knight-prisoner" is used in a somewhat complimentary fashion as the epithet of a prisoner of war, not a common criminal. The claim for Thomas Malory of Studley and Hutton rests on these grounds.

Other candidates have been proposed as the author of *Le Morte d'Arthur*, but few can be considered seriously. Thomas Malorys appear in the records of English courts and parishes as laborers, armigers—and one as a member of parliament (though he is mentioned only once, and nothing else is known about him). What is known for certain about the author of *Le Morte d'Arthur* can only be gleaned from the text of the work itself, and then verified—with much conjecture—by searching the records of fifteenth century England.

ANALYSIS

The modern reader approaching Sir Thomas Malory's *Le Morte d'Arthur* may be perplexed at first reading, for while the story of Arthur and his knights has the appearance of a novel, it is certainly far removed from representatives of the genre with which today's reader is more familiar. Though there is an overarching structure to the work, provided by the chronology of Arthur's reign, individual stories often seem mere appendages that add little to the major plot and seldom seem to have concrete beginnings or endings themselves. The "fault" for this apparent lapse into chaos lies not so much with Malory (though too close a reliance on his sources does tend to cause the story to branch off in several directions that lead nowhere), but rather with the reader who is not familiar with medieval techniques of storytelling. It is not uncommon to find medieval romances that simply begin *in medias res* and seem to end there as well. That form of narrative technique has been supplanted in today's literary world by the "well-made story," whose beginning, middle, and end are clearly defined, and whose parts are clearly integrated into

the whole. The medieval audience demanded neither tight concentration on a single story line nor analysis of cause-and-effect relationships; to appreciate Malory and his achievement in the chain of events leading to the modern novel one must first appreciate that for writers before him, and for Malory himself, emphasis on the event itself, rather than on its consequences or on the role of characters, was of primary importance. Malory, in fact, was one of the first writers to delve into the minds of his characters and achieve a certain degree of verisimilitude in presenting the people who appear in his story.

Malory lacks originality in the modern sense, since almost everything he recounts in *Le Morte d'Arthur* is taken from medieval romances popular for centuries before his. His accomplishments as a storyteller and his claim to literary greatness lie in the artistry with which he wove together the elements of the Arthurian legend and in the insight he presents into the meaning of the story both for his contemporaries and for readers throughout the centuries. Beneath the surface chaos of the tales that make up the work, Malory has presented a unified vision of a society in triumph and in decay; his is a complex work with a complex purpose. As D. S. Brewer explains in his introduction to *Malory: The Morte Darthur* (1968), the work was "a part of the movement that transformed the medieval knight into the English gentleman." Through this story of the "ideal society," Malory presents the enduring dilemma of man's attempt to reconcile individual demands with those of the society in which he lives and those of the God he worships.

LE MORTE D'ARTHUR

Le Morte d'Arthur consists of eight tales, which Caxton divided into twenty-one books in his edition. The story itself divides into three large sections. The first, consisting of books 1 through 5 in the Caxton text, details the coming of Arthur and the establishment of the Round Table. It begins with the adulterous conception of the King, tells the now popular story of the sword in the stone, and continues with an account of the early battles and adventures of Arthur and his knights in their effort to subdue external threats to the realm. Always the careful craftsman where larger issues of plot and motivation are concerned, Malory skillfully interweaves into this larger story details that become important in later episodes: the "dolorous stroke" wielded by Balin that initiates in a curious way the Holy Grail quest, the hatred felt by Morgan le Fay for her brother Arthur, and the power of Excalibur and its symbolic significance. In the final book of this section, Arthur is hailed as the conqueror of Rome and welcomed into the city by the pope himself; the last great external challenge to this new order of society has been met and overcome.

The main books of *Le Morte d'Arthur* (11-17) deal with the adventures of Arthur's knights. Included are tales of the prowess of Sir Lancelot, the dedicated idealism of Sir Gareth ("Beaumains"), and the accomplishments and deceptions of Sir Tristram and his paramour, La Beal Isould. In these accounts, the court of King Mark is established as a kind of counterculture to that of Arthur, and the reader is made to feel the imminent doom that awaits Arthur's kingdom should the knights falter in their loyalty to their leader and the virtues he upholds. The final books of this section recount the quest of the Sangreal (Holy Grail), a devastating undertaking that strips Arthur of many of his knights and exposes the shortcomings of many of those considered the best in the realm. The quest marks the beginning of the end of the Round Table, for through vain pursuit of this holy artifact, the knights reveal their spiritual imperfection and perhaps their inherent imperfectability.

The third and final section of the work tells of the decay of Arthur's kingdom, a process that begins when the knights return from the unsuccessful Grail quest. Lancelot, by his actions, reveals that his dedication to the Queen is greater than his devotion to God, his personal needs more important than his public duties. Arthur becomes unable to effect a suitable compromise between public and private life, and as incident after incident forces him to choose between his queen and his knights, he reluctantly is forced to opt for the latter. His sad statement after the civil war has begun in his kingdom reflects his inability to maintain a balance between his private and public lives: "Much more I am sorrier for my good knights' loss than for the loss of my fair queen; for queens I might have enough, but such a fellowship of good

knights shall never be together in no company." This conflict between public and private virtues, a universal condition of humankind that Malory perceived at the heart of the Arthurian tale that he was transcribing, is the cause of the tragic development in the story.

The essence of the conflict Malory portrays in *Le Morte d'Arthur* has been described by D. S. Brewer as "the divergence of the values of honour and goodness from each other." The concept of honor is the paramount public virtue, informing the code of chivalry and motivating actions of those who were proponents of knighthood. Goodness, on the other hand, is a private virtue, and in *Le Morte d'Arthur* it is specifically identified as a Christian attribute. Hence, the conflict between honor and goodness is elevated beyond the level of individuals struggling within themselves to choose the proper path in life; it becomes, under Malory's skillful handling of individual tales from Arthurian romances, a larger conflict between two modes of living—the way of the good knight and the way of the good Christian.

The public virtue of honor had been the hallmark of chivalry for centuries before Malory brought it under scrutiny in *Le Morte d'Arthur*, and his characters all place great emphasis on winning and maintaining it. The promise of honor brings the knights to court; the chance to increase one's honor motivates them to accept the most impossible quests and to battle against the most insurmountable odds. The preservation of honor demands strict obedience to one's lord, unswerving fidelity to one's lady, and unshakable loyalty to one's brother knights. By striving for honor, the knights make the Round Table great, and paradoxically, by striving to maintain their honor, they destroy it.

In the society that Malory's Arthur imagines and attempts to build, honor and goodness are inseparable. In a passage not in any of Malory's sources, the King charges all his knights "never to do outrageousity nor murder, and always to flee treason [that is, to avoid committing it]; also, by no mean to be cruel, but to give mercy unto him that asketh mercy, upon pain of forfeiture of their worship . . . and always to do ladies, damosels, and gentlewomen succour, upon pain of death." By their honor, the knights are committed to doing good deeds. As the story progresses, however, the requirements of honor and goodness begin to diverge, and the inability of the knights and ladies to reconcile the two leads to the tragic demise of Arthur's society.

Malory highlights the growing divergence throughout a number of stories in *Le Morte d'Arthur*, but in none more clearly than "The Poisoned Apple" (book 18, chapters 1-7). In this vignette, Guinevere is accused by Sir Mador of poisoning Sir Patrice, his cousin. Mador demands justice: Either the queen is to be executed, or her champion must defeat Mador in battle. Arthur cannot fight, as he is to sit in judgment of the case, and Lancelot is not at court. Clearly this is a matter of honor—the king's lady is to be shamed, bringing dishonor on the entire court—and yet all of the knights present at court suspect Guinevere and refuse to fight in her behalf. In desperation, Arthur and Guinevere send for Sir Bors. They appeal to him to champion the queen not because she is to be shamed, and through her the court, but rather because he has an obligation to uphold the honor of his kinsman Lancelot, who no doubt would fight for the queen were he at court. Bors tells Arthur he will fight "for my Lord Luancelot's sake, and for your sake." Bors then appeals to other knights, claiming that "it were great shame to us all" should the wife of Arthur be "shamed openly"; he is rebuked by many who, while acknowledging their respect for the king, have no love for Guinevere because she is a "destroyer of good knights." Though Lancelot eventually arrives in time to fight for Guinevere and save her from this charge, of which she is innocent, the implication here—borne out later in *Le Morte d'Arthur*—is that the prowess that wins honor may also allow one to win when the cause for which one is fighting is on the wrong side of justice; it might may indeed prevail for evil instead of goodness.

This sad fact is brought home to the reader in Malory's account of Lancelot's battles for the queen when she is accused of adultery. Lancelot is forced to come to Guinevere's rescue, even at the expense of creating strife within Arthur's realm, because his honor is at stake. "Whether ye did right or wrong," Bors advises him, "it is now your part to hold with the queen, that she be not slain . . . for and she so die the shame shall be yours." In the final chapters of *Le Morte d'Arthur*, Malory presents Lancelot fighting reluctantly against truth to preserve his honor. Arthur, too, fights reluctantly, even though he is on the side of truth, for he would rather preserve his noble society of knights than save his queen, and he appears willing to be cuckolded rather than have the Round Table destroyed by internal strife.

The clear dichotomy between knightly and Christian virtues is made evident at several points in *Le Morte d'Arthur*, but Malory makes his most forceful statement about the problem in "The Maid of Astolat" (book 18, chapters 9-20). Lancelot, fighting in disguise against his own kinsmen and the other knights of the Round Table, is wounded and taken to a hermitage to heal. The hermit attending him asks who this knight is, and when he learns it is one who fought against Arthur, remarks: "I have seen the day . . . I would have loved him the worse because he was against my lord, King Arthur, for sometime I was one of the fellowship of the Round Table, but I thank God now I am otherwise disposed." The hermit has renounced his former calling, perhaps because he has seen where the path of honor leads and has adopted a new path and a new Lord. Lancelot, who recovers from his wound while at the hermitage, comes to a momentary realization of his folly and bitterly acknowledges that his "pride" has led to his being thrown into this lowly condition. Only much later, however, does he abandon the pursuit of honor through the chivalric code, and by then Arthur is dead, Guinevere has entered a nunnery, and the kingdom is in ruins. The sense that one gets from reading Malory's account of the last days of Arthur's realm is that even the most chivalric society is doomed to failure, and that humanity's only hope lies in adopting values and goals that transcend worldly ideals.

What, then, has Malory accomplished in telling this tale? In the strife that tears Arthur's kingdom apart, fifteenth century readers saw mirrored their own griefs over the demise of feudal England, ravaged by the bloody struggle for the English throne that became known as the Wars of the Roses. *Le Morte d'Arthur* offered these readers faith, in a curious way, because in his work Malory has shown that, despite the collapse of an ideal society, lives and societies continue.

Even in their failures, the characters of *Le Morte d'Arthur* appear as larger-than-life personages who speak to the reader of the potential greatness of humankind. If honor can somehow be wedded to goodness, if the public virtues that gave the knights their sense of purpose can be married to the private virtues that cause man to rise above societal bonds when necessary, the ideal society can be created. To his contemporary readers, Malory's story no doubt offered this note of special hope. Thus, *Le Morte d'Arthur* speaks not only to its fifteenth century readers, but through the story of Arthur and his knights, Malory also speaks to all peoples of all nations and times of the possibility of greatness, the inevitability of failure, and the glory that humankind achieves by striving for the impossible.

Laurence W. Mazzeno and Sarah B. Kovel

BIBLIOGRAPHY

Archibald, Elizabeth, and A. S. G. Edwards, eds. *A Companion to Malory.* Woodbridge, England: D. S. Brewer, 1996. Part of the Arthurian Studies series, this volume examines the Arthurian legend in Malory's seminal work. Includes bibliographical references and an index.

Field, P. J. C. *The Life and Times of Sir Thomas Malory.* Cambridge: D. S. Brewer, 1993. A very detailed, scholarly retelling of Malory's life. Recommended for advanced students and scholars.

Ihle, Sandra Ness. *Malory's Grail Quest: Invention and Adaptation in Medieval Prose Romance.* Madison: University of Wisconsin Press, 1983. Examines "The Tale of the Sangreal" from *Le Morte d'Arthur,* looking both to its thirteenth century French source and to Malory's own structural and thematic adaptation. Gives insight into medieval literary theory and the underlying intentions of Malory's distinctive Grail quest.

McCarthy, Terence. *An Introduction to Malory.* Reprint. Cambridge, England: D. S. Brewer, 1991. McCarthy provides very ample discussions of how to read Malory, exploring, in depth, characters such as Lancelot, Tristram, and Arthur and the world of romance that Malory creates. McCarthy takes many different critical approaches, and he includes a section of background and biography as well as a very useful bibliographical essay.

_____. *Reading "The Morte Darthur."* Cambridge, England: D. S. Brewer, 1988. A study intended to assist the newcomer to Malory's work. Follows Eugène Vinaver's division of this work into eight books. Presents various contexts through which to view *Le Morte d'Arthur.* A useful and accessible reader.

Merrill, Robert. *Sir Thomas Malory and the Cultural Crisis of the Late Middle Ages.* New York: Peter Lang, 1987. An original inquiry into the psychology of the knights of Arthurian romance and the impact of the Round Table on their lives. Traces the formation of medieval institutions and explores the personal and social tensions in the Middle Ages that led to the Protestant Reformation.

Parins, Marylyn Jackson. *Malory: The Critical Heritage.* New York: Routledge, 1988. An important collection of early criticism and commentary on Malory's *Le Morte d'Arthur* in chronological order, beginning with William Caxton's preface to the first edition and ending with remarks by influential literary critic George Saintsbury in 1912.

Riddy, Felicity. *Sir Thomas Malory.* New York: E. J. Brill, 1987. An excellent critical commentary that examines *Le Morte d'Arthur* from a number of perspectives. This scholarly work contains much useful information.

DAVID MALOUF

Born: Brisbane, Australia; March 20, 1934

PRINCIPAL LONG FICTION

Johnno, 1975

An Imaginary Life, 1978

The Bread of Time to Come, 1981 (also known as *Fly Away Peter,* 1982)

Harland's Half Acre, 1984
The Great World, 1990
Remembering Babylon, 1993
The Conversations at Curlow Creek, 1996

OTHER LITERARY FORMS

Because literary recognition came to him first for his verse collections, for quite some time David Malouf was regarded primarily as a poet. His first published writings were poetry, and in addition to contributions to works featuring several authors, efforts such as *Bicycle and Other Poems* (1970; also known as *The Year of the Foxes and Other Poems*, 1979), *Neighbours in a Thicket* (1974), *Wild Lemons* (1980), and *First Things Last* (1981) have sustained his reputation in this genre. Some critics have discerned varying levels of sophistication when his earlier is compared with his later verse.

Malouf has experimented with the writing of short stories, an autobiographical narrative, and drama. His stories "Eustace" (1982) and "The Prowler" (1982) concern isolated and apparently unsociable characters who seem misplaced yet oddly adapted to Australian settings. The collection *Antipodes* (1985) comprises short stories which in the main deal with the troubles of immigrants and problems of adjustment in Australia as well as the culturally ambivalent situation of Australians in Europe. Malouf has set down some of the personal sources behind themes and images in his fiction with the publication of *12 Edmondstone Street* (1985), a memoir that deals in part with the writer's childhood years in Brisbane and in part, somewhat impressionistically, with work and travel during the 1980's. He also wrote the libretto for *Voss* (1986), based on Patrick White's novel. Another line of creative interest was explored in his play *Blood Relations* (1988). Interviews and other writings of his have been published in periodicals in Australia and abroad.

ACHIEVEMENTS

Many of David Malouf's works have won awards in his native country. For the poetry collection *Neighbours in a Thicket*, he received the Grace Leven Prize and the Australian Literature Society's Gold Medal,

(Jane Bown)

as well as an award from the James Cook University of North Queensland. He held an Australian Council fellowship in 1978, and his novel *An Imaginary Life* won the New South Wales Premier's Fiction Award in 1979. The short novel *The Bread of Time to Come* (published in Great Britain as *Fly Away Peter*) won two awards offered by the publication *The Age* in 1982, and his fiction was again honored with the Australian Literature Society's Gold Medal in 1983. His short stories won the Victoria Premier's Award in 1985, and his play *Blood Relations* received the New South Wales Premier's Award for drama. *The Great World* received the Commonwealth Writers' Prize in 1991. *Remembering Babylon*, which was considered for the Booker Prize, won the inaugural IMPAC Dublin Literary Award in 1996. In addition to honors of this sort, Malouf frequently has been considered an important literary spokesman for his country, and much of his writing has been regarded as significant in indicating new trends in creative work.

THE BREAD OF TIME TO COME

Much of Malouf's writing has a retrospective tendency, where events from earlier portions of the twentieth century are called back in an effort to delineate the effects of historical change and upheaval on Australia and its people. *The Bread of Time to Come* concerns two young men in their early twenties, Ashley Crowther and Jim Saddler, who are drawn together by a common interest in the birds that gather at a local refuge. Strange, exotic birds of every sort, from as far away as Siberia and Norway, put in an appearance in the course of their elongated migratory flights. Just as it has become a destination for such journeys from afar, the island continent seems isolated yet a part of the greater pattern of events in the world at large. The outbreak of World War I in Europe sets in motion a delayed reaction in Australia. The men are packed off to the Western front in France, feeling perhaps at first some tug of patriotism; but the harsh realities of trench warfare leave them troubled and hardened. After one soldier, as part of a foolish bet, shows himself to snipers and is shot down, and an enemy shell leaves others dead or maimed, the grim, mindless, and destructive underside of armed conflict becomes apparent to them. When it is learned finally that, in another engagement, Jim has been killed and Ashley wounded, the news, when it reaches Australia, brings home finally the senseless and brutal wastefulness the war has brought.

HARLAND'S HALF ACRE

One of Malouf's most highly regarded works of fiction is *Harland's Half Acre*, which portrays the development of an Australian artist against a historical backdrop that embraces much of the twentieth century. The title character, Frank Harland, is a crotchety, reclusive person who wears his aspirations lightly. Harland is loosely based on the life of Ian Fairweather (1891-1974), a painter who settled on an island off the coast of Brisbane. Like Harland, he was reclusive and ignored the demands of fame. During the earlier portions of his career, when he has been beset by economic hardships, he finds odd ways to support himself during the difficult years of the Great Depression. He also becomes acquainted with others who have become impoverished by the onset of hard times. Later, during World War II, he comes to know refugees who have left Europe and learns that older established nations have cultural traditions with historical dimensions that Australia cannot yet share; on the other hand, Europe is also subject to political turmoil and upheaval that has not affected the island continent. Much of Harland's story is told indirectly, through the accounts of others who have known him. It would appear that he has remained fiercely independent and stubbornly dedicated to his efforts at painting, during bad times and good; much of his later work is done on a small plot of land where he can preserve some sense of solitude. He has, however, acquired land elsewhere, partly in an effort to regain holdings that one of his ancestors, during the nineteenth century, lost in a card game. At times some of Harland's paintings are sold for relatively little; even toward the end, when he has become well known and his works have become collector's items with some value to investors, he does little to exploit the reputation he has earned. Critics have taken his story as in some way symbolic of the problematical position of creative art in Australia, which began with little legacy of its own. It seems likely as well that Malouf intended his title character's situation in some sense to suggest the personal isolation that may accompany any creative quest.

THE GREAT WORLD

The Great World takes up various themes again in depicting the response to historical change that is felt among Australian men who grew up before World War II. Their uncomplicated existence is abruptly altered when war with Japan brings the men to Malaya with other Australian fighting forces. After their units have surrendered, the men, who have been trained in combat, are ill prepared for captivity, and waves of memories from the past sweep over them during the difficult early days of their confinement. Their lot is hard but not quite unbearable, though there are numerous discomforts and indignities. One of them fights with a guard and a full-scale riot erupts; even then, they are not mistreated as seriously as they had feared. Even wearying labor in a work camp set up along the lines of a railway into Burma does not daunt them entirely, though others among them fall victim to any of a multitude of diseases. In time, however, exhaustion and fevers begin to tell on them, and their life seems reduced to a few relatively simple elements. The men feel a common bond with one another; they also cherish the few letters they have received from the outside world. Toward the end of the war, weakened by privations and troubled that they have become little more than coolie labor for their captors, they have nearly lost track of the passage of time, and when peace comes, they are somewhat taken by surprise. Even after they have been repatriated, afterimages from their years of ordeal haunt them occasionally. Nevertheless, there is also a sense of tedium and sameness to the routine into which they are cast in their civilian work. Renewing old acquaintanceships holds some fascination for them, but even this becomes tiresome after a while. Settled patterns of doing things eventually become habits that are followed almost instinctively. After the war, time seems to pass quickly and stealthily, sometimes in leaps of years at a time, and change engulfs Australia in odd, ironic ways. The Japanese, once feared as enemies, have become known now for their commercial acumen; another war, in Vietnam, comes and goes; and business expansion takes hold for a while. Toward the end, the two men who began as friends some decades before can look back on a bewildering array of images from the past even as financial reverses seem to have laid them low.

REMEMBERING BABYLON

Malouf returns to the Australian colonial period in *Remembering Babylon*, which recounts the lives of Scottish pioneers in a remote settlement. Their hardscrabble but contented existence in the Northern Queensland tropics is disrupted by the appearance of a near-naked Englishman named Gemmy Fairley, who has spent sixteen years with an Aborigine tribe. When confronted by the stalwart Scots, he shouts: "Do not shoot . . . I am a B-b-british object!" Gemmy gains a reluctant acceptance in the community until two of the tribesmen visit him. The deep-seated fear of the Aborigines and of someone tainted by them is so strong that the settlers eventually drive Gemmy back to the bush, where he is killed during a raid

on the tribe he has joined. The narrative also follows into adulthood some of the children who knew Gemmy and reveals how their contact with this exile affected their lives.

Fragmented in structure and abbreviated in its development, the novel falters as a precise depiction of pioneer life and as a sympathetic account of the hapless Gemmy. Instead, it has been read as a symbolic representation of exile—in particular, artistic and linguistic exile, which brings to mind the earlier books *An Imaginary Life* and *Harland's Half Acre*. On this level, the narrative questions obliquely through the experiences of the pioneers how the Australian artist can grasp the fresh experience that the new continent offers and reshape it in untried forms apart from inherited European culture. Gemmy appears to represent the artist's answer to this dilemma. He realizes that there exists a connection between language and landscape. At least metaphorically, by forgetting his English and replacing it with a native language, he is better able to reach an understanding of the new world.

THE CONVERSATIONS AT CURLOW CREEK

In *The Conversations at Curlow Creek*, Malouf again finds a rich source of metaphor in colonial Australia and the great emptiness of the continent. The conversations take place between Michael Adair, a policeman, and Daniel Carney, a bush ranger. They meet in a desolate area, where Carney, the remaining member of a gang, awaits hanging. The two men spend the night before the execution in a hut, intermittently talking, remembering, sleeping, and dreaming. About half of the book is devoted to actual conversations, the rest to flashbacks of the two men's lives in Ireland. Although the direct exchanges are stronger than the extended forays into memory, revelation of their disparate backgrounds intensifies the immediate situation. The two men take opposite views of the colony, reflecting a dichotomy that has long dominated Australian thinking. The doomed one sees the barren land as a source of punishment, a place that makes life hard, while the policeman imagines settlers prospering there. Along with this exploration of colonialism, the novel focuses on a timeless question: Which takes precedence in human affairs,

Malraux's novels, including *Man's Hope*—based on the Spanish Civil War, in which Malraux himself actively participated—are not vehicles for political ideology. Indeed, the realistic political struggle portrayed in his fiction is now viewed as only a backdrop for the metaphysical conflict confronting Malraux's characters. In short, Malraux's portrayal of humankind is what is most valued by serious readers of today; this compelling picture calls up questions that critics and thinkers may ponder for a long time to come.

BIOGRAPHY

Georges André Malraux was born in Paris, France, on November 3, 1901, the only child of young working-class parents. When Malraux was about eight years old, his parents separated, and his mother took him with her to live with her mother and sister above a grocery store in Bondy, a northeastern suburb of Paris. One of Malraux's favorite pastimes was reading, and the close proximity of Paris and the Louvre allowed him to discover art at a fairly early age. For a time, Malraux commuted to school in Paris. He was judged to be an exceptionally good student, but, when he turned eighteen, he abruptly lost interest in formal education. He dropped out of school and rented an apartment in Paris. To supplement the allowance given him by his father, Malraux worked for a bookstore, buying rare books. Gradually, he turned to writing articles for magazines, and his interests drew him into Parisian literary circles. At the age of twenty, he met and married Clara Goldschmidt, an intelligent woman, somewhat older than he, from a wealthy Jewish family. Their impetuous wedding and liberal marriage were like a romantic adventure. What appears to have united Malraux and Goldschmidt was their mutual interest in art and their desire to travel around the world. All

the women who were closely associated with Malraux were writers or artists; all were intelligent and endowed with dynamic personalities. Goldschmidt spoke German, French, English, and Italian and would later write six volumes of memoirs about her life with Malraux, entitled *Le Bruit de nos pas* (1963, 1966; *Memoirs*, 1967).

In 1923, the young married couple undertook an archaeological trip to Indochina. This expedition led to Malraux's arrest for trying to take bas-reliefs from a Khmer temple. Eventually, Malraux was released, however, as a result of the protestations of many French writers, including Louis Aragon, André Breton, André Gide, Max Jacob, and François Mauriac. In a second trip to Indochina, Malraux and Clara attempted to publish a French-language, antigovernment newspaper in Saigon. When one newspaper, *L'Indochine*, was forced out of business; another, *L'Indochine enchaînée* (Indochina in chains), was started, only to be suppressed by the government in 1926. Malraux's first four novels are based on his readings about Asia and some of his experiences there.

In 1936, a year before the publication of *Man's Hope*, Malraux volunteered to fight in the Spanish

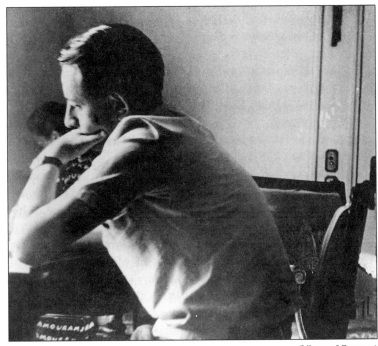

(Library of Congress)

Civil War, in which he commanded an international air squadron. Subsequently, Malraux and Clara officially separated; their marriage had been strained for some time. Clara, who had given birth to their daughter, Florence, did not want a divorce.

After his separation from Clara, Malraux had a seven-year liaison with Josette Clotis, a young, vivacious writer who, when he met her, was working for *Marianne*, a magazine for which Malraux was writing at that time. During World War II, Malraux enlisted in a French tank regiment; he was taken prisoner in Sens in 1940 but escaped. Later, he worked for the Resistance movement. Josette bore Malraux two sons, Pierre-Gauthier and Vincent. When the children were still quite young, in 1944, Josette was killed when she accidentally fell in front of a moving train.

In 1945, Malraux became minister of information for the first de Gaulle government. Now that the war, with its persecution of Jews, was over, the divorce from Clara could finally be settled. In 1950, Malraux married again, to Madeleine Lieux Malraux. The widow of Malraux's half brother, Roland, who had been killed in the war, Madeleine had been a concert pianist.

From 1959 to 1969, Malraux became minister for cultural affairs in the second de Gaulle government. During this time, he made several trips to European countries, the United States, China, and parts of Asia to give speeches on culture and art and to talk with foreign dignitaries such as John F. Kennedy, Mao Tse-tung, and Indira Gandhi.

In 1961, the two sons that Malraux had with Josette Clotis were killed in an automobile accident. A period of depression followed this event, but in 1966, when Malraux was sixty-five years old, he met an old acquaintance, Louise de Vilmorin, who subsequently changed his life. She and Malraux had had an affair in 1933. A romantic, aristocratic woman, she was also a poet and a novelist. Despite their age, their reunion sparked off all the madness of a first love. After Louise's death in 1969, Malraux stayed at the Vilmorin family estate, located not far from Paris, in Verrières, where he spent his later years writing. When he died of a pulmonary embolism on No-

vember 23, 1976, André Malraux was given national homage at the Louvre.

ANALYSIS

André Malraux's novels immediately come alive by means of their style. The literary text gives one the impression of capturing a series of fleeting moments as a recent newspaper headline, a dispatch, a radio transmission, or a telephone call is urgently related. Passing time is often officially noted by date and time. Scenes are cinematically condensed. Malraux's heroes are already enmeshed in a struggle in which they have chosen to fight. Even the most insignificant gestures and movements are now powerful and carry with them the urgency of a crisis. When events occur or communiqués are released, Malraux's characters grope to understand what is really happening in the conflict surrounding them—what is false and what is true. With Malraux's heroes, the reader plunges into a void of uncertainty that encompasses not only the happenings related in the novel but also the inner turmoil of the heroes themselves.

In this crucial situation, Malraux's protagonists experience a loss of equilibrium and ask themselves questions that, under normal circumstances, they would not ask. Why are they fighting, who is the enemy, and who are they? Regarded by many critics as a precursor of the existentialists, Malraux often causes his heroes to confront death—an important theme in his fiction, because the novelist can thereby question the very essence of humanity.

According to Malraux, the greatest tragedy of human destiny in the contemporary world is not the meaninglessness of his existence, doomed to be defeated by death. Rather, Malraux believes that humanity's real tragedy lies within people themselves and, more specifically, in modern notions of individualism. The novelist's brief encounter with the Surrealist movement proved to him that the individual does not know himself or herself. Contrary to Surrealist thought, however, Malraux believed that one's inner being could never be understood. Thus, the ego of Malraux's characters is portrayed as an incongruous monster. Moreover, his protagonists' preoccupation with themselves as individuals only leads them to draw closer to madness and increasingly to isolate themselves from others. Individualism, then, is at the heart of the most significant theme of Malraux's fiction, solitude. Absolute solitude, in which one becomes alienated from others as well as from oneself, represents, for Malraux, the most tormenting of human conditions.

To counteract human solitude and give meaning to human existence, faced by the inevitability of death, another theme appears in Malraux's fiction: *fraternité virile*, or virile fraternity, a term that denotes a special bond between human beings, a solidarity with others of such strength that individual solitude and metaphysical anguish are overcome. Malraux's service during World War II and in an air squadron in the Spanish Civil War confirmed his conviction that the comradeship between soldiers can sometimes approximate this ideal of fraternal love.

Himself an avowed agnostic, Malraux painted in his fiction the tragic picture not of humanity's loss of God, but rather of the loss of man's belief in man. Particularly in *Man's Fate* and *Man's Hope*, Malraux proposed that man can recapture the latter conviction through what may be termed a personal revolution. When some of Malraux's heroes revolt against the dominance of the ego and succeed in defeating its power over them, their unity with others shows that mutual love between human beings is possible.

THE CONQUERORS

Published in 1928, *The Conquerors* introduced the journalistic style that became characteristic of Malraux's fiction. The novel begins with a radioed news flash, "A general strike is decreed in Canton," and updates about political upheaval in Canton and Hong Kong punctuate the entire book. From the beginning, the narrator—who remains nameless—writes down dates, places, and whatever factual impressions he can record. In the first part of the novel, his boat draws near Canton, where he intends to meet and work with an old friend, Pierre Garin, now called Garine. The narrator has not seen Pierre for five years; when he comes across verbal and written reports about him, he strives to find once again the man he used to know so well. Garine, however, has become so different that he might as well be a stranger.

Garine had always been a gambler and an adventurer; now, in charge of the propaganda bureau in Canton, he is obsessed by a power struggle over the expulsion of the British from Hong Kong.

When the narrator finally sees Garine face to face, it is obvious that the latter can think of nothing but his struggle for power and his enigmatic adversary, Tcheng-Daï. The latter is an old Chinese leader whose conservative, altruistic philosophy opposes the liberal individualism of Garine. In a way, Malraux continues in *The Conquerors* a debate that was at the heart of his philosophical tale *The Temptation of the West*, in which the letters exchanged between a European in China and a Chinese traveler in France contrast Western and Eastern philosophical beliefs. More important in *The Conquerors* than the revealing questions to which such a contrast leads, however, is the notion of solitude, which Malraux presents primarily through his hero, Garine.

Probably the most compelling theme in Malraux's fiction, solitude is often portrayed, as Malraux depicts it in *The Conquerors*, as the result of a break of ties to another—a break caused by an individual's personal ambition and by the egocentric image he has of himself. It is significant that, before going to China, Garine had already totally rebelled against society as a result of a brush with the law. The brief account of the trial in which Garine was found guilty of financing illegal abortions, although undoubtedly based on Malraux's own trial for having attempted to take several bas-reliefs of an Indochinese temple out of the country, also prefigures in many ways Albert Camus's well-known novel *The Stranger* (1942). Like the trial of Camus's hero, Meursault, Garine's court judgment is shown to be an absurd ritual. In Garine's eyes, his trial was a ludicrous comedy, since the process of "judging" him only proved the refusal of the jurors to understand what he had done. Although Garine knew that what he had done was not legal, he had spent his own money to help destitute women pay for their abortions.

Since the trial, Garine's hatred for society has led him to think only of himself. With pride, he declares to the narrator at one point that he is completely asocial and hates all humanity, including himself. What his ego demands is power. Even the political struggle in which Garine is now engaged, where it is a question of the expulsion of the British from Hong Kong, is a highly personal fight in which he sees himself as having to emerge as conqueror. This image of himself has isolated him not only from the social establishment but also from himself. Dominated by his quest for power, Garine willfully ignores the signs of tropical disease that he knows is slowly eroding his vitality and about which his doctor has alerted him in vain. Garine will get necessary medical help later.

Finally, the friendship between Garine and the narrator has likewise broken down because of Garine's obsession. Malraux shows by his narrator's continual physical presence during nearly every minute of Garine's day—logically explained by the fact that he is Garine's secretary and Chinese interpreter—that the bond of friendship that united them in the past has been destroyed. The narrator's cautious attempts to reach Pierre Garin are only rebuffed.

It is somewhat ironic that a secondary character in the novel, Hong, who is as obsessed with terrorism as Garine is by political power, should, in one scene, explain to a group of shocked observers—which includes Garine and the narrator—that he kills, not for politics or to change the social order, but rather to prove something to himself.

In the final pages of the novel, Malraux suggests the need for fraternal love when Garine, upon learning of the successful advance of the Red Army, spontaneously embraces the narrator. This embrace causes all the latent fraternal emotions of the narrator to burst forth, but when he looks at Garine again, the latter seems to be as distant as ever. Although Garine is now closer than ever to death, he is already thinking about going to England to continue his conqueror's fight.

THE ROYAL WAY

Even though Malraux had not yet visited China when he wrote about it in *The Conquerors*, the Cambodian jungle where he situates the characters of *The Royal Way* was all too familiar to him. Published in 1930, *The Royal Way* is linked to the author in two ways.

First, through one of his protagonists, Claude Vannec, Malraux retraces his own footsteps to Indo-china, where he had uncovered stone engravings and tried to remove them. Malraux conceals the motivations of his hero and also his own when two different arguments are proposed for the dangerous archaeological trip. Claude is aware that the bas-reliefs he secures will yield him a fine sum of money, but, even so, it is difficult to conclude that he is nothing more than a fortune hunter, because of the argument he makes to the director of the French Institute in Saigon. His venture, Claude explains, will ultimately benefit all humankind. Someone must uncover the bas-reliefs and statues of Khmer art so that they can be preserved for history. The government does not propose to track them down; other adventurers are turned away by the perilousness of the enterprise. It is therefore possible to conclude that Claude is a courageous man, willing to risk his life for the sake of art.

Through his second protagonist, Perken, Malraux portrays a legendary middle-aged hero, supposedly modeled after the adventurer David de Mayrena, who, in the tradition of Lawrence of Arabia, had made himself king of the Sedangs. The link between Perken and the author occurs through the theme of death, which dominates the novel and which is clearly associated with Perken.

It is probable that Perken—a man who is faced by an inevitable death—is, to some extent, a fictionalized shadow of Malraux's own father, who, only a year before the publication of *The Royal Way*, had suffered a massive stroke. The relationship between the two protagonists of Malraux's book can be seen as a mythical association—perhaps as much imaginary as real—between the novelist and his father. Claude strongly admires Perken, not only for what he has done but also for the aura of grandeur that seems to surround him. Moreover, Claude feels a strong affinity between himself and Perken, Malraux explaining, for example, that Claude, like his older companion, has been obsessed with death ever since his grandfather accidentally killed himself with an ax (Malraux's own grandfather had died in this way).

Near the end of the book, when Perken is slowly dying from having fallen on an arrowhead planted in the ground by Stieng warriors, Claude has the choice

OTHER MAJOR WORKS

SHORT FICTION: *Lunes en papier*, 1921; *Le Royaume farfelu*, 1922, 1928.

NONFICTION: *La Tentation de l'Occident*, 1926 (criticism; *The Temptation of the West*, 1961); *Le Musée imaginaire*, 1947 (*Museum Without Walls*, 1949); *La Création artistique*, 1949 (*The Creative Act*, 1949); *La Monnaie de l'absolu*, 1950 (*The Twilight of the Absolute*, 1950; rev. as *Les Voix du silence*, 1951 [*The Voices of Silence*, 1953]); *La Psychologie de l'art*, 1947-1950 (collective title for previous 3 works; *The Psychology of Art*, 1949-1950); *Saturne: Essai sur Goya*, 1950 (*Saturn: An Essay on Goya*, 1957); *La Statuaire*, 1952; *Des bas-reliefs aux grottes sacrées*, 1954; *Le Monde chrétien*, 1954 (previous 3 titles collectively known as *Le Musée imaginaire de la sculpture mondiale*); *Le Surnaturel*, 1957 (*The Metamorphosis of the Gods*, 1960); *Antimémoires*, 1967 (*Anti-Memoires*, 1968); *Les Chênes qu'on abat*, 1971 (*Felled Oaks: Conversation with de Gaulle*, 1972); *L'Irréel*, 1974; *La Tête d'obsidienne*, 1974 (*Picasso's Mask*, 1976); *Lazare*, 1974 (*Lazarus*, 1977); *Le Miroir des limbes*, 1976 (collective title for *Antimémoires*, *Les Chênes qu'on abat*, *La Tête d'obsidienne*, and *Lazare*); *L'Intemporel*, 1975; *La Métamorphose des dieux*, 1976 (collective title for *Le Surnaturel*, *L'Irréel*, and *L'Intemporel*); *L'Homme précaire et la littérature*, 1977.

BIBLIOGRAPHY

Bloom, Harold, ed. *André Malraux*. New York: Chelsea House, 1988. Essays on Malraux's major novels, on Malraux and his critics, on his creation of a Bolshevik hero, on his philosophy of art, and on his treatment of violence and of Asian man. Includes introduction, chronology, and bibliography.

Cate, Curtis. *André Malraux: A Biography*. New York: Fromm International, 1995. A solid, scholarly effort. See the helpful preface in which Cate assesses previous biographies. Includes detailed notes and bibliography.

De Courcel, Martine, ed. *Malraux: Life and Work*. New York: Harcourt Brace Jovanovich, 1976. Divided into sections on Malraux's life and work.

The first section includes essays on his early novels and his experience in Indochina and in Spain. The second section explores Malraux's "unity of purpose through art and action," the myth he established of himself as a writer, and his philosophy and creative process. With a chronology, notes, and bibliography.

Harris, Geoffrey T. *André Malraux: A Reassessment*. New York: St. Martin's Press, 1996. A good, updated look at Malraux's works. Includes bibliographical references and an index.

Hewitt, James Robert. *André Malraux*. New York: Ungar, 1978. A short, clear introduction to Malraux's life and work. Contains a useful bibliography.

Jenkins, Cecil. *André Malraux*. New York: Twayne, 1972. Chapters on the writer and the myth, on Malraux's career as an anti-Fascist, and on his major novels and memoirs make this a very useful introduction. Provides chronology, notes, and an annotated bibliography.

Lewis, R. W. B. *Malraux: A Collection of Critical Essays*. Englewood Cliffs, N.J.: Prentice-Hall, 1964. See the useful introduction, "Malraux and His Critics," as well as essays on Malraux's image of humans and their view of art and the intellect. An especially good collection with representative work of Malraux's best critics. Includes chronology and bibliography.

Romeiser, John Beals. *André Malraux: A Reference Guide, 1940-1990*. New York: G. K. Hall, 1994. Indispensable for the student of Malraux. With indexes.

THOMAS MANN

Born: Lübeck, Germany; June 6, 1875
Died: Zurich, Switzerland; August 12, 1955

PRINCIPAL LONG FICTION

Buddenbrooks: Verfall einer Familie, 1901 (English translation, 1924)

Tonio Kröger, 1903 (novella; English translation, 1914)

Tristan, 1903 (English translation, 1925)

Königliche Hoheit, 1909 (*Royal Highness*, 1916)

Der Tod in Venedig, 1912 (novella; *Death in Venice*, 1925)

Der Zauberberg, 1924 (*The Magic Mountain*, 1927)

Unordnung und frühes Leid, 1926 (novella; *Disorder and Early Sorrow*, 1929)

Die Geschichten Jaakobs, 1933 (*Joseph and His Brothers*, 1934; also as *The Tales of Jacob*, 1934)

Der junge Joseph, 1934 (*The Young Joseph*, 1935)

Joseph in Ägypten, 1936 (*Joseph in Egypt*, 1938)

Joseph, der Ernährer, 1943 (*Joseph the Provider*, 1944)

Joseph und seine Brüder, 1933-1943 (collective title for previous 4 novels; *Joseph and His Brothers*, 1948)

Lotte in Weimar, 1939 (*The Beloved Returns*, 1940)

Die vertauschten Köpfe: Eine indische Legend, 1940 (novella; *The Transposed Heads: A Legend of India*, 1941)

Doktor Faustus: Das Leben des deutschen Tonsetzers Adrian Leverkühn, erzählt von einem Freunde, 1947 (*Doctor Faustus: The Life of the German Composer Adrian Leverkühn as Told by a Friend*, 1948)

Der Erwählte, 1951 (*The Holy Sinner*, 1951)

Bekenntnisse des Hochstaplers Felix Krull: Der Memoiren erster Teil, 1954 (*Confessions of Felix Krull, Confidence Man: The Early Years*, 1955)

(The Nobel Foundation)

OTHER LITERARY FORMS

Thomas Mann presents a complex intellectual and aesthetic physiognomy, primarily in the area of long and short fiction, though for many he is equally powerful as an autobiographical, literary-critical, or political essayist. Alongside his novels and novelettes stand his novellas and short stories; the two types of fiction are often mixed in collections such as *Ausgewahlte Erzählungen* (1945). A true twentieth century classical author, Mann spanned all the restless philo-

sophical issues of his day, obsessed with the notion of decay and nothingness, with the concept of beauty superhumanly understood and melancholically associated with death, and with the shifting verities of political, social, and moral existence in a decadent world. On one hand, with the exception of the World War I period, during his early and middle years he guarded jealously his posture of intellectual independence and impartiality before historical events, retaining the objectivity of a witnessing spectator and artist, either acquiescing or rejecting (and doing so often, given the distance he maintained) with ironic glances. On the other hand, this stance did not preclude (particularly toward the end of his life) a strong ideological, idealistic commitment. These qualities of fundamental impartiality and occasional engagement spilled over into his noncreative writing, from the essays later collected in *Adel des Geistes: Sechzehn Versuche zum Problem der Humanität* (1945;

Essays of Three Decades, 1947) and *Neue Studien* (1948) to more openly political tracts and those pieces collected in *Altes und Neues* (1953). The latter collection contains some of Mann's best autobiographical and autocritical writings. The intimate relationship between some of his nonfiction and his fiction creates a thought network that unifies his total production, which is that of an author less interested in conventional narrative than in analytical discourse. Thus, Mann's thoughts on writers Johann Wolfgang von Manzoni and Leo Tolstoy relate to *The Magic Mountain*, as those on philosopher Friedrich Nietzsche and writer Fyodor Dostoevski relate to *Doctor Faustus* or as, conversely, his autocritical comments on the tetralogy *Joseph and His Brothers* grow out of a lecture on psychoanalyst Sigmund Freud. As a result, Mann's narrative fiction contains little plot, as plot is narrowly understood. A document that stands on its own is *Betrachtungen eines Unpolitischen* (1918; *Reflections of a Nonpolitical Man*, 1983), with its self-examining reflections mingled with a polemic against Western civilization and democracy (note the war-year dates). Finally, to round out his writer's profile and not to be overlooked are pieces such as the short prose idyll about his mongrel Bauschan, "Herr und Hund" (1918; "A Man and His Dog," 1936); his charming and sentimental (if unsuccessful) attempt at poetry, "Gesang vom Kindchen" (1919), on the occasion of the birth of his last child; his letter about matrimony, "Über die Ehe: Brief an den Grafen Keyserling" (1923), affirming the moral and religious validity of the institution; and his one attempt at drama, *Fiorenza* (1906), dealing with the supposed confrontation between the paganizing, artloving Lorenzo de' Medici and the moralistic, religious fanatic Girolamo Savonarola. In 1956, one year after his death, Mann's *Nachlese* appeared.

ACHIEVEMENTS

While concerned primarily with the problem of Germany, however socially, politically, artistically, or morally perceived, Mann's focus always benefited from an awareness of spatial and temporal considerations, from the geographical and the historical. Holland and London, Valparaiso and Florence, Russia

and Venice, Palestrina and Switzerland, Italy and the Near East, Mesopotamia and Egypt, Torre di Venere and Davos, India and Lisbon—all these settings round out a worldview that is in no way restricted to the Rhineland or Thuringia or Munich or Lübeck, Hamburg, Weimar, or Bremen. Similarly, the historical dimension shifts broadly, from the Napoleonic wars in *Buddenbrooks* and the Italian Renaissance in *Fiorenza* or the Lutheran Reformation in *Betrachtungen eines Unpolitischen* to medieval society in *The Holy Sinner*, the Greek civilization in passages from *Death in Venice*, the Judeo-Egyptian world in *Joseph and His Brothers*, even the prehistorical world, in passages from *Confessions of Felix Krull*. All was designed to arrive at a better understanding not only of Germany but also of the human condition, of what it means to be human.

The sheer breadth of his perspective facilitated, perhaps even inspired, one of Mann's major analytical devices: contrast and antithesis. The Dionysian of Italy and the arts, of profane love and the irrational, is juxtaposed to the Apollonian of Germany and the mercantile, of sacred love and the rational. Like Goethe and many other "Teutons" before him, Mann felt acutely the lure of southern Europe, the so-called *Drang nach Süden*, whereby Italy (and Greece, sometimes translated into what is Latin, French, or even Russian) beckons like a Siren of art, music, and poetry the efficient and practical will of the northerner. The Bohemian attracts the bourgeois. With the attraction, interwoven with the whole question of genius or the superior creative spirit, come the notions of disease, sickness, and death as they counterbalance soundness, health, and life.

If the names and origins of the characters mislead at times in this regard, the antithetical premise remains the same. Tonio Kröger (Italian-German)—like the German engineer Hans Castorp in *The Magic Mountain*, who falls in love with the French-named Russian Clavdia Chauchat—is torn between the two poles, very much like the author himself. The Germanic Hans Hansen and Ingeborg, in *Tonio Kröger*, are juxtaposed to the Slavic and more romantic Lisabeta Ivanovna; in *The Magic Mountain*, the rational Italian humanist scholar Settembrini opposes the mystical, Jesuit-trained Jew Naphta; and in *Doctor Faustus*, the staid, conservative bourgeois Professor Serenus Zeitblom contrasts only too obviously with the genial hedonist composer Adrian Leverkühn. The same kind of dialectic obtains outside Mann's novels and novellas, for example, in "Gesang vom Kindchen," with the Nordic father and the southern/eastern mother; in *Fiorenza*, with the hedonistic Lorenzo and the ascetic Savonarola; indeed, even in "A Man and His Dog," with the mongrel Bauschan and the purebred Percy. This contrasting technique usually makes for character delineations that project Mann's own views through the protagonists or that portray eccentricities through the secondary characters.

Most often we are dealing with artist figures, creators concerned with beauty, and the sound of music is generally audible. According to the nineteenth century philosopher Arthur Schopenhauer, music is the central energy of life; according to Nietzsche, it gives birth to the spirit of literature. Along with Goethe, Freud and Carl Jung, Tolstoy and Dostoevski, and the aestheticist Stefan George, Nietzsche in particular moved Mann to a number of speculations. For Mann, the superior artist is touched with madness and the devil, ecstasy and disease; isolated, he does not achieve the modest comforts and simple expectations of life—not even the love of a woman. One of Mann's finest achievements lies in his representation of this concept in *Doctor Faustus*, a novel that readers and critics, unless they are versed in the art of music, will never fully understand. With its analyses of Johann Sebastian Bach, Franz Joseph Haydn, Ludwig van Beethoven, Frédéric Chopin, twelve-tone composition, and modern music generally, it is a culmination of a process that had begun years before, with the later generations in *Buddenbrooks*, the Wagnerian presence in *Tristan*, and the musical observations in *The Magic Mountain*, and which had been abetted by Mann's association with conductor Bruno Walter and composer Arnold Schönberg. More than Honoré de Balzac, E. T. A. Hoffmann, Romain Rolland, or Gabriele D'Annunzio, whose utterances on music have left a mark in novelistic history, Mann developed a unique facility to grasp the essence of the musical experience, theoretically and historically,

and to communicate it in a way the art of the novel has never known before or since (Alejo Carpentier notwithstanding). Though associated with disease and therefore inhabited by a diabolism that places the mystique-powered Richard Wagner and Gustav Mahler at the threshold of Nazism, music, however suspect to Mann, is nevertheless the centrifugal core of the free human impulse.

Mann preferred opportunities to meditate to opportunities to contemplate. Music is meditation, a landscape is contemplation, and it has often been noted that, outside the mountain (see *The Magic Mountain*) and the sea (see *Death in Venice*), Mann rarely paints landscapes, despite *Joseph and His Brothers*. What he excels in depicting is human nature, the portrait over the landscape, in all of its most intricate and elusive details—a talent that made him appreciate Albrecht Dürer, as Leverkühn's soulful fascination with the painter clearly indicates.

Mann's other achievement lies in his penetrating understanding of all that is human, the vagaries of sublimity and grotesqueness, of hedonism, passion, and violence, and of measure, Puritanism, and gentility. He discovers the stimulation of sickness and the relation between disease and genius, and he combines his observations with a keen interest in myth (there are archetypal reminiscences in all of his works) and its recurrence in the human experience; most obviously, the Faust archetype reemerges in *Doctor Faustus*. In line with Mann's psychological/ psychoanalytical preoccupations, one must mention his concern with eroticism, an almost *sui generis* eroticism, not one of pseudopornographic titillation but one derived from Nietzsche's, and then Freud's, views on erotic phenomena. Concealed at first, in such works as "Der kleine Herr Friedemann" (1897; "Little Herr Friedemann," 1936) and *Confessions of Felix Krull* (which was actually begun as early as 1911), sensual love surfaces finally in *The Magic Mountain*, when, upon contracting tuberculosis, Hans Castorp develops a passionate love for Clavdia Chauchat, just as Leverkühn achieves stature as a composer after contracting syphilis. *The Transposed Heads* and *The Holy Sinner* (here we are dealing with incest) sink even deeper into the erotic. If the psycho-

of American culture, as he saw it, chilled him; indeed, he said that in the New World he felt an imposition on his freedom. He returned permanently to Europe, to Switzerland, in 1953, living first in Erlenbach, then in Kilchberg, and finally in Zurich. Not to leave anything undone, he returned to work on *Confessions of Felix Krull, Confidence Man*, begun more than two score years before and temporarily resumed in 1923, which he finally finished in 1954—the lighthearted story of a handsome and intelligent man who lives day by day and derives maximum pleasure from his attributes. On the threshold of his eightieth year, Mann fittingly composed his last work for the May 9, 1955, anniversary of Friedrich Schiller's death, commemorated on both sides of the Iron Curtain, *Versuch über Schiller*—fitting because this poet, too, as the critic Bonaventura Tecchi suggests, had ultimately found an abiding solace not in dialectics but in the ideal, not in intellectual play but in human duty. After a brief illness, Mann died in Zurich three months later. In the long run, then, Mann remains the classical modern writer because he was able to dissect the neuroses and reveal the inquietudes of the human condition of the twentieth century by staying close to it.

ANALYSIS

In *Meine Zeit* (1950), Thomas Mann wrote:

> If Christian means to consider life, one's own life, as a guilt, a debt, an invoice to pay, as a subject of religious uneasiness requiring immediate remission, redemption, and justification, then those theologians who see me as the type of un-Christian author are not at all correct. For rarely has the work of a lifetime, even when it appeared to be a skeptical, artistic, and humorous game, been born totally and from the outset of an anxious desire for reparation, for purification, and for justification as was my personal—and so modestly exemplary—attempt to practice the art.

More than that of most writers, Mann's own literary production can come under the heading of a quest.

BUDDENBROOKS

As its German subtitle indicates, *Buddenbrooks* tells of the decadence of a family—by extension, the nineteenth century bourgeoisie, which socially and politically lost to the lower classes it had worked to advance, and aesthetically so enriched the spirit with inner life that no practical energy was left for the outer life of action. In 1835, in Hanseatic Lübeck, the clan of the old grain merchant Johann Buddenbrook appeared wealthy and solid when it inaugurated its economic prominence with a grand banquet (Mann describes it in no fewer than sixty pages) in its seventeenth century palace on Mengstrasse, with offices on the ground floor. Four generations later, the process of weakening and disintegration ends, in 1876, when the delicate and artistic Hanno dies of typhus in a modest house outside Porta.

The decadence, like an uncontrollable germ inside the family body organism, is ineluctable. Mann does not present what is commonly referred to in Marxist terms as class struggle, nor does he base his perspective either on the French, naturalistic tradition or on the historical manner that informs John Galsworthy's *The Forsyte Saga* (1922). There is something less scientific or legendary than personal about *Buddenbrooks*, for it was the chronicle of Mann's own family as seen by him, an aesthete doting on the fantasies of the inner life yet a bourgeois with a keen sense of reality and of observation. Hence, Mann's sensibility and understanding are interpenetrated with his irony and detachment. Men and women, relatives and friends, their conversations and values, dress and habits, food and furniture provoke the author's sarcastic smile, but at the same time he senses in them something solid and virtuous. The banquet sets the stage, like a skillful overture adumbrating many coming themes. Not many events occupy the novel's six hundred pages, but a whole way of life does.

Johann Senior is orderly and self-assured; Johann Junior (the Consul) is self-satisfied, without his father's daring and vision; his older brother Gotthold, whose marriage has never received his father's sanction, finds himself nearly dispossessed. Of the Consul's children, only Thomas keeps up the family name by being made consul and elected senator, but, though intelligent and elegant, he continues the business lazily and irresponsibly, without self-criticism, dabbling in aesthetics and philosophy, morbidly and nervously concerned with "subconscious needs," and in the long run ruinously alone in his palace, his wife, business, and future gone. His brother Christian has some of the old Buddenbrook energy, but he cannot harness it, failing repeatedly in business ventures, trying to "find somehow his place in the world," and finally becoming insane. Their sister Annette inspires no assurance with her impulsiveness and frivolousness. She does not marry the older, unattractive Herr Grünlich, but her elder sister, Tony, who fills the novel, develops both interest and pride in the family genealogy, does not wait for the medical student, Mortens, with whom she has fallen in love at the beach, and marries Grünlich, who turns out to be a self-seeking bankrupt. Tony, on the other hand, is a fine echo of the good bourgeois, sentimental and dutiful, vivacious and supportive, but she must undergo divorce, another marriage, and another divorce, and see her daughter Erika do the same (Erika's man is jailed for fraud). The other marriage was to Herr Permaneder, a man "as good as bread" but who does not have enough "for home and beer"; he is caught with his arms around the cook Babette, and all breaks up again.

Tony's school-year friend is the Dutch Gerda, whom her brother Thomas married in Holland and who thinks only about her attractiveness, music (Bach and Wagner), and her relationship with the impetuous Lieutenant von Trotha, who is equally interested in music. The semblance of riches continues; Thomas acquires an even grander mansion, on Fischerstrasse, but, as he tells Tony: "Often the outward and visible material signs and symbols of happiness and success only show themselves when the process of decline has already set in." Even the tender devotion of the "eternal tutor" of three generations of Buddenbrooks, Ida Jungmann, or the correct and attentive teacher of all proper young ladies in town, Sesemi Weichbrodt (whom Mann has conclude the novel with a philosophical observation about life after death: "Es ist so!"—"So it is!"), cannot stem the creeping disintegration. When the last of Thomas's children, Johann (known familiarly as Hanno), comes along, he is frail and dreamy, musically gifted, a violinist, and he dies in young manhood.

In this context, a natural event such as death assumes symbolic proportions, and retrospectively, through its recurrence, functions almost as a leitmotif. As each character lives his or her life, so does each die his or her death: Johann Senior quietly, with dignity; his daughter Klara, ingenuously; Johann Junior, unexpectedly; Johann Junior's wife, Elisabeth, deliberately and slowly (the agony takes twenty pages); Consul Kröger, on his outdoor marble steps; Senator Thomas, on the pavement, where two passersby recognize him; and Hanno, exhausted and drained of the little vitality that his music had afforded him. This atmosphere cuts through all social strata encountered in the novel, and through it, the novel rises philosophically above the narrower confines of the decadence of Thomas Mann's own family.

TONIO KRÖGER

The story of *Tonio Kröger* is related to that of *Buddenbrooks*; even the protagonist's surname derives from the earlier novel. Unlike Hanno, however, Tonio is a vigorous young writer, strongly reminiscent of Mann; indeed, the autobiographical thrust of the story is only too clear: a temperamental, artistic mother; a practical Lübeck businessman for a father; and a shy, sensitive adolescent poet who feels "inferior" to his companions, such as the normal, healthy, athletic, and popular Hans Hansen, who, though a fine scholar, is not interested in Schiller's *Don Carlos* and is far more at ease, and less awkward, on the dancing floor with the Germanic blonde Ingeborg Holm, whom Tonio would like to befriend—this is the basic situation. Years later, well-known in Munich, Tonio is rejected by the romantic young painter Lisbeta Ivanovna, who deems him incapable of shedding his middle-class background. Several queries plague him: Can a true artist ever feel like a normal, honest person? How can modern art reach simple folk? What is it to be an artist? Disillusioned, he returns to Lübeck, where, as a result of the family's financial woes, the ancestral home has been sold; after he is almost arrested, he continues to Denmark where, in an isolated hotel, Hans and Ingeborg arrive on their honeymoon. Tonio sees his life as a failure; deprived of the simple joys and "tired out with envy," he gives up the possibility of living in order to understand it.

Most of this sounds familiar, but the narration is less naturalistic and more impressionistic than in *Buddenbrooks*, and the artistic motif is more pronounced: the contrast between the modern artist's need to transcend the human dimension and his attachment to safer and more traditional ways. Tonio is destined to wander forever between these two poles. Corresponding to Tonio's nature, a musical sense underscores the wandering, displaying Mann's strong musical consciousness. The work is structured along the lines of the A-B-A sonata form, while being punctuated with many nearly word-for-word repetitions of descriptive phrases serving as leitmotifs: a "gentleman with the wild-flower in his buttonhole" (the father); "not being gypsies living in a green wagon" (a metaphor for propriety).

TRISTAN

What Mann later referred to as "a certain fascination with decadence" continued in *Tristan*, which also derived spiritually from *Buddenbrooks*—from the whole *fin de siècle* syndrome in relation to the effect that Wagnerian music can have on society— while presaging *The Magic Mountain* with its sanatorium atmosphere of doctors, attendants, guests, visitors, isolation, and quiet, and the Directress, Fraülein von Osterloh. In *Tristan*, the monotony of the Einfried Sanatorium for consumptives is broken when the prosperous, robust merchant Klöterjahn takes his fragile, lovely wife there—a pianist and the daughter of a patrician of Bremen who is a violinist and whose high culture suggests, in Mann's context, a setting of decadence. She became enfeebled giving birth to a sound son, Anton. In her, a melancholy writer, seeker of beauty, and neurotic intellectual named Detlev Spinell, who cannot shake off, as he would like to, his bourgeois ties, sees a wonderful woman living an ill-designed life with her merchant husband. He induces her, against the doctors' stern orders, to play the piano; the score of Wagner's *Tristan und Isolde* is intoned, exuding the voluptuousness of death. Now she becomes herself, not just "the wife of Herr Klöterjahn," but Gabriele Eckhof. Thereafter, however, her health deteriorates rapidly. Spinell infuriates Klöterjahn by suggesting that at least now Gabriele may die basking in her musical beauty, and he exits into the garden, humming the *Sehnsuchtsmotiv* that accompanies the death of Tristan, though nauseated at the sight of the healthful, "sheer animal spirits" of Anton.

DEATH IN VENICE

No more decadent piece can be found among Mann's works than *Death in Venice*. Another Mann-like protagonist and (successful) writer, Gustav von Aschenbach, exhausted by his labors and his art's artifice, journeys to Venice to seek invigoration and renewal. On the beach and in a Lido hotel lounge, he notices four Polish children with a governess, the sole boy, Tadzio (about fourteen years old), "astonishing, even terrifying" him with his "really godlike beauty." He felt an "unending delicate appeal to his senses" as he devised all kinds of ways to espy him, in the hotel and streets, on boats and sand. All of this takes place without a word of communication between them. The lad who naturally stands for beauty contrasts with the writer who has to strain to create it; Homer and Plato are invoked to help explain Aschenbach's insane love for the boy (he resorts to cosmetics to look younger); rather than invigoration, Aschenbach cultivates a further weakening of his being. Learning of an outbreak of cholera in the city, he neither informs the Polish family nor departs to safety. He falls victim to the disease, and on the day the family is due to leave and Tadzio is dipping a final time into the sea, waving as if beckoning to him, Aschenbach dies.

Mann's exceptionally symbolic, even precious style drags the Greek gods into Byzantine Venice (Dionysus ultimately dispatches Aschenbach), makes Tadzio represent degeneration and death, and plays fluidly with antitheses: youth and old age, Christianity and classicism, Germany (the north) and Italy (the south), health and disease, voluptuous aestheticism and moral conscience, love and death.

THE MAGIC MOUNTAIN

Symbols, motifs, and antitheses interweave in the unusual and complex novel of life and treatment in a sanatorium, *The Magic Mountain*, which moves toward a greater equilibrium and understanding with reference to the totality of living, including its simpler aspects, by stepping away somewhat from the gravitational themes of decadence and dissolution. Hans Castorp, a German engineer from Hamburg, visits his cousin Joachim (who dies after leaving and returning to the institution) in the Alpine valley at Davos, Switzerland. Feeling fatigued with a slight chest oppression in this "magic" realm, Castorp decides to take the cure, extending his sojourn of three weeks to a stay of seven years, losing all track of time until the 1914 "thunderclap" of World War I breaks the spell. In the end, the author hints that Castorp lost his life as a soldier. Yet the magic spell opens up to him a new world of spirit as he comes in contact with various people representing various living forces; in the aggregate, his mountaintop experience brings into view all shades of European culture.

The Magic Mountain has been called a *Bildungsroman*, that is, a novel of individual development; more than this, however, it is a novel of ideological adventure (through long discussions on every conceivable subject, Mann attempts a *summa* of modern knowledge—impossible, of course, but still impressive). It functions on various levels. To begin with, there is the naturalistic description of pathological realities revolving around the illnesses, as well as the presence of many European nationalities, which together suggest embryonically a future society, thanks to the institution's isolated elevation. Then there is the evolution of Castorp as he undergoes many influences: his erotic awakening, immaturely with Pribislav Hippe and passionately (though Mann never had a flair for overwhelming passion) for the sensual and divine Russian redhead, Clavdia Chauchat, representing Eastern eroticism; the intellectual discourses with the Enlightenment humanist and nineteenth century libertarian, the clear rationalist Settembrini, as opposed to the irrational, instinctive, medievally mystic and romantic "apostle of darkness," Naphta, the lawyer who wins the arguments. Naphta shoots himself in a duel with Settembrini. Castorp does not choose between them; they are less characters than ideas in dialogue, ideas blowing through Germany at the time, and their duel was to rend the world.

There is also the unsavory psychiatrist Dr. Krokowski, who probes the recesses of the mind, and the Director, Dr. Hofret Behrens, detached and cynical

with his explanations of human anatomy; these influences shape the intellectual and emotional mosaic of Castorp's formation. Finally, there is Time, which emerges as a passive yet instrumental force whose rhythm beats at a different pace (it nearly stands still) amid the rarefied snows and allows ideas to acquire personalities, as if they were characters.

In this shuttling back and forth between life and death, Castorp would not be able to take stock of himself and his position in the world without the constant drama of oppositions and without being surrounded by all types of personalities. This includes the magnificent and grotesque Dutchman, the friend of Madame Chauchat, Mynherr Pepperkolm, who becomes the ruling spirit of the group but burns himself out in Dionysian fervor. Thanks to all these "events," Castorp gains experience of the world and a balanced view of it, as in the revelation in chapter 5 ("Snow"), when, drowsy in a snowstorm, he dreams of the Apollonian "people of the Sun" (the Greeks), whose moderation and serenity counterbalance the concealed but coexisting Dionysian, elemental, evil forces of life; the dream sets forth the dual structure underlying civilization and art.

THE TALES OF JACOB

Dreams assume prominence in the tetralogy *Joseph and His Brothers*. Mann's familiarity with Freud's theories of the subconscious and dreams, with Jung's archetypes, with Goethe's primal types, and with Nietzsche's Eternal Return was brought to bear on the Genesis story of Joseph—very faithfully retold, but with a clear concern for its mythological import. Thanks to his intellectual mentors, Mann was able to retell the story for the moderns and for future generations, humanize the myth, and make it contemporary. A "prelude" to the first volume, *The Tales of Jacob*, establishes the mythological motifs. Then comes the story, without particular concern for chronology: Jacob's special love for Joseph, God's favorite; Jacob's reverence for the God (Adonai) who subjects him to many trials; Jacob's seven years' work to obtain the hand of Rachel from the "devilish" Laban; the nuptial-bed substitution of Leah for Rachel; Jacob's acquisition of the birthright from Esau; his childbearing relationships with Laban's daughters

1938; *Dieser Friede*, 1938 (*This Peace*, 1938); *Vom künftigen Sieg der Demokratie*, 1938 (*The Coming of Victory of Democracy*, 1938); *Deutsche Hörer!*, 1942 (*Listen, Germany!*, 1943); *Order of the Day: Political Essays and Speeches of Two Decades*, 1942; *Adel des Geistes: Sechzehn Versuche zum Problem der Humanität*, 1945 (*Essays of Three Decades*, 1947); *Neue Studien*, 1948; *Die Entstehung des "Doktor Faustus": Roman eines Romans*, 1949 (*The Story of a Novel: The Genesis of "Doctor Faustus,"* 1961); *Altes und Neues: Kleine Prosa aus fünf Jahrzehnten*, 1953; *Versuch über Schiller*, 1955; *Nachlese: Prosa, 1951-1955*, 1956; *Last Essays*, 1958; *Briefe*, 1961-1965 (3 volumes; partial translation *Letters of Thomas Mann, 1889-1955*, 1970); *Addresses Delivered at the Library of Congress*, 1963; *Wagner und unsere Zeit*, 1963 (*Pro and Contra Wagner*, 1985); *Reden und Aufsätze*, 1965 (2 volumes); *Essays*, 1977-1978 (3 volumes); *Tagebücher*, 1977-1986 (6 volumes; partial translation *Diaries 1918-1939*, 1982); *Goethes Laufbahn als Schriftsteller: Zwölf Essays und Reden zu Goethe*, 1982; *Frage und Antwort: Interviews mit Thomas Mann 1909-1955*, 1983; *Thomas Mann's "Goethe and Tolstoy": Notes and Sources*, 1984.

MISCELLANEOUS: *Gesammelte Werke*, 1956 (12 volumes; includes critical writings in volumes 10-11); *Gesammelte Werke*, 1960-1974 (13 volumes; includes critical writings in volumes 9-11); *Werkausgabe*, 1980-1986 (20 volumes; includes 3 volumes of critical writings).

BIBLIOGRAPHY

Berlin, Jeffrey B., ed. *Approaches to Teaching Mann's "Death in Venice" and Other Short Fiction*. New York: The Modern Language Association, 1992. Part 1 (materials) focuses on general introductions, reference works, and critical studies. Part 2 (approaches) contains in-depth essays on Mann's handling of many themes and his approach to comedy, tradition, modernism, Sigmund Freud, and other thinkers and writers. Includes an extensive bibliography.

Bloom, Harold, ed. *Thomas Mann*. New York: Chelsea House, 1986. Essays on all of Mann's major long fiction, exploring his use of myth, the historical novel, irony, autobiography, and character. A very comprehensive volume with essays by distinguished critics and a bibliography.

Ezergailis, Inta M., ed. *Critical Essays on Thomas Mann*. Boston: G. K. Hall, 1988. A wide-ranging selection of essays, with a comprehensive introduction. No bibliography.

Heilbut, Anthony. *Thomas Mann: Eros and Literature*. New York: Knopf, 1996. The most commanding biography of Mann in English, with a carefully detailed narrative of his life and work. Provides detailed useful notes and an extensive bibliography.

Ridley, Hugh. *Thomas Mann: "Buddenbrooks."* Cambridge, England: Cambridge University Press, 1987. Very useful study guide, with a chronology of Mann's life, a chronology of the novel, a discussion of his life and work, an exploration of his relationship with the nineteenth century novel, and the themes and narrative techniques of *Buddenbrooks*. Contains a very helpful annotated bibliography.

Travers, Martin. *Thomas Mann*. New York: St. Martin's Press, 1992. An excellent, short introductory study, with chapters on Mann's life; the autobiographical elements of his first novels and early stories; and separate chapters on *Death in Venice*, *The Magic Mountain*, the *Joseph* tetralogy, *Doctor Faustus*, and *Confessions of Felix Krull, Confidence Man*. A concluding chapter assesses Mann as a modern novelist. With notes and very useful annotated bibliography.

Alessandro Manzoni

Born: Milan, Italy; March 7, 1785
Died: Milan, Italy; May 22, 1873

PRINCIPAL LONG FICTION

I promessi sposi, 1827, revised 1840-1842 (*The Betrothed*, 1828, revised 1951)

(Library of Congress)

OTHER LITERARY FORMS

Alessandro Manzoni's vast range of intellectual endeavor is astonishing. He was a scholar and thinker in the best sense of the words, respecting thoroughness of documentation and clarity of analysis. His novel maintains an epic quality throughout, not simply because of the constantly expanding tableaux and narrative but also because of the breadth of knowledge that informs it. It is a historical novel because Manzoni was a historian, the author of such works as the *Discorso sopra alcuni punti della storia longobardica in Italia* (1822), the *Lettre à Alphonse de Lamartine* (1848), and the jurisprudential and humanitarian *La storia della colonna infame* (1842; *The Column of Infamy*, 1964). The best known of his philosophical and religious works include *Lettre à Victor Cousin* (1829), *Dell'invenzione* (1850), and *Osservazioni sulla morale cattolica* (1819). His two historical tragedies, *Il conte di Carmagnola* (1820) and *Adelchi* (1822), were much admired by Charles-Augustin de Sainte-Beuve and Johann Wolfgang von Goethe. To round out his accomplishments, it must

be added that as an agronomist he performed a number of experiments at his country retreat in northern Lombardy, some of which yielded positive and enduring results. For all these reasons, his published correspondence, *Epistolario* (1882), makes fascinating reading.

Finally, as a poet, his fame rests primarily on his religious poetry, the *Inni sacri* (1812-1815; *The Sacred Hymns*, 1904), an occasional political piece such as "Marzo 1821" (1821, 1848), and "Il cinque maggio" (1821; "The Napoleonic Ode," 1904), the historico-philosophico-religious ode on the emperor Napoleon Bonaparte, perhaps the most dispassionate view (compared to the poems of Victor Hugo and Henrik Wergeland on the same subject) of the emperor.

ACHIEVEMENTS

Manzoni understood many of his era's religious and moral, historical and political, and aesthetic and linguistic problems, all of which he synthesized in different ways in his various works, particularly in his salient achievement of *The Betrothed*, judged by literary critics around the turn of the century in Geneva to be the greatest novel of the 1800's. In its pluralism of modes, it surpasses generic classification: It is at once historical, philosophical, sociological, metaphysical, psychological, realistic, naturalistic, idealistic, lyric, epic, dramatic, religious, optimistic, pessimistic, moralistic, ironical, oratorical, and both classical and Romantic—in short, universal. For the first time (aside from the picaresque, which exists in a class by itself), the "heroes" are peasants who are battered by historical events and yet around whom all historical events turn. Along with this, it may be said with justification that after Dante's *The Divine Comedy* (c. 1320), *The Betrothed* established the literary Italian language, for there has been no better stylist to dispute this claim. As a playwright, Manzoni has been credited with composing, in *Adelchi*, a truly Christian tragedy, regardless of the pronouncements of theorists that such a tragedy amounts to a contradiction in terms. *The Column of Infamy* stands out as a remarkable example of that two-edged combination of legal literature and literary

his death in Milan on May 22, 1873, and the event inspired composer Giuseppe Verdi to return to work on the *Messa da Requiem*, which he had put aside; it was dedicated to Manzoni and performed in Milan's Church of San Marco on the first anniversary of his death.

Analysis

The premise of Alessandro Manzoni's only novel is a timeworn one: The author claims to have discovered an interesting, but primitive, anonymous manuscript of the seventeenth century dealing with the war, famine, and pestilence occasioned by the occupation of Lombardy by Spanish troops; because this narrative is poorly written, he has decided to retell the story in his own words.

The Betrothed

Somewhere in the Milanese, the story begins, around Lecco and Lake Como, two young peasants wish to marry and seek the services of the village priest. Renzo Tramaglino and Lucia Mondella are good, honest people, and at first they cannot understand Don Abbondio's equivocation followed by a refusal, until it becomes known that the local tyrant, the evil and feared Don Rodrigo, wants Lucia for his own pleasures and through his *bravi* (ruffians) has threatened the priest accordingly. Eight hundred pages later, the two finally marry. The epic of *The Betrothed* lies in between.

From the microcosm of Lecco, the events swell into a macrocosmic panorama of life itself, with all its confusion and wandering, suffering and barbarism, death and destruction. The simple threads of private events weave into ever more complex fabrics until the tapestry of calamities reaches fateful public proportions. The lives of Renzo and Lucia fork at the outset. Fra Cristoforo, a sternly upright monk, arranges for the latter to leave her town and seek shelter in a convent directed by a nun with a dark past, Sister Gertrude, whose story shows Manzoni to be one of the finest psychologists in literature. For his part, Renzo looks for help from a crooked lawyer, Azzeccagarbugli; travels to Milan, where he is greeted by bread riots and other difficulties; and escapes to the Adda River after talking too long at an inn. Meanwhile, angry Don Rodrigo requests assistance in his wrongdoing from a powerful and enigmatic figure, a kind of regional overlord whose name is never told but who goes under the appellation of the Unnamed (*l'innominato*). This spirit of evil (and as such he acquires impressive literary stature, to be considered along with Honoré de Balzac's Vautrin, William Shakespeare's Iago, and the like) has Lucia kidnapped and brought to his secluded castle. One of the most debated issues in literature occurs here: the conversion of this formidable figure to good, seemingly occurring overnight in the presence of the purity and radiance of the innocent peasant girl, but which actually occurred over a period of time preceding the novel's action. A famous colloquy takes place between him and the historical cardinal of legendary sanctity, Federico Borromeo.

The ills continue, however—indeed, multiply: drought, famine, war (a ramification of the Thirty Years' War), infection introduced by the Spanish army, and the devastating plague of 1630, which decimated the population of the Milanese, whose bodies were carried off by hooded *monatti* to the hospital camp known as the *lazzeretto* or to burial ditches. Manzoni's description of the terror of the "greasers," or *untori*, the supposed spreaders of disease, and of the horrible plague itself, must be considered literary landmarks. Many characters perish: Don Rodrigo; his henchman, Il Griso; Fra Cristoforo; the village priest's gossipy housekeeper, Perpetua; the ostentatious intellectual, Don Ferrante; and his wife, Donna Prassede. Lucia recovers miraculously, and her mother, Agnese, is spared. Fires burn the evil out, rains purify the land, and Renzo and Lucia are finally united in humble marriage.

The novel blends aesthetico-poetic and ethico-religious elements in a creative synthesis that conceals Manzoni's concern to separate artistic invention from historical document. History is not a convenient mold into which to pour the vicissitudes surrounding the lives of Renzo and Lucia but a vehicle to expand the reader's humanitarian consciousness, which must then outweigh narrowly political, social, or economic issues. Rocco Montano put it this way: The unity of the novel consists in its universality, which on the level of moral vision absorbs the historical and realistic particular; it consists in the profound accord between man's autonomy and the existence of an Absolute which transcends us; it consists in the dialectic of historical truth, which becomes myth and with which corresponds that other dialectic of feeling and linguistic objectivity.

Critics have put a great deal of emphasis—possibly too much emphasis—on Manzoni's Catholic persuasion and have thereby failed to grasp his true universality. There is no denying his religious conviction, but this conviction never reached such doctrinaire proportions as to preclude a transcending commitment to poetry, in the broadest sense of the word. If the ending of the novel suggests the working of Providence, the fact is that, as in *Adelchi*, Providence comes not from without but from within and is something that people work out for and by themselves. If the Unnamed converts, he or she does so after long self-questioning that emerges from an existential anguish of loneliness and dread and self-doubt. If Fra Cristoforo appears at times hard to believe in his total unselfishness, like Victor Hugo's Bishop Myriel in *Les Misérables* (1862), it is because, unlike Myriel, he is atoning for his former sinful ways, driven by a guilty conscience. More than anything else, Manzoni embraced closely the fundamental attitudes of the Christian tradition—love, humility, forgiveness, and charity—in such a way as to seem to make Christianity itself a metaphor for the superior life of the spirit, the universal spirit. This was his true Absolute, a moral vision which, in the context of art, becomes poetic, even mythical. More than a "religious" novel, then, *The Betrothed* is a human novel, well worth its place in the original Harvard Classics series.

Hence Manzoni's profound feeling for the humble and the suffering who give history a *common* sense; hence, too, the absence of any protagonist of exalted individualism. Manzoni "deheroizes" the novel, yet every character stands out with recognizable humanity: Renzo, candid, ingenuous, excited, generous, like the perdurance of the human race; Lucia, pious, sensible, good, like a creature of light; Agnese, enterprising, affectionate, energetic, a woman of the people; Perpetua, protective, brash, the perpetual gossip;

Don Abbondio, fearful, confused, vacuous, the model of a coward; Don Rodrigo, mean, capricious, vainglorious, an impenitent rascal; Fra Cristoforo, altruistic, concerned, impulsive, a fiery saint; the Unnamed, mysterious, awesome, demoniac, like an emanation of evil; Cardinal Borromeo, exemplary, firm, a noble figure of persuasive serenity; Sister Gertrude, proud, agonized, gloomy, a tragic victim of misguided parents; Azzeccagarbugli, false and niggardly; Don Ferrante and Donna Prassede, the pedant in his artificial world and the presumptuous Christian. All these characters need more than a few adjectives to describe them, for not one of them is two-dimensional. Each is greater than the sum of his or her parts, each is portrayed with the understanding and compassion of an author who has long observed humankind, and each is subjected to a delicately comic assessment. Manzoni's is an art of indulgence.

This art is expressed in exquisite prose, highly sophisticated and precise. Action, commentary, soliloquy, dialogue—all are finely honed to the needs of analysis, humor, irony, or moral example. The style engages many tonalities—"rather a chorus," says Giorgio Petrocchi, "a concert of languages." Many passages have remained classics, such as the opening paragraph (an interesting adumbration of the novel in imagistic terms), Lucia's farewell to her hometown as she escapes to the convent, Don Abbondio's humorous donkey ride up the mountainside to the Unnamed's castle, the bread riots in Milan (Manzoni handles crowds adroitly), and the agony of death in the throes of the plague. In Manzoni's prose, the word has a communicative vitality, always contained, fitting, and significant. This virtue more than makes up for the repeated digressions, which have not gone uncriticized, even if they ultimately fit the tale's epic dimensions, completing the background of the events, and are presented in a style consistent with the tenor of those events. Furthermore, images planted here and there structure the novel expressively and create desired tonalities. Individual words become word-symbols that interrelate within the novel, stimulating in the reader an associative process that gives certain images their own "plot." (Bread, as juxtaposed to wine, is one such image.) They become the lifeblood

Reluctant to participate at first, Avey eventually joins in the ritual and discovers the meaning of her recurring dream. The landing of the Ibos in South Carolina and their return to Africa by the mythic walk on water symbolize the link between Africa and all black people of the diaspora. In participating in this ritual, Avey becomes aware that she can achieve wholeness only if she becomes reconnected to her African roots.

DAUGHTERS

Like the protagonists of most of Marshall's other novels, the protagonist of *Daughters*, Ursa MacKensie, is a woman caught between two cultures: the African American culture of her mother, Estelle, and the Caribbean culture of her father, Primus. The action of the novel is divided almost equally between New York City, where Ursa lives, and Triunion, the West Indian island where her parents reside, her father being a leading politician, known from his boyhood as the PM (prime minister). Although firmly rooted in the urban culture of New York, where she is pursuing a career as a young black professional, Ursa keeps one foot planted in the small Caribbean island through her relationship with her doting father, a relationship strengthened by frequent letters and periodic visits.

In this novel, Marshall again explores the themes of identity and the attempt to bridge the gap between two cultures. The novel addresses the integration of the two cultures on several levels, the first being the marriage of Ursa's parents—her African American mother to her West Indian father. The second is the birth of their daughter, Ursa-Mae, who physically integrates the two cultures. Then, the African American and West Indian cultures are geographically and spiritually linked as Ursa's mother moves to Barbados with her husband and becomes integrated into that community.

As in *The Chosen Place, the Timeless People*, much of the novel is devoted to the workings of Triunion politics and their effect upon the Triunion people, the marriage of Primus and Estelle, and Ursa. Its setting and wide array of characters provide Marshall the opportunity to explore the theme of self-discovery from a number of perspectives.

Gladys J. Washington

OTHER MAJOR WORKS

SHORT FICTION: *Soul Clap Hands and Sing*, 1961; *Reena and Other Stories*, 1983; *Merle: A Novella and Other Stories*, 1985.

BIBLIOGRAPHY

Christian, Barbara. "Paule Marshall: A Literary Biography." In *Black Feminist Criticism: Perspectives on Black Women Writers*. New York: Pergamon Press, 1985. This essay traces the development of themes in Marshall's fiction from *Brown Girl, Brownstones* through *Praisesong for the Widow*.

Collier, Eugenia. "The Closing of the Circle: Movement from Division to Wholeness in Paule Marshall's Fiction." In *Black Women Writers (1950-1980): A Critical Evaluation*, edited by Mari Evans. New York: Doubleday, 1984. This essay is an excellent source of information on Marshall's treatment of the theme of racial identity and characterization in her novels.

Coser, Stelamaris. *Bridging the Americas: The Literature of Paule Marshall, Toni Morrison, and Gayl Jones*. Philadelphia: Temple University Press, 1995. Compares and contrasts the fiction of the three authors, taking their cultural heritage into consideration.

DeLamotte, Eugenia C. *Places of Silence, Journeys of Freedom: The Fiction of Paule Marshall*. Philadelphia: University of Pennsylvania Press, 1998. Studies Marshall's oeuvre, focusing on her Caribbean roots.

Denniston, Dorothy Hamer. *The Fiction of Paule Marshall: Reconstructions of History, Culture, and Gender*. Knoxville: University of Tennessee Press, 1995. Reviews Marshall's novels, concentrating on her dominant theme in each. Examines cultural expansion, personal and political liberation, diasporan connections, and transformation of female identity.

Kapai, Leela. "Dominant Themes and Techniques in Paule Marshall's Fiction." *CLA Journal* 16 (September, 1972): 49-59. Examines prominent themes in Marshall's works.

Washington, Mary Helen. Afterword to *Brown Girl,*

Brownstones. New York: Feminist Press, 1981. An excellent critical commentary on the novel.

(The Nobel Foundation)

ROGER MARTIN DU GARD

Born: Neuilly-sur-Seine, France; March 23, 1881
Died: Bellême, France; August 22, 1958

PRINCIPAL LONG FICTION

Devenir!, 1908
L'Une de nous, 1910
Jean Barois, 1913 (English translation, 1949)
Le Cahier gris, 1922
Le Pénitencier, 1922
La Belle Saison, 1923
La Consultation, 1928
La Sorellina, 1928
La Mort du père, 1929
L'Été 1914, 1936
Épilogue, 1940
Les Thibault, 1922-1940 (collective title for previous 8 novels, *Le Cahier gris* through *Épilogue*; *The World of the Thibaults*, collective title for *The Thibaults*, 1939 [parts 1-6] and *Summer 1914*, 1941 [parts 7-8])
Lieutenant-Colonel de Maumort, 1983 (English translation, 1999)

OTHER LITERARY FORMS

Roger Martin du Gard published three plays: *Le Testament du père Leleu* (old Leleu's will), in 1914; another farce, *La Gonfle* (the swelling), in 1928; and *Un Taciturne*, in 1932. He also published the short-fiction work *Confidence africaine* (1931; African confession) and sketches of provincial life, *Vieille France* (1933; *The Postman*, 1954). All these works are available in the two-volume Pléiade edition of Martin du Gard's complete works. In 1951, a portion of his extensive journal was published under the title *Notes sur André Gide* (*Recollections of André Gide*, 1953). Of his letters, only his exchanges with Gide and Jacques Copeau have appeared.

ACHIEVEMENTS

Success came rather early to Roger Martin du Gard. Even his first novel, *Devenir!*, published in 1908, earned for him a *succès d'estime* at the age of twenty-seven. The publication of *Jean Barois*, in 1913, and the reception of his first play, *Le Testament du père Leleu*, in 1914, earned the esteem of the new literary establishment developing around *La Nouvelle Revue française*. After World War I, when he began to publish the eight volumes of *The World of the Thibaults*, his readership continued to grow steadily.

Although leading a discreet life and shying away from the Parisian literary scene, Martin du Gard maintained at least an epistolary contact with numerous confreres among the established and the young, who frequently sought and received his advice. He was respected by all for his integrity, moderation, and

the concierge's daughter. While having an affair with her, Antoine urges her to initiate his brother. The latter, however, begins by having a Platonic infatuation with her. Erotic awakening at the beginning of *Le Pénitencier* is associated with adolescent rebellion, and sexual initiation with the beginning of maturation and socialization. In this novel on adolescence, Martin du Gard does not abandon one of his major themes and biases, namely, the evils and consequences of religious faith: Father Thibault founded the reform school with the approval of the Paris archbishop, and the fanatical Protestant minister preaches to Madame Fontanin to forgive her husband's extreme infidelity. These elements are contrasted with Antoine's humane attitude, which derives from his faith in science and reason.

LA BELLE SAISON

La Belle Saison (the beautiful season) is the longest volume of *The World of the Thibaults* before *L'Été 1914*. Focused on two families, the Thibaults and the Fontanins, it is also complex and includes a great deal of action. Each of the two families owns a summer home in Maisons-Lafitte, which becomes the point of departure and return for many episodes. The three young men, Daniel, Jacques, and Antoine, have leading roles. They have become adults and now encounter a variety of people through their discoveries, and through them the author broadens his exploration of society. It is the beautiful season because it is the season of youth, which holds out limitless possibilities for the young men. They will not approach these possibilities, however, with total freedom. Again, heredity manifests itself as an important force, as does the conditioning of their respective childhoods. Daniel clearly has artistic talent but is a philanderer like his father. Jacques, who wins admission to the École Normale Supérieure, a door to professional and social success, is elated. Instead of pursuing this promising path, he is drawn to socialism, which, interestingly, is his own extension of his father's preoccupation with philanthropy. For most of the novel, however, he is searching for himself and remains confused both about his attraction to Jenny and her rejection of him. Antoine emerges as a liberated positivist, a man of science who exercises his

profession most competently. In the eyes of the reader, he is adorned with the prestige of one who saves lives. The protection of human life was for Martin du Gard a fundamental value. While saving a child's life, Antoine meets Rachel, with whom he has a genuine and beautiful love affair. In the end, however, she returns to her former lover, Hirsch, to whom she is irresistibly drawn despite his bizarre character and sordid past.

As a departure from his usual thematic concerns, Martin du Gard treats in this volume the influence a literary work may have on its readers. Jacques becomes enthralled by André Gide's *Les Nourritures terrestres* (1897; *Fruits of the Earth*, 1949). Both he and Daniel are drawn to Gide's urging to reject bourgeois morality and family. It is not purely coincidental that none of the three young men will found families. For that, their fathers bear some responsibility: Jérôme de Fontanin for having neglected all of his responsibilities toward his family, and Oscar Thibault for having placed the interests of religion and society above paternal love.

LA CONSULTATION

Antoine, the medical doctor, is at the center of *La Consultation* (the doctor's visit) and dominates the action even more than Jacques did in *La Belle Saison*. He is presented during a day of consultation, October 13, 1913. The day begins for him with a visit to his father, who is critically ill. Not only does Antoine struggle to sustain life, but he also must face the question of whether to hasten death. These alternatives, within the power and responsibility of doctors, appear as goals of science and the culminating point of philosophy. In all professional circumstances, Antoine is prepared to do what he believes to be right; thus he accepts the possibility of euthanasia, without reference to the dictates of religion or even medical ethics.

Throughout this phase, Antoine's life is dominated by medicine and his service to others. He appears somewhat interested in Gise. His major concern, however, is Jacques's disappearance. Depicting the way Antoine spends his time enables Martin du Gard to present him as the mature man and professional he has become. Although he leads a quieter and even more prosaic life, Antoine is assuming a more important role in the novel.

Antoine's friendly concern for two adolescent brothers who struggle to survive alone, without the support of a family, is the means through which the reader catches a glimpse of the harsh economic conditions faced by the working class. Similarly, through his conversation with his patient Rumelles, who works at the Foreign Ministry, the reader becomes aware of the intensifying crisis about to culminate in World War I.

LA SORELLINA

La Sorellina, a somewhat longer volume, relates the events of one week. Monsieur Thibault continues to decline after the serious operation he has undergone. His desire to die in an edifying manner makes him appear ridiculous. It is at this time that Antoine discovers a story, "La Sorellina," written by Jacques. As he reads it, he soon understands that it is based on circumstances in Jacques's life. Through "La Sorellina," the reader learns that Jacques did not commit suicide, as his father thought; that he loved both Jenny and Gise; and why he disappeared. As soon as he learns of his brother's precise whereabouts in Lausanne, Antoine goes there to bring Jacques back to their father's deathbed. As the two brothers converse, Jacques rectifies some of the inaccuracies in Antoine's interpretation of events in his life as seen transposed in "La Sorellina."

LA MORT DU PÈRE

In *La Mort du père* (the death of the father), Antoine, on returning from Lausanne, discovers that his father's condition has worsened. Martin du Gard is not only precise but also quite technical in his description of Thibault's illness and of its treatment. Death becomes the focal point of Thibault's thoughts and of life itself. As he rejects the consolation of religion, it is clear that Thibault does not accept death, that he desperately wants to live. Seeing their father suffer to a degrading extent, "like an animal," his sons agree to resort to euthanasia.

After Thibault's death, Antoine's attitude toward him changes, especially as he discovers, by reading his father's papers, how humane he had been. Too late, Antoine realizes that he could have understood

and loved his father. On the other hand, Jacques's attitude does not change. He continues to hate his father, and he remains awkward toward Gise. Again, thoughts of suicide and destruction increase his violent and nihilistic sentiments.

As they travel back to Paris after the funeral, Abbé Vécard and Antoine engage in a discussion on religious faith. Martin du Gard strives to advance the strongest arguments on each side. In the end, while not conceding, Antoine simply admits that he may lack a religious sense—as Martin du Gard felt he himself did.

L'ÉTÉ 1914

L'Été 1914 deals in detail with events that took place between June 28, 1914, the date of the assassination of the Austrian Archduke Ferdinand in Sarajevo, and August, 1914. This volume is almost as long as all previous volumes together. For all the major characters, the outbreak of World War I is a climactic event, as indeed it was for all Europeans. Although Martin du Gard wrote at least a decade after that war, he respects the perspective of his characters. As the diplomatic tension intensifies and the threat of war grows, people become increasingly preoccupied with the crisis. In *L'Été 1914*, the psychological analysis of adolescents or young adults and the study of tensions within middle-class families are overshadowed by the focus on national and international tensions of vast proportions. The change of viewpoint corresponds to a natural evolution from personal concerns to the broader spheres of the momentous crisis.

At the beginning of *L'Été 1914*, the reader resumes contact with Jacques, who lives in the cosmopolitan Socialist milieu in Geneva. The total commitment of the young bourgeois to the Socialist cause may first seem surprising. In spite of Martin du Gard's long and keen interest in socialism, his emphasis on the movement in that chronological framework was probably increased by subsequent events. Like most intellectuals of the 1920's and 1930's, he was convinced that the coming to power of socialism in at least one major country on the globe, Russia, was the single most important event of the first half of the century.

Jacques is observed within a cross section of revolutionaries. Their respective ideas and plans on the eve of the war are studied from their perspective. Jacques's return to Paris on a special mission coincides with Jérôme de Fontanin's suicide. Jacques also finds Antoine preoccupied by his affair with Anne de Battaincourt. The doctor appears rather out of touch and unconcerned with the alarming political situation threatening Europe. By temperament and habit, however, he opposes Socialist ideals.

While paying a visit to the dying Jérôme, Jacques sees Jenny—four years after his unexplained departure. This encounter does not bring about a reconciliation. At first, Jenny, who has suffered much from the separation, feels resentful toward Jacques. In subsequent days, they see each other frequently, and Jacques explains to her his feelings about the past and his present commitment to socialism and pacifism. Jenny comes to share his idealism and his commitment. Perhaps Martin du Gard knew that Jenny was also the name of one of socialist Karl Marx's daughters; his choice of such an un-French name is significant.

In the meantime, the political situation worsens, and Jacques accomplishes clandestine liaison missions in Paris, Antwerp, Berlin, and Brussels for his revolutionary leader, Meynestrel. The reader becomes aware of the lack of a unified view among Socialists on such vital issues as whether to try to prevent war or to hope war will result in progress for socialism. Martin du Gard succeeds in re-creating the tension and the confusion in the days preceding the declaration of war. Antoine's belief that reason and science are the foundations of life is pushed aside by the momentum of the war movement. Jacques decides to give his inheritance to the Socialist Party andplans to refuse to be conscripted. He still hopes French and German Socialists will be able to organize a general strike to prevent the war. At this critical point, Jacques and Jenny witness the assassination of Jean Jaurès, the only leader capable of inspiring a strong pacifist following.

Before departing, Jacques tells Antoine of his love for Jenny. This causes the two brothers to quarrel in very unfortunate circumstances. The same day, war is declared by Germany on Russia. During that night, Jacques and Jenny consummate their love, but not very happily. Perhaps as a result of her puritanical upbringing, Jenny feels humiliated, while Jacques feels remorse for having drawn her into his tragic destiny. Jenny's mother is strongly opposed to their marriage. As a consequence of an argument with her mother, Jenny decides to postpone settling in Geneva with Jacques. That suits him well, for he has decided to make an ultimate attempt to interrupt the war. With Meynestrel, he plans to drop a million leaflets urging soldiers and workers not to fight. The mission, however, fails pathetically. Their plane crashes, the leaflets are burned, the two Socialists are killed, and the war continues. In spite of his useless death, Jacques appears as a hero who embodies an ideal of justice and the vision of a better world.

ÉPILOGUE

The World of the Thibaults could have ended with Jacques's death, as it begins with his misadventure. Accustomed, however, to the regular reappearance of all major characters, readers do not expect to know about their fate—especially that of Antoine, the other known heir of the Thibault spirit. The final volume, *Épilogue*, picks up the thread of history in the spring of 1918 as Antoine is being treated for toxic gas inhalation in a hospital in the south of France. He spends all of his time reflecting on his own condition and the human condition in general. On a visit to Paris, he returns to the family house there and the summer home in Maisons-Lafitte; he sees Jenny and Gise, both caring for Jean-Paul, Jenny's child by Jacques. Daniel has been completely transformed by a castrating wound. He has lost all interest in life and contemplates suicide. Antoine also pays Dr. Philip a visit. After his professor has examined him, he realizes he will not recover.

Épilogue ends with letters and Antoine's journal. During the last four months of his life, Antoine has kept a diary. Through it readers learn of his anguish and the solitude of his ending life. He takes a keen interest in the Allies' progress, although he will die a week after the Armistice. His attitude alternates between despair at the thought of his death and his thoughts of Jean-Paul's future in a world of peace that is full of possibilities. He hopes that when his nephew reaches full manhood—ironically, in 1940—

it will be a more propitious time. Finally, Antoine refuses the consolation of religion and hastens his own death. In spite of his cruel fate, however, he dies believing in human progress.

The World of the Thibaults is something of an anomaly in twentieth century literature. Like the even more ambitious *roman-fleuve* by Jules Romains, *Les Hommes de bonne volonté* (1932-1936; *Men of Good Will*, 1933-1946), it recalls the sweeping vision of Honoré de Balzac and Émile Zola. Martin du Gard, however, lacks Balzac's energy, psychological acuity, and sheer narrative genius, and his treatment of social issues cannot match Zola's brutal force. Time has not been kind to writers who, in the first half of the twentieth century, wrote as if they were living in the nineteenth.

Jean-Pierre Cap

OTHER MAJOR WORKS

SHORT FICTION: *Confidence africaine*, 1931; *Vieille France*, 1933 (*The Postman*, 1954).

PLAYS: *Le Testament du père Leleu*, pr. 1914; *La Gonfle*, pb. 1928; *Un Taciturne*, pb. 1932.

NONFICTION: *Notes sur André Gide*, 1951 (*Recollections of André Gide*, 1953); *Correspondance, 1913-1951*, 1968; *Correspondance*, 1972.

MISCELLANEOUS: *Œuvres complètes*, 1955 (2 volumes).

BIBLIOGRAPHY

Boak, Denis. *Roger Martin du Gard*. Oxford, England: Clarendon Press, 1963. Still one of the best critical studies, thorough and authoritative, sympathetic and sensitive. Includes a detailed bibliography.

Brombert, Victor. *The Intellectual Hero: Studies in the French Novel, 1880-1955*. Chicago: Phoenix Books, 1960. Contains a very good chapter on *Jean Barois* concentrating on the novel's structure and its handling of ideas and history. Brombert is one of the most distinguished critics of French literature.

Gibson, Robert. *Roger Martin du Gard*. New York: Hillary House, 1961. Succinct appraisal with many excellent insights.

Lukacs, Georg. *Realism in Our Time*. New York: Harper & Row, 1964. Although Lukacs's Marxist bias must be carefully considered, he provides a learned discussion of Martin du Gard's place in the context of European realism.

Peyre, Henri. *The Contemporary French Novel*. New York: Oxford University Press, 1955. A distinguished French critic, Peyre deems *Jean Barois* one of the most significant novels of 1910-1930. Peyre is particularly appreciative of Martin du Gard's traditional qualities.

Ru, Yi-ling. *The Family Novel: Toward a Generic Definition*. New York: Peter Lang, 1992. Examines the Thibault series as well as John Galsworthy's Forsyte novels and Chin Pa's fiction.

Savage, Catharine. *Roger Martin du Gard*. New York: Twayne, 1968. Chapters on the writer's career, his early work, his major fiction, the naturalism of his short fiction and plays, values, and the novel. Includes a chronology, notes, and a very useful annotated bibliography.

Schalk, David L. *Roger Martin du Gard: The Novelist and History*. Ithaca, N.Y.: Cornell University Press, 1967. Chapters on the novel as history, *Jean Barois* and the Dreyfus Affair, Martin du Gard's years of optimism and productivity, his development of historical consciousness, and his politics. With detailed notes and extensive bibliography.

Stern, Richard Clarke. *Dark Mirror: The Sense of Injustice in Modern European and American Literature*. New York: Fordham University Press, 1994. Contains a perceptive section on *Jean Barois*.

PETER MATTHIESSEN

Born: New York, New York; May 22, 1927

PRINCIPAL LONG FICTION
Race Rock, 1954
Partisans, 1955
Raditzer, 1961

At Play in the Fields of the Lord, 1965
Far Tortuga, 1975
Killing Mister Watson, 1990
Lost Man's River, 1997
Bone by Bone, 1999

OTHER LITERARY FORMS

Peter Matthiessen is perhaps better known, and certainly far more prolific, as a writer of nonfiction than as a novelist. He has produced numerous volumes of nonfiction, beginning with *Wildlife in America* (1959). Many are chronicles of Matthiessen's trips to distant and barely accessible areas of the earth: *The Cloud Forest: A Chronicle of the South American Wilderness* (1961), *Under the Mountain Wall: A Chronicle of Two Seasons in the Stone Age* (1962), *Oomingmak: The Expedition to the Musk Ox Island in the Bering Sea* (1967), *Blue Meridian:*

(Nancy Crampton)

The Search for the Great White Shark (1971), *The Tree Where Man Was Born: The African Experience* (1972), *The Snow Leopard* (1978), *Sand Rivers* (1981), and *African Silences* (1991). *The Shorebirds of North America* (1967) is straight natural history, and *Sal Si Puedes: Cesar Chavez and the New American Revolution* (1970) is a biographical essay and political commentary on the California labor leader.

Among his other works of nonfiction are *In the Spirit of Crazy Horse* (1983), *Indian Country* (1984), *Nine-Headed Dragon River: Zen Journals 1969-1982* (1985), and *Men's Lives: The Surfmen and Baymen of the South Fork* (1986). Matthiessen has published two volumes of short fiction: *Midnight Turning Gray* (1984) and *On the River Styx* (1989); the former is a small press publication, the contents of which overlap with the latter.

ACHIEVEMENTS

Matthiessen's achievements lie in two distinct but interrelated genres—that of the personal essay, similar in many respects to the writings of Henry David Thoreau, and that of the novel. His most distinguished works of fiction—*At Play in the Fields of the Lord* and *Far Tortuga*—both draw heavily on the author's evocation of the natural world, that of the Amazon rain forest in the first case and the open sea and Caribbean islands in the second. Both novels are extended studies of humanity's interrelation with these wild environments, and much of their effectiveness lies in Matthiessen's ability to place the reader within the primeval setting, projecting the smell, taste, and feel of the jungle and the sea. Similarly, Matthiessen's nonfiction relies for its power on transporting the reader to a remote natural world and making that world live, impressing indelibly nature's importance on the reader. Matthiessen stresses the value of nature to humankind, as a fountainhead of fundamental impulses and as an avenue of self-exploration, a means of cutting away the confusions of the "civilized" world and probing the essential elements of human nature. Matthiessen is not, however, a naïve romantic, finding in nature a Rousseauistic panacea for all the ills of society. His essays, whether book-length or merely brief sketches, have a gritty objectivity that precludes any superficial romanticizing of the natural world.

Matthiessen has won such awards as the Ambassador Award for *Killing Mister Watson*, and both the American Book Award and the National Book Award for *The Snow Leopard*. He received the John Burroughs medal and the African Wildlife Leadership Foundation Award for *Sand Rivers*, another nonfiction work on Africa. His nonfiction book *Wildlife in America* can be found in the White House's permanent collection.

BIOGRAPHY

Peter Matthiessen was born in New York City on May 22, 1927, of a well-to-do, if not wealthy, family. His father, Erard A. Matthiessen, was a well-known architect and for many years a trustee of the National Audubon Society. His interest in nature and conservation was passed on to his son, and many of Peter Matthiessen's essays were eventually published in the Society's magazine, *Audubon*. From childhood, Matthiessen was exposed to the New York world of literature and the arts. By the time he was sixteen, he had decided to become a writer. Following the path of many boys from prominent families, he was first educated at the Hotchkiss School, then at Yale University. He spent many of his summers on the Connecticut shore in the relatively exclusive society of friends from the New York intellectual world. "My first story," he later said casually, "was published by my girl's father"—Cass Canfield, then editor of *Harper's* magazine.

Late in World War II, Matthiessen interrupted his education to join the navy, an experience of mixed success, since he was demoted for disciplinary reasons, but one which gave him his first real experience of the life of common men. He returned to Yale in 1947, continued his creative writing, and wrote about hunting and fishing for the Yale *Daily News*. He was graduated from Yale in 1950, spent a year there as an instructor in creative writing, and moved to Paris, by then married to Patsy Southgate, the daughter of a socially prominent diplomat. The Matthiessens soon became the center of a glittering crowd of American expatriate intellectuals, including William Styron,

James Jones, George Plimpton, James Baldwin, and Irwin Shaw. In 1951, with Harold L. Humes, Matthiessen founded the *Paris Review*, which became one of the most influential postwar literary magazines; for four decades Matthiessen served as fiction editor.

Matthiessen's first novel, *Race Rock*, was written in Paris. It looks back to the world of Matthiessen's youth: The characters are a group of disillusioned, upper-middle-class young people living on the New England coast. Aimless and confused by their meaningless lives, they stagnate, wallowing in their angst and neuroses. A reunion of childhood friends degenerates into an overflow of emotions and finally violence. Sadder but wiser, the survivors face an uncertain future, vowing to profit from their past mistakes and show maturity in the future.

In 1953, the Matthiessens returned to the United States and settled in East Hampton, Long Island, where Matthiessen divided his time between writing in bad weather and commercial fishing in good. His second novel, *Partisans*, appeared in 1955. It was an obvious product of Matthiessen's knowledge of the avant-garde left wing that infested expatriate intellectual circles in the 1950's. (Ironically, in the light of his later political commitments, it was rumored among the *Paris Review* crowd that Matthiessen was a CIA agent, which would hardly have been surprising, considering his background and contacts.) The protagonist of *Partisans* is Barney Sand, a young American journalist and son of a diplomat, searching for a cause to which he can commit himself. With the pure idealism of a grail knight, he scours the Paris slums seeking Jacobi, an old and deposed revolutionary who has been rejected by the Communist party, but who is the emblem of purity and integrity to Sand. Like *Race Rock*, *Partisans* is a kind of *Bildungsroman* in which a young person grows into maturity, in this case coming to realize that his naïve vision is unattainable.

The Matthiessens' marriage ended in divorce in 1957, but by that time Matthiessen had already begun the series of "world wanderings" that would provide him with the subject of his major works. With little formal scientific training, he spent three years studying American animals and birds, with particular attention to endangered species. The result was *Wildlife in America*, a book widely praised for showing, as one reviewer wrote, "the skill of a novelist and the accuracy of a zoologist." In 1959 and 1961, he made the two difficult journeys which eventually provided him with the setting for *At Play in the Fields of the Lord*, the first to South America and the second to New Guinea. On both expeditions, Matthiessen penetrated the wilderness as deeply and thoroughly as possible, at times at considerable personal risk, and lived with the native tribesmen in an effort to come to known them.

Between these travels, Matthiessen produced a third "conventional" novel, *Raditzer*, drawing this time on the navy experience of his young manhood for material. The novel is the study of a pariah, Raditzer, a sailor who embodies virtually every human vice. A product of the slums, Raditzer is dishonest, paranoid, sadistic, servile, and bullying by turns—a more unpleasant version of James Wait of Joseph Conrad's *The Nigger of the "Narcissus"* (1897); Matthiessen has pointed to Conrad and Fyodor Dostoevski as two important influences on his fiction. An instinctive parasite, Raditzer attaches himself to the hero, a young intellectual sailor of good family, who, like the protagonists of *Race Rock* and *Partisans*, bears considerable resemblance to the author as a young man. When Raditzer becomes such a Jonah that his shipmates plot to kill him, the sailor-hero finds himself in the disagreeable position of having his courage tested in the defense of a man he loathes. He comes to realize—as Barney Sand did, despising the poor whose cause he championed—that moral action does not come in neat, sanitized packages, and that good and evil are peculiarly muddled in the real world. Unlike most of Matthiessen's works, *Raditzer* does not concern itself integrally with nature, and it is particularly interesting for the success with which it explores the lives of common working men, a topic of increasing interest to the author.

At Play in the Fields of the Lord signaled Matthiessen's coming of age as a writer and thinker. In it, and in the rest of his mature work, he fuses the speculative insight of a philosopher, the lyricism of a poet, and the scrupulous observation of a scientist to produce a broad statement about the relationship between humanity and the natural world as profound as any in Western literature. His fifth novel, *Far Tortuga*, published in 1975, is a stylistic and structural tour de force as well as a profoundly moving elegy for the doomed world of the Caribbean turtle fishers. It followed a remarkable book-length essay, *The Tree Where Man Was Born: The African Experience*, an extended philosophical commentary on life and death in East Africa that contains some of Matthiessen's finest and most thoughtful observations concerning humanity's place in the natural world.

Matthiessen remarried in 1963, but his second wife, Deborah Love Matthissen, died ten years later after a long struggle with cancer. Toward the end of her life, both she and her husband had been moving deeply into a study of Zen, convinced that it offered an alternative to the emptiness of the modern world. After his wife's death, Matthiessen undertook a difficult and dangerous trip on foot into the heart of Nepal to visit the Crystal Monastery, a center of Zen meditation and reverence; his companion on the trip was the noted naturalist George Schaller, who was studying Nepalese blue sheep. Matthiessen was specifically hoping for a sight of the real but mystical snow leopard, an animal so rarely seen that is has become a Zen symbol for everything possible and unattainable. *The Snow Leopard*, based on his journey, was published in 1978. It is Matthiessen's very personal account of his spiritual pilgrimage in the Himalayas and was awarded the National Book Award.

In the early 1980's, Matthiessen published two books dealing with the fate of the American Indian: *In the Spirit of Crazy Horse* and *Indian Country*. The former, which argues for the innocence of Leonard Peltier, a member of the American Indian Movement convicted of murdering two agents of the Federal Bureau of Investigation, embroiled Matthiessen and his publisher, Viking Press, in two libel suits that lasted for six years. The result was the virtual suppression of the book, despite the fact that the suits were ultimately found to be without merit.

In 1990, Matthiessen published his first novel in fifteen years, *Killing Mister Watson*, which was the beginning of an ambitious trilogy, or one "monster novel," as Matthiessen referred to it. The second part, *Lost Man's River*, was published in 1997, and the third, *Bone by Bone*, was released in 1999. A film adaptation of Matthiessen's book *At Play in the Fields of the Lord* was finally released in 1991, twenty-five years after it was first optioned in 1966 and after passing through the hands of many celebrated directors, producers, and actors, including John Huston, Paul Newman, and Richard Gere.

Matthiessen settled in New York with his third wife, Maria, whom he married in 1980. He is a monk in Zen Buddhism (ordained in 1981) and is a frequent speaker on the topics of ecology and writing.

ANALYSIS

Peter Matthiessen is America's twentieth century Henry David Thoreau. There are other fine contemporary nature writers, such as Edward Hoagland and John McPhee, but there is no one else who brings to his observation of the natural world and humankind's place in it Matthiessen's philosophical depth and poetic command of the language. His two finest novels, *At Play in the Fields of the Lord* and *Far Tortuga*, combine his experience as a naturalist with the felt immediacy that only a deeply persuasive work of fiction can provide.

Matthiessen's first twenty years as a novelist must really be divided into two phases, one comprising his first three novels—*Race Rock*, *Partisans*, and *Raditzer*—and the other, his two major works, *At Play in the Fields of the Lord* and *Far Tortuga*. The first three are thoroughly competent novels, and they certainly show the promise of the writer Matthiessen became. All exhibit a young man's fascination with the maturing process and the loss of innocence—with "rites of passage." All center on protagonists who are obviously surrogates for the author himself, idealistic but troubled young men of good family, aimless and seeking direction and commitment in a world of inexplicable evil and suffering. Although *Race Rock*, in particular, is rather complex in its presentation of multiple levels of time, all three books are essentially traditional narratives, accomplished but unextraordinary.

Matthiessen's next two novels, however, are fundamentally philosophical meditations on the human condition. As such, they join the company of Herman Melville's *Moby Dick* (1851), Joseph Conrad's *Heart of Darkness* (1902), and Stendhal's *Le Rouge et le Noir* (1930; *The Red and the Black*, 1898), all works in which the narrative impulse, however strong, is essentially a vehicle for metaphysical statement; Matthiessen is concerned with *things*, but he is more concerned with the meaning of things. This is hardly to say that he is a didactic writer (although unequivocal pleas for environmentalism fill his nonfiction), but he is insistently an explorer of the meaning of life. In both *At Play in the Fields of the Lord* and *Far Tortuga*, that meaning is manifested in terms of humanity's place in the continuum of natural life on earth. In the former, Lewis Meriwether Moon deliberately and consciously projects himself into the world of the Niaruna, and his discovery of his identity as a natural man is the result of an act of will. In contrast, Raib Avers and the crew of the *Lillias Eden*, of *Far Tortuga*, are in harmony with the sea and its creatures but have little opportunity to determine the lives they lead.

Unlike most philosophical writers, who persistently project humankind as purely social or psychological beings, Matthiessen insists that people are animals, although not primarily in the naturalistic terms of Theodore Dreiser or Jack London, who write of people as victims of fate, the pawns of uncontrollable chemical and biological impulses. Matthiessen's human beings, as animals, share a common heritage and destiny with all the living world. Both *At Play in the Fields of the Lord* and *Far Tortuga* do exhibit a fatalism, however, that suggests affinities with literary naturalism. An unavoidable destruction hangs over and overtakes the Niaruna, regardless of the efforts of the missionaries and Moon. Similarly in *Far Tortuga*, the last voyage of the *Lillias Eden* has a predestined quality about it, and the novel is full of omens and foreshadowings. There is, in Matthiessen's art, an ominous skepticism about the possibility of survival for traditional patterns of life. Men such as Moon and Avers, who cast their lot with the natural world, through choice or chance, are destined to go down with the ship; the smug, technocratic modern society has little place or tolerance for them. Still, there are survivors. These two novels are too open-ended to be tied up with certainties and happy endings, but both also hold out the possibility of hope. Moon soldiers on, "in celebration of the only man beneath the eye of Heaven," himself. Speedy, the most decent and heroic of the turtlers, survives the wreck, like Melville's Ishmael. The reader is unsure that he will live but sure that the novel does not explicitly have him die with the rest of the crew.

Both *At Play in the Fields of the Lord* and *Far Tortuga* present the possibility of human fulfillment through the apprehension and acceptance of humanity's proper role in the natural world. That world is constantly threatened, however, by the values of "civilization." Still, Matthiessen believes, there is a chance of avoiding the spiritual damnation implicit in the destruction of the Niaruna and the turtlers. "I hope we'll be forced into a new value system," he said. "But I think we're going to be forced to the edge of the cliff first. It's going to be so close."

At Play in the Fields of the Lord

More than a decade after he published *At Play in the Fields of the Lord*, Matthiessen remarked that he thought of it as a "conventional novel . . . full of fine writing." The critics, however, saw the novel as extraordinary in theme, structure, and style, as well as in quality. "A most unusual novel," wrote Emile Capouya in *The New York Times*; Granville Hicks wrote of the book's "power over the imagination" and its "astonishing assortment of characters." More than any other work, *At Play in the Fields of the Lord* established Matthiessen, in fellow novelist and poet Jim Harrison's words, as "our most eccentric major writer."

Superficially, the novel is an obvious outgrowth of Matthiessen's years as a wandering naturalist in obscure areas of the world. He had already produced two nonfiction studies of the tropical wilderness and its native inhabitants, both of which explored in depth the implications of the contact between the "civilized" world and the "primitive." *At Play in the Fields of the Lord* is set in the Amazon, and it is a study of the interpenetration, and ultimately the irreconcilability, of cultures.

At the center of the novel, more a presence than a group of characters, are the Niaruna, a tiny Stone Age tribe precariously clinging to life on the banks of a jungle river. Matthiessen does not romanticize the natives. They are crude, unthinking, dirty, and addicted to drugs and occasional violence; there are no noble savages here. Still, there is a kind of purity and integrity in their lives which the more "civilized" characters lack. The greatest threat to the Indians' existence is the local governor, Guzman, "El Comandante," a petty dictator with a handful of bestial troops at his disposal. This vanguard of civilization is engaged in a "pacification" of the Niaruna bordering on genocide; only drinking and whoring in the squalid fleshpots of Madre de Dios, the little jungle town that provides much of the novel's early locale, and self-indulgent incompetence have kept these representatives of law and order from exterminating the Indians long since. A third cultural block is formed by an earnest pair of American missionary families, the Hubens and the Quarriers. Humorless hustlers for God's will as they see fit to interpret it, the missionaries seek to convert and uplift the Niaruna before El Comandante uses the tribe's savagery as an excuse for its liquidation or dispersal. For the missionaries, the salvation of the Niarunas' souls, as well as their bodies, is synonymous with the abandonment of the tribe's primitive, natural culture.

Caught between these groups, and emphatically not of any of them, are Lewis Meriwether Moon and his partner Wolfie. These two American soldiers of fortune are stranded in the jungle after El Comandante impounds their small plane, gaudily plastered with a sign reading "Wolfie and Moon, Inc.—Small Wars and Demolition." When Martin Quarrier sees it, he says, disbelieving, "It's a joke." So it is, and one of the aspects of *At Play in the Fields of the Lord* most frequently ignored is the pervasive comic irony of the novel. Wolfie is only a richly sketched bit player in the panorama of the novel, but Moon is the most thoroughly developed and complex character in all Matthiessen's fiction, and one of the most interesting in modern American writing; it is his novel. Part American Indian and something of a cynical philosopher, Moon masquerades as an amoral pragmatist. In fact, he is a closet mystic who practices introspection that borders on meditation (foreshadowing Matthiessen's own developing interest in Zen, which culminated in *The Snow Leopard*). El Comandante wants Moon and Wolfie to bomb the Indians for him, and at first Moon is tempted. Gradually, though, circumstances and powerful but obscure forces in his own psychology impel him to cast himself in the role of a savior to the tribe. The native hallucinogen *ayahuasca* projects Moon into a weird and frightening drug trip, an exploration into the depths of his psyche, rendered with astonishing effectiveness by Matthiessen's surrealistic prose. (Matthiessen may have used his own experiences with hallucinogens to inform this scene.) Moon goes to live among the Indians, his civilized persona dissolving as he adopts their simple ways. As he sheds his Western cultural skin and melds himself into the ethos of the tribe, Moon also discovers a new self lurking under his civilized mask—that of the Indian he comes to believe he truly has always been.

Walls of misunderstanding rise between the characters of this novel. Each group struggles against what it perceives to be the challenges of the others, crippled by a myopia that makes it impossible for any character but Moon to see beyond his own values. Doomed by their lack of knowledge and by the narrowness of their specialized world, the Niaruna tremble on the brink of extinction. Blinded to their own bigotry by their faith and by the arrogance of religious Babbittry, the missionaries seek to do everything for the Indians at Niaruna Station but understand and accept them for what they are. The missionary leader, Les Huben, is, in his own way, nearly as sinister an embodiment of progress as the soulless and corrupt representatives of the state, who are at least more candid in acknowledging their desire to destroy the Indians.

Society, whether the elemental one of the Niaruna tribe or the neurotic and more complex one of the other characters, is only one pole of the action of *At Play in the Fields of the Lord*. The human world is counterpointed throughout by the natural world. The jungle hangs persistently about the characters,

purifying some, driving others to the verge of insanity. The lushness of Matthiessen's rhetoric (which eventually led him to describe the novel as "ornate") complements the scrupulous accuracy of his observations, so that the forest is rendered with a rich immediacy unmatched in modern fiction. Matthiessen's jungle is *alive*, and the equal of the jungles of Conrad or of Melville in *Typee* (1846). So vividly is the natural world painted that it assumes a thematic weight and aesthetic value that makes it superior to its foil, the world of society and civilization. At the end of the novel, appropriately, the Niaruna are all killed or scattered, and Moon finds himself alone and naked in the jungle. Momentarily, at least, civilization has fallen away and the forest primeval has reassumed the land.

The jungle for Matthiessen is much more than simply a setting. So great is the power of his evocation of it that it becomes almost a character, and a character with a particular personality. It is schizophrenic—alternately rich and nurturing, then corrupt and threatening. The life with which it swarms is emblematic of degeneration and filth to Hazel Quarrier but represents vitality and sustenance to the life-affirming Niaruna. As their chief says, "We have our river and our forest, we have fish and birds and animals to eat. . . . Surely we are living in a golden time!"

The jungle setting gradually absorbs, or rather subsumes, the other elements of the novel. The psychological, social, political, and religious forces that seethe through the early pages subside, replaced by an almost beatific peace that Moon finds by withdrawing into the forest life of the Indians. Certainly, the threat of annihilation from outside society hangs over the book to the end, but it becomes a threat external to the organic integrity of the jungle life. By the time the Niaruna have been dispersed, all the characters have faded, and only the jungle earth remains.

The jungle earth remains, and Moon tenaciously endures. He finds himself with only his own soul for sustenance in the face of the awesomeness of nature. It is he alone, and not the Niaruna, who represents the force that counterpoints the rich, beautiful, but inhuman breadth of nature: the individual human mind. Matthiessen's fundamental apposition is not the traditional one between nature and society, but between the individual human consciousness and the great natural world within which it exists. Matthiessen maintains, in fact, that the true genesis of *At Play in the Fields of the Lord* was an image of isolation in nature: "I wanted to get at what I consider to be the essential human condition, which is solitude under a big sky. I think it's when we run away from that that we miss the whole reverberation of life."

This basic "reverberation of life" is the ultimate subject of the novel. In the end, Moon and the natural world vibrate to a common chord. Thematically, the civilized world falls away, and the individual human psychology forms a continuum with the natural world it inhabits. In this sense, *At Play in the Fields of the Lord* is a Romantic novel, with overtones of William Wordsworth and Percy Bysshe Shelley. Humanity for Matthiessen becomes something like the "mind that feeds upon infinity" of Wordsworth's *The Prelude* (1850), and nature assumes its traditional Romantic role as the path to transcendental experience.

In his developing power to interpret that experience, Moon becomes a priest of nature without portfolio, or, to use one of Matthiessen's favorite words, a shaman. Ultimately, *At Play in the Fields of the Lord* is a novel of religious conflict. On one side is the sterile and lifeless theology of the missionaries, on the other the natural celebration of life, biological and spiritual, practiced daily by the Niaruna. For the Indians, the jungle and their existence therein is truly sacramental—the external and visible manifestation of an inward and invisible state of grace. For the missionaries, God is extrinsic to the corrupt world of the tropical wilderness. Martin Quarrier, the most decent and conscientious of the group, tries to come to grips with natural instinct as embodied both by the Indians and by his own lust for another missionary's wife, but he cannot bridge the gap between his rigid intellectualized Western mind and the elemental life of the jungle world. Only the part-Indian Moon can gain the natural world and not lose his individual soul in the process.

FAR TORTUGA

If Matthiessen could claim of *At Play in the Fields of the Lord* that it was a conventional novel, he could hardly say the same of the radical *Far Tortuga*, which novelist James Dickey called a turning point in the evolution of the novel, "creating a new vision." *Far Tortuga* was widely hailed at its publication for its experimentalism in style and structure, reaping high praise even from the reclusive novelist Thomas Pynchon. If not entirely unique, its departures from conventionality marked it as an impressionistic tour de force. Going beyond even the metaphor-free, plain style of writers such as Ernest Hemingway, Matthiessen trimmed his book of superfluities. Quotation marks, indicators such as "he said" and "there was," adjectives, and adverbs were left out. Further, he used the physical form of the book itself and of words and sentences on the page to create a visual impression analogous to the typographic effects of e. e. cummings. At times, the verbal yields to the ideographic in *Far Tortuga*: a black smudge represents the death of a man, a meandering line marks the horizon or the edge of the sea. Often, words or lines are accented by sweeps of empty white paper, and Matthiessen said that if he had the novel to do over, he would have written it even more like a musical score or an illuminated manuscript, with a much larger format and more dramatic utilization of space.

The form of the novel was an organic outgrowth of its subject, the dying world of a Caribbean turtle-fishing boat on its last voyage. The crew's world is a primitive one, like that of the Niaruna, an unintellectual existence of sea and sky, of superstitions, myths, and folktales, and of a rich cultural tradition succumbing to the modern world. The objective particulars of the turtlers' lives—the boat, the creatures of the sea, the shifting weather—parade through the novel without authorial comment, producing a stark, powerful texture that gives an impression of overwhelming physicality.

Like the cetology sections of *Moby Dick*, the action of *Far Tortuga* is rooted in a solidly constructed core of informational specifics delineating the turtlers' trade. The characters themselves, the doomed sailors of the decrepit boat *Lillias Eden*, live only in their speech and their actions, for Matthiessen never penetrates their minds. The novel's unique oral quality derives from its swell of dialect that seems increasingly natural as the book progresses. Rhythm is everything in *Far Tortuga*, rhythm and basic image (there is only a single simile in the entire work). As on the pages of Walt Whitman, Ezra Pound, or Charles Olsen, the basic elements of poetic evocation, words, raise up their images as *things*, hung together with a kind of narrative glue, the speech and stories of the turtlers. The dialogue is of a rich and variegated texture. As William Kennedy observed, the great strength of *Far Tortuga* is its use of detail, and both the dialogue and the narrative swarm with a wealth of objective particulars.

Like Matthiessen's Amazonian rain forest, this Caribbean setting is a singular one. Again, the book presents a simple people living close to nature and comfortable with it. Again, the protagonists' culture is threatened, on the brink of extinction. "The Modern World," as the turtlers bitterly call it, is a more distant enemy in this book, lurking outside the visual and verbal matrix that defines the narrative space of *Far Tortuga*, but the reader is well aware that it will soon bring the end of this culture. Modernity is distant only because, within the context of this novel, what is, and what is done, and what is said on the *Lillias Eden* is everything. On one hand are the specific objects and actions that define activity on the boat. On the other hand, there is a kind of spirit-world bodied forth in the talk of the men. Legends, ghost stories, and most of all tales of the past give the sense of an existence lived always in the shadow of the unseen. For these men, the sea turtle itself, like all animate and inanimate nature, is imbued with a spiritual character, akin to a soul. The line "Green turtle very mysterious, mon" runs through the novel like a chorus. Very mysterious, indeed: sacred, in fact.

The characterization in *Far Tortuga* is one of Matthiessen's most remarkable achievements. As the novel progresses, the reader is able to distinguish among the various speakers, and, gradually, individual personalities emerge. The sailors are rendered only in terms of their verbal expression of the world in which they work and live. There are no narrative threads or subplots unrelated to the immediate action of the book. One character stands out, the captain of the *Lillias Eden*, "Copm" Raib Avers. He is a full-bodied creature, irascible, arrogant, and energetic. He is also the embodiment of the integrity of the turtlers' trade, for he is rightfully proud of his skill as a sailor and passionate in his desire to be as good as "de copms of old"—men to whom sailing and turtle fishing were a calling rather than a way of just getting by. Avers's character is totally a function of the sea-swept world in which he lives. He seems to be related to half the people in the story, and his speech is a continual tale of the folk. To listen to him is to hear a kind of cultural history of the Caribbean, in which the living and the dead, the real and the fanciful, the past and the present are interwoven to create a vivid tapestry. Avers is the voice of the *paideuma*, the wisdom, knowledge, and heritage of his people. "I really do know what working men talk like," Matthiessen said once. In *Far Tortuga*, he proves it.

If Avers is the mouthpiece of a communal voice, he is also, like Moon, an individual voice. Doomed to defeat and death, each man on the *Lillias Eden* shares a common fate. If Avers's voice stands out, it is still the choral effect that dominates the novel. The group of men moves as a unit toward its destiny, borne relentlessly by the tides and their own impulses, like the characters in a Greek tragedy. Avers repeatedly asserts his belief that he is the master of his fate and captain of his soul as well as of the ship. He is more aggressive and less introspective than Moon, more of an activist, and he sees his role in the natural world as confrontational, a constant struggle between himself and the sea. He accepts the struggle, even celebrates it in his rough way, but he does not dominate the novel. Ultimately, his life and death are merged into the total picture of the turtlers as a group.

Avers is not even the last to survive the wreck of the *Lillias Eden* after the ship strikes a reef and sinks. The last forty pages of the novel are a remarkable finale in which the turtlers, adrift and unprotected in catboats, die one by one. The furious, frenetic rush of sounds and images subsides as the life goes out of the men. Finally, only a few hesitant words scattered on otherwise empty pages remain, and finally only

used the pseudonym of Dennis Jasper Murphy, publishing three novels under that name. When it was discovered that he was the author of the play *Bertram*, a play involving adultery and an amoral hero, he was for a time in danger of losing his curacy. Apparently, friends intervened to soothe the necessary bishops. After this incident, since his identity was known, he published his next novels and plays under his own name. It is quite possible that his literary activities did prevent his advancement in the clerical profession. There were those who interpreted the beliefs of his characters, some of which were atheistic and heretical, as Maturin's own.

His novels did gain him one very influential friend, Sir Walter Scott. In 1810, Scott wrote a generally favorable review of *Fatal Revenge* for *The Quarterly Review*. Encouraged, Maturin wrote to him, and a correspondence was begun which lasted until Maturin's death. Although the two men never actually met, Scott did assist Maturin with encouragement and advice, and he was instrumental in Maturin's one financial success; he recommended *Bertram* to George Gordon, Lord Byron, who was then responsible for play selection at Drury Lane Theatre. Byron was favorably impressed, and the famous actor Edmund Kean agreed to play the lead. The play's success earned Maturin one thousand pounds, most of which paid a relative's debt. Earlier, Maturin had been able to sell the copyright of his third novel, *The Milesian Chief*, for eighty pounds (the first two novels he had printed at his own expense), and later he was advanced five hundred pounds for *Melmoth the Wanderer*, but his literary efforts never brought the long-sought and often desperately needed financial stability. Up until his death, he continually tried to write in a style that would sell. *The Albigenses* is a historical romance, a type Scott had established and made quite popular. This novel was the first in what was to be a trilogy depicting European manners in ancient, medieval, and modern times. Soon after *The Albigenses* was completed, Maturin died in his home on October 30, 1824, apparently after a long period of ill health. The exact cause of his death is not known. He left a wife and four children who were still in desperate need of financial assistance.

ANALYSIS

In his preface to *Fatal Revenge*, Charles Robert Maturin stresses the fear of the unknown as essential in man's emotional and spiritual life: "It is *not* the weak and trivial impulse of the nursery, to be forgotten and scorned by manhood. It is the aspiration of a spirit; 'it is the passion of immortals,' that dread and desire of their final habitation." In one of his sermons, he focuses on the same theme:

> The very first sounds of childhood are tales of another life—foolishly are they called tales of superstition; for, however disguised by the vulgarity of narration, and the distortion of fiction, they tell him of those whom he is hastening from the threshold of life to join, the inhabitants of the invisible world, with whom he must soon be, and be for ever.

These quotations indicate a major aspect of Maturin's perception of human existence; the haunted and the sacred are interwoven and share a common ground. Human fascination with the supernatural, the world of demons and ghosts, springs from the same source as the desire to believe in salvation and a return to paradise. In fact, the road to salvation leads through the dark places of the soul where individuals must admit their fallen state, their own guilt. The theme of guilt is common in all of Maturin's novels. His major characters must struggle with the serpents in their own hearts, their own original sin. In keeping with this theme, the settings of his novels are generally those of a fallen world; dungeons and underground passages are common backgrounds for the action. Even in those novels that contain descriptions of more natural surroundings, storms and earthquakes are common occurrences, always reminding people that they have been exiled from paradise. Harmony with nature, with humanity, and with God has been lost.

Maturin develops this theme of guilt, which brings exile and separation, through his handling of character. The divided nature of humanity is represented by the pairing of characters, especially brothers: Ippolito and Annibal in *Fatal Revenge*, Connal and Desmond in *The Milesian Chief*, Paladour and Amirald in *The Albigenses*. These brothers are described in such a way as to suggest one identity fragmented into two opposing selves. Ippolito is passionate, Annibal rational; Desmond is the soft flower, Connal the proud oak. Often a character is torn in two opposing directions and does not know how to reconcile them: Connal between his Irish pride and his realization that the Irish peasants are not yet ready to govern themselves; Charles in *Women* between his love for Eva, a shy quiet girl, and Zaira, a worldly and more accomplished woman. At times, a character seems pursued by a dark, sinister double: Montorio by Schemoli in *Fatal Revenge*; Alonzo by the parricide in *Melmoth the Wanderer*. By far the most striking and powerful example of this is the character of the wanderer himself. Melmoth represents the potential for evil which can be found in all humans. In developing Melmoth's character, Maturin echoes the warning in Genesis against too much curiosity about the tree of knowledge of good and evil. Melmoth has sold his soul for increased knowledge; his sin is one of "pride and intellectual glorying," the sin of Lucifer and of the first mortals.

As Maturin's characters wander in a fallen world, little guidance is provided. Especially weak and ineffective are the parental figures. In fact, a distinguishing trait of this fallen world is the disintegration of the family. In all of Maturin's six novels, there are parents who are woefully irresponsible. They are often self-centered, putting their own greedy desires before their children's welfare, or they seek to expiate their own guilt by placing the burden of their sin upon their children. This selfish turning inward and transference of guilt to another is also found in Maturin's representations of larger structures of authority, especially the Catholic Church. As the divided soul wanders in a fallen world, parent and church offer little hope.

Maturin reserves the role of spiritual guide for the female characters who either love or are loved by the hero (such love is not always fulfilled or requited). Often his women are idealized creatures who can reconcile within themselves all conflicting opposites: in *Melmoth the Wanderer*, Immalee embodies passion and purity; in *The Albigenses*, Genevieve is a "mixture of strength and purity that is never to be found but in woman." Even if a woman finds herself hurled into a world of experience and corruption, as Zaira is in *Women*, her heart remains pure. At times, Maturin uses his female characters to symbolize self-sacrificing love that, although never placing the beloved before God, does place the beloved before the self. Despite Maturin's emphasis on such redeeming love, however, when domestic happiness is found by his characters it seems contrived and imposed upon them by others. Maturin is undoubtedly at his best when depicting people lost and searching for wholeness, not in actually finding it.

FATAL REVENGE

Maturin titled his first novel *The Family of Montorio*, but the publisher changed the title to *Fatal Revenge*, hoping to attract readers who would be interested in a gothic tale. The novel is definitely written in the style of Ann Radcliffe—one of its central figures, a ghostlike monk who calls himself Schemoli, is clearly patterned after Radcliffe's Schoedoni in 1797's *The Italian*—but Maturin uses what he borrows to develop his own characteristic theme with originality. Although he follows Radcliffe's technique of revealing the supernatural events as merely the result of disguise and charade, his descriptions of aberrant states of mind, to which all are subject, go beyond her handling of evil, and beyond the mere cataloging of grotesque horrors used by those writers who chose to imitate the more sensational style of Matthew Gregory Lewis. Annibal concludes after a brief period of solitary confinement that an "inward acquaintance" delights one not with tranquillity but, on the contrary, with "the grave of the mind." In describing the anguish of his guilt, Montorio cries, "the worm within me never dieth; and every thought and object it converts into its own morbid food." In Maturin, the evil within is quite real.

The plot of this novel is complicated, and Maturin's narrative is at times twisted and confusing. The tale relates the vengeful machinations of Schemoli, the once noble Count Montorio. He is seeking revenge for the wrongs his younger brother committed against him by manipulating Ippolito and Annibal, two young men he believes are his brother's sons, into believing that they are fated to murder their father. In part, the novel's convoluted structure works

able for the images of evil and suffering that populated his own mind, a mind repeatedly drawn to the
problems of human guilt and the divided soul. The
body of Maturin's work, although uneven, offers ample proof of his ability to shape these dark themes
with power and originality.

Diane D'Amico

OTHER MAJOR WORKS

PLAYS: *Bertram: Or, The Castle of St. Aldobrand*,
pr., pb. 1816; *Manuel*, pb. 1817; *Fredolfo*, pb. 1819.

BIBLIOGRAPHY

Bayer-Berenbaum, Linda. *The Gothic Imagination:
Expansion in Gothic Literature and Art.* Rutherford, N.J.: Fairleigh Dickinson University Press,
1982. A sympathetic study of gothicism, the essence of which is its confrontation with evil and
feelings of doom. Contains chapters on literary
gothicism and gothic art and its relationship to literature, as well as focused analyses of particular
works of literature. As one of the central writers
of gothicism, Maturin is given considerable attention, including an extensive analysis of *Melmoth
the Wanderer* that examines the novel as a pattern of expulsions and expansions. The conclusion sees a correlation between the gothic urge for
expansion and its style of intensification. Includes
a bibliography and index.

Kiely, Robert. *The Romantic Novel in England.* Cambridge, Mass.: Harvard University Press, 1972.
An important book on Romantic prose fiction, including Maturin's gothic romances, which analyzes in depth twelve Romantic novels to define
the intellectual context of the era. Notes that concepts of reality were tested and changed by Romantic novels and Edmund Burke's ideas of the
sublime modified aesthetic forms. Maturin has an
important place in this general thesis, and *Melmoth the Wanderer* is analyzed in detail as the
focus of his chapter. Finds this novel more emotionally involved with Roman Catholicism and
rebellious against authoritarian political systems
than other gothic fiction, believing it to be a journey into the darkness of the mind. Finds a common drift toward death in most novels of this
genre. Includes a set of notes and an index.

Kramer, Dale. *Charles Robert Maturin.* New York:
Twayne, 1973. Analyzes Maturin's personality,
describes the conditions of his life, and indicates
his innovations in the gothic tradition. Examines
his early novels from *Fatal Revenge* to *The Wild
Irish Boy*, then looks at Maturin's experiments on
the stage, where he achieved popular success with
Bertram but hardly any with *Manuel* and *Fredolfo*. Analyzes *Women*, Maturin's novel of "real
life," and devotes a chapter to *Melmoth the Wanderer* as his most successful writing, favorably
comparing it to Mary Shelley's *Frankenstein* and
William Godwin's *Adventures of Caleb Williams*.
Also examines *The Albigenses* as a descendant of
Sir Walter Scott's historical romances and sketches
Maturin's place in the history of literature. A
chro4nology, notes and references, a selected annotated bibliography, and an index are included.

Lougy, Robert E. *Charles Robert Maturin.* Lewisburg, Pa.: Bucknell University Press, 1975. An insightful review of Maturin's life and writings,
dividing his career into early, middle, and later
years. *Fatal Revenge* is analyzed for his characteristic themes: fear and guilt. His other writings are
placed in the context of his biography but also receive critical attention in comparison with one another, as well as with other works in the gothic
and Irish traditions. Focuses on *Bertram*, which
benefited from the popularity of Lord Byron's
Childe Harold's Pilgrimage, and concentrates on
Melmoth the Wanderer as a unique adaptation of
the legends of the Wandering Jew and Faust. Although *The Milesian Chief* and *Women* deserve
credit and Maturin's other writings are given
some attention, his reputation rests on *Melmoth*.
Includes a chronology and a selected bibliography
of primary and secondary works.

Tinkler-Villani, Valeria, Peter Davidson, and Jane
Stevenson, eds. *Edited by Candlelight: Sources
and Developments in the Gothic Tradition.* Am-
sterdam: Editions Rodopi, 1995. See Anthony
Johnson's essay, "Gaps and Gothic Sensibility:
Walpole, Lewis, Mary Shelley, and Maturin," for

a learned and clear discussion of how Maturin handles the gaps in reality that gothic fiction exploits.

W. SOMERSET MAUGHAM

Born: Paris, France; January 25, 1874
Died: Saint-Jean-Cap-Ferrat, France; December 16, 1965

PRINCIPAL LONG FICTION

Liza of Lambeth, 1897
The Making of a Saint, 1898
The Hero, 1901
Mrs. Craddock, 1902
The Merry-Go-Round, 1904
The Bishop's Apron, 1906
The Explorer, 1907
The Magician, 1908
Of Human Bondage, 1915
The Moon and Sixpence, 1919
The Painted Veil, 1925
Cakes and Ale, 1930
The Narrow Corner, 1932
Theatre, 1937
Christmas Holiday, 1939
Up at the Villa, 1941
The Hour Before Dawn, 1942
The Razor's Edge, 1944
Then and Now, 1946
Catalina, 1948
Selected Novels, 1953

OTHER LITERARY FORMS

A professional man of letters whose work spanned more than six decades, W. Somerset Maugham published in a wide range of literary forms, the significant exception being poetry. He first won success, fame, and wealth in the theater; his most acclaimed dramas were performed on the London stage during the first three decades of the twentieth century. He produced more than a hundred short stories, largely written during the period from 1921 to 1950; his collected short stories include four of the best-known stories of the twentieth century: "Rain," "The Outstation," "The Letter," and "The Colonel's Lady." Fifteen or more additional volumes are devoted to autobiography, literary and aesthetic criticism, and travel. Among these, the most useful for students are *The Summing Up* (1938), *Great Novelists and Their Novels* (1948), and *A Writer's Notebook* (1949).

ACHIEVEMENTS

Maugham's twenty novels are exceptionally uneven; the first eight, though interesting, suggest the efforts of a young novelist to discover where his talent lies. From the publication of *Of Human Bondage* (1915) through *The Razor's Edge* (1944), he produced his most significant prose works. During this period, he was a world-famous man of letters with a following of many thousands who would buy and read anything he wrote; however, a few novels that he produced, such as *Then and Now* and *Up at the Villa*, were not in his best vein.

(Library of Congress)

The novels brought Maugham acclaim and recognition both from a general audience and from the intelligentsia. Among common readers, he was perhaps the most successful English novelist of the twentieth century, and, as Samuel Johnson pointed out, the common reader is not often wrong. Yet, it must be admitted that Maugham's detractors, such as Edmund Wilson, present valid criticism: One expects a serious artist to exert an important influence, either thematic or formal, upon his medium. The symphony was forever altered by Ludwig van Beethoven; no similar statement can be made about Maugham and the novel. He sought to tell a story with clarity and grace, to embody a set of attitudes and values, and to entertain his readers with insights into character and life.

BIOGRAPHY

William Somerset Maugham, son of an English solicitor, was born in the British Embassy in Paris and spent his early childhood in France, learning French as his first language. Following the early death of both parents, Maugham went at age ten to England to live with his uncle, the Reverend Henry Maugham, Vicar of Whitstable, and his German-born wife. The rigid routine and disciplined family life of the Whitstable rectory contrasted with the casual, carefree existence and close warmth that Maugham had known in France. He was enrolled in the King's School, Canterbury, where he spent several unhappy years. A permanent stammer that developed during this period of his life destroyed any possibility of following the profession of his father and two of his brothers. Instead of enrolling in a university, Maugham chose to travel abroad to Germany, where at Heidelberg he saw Henrik Ibsen's dramas and attended lectures by Kuno Fischer on the philosophy of Arthur Schopenhauer. Returning to London, he enrolled in the medical school at St. Thomas's Hospital, where he received his M.D. in 1897.

Maugham's stronger interests, however, were literary and aesthetic, and when his first novel, *Liza of Lambeth*, achieved a modest success, he resolved to enter upon a career as a writer. None of the novels that Maugham wrote during the following decade repeated the success of *Liza of Lambeth*, yet he achieved sudden and unexpected acclaim through a series of plays, modern comedies of manners, beginning with *Lady Frederick* (1907). In 1908, four of his plays were running in London simultaneously. During World War I, Maugham served with British Intelligence in Switzerland and Russia. In 1915, he married Syrie Bernardo Wellcome, a marriage that ended in divorce in 1927. Following World War I, Maugham traveled to more remote areas of the world: the South Seas, Southeast Asia, and America, accompanied by his secretary, a gregarious American named Gerald Haxton, who aided the author in finding material for his fiction. Maugham acquired the Villa Mauresque on the French Riviera in 1928, an estate that became his home for the remainder of his life, though he continued his frequent travels and spent several years during World War II living in the United States. Creative work during his later years centered principally upon short stories, novels, and autobiography.

ANALYSIS

W. Somerset Maugham's novels are written in a style highly idiomatic and fluent, revealing the qualities of simplicity, lucidity, and euphony which the author sought to attain. Content to narrate an interesting story from his own unique angle of vision, he brought to the genre a gift for creating interesting characters who reflect life's ironies. In his later works, Maugham's narrative persona is a character interested in people, yet detached and somewhat clinical in his analysis of their actions and motives. The narrator demonstrates an unusual degree of tolerance for human peccadillos and incongruities and is reluctant to judge the actions of human beings. He writes primarily of adults in conflict with one another and with social mores. Frequently, his characters grow in tolerance and acceptance of human life, which is portrayed somewhat pessimistically. Maugham based his characters upon people whom he had known or whose lives he had somehow come to know; their actions are presented with consummate realism. They are motivated by their passions or emotions and by their attempts to control their destinies, not by an ideology or set of ideals. Though they may experience inner turmoil and conflict, they are seldom tormented by such emotions. Like their creator-narrator, the characters often have the ability to view themselves with clinical detachment and objectivity, to cast a cold eye on life.

LIZA OF LAMBETH

Among the early novels of Maugham, *Liza of Lambeth*, published when the author was only twenty-three, is probably the best known. Set in the Lambeth slum along Vere Street, London, it depicts naturalistically the lives of people in a state of poverty, characters such as those whom the author had come to know at first hand as an obstetric clerk at St. Thomas's Hospital. In its depiction of character, *Liza of Lambeth* fits the tradition of the naturalistic novel, somewhat in the manner of George Gissing, whose work Maugham knew well. The Cockney dialogue that pervades the novel is accurately represented, both in its pronunciation and in its slang or colloquial expressions. As is typical of naturalistic fiction, the characters are generally without hope, yet even in a naturalistic tradition Maugham reveals an original perspective. Unlike much naturalism, *Liza of Lambeth* does not urge social reform; the characters exhibit more hostility toward one another than toward any system. They generally accept their lot, which would be bearable but for their own mistakes. Liza Kemp's friend Sally enters marriage with hope, only to find her chances for happiness shattered owing to her husband's bad temper following drinking bouts, a weakness he had previously concealed. Liza, brimming with life and energy, spurns the devotion of a staid suitor, Tom, and finds excitement in an affair with an older, married neighbor, Jim Blakeston. By allowing passion to dominate their lives, the characters create undue hardships for themselves. This theme is commonly found in Maugham's work.

Just as *Liza of Lambeth* represented an effort at producing a naturalistic novel, Maugham's other early novels give the impression of deliberate attempts at imitating well-established forms. In *The Making of a Saint*, he wrote a brief historical novel with a late fifteenth century Florentine setting. A story of intrigue, assassination, and revenge, it is derived from a brief passage in a work by Niccolò

Machiavelli. *Mrs. Craddock* is set in rural England of the late nineteenth century, a novel of manners depicting provincial life, much in the manner of Arnold Bennett; *The Merry-Go-Round* belongs to a similar tradition. In *The Magician*, Maugham incorporates the conventions of the gothic genre, though there is perhaps too much realism for this work to be designated a true gothic novel.

OF HUMAN BONDAGE

In *Of Human Bondage*, Maugham's longest novel and his masterpiece, he turned to the well-known form of the *Bildungsroman*, the novel of a young person growing to maturity. *Of Human Bondage* is highly autobiographical, although it departs significantly from autobiographical accuracy in places. With the aid of an omniscient narrator, the reader follows the life of Philip Carey from his mother's death when he was only nine until he becomes a doctor and resolves to marry. Numerous characters in the novel are based upon people the author knew. The Reverend William Carey and his wife Louisa are based upon Maugham's uncle and aunt with whom he lived; Lawson is his friend Sir Gerald Kelly; Cronshaw derives from the eccentric poet Aleister Crowley, who had also been the model for Oliver Haddo in *The Magician*; and Hayward is based upon Maugham's friend Ellington Brooks. In a similar manner, Maugham incorporates descriptions of places that he knew well, with names only slightly altered (Whitstable to Blackstable, Canterbury to Tercanbury) or not altered at all, as the countryside of Kent or the cities of London and Paris.

In *Of Human Bondage*, Maugham sees three forces impinging upon Philip, shaping and influencing his life, forces that the novel emphasizes strongly: passion, disillusionment, and the quest for purpose in life. Philip is ill-equipped to cope with passion. Having been born with a clubfoot, which becomes a source of ridicule among school boys, and having lost both parents in childhood, he becomes overly sensitive. He takes pleasure in the solitary pursuit of reading and is less in the company of others than most boys; as a result, he has little understanding of the world at large. He finds that women who adore him arouse in him no passion in return, whereas he

study with such unguarded comments as the famous opening, "I have never begun a novel with more misgiving," and such wry asides as "I feel it right to warn the reader that he can very well skip this chapter without losing the thread of [the] . . . story. . . . I should add, however, that except for this conversation I should perhaps not have thought it worthwhile to write this book." Usually "Mr. Maugham" limits his involvement to conversation; his own actions, where they are noted (as when he withdraws to write a novel or takes his boat to Toulon), do not advance the plot. Occasionally, he does involve himself in the plot in some minor way. He contrives for the dying Elliott Templeton to receive an invitation to a party given by the Princess Novemali after she had deliberately snubbed Elliott, and he is on hand to identify the body of Sophie Macdonald.

"Mr. Maugham" reports the story as the major characters reveal it in their conversations. Isabel Bradley is in love with Larry Darrel but sensibly marries the successful Gray Maturin, only to find that after Gray loses his assets during the Depression, she and her husband and their two daughters must live on the generosity of her uncle Elliott. Larry, whose main interest in life is the study of philosophy and religion, attempts to marry Sophie Macdonald to save her from a dissolute life, an effort which Isabel shrewdly thwarts. Larry goes to a Benedictine monastery in France, later leaving it to study the Hindu religion in India. Returning from India at the end of the novel, he gives up his independent income and resolves to find work in New York driving a taxi. The Maturins move from Paris to Dallas, where Gray has secured an executive position in an oil company. The plot covers more than a decade, with the settings in France, England, and America. "Mr. Maugham," like the young Philip Carey, seeks a pattern in the lives of those he has met, and he finds that each life in *The Razor's Edge* has been a success. Even Sophie Macdonald, whose trauma caused her to seek death, found what she was seeking.

Maugham's three most significant novels following *Of Human Bondage* explore ideals that he considered in the final chapters of his autobiography, *The Summing Up*—truth, beauty, goodness. In *The Moon and Sixpence*, Charles Strickland represents the true genius whose work survives and speaks to posterity, even though his talent surfaced late in life and he violated accepted standards to advance it. In him, truth is neither obvious nor pleasant, but its existence can be confirmed by those who have felt the power of his work. Even the wife he abandoned displays reproductions of his paintings in her home and takes pride in his attainments. In *Cakes and Ale*, the ideal is beauty, which readers and critics find in the style, characters, and descriptions of Edward Driffield's novels. The narrator Willie Ashenden rejects this aesthetic beauty in favor of a more realistic beauty. He discovers the ideal in the warmth and charm of Rosie Gann, Driffield's first wife, who possessed neither fidelity nor business ethics but whose character brought others a wholesome sense of well-being. In *The Razor's Edge*, Larry Darrel reveals a basic goodness, a difficult quality to depict, partly because it may be attributed to the absence of either appetites or temptations. Though not an ascetic, Larry keeps passion and ambition in check and pursues his own spiritual development. He readily sacrifices himself for others, making a futile effort to save Sophie Macdonald from self-destruction through an offer of marriage, yet his sacrifices do not appear quixotic. A generous amount of modesty enables him to make the best of a life that reveals only goodness as an extraordinary element.

In each character, the ideal is neither obvious nor probable in the conventional sense. Its existence is ironic, and it might be overlooked were not the Maugham persona on hand to define it. Not even the narrator, however, can explain or account for it; the reader savors its presence without fully understanding its origin.

Among the remaining novels of Maugham, one finds works of literary merit and appeal, though they represent lesser achievements. A reader of Maugham would not want to miss novels such as *The Painted Veil* and *The Narrow Corner*, which narrate suspenseful and intense conflicts. Works such as these differ from the better-known novels in several important respects. First, the Maugham persona is either absent or less intrusive. In *The Narrow Corner*, for example, the author's viewpoint is usually expressed through Dr. Saunders, who lives on a Pacific island and has no literary interests or ambitions. Further, the settings are usually foreign or exotic—European or Asian rather than American or English. Instead of spanning decades, the plots narrate events that occur during a few months; novels such as *Up at the Villa*, for example, differ little from some of Maugham's short stories.

Significantly, in Maugham's major novels, the important characters—Philip Carey, Larry Darrel, Rosie Gann, and Charles Strickland—either embody an ideal or achieve some measure of success in pursuit of an ideal, whereas idealism in the minor works is usually crushed and defeated. Fred Blake and Erik Christensen in *The Narrow Corner* find only disappointment, disillusionment, and early death, as does the unfortunate Karl Richter in *Up at the Villa*. Those who survive are worldly-wise and detached characters who can regard life as Maugham's spokesman Dr. Saunders does:

> Life is short, nature is hostile, and man is ridiculous but oddly enough most misfortunes have their compensations and with a certain humour and a good deal of horse-sense one can make a fairly good job of what is after all a matter of very small consequence.

The minor works reward the reader with their depiction of the ironies of human life, the eccentricities of human beings and the unusual settings and universal conflicts, yet, however rewarding, they lack the thematic richness and emotional concentration of Maugham's best novels.

Stanley Archer

OTHER MAJOR WORKS

SHORT FICTION: *Orientations*, 1899; *The Trembling of a Leaf: Little Stories of the South Sea Islands*, 1921; *The Casuarina Tree: Six Stories*, 1926; *Ashenden: Or, The British Agent*, 1928; *Six Stories Written in the First Person Singular*, 1931; *Ah King: Six Stories*, 1933; *East and West: The Collected Short Stories*, 1934; *Cosmopolitans*, 1936; *The Favorite Short Stories of W. Somerset Maugham*, 1937; *The Round Dozen*, 1939; *The Mixture as Before:*

Short Stories, 1940; *Creatures of Circumstances: Short Stories*, 1947; *East of Suez: Great Stories of the Tropics*, 1948; *Here and There: Selected Short Stories*, 1948; *The Complete Short Stories*, 1951; *The World Over*, 1952; *Seventeen Lost Stories*, 1969.

PLAYS: *A Man of Honor*, wr. 1898-1899, pr., pb. 1903; *Loaves and Fishes*, wr. 1903, pr. 1911; *Lady Frederick*, pr. 1907; *Jack Straw*, pr. 1908; *Mrs. Dot*, pr. 1908; *The Explorer*, pr. 1908; *The Noble Spaniard*, pr. 1909; *Penelope*, pr. 1909; *Smith*, pr. 1909; *Landed Gentry*, pr. 1910 (as *Grace*); *The Tenth Man*, pr. 1910; *The Land of Promise*, pr. 1913; *Caroline*, pr. 1916, pb. 1923 (as *The Unattainable*); *Our Betters*, pr. 1917; *Caesar's Wife*, pr. 1919; *Home and Beauty*, pr. 1919 (also known as *Too Many Husbands*); *The Unknown*, pr., pb. 1920; *The Circle*, pr., pb. 1921; *East of Suez*, pr., pb. 1922; *The Constant Wife*, pr., pb. 1926; *The Letter*, pr., pb. 1927; *The Sacred Flame*, pr., pb. 1928; *The Breadwinner*, pr., pb. 1930; *The Collected Plays of W. Somerset Maugham*, pb. 1931, 1952 (3 volumes; including 18 plays); *For Services Rendered*, pr., pb. 1932; *Sheppey*, pr., pb. 1933.

SCREENPLAY: *Trio*, 1950 (with R. C. Sherriff and Noel Langley).

NONFICTION: *The Land of the Blessed Virgin: Sketches and Impressions in Andalusia*, 1905 (also known as *Andalusia*, 1920); *On a Chinese Screen*, 1922; *The Gentleman in the Parlour: A Record of a Journey from Rangoon to Haiphong*, 1930; *Don Fernando*, 1935; *The Summing Up*, 1938; *Books and You*, 1940; *France at War*, 1940; *Strictly Personal*, 1941; *Great Novelists and Their Novels*, 1948; *A Writer's Notebook*, 1949; *The Writer's Point of View*, 1951; *The Vagrant Mood: Six Essays*, 1952; *The Partial View*, 1954 (includes *The Summing Up* and *A Writer's Notebook*); *Ten Novels and Their Authors*, 1954 (revision of *Great Novelists and Their Novels*); *The Travel Books*, 1955; *Points of View*, 1958; *Looking Back*, 1962; *Purely for My Pleasure*, 1962; *Selected Prefaces and Introductions*, 1963.

BIBLIOGRAPHY

Cordell, Richard A. *Somerset Maugham, a Writer for All Seasons: A Biographical and Critical Study.*

2d ed. Bloomington: Indiana University Press, 1969. A valuable discussion of Maugham's philosophy, which Cordell finds in the "writings of wise men of all ages." Considers both sides—sympathetic and unsympathetic—to Maugham while focusing on his novels, short stories, plays, and nonfiction (briefly). The best of his work is *Of Human Bondage, The Moon and Sixpence*, and *Cakes and Ale*. Indexed.

Holden, Philip. *Orienting Masculinity, Orienting Nation: W. Somerset Maugham's Exotic Fiction*. Westport, Conn.: Greenwood Press, 1996. Examines the themes of homosexuality, gender identity, and race relations in Maugham's works.

Loss, Archie K. *"Of Human Bondage": Coming of Age in the Novel*. Boston: Twayne, 1990. One of Twayne's masterwork studies, this is an excellent analysis.

Maugham, Robin. *Somerset and All the Maughams*. New York: New American Library, 1966. Maugham's complex personality is illuminated in this intriguing study of his ancestors and immediate family members. An index is included.

Morgan, Ted. *Maugham*. New York: Simon & Schuster, 1980. The first full-scale biography of Maugham and therefore an essential text in all studies of the man and his work. Unlike previous biographers, Morgan enjoyed the cooperation of Maugham's literary executor and, therefore, is able to correct many distortions in previous studies. Offers the most comprehensive account yet of the private man, including photographs, a complete primary bibliography, and an index.

Naik, M. K. *William Somerset Maugham*. Norman: University of Oklahoma Press, 1966. Argues that a conflict between "cynicism" and "humanitarianism" kept Maugham from literary success. Only in *Cakes and Ale*, his short stories, and his travel books does he balance the two points of view.

Rogal, Samuel J. *A William Somerset Maugham Encyclopedia*. Westport, Conn.: Greenwood Press, 1997. Contains information on Maugham's life as well as his works. Includes bibliographical references and an index.

HERMAN MELVILLE

Born: New York, New York; August 1, 1819
Died: New York, New York; September 28, 1891

PRINCIPAL LONG FICTION

Typee: A Peep at Polynesian Life, 1846
Omoo: A Narrative of Adventures in the South Seas, 1847
Mardi, and a Voyage Thither, 1849
Redburn: His First Voyage, 1849
White-Jacket: Or, The World in a Man-of-War, 1850
Moby Dick: Or, The Whale, 1851
Pierre: Or, The Ambiguities, 1852
Israel Potter: His Fifty Years of Exile, 1855
The Confidence Man: His Masquerade, 1857
Billy Budd, Foretopman, 1924

OTHER LITERARY FORMS

After the financial failures of *Moby Dick* and *Pierre*, Herman Melville, as if turning a new corner in his literary career, began a series of short stories. Published between 1853 and 1856, either in a collection (*The Piazza Tales*, 1856) or individually in journals such as *Putnam's Monthly Magazine* and *Harper's Monthly* magazine, the tales present an enigmatic addition to Melville's artistry. Melville had difficulty with the short forms, and he seemed unable to work out the plot and characters in the space required. His best stories are novella length: "Benito Cereno," "The Encantadas," and "Bartleby the Scrivener." With the publication of *The Apple-Tree Table and Other Sketches* (1922), all of Melville's stories became available in collection.

Melville also wrote poetry, which suffers from the same unevenness that plagues his short fiction. A handful of poems, gathered selectively from *Battle-Pieces and Aspects of the War* (1866), *John Marr and Other Sailors* (1888), and *Timoleon* (1891), are worthy of being anthologized with the best poetry of the nineteenth century. His worst poem, *Clarel: A Poem and Pilgrimage in the Holy Land* (1876), a long, flawed reflection on Melville's travels in the Holy

Land, continues to be of interest only for its revealing autobiographical and philosophical content. "Hawthorne and His Mosses," Melville's only serious attempt at criticism and analysis, is important as an assessment of Hawthorne's first important sketches.

ACHIEVEMENTS

Melville's achievements, before the discovery of *Billy Budd, Foretopman* and the subsequent revival of Melville studies, were viewed simply as writings from "a man who lived among the cannibals." He was remembered only for *Typee* and *Omoo*, his slight but extremely popular South Seas adventures. While important as the beginnings of the popular tradition of exotic romances, *Typee* and *Omoo* are not classics. Only with the publication of *Billy Budd, Foretopman*, and the critical scrutiny that its publication encouraged, were *Moby Dick, Pierre*, and the rest reassessed, and Melville's reputation as a leader among giants affirmed.

Apart from introducing the South Seas tale to the American public, *Pierre* is arguably the first important work of psychological realism, and *Moby Dick* is a masterpiece of metaphysics, allegory, philosophy, and literature. The assessment of Melville's work was not realized until years after his death and almost seventy years after Melville had given up the novel form for the quick money of short stories, the personal introspection of poetry, and the security of a government post in the New York customs office. Melville was never psychologically or ideologically attuned to the demands of his public, and, thus, popularity eluded him in his lifetime.

BIOGRAPHY

Herman Melville was born in New York City, August 1, 1819, the third child of a modestly wealthy family. His father, a successful merchant, traced his lineage back to Major Thomas Melville, one of the "Indians" at the Boston Tea Party. His mother, Maria Gansevoort Melville, was the only daughter of General Peter Gansevoort, also a revolutionary war hero. Melville had a happy childhood in a home where there was affluence and love. He had access to the arts and books, and he was educated in some of the

city's finest private institutions. His father, however, considered young Melville to be somewhat backward, despite his early penchant for public speaking, and marked him for a trade rather than law or a similar professional pursuit.

The prosperity that the Melvilles enjoyed from before Herman's birth came to an end in the economic panic of 1830. Unable to meet creditors' demands, despite the financial aid of his family, Melville's father lost his business and was forced into bankruptcy. After attempts to save the business, he moved the family to Albany and assumed the management of a fur company's branch office. The move seemed to settle the Melvilles' financial problems until the cycle repeated itself in 1831. Melville's father again suffered a financial reversal, went into physical and mental decline, and died on January 28, 1832.

After his father's death, Melville became, successively, a bank clerk and accountant, a farm worker, a schoolteacher, and, after another economic failure—this time his brother Gansevoort's fur business—an unemployed, but genteel, young man seeking a job in

(Library of Congress)

New York City. With the aid of his brothers, Melville secured a berth on a Liverpool packet and thus launched his sea career, and indirectly, his literary fortunes. After one cruise, however, Melville returned to schoolteaching. When the school closed for lack of funds, he and a friend determined to go West to visit Melville's uncle in Illinois, hoping to find some type of financially satisfying arrangement there. Failing to find work, Melville returned to New York City and signed aboard the *Acushnet*, a new whaler making her maiden voyage. From 1841 to 1844, Melville was to participate in seafaring adventures that would change American literature.

On his return to New York in 1844, he found his family's fortunes somewhat improved. He also found that the stories he had to tell of his travels were enthusiastically received by his friends and relatives. Finally persuaded to write them, he produced *Typee* and published it in 1846. The immediate success and acclaim which followed the publication assured Melville that he had finally found his place in life. He followed *Typee* with its sequel, *Omoo*, which achieved a similar success, and resolutely set out to make his living by his pen. He found the financial return of two popular novels was not sufficient to support him, however, and he applied for a government position and was rejected. Melville married Elizabeth Shaw, moved to New York City with most of his family, and started a third novel that became *Mardi, and a Voyage Thither.*

The visionary and allegorical structure of *Mardi, and a Voyage Thither* did not appeal to the readers of his previous successes, and its failure frustrated Melville. In need of ready funds, he began two "potboilers" in order to produce those funds. After the publication and success of *Redburn* and *White-Jacket*, Melville moved his family to a farm in the Berkshires, which he dubbed "Arrowhead" because of Indian artifacts he found there, and assumed the life of a country gentleman and a member of the loosely knit literary society that included Oliver Wendell Holmes, Nathaniel Hawthorne, and others living in the vicinity of Pittsfield, Massachusetts.

How Hawthorne and Melville met is not known, but that they met is witnessed by the production of *Moby Dick*. It was likely that Hawthorne encouraged Melville to write as he saw fit, not as the public demanded. Their correspondence reveals an intense, cordial friendship that was of immense value to Melville during this time of his greatest personal, emotional, and artistic development. Hawthorne was one of the first, not to mention the few, to praise Melville's whaling story. Despite Hawthorne's praise, *Moby Dick* was a financial and critical failure. *Pierre*, the "rural bowl of milk" that followed *Moby Dick*, defied Melville's predictions for its success and was also a failure. The dual failure caused Melville considerable pain and bitterness. As a result of the failures and the debt to his publishers, Melville turned away from the novel to the short-story form.

He was to publish two more novels in his lifetime, but neither was commercially successful. Melville began writing poetry in addition to the short story, but his poetry was even more introspective than his fiction, and by the time he was appointed to the customs office of New York City in 1866 he had virtually stopped publishing for public consumption.

The security of the customs office eliminated Melville's need for the slim financial return of publication, and he no longer felt compelled to write for an unwilling public. Yet, he continued to write. At his death, he left a box full of manuscripts of his unpublished work during the years from 1866 to his death (he had published some poetry). When the box was opened, it was found to contain one more novel. *Billy Budd, Foretopman*, published in 1924, was the final piece of Melville's frustration. He never finished it and never attempted to publish it, but since its discovery and publication it has been recognized as one of Melville's masterpieces. When Melville died in 1891, his obituaries recalled him not only as a man who wrote novels of adventure but also one who had "fallen into a literary decline." It was left for another generation to appreciate and revere him.

Analysis

Herman Melville's career as a novelist breaks down, somewhat too neatly, into a three-part voyage of frustration and disappointment. The first part of his career is characterized by the heady successes of

Typee and *Omoo*, the second by the frustrating failure of, among others, *Moby Dick*, and the third by his increasing withdrawal from publication and the final discovery of and acclaim for *Billy Budd, Foretopman*, thirty-two years after Melville's death. After the initial successes of *Typee* and *Omoo*, Melville never again achieved anything approaching popular success, but it was the acclaim over those two novels that assured Melville that he should attempt to make his way as a novelist. It probably did not occur to Melville at the time, but he was introducing a new genre into American literature.

Typee struck the American public like a ray of sunshine falling into a darkened room. The fresh descriptions and intriguing narrative of an American sailor trapped among the Rousseauesque natives of the Marquesas Islands were hailed on both sides of the Atlantic Ocean, and its sequel, *Omoo*, was received even more enthusiastically. The problems inherent in Melville's harsh treatment of missionaries and imperialism and the general disbelief of the veracity in the author's tale aside, the works satiated a public thirst for exotic places. That *Typee* and *Omoo* have survived in the estimation of critics is testimony to Melville's art even in those early stages of his development.

TYPEE

Whether it is the simple narrative or the dramatic suspense of impending doom that holds the reader, *Typee* offers a flowing romantic atmosphere of timeless days, pointless endeavor, and mindless existence. The Happy Valley in which Melville's Tommo finds himself trapped is an idyllic setting for the lovely Fayaway and Tommo to live and love. In *Typee* there is none of the agonizing speculation on life, humanity, philosophy, or the cosmos, which readers later came to expect of Melville. With only slight exaggeration and minimal research, Melville created the picture of a world beyond the ken of his readers but which would never die in his memories.

OMOO

Omoo, a sequel to *Typee*, is only an extension of that idyll. There is a basic difference between *Typee* and *Omoo*, however; *Typee* is a tightly woven dramatic narrative, incorporating the day-to-day suspense of whether Tommo would be the Marquesan cannibals' next meal; *Omoo* is a more picaresque representation of the events, the charm in *Omoo* depending solely on the loosely tied chain of events encountered by the narrator and his companion, Dr. Long Ghost, among the natives of Tahiti. There is no threat hanging over them, as in *Typee*, and there is no necessity for escape. *Omoo* also differs in that it takes place in a tainted paradise. Tahiti has been, in *Omoo*, Christianized and settled and, thus, the natives are familiar with the white sailor and his games. This reduction of innocence colors *Omoo* in a way not reflected in *Typee*.

There is an inescapable glow of romance throughout Melville's two Polynesian novels. The record of missionary abuse and the encroachment of civilization does not make an overbearing appearance, but it does lay the groundwork for the reflections of Melville's despair and convoluted indictments of man and his world in later, more mature works.

Mardi, *Redburn*, and *White-Jacket* rapidly followed Melville's early successes. *Mardi*, opening like a continuation of *Typee* and *Omoo*, shocked readers when it lapsed into philosophical allegory. *Mardi*'s subsequent failure prompted Melville, in search of fame and funds, to return to sea narrative in *Redburn* and *White-Jacket*, but despite their modest successes, Melville reviled them as hackwork.

MOBY DICK

In *Moby Dick*, there is evidence that Melville intended it to be little more than a factual account of the whale fisheries in the South Pacific detailed with firsthand tales of adventures on a whaler. When completed two years after its beginning, it was a puzzling, intricately devised literary work in which a white whale is the central character. Around this central figure, Melville weaves symbolism, speculation, philosophy, and allegory on life, God, man, and the human condition. In short, Melville had created an epic romance that stood at the brink of becoming mythology.

The plot of *Moby Dick*, when not interrupted by authorial asides and digressions, is relatively direct. A young man, Ishmael, comes to the sea seeking a berth on a whaling ship. He finds the *Pequod*; falls into a friendship with the cannibal harpooner Queequeg; discovers that the ship is captained by a madman, Ahab, who is driven to wreak vengeance on the white whale that took his leg off on a previous voyage; finds himself in a crew that is a microcosm of the world's peoples; watches as Ahab drives the ship and crew in pursuit of Moby Dick; and is the sole survivor when Ahab is killed in a direct confrontation with the whale. By itself, the plot is thrilling but does not have the ingredients of greatness. The layers of fiction—the levels that the reader must traverse in order to rend the novel for all its substance—make the work magnificent. To the surface adventure, Melville adds gleanings from volumes of cetological and marine lore, his own observations on the psychology of man, and, finally, his ultimate speculations on good and evil—the basic morality of man and of man's place in the universe.

Melville's frequent displays of marine erudition are often cursed as flaws in an otherwise closely woven fabric. They seem to do little for the on-rushing spectacle of Ahab and his monomania, and they almost function as literary irritants designed to interrupt the reader's chain of thought. They are not intended to enhance the characterization of Ahab or his crew, nor are they an integral part of the narrative; they are, however, the essence of the novel's central character, the whale. Without Melville's lore, there is no reality to the ominously ethereal presence of Moby Dick. The periodic chapters of information and background are the author's reminders to the reader of the whale's presence and that the whale drives the story forward. The lore is also the foundation of belief in the whale. It promotes and maintains the physical presence of the whale by the sheer weight of scientific or pseudoscientific data. When the whale finally appears, the reader has been sufficiently educated and prepared. Melville creates the whale, vicariously, with his lore and trivia and sets the stage for its appearance.

In describing Ahab, his ship, and the crew, Melville employs a nonnarrative form of characterization, where each individual is the subject of an inquiry or is an example of a human type. Of the major characters, Ahab is the most complex, but the others

form a society in which that complexity can best be displayed. Starbuck, the first mate, Stubb, the second mate, and Flask, the third mate, are only the closest of several layers of the crew around Ahab. Queequeg, Tashtego, and Daggoo, the harpooners, form the next layer, and the rest of the crew fill out Ahab's world. Like Fleece, the ship's cook, and Pip, the mad cabin boy, they all perform vignettes that enlarge and enhance the magnitude of Ahab and his quest. For example, Ahab feels compelled to explain the real reasons behind his insane search for the white whale only to Starbuck, the conscientious, scrupulous first mate. Rather than simple revenge, as Starbuck supposes it to be, Ahab proposes to strike through the "pasteboard masks" of reality by striking at the whale. In his reasoning with Starbuck, Ahab demonstrates a side of himself which is otherwise hidden; there is purpose, calculation, and preparation in his madness. Ahab's insanity, thereby, becomes a divine sort of madness, and he transcends mere earthly logic to become an epic madman jousting with creation. It is through Starbuck and the others that the reader learns most about Ahab, and it is in such relationships that one sees the mastery of Melville's artistry.

Ahab becomes more than a simple villain when viewed against the backdrop of Starbuck and the other characters. He becomes a monolithic character testing a universe that he sees as perverse and unkind toward human existence. He dares to confront nature itself and to challenge it to single combat. It is Queequeg who unwittingly provides the clues to the venture's outcome. He has a coffin built when he fears he will die of a fever, and when Moby Dick rams the *Pequod*, it is the coffin that supports Ishmael, the only survivor. The coffin becomes the symbolic remainder of Ahab's world. Humans and their science cannot stand against nature and hope to survive. It is Ahab's hamartia to believe that he can survive, and his belief is the final sign of his ultimately evil nature.

Ahab would, he tells Starbuck, "strike the sun if he offended me," and he considers himself as the equal of any other force in nature. He forgets that he is limited by human frailty—or he believes he is no longer subject to the laws of temporal existence or his own physical shortcomings. He is, in one sense, a blighted Prometheus who can offer nothing but his vision to his fellow men, and they blindly accept it. Ahab's greatest evil is the corruption of his relatively innocent world, and its ultimate destruction is his sole responsibility.

Melville used many symbols and devices in *Moby Dick*, and they are important strands by which the story is held together. The names alone are important enough to demand attention. The biblical significance of Ishmael and Ahab, and of Jereboam and Rachel, needs no explanation. Starbuck, Stubb, and Flask all have significance when examined symbolically. The mythical ramifications of a voyage beginning on Christmas night enlarge as the story unfolds. The ultimate device is Ishmael himself. Ostensibly the story's narrator, he only appears in about every fourth chapter after the first twenty-five. When he does appear, it is difficult to keep track of whether the narrator or author is speaking. Ishmael, however, is never used in an omnipotent, obtrusive manner that would belie his place on the *Pequod*, and, thus, the point of view remains clear. Ishmael opens the novel and announces "and I only am escaped alone to tell thee," but he is there primarily to provide a frame for the story. This very flexible point of view is an adroit device by which the author can distance himself from the story while still involving himself in a story as few authors have or will. When Melville finds Ishmael to be an encumbrance, he sheds him and speaks for himself. It remains an open question whether the story is Ishmael's, Ahab's, the whale's, or Melville's. It is not necessary, however, that the dilemma be resolved in order to appreciate and acknowledge the massive achievement in *Moby Dick*.

BILLY BUDD, FORETOPMAN

After the failure of *Moby Dick* to be a commercial success, Melville's increasingly sour approach to novel-writing produced *Pierre*, perhaps the first psychological novel in American literature but also a miserable failure; *Israel Potter*, a rewriting and fictionalizing of a Revolutionary War diary; *The Confidence Man*, a sardonic, rambling, loosely constructed allegory on American society; and *Billy Budd, Foretopman*. The last of Melville's attempts in the novel

form, *Billy Budd, Foretopman* was never offered for publication by the author and was discovered and published in the mid-1920's. Despite its checkered publication history (it has appeared in any number of flawed or badly edited forms), *Billy Budd, Foretopman* has come to be recognized as Melville's final word on the great problems with which he first grappled in *Moby Dick*. Its form and simplicity make it the perfect companion for the epic proportions of *Moby Dick*. Its message is such that it seems Melville created it as a catharsis for the unanswered questions in the greater work.

Billy Budd, Foretopman is a masterful twisting of historical event into fiction in order to maintain the tension of a gripping story. While so doing, Melville explores the stirring, but somewhat less exciting, problems of the conflict between man, good and evil, and the law. Melville uses a blend of the historically significant British mutinies of the *Nore* and at Spithead in 1797 and the 1842 execution of three alleged mutineers of the United States ship *Somers*, in which his cousin Guert Gansevoort played a significant part, to mold the setting and motive for his story leading to the trial and execution of the "handsome sailor." The events leading to the trial are relatively unadorned, and there is little question prior to the trial where the reader's sympathies should be and which characters embody which attributes of human nature.

There is a slightly melodramatic air about the principal characters in *Billy Budd, Foretopman*. Claggart, by shrewd characterization and description, is the evil master-at-arms who is in direct conflict with the innocent, pure, guileless Billy Budd. Melville never makes clear why Claggart develops his seemingly perverse prejudice against Billy, but a definite line of good and evil is drawn between the two men. The evil is magnified by the mysterious impetus for Claggart's antipathy toward Billy; the good is intensified by Billy's naïve ignorance of Claggart's malice, even though the entire crew seems to know of it and understand the reasons for it, and by his cheerful mien not only in the face of Claggart's bullying but also in spite of the circumstances that brought him to the *Indomitable*.

PRINCIPAL LONG FICTION

The Shaving of Shagpat, 1855
Farina, 1857
The Ordeal of Richard Feverel, 1859
Evan Harrington, 1861
Emilia in England, 1864 (as *Sandra Belloni: Or, Emilia in England*, 1886)
Rhoda Fleming, 1865
Vittoria, 1867
The Adventures of Harry Richmond, 1871
Beauchamp's Career, 1874-1875 (serial), 1876 (book)
The Egoist, 1879
The Tragic Comedians, 1880
Diana of the Crossways, 1885
One of Our Conquerors, 1891
Lord Ormont and His Aminta, 1894
The Amazing Marriage, 1895
Celt and Saxon, 1910 (unfinished)

OTHER LITERARY FORMS

Ironically, George Meredith, one of nineteenth century England's greatest novelists, actually considered himself a poet. Regrettably, the several volumes of poetry he published during his lifetime went largely unnoticed. Even though Alfred, Lord Tennyson, praised "Love in the Valley," published in his first volume, *Poems* (1851), dedicated to his then father-in-law, Thomas Love Peacock, it was as a novelist that Meredith achieved recognition in his own time. Undaunted, nevertheless, Meredith continued to write poems and, in keeping with his stated vocation and with his aspiration, both his first and his last published books were collections of poems.

Modern Love and Poems of the English Roadside (1862) represents Meredith's lyric and dramatic power at its height, especially in the sequence of fifty sixteen-line lyrics, *Modern Love*. In these poems, Meredith traces the dissolution of a mar-

riage with an unrestrained candor that is more like the attitudes toward marital relationships of the late twentieth century than the straight-faced, closed-lipped Victorian notions. At the lowest point in the sequence, the persona exclaims, "In tragic life, God wot,/ No villain need be! Passions spin the plot;/ We are betrayed by what is false within." Herein Meredith seems to capture with great precision the essence of tragedy. Meredith's poetic vision is not always dark; light imagery, in fact, plays a significant role in his poetry.

The thinking man appears often in Meredith's works, but he is perhaps most prominent in the 1877 essay "The Idea of Comedy and the Uses of the Comic Spirit." This essay is significant enough to be included in many contemporary collections of criticism, especially in those that pertain to drama. Acknowledging that the muse of comedy has never been "one of the most honored of the Muses," Meredith submits that it is the "Comic Spirit" that civilizes man. By means of thoughtful laughter, the Comic Spirit corrects and checks the foibles of all the men who exceed the bounds of temperance and indulge by excessive behavior. Although Meredith opened himself to censure in his own day, his ideas about women and their roles in comedy are particularly interesting

(Library of Congress)

to today's readers. Indeed, comedy, "the fountain of common sense," teaches that men and women are social equals and that women are often men's superiors.

ACHIEVEMENTS

In the late nineteenth century, Meredith achieved the status of a literary dictator or arbiter of taste. The path toward this recognition was, however, a long and arduous one. For years, Meredith received little to no recognition, and he had to wait for the publication of *The Ordeal of Richard Feverel* before he enjoyed the limited appreciation of Algernon Charles Swinburne, Dante Gabriel Rossetti, and others among the pre-Raphaelites. Not until the appearance of *The Egoist* in 1879 did Meredith's literary reputation reach its zenith.

During his last years, Meredith received many awards and honors, including the succession of Alfred, Lord Tennyson, as the president of the Society of British Authors and election as one of the original members of the Order of Merit. Within twenty years after Meredith's death in 1909, nevertheless, his literary reputation began to suffer a partial eclipse, from which it began to recover in the 1970's. One explanation for Meredith's decline in reputation is simple: His turgid style and complex plots demand more from the average reader than he or she is often willing to give. C. L. Cline's three-volume edition of *The Letters of George Meredith*, which appeared in 1970, and Phyllis B. Bartlett's two-volume, collection of *The Poems of George Meredith* (1978) have done much to reawaken interest in Meredith's work, particularly in his poetry, which seems to appeal to modern readers much more markedly than it had to those of his own time. Even so, the influence of Meredith the novelist on such younger writers as Thomas Hardy was decisive, and Meredith's theory of the Comic Spirit as the civilizing force of all thoughtful men speaks to all cultures of all times.

BIOGRAPHY

Born the son and grandson of tailors, George Meredith appears to have rejected his humble origins. Indeed, he once threatened that he would "most horribly haunt" any who attempted to reconstruct his biography. Despite his modest heritage, legacies from his mother and an aunt permitted him to attend private schools, St. Paul's Church School, Southsea, and the Moravian School of Neuwied, Germany. His objective in formal training was to become a lawyer, and he was apprenticed to a London solicitor in 1845. Young Meredith soon became dissatisfied with the legal profession, however, and began to seek a career as a journalist, a vocation which he pursued throughout most of his life, since he was never quite able to survive financially as an author of novels and poems.

From at least 1845 until his marriage in 1849 to Mary Ellen Nicolls, a widow and the daughter of Thomas Love Peacock, Meredith appears to have read widely and deeply in the literature of Greece, Rome, Germany, France, and England. The first few years of his marriage appear to have been ones of continued intellectual growth. The Merediths lived either with or near the aspiring young author's famous father-in-law. Meredith made good use of Peacock's extensive and often arcane library, whose shelves included volumes on such Near Eastern religions as Zoroastrianism, a faith that was later to have a profound influence on Meredith's novels and poems.

The first few years of apparent bliss were soon terminated, however, when Mary eloped in 1858 with the painter Henry Wallis to the isle of Capri. Meredith was consequently left alone to rear his son Arthur; the author later wrote about these unhappy times both in the novel *The Ordeal of Richard Feverel* and in the lyric sequence *Modern Love*. After Mary's death in 1861, Meredith married, within three years, Marie Vulliamy; this match proved to be both enduring and much happier. After serving as war correspondent, he and his new wife moved to Flint Cottage, Box Hill, Surrey, where he lived the remainder of his life. Box Hill is where admiring and enthusiastic young authors went to seek Meredith's sage counsel.

ANALYSIS

Although George Meredith's works all emphasize the corrective, civilizing influences of the Comic Spirit, his novels, as well as his poems, forcefully

to "save the world." He joins a radical political party in order to battle the more conservative Tory Party and to oppose the vehement objections of his Uncle Everard Romfrey, a hater of radicals. After Nevil loses an election for a seat in Parliament, he comes under the tutelage of Dr. Shrapnel, a professed Fire-worshipper.

Since "Fire-worshippers" is a name that Zoroastrians were often mistakenly called, when Dr. Shrapnel testifies "I am a Fire-worshipper," the reader perceives already an element of Meredith's comedy. Dr. Shrapnel, whose name calls to mind a number of images, all of which indicate either potential destruction or active destruction, has obviously become enamored of the mystic, esoteric nature of the religion and hence has adopted certain of its tenets to his own philosophy. Basically Shrapnel's personal doctrine is, in his own words: "That is our republic: each one to his work; all in union! There's the motto for us! *Then* you have music, harmony, the highest, fullest, finest!"

Admittedly, Shrapnel's philosophy is good, or superior in its idealism, and it represents a direct restatement of Meredith's own philosophy (expressed in many of his poems). At this point in the novel, however, the philosophy is stated by an extremist; hence, there is a touch of the comic which becomes more apparent as the novel progresses. Meredith's infrequent use of the exclamation point and his almost negative use of italics make this particular passage stand out as the radical view of an extremist.

Rosamund Culling, the future wife of Nevil's uncle, thinks of Shrapnel as "a black malignant . . . with his . . . talk of flying to the sun." As may be expected from Rosamund's tone, Dr. Shrapnel has at some time in her company been overzealous in the expression of his republican sentiments. News of Dr. Shrapnel's inflammatory radicalism soon reaches Nevil's Uncle Romfrey, who proceeds to horsewhip Shrapnel to the point of severe injury. Lack of understanding by his fellowman appears to be Shrapnel's failing and provides the occasion for comment from the Comic Spirit, who judges that Shrapnel must suffer for his intemperance, for his imbalance. Compromise should be man's objective.

Both in *The Egoist* and in *Diana of the Crossways*, the part played by Zoroastrian imagery is greatly reduced from that which it played in *The Ordeal of Richard Feverel* and *Beauchamp's Career*. Meredith's Comic Spirit, however, comes to the front in full array; the increased subordination of Zoroastrian imagery to Meredith's portrayal of his Comic Spirit indicates that Meredith's theories and understanding of the purpose of his literary art were expanding and maturing. In the later novels, Meredith's Zoroastrian and classical images become frequently and inseparably fused, a combination which further exemplifies Meredith's artistry and more significantly indicates that Meredith's philosophy was progressively becoming more distinct. His thinking was beginning to become a cultivated doctrine.

THE EGOIST

The Egoist characterizes the egocentric element in Meredith's theory of high comedy. Sir Willoughby Patterne, who thinks himself the epitome of goodness and excellence in the world, surrounds himself with admirers and sycophants who satisfy his compulsion to be adored. In creating Patterne, Meredith has taken the next logical step from his production of Beauchamp. Patterne does not merely aspire to goodness and excellence; he actually believes himself to be the embodiment of these qualities.

Patterne attempts to satisfy his ego chiefly by involving himself with three women whom he manipulates with promises of marriage. His first "pretender," Constance Durham, sees through Patterne's facade of greatness with some degree of alacrity and leaves him. The lovely Clara Middleton, however, is not so insightful. She experiences a great deal of emotional turmoil, first in ascertaining the truth of Patterne's pose and then in distinguishing the light of "her sun" from that of Patterne's less self-assured cousin, Vernon Whitford, "a Phoebus Apollo turned Fasting Friar."

Here, Meredith gives more attention to extravagances so that he may better reveal the necessity for the corrective influence of his Comic Spirit. Sir Willoughby Patterne burns; he does not merely reflect. His fire is the product of his own egotism, which burns with an outer brilliance but promises no inner flame. Meredith may well be recalling satirically the Western world's traditional misconception of the importance of fire to the Zoroastrians, who do not worship fire for itself but only as a symbol of the light of the inner spirit.

The character of Vernon presents a striking contrast to that of Patterne. His light is the light of Apollo, who is not only the Greek god of poetry but also the classical god of the sun. Meredith has fused classical allusion with the Zoroastrian importance placed upon fire. Vernon's flame is one of inner strength, for he burns with the light of poetic truth as well as with physical fire. He is also a Fasting Friar, however, a characteristic that raises doubt about the nature of his fire, since Meredith was not an ascetic. In effect, he has achieved in the characterization of Vernon the moderation that Dr. Shrapnel's explosive goals denied him, since Vernon's flame is tempered with some degree of asceticism. Vernon has measured life for what it is, but he has not given up the light of hope for what life can become. Meredith has achieved in his image of the contrast of the two fires the blending of Zoroastrian, classical, and Christian elements.

Laetitia Dale, the third of Patterne's "adorers," presents an interesting foil to Patterne's character. At the beginning of the novel, she is described as a delicate, misled woman, a "soft cherishable Parsee." The Zoroastrian connection is obvious: The Parsees are a modern sect of the Zoroastrians. Indeed, within Meredith's comic framework, Laetitia worships "her sun" much as the Parsees were reputed to worship a "god of fire."

Laetitia gradually becomes a strong, practical Parsee, however, as she, like the other two women in Patterne's egotistic design, begins to see that the source of Patterne's fire is not from within. Patterne is left in the end with Laetitia and is forced to accept her on her own terms. No reader of *The Egoist* can claim its conclusion as romantic or condemn it as pessimistic; rather, Meredith has achieved a noble expression of the corrective power of his Comic Spirit.

Diana of the Crossways

Meredith creates in *Diana of the Crossways* a character who faces decisions similar to those of the

women in *The Egoist*. Even Diana's superior wit and intellect do not prevent her from battling the forces of darkness. Meredith prepares the reader for Diana's struggle in the introductory chapter of the novel. He develops a light image, "rose pink," which "is rebuked by hideous revelations of filthy foul," a likeness of darkness. Meredith opens this novel with a discussion of the same subject he had treated in his other novels. For man to think himself already a part of the celestial light at his present step on the evolutionary ladder is surreptitious folly. The future holds for him only "hideous revelations of filthy foul." The narrator further asserts that it is not within the capacity of man to suppress completely the evil forces of darkness. The duality of good and evil inevitably creeps into life.

Having established an atmosphere of foreboding, the narrator sets out to explore Diana's mental processes. Diana quickly becomes disillusioned by a mismatched marriage. Her husband, Warwick, is a man of limited intelligence. As a consequence, Diana becomes drawn to ideas outside the rigid, Victorian system of mores. Her desires strongly urge her to take leave of her witless, insensitive husband, who has accused her of infidelity. She experiences a night of conflict in which she fights like "the Diana of the pride in her power of fencing with evil."

Meredith's presentation of the strife between good and evil by his mixing of classical mythology with overtones of the Zoroastrian duality creates a sense of the universal nature of Diana's struggle. Diana must decide whether to remain loyal to her marriage vows or to strike out on her own and obey her inner compulsions. She finds the impetus for her escape in Dacier, a character who is associated with devil imagery. Indeed, Dacier is the embodiment of Meredith's assertion that there is "an active Devil about the world."

Dacier is a lure to Diana in her desire to escape. His devilish character, however, is ironically exposed by his sanctimonious friend, Sir Lukin. Lukin declares that no man should be fooled by masks of goodness that seem to cover the bad in the world. Dacier, who presents every indication of virtuous conduct, is compared to the old Jewish Prince of

Devils, Asmodeus, who spurs on appetite and uproarious activities of all sorts. Although the name Asmodeus appears in the Apocrypha, it also bears connotations to Eshina-Dewa, a wicked spirit of ancient Persian mythology. This is one of Meredith's clearest fusions of Zoroastrianism with Christianity.

Dacier is thwarted in his evil intentions to seduce Diana. An acceptable guide appears for Diana in Thomas Redworth, a character capable of controlling Diana's energetic impulses. Dacier does obtain a prize, however, in the lovely but naïve Constance Asper. Constance is "all for symbols, harps, effigies, what not" and believes that brains in women are "devilish." Constance is perhaps the ideal mate for *The Egoist*'s Sir Willoughby Patterne, and she presents no problems for Dacier's devious motivations. Constance, along with Dr. Shrapnel and Patterne, has failed to see the smoke for the fire. All three are so enamored of the physical brilliance of the flames that they cannot see the subtle glow of spiritual truth within the heart of the blaze.

In *Diana of the Crossways*, Meredith suggests that the endurance of life is perhaps more replete with task than with play. The individual is forced to make a distinction between good and bad, which life seldom presents in a clear-cut fashion. Constance and Dacier somewhat ironically indulge each other in their ostensibly opposing forces. The subtle comment of the Comic Spirit is that both approach life with attitudes of excess; hence, both have lost contact with the steady movement toward self-improvement. Diana and Redworth offer hope to the reader, however, because they have accepted the moderation that the Comic Spirit has taught them and that is necessary for the future success of the human spirit.

These novels present Meredith's concern with the inevitability of "The Magian Conflict" in the life of each man. They also present Meredith's keen observation that this conflict is never one from which one emerges successfully with ease. The struggle makes man's attempt to choose an acceptable path—a way which is acceptable both to him and to his society—extremely difficult. The conflict is presented in terms of Zoroastrian, Christian, and classical myth; Meredith borrows from each in order to make his presenta-

tion of this undeniable, unavoidable battle assume universal dimensions. Meredith's Comic Spirit attempts to aid man in his struggle, but it is not always successful in exposing man's shortcomings, excesses, and refusal to see himself in a true light. In the fullest meaning of Meredith's doctrine, however, the individual is also instrumental in the greater, universal struggle of humankind to move up the evolutionary ladder.

Meredith demonstrates in his attitude toward humankind and nature the belief that humans can achieve their evolutionary destiny by conforming to the lessons and demands of nature. His philosophy is universal in scope and implies a comprehensive fusion of nearly all the ethical ideals that people have gathered from the beginning of time. Although Meredith does not discard all the dogma or the moral ideals of the many religious philosophies he studied, he does select with careful scrutiny those elements that he feels contribute to his own doctrines. Indeed, he demonstrates that he is vitally affected by all the religious thought known to him.

John C. Shields

OTHER MAJOR WORKS

SHORT FICTION: *The Case of General Ople and Lady Camper*, 1890; *The Tale of Chloe*, 1890.

POETRY: *Poems*, 1851; *Modern Love and Poems of the English Roadside*, 1862; *Poems and Lyrics of the Joy of Earth*, 1883; *Ballads and Poems of Tragic Life*, 1887; *A Reading of Earth*, 1888; *Selected Poems*, 1897; *A Reading of Life, with Other Poems*, 1901; *Last Poems*, 1909; *The Poems of George Meredith*, 1978 (2 volumes; Phyllis B. Bartlett, editor).

NONFICTION: *On the Idea of Comedy and the Uses of the Comic Spirit*, 1877; *The Letters of George Meredith*, 1970 (3 volumes; C. L. Cline, editor).

BIBLIOGRAPHY

Beer, Gillian. *Meredith: A Change of Masks.* London: Athlone Press, 1970. Attempts one of the first modern appraisals of Meredith's art, seeing him as a novelist anticipating twentieth century concerns and techniques, as well as questioning Victorian certitudes. Includes an index.

Muendel, Renate. *George Meredith*. Boston: Twayne, 1986. Chapters on Meredith's poetry, his early fiction, his novels of the 1870's and 1880's, and his last novels. A beginning chapter sums up his biography. Includes chronology, notes, and an annotated bibliography.

Pritchett, V. S. *George Meredith and English Comedy*. Toronto: Clarke, Irwin, 1970. A very readable introductory account of Meredith, constituting the five Clark lectures for 1969.

Roberts, Neil. *Meredith and the Novel*. New York: St. Martin's Press, 1997. A good study of Meredith's long fiction. Includes bibliographical references and an index.

Shaheen, Mohammad. *George Meredith: A Reappraisal of the Novels*. Totowa, N.J.: Barnes & Noble Books, 1981. Suggests that traditional Meredith criticism has viewed his fiction too much in the light of *The Egoist*. Concentrates on Meredith's other major works as more representative of his true independent mind and specifically explores how character expresses theme for Meredith. Contains selected bibliography.

Stevenson, Lionel. *The Ordeal of George Meredith*. London: Peter Owen, 1954. A straightforward, readable biography of Meredith. Includes a bibliography.

Williams, Ioan, ed. *Meredith: The Critical Heritage*. London: Routledge & Kegan Paul, 1971. A collection of reviews and essays showing the critical reception of Meredith's work from 1851 through 1911. Contains indexes of his work, periodicals, and newspapers.

JAMES A. MICHENER

Born: New York, New York(?); February 3, 1907(?)
Died: Austin, Texas; October 16, 1997

PRINCIPAL LONG FICTION

Tales of the South Pacific, 1947
The Fires of Spring, 1949
The Bridges at Toko-Ri, 1953
Sayonara, 1954
The Bridge at Andau, 1954
Hawaii, 1959
Caravans, 1963
The Source, 1965
The Drifters, 1971
Centennial, 1974
Chesapeake, 1978
The Covenant, 1980
Space, 1982
Poland, 1983
Texas, 1985
Legacy, 1987
Alaska, 1988
Journey, 1988
Caribbean, 1989
The Eagle and the Raven, 1990
The Novel, 1991
Mexico, 1992
Recessional, 1994
Miracle in Seville, 1995

OTHER LITERARY FORMS

Although James A. Michener considered himself primarily a novelist, he was also an accomplished short-story writer, esssayist, art historian, and editor. Major themes in his nonfiction are travel and American politics. *The Voice of Asia* (1951) is also in that tradition. *The Floating World* (1954) is a philosophical essay on Japanese art, a theme he treats in four other works, most notably in *Japanese Prints from the Early Masters to the Modern* (1959).

ACHIEVEMENTS

In the early 1950's, Michener was heralded as the new voice in American fiction. Still basking in the considerable praise that followed his first book, *Tales of the South Pacific*, and the Pulitzer Prize that accompanied it, he shared the reflected glow of Richard Rodgers and Oscar Hammerstein's musical adaptation, *South Pacific* (1949). Although critics objected to the romantic cast of his early novels, they also found much to praise. Critical reaction to his later novels has also been mixed: While some consider

Swarthmore College, from which he was graduated summa cum laude in 1929. For ten years, he taught at a variety of schools and universities, including the School of Education at Harvard, and in the early 1940's he became an editor at Macmillan. Although as a practicing member of the Society of Friends (Quakers) he might have been exempted from combat, in 1942 he volunteered for active duty in the United States Navy and was sent to the Pacific. Royalties and a small percentage of ownership in the musical *South Pacific*, which opened in April, 1949, assured him financial freedom to travel and write. Michener thus became an independent writer and scholar, publishing more than forty books, and an even greater number of articles, from his home base in Bucks County, Pennsylvania. He also wrote shortened versions of many of his novels for inclusion in the *Reader's Digest* series of condensed books.

them brilliant for their sweeping panoramic scope, others have condemned the novels for their mass of information, undeveloped characters, and lack of depth. Despite the doubts of literary critics as to the merits of Michener's novels, an eager public has responded to them enthusiastically.

In addition to the Pulitzer Prize, Michener's writing earned for him a number of honorary degrees and awards, including the appointment to several government committees. His work on two of these committees—the Centennial Commission and the National Aeronautics and Space Administration (NASA) Advisory Council—contributed to research for his fiction. In 1977, President Gerald Ford awarded Michener the Medal of Honor, America's highest civilian award.

BIOGRAPHY

Although standard references state that James Albert Michener was born on February 3, 1907, in New York City to Edwin and Mabel Michener, the facts of his birth are unknown; he was a foundling whom Mabel Michener reared from birth, moving at times to the county poorhouse to help the family through poverty and illness. On a scholarship, he attended

Overcoming serious heart problems in the 1980's, Michener remained active until his death, writing and traveling. In addition, he was generous in support of literature and the arts, endowing a fellowship for young writers and contributing in many other ways to the benefit of individual artists and arts institutions. In particular, Michener donated more than one million dollars to the Bucks County, Pennsylvania, Free Library, more than three million dollars to the James A. Michener Art Museum in Doylestown, and more than seven million dollars to his alma mater, Swarthmore College, part of which was used to teach students discipline-specific ways of writing. For his numerous contributions to benefit humanity, Michener was named Outstanding Philanthropist in 1996 by the National Society of Fund-raising Executives.

Michener built a legacy as a storytelling phenomenon. He was a world traveler who was at home on virtually every continent, having reportedly lived in 121 different states and countries where he gathered background for his novels. His secrets to success were determination, hard work, self-reliance, and an incredible memory. Unlike many other novelists who write by pulling plots and characters out of their heads, Michener was a meticulous researcher, a craftsman who would not begin to write until he had absorbed the details of the culture, the history, the geography, and the people of the country he had chosen for his next work.

In his books, Michener emphasized the importance of harmonious relationships among people and the continuing need to overcome ignorance and prejudice. While the critics were often unkind to Michener, he was adored by the public, who have bought an estimated seventy-five million copies of his books. Plagued by numerous health problems in the 1990's, Michener died on October 16, 1997, after declining to continue receiving dialysis treatments for kidney failure. Up until the end, Michener remained productive, completing *This Noble Land* in 1996 and *A Century of Sonnets* in 1997.

ANALYSIS

In almost all of James A. Michener's novels, the story line is a loosely woven thread, a framework, a context in which to tell tales and provide geographic and historic detail. Although in his notes on *Centennial* Michener explains four different narrative devices he developed in the course of his writing career, each is still a framing device for a series of related events or information. Throughout all of his work Michener is the social science editor and teacher, using quantities of well-researched data and imaginative incidents to explain issues from his particular point of view. In many of his writings, it is apparent that Michener is not only a very competent writer, historian, and geographer, but also a competent psychologist and geologist. While each of his novels has a historical basis that covers hundreds or thousands of years, each is rooted in its own time as well.

Much of Michener's writing, both fiction and nonfiction, is journalistic in style, but his staccato rhythms are interrupted from time to time by florid descriptions and precise diversions, such as recipes and statistical contrasts. All of his writing is permeated by an unmistakable creed that affirms human

values and a deep concern for America. The harsh facts of his early life shaped Michener's career, and his writing is that of a grateful man driven to repay society for the chances he was given in life. There is more to his writing, however, than a need to express gratitude: His broad panoramas are peopled with Dickensian characters from every part of society, although his sympathies remain with the sad and the unfortunate—even rogues such as Oliver Wendell in *Centennial* and Jake Turlock in *Chesapeake*—who can get by on their wits. Underscoring all of Michener's work is a strong statement of human courage and human tolerance, coupled with a driving concern for humanity's relationship with its environment. Many of his novels focus on racial discrimination of some kind, and each teaches the value of hard work and the necessity for change. As in his nonfiction, Michener does not hesitate to portray society's weaknesses. While critics have frequently panned both his style and the values it embodies, particularly in his later work, these same late novels have consistently been best-sellers.

TALES OF THE SOUTH PACIFIC

Ironically, *Tales of the South Pacific* was not a best-seller, even though of all Michener's works it is perhaps the most familiar. Although it continues to sell as many copies today as when it was originally published and has won the Pulitzer Prize, the book was first printed on the cheapest paper with the poorest binding available—so little did the publisher think of its chances—and new chapters did not even begin at the tops of new pages. Even after its award, the novel would have continued to die a slow death were it not for the musical comedy based on it. Few successful writers have had a less auspicious beginning.

Tales of the South Pacific is a framing story that sets up many of Michener's themes; with it the author began a literary romance with the Pacific islands that would last for more than fifteen years and characterize much of his work. In this work, nineteen related episodes tell the story of America's commitment to the Pacific theater during World War II. The treatment of character as well as setting is significant to the body of Michener's work. No one character can

dom. In ironic contrast, both the Steeds and the Pax-mores own slaves. The final struggle for black free-dom comes at the start of the twentieth century, with an amendment to the Maryland constitution in-tended to disenfranchise blacks. Although the Steed and Turlock clans support it, Emily Paxmore champi-ons the defeat of the bill by arguing that it can be ap-plied equally to all European immigrants after 1869, and the campaign becomes her own personal Arma-geddon.

Chesapeake is a big novel (it includes even a rec-ipe for oyster stew). The fragments that fill the end are the unresolved conflicts of modern time—except for an account of the passing of Devon Island. As the scene of much of the action slips into the sea, Michener affirms that it will come again and again until at last the "great world-ocean" reclaims it.

SPACE

Although his other novels touch on the twentieth century, *Space* and *Recessional* are Michener's two pieces of fiction that concentrate solely on life in twentieth century America. In *Space*, he chronicles the space program from its inception in 1944 to an ebb in 1982 through a series of incidents that connect neatly to his work before and after it. The novel be-gins on October 24, 1944, with scenes that introduce four major characters. The first is Stanley Mott, an American engineer, in London at the request of the American president, whose job it is to see that the German installation at Peenemunde is not bombed before three of the chief scientists can be captured alive. The second is Norman Grant, drawn much like Harry Brubaker, in the climactic naval battle of Leyte Gulf. The third is John Pope, a seventeen-year-old football hero from Grant's hometown of Clay. Finally, there is Dieter Kolff, one of the scientists whom Mott must rescue, who survives the bombing because he is with his girlfriend. The next part of the novel introduces the women who are loved by these men and advances the story through them. Because of the ingenuity of a Nazi officer who later becomes a leader of the American aerospace industry, Dieter Kolff and Leisl come to the United States, shep-herded by Mott and his wife, Rachel. Pope gets appointed to Annapolis, on the recommendation of

Grant, who has become senator from the state of Fremont; Pope's wife, Penny, earns a law degree and goes to work for Grant when he is appointed to the space committee; Grant's wife, Elinor, preoccupied with little green men, becomes the principal sup-porter of Leopold Strabismus and the Universal Space Associates.

These characters, and those who flesh out their sto-ries, create the substance of the novel. While Miche-ner's focus is on the space program, these people are among the most fully developed in all of his work. Systematically moving through the various stages of America's efforts in outer space, he keeps the weight of his research in careful balance with the stories of human lives. This is particularly true in the second half of the novel, which centers on six fictional astro-nauts (Pope among them). While the reader is drawn into the explorations (particularly the Gemini flight, which Pope shares with his likable opposite, Randy Claggett, and their adventures on the dark side of the moon), one's interest is held by the characters at least as much as by the technology. This is particularly true of the capable con man Strabismus.

At first Strabismus seems an unnecessary diver-sion—similar to the recipes Michener offers for Pol-ish sausage or oyster stew—but as the story builds, he becomes an integral part of the work. Playing off the initials U.S.A., Strabismus moves through a se-ries of lucrative rackets until he sets himself up as a preacher with the United Salvation Alliance. As he panders to the fears of the uneducated, he crusades against "atheistic humanism" and advocates a return to fundamentalism that will prohibit the teaching of evolution and forbid national park rangers from describing the geological history of their areas. He launches impassioned attacks on homosexuals and fosters a virulent anti-Semitism. Michener clarifies his point of view in the final confrontation between Strabismus and the "heroes" of his novel. Finally, Michener suggests, the conflict is part of the long march of history and will continue thousands of years hence.

POLAND

Two massive novels are representative of Miche-ner's later works: *Poland* and *Texas*. The first is a well-researched chronicle of Polish history that moves backward and forward, connecting the Communist country of modern time to the thirteenth century raids of Genghis Khan through the development of three fictional families. In the acknowledgments, in which the author explains his reasons for choosing this particular subject, he sounds very much as he did three decades before, when clarifying his interest in Asia. In both instances, the geographical and ideological positions of the areas indicate that they will become political focal points. Again, Michener is using his fiction to educate readers of his time, moving through history to explain the present.

TEXAS

Texas is perhaps Michener's largest novel: More than two hundred characters are involved in its story, a number of whom are historical figures, and dialogue is the primary vehicle through which their story is told. Michener tracks the major events in Texas history, including the struggle for independence from Mexico. The battles of the Alamo, Goliad, and San Jacinto form the backdrop for fictional characters who illustrate the migrations of the Spanish, Europeans, and Americans to Texas. With its narrative framework and blending of fact and fiction, the novel compares neatly with many of its predecessors. Despite its scope, however, one would be hard-pressed to claim that *Texas* is among the finest of Michener's works.

MEXICO

Mexico traces the history of Mexico from fictional pre-Columbian Indians to modern Mexico through the eyes of an American reporter. Begun by Michener in the 1950's, *Mexico* was set aside because of negative comments by the publisher, eventually was lost, and then was rediscovered and completed by Michener in 1992. The narrative's structure differs from Michener's previous novels, with more concentration on the present than the past. Norman Clay, the central character, is a Princeton-educated Virginian whose family roots have been in Mexico since the 1840's. Clay is sent to Mexico as a Spanish-speaking journalist to cover a series of bullfights between two celebrated matadors, Victoriano Leal and Juan Gomez. Through Clay's eyes, the readers discover Mexico, its turbulent history, and the part that Clay's family

played in it. A variety of conflicts are portrayed, including Spaniard versus Indian, Catholic versus pagan, the quest for the exploitation of gold and silver, war, civil war, and revolution in the twentieth century.

A gripping story unfolds that becomes a vivid portrait of a fascinating country. The cultural conflicts of a class-torn society are epitomized through the tale of the sad, bitter, dirty, sometimes lucrative business of being a matador. In Mexico, bullfighting is not only a sport, but it is also an art form, big business, and festival, mirroring the sordid, grisly, and violent aspects of the Mexican culture. *Mexico* shows that Michener had not lost any of his ability to tell a great story while providing his readers with interesting information about how different cultures live, think, and interact.

MIRACLE IN SEVILLE

As in *Mexico*, Michener uses a journalist as the narrator and participant in *Miracle in Seville*. The narrator, Shenstone, is sent by his editor to Seville, Spain, to write the story of Don Cayetano Mota, owner of a famous ranch where fighting bulls have been raised for decades. However, Shenstone never writes the story, because he believes that he will lose his credibility as a journalist if he reports the unbelievable events that he witnessed while in Seville.

By using a journalist as the narrator, Michener provides a realistic framework for detailing the classical Spanish bullfight with its four distinct parts, as well as the context for describing the appearance, personalities, and techniques of four matadors who will fight in Seville after Easter. Michener places the reader in Seville, seeing, smelling, hearing, and experiencing the bullfights, the processions, and the parade. Character development becomes secondary in the narrative, as Michener is much more interested in telling the story of Don Cayetano, who is seeking to restore the lost honor and glory of his ranch with the help of the Virgin Mary. Through Shenstone, Michener paints a portrait of Spain as a country where bullfighting is an art form, where religious faith is sincere and often dramatic in its expression, and where constant effort is required to sustain personal and family honor.

Miracle in Seville stands apart from Michener's other novels. Although it resembles his previous novels in its focus on the culture of a particular place, it is his only novel that presents events that cannot be rationally explained, creating a strong aura of fantasy. However, even though it is an adult fairy tale, this novel exhibits a well-developed story and a vivid sense of location.

Whatever the critical verdict on Michener the novelist may be, it is clear that Michener the educator- through-fiction has been a great success. To a popular audience numbering in the millions, he has communicated the uniquely modern sense of the long view of history.

Joan Corey Semonella, updated by Alvin K. Benson

OTHER MAJOR WORKS

SHORT FICTION: *Return to Paradise*, 1951; *Creatures of the Kingdom: Stories of Animals*, 1993.

NONFICTION: *Proposals for an Experimental Future of the Social Sciences: Proposals for an Experimental Social Studies Curriculum*, 1939 (with Harold Long); *The Unit in the Social Studies*, 1940; *The Voice of Asia*, 1951; *The Floating World*, 1954; *Selected Writings*, 1957; *Rascals in Paradise*, 1957 (with A. Grove Day); *Japanese Prints from the Early Masters to the Modern*, 1959; *Report of the County Chairman*, 1961; *The Modern Japanese Print: An Appreciation*, 1962; *Iberia: Spanish Travels and Reflections*, 1968; *Presidential Lottery: The Reckless Gamble in Our Electoral System*, 1969; *The Quality of Life*, 1970; *Facing East: The Art of Jack Levine*, 1970; *Kent State: What Happened and Why*, 1971; *A Michener Miscellany, 1950-1970*, 1973; *About "Centennial": Some Notes on the Novel*, 1974; *Sports in America*, 1976; *In Search of Centennial: A Journey*, 1978; *Testimony*, 1983; *Collectors, Forgers, and a Writer: A Memoir*, 1983; *Six Days in Havana*, 1989; *Pilgrimage: A Memoir of Poland and Rome*, 1990; *My Lost Mexico*, 1992; *James A. Michener's Writer's Handbook: Explorations in Writing and Publishing*, 1992; *The World Is My Home: A Memoir*, 1992; *Literary Reflections: Michener on Michener, Hemingway, Capote, and Others*, 1993; *William Penn*, 1994; *This Noble Land*, 1996; *A Century of Sonnets*, 1997.

EDITED TEXT: *The Hokusai Sketchbooks: Selections from the Manga*, 1958.

BIBLIOGRAPHY

Becker, George J. *James A. Michener*. New York: Frederick Ungar, 1983. Part of the Literature and Life series, this book examines the life of Michener through the early 1980's. Contains critical analysis of Michener's writings, including some negative comments about *Centennial*. Discusses thematic considerations of Michener. Includes a bibliography.

Groseclose, Karen, and David A. Groseclose. *James A. Michener: A Bibliography*. Austin, Tex.: State House Press, 1996. A detailed chronology of Michener's life, including the most important events, his publications, honors, awards, and his contributions to society, education, and politics. Contains a comprehensive bibliography about Michener and presents an informative synopsis of each of Michener's novels, as well as a compilation of Michener's works.

Hayes, John P. *James A. Michener: A Biography*. New York: Bobbs-Merrill, 1984. Hayes conducted more than twenty-five interviews with Michener, providing rich biographical material for this meticulous work that was ten years in the making. Covers his prolific writings, from *Tales of the South Pacific* to *Space*, and praises *Centennial*, even though it was rejected by the literary community. Most useful for background information and anecdotes on Michener.

Roberts, F. X., and C. D. Rhine, comps. *James A. Michener: A Checklist of His Works*. Westport, Conn.: Greenwood Press, 1995. As part of the series on Bibliographies and Indexes in American Literature, Roberts and Rhine have compiled a comprehensive list of Michener's writings. Excellent reference work that contains a selected, annotated bibliography.

Severson, Marilyn S. *James A. Michener*. Westport, Conn.: Greenwood Press, 1996. Severson's book, part of the series of Critical Companions to Popular Contemporary Writers, presents a complete overview of Michener's life, including his writing style, themes, ideas, and concerns. Also provides an excellent, detailed analysis of nine of Michener's forty-eight books. Includes a partial bibliography of works by Michener, of information and criticism about Michener, and of reviews of some of Michener's books.

HENRY MILLER

Born: New York, New York; December 26, 1891
Died: Pacific Palisades, California; June 7, 1980

PRINCIPAL LONG FICTION

Tropic of Cancer, 1934
Black Spring, 1936
Tropic of Capricorn, 1939
The Rosy Crucifixion 1949-1960, 1963 (includes
    Sexus, 1949, 2 volumes; *Plexus*, 1953, 2 volumes; *Nexus*, 1960)
Quiet Days in Clichy, 1956

OTHER LITERARY FORMS

In an interview, Henry Miller once described himself as one part a writer of tales and one part a man electrified by ideas. This simple dichotomy provides a way to classify Miller's work, but, in truth, his whole canon is autobiographical. The many collections of his shorter pieces—portraits, essays, stories, travel sketches, reviews, letters—are all of value in ascertaining the truth of his life, his admitted literary goal. For example, *The Colossus of Maroussi: Or, The Spirit of Greece* (1941), Miller's first book about Greece, is ostensibly about George Katsimbalis, a leading figure in modern Greek letters. Katsimbalis, however, turns out to be Miller's alter ego, a fascinating monologuist, and the book becomes the record of Miller's attaining peace of heart through the elemental beauty of Greece. *The Time of the Assassins: A Study of Rimbaud* (1956) is less about Arthur Rimbaud than about the romantic affinities between Miller's and Rimbaud's lives. In Miller's books, all things become translated into images of his own mental landscape.

ACHIEVEMENTS

When Miller repatriated in 1940, only *The Cosmological Eye* (1939), a collection of short pieces drawn from *Max and the White Phagocytes* (1938), had been published in the United States; all of his fiction was deemed too obscene for publication. In France, *Tropic of Cancer* and *Tropic of Capricorn* had been seized in 1946, and Miller was convicted as a pornographer. After an outcry of French writers, this conviction was reversed, but in 1950, *Sexus* was banned in France, and in 1957, it was condemned as obscene in Norway. When *Tropic of Cancer* was finally published in the United States, in 1961, by Barney Rosset of Grove Press, more than sixty suits were instituted against Miller and the book. Miller became the most litigated-against author in history, and the book was only allowed to circulate after a Supreme Court decision in 1965. The furor over his books' alleged obscenity prevented dispassionate evaluation of his literary merit for many years, and Miller feared that he would be dismissed as the "King of Smut." He

(Larry Colwell)

2253

was, however, inducted into the National Institute of Arts and Letters in 1957, and he received a citation from the Formentor Prize Committee, in France, in 1961 and the French Legion of Honor in 1975.

These memberships and citations, however, do not mark Miller's true achievement. His true quest and calling was to narrow the gap between art and life. That he—or his public persona of Paris expatriate, Big Sur prophet, desperado, clown, artist-hero, satyr—was the focus of critical attention throughout his life, rather than his books, testifies to the measure of success he achieved. Miller wanted to become free, as free as the young boy of the streets he had been in his childhood, in the face of a culture he saw as sterile, mechanical, and death-driven. He also wanted to discover and embody the truth of his life in art, in his "autobiographical romances." His defiant spit in the face of art in his first book, *Tropic of Cancer*, prompted critics to label his works as "antiliterature." Rather than deprecating literature, however, Miller saw art as a means to life more abundant. He conceived of his work as enlightening, as offering his vision of reality. Often described as a *roman-fleuve* of the life of Henry Miller, his fiction is neither strictly autobiographical nor realistic in method. As an artist, he notes in *The Wisdom of the Heart* (1941), he must give his reader "a vital, singing universe, alive in all its parts"; to accomplish this, he relied on the verbal pyrotechnics of Surrealism and the temporal discontinuities of stream of consciousness. The result was a series of works full of contradictions, repetitions, incongruities, and rhetorical flights, all documenting his growth as a man and as an artist.

Biography

Henry Valentine Miller was born on December 26, 1891, in the Yorkville section of New York City. Both of his parents were of German stock: His father, a gentleman's tailor, came from jovial people; his mother and her family typified the austere, industrious, respectable bourgeois life against which Miller was to rebel so vehemently. For the first nine years of his life, the family lived in the Williamsburg section of Brooklyn, the Fourteenth Ward. For Miller, this was a child's paradise. When he was ten, his family moved to Decatur Street, the "Street of Early Sorrows," in Brooklyn's Bushwick section. His teenage experiences there helped form his attitudes on life, literature, and women. Miller was an affable young man; his special friends at this time were members of the Xerxes Society, a musical crowd. Male conviviality would be important to Miller throughout his life.

Miller was a model student and was graduated as salutatorian from high school, but his formal education ended after a few months at the City College of New York. Always an avid reader—he had read through the Harvard Classics as well as many romantic and adventure tales—Miller became an autodidact. By the time he was twenty, he had devoured such diverse authors as Joseph Conrad, Madame Blavatsky, and François Rabelais and had decided that he wanted to be a writer—about what, he did not know. Besides frequenting theaters in New York and Brooklyn, Miller was often seen at burlesque shows and in brothels. If his mother seemed cold and difficult to please, these women were open for sexual pleasure. Despite these experiences, Miller developed an intense idealism about love and the perfect woman, centering his longing on a school classmate, Cora Seward. At the same time, though, he began in 1910 an affair with a widow, Pauline Chouteau, closer to his mother's age.

In an effort to escape this passionate entanglement, Miller went to California in 1913, winding up miserable as a ranch hand near Chula Vista. Only hearing Emma Goldman in San Diego, extolling anarchism, redeemed the trip. The next year Miller was back in New York, working in his father's tailor shop (described in *Black Spring*) and reading omnivorously. He was attracted to universalizing ideas and grander interpretations of the meaning of life than those of his Brooklyn milieu. During the years 1914-1915, Miller began to study piano seriously; through this enthusiasm, he met Beatrice Sylvas Wickens, whom he married in 1917. Their stormy courtship and marriage is depicted graphically in *The World of Sex* (1940, 1957), *Tropic of Capricorn*, and *Sexus*. Drifting through many jobs, Miller found his way to the bottom—Western Union. His experience as a messenger employment manager opened his eyes to the underlying misery in America. His sympathy with these victims, adrift in a dehumanized urban landscape, was responsible for his unpublished first novel, *Clipped Wings*, dedicated to Horatio Alger. Miller's disillusionment with the American Dream came at a time when his marriage was also foundering. His response, rather than despair or self-pity, was to begin keeping a journal and extensive files of material for later use. He was beginning to become a writer, establishing an aesthetic distance from life and from himself.

His delivery as a full-fledged artist was through the agency of June Edith Smith, the Mona, Mara, "She," or "Her" of his fiction, his second wife, whom he met at a Broadway dance hall in 1923 and married the next year. June was a creative artist—of herself and her life story—who showed Miller the bridge between life and the imagination. Convinced that he was a great writer, she made him quit his job and devote his life to his work. This metamorphosis is recorded in *Tropic of Capricorn* and *Plexus*. To relieve their desperate poverty, June began peddling a series of brief prose sketches Miller had written called "Mezzotints," signed "June E. Mansfield." Miller might have freed himself from a conventional American life, but June—her schemes, her stories, her lovers, herself—held him completely in thrall. When June eloped with her lover Jean Kronski to Paris in 1927, Miller began to record notes of his obsessional attachment to her. His life with June was to be the book he tried to write throughout his life, culminating in *The Rosy Crucifixion*. His second unpublished novel, *Moloch*, the story of Miller's experiences in the year 1923, was written under unique pressure: One of June's admirers promised her a year in Europe if she completed a book. *Moloch* was their ticket to Paris.

Their trip to Paris in 1928-1929 was unproductive; Miller painted watercolors instead of writing books. Only when he returned alone to Paris in 1930 and ran out of resources did he begin to live and write truly. Living a marginal life, he not only completed his novel about June and Jean, *Crazy Cock*, but he also discovered "Henry Miller," the voice and main character of his "autobiographical romances." Alfred Perlès, "Joey," contributed his bohemian lifestyle and

epicurism to Miller's new persona. The French Surrealists gave artistic form to Miller's sense of incongruity. The photographer Brassai helped him see the poetry of the sordid side of Paris. Walter Lowenfels and Michael Fraenkel converted him to the "death school"—although Miller knew that he, for one, remained very much alive. Anaïs Nin became his ministering angel. Her love restored his faith in both himself and womankind. Her own journals confirmed him in the belief that his true subject was himself. Through her, he met the psychoanalyst Otto Rank: Miller's interest in psychology (and Nin) brought him back to New York for a brief period in 1936 to work as an analyst, but more important, it helped him understand his past and himself, which were to become the central concerns of his life. He kept a "dreambook" in this period, some of which reappears in his fiction. *Tropic of Cancer* and *Quiet Days in Clichy* draw on Miller's first two years in France. By 1936, Miller's apartment in Villa Seurat had become the center of an industrious artistic circle, which was joined in 1937 by Lawrence Durrell, Miller's first disciple. Far from Wambly Bald's Paris *Tribune* picture of the great American hobo artist, Miller in his Paris years worked with Germanic regularity and thoroughness on his fiction and essays.

By 1939, Miller was able to finish *Tropic of Capricorn*. With its completion, Miller's furious literary activity abated. He began to lose interest in the narrative of his life and became engrossed in spiritual literature—astrology, Zen, Theosophy, Krishnamurti, the I Ching. When he left Paris in 1939, at the advent of World War II, to visit Durrell in Corfu, Greece, the stage was set for his third metamorphosis. He records in *The Colossus of Maroussi* that in Greece he discovered a new goal in life: not to be a writer, but simply to be. Images of simplicity—the land, sea, and silences of Greece—awakened in Miller, the city man, a response to the allure of nature.

Back in America in 1940, Miller continued his autobiographical saga, but his only major fictional endeavor in the next forty years was to be *The Rosy Crucifixion*, written between 1942 and 1959, in which he tried to capture the elusive truth of his relationship with June. Most of his writing during this period was nonfiction. On an advance from Doubleday, Miller and the painter Abraham Rattner went on a tour of the United States from 1940 to 1941. The resulting book, *The Air-Conditioned Nightmare* (1945), turned out to be a jeremiad rather than a travelogue.

In 1942, Miller moved to California, settling into a cabin at Big Sur in 1944. There, amid its natural splendor, he found his Walden. Miller was again the center of a circle of painters and writers, a group that came to national attention through a 1947 *Harper's* magazine article, "Sex and Anarchy in Big Sur." Life, however, was not an orgy for Miller. He still remained in poverty, supporting himself by selling his watercolors and begging from his friends. In 1944, he married his third wife, Janina M. Lepska, who attempted to introduce domestic order into his life, but by 1948, she had left him. She and Conrad Moricand, an astrologer friend from his Paris days, were castigated as "devils" in his account of his life at Big Sur, *Big Sur and the Oranges of Hieronymous Bosch* (1957). In 1953, he married Eve McClure; their marriage was dissolved in 1962. In 1967, he married Hiroko "Hoki" Tokuda, a twenty-nine-year-old cabaret singer from Tokyo; that marriage ended in divorce in 1978. His later travails in love are described in *Insomnia: Or, The Devil at Large* (1970). Indeed, his later works seem to have been written to cleanse himself of the demons that possessed him. His final days were spent in Pacific Palisades, California. The acclaimed father of the sexual revolution of the 1960's died on June 7, 1980. He was eighty-eight years old.

ANALYSIS

Henry Miller's books, in their frank sexual description, pushed back the last frontier of American literary realism. Sex was, for Miller, a means by which to study the cosmos: He noted in *The World of Sex* that "to enter life by way of the vagina is as good a way as any. If you enter deep enough, remain long enough, you will find what you seek. But you've got to enter with your heart and soul—and check your belongings outside." Whatever he sought, women became his connection to the universal. Although women are often depicted as sexual objects in his fic-

tion, sex, he insisted, is "an elemental force. It's just as mysterious and magical as talking about God or the nature of the universe." The way in which Miller used obscenity against the bourgeoisie is telling: that sex was considered "dirty" reflected the puritanical nature of the culture he was attacking.

Because of his use of the obscene, the world of Miller's books is often repulsive and degrading, filled with grotesque characters living on the margin of society. The harsh reality of life must be accepted, he felt, before it could be transcended. In *My Life and Times* (1971), he explained, "The only way you can prove you are not of it is by entering into it fully. . . . When you fully accept something, you are no longer victimized by it." Savoring the dregs of civilization, Miller castigated its pretensions with anarchic glee. Indeed, Miller's value lies not in a depiction of some salvific vision (reality always remains a bit hazy in his fiction), but in his searing indictment of the modern world's impoverishment of "soul life." Miller shared D. H. Lawrence's horror of the mechanical modern world and endorsed Lawrence's response— the instinctual life—yet for all his apocalyptic prophecies, Miller was no Lawrentian messiah. Indeed, the "Henry Miller" of the novels is a *flâneur*, an American picaro.

TROPIC OF CANCER

Ernest Hemingway's *The Sun Also Rises* (1926), Miller admitted in an interview at age eighty-four, was the impetus for his journey to Paris, the artists' mecca. What Miller found there in the 1930's forms the basis of his first and best novel, *Tropic of Cancer*: Paris provided both the impetus and the substance of his disjointed narrative. Paris, Miller writes, is like a whore, "ravishing" from a distance, but "five minutes later you feel empty, disgusted with yourself. You feel tricked." Whores—Germaine, Claude, Llona, and others—and their hangouts dominate Miller's Paris, suggesting the debunking of romantic ideals, which was necessary for Miller before he could write. This is apparent in the evolving nature of his relationship to his wife Mona in the book. It begins with his anticipation of their reunion, which proves blissful but short-lived. Although he claims that "for seven years I went about, day and night, with only one thing in my mind—*her*," after she returns to America, her image—like all the rest of his old life—"seems to have fallen into the sea," until he can only wonder "in a vague way" at the novel's conclusion whatever happened to her. Paris has replaced her as the center of his attention, and Paris makes far fewer demands on his inner self. Like his superficial relationships with whores, his stay in Paris is a fruitful form of self-destruction out of which a new self emerges.

The predominant metaphor in *Tropic of Cancer* is that of the river, of all that flows, in contrast to the stultifying conceptions and conventions of modern civilization. Early in the book, the sight of the Seine, and the great unconscious life that it represents, is inspirational. He later learns to see the world without "boundaries" or preconceived notions and recognizes it "for the mad slaughterhouse it is." His two trips outside Paris demonstrate his acclimatization and the death of his illusions. Returning from Le Havre, he recognizes the essential attraction of Paris for him, and he demonstrates in his outwitting of a whore his adjustment to the scene. Returning from Dijon, that bastion of medievalism which reminds him of the North (a bad place in Miller's geography, redolent of the coldness and sterility of his German ancestors), where everybody is constipated and even the toilet pipes freeze, he recognizes his previous dependency upon women, "a fear of living separate, of staying born." This realization enables him to free Fillmore from the clutches of the rapacious Ginette and himself from Mona. The climax of the episode, and of the book as well, takes him again to the River Seine. He has already announced his love for everything that flows—"rivers, sewers, lava, semen, blood, bile, words, sentences"—and in this climax, he surrenders himself with religious intensity to the flux of time and space: "I feel this river flowing through me—its past, its ancient soul, the changing climate."

While a parade of other displaced persons in Paris passes through the book, they are all, like Moldorf, a "sieve through which my anarchy strains, resolves itself into words." Unlike the Jews Boris and Moldorf, the reborn Miller enjoys his suffering, because it confirms his sense of this world as a "putrid sink." Van Norden exists as a foil to Miller, both in relation to

women and to himself. Van Norden is a neurotic egotist who uses women to try to forget himself, personifying the lovelessness of the modern world, where passion is removed from sex. As he watches Van Norden and his fifteen-franc whore grinding away, Miller compares him to a runaway machine or a maimed war hero: The human reality that gives meaning to the act is missing. Fillmore is another foil to Miller; like the typical American expatriate, he has come to France for wine, women, and song. Miller helps him escape Ginette and a marriage into the French bourgeoisie, and he returns to America disillusioned. Miller stays behind, his illusions gone, replaced by an appetite for life. The women characters of the book are negligible—with Mona's disappearance from his world, the woman has been replaced by her pudendum.

Tropic of Cancer is Miller's gleeful song over the corpse of the twentieth century: "I will sing while you croak." The comedy, sexual and otherwise, is at the expense of everyone, himself included. The novel played a decisive role in Miller's career: In it, he found the distinctive voice that he never thereafter abandoned. Miller describes the realization of the insufficiency of all ideas and the justification for the abandonment of conventional beliefs: "I am only spiritually dead. Physically I am alive. Morally I am free. . . . The dawn is breaking on a new world." The book ends on this note of openness to a better life.

Tropic of Capricorn

Tropic of Capricorn is Miller's *Künstlerroman*, depicting his own development as an artist. It records his struggle to achieve detachment from America and from his past life and become an angel, "pure and inhuman," in possession of his spiritual core. It is written from the perspective of one who has awakened from the "nightmare" of history, an achievement at first inspired by his friend Ulric and by the works of D. H. Lawrence and Fyodor Dostoevski, and later catalyzed by "Her," Mara.

The book opens "on the ovarian trolly," when the persona of Miller is still unclear, mired in the chaos of his surroundings. America is a "cesspool of the spirit," and its statistical wealth and happiness is a sham: Everywhere, there is testimony to man's inhu-

tobiography in America." Brown writes with clarity and knows the material well. Includes a chronology of the events of Miller's life, a bibliography of his writing through 1980, and useful sections listing interviews, bibliographical collections, biographies, and selected criticism.

Ferguson, Robert. *Henry Miller: A Life.* New York: Norton, 1991. A full and sensitive treatment of Miller's life and work. See especially the first chapter for the problems involved in interpreting Miller, the response of feminist critics, and the difficulties of evaluating Miller's memoirs. Includes notes and bibliography.

Gottesman, Ronald, ed. *Critical Essays on Henry Miller.* New York: G. K. Hall, 1992. Divided into sections on the early Miller (includes biographical material and book reviews); the "phallic" Miller (including conflicting interpretations by Norman Mailer and Kate Millett); the "orphic" Miller; the "American" Miller; and various retrospectives of his life and career, including memoirs. Includes introduction and bibliography.

Lewis, Leon. *Henry Miller: The Major Writings.* New York: Schocken Books/Random House, 1986. Concentrates on the seven books regarded as the heart of Miller's achievement as a writer, offering detailed critical analysis of each book as well as a comprehensive estimate of Miller's entire life as an artist. Relates Miller to the American writers he admired and to Albert Camus and the surrealists of the 1920's to locate him within literary and cultural traditions. Includes a bibliography and related criticism.

Mathieu, Bertrand. *Orpheus in Brooklyn: Orphism, Rimbaud, and Henry Miller.* Paris: Mouton, 1976. Mathieu is an expert on the work of Arthur Rimbaud, and his study focuses on the parallels between Miller and the French poet, particularly in regard to Miller's *The Colossus of Maroussi* (1941). Mathieu is very knowledgeable, writes with energy and insight, and offers the useful thesis that Miller's work is constructed on a plan similar to Dante's *The Divine Comedy.*

Mitchel, Edward, ed. *Henry Miller: Three Decades of Criticism.* New York: New York University

Press, 1971. A representative compilation which indicates just how much controversy and personal response Miller's work elicited during the first three decades after *Tropic of Cancer* was published. A good companion volume is George Wickes's collection *Henry Miller and the Critics* (Carbondale: Southern Illinois University Press, 1963).

Widmer, Kingsley. *Henry Miller.* Rev. ed. Boston: Twayne, 1990. Updates Widmer's 1962 work, taking into account the final years of Miller's career and the criticism that appeared after Widmer's study. A succinct yet comprehensive introduction. Includes chronology, notes, and annotated bibliography.

YUKIO MISHIMA
Kimitake Hiraoka

Born: Tokyo, Japan; January 14, 1925
Died: Tokyo, Japan; November 25, 1970

PRINCIPAL LONG FICTION

Kamen no kokuhaku, 1949 (*Confessions of a Mask,* 1958)

Kinjiki, 1951, and *Higyo,* 1953 (combined as *Forbidden Colors,* 1968)

Shiosai, 1954 (*The Sound of Waves,* 1956)

Kinkakuji, 1956 (*The Temple of the Golden Pavilion,* 1959)

Kyōko no ie, 1959

Utage no ato, 1960 (*After the Banquet,* 1963)

Gogo no eikō, 1963 (*The Sailor Who Fell from Grace with the Sea,* 1965)

Haru no yuki, 1969 (*Spring Snow,* 1972)

Homba, 1969 (*Runaway Horses,* 1973)

Akatsuki no tera, 1970 (*The Temple of Dawn,* 1973)

Tennin gosui, 1971 (*The Decay of the Angel,* 1974)

Hōjō no umi, 1969-1971 (collective title for previous 4 novels; *The Sea of Fertility: A Cycle of Four Novels,* 1972-1974)

OTHER LITERARY FORMS

In addition to serious novels and his lighter fictional "entertainments," Yukio Mishima wrote a number of works in a variety of genres and styles. His short stories, particularly "Yūkoku" ("Patriotism"), written in 1961, are among his most sharply etched and emotionally charged works of narrative fiction. Mishima's writing for the stage earned for him an important reputation as a dramatist in Japan, both in the older forms of twentieth century drama such as *shimpa* (a hybrid between Kabuki and modern theater), for which he created a masterful melodrama of nineteenth century Japan, *Rokumeikan*, in 1956, and in the contemporary theater, perhaps most effectively for the play *Sado kōshaku fujin* (1965; *Madame de Sade*, 1967). He also wrote dramas specifically composed for performance by traditional *bunraku* puppet troupes. Mishima's modern versions of traditional Japanese No plays, reconceived for modern actors, have also been widely admired.

Mishima also earned considerable fame as an essayist, particularly for his confessional *Taiyō to tetsu* (1968; *Sun and Steel*, 1970), in which he explored his newfound commitment to and trust in his body, superseding what he had come to see as the limitations inherent in the life of the mind.

ACHIEVEMENTS

Many Japanese readers and critics, and a large number of enthusiastic readers of Mishima in translation, are willing to place him at the forefront of postwar Japanese writers, perhaps even among the best writers of the entire modern period in Japanese literature. Yet there remains a certain disparity between foreign and Japanese views of Mishima and his accomplishments. For many intellectuals in Japan, Mishima's talents and attitudes are looked on with a certain reserve. For many Japanese, Mishima's flamboyant life and death lacked the dignity appropriate to a great writer; yet, his often sensational subject matter (homosexuality, right-wing patriotism, mental derangement) was not necessarily frowned upon per se. Nevertheless, the posture frequently adopted in Mishima's writings of the novelist/narrator as a kind of voyeur seemed to some critics self-indulgent and

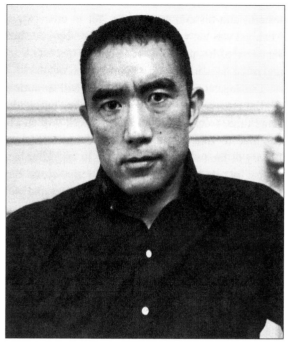

(CORBIS/Bettmann)

inappropriate. It should be noted, however, that the very levels of emotional and erotic life that Mishima sought to chronicle were and are a part of human, specifically Japanese, mentality, and he bears genuine witness to aspects of Japanese life that may well make his novels and other works outlive their first popularity and attain a classic status.

One Japanese critic has remarked that Japan needed Mishima in the same way that Victorian England needed Oscar Wilde: Both writers used the beauty of the perverse to reveal crucial aspects of life in their societies that were tacitly banned from examination or open discussion. In many ways, Mishima was a man living out of his time, particularly because of his seemingly total lack of interest in social and political issues. The postwar literary scene in Japan has had at its center a considerable number of distinguished writers who show a genuine social commitment, often of a Marxist orientation. To such writers, Mishima merely seemed self-absorbed and narcissistic. The fact that Mishima, toward the end of his life, combined his aesthetic responses to life with a highly charged personal sort of homoerotic militarism, which resulted in his own suicide, remains dis-

rounding the candidacy of a prominent Socialist politician, who, because of his attachment to the proprietress of a fashionable restaurant, suffered a good deal of criticism and, among other things, lost the election. The novel caused a considerable scandal itself because of the supposedly relevatory nature of certain details in his account, but again, Mishima used the materials he had at hand to evoke his own authentic image of a contemporary Japan, catching both crucial details of the milieu and a beautifully realized delineation of the psychology of his two main characters, the stiff politician Noguchi and the earthy, yet somehow winning, Kazu, the owner of the restaurant.

The novel offers as revealing a glimpse into the somewhat despoiled yet remarkably vigorous life of politicians in Tokyo as any postwar author has been able to manage. The success of the novel results in part from the fact that Mishima's thrust is psychological, not political; he espouses no causes but plays instead the role of a humane and astute observer. The moral of the novel lies thus within the structures of the narrative itself. The development of the relationship between the pair, in which money and opportunity signally affect the changing nature of the affection each feels for the other, make *After the Banquet* perhaps the most objectively rendered and humanly satisfying of Mishima's novels.

THE SOUND OF WAVES

Mishima's attraction to European literature is particularly apparent in his novel *The Sound of Waves*, published in 1954 after his European trip four years earlier. Here Mishima drew directly on the Greek pastoral romance of Daphnis and Chloë (used also in the twentieth century by Maurice Ravel in his celebrated 1911 ballet), couching the famous account of the antique shepherd and shepherdess in Japanese terms. Quite popular at first, and immediately a success abroad when translated into English, the work has not worn well. The style is doubtless brilliant, yet the world of classical Greece and timeless, rural Japan are too far apart to merge effectively. The result now seems a sort of artificial pastiche. On the other hand, Mishima could blend classical Japanese sources into his work with enormous skill. A work

such as the modern No play *Dōjōji* (1953; English translation, 1966) shows a remarkable blending of ancient form and subject matter with a thoroughly modern sensibility. In Mishima's version, a young woman, spurned in love, decides to take her revenge in a fashion that, while paying homage to the medieval play, allows a thoroughly contemporary and, for the reader or spectator, altogether intimidating moment of psychological truth.

THE SEA OF FERTILITY

Mishima's tetralogy *The Sea of Fertility*, which occupied him from the mid-1960's until his death in 1970, was to be for him the summing up of his life, art, and belief. Although the tetralogy has been widely read in the original and in translation, the critical response to these four books has remained mixed. The highest praise has been reserved for the first volume, *Spring Snow*, which begins an account of a reincarnation in four separate personalities, all to be witnessed by Honda, a subsidiary character whose own growth of self-awareness and spiritual insight stands as one of the accompanying themes of this vast fable.

In *Spring Snow*, Honda is shown as a friend and confidant of Kiyoaki, a beautiful and willful young man who only manages to fall in love with his fiancée Satoko when he finds it necessary to force his way to see her in secret. At the end of the novel, Satoko flees their difficult situation and becomes a Buddhist nun. Kiyoaki dies, with an intimation that he and his friend Honda will meet again. The novel is elegiac in its emotional tone and contains a moving re-creation of the atmosphere of late nineteenth century Japan that can surely stand among Mishima's finest accomplishments.

The three remaining volumes find Kiyoaki reborn as a young fencer turned political extremist in *Runaway Horses*, then reappearing as a Thai princess in *The Temple of Dawn*, and, in the final volume, *The Decay of the Angel*, as a selfish, and perhaps empty-spirited, working-class youth. The plan and conception of this work is surely grand, perhaps grandiose. Some readers find the series, with the increasingly powerful Buddhist references, too far removed from the realities of the present-day Japanese consciousness. Some critics have also commented on the fact that the later volumes are spottily written. In any case, it is still too soon to say if this last and most ambitious effort on Mishima's part will take its place at the head of his oeuvre or will merely remain a last ingenious experiment in the career of this gifted, adventuresome, and sometimes perverse genius of modern Japanese letters.

J. Thomas Rimer

OTHER MAJOR WORKS

SHORT FICTION: *Kaibutsu*, 1950; *Tōnorikai*, 1951; *Manatsu no shi*, 1953 (*Death in Midsummer and Other Stories*, 1966).

PLAYS: *Kantan*, wr. 1950, pb. 1956 (English translation, 1957); *Yoro no himawari*, pr., pb. 1953 (*Twilight Sunflower*, 1958); *Dōjōji*, pb. 1953 (English translation, 1966); *Aya no tsuzumu*, pr. 1955 (*The Damask Drum*, 1957); *Aoi no ue*, pr., pb. 1956 (*The Lady Aoi*, 1957); *Hanjo*, pb. 1956 (English translation, 1957); *Sotoba Komachi*, pb. 1956 (English translation, 1957); *Kindai nōgakushū*, pb. 1956 (includes *Kantan*, *The Damask Drum*, *The Lady Aoi*, *Hanjo*, and *Sotoba Komachi*; *Five Modern Nō Plays*, 1957); *Tōka no kiku*, pr., pb. 1961; *Sado kōshaku fujin*, pr., pb. 1965 (*Madame de Sade*, 1967); *Suzakuke no metsubō*, pr., pb. 1967; *Wagatomo Hittōra*, pb. 1968 (*My Friend Hitler*, 1977); *Chinsetsu yumiharizuki*, pr., pb. 1969.

NONFICTION: *Hagakure nyumōn*, 1967 (*The Way of the Samurai*, 1977); *Taiyō to tetsu*, 1968 (*Sun and Steel*, 1970); *Yukio Mishima on "Hagakure": The Samurai Ethic and Modern Japan*, 1978.

EDITED TEXT: *New Writing in Japan*, 1972 (with Geoffrey Bownas).

MISCELLANEOUS: *Hanazakari no mori*, 1944 (short fiction and plays); *Eirei no Koe*, 1966 (short fiction and essays).

BIBLIOGRAPHY

Napier, Susan J. *Escape from the Wasteland: Romanticism and Realism in the Fiction of Mishima Yukio and Oe Kenzaburo*. Cambridge, Mass.: Harvard University Press, 1991. Explores Mishima's handling of myth, the metaphor of the wasteland, eroticism, religion, postwar and modern Japan. With notes and bibliography.

Nathan, John. *Mishima: A Biography*. Boston: Little, Brown, 1974. A solid scholarly biography. See especially the preface, which relates Mishima's suicide to his writing. Includes notes and illustrations, but no bibliography.

Scott-Stokes, Henry. *The Life and Death of Yukio Mishima*. New York: Farrar, Straus & Giroux, 1974. Rev. ed. New York: Noonday Press, 1995. See the beginning for the biographer's personal impression of Mishima. Scott-Stokes complements Nathan's biography, providing a somewhat more thorough book, with a glossary, chronology, and bibliography.

Starrs, Roy. *Deadly Dialectics: Sex, Violence, and Nihilism in the World of Yukio Mishima*. Honolulu: University of Hawaii Press, 1994. Divided into three parts: Mishima as a philosophical novelist; sex, psychology, and anti-psychology; Mishima's gravitation toward violence. Starrs explores Japanese literary and intellectual traditions, Mishima's novels in a Western context, and a discussion of the novelist's connection to Friedrich Nietzsche. Contains notes and bibliography.

Ueda, Makota. *Modern Japanese Writers and the Nature of Literature*. Stanford, Calif.: Stanford University Press, 1976. Provides a chapter with an excellent overview of Mishima's career.

Wolfe, Peter. *Yukio Mishima*. New York: Ungar, 1989. A good introductory study covering all of Mishima's major work in addition to a chronology, notes, and bibliography.

Yourcenar, Marguerite. *Mishima: A Vision of the Void*. Trowbridge, United Kingdom: Aidan Ellis, 1986. A searching essay of the writer's work by one of the twentieth century's great novelists.

BRIAN MOORE

Born: Belfast, Northern Ireland; August 25, 1921
Died: Malibu, California; January 11, 1999

PRINCIPAL LONG FICTION

Judith Hearne, 1955 (pb. in U.S. as *The Lonely Passion of Judith Hearne*)
The Feast of Lupercal, 1957
The Luck of Ginger Coffey, 1960
An Answer from Limbo, 1962
The Emperor of Ice-Cream, 1965
I Am Mary Dunne, 1968
Fergus, 1970
Catholics, 1972
The Great Victorian Collection, 1975
The Doctor's Wife, 1976
The Mangan Inheritance, 1979
The Temptation of Eileen Hughes, 1981
Cold Heaven, 1983
Black Robe, 1985
The Color of Blood, 1987
Lies of Silence, 1990
No Other Life, 1993
The Statement, 1996
The Magician's Wife, 1997

(Doubleday)

OTHER LITERARY FORMS

In addition to his novels, Brian Moore wrote a travel book, *Canada*, with the editors of *Life* magazine in 1963. A number of his works were regarded by Moore himself as hackwork, written to support his serious fiction; these include romances and mysteries, some published under the pseudonym "Michael Bryan." His dozens of short stories appeared in a wide range of periodicals, from *Weekend Review* to *The Atlantic*, and in anthologies including *The Irish Genius*, edited by Devin A. Garrity (1960), *Canadian Writing Today*, edited by Mordecai Richler (1970), and *The Best American Short Stories, 1967* (1967), edited by Martha Foley and David Burnett. Throughout his writing career, he published many articles and reviews. Several of Moore's books have been adapted for films and television, and he wrote screenplays and teleplays produced in the United States, Canada, and Great Britain.

ACHIEVEMENTS

Moore's first novel, published both as *Judith Hearne* and as *The Lonely Passion of Judith Hearne*, established him as a contemporary novelist of the first order. He has appealed to many readers as a novelist who writes without embarrassment in the realistic tradition of the Victorians about distinctively modern topics: spiritual and erotic crises, the reality of the objective world, ethnic conflict, relationships between men and women, and the place of women in the societies of the old world and the new. Modern themes of alienation and estrangement are rooted firmly in Moore's work by a sense of place and of time. His evocation of Montreal in *The Luck of Ginger Coffey* has been compared to James Joyce's portrayal of Dublin on "Bloomsday." The bleak urban environment of Belfast of the earlier works and the windswept Irish coast of *The Mangan Inheritance* strike responsive chords in readers conditioned to the blank landscapes of much modernist literature. Just as Moore's geographical terrain changes, however, so do his characters and his stylistic formats. From the almost naturalistic treatment of the unfortunate Judith Hearne to the ghostly dialogues of *Fergus* and the magical creation of *The Great Victorian Collec-*

tion, from the Jesuit missionaries in *Black Robe* to the terrorists in *Lies of Silence*, Moore's unpredictable inventiveness and his sure hand in storytelling and character development kept him in the forward ranks of late twentieth century novelists.

Among the honors Moore received were a Guggenheim Fellowship, an award from the American National Institute of Arts and Letters, a Canada Council Fellowship, the Author's Club of Great Britain First Novel Award, the Governor-General Award of Canada for fiction, and honorary literature degrees from Queens University, Belfast (1989) and National University of Ireland, Dublin (1991). He was three times shortlisted for the Booker Prize, for *The Doctor's Wife*, *The Color of Blood*, and *Lies of Silence*. *Catholics* won the W. H. Smith Award in 1973, and *The Great Victorian Collection* was winner of the James Tait Black Memorial Prize in 1975. *Black Robe* was given the Heinemann Award from the Royal Society of Literature in 1986.

BIOGRAPHY

The basic facts of Brian Moore's life are familiar to anyone who knows his work, for he has mined heavily his own experiences for his novels. Moore was born in Belfast, in 1921, to James Bernard Moore, a fellow of the Royal College of Surgeons, and Eileen McFadden Moore. His childhood was a stable and fundamentally happy one; the warm and well-ordered O'Neill family in *Judith Hearne* was in fact identified by Moore in an interview as "a sort of facsimile of my own." Although his work reveals a continuing ambivalence about the order and protection of the family, as about other highly ordered forms of community, he clearly finds much to admire in the sort of family structure that provided his early nurturing.

Moore was educated in Catholic schools, leaving St. Malachi's College, Belfast, in 1940 to join the Air Raid Precautions Unit in Belfast. He served with that unit until 1942, when he left Belfast to serve as a civilian employee of the British Ministry of War Transport in North Africa, Italy, and France. Immediately after the war, he served as a port officer in Warsaw, and then remained for some time in Scandinavia,

where he was a freelance reporter in Sweden, Finland, and Norway until he emigrated to Canada in 1948. From 1948 to 1952, he continued his career as a journalist in Montreal. His Canadian newspaper career began humbly; he was first a proofreader for the *Montreal Gazette*. He was promoted to reporter, an occupation he continued until he began writing pulp fiction to finance his serious work. Although some of his serious short fiction was published in the early 1950's, Moore was forced to continue to write pulp fiction until the appearance of *Judith Hearne* in 1955, and even after, under the pseudonym "Michael Bryan."

The early stages of Moore's life and work essentially came to a close two years after the publication of *Judith Hearne* with the appearance of his second novel, *The Feast of Lupercal*. Shortly thereafter, he moved to the United States from Canada, and in 1959, received the Guggenheim Fellowship that allowed him to complete one of his most highly regarded works, *The Luck of Ginger Coffey* (1960). Between 1960 and the publication of *The Emperor of Ice-Cream* in 1965, he published *An Answer from Limbo*. Moore said, in an interview with Hallvard Dahlie, that a dramatic change in his life occurred in the years between the publication of the latter two novels: "I am much happier now than I was when I was thirty-five or forty. *Emperor* was written at a crucial time in my life—it was the first book after I changed." That change was demonstrated also in his personal life during the year of *The Emperor of Ice-Cream*'s publication. In 1966, Moore married his second wife, Jean Denny, his first marriage having been to Jacqueline Sirois.

From 1966 until his death in 1999, Moore continued to publish at the rate of a novel every one to three years. Although he maintained Canadian citizenship, he continued to live in the United States, in a house overlooking the Pacific Ocean, near Oxnard, California.

ANALYSIS

Although he became increasingly cosmopolitan in his adult life, Brian Moore's work is very much rooted in the place of his origin—Northern Ireland—

Una remained a "hot Protestant," a representative of the sex who were "mockers, character assassins, every single one of them," the simple equations upon which Moore's Catholic Ireland rests could be sustained. "Fancy putting yourself in a position where a woman could laugh at you. An intimate moment, a ridiculous posture—a declaration of love, for instance. Or on your wedding night, to hear a girl laugh at you." In the tradition of the early Church Fathers, man is the spirit and woman the body—the defiling physical presence. The sight of a real and vulnerable young woman, however, undoes the myth, and him, in a culturally caused sexual dysfunction suffered by heroes throughout Moore's work.

Dev makes the "Irish choice," retreating from actuality. Afraid of censure from the hierarchy of the fathers, who are embroiled in a power struggle of their own that threatens Dev, he abandons Una to the consequences of the morally compromising position in which he has placed her, and resigns himself to his narrow and deprived existence. The "boy who dreamed of marrying Madeleine Carroll, the film actress, and taking her to the Riviera where they would commit unknown flesh sins the priests warned about in sermons . . . [was] now a man of thirty-seven [who] had not lived a real life; he had been dreaming."

THE LUCK OF GINGER COFFEY

Moore's third novel, *The Luck of Ginger Coffey*, is set in Montreal, and its title character is a man who has nominally extricated himself from the ties of religion, family, and community that bind Judith Hearne and Dev. Still very much a son of Ireland, however, Ginger dreams of success in the New World, just as Judith dreams of love and marriage and Devine fantasizes sexual conquest. The affliction of the "Irish choice" makes Ginger a man for whom, as for Dev, real life is obscured by dreaming.

In Moore's later expatriate novels—and even at the end of *The Emperor of Ice-Cream*, when young Gavin Burke decides to leave Belfast—there is hope of fulfillment for his dreaming Irish men and women. Tierney in *An Answer from Limbo*, and the confused *poète maudit* of *The Mangan Inheritance*, Jamie Mangan, are endowed with the potentially transform-ing and liberating force of imagination. They are possessed of a creative power denied Ginger Coffey, as it had been denied to Judith and Dev.

Trapped in a series of cheap fictional images of success rooted in his Irish past, Ginger affects a Dublin squire look, and he thinks of himself as being in his soldierly prime, handsomely mustachioed and booted. A Canadian employer to whom he appeals sees him otherwise: "A limely type . . . with his tiny green hat, short bulky car coat and suede boots." Nor is he otherwise successful in adapting to his adopted country. The uniform of a diaper service delivery man is a mockery of his early dreams of military adventure. His dreams of an adventurous career as a journalist shrink in the cellar of the building where he works as a proofreader, and evaporate finally in the words of a dying co-worker: "Irish. An immigrant same as you," the dying man tells him. Nearly forty, he looks at his dying compatriot and realizes what he has abandoned, and how little he has gained. Will he so end his days, "his voice nasal and reedy, all accent gone"? Coffey denies such a fate: "Yes, I'm Irish. James Francis Coffey. Fine Irish name."

In the end, though, Coffey is a man without country or community, and a man nearly without family, as his wife and daughter yield to the attractions of the vulgar materialism of the country to which he has brought them, in which he has insisted they stay, and where at last he resigns himself to life with them in "humble circs." His marriage to Veronica, née Shannon, whom he calls by a name for Ireland, "Dark Rosaleen," is his only tie to his native land. He must pay a dear price to sustain that tie, his only protection from the chaos that threatened Judith Hearne, and that Dev could not even contemplate. The price is to be what he most feared—an Irish failure, living with a wife he no longer wants, and working at a job worse than the one he left behind in the scorned Ulster.

AN ANSWER FROM LIMBO

Ginger Coffey represents to Moore, as he told Robert Fulford, "what I was terrified would happen to me. I've always felt myself to be a misfit, I still do." By contrast, Brendan Tierney, the protagonist of *An Answer from Limbo*, is the first of Moore's protagonists to possess the creative power that seems to have been Moore's salvation. Curiously, however, Tierney is a less sympathetic character than any of the three doomed and powerless protagonists who precede him in Moore's work. The hapless Judith, who suffers a woman's fate along with the burden of the Irish cross; the tragicomic Dev; and the feckless Ginger, who befriends the lonely child of his landlady in the midst of his troubles—all are caught in the grip of social circumstances, and all struggle to maintain dignity and humanity in spite of those circumstances. That humanity is absent in Brendan Tierney. The theme of *An Answer from Limbo*, repeated in *Fergus* and in *I Am Mary Dunne*, is a problematic repudiation of the Irish past with its shackles of family, religion, and community in favor of a freer identity, shaped by the personal power of the imagination. Moore's disapproval of Tierney, as of later artist heroes, warns the reader, however, not to expect simple solutions to the conflict.

No childlike victim, no futile fantasizer, Brendan Tierney is a hard-eyed young writer who seems destined to achieve the success and fame for which he hungers. Replete with the self-confidence absent in Judith and Dev, and possessed of talent and purpose sadly lacking in Ginger, Brendan expects his future work to find a place among the ranks of "Kierkegaard and Camus, Dostoyevsky and Gide." As John Scanlan has observed, the theme here is Faustian. Tierney is the artist who sacrifices not only his own happiness for his art, but also the well-being of those who have loved him or depended upon him in the past. He drives his wife Jane into miserable infidelity; his rejected mother dies alone, waiting to return to Ireland. Mrs. Tierney is effectively "killed" by Brendan, who rejects her overtly and puts her out of his mind. In his single-minded devotion to his art, Brendan denies his past, the emotional solace and protection offered by Ireland, his family, and his religion. At the novel's end, he is overcome by the self-loathing that even Ginger Coffey was spared. Ginger was able to say at least, as he sought to reconcile himself to his failures, "Life itself is a victory." Brendan, even with the real prospect of attaining his dreams of success, is left with the knowledge that "I

have altered beyond all self-recognition. I have lost and sacrificed myself."

I AM MARY DUNNE

I Am Mary Dunne marked a shift in direction for Moore. Having achieved a kind of resolution of his old material with the altered—and happier—perspective of *The Emperor of Ice-Cream*, Moore was ready in this sixth novel to move into new territory. It is significant that the protagonist of the first novel in this less traditional phase is, like that of his first novel, a woman. Just as he wanted to ensure that his first major character "wasn't me—could never be mistaken for me," so *I Am Mary Dunne* is determined to avoid the appearance of autobiography. Despite its innovative style, the novel takes up many of Moore's familiar themes. Mary is an artist—a failed one, perhaps—and an Irish expatriate whose haunted past is full of the old ghosts of religion, a troublesome father, and an identity and community that elude her in both Canada and New York.

Moore, whose insights into feminine psychology as well as sexual politics were demonstrated in *Judith Hearne*, makes clear the importance of Mary's sex in her search for identity. She has fitted herself to each of her husbands, adopting a new identity with each name-change. The novel's epigraph from Yeats is apt: It is no longer possible for Mary to tell the "dancer from the dance." She is threatened by the void that froze the earlier Moore characters into childhood, and drives the quest of the later characters for meaning through acts of the imagination. For Mary, though, the possibilities of the creative imagination have been discarded; her life as an actress is over, her potential as a writer and a painter lie fallow. Her current identity is defined by the successful playwright to whom she is now married. Thus, she tries to find herself by remembering who she once was—her mother's daughter, Mary Dunne.

CATHOLICS

In *Catholics*, Moore's eighth novel and one of his best, the religious commitment that was a major hedge against the void for the victimized early characters regains center stage. For the first time, however, the struggles are sexless. Neither the relationship between men and women nor the exercise of sexual power is at issue here. The confrontation with the empty tabernacle is drawn pure and simple. On a remote rocky island in Kerry, a priest's personal crisis of faith is played out against the clinical relativism of a twenty-first century world, represented by James Kinsella, a young priest sent by Rome to obliterate the last vestiges of the old order to which the priests and parishioners of Muck Abbey still cling.

Unlike Judith Hearne, whose ultimate capacity for childlike fantasy offered her protection against the void, the Abbott has no defenses. He had chosen long ago to forsake all else for his God, and now he has found that "there is no Father in Heaven." When he tries to pray, he "enters null." When the young priest, Kinsella, arrives, the Abbott has not prayed in years. He sees his role as a manager of the Abbey, and also as a human bulwark for others against the void he has confronted. The Abbott knows, just as the behaviorist friend of young Kinsella knows, that "People don't want truth or justice. They want certainties. The old parish priest promised them that." Thus, the Abbott tries to deliver certainty, although it is lost to him. The past, however, is irredeemable. Its loss began long ago with "that righteous prig at Wittenberg nailing his defiance to the church door." The Abbott's attempt to recall it is doomed, as is he.

While those last lines absolve Moore of any suspicion of romanticizing the past of which he once despaired, the earlier faith in the possibilities of the imagination to liberate and to create its own enduring reality seems all but lost here. *The Great Victorian Collection*, Moore's next novel, continues that dark view of the power of the individual spirit and the creative imagination.

THE GREAT VICTORIAN COLLECTION

Moore's increasingly pessimistic vision is expressed in the central conceit of *The Great Victorian Collection*: Anthony Maloney, an undistinguished young professor and student of Victorian life, dreams into existence an authentic and unprecedented collection of Victoriana, an opportunity for the creative synthesis of past and present, of tradition and the imagination, that would resolve the fundamental conflict Moore presents. Significantly, however, the Collection is dreamed into existence in California, a land

of hollow dreams. Moreover, it appears in a motel parking lot in that precious California tourist mecca, Carmel-by-the-Sea, with its "galleries filled with local paintings, arcade shops selling homemade candles, and bookstores displaying the complete works of Kahil Gibran."

The California tourist town becomes, in this most imaginative of Moore's novels, a world that, however far in form and principle from Belfast, has an equivalent capacity to thwart the individual spirit and to stultify the creative process. Tony is trapped by the Collection, which begins to deteriorate as he allows his attention to waver from it. Trapped in the dilemma of the successful artist, he must involve other people in his work. Other people include, notably, a commercial agent whose efforts to "market" the Collection lead to great commercial success, but the real "success" is a facsimile of the Collection at a place and in a form more palatable to the public. Tony's own investment in his creation becomes increasingly detached, until the pieces of it become artificial, and his caretaking is mechanistic. His dreams are reduced to soul-deadening surveillance by a black-and-white television camera. Finally, he tries to destroy his deteriorated creation, but it has assumed a life of its own and is indestructible.

This parable of the failure of the imagination to liberate or to sustain the spirit includes Moore's familiar erotic crisis. The creation of The Great Victorian Collection seems to be connected with Maloney's relationship with the beautiful young girl who comes into his life almost immediately after the Collection appears. A Dutch clairvoyant warns him that she is important to what has happened, and indeed, Mary Ann McKelvey soon emerges as Tony's anchor to reality in the feverish life of the imagination in which he finds himself. In a scene highly reminiscent of Moore's early works, their first and only sexual encounter ends in disaster, with Mary Ann thinking she has "failed" Tony. In fact, as with Dev, the apprehension of Mary Ann as a real woman "undid him." Tony "was, and always would be, a dreamer. . . . No longer a man and maid in those far-off wicked times, they were now equals, contestants, almost enemies." Unable to live with the human challenges of the real world or with women who are real people, and faced in his life as an artist with a choice between commercial exploitation of his gifts or the caretaking of deteriorating museum pieces, Maloney chooses to end his own life.

THE MANGAN INHERITANCE

The connection between Moore's concern with a particular male inability to form adult sexual relationships and the failure of the imagination to craft a synthesis of tradition and the individual creative spirit is treated most directly in his two most recent novels. In *The Mangan Inheritance*, the connection, at least in outline, is simplistic. Jamie Mangan, failed poet, failed husband, perhaps even failed son, uses the windfall from his wife's sudden death to try to bury his failures in a return to a romanticized past. His search in the Irish village of his ancestors for confirmation of his relationship to the nineteenth century *poète maudit* James Clarence Mangan is a search for validation by the past, and is as doomed to failure as that of the Abbott in *Catholics*.

Unlike some of Moore's previous protagonists, however, Jamie is able to acknowledge his failures and learn from them. He refuses to succumb to the romantic fantasies that have spoiled the lives of past and present members of his Irish family. The excesses of the *poète maudit* are revealed to him in their sordid reality in the lives of his Irish cousins. He even comes to see his sexual infatuation with the beautiful but slovenly teenage Kathleen for the destructive fantasy it is in the light of the story of incest and sexual abuse he hears from his Irish *Doppelgänger*, Michael Mangan. In the end, Jamie is able to repudiate his fantasies, literary and sexual, and return to his dying father and to responsibility to a future generation. In the daguerrotype of James Clarence Mangan lying smashed beyond repair against the stones of a ruined Irish castle, Jamie sees the features of his dying father and "wished that those features were his own." Implicit is the promise that his father's unborn child, whom he has promised to protect, will be welcomed into a family free of romantic illusion about itself, and that Jamie has a chance at fulfillment in the real world. The resolution is not unshadowed, however, for Jamie was a poet, and apparently will be no longer.

THE TEMPTATION OF EILEEN HUGHES

The note of guarded optimism on which *The Mangan Inheritance* ends is not repeated in Moore's next novel, *The Temptation of Eileen Hughes*. Bernard McAuley, the novel's "artist," is a strange admixture of Moore's earlier protagonists. Sexually paralyzed, though married to Mona, a beautiful woman who loves him, Bernard searches for identity and meaning in his life, ranging from "offering [himself] to God" as a priest and finding he "wasn't wanted," through studies of history, art, music, and business, and finally to his bizarre attempt to force his strangely celibate relationship with young Eileen Hughes into his sordid household.

The themes of sexual power and the act of the imagination attain a distorted unity in this novel. Bernard enacts an evolution into decadence, and in a confirmation of Moore's recurrent tendency to find healthy self-knowledge in women targeted as victims by male identity-seekers, Eileen ultimately understands the manipulative and powerful McAuleys: "It was not she who had been in their power but they in hers. She had escaped them. Would they escape her?" Like Mary Ann McKelvey, or Diarmud Devine's Una, Eileen is anchored in a reality to which men such as Bernard (and the women whose lives they steal) will be forever denied admission.

The four novels that followed *The Temptation of Eileen Hughes* are diverse in setting and character, yet they are linked both stylistically and thematically; together they mark a new phase in Moore's work. In three of the four—*Cold Heaven*, *The Color of Blood*, and *Lies of Silence*—Moore adopts the plot-scaffolding and many of the generic conventions of the thriller, while in *Black Robe*, set in the 1630's in the Canadian wilderness, he adopts the conventions of the historical adventure novel.

Some reviewers have seen in this shift an attempt on Moore's part to win a larger audience. If that is the case, the attempt must be judged a failure, for while these works have been well received by critics, they did not make Moore a best-selling author. It seems just as likely, though, that Moore turned to the thriller for other reasons. In *Black Robe*, which centers on the physical hardships and spiritual conflicts

Ulick and Soracha, 1926
Aphrodite in Aulis, 1930

OTHER LITERARY FORMS

George Moore was man of letters rather than purely a novelist. He published seven collections of short fiction, and all but the first of his eight plays were produced in London or Dublin. He published two volumes of poetry in 1877 and 1881. Moore published numerous nonfictional works and more than one thousand of his periodical writings have been located in English, Irish, French, and American journals. In addition, he published a notable translation of Longus's *Daphnis and Chloë* in 1924.

ACHIEVEMENTS

Moore's fiction was at all times innovative and influential. Amid much controversy in the early 1880's, he adapted the methods of French realism to the English novel. His earliest goals were to liberate the novel from Victorian conventions of subject and treatment and from commercial constraints imposed by a monopolistic book trade.

By the middle 1880's, he began to turn from realism to aestheticism. Under the influence of his friend Walter Pater and the rising Symbolist poets of France, Moore anticipated the "decadence" of the 1890's by eschewing the conflict between realism and popular Romanticism which had formerly absorbed him. He realized that these schools of writing were generally organized and evaluated on moral and social grounds. In regard to prose narrative, Moore's increasing and then sole preoccupation became literary art.

As an aesthete in the early 1890's, he composed his masterpiece *Esther Waters*. He also wrote some of the short stories that later contributed to his reputation as an inventor of modern Irish fiction. The large income generated by his books allowed him to quit his second career as one of England's leading art critics. He cofounded the Independent Theatre and Irish Literary Theatre and by the turn of the century he became a leading polemicist of the Irish revival.

The major achievement of Moore's Irish involvement was the composition of *Hail and Farewell: A Trilogy* (1911-1914). In the tradition of Laurence Sterne, Thomas De Quincey, and George Borrow, Moore wrote the story of his life using the conceptual framework of fiction rather than history. The trilogy contains an account of artistic movements of the late Victorian era, but attention is concentrated on the intellectual life of Dublin in the early years of the twentieth century.

During the 1910's and 1920's, Moore retreated from the popular literary market to the composition of prose epics. Biblical history in *The Brook Kerith*, medieval history in *Héloïse and Abélard*, and classical history in *Aphrodite in Aulis* offered structural premises for a new exploration of human problems and for the development of a modern, rarefied aestheticism. Reviewers greeted the novels as exemplars of composition and elevated Moore to the status of England's senior man of letters.

BIOGRAPHY

The Moores of Moore Hall were a prominent Catholic family in the west of Ireland. Their home, a large gray stone mansion presiding over 12,500 acres, was built in 1795 by George Moore, the novelist's great-grandfather. The founder of Moore Hall was a businessman. His eldest son Peter was certified insane for most of his life; the second son John was martyred in the 1798 rebellion (see Thomas Flanagan's novel *The Year of the French*, 1979); the youngest son George, the novelist's grandfather, was a scholarly historian. George inherited the estate and through marriage established an intimate connection with the Brownes of Westport. His eldest son was George Henry Moore (1810-1870), a keeper of excellent racing stables and member of Parliament for the nationalist cause. In 1851, he married Mary Blake (1829-1895), daughter of a neighboring landlord.

George Augustus Moore, the eldest of G. H. Moore's five children, was born at Moore Hall on February 24, 1852. He was a robust but rather backward child: a late talker, then an endearing but poor pupil under a succession of governesses. Beginning in 1861, he attended Oscott College, Birmingham, a famous preparatory school designed as the Catholic complement of Eton or Harrow. He remained at Oscott until 1868, when his learning disabilities finally convinced the headmaster that further attempts at instruction would be futile.

After leaving Oscott, Moore lived with his parents in London while Parliament was in session. His time was divided between military tutors and amusements, including betting shops, music halls, and painting studios. When his father died suddenly in 1870, the quest for an army commission was dropped, and soon Moore was devoting most of his energy to the study of painting.

From 1873 until 1879, he lived mostly in Paris, first as a student painter at the École des Beaux Arts and Académie Julian. Before setting aside his brushes in 1875, he had received instruction from James Whistler, John Millais, Alexandre Cabanel, and several less famous painters in France and England. Education did not make a painter of him, but it did help make him a sensitive art critic later in life. His first steps in literature during the later 1870's were likewise tentative. He was enraptured with French Romantic drama and Parnassian poetry. By the time the income from his property suddenly failed and he was forced to leave France, he had published two volumes of exotic juvenile verse and a large Romantic drama which was intended for but declined by Henry Irving.

Moore's literary career properly began in London in 1881. He was then settled in inexpensive rooms near the Strand and determined to make a living by his pen. While developing the plan of a naturalistic novel, he contributed paragraphs and reviews to the weekly press. Among his friends he numbered several poets and critics of the Pre-Raphaelite Circle, but these receded as his friendship with Émile Zola became a discipleship. "When I attacked the Philistine," Algernon Charles Swinburne commented after reading *A Mummer's Wife*, "it was not with a chamber pot for a buckler and a dung fork for a spear." Moore's first two novels and his early journalism, though consonant with the ideals of the French avant-garde, drew charges of indecency from English readers. Though he moderated his style as his aestheticism changed, the reputation he earned at the start of his career remained with him, and all of his fiction until

the turn of the century was banned from the circulating libraries.

Moore continued to live in the vicinity of the Strand until 1886, when he moved to a village near Brighton and afterward to a house atop the Sussex downs. In the English countryside he found an almost idyllic refuge from the distractions of London. His fiction of the period shows an increasing tolerance of ordinary life, and his literary theories, which he collected for *Confessions of a Young Man* (1888), reveal a firmer, more self-reliant mind than was evident before. He returned to London in 1889, engaged to write art criticism for his brother's magazine *The Hawk* and, more important, with the plan for a novel which became *Esther Waters*.

From 1889 until 1895, Moore contributed columns of art criticism briefly to *The Hawk* and then to *The Speaker*, both weekly reviews of politics and the arts. He was the first Impressionist art critic in England. Aside from writing fiction and criticism, he became deeply involved in theater reform and in 1890 cofounded the Independent Theatre, where Henrik Ibsen and George Bernard Shaw had their London premieres. With the publication of *Esther Waters*, he was soon able to leave the staff of *The Speaker*.

During the rest of the 1890's, Moore was prominent among the aesthetes and Decadents generally associated with *The Yellow Book*. He also took a publicized interest in the revival of early music, begun by his friend Arnold Dolmetsch, and in Wagnerism. His annual pilgrimage to Bayreuth began at this time, and his last novel of the century is permeated with musical theory. Drawn by the ideas of William Butler Yeats and others concerning the artistic possibilities of Gaelic, he also became involved in the Irish revival. With Yeats and Edward Martyn he founded the Irish Literary Theatre (precursor of the Abbey). In 1901, enamored of the "new Ireland" and bitterly depressed by British conduct of the Boer War, Moore leased a house in Upper Ely Place, near St. Stephen's Green in Dublin. He remained there until 1911.

Owing mainly to aesthetic and religious convictions, Moore's return to Ireland was characterized more by frustration than success. Having learned his profession in Paris and London, he could feel little sympathy for the relatively parochial challenges that writers of the movement faced. His advocacy of intellectual freedom for the artist was inappropriate to prevailing ideology. Worse, his notion that a politically free Ireland was one that would disown both Westminster and the Vatican virtually exiled him from the cause he tried to embrace. Though he made several friends among literary Dubliners, wrote polemics in the Irish press, and published important fiction, his greatest achievement was the comic indictment of the movement that appeared, after he left Dublin, in *Hail and Farewell*.

From 1911 until his death, Moore lived in Ebury Street, London. For the first time he was associated with no movement but instead practiced his art purely as an individual. His fiction and books of theory were welcomed by an elite readership of a few thousand. His best friends were the English Impressionist painters who lived in nearby Chelsea. Turning about-face on the six-shilling format he had invented with publisher Henry Vizetelly in 1884, he issued his books in limited, sometimes elegantly illustrated editions that took him entirely out of the popular market. He died in his home on January 21, 1933, and was buried on an island in Lough Carra, in front of Moore Hall. Because the rites of burial were pagan, a police guard was called to protect the funeral. George Russell composed the oration and the epitaph of George Moore: "He forsook his family and friends for his art. But because he was faithful to his art his family and friends reclaimed his ashes for Ireland. VALE."

ANALYSIS

Thirty of George Moore's fifty years as a novelist postdate the Victorian era, yet he is not generally remembered as a modern writer. To some extent this is because his aestheticism was the outcome of inspiration rather than experiment. "I desire above all things," he wrote in 1892, "to tell the story of life in grave simple phrases, so grave and simple that the method, the execution would disappear, and the reader, with bating breath, would remain a prey to an absorbing emotion."

Complexity and diversity are striking characteristics of the Moore corpus. He told "the story of life" ranging from classical Greece (*Aphrodite in Aulis*) to industrial England (*A Mummer's Wife*). His changing style reflected the influence of diverse writers, including Gustave Flaubert, Ivan Turgenev, and Walter Pater. Confused by such diversity, Arthur Symons reached the conclusion that Moore had no style, and James Whistler believed that he had no conscience. In a curious way this is true. He achieved not style, but expression. As an artist he avoided moral judgments and ceased his endeavors after discovering the soul in the body, the idea in action. The nature of his critical theories and the evolution of his fiction confirm that he was not a modernist, but a classicist.

A MODERN LOVER

Moore's first novel, *A Modern Lover*, like his last, is a study of artistic temperament. The chief protagonist is Lewis Seymour, a young painter of middling talent whose problem is to advance his career. He is attracted to a fraternity of avant-garde artists called "the moderns," who advocate a radical departure from academic painting. However, he realizes that to achieve success in the sense of worldly recognition, he must be conventional and flatter the tastes of an ignorant public. The narrative traces Lewis's development as a painter with a "market" that expands in proportion to the distance between himself and personal integrity.

A Modern Lover represents the first conscious attempt to write a naturalistic novel in English. Reviewers noticed its power. In addition to its literary qualities, the novel offers an account of conflicting trends in art: "The moderns" are painters modeled after the French Impressionists; "the medievalists" are modeled after the Pre-Raphaelite Brotherhood; the Royal Academy appears as a copy of the original. Through the character of John Harding, Moore expounded his own views as a critic of Victorian culture and advocated reforms that prepared the way for a new definition of modern art.

Susan Mitchell noted in her study of Moore that he had an uncanny ability to understand women. *A Mummer's Wife* and *A Drama in Muslin* may be regarded as portraits of women: the first novel rather sinister and tragic, the second almost feminist and deeply encouraging.

A MUMMER'S WIFE

Kate Ede is introduced in *A Mummer's Wife* as the wife of a shopkeeper living in the industrial town of Hanley. She is a young woman of sober character and dry religious convictions. Dick Lennox, the actor-manager of a touring company, rents lodgings in her house and seduces her. She is persuaded to leave her unhappy marriage and to accompany Dick on his travels. Moravia, Kate's self-discipline gives way to a sensuous dreaminess. After becoming an actress, she marries Dick and has a baby by him, but her course runs steadily downward. As the moral underpinnings of her life are loosened, she slips almost unawares into depravity and dies in the end, an alcoholic among prostitutes.

A DRAMA IN MUSLIN

Alice Barton, the heroine of *A Drama in Muslin*, is the daughter of an Irish landlord. She is an intellectual girl and rather homely; consequently she is unfitted for the grotesque "marriage market" of the Castle season in Dublin. Her sister and acquaintances spend their energy and sometimes dignity in preparing for the most important event of their lives: the entrapment of a moneyed young man in matrimony. All the innocence, loveliness, and promise of girlhood are publicly and somewhat brutally bartered for the passing illusions of title and fortune. Alice remains aloof, quietly preparing herself for a literary career. In the end, because of her intelligence and self-reliance, she alone makes a happy marriage.

Apart from many distinguishing features, the one shared by Kate Ede and Alice Barton is a departure from the common rut of experience. When Kate becomes the mummer's mistress, she breaks free from the paralyzing control of her husband and mother-in-law. During the months before conscience prods her to become the mummer's wife, she achieves sexual and emotional fulfillment and finds herself on the verge of a career and independence. Kate's is not a social tragedy: The opportunity to change her life was offered, but for personal reasons she neglected it. Alice's success is likewise of her own making. The reader finds soon after beginning *A Drama in Muslin* that the heroine is set apart less by her lack of beauty than by her strength of character. By virtue of a cor-

rect perception of Vanity Fair, Alice disentangles herself from the fatal bonds of family, class, and background to secure a hopeful future.

ESTHER WATERS

Esther Waters, properly regarded as one of the greater novels in English literature, is also one of the least understood. From the year of its publication, reviewers and scholars have persisted in classing it as a realistic novel, using "realism" to mean an imitation of nature. Moore explained in "Exteriority" (*The Speaker*, June 22, 1895) that though he deferred to realism in regard to subject matter, the book was formed on higher, more subjective principles. Returning to an argument published earlier in *The Speaker* (October 8, 1892), he observed that all art should contain truth and beauty, but these were separate attributes. Truth he associated with nature, so to be truthful the novelist chooses a realistic subject. Beauty he associated with imagination. To achieve beauty, the novelist permeates nature with his personal vision. Through the quality of expression, or literary form, he succeeds in conveying images to and from the soul and hallows nature with the spirit of art.

Esther Waters has been bound in its reputation of realism because Moore's choice of a subject from nature was powerful enough to be blinding. His protagonists were servants, characters whose place in English fiction had been confined to doing odd jobs and providing comic entertainment. Now they were comprehended as full human beings and their vast subculture moved from the periphery to the center of consciousness. The force of Moore's decision to write about servants was increased by the novel's central problem: the struggle of an unmarried mother to rear her child. By making Esther Waters his heroine, Moore overturned an array of Victorian sexual mores and political assumptions.

It is not surprising that the controversy that greeted publication of the novel distracted readers from its artistic merits. It must be emphasized, however, that Moore was no champion of the working class; he was neither a sociologist nor a philanthropist. He was only what he claimed to be: an artist. Essentially, he was no more interested in servant girls than his friend Edgar Degas was interested in balleri-

Moore and his work from a variety of perspectives: his Irish background and the Irish Literary Renaissance, his connections with Samuel Beckett, and his relationship to James Joyce. The appendix includes a bibliographical essay by Edwin Gilcher. A valuable contribution to the criticism on Moore.

Farrow, Anthony. *George Moore*. Boston: Twayne, 1978. A helpful study of Moore for the beginning reader, but somewhat restricted in format. An appreciative approach to Moore that places him at a high level of literary distinction, despite the fact that his novels remain largely unread. Includes a selected bibliography.

Fratantaro, Sal. *The Methodology of G.E. Moore*. Brookfield, Vt.: Ashgate, 1998. Part of the Avebury Series in Philosophy, this volume examines Moore's contributions to long fiction in methodology.

Gray, Tony. *A Peculiar Man: A Life of George Moore*. London: Sinclair-Stevenson, 1996. A good, updated biography of Moore that takes into account his different vocations, such as art critic and landowner. Includes a short bibliography.

Grubgeld, Elizabeth. *George Moore and the Autogenous Self: The Autobiography and Fiction*. Syracuse: Syracuse University Press, 1994. As Grubgeld's title suggests, she explores the interdependence of Moore's fiction and autobiography. See especially chapter 8 for her discussion of narrating and remembering. Includes detailed notes and extensive bibliography.

Langenfeld, Robert. *An Annotated Bibliography*. New York: AMS Press, 1987. The most up-to-date and comprehensive bibliography on Moore. Gives credit to Gilcher's pioneering bibliography, and the introduction assesses Moore's reputation, past and present. An excellent resource.

Seinfelt, Frederick W. *George Moore: Ireland's Unconventional Realist*. Philadelphia: Dorrance, 1975. A full-length study that examines Moore's treatment of men and women in his novels. Seinfelt argues that Moore saw the two sexes as separate and incompatible, and that his works show "remarkable insight" into the state of marriage and male-female relationships. Includes an essay on the Wagnerian elements in Moore's writing, also referring to other influences on his work.

ALBERTO MORAVIA

Born: Rome, Italy; November 28, 1907
Died: Rome, Italy; September 26, 1990

PRINCIPAL LONG FICTION

Gli indifferenti, 1929 (*The Time of Indifference*, 1953)

Le ambizioni sbagliate, 1935 (*The Wheel of Fortune*, 1937; also known as *Mistaken Ambitions*)

La mascherata, 1941 (*The Fancy Dress Party*, 1947)

Agostino, 1944 (English translation, 1947)

La romana, 1947 (*The Woman of Rome*, 1949)

La disubbidienza, 1948 (*Two Adolescents*, 1950; also known as *Disobedience*)

L'amore coniugale, 1949 (*Conjugal Love*, 1951)

Il conformista, 1951 (*The Conformist*, 1952)

Il disprezzo, 1954 (*A Ghost at Noon*, 1955)

La ciociara, 1957 (*Two Women*, 1958)

La noia, 1960 (*The Empty Canvas*, 1961)

L'attenzione, 1965 (*The Lie*, 1966)

Io e lui, 1971 (*Two: A Phallic Novel*, 1972)

La vita interiore, 1978 (*Time of Desecration*, 1980)

1934, 1982 (English translation, 1983)

L'uomo che guarda, 1985 (*The Voyeur*, 1986)

Il viaggio a Roma, 1988 (*Journey to Rome*, 1990)

OTHER LITERARY FORMS

Though he is known primarily as a novelist, especially outside Italy, Alberto Moravia was equally productive as a short-story writer. Not available in translation until the 1950's, Moravia's short stories brought him considerable recognition in his own country. The majority of Moravia's short stories appeared in collected form, usually after an initial publication in a literary journal or newspaper, in the following volumes: *La bella vita* (1935), *L'epidema*

(1944), *Due cortigiane* (1945), *Racconti romani* (1954; *Roman Tales*, 1956), *Nuovi racconti romani* (1959; *More Roman Tales*, 1963), *L'automa* (1963; *The Fetish*, 1964), *Una cosa è una cosa* (1967; *Command and I Will Obey You*, 1969), *Il paradisio* (1970; *Paradise and Other Stories*, 1971; also as *Bought and Sold*, 1973), *Un'altra vita* (1973; *Lady Godiva and Other Stories*, 1975; also as *Mother Love*, 1976), and *Boh* (1976; *The Voice of the Sea and Other Stories*, 1978). Two useful comprehensive editions of Moravia's stories are *I racconti, 1927-1951* (1952) and *I racconti di Alberto Moravia* (1968), though they must be supplemented by the collections published subsequently.

In addition to his fiction, Moravia also published and produced a number of plays, including dramatic versions of *Gli indifferenti* (1948) and *La mascherata* (1954), as well as several original dramas: *Beatrice Cenci* (1955; English translation, 1965), *Il mondo è quello che è* (1966), *Il dio Kurt* (1968), and *La vita è gioco* (1969). The collected edition of his plays is published as *Teatro* (1958, 1976).

Moravia's travel essays appeared in four collections: *Un mese in U.R.S.S.* (1958), *Un'idea dell'India* (1962), *La rivoluzione culturale in Cina* (1967; *The Red Book and the Great Wall*, 1968), and *A quale tribù appartieni?* (1972; *Which Tribe Do You Belong To?*, 1974).

Moravia also wrote a large body of polemical essays on literature, politics, religion, and other topics. These appear in *Saggi italiani del 1959* (1960) and *L'uomo come fine e altri saggi* (1964; *Man as an End*, 1965). They are collected in a comprehensive edition, along with other, previously uncollected, polemical writings, in *Impegno controvoglia: Saggi, articoli, interviste* (1980).

Numerous film adaptations of Moravia's work have been made, not only in Italy but also in other countries, by some of Europe's leading filmmakers. Among the best-known of them are Vittorio De Sica's *La ciociara* (1960; *Two Women*, 1961), Michaelangelo Antonioni's *L'avventura* (1960), Damiano Damiani's *La noia* (1964; *The Empty Canvas*, 1964), Jean-Luc Godard's *Le mépris* (1964; *Contempt*, 1964), Bernardo Bertolucci's *Il conformista* (1969; *The Con-*

formist, 1970), and *L'amore coniugale* (1970), directed by Moravia's wife, Dacia Maraini.

ACHIEVEMENTS

Alberto Moravia is an important figure in the history of modern Italian literature for several reasons. First, and for some literary historians most important, is Moravia's popularity with a large, widely dispersed international reading audience. He is, by far, the most widely translated modern Italian novelist. Every one of his novels has been translated into English, for example, as well as nearly all of his shorter fiction. This international popularity is, no doubt, helped by the frequent practice of marketing his works as soft-core pornography in paperback editions, so that his work is made to appeal to an audience much wider than those who would read it solely for its literary qualities. This practice is made possible by the prominence of sexuality in Moravia's fiction, but it would be misleading to think of this erotic content as an end in itself.

(Library of Congress)

tive and positive responses. Those who dislike this element of Moravia's work point to the sameness of his alienated middle-class male protagonists, who go through a predictable pattern of development that is always essentially the same. To these critics, Moravia's work seems to lack the dynamism that arises from a hero who is capable of growth and change. More sympathetic critics have shown, however, that the dynamism of Moravia's novels lies not within the protagonists themselves but in the conflict between characters who are capable of making choices and gratifying their desires through physical action and those who are caught up in narcissistic reflection that does not lead to action and therefore cannot change their situation in the world. More important than the description of this pattern of conflict, however, is the fact that Moravia's characters rarely come to any recognition themselves; the recognition almost always takes place within the reader, who reflects upon the meaning of the characters' successes and failures in the novel.

Two other aspects of Moravia's characterization that are frequently commented upon are his portrayal of women and of human sexuality. By unsympathetic critics, he is accused of creating nothing but mindless women whose sole trait seems to be a powerful erotic drive. Sympathetic critics see these flat women as catalytic agents whose function is to expose the hero's character. The same is true of Moravia's use of sexuality. To unsympathetic critics, it is simply exploitative titillation or an unwitting reflection of the author's own prurient or voyeuristic sensibility. To sympathetic critics, such as Donald Heiney, however, sex is an "encounter in which the conflict of human egos is seen more simply," while for others it assumes the status of a symbol for the alienation of modern man, a demonstration of the fundamental isolation from others that characterizes the life of individuals in modern industrial societies.

One of the most distinctive elements of Moravia's fiction is his narrative style and form. The unnamed narrators who dominate Moravia's early work speak in an unadorned, journalistic style that has frequently been compared to Ernest Hemingway's in its emotional reticence, objective detachment, and avoidance

of value-laden diction. The narrative stance in these works often seems to approach the extreme objective detachment of Hemingway's famous story "The Killers," which Moravia translated in 1934.

Following World War II, Moravia began to abandon the omniscient perspective in favor of first-person narrators. *The Woman of Rome* and *Conjugal Love* are both told from this new perspective, as are all the seven novels following *The Conformist*, which uses the omniscient point of view. The reasons for this change in strategy are complex, as are its effects. Beginning with *The Woman of Rome*, Moravia's principal subject—the analysis and critique of middle-class life in modern Italy—is rivaled by a growing interest in the lives of the lower class. Moravia himself said this change of interest was stimulated by his experiences with the peasants among whom he and his wife lived during the German Occupation. An equally strong influence, however, was the developing neorealist aesthetic, which encouraged the employment of participating narrators speaking in the informal diction of regional vernaculars as a much-needed relief from the convention-bound *lingua pura* dialect traditionally employed in literary works.

Another aspect of Moravia's work that has elicited mixed reaction from his critics is the repetitiveness of subject and theme. Moravia himself acknowledged this aspect, but he saw it as an artistic necessity, not a creative shortcoming: "Good writers are monotonous, like good composers. Their truth is self-repeating. They keep . . . trying to perfect their expression of the one problem they were born to understand." The central theme of Moravia's work is the human relationship to reality, which he sees as "the fundamental problem of our time." In Moravia's work, the relationship of people to the world and to others is an amoral one, for clearly defined conceptions of good and evil based on traditional ethics no longer apply to these relationships. In the modern world, humankind, according to Moravia, "is no longer the end but the means," and in the face of this, it adopts the attitude of indifference, becoming alienated from the external world.

Modern human alienation is expressed in many ways in Moravia's work. One of the most prominent of these methods is his portrayal of the decadence and irresponsibility of the affluent Italian middle class, whose desire to protect their vested interests in a world of crumbling social, political, and economic values paved the way for the rise of Fascism in Italy. Many of Moravia's protagonists, being intellectuals, come from this class, as did Moravia himself. As Jane Cottrell says, "Painfully aware of the hypocrisy and false values of middle-class society, the Moravian hero rejects his own class and turns to the lower classes, which he sees as more authentic." This myth of the lower classes is an important theme that recurs throughout the course of Moravia's career.

Another symptom of modern alienation is expressed in Moravia's portrayal of the family. Like capitalistic economics and totalitarian politics, the institution of the family, in Moravia's analysis, robs people of their freedom, making them an end instead of a means. In a 1965 essay, he stated the thoughts that are often voiced less coherently by his alienated protagonists: "The most mistaken teachings are those given by the family . . . worship of such divinities as Prudence, Self-interest, Ignorance, Hedonism. . . . Any school at all, even the worst, is better than the family."

Underlying Moravia's central concerns is his particular philosophical orientation toward the world, which mingles elements of Freudianism, Marxism, existentialism, and phenomenology. In Freudian thought, Moravia found a confirmation of the idea of the primacy of sexual experience in humanity's relation to the world. Marxism, as Heiney says, "provided Moravia with an explanation of the decadence of his own social class," helping him to put his analysis of modern human position in the world into a historical framework. In existentialism, he found a philosophical context for his own conception of people's alienation from the world, which he had formulated—not by systematic reasoning but by the unconscious processes of intuition—years before it was elaborated by Jean-Paul Sartre. In phenomenology, he found confirmation for the idea of the intentionality of consciousness, which is reflected in the method of exhaustion employed in his work. These basic patterns of thought inform Moravia's fictional world.

THE TIME OF INDIFFERENCE

Alberto Moravia wrote *The Time of Indifference*, his first published novel, between October, 1925, and March, 1928. It was Moravia's third attempt at the genre, according to him, for he had already completed two novels that failed because "they were imitations of this or that author with whom I had become infatuated as I went along." *The Time of Indifference* is certainly not open to this charge; it contains many of the distinctive characteristics of Moravia's subsequent work. Despite its remarkable maturity and originality, the novel was turned down by three reputable publishers before being accepted by Alpes, an obscure publishing house in Milan, which issued the novel at Moravia's expense in July of 1929. The novel was an immediate popular success and received high praise from many critics. By the following year, Moravia was already being identified as one of the leading innovators of the developing neorealist aesthetic in literature. Though the novel was strongly attacked by the Fascist press for its negative portrayal of the life of comfortable affluence led by the Italian middle class, to other critics this was precisely the value of the novel—its portrayal of the moral corruption and social irresponsibility of the middle class for the first time in an unsentimental and realistic way.

The novel's protagonist, Michele Ardengo, suffers from that form of modern alienation that Moravia calls "indifference." Michele observes, from this position of detachment, the struggles of his mother, Mariagrazia, to hold on to her bored lover, Leo Merumeci, and the growing willingness of his sister, Carla, to sacrifice her innocence to Leo in order to assure the continued affluence of the family in the face of their sagging fortunes. As the narrator's description of her thoughts reveals, Carla's own actions arise from this same feeling of indifference: "Why should she refuse Leo? Virtue would merely throw her back into the arms of boredom." Helpless to escape his detachment from life, Michele is only able to protest feebly the absurdity of his own condition. In this novel, Moravia's critique of the family as an institution for the perpetuation of decadent social values is prominent.

The Time of Indifference is also an important example of Moravia's use of novelistic form. Like *Mistaken Ambitions, The Fancy Dress Party, Agostino,
Two Adolescents*, and *The Conformist*, this first
novel employs the objective detachment of third-person narrative. His later shift to first-person narration
marks an important division in his work and arises in
part from the radical questioning of the objective nature of reality that is first expressed through the
thoughts and actions of Michele Ardengo.

In its use of the alienated protagonist-hero, the
middle-class Roman background, and the objectification of reality through the omniscient point of view,
The Time of Indifference is perhaps the best representative of the work Moravia published before the end
of World War II.

THE WOMAN OF ROME

The Woman of Rome marks the next, and for many
critics the most important, step in Moravia's development as a literary artist, for this novel was the first
work in which he employed the first-person narrative
perspective that dominates his later fiction. Moreover, the novel was his first to be written in the Roman vernacular. In this respect, it is related to his
Roman tales, in which he brought the use of the
lower-class vernacular narrator to stylistic perfection.
The Woman of Rome marks the beginning of this
phase of Moravia's work, which concluded with *Two
Women*, the last of his novels written in the vernacular.

The Woman of Rome, which Moravia began writing shortly after his return to Rome in 1944, grew
from its original conception as a short story to a massive, five-hundred-page novel comprising the "memoirs" of a Roman prostitute, Adriana. This expansion
of scope, and the perspective from which the novel is
told, indicated an important change of orientation in
Moravia's aesthetic, which he later expressed in an
interview: "The third person is a way of telling a
story of a time when people believed in objective reality. Nowadays we believe in subjective reality. Everybody is his own reality and your reality is not
mine."

This novel also marked the beginning of Moravia's re-creation of the authentic, uncorrupted life of
the lower classes. Adriana, the working-class heroine
of this novel, is unlike the alienated middle-class
heroes of his early work in that she represents "a
triumph of the life force," as Luciano Rebay has put
it. To a large degree, the great popular success the
novel enjoyed resulted from the vitality of its heroine. Moravia himself later said that "in identifying
myself with Adriana I thought for a while that I had
found the key to my own rapport with reality, with
life." This myth of the renewing vitality of the life
of the lower classes, as well as his interest in the
Roman vernacular, was stimulated by his experiences at Fondi during the period he spent in hiding
from the Fascist authorities. Here, for the first time,
Moravia was removed from the social milieu and
material comforts of the affluent middle-class existence he had always known. Though it is certain
that, given a choice, Moravia would not have spent
this period of nine months living in a peasant's stable, it is also certain that without this experience, *The
Woman of Rome, Two Women*, and the Roman tales
that won him the Strega Prize would never have been
written.

Moravia had become accustomed to portraying in
his fiction, for almost twenty years, the life of the affluent middle class. Because this social milieu was
identical with his own experience, his use of an educated, literate narrator speaking in the third person
seemed unobtrusive enough; it created little conflict
between the omniscient consciousness and the mentality of the principal characters. The literate style
would seem very artificial in presenting the experiences and thoughts of his uneducated, working-class
heroine, however, and it is most likely for this reason
that Moravia finally decided to cast the novel into the
form of a memoir, allowing Adriana to tell her own
story in her own speech, employing the vernacular
with which he had become familiar during his stay at
Fondi.

The abandonment of the omniscient point of view
also reflects, in retrospect, a more radical shift in
Moravia's conception of fictional representation,
which was retained even in the later novels which return to portraying the alienation of the Italian middle
class. In "Notes on the Novel," an essay later col-

lected in *Man as an End*, Moravia argued that "the omniscience of the nineteenth-century novelist turned finally into a trick, a lifeless convention. Today we can no longer write 'He thought.' . . . We can only write 'I thought.'" Elaborating on Moravia's statement, Heiney observes that the omniscient perspective does not correspond to the epistemological need of the modern novel to be realistic, because it does not correspond to the radically subjective way in which modern man regards the phenomena of consciousness or the external world. It is above all this particular aesthetic principle that is retained and developed in Moravia's subsequent fiction.

THE CONFORMIST

To many critics, *The Conformist* is an embarrassing anachronism in Moravia's oeuvre, because it employs the third-person omniscient narrative perspective he had abandoned four years earlier in *The Woman of Rome*. Though it is true that Moravia did not return to the objective point of view that he used in *The Conformist*, the novel is not by any means the miserable failure that many critics, in an effort to mold Moravia's technical development into a neat but oversimplified pattern, have asserted.

There are, in fact, a number of conditions in this particular case which make the omniscient perspective an effective choice. The first is Moravia's desire to put the totalitarian era, with which the novel deals, into a historical perspective, so that he can explore and analyze its effects on particular types of individuals. In addition, *The Conformist* employs irony very differently from the way it is used in most of Moravia's other work. The novel has as its central character a hero who is exceptional, not representative, whom the reader is expected to dislike and from whom he is expected to distance himself—not one with whom the reader can sympathize and identify. The irony is conveyed by the comments of the omniscient narrator, who condemns and satirizes Marcello's behavior.

Unlike the heroes and heroines of his other novels, who usually suffer from an excess of self-consciousness, Marcello does not reflect at all but only responds mechanically to external stimuli. In *The Conformist*, unlike most of Moravia's other nov-

els, it is the narrator rather than the characters who does most of the thinking. For these reasons, *The Conformist* is not only Moravia's most uncharacteristic novel but also the one most suited to the use of third-person narrative. The objectification Moravia achieves through the use of viewpoint is reinforced by the form of the novel, which—as several critics have pointed out—resembles that of a classical tragedy. Cottrell has even attempted to show the similarity of Marcello's fate to that of Oedipus.

Undeniably, *The Conformist* has faults. This is so mainly because of the same devices of objectification, which Moravia used effectively to help guide the reader's response to the material. The hero, Marcello, who becomes a Fascist agent out of a desire to prove himself "normal" through submission and conformity, is, in fact, so "spineless"—as one critic put it—that it is difficult for the reader to care much about his fate. There is an unsettling discontinuity between the various parts of the novel, which cover events ranging from 1920 to 1943, as well as the artificiality of the *deus ex machina* ending. The events of the prologue, which covers Marcello's childhood, often remind one of the sensational case histories Freud recounted in formulating his theory of infantile sexuality. The intrusive moralizing of the narrator, while seen by some critics as an artistic defect, seems more a matter of personal taste, because it does serve a useful function in the narrative.

Despite these shortcomings, the novel does effectively present to the reader an analysis of the phenomenon of conformity—the roots from which it arises and the effects it has upon the relation of humans to the world. In this respect, *The Conformist* is not a failure at all, since it addresses one of the central ethical dilemmas of the modern era.

THE EMPTY CANVAS

In *The Empty Canvas*, Moravia returned to the portrayal of the alienated, middle-class hero, yet in this mature novel, there are two new elements present: the subjective narrative perspective afforded by the use of the first-person point of view and the close relationship of the thoughts of the hero, Dino, to those of the author himself. This latter characteristic led some critics, following Moravia's own use of the

ravian sexuality," the absurd, nihilism and crime, self-delusion or bad faith, and conversion. Includes notes but no bibliography.

Wood, Sharon. *Gender, Discourse, and Politics: Woman as Object—Language and Gender in the Work of Alberto Moravia.* London: Pluto Press, 1990. Examines Moravia's treatment of female characters in his works. Includes bibliographical references and an index.

WRIGHT MORRIS

Born: Central City, Nebraska; January 6, 1910
Died: Mill Valley, California; April 26, 1998

PRINCIPAL LONG FICTION

My Uncle Dudley, 1942
The Man Who Was There, 1945
The Home Place, 1948
The World in the Attic, 1949
Man and Boy, 1951
The Works of Love, 1952
The Deep Sleep, 1953
The Huge Season, 1954
The Field of Vision, 1956
Love Among the Cannibals, 1957
Ceremony in Lone Tree, 1960
What a Way to Go, 1962
Cause for Wonder, 1963
One Day, 1965
In Orbit, 1967
Fire Sermon, 1971
War Games, 1972
A Life, 1973
The Fork River Space Project, 1977
Plains Song, for Female Voices, 1980

OTHER LITERARY FORMS

Several of Wright Morris's books, including *The Inhabitants* (1946), *God's Country and My People* (1968), and *Love Affair: A Venetian Journal* (1972), are "photo-texts." They feature photographs ac-

companied by brief prose passages. In the first of these, Morris describes the "inhabitants" of America from coast to coast through photographs of their structures—buildings which have affected the "indwellers." Pictures of porch fronts in the West, for example, reveal New England influences, as do the inhabitants of the dwellings. The photographs, although not synchronized with the text, appear on facing pages and combine with it to make a larger statement than would be possible from either medium used alone—a statement about America and its people and their place in the changing world. Fences, privies, and churches are among the other artifacts pictured on unnumbered pages and bearing a poetic relationship to the human characters described in the text; it is up to the reader to determine the truths thereby conveyed.

God's Country and My People, more autobiographical yet less nostalgic than its predecessors, suggests present-day values and their usefulness to a later generation. *Love Affair*, utilizing color photographs taken in Venice in 1969, presents the problem of "shouting" that everything is of interest, while the black and white pictures of the photo-texts of the plains are more selective in their emphasis. Morris has also published several collections of photographs: *Wright Morris: Structures and Artifacts, Photographs, 1933-1954* (1975), *Photographs and Words* (1982), and *Picture America* (1982). A meditation on photography and writing, *Time Pieces: Photographs, Writings, and Memory*, appeared in 1989.

Morris's books of essays include *The Territory Ahead* (1958, 1963), a work of criticism expressing his admiration for the artistry of Henry James and the vitality of D. H. Lawrence, and his concern about the misuse of the past by sentimental illustrators or writers. *A Bill of Rites, a Bill of Wrongs, a Bill of Goods* (1968) contains more critical essays deploring the practices of professional reviewers, of speed readers, and of symbol hunters, and the passing of the reader who simply wants to establish a dialogue with the writer. The writer's duty, says Morris, is to bring the real world into a field of vision that will give it meaning and to stir the readers' imagination. In this sometimes angry book, Morris also denounces advertising, which has created the consumer culture with its longing for possessions, and technological expertise, which allows humankind to explore space without at all improving life on Earth. In his third book of essays, *About Fiction* (1975), Morris describes the ideal reader, discusses point of view, and compares realism with "fabulation"—a more artistic, shapely, idea-filled narrative, exemplified by the works of John Barth, Thomas Pynchon, and Vladimir Nabokov. *Earthly Delights, Unearthly Adornments* (1978) surveys his own career and the course of American writing through quotations, recollections, and pictures. Perhaps the best summation of these books of essays is to be found in the subtitle of *About Fiction*, *Reverent Reflections on the Nature of Fiction with Irreverent Observations on Writers, Readers, and Other Abuses.*

Morris's other works include an anthology, *Wright Morris: A Reader* (1970), which contains two short novels, *The Works of Love* and *The Field of Vision*, two short stories, and selections from eight other novels. *Real Losses, Imaginary Gains* (1976) is a collection of thirteen short stories; another volume of Morris's short fiction appeared in 1986, *Collected Stories: 1948-1986*. The memoir *Will's Boy* (1981) was followed by two other autobiographical works: *Solo: An American Dreamer in Europe, 1933-1934* (1983) and *A Cloak of Light: Writing My Life* (1985).

ACHIEVEMENTS

While a few of Morris's books have European settings, he is most effective when writing about his native Nebraska and characters returning home to try to recapture memories or relive the past. That Morris was unusually concerned with his craft is evidenced by his several books of essays on the writing of fiction and the readers thereof. A prolific writer, Morris was primarily a delineator of character, rather than a constructor of intricate plots. He pays considerable attention to the "artifacts" of his characters' worlds and to the workings of their minds, most particularly to the kinds of thoughts that are never expressed aloud.

Morris is inevitably compared to both James Agee and Walker Evans because of his poetic, reflective prose about the dignity of rural life and because his

(Jo Morris)

photography is reminiscent of Evans's in *Let Us Now Praise Famous Men* (1960). Morris combines the talents of both men in his photo-texts, conducting a search for the meaning of America through word and picture.

Although Morris always received critical acclaim, he did not enjoy a popular success. Robert Knoll suggested that the reason may be Morris's failure to involve the reader in the exciting events of his fiction. He rather invites the reader casually, as did Robert Frost, to come along and clear the leaves away. His poetic style is as far removed as prose can be from the popular journalistic narrative mode. Although Morris knew that readers do not want fictive distance, he created novels that question rather than confess, that disturb rather than reassure.

Morris received three Guggenheim awards, two of them for photography and the third for fiction (*The Deep Sleep*), the National Book Award for *The Field of Vision* and *Plains Song, for Female Voices*, and the National Institute for Arts and Letters Award for *Ceremony in Lone Tree*. He received a National Institute Grant in 1960 and was fiction judge for the National Book Award in 1969.

BIOGRAPHY

After his birth in Central City, Nebraska, Wright Marion Morris lived with his father in Schuyler, Kearney, and other small Nebraska towns along the Platte River before moving to Omaha. (His mother died six days after his birth.) He worked for two summers on his uncle Harry's farm in Norfolk, Nebraska, but the move to Chicago in 1924 brought him a different kind of employment at the YMCA. He attended college in California for five weeks, then worked for several months on the Texas ranch of his uncle Dwight Osborn. He entered Pomona College in Claremont, California, but withdrew to spend a year in Austria, Italy, Germany, and France. He had written some brief prose sketches while at Pomona, and he returned to California to begin his first novel.

Morris married Mary Ellen Finfrock of Cleveland, Ohio, in 1934. Between 1935 and 1938, he wrote two novels and the sketches for *The Inhabitants* and developed the interest in photography which flourished during two summers at Wellfleet, Massachusetts. In 1940-1941, he toured the United States, taking pictures to be used in *The Inhabitants*. He lived in California two more years before moving to Haverford, Pennsylvania, in 1944. In 1954, he began spending more time in Venice, Italy, Mexico, and Greece, returning intermittently to California. He lectured at the University of Southern California and at Amherst College and taught at California State University, Los Angeles. He was a professor of English at San Francisco State University from 1962 until his retirement in 1975.

In 1961, he and his first wife were divorced, and Morris married Josephine Kantor. He was selected in 1983 to occupy the Visiting Writers' Chair at the University of Alabama. In 1992, an exhibit of Morris's photography was held in San Francisco. Morris died of unreported causes in Mill Valley, California, where he had lived since the early 1960's, on April 26, 1998. In the obituary in *The New York Times*, Ralph Blumenthal noted that Morris is "often called one of the nation's most unrecognized recognized writers."

ANALYSIS

A novelist who has been read more—and surely appreciated more—in Europe than in his own country, Wright Morris explored the legacies of heroism and nostalgia, the dreams and delusions examined by earlier twentieth century American writers. Another concern of Morris, whose novels seldom display violence, is the rise of violence in America. His narratives often take place within a twenty-four-hour time period, suggesting the capture of a finite period of time as the photographer captures a finite space with his camera. This limitation of time unifies Morris's novels, which are more intimately related by the device of recurring characters. Indeed, David Madden and other critics have suggested that one must read Morris's entire canon in order to understand any one novel.

The spirit of place, whether it be the central plains, a California beach, a Philadelphia suburb, or an Alpine chateau, is central to Morris's novels, and the impingement of objects or places upon humanity a major facet of Morris's imagination, as they had been to Henry James, who believed that places gave out a "mystic meaning." Admittedly influenced by James and by D. H. Lawrence, Morris was his own man for five prolific decades. Fortunate to have as his birthplace the "navel of the universe," the central United States, from that vantage point he "salvaged" meaningful artifacts that represent an earlier American life and, concomitantly, the values of that life.

Accused by Alfed Kazin of overloading his fiction with symbols, Morris disavowed any conscious symbolic creation, noting that symbols may appear without the author's deliberate intent in any good work of fiction. Obsessed by the cliché, which he considers a dead repository for something once alive, he peoples his fiction with stereotypes and challenges himself to bring them back to life. Wayne Booth described Morris's transformation of clichés as "toying" with them. David Madden saw the characters' coming to terms with clichés as absolutely essential to their knowledge of the enjoyment of love, sex, their bodies—even of travel. He added that after Morris, clichés are never the same, because they are killed and resurrected in the same moment, reappearing in an improved form.

It is not easy to generalize about an oeuvre as varied as Morris's, but he does frequently disregard chronology, an attempt to possess time and understand it being one of his obsessions. A recurring relationship, as Madden pointed out, is that of the hero and his "witnesses"—the characters who are transformed because their lives have intersected his. The contact, strangely enough, is often more meaningful after the death of the hero. Wayne Booth noted that the novels of Morris begin with a problem or a misunderstanding and conclude with a solution or a clarification. While this statement could be made about most plots, it is not the beginnings and the endings that occupy Morris's inventive mind, but what is in between. The resolutions that he works toward require especially appropriate intervening incidents that require "a lot of doing." Morris, added Booth, thinks of his introductions not as promises to the reader, but as problems to be solved by the author himself. What is important in this kind of plot progression is the quality of the middle, and here Morris excels.

Believing that the fiction writer must do more than reproduce facts, Morris transmutes his raw material, particularly his experience of the Midwest, through his imagination into something that he sees as more real than life itself.

MY UNCLE DUDLEY

My Uncle Dudley, Morris's somewhat autobiographical first novel, concerns an odyssey in an old Marmon touring car from California to the banks of the Mississippi. The central character, Uncle Dudley, a cross between a modern-day Odysseus and Don Quixote, describes himself as a "horseless knight." His impossible dream of committing one single audacious act is realized when he spits a stream of brown tobacco juice accurately into the eye of a sadistic, perverted policeman.

What is experimental about this novel is the use of the unnamed adolescent narrator, known only as the Kid, who records no emotion at all, thereby enabling the author himself to remain detached. As Madden noted, the heroic act requires a witness. The Kid is Uncle Dudley's witness, through whose imagination the reader recognizes heroism and an unexpressed affection.

Morris acknowledges a debt to Mark Twain's *The Adventures of Huckleberry Finn* (1884), although he had not then read the Twain work "as a writer." The Kid is the Huck figure, Uncle Dudley the Jim-father, and the journey in the Marmon a flight from repressive civilization similar to the downriver trip of the raft. The unifying element in Morris's narrative is not the river or the road, however, but Uncle Dudley himself, whose final foolhardy act qualifies him as the first in a long line of heroes.

THE MAN WHO WAS THERE

Agee Ward, the "protagonist" of *The Man Who Was There*, has gone to war and has been reported missing in action; he makes his presence felt through his absence, and is a hero not of action, as was Uncle Dudley, but of imagination. In the novel's first section, he is remembered at Grandmother Herkimer's funeral by Private Reagan, a boyhood friend, whose stare causes the minister to change his sermon subject to the desire for immortality. The middle section of the book, entitled "The Three Agee Wards," represents the hero through the media of family photographs, sketches, and letters, through knowledge about his ancestors, and through the mind of the village barber, who has seen him in the eyes of his now deceased mother. Her gravestone inscription announces, "She died that he might live."

The unity of the novel results from the hero's power to transform others. Agee has become a painter and a writer, whose notebooks contain drawings of such artifacts as a pump and a privy; his perspective is faulty because his memory fails and because he cannot reconcile the real and the imaginary in his own mind.

The last witness to be transformed is his spinster landlady Gussie Newcomb, who becomes Agee's symbolic next-of-kin when she is notified by the War Department that he is missing. She barely remembers her lodger, but when the people who do remember him want to look at his belongings, Gussie moves into the apartment herself. Peter Spavic, who has kept up Agee's album, and who is obviously a witness, enables Gussie to absorb Agee's personality, the transformation assisted by her communion with the missing man's personal artifacts. Gussie begins to drink, to tell Agee jokes, to dress in some of his costumes, and to take the initiative in her relationship with her suitor, Mr. Bloom. She sits in the dark, as Agee had sat, and she agrees with Peter to name his first son Ward while she will name her first child Agee.

The book explores an idea which was then a cliché: the effect of a dead or missing-in-action soldier on those left at home. Agee, a hero in the literal sense because he actually wants to combat Fascism, transforms his witnesses by his very absence, at the same time suggesting the problems of an artist who tries to filter reality through his imagination.

MAN AND BOY

The first few chapters of Morris's novel *Man and Boy* have been widely anthologized, with slight changes, as the short story "The Ram in the Thicket." The first of Morris's novels to depart from the plains tradition, *Man and Boy* takes place in Philadelphia and New York and describes a single day in the life of the remnants of a family. The Navy is to name a destroyer in honor of the Boy, who has died a hero. His father Warren recollects the day he gave the Boy an air rifle, a gift which caused his mother to abolish Christmas henceforth and the Boy to become a hunter, who perhaps wanted to die. Recalling the diverse impressions of Agee Ward in *The Man Who Was There*, the Boy Virgil appears to his parents in different ways, transforming them both, but not improving their relationship.

Warren Ormsby, the Man, is a westerner who boasts that his pioneer grandfather used to eat three rabbits as a meal. He soon learns, however, that his wife Violet is not very "feminine." She has, in fact, appropriated to herself the virtues once attributed to pioneer men. Warren has to call her "Mother" and allows her to dominate the household. She rids the house of germs and bathroom sounds, and even of conversation. While Ormsby cares for the birds in a way that is to him a form of worship, a "Eucharist," Mother insists on calling them by their Latin names. After the Boy is dead, he appears to his father in a dream, wearing "bright, exotic plumage" and accompanied by a flock of birds. When the father tries to join the birds, they attack him. Even in his dream, he

recognizes the Mother's effort to destroy the Boy's love for his father, who has been systematically unmanned by Mother.

Indirectly responsible for her son's death, Mother is selected to christen the boat named for her son; thus ironically ensuring the continuation of killing, to which she has been so opposed. The Boy lives on in the imagination of the Man, but Mother's power may extend over that realm eventually; it has embodied the sanitized house and defeated the United States Navy on the day of the ceremony.

THE WORKS OF LOVE

Morris has admitted that he gave an inordinate amount of time to writing *The Works of Love*. In his first novel, he had set out to make a hero of a nonheroic figure, in the second to allow a man who was not present to dominate the action, and in the third, to allow a man to be dominated by a ruthless female, who finally won his grudging respect, if not admiration. In the fourth novel, the protagonist, Will Brady, learns to love in a prodigious, self-conscious, almost methodical manner, even though he has not himself been loved or found suitable recipients for his own works of love. The self-centered women in his life have not appreciated his fumbling, inarticulate efforts at communication. Two of them have been prostitutes, one of whom laughed when he proposed marriage; the other ran away and mailed him another man's baby son to adopt. After his marriage to the widow Ethel Bassett, who sleeps like a mummy tightly wrapped in a sheet, he lies beside her listing in his incipiently loving mind her reasons for doing so. The last woman to whom he tries to become a father-husband is a cigar-counter girl turned alcoholic streetwalker. In an effort to understand and grow closer to his adopted son Willy, Will searches the pages of Booth Tarkington's *Penrod* (1914) and Mark Twain's *The Adventures of Tom Sawyer* (1876) for enlightenment. His final role, that of a department store Santa Claus, allows him to touch and love little children, at the same time distributing some of the works of his abundant love.

Will handles the eggs that he sells with the same gentle touch that he reserves for women, sensing perhaps that both species contain the miracle of life. He is more at home, however, with the eggs than with the women, always a stranger in his own house. In his pursuit of love, he finally cuts himself off from all Midwestern, rural roots and heads for Chicago on a quest to fill his emotional void. His incapacity to receive love, his failure to understand himself, and especially his inability to communicate his feelings have set up an almost insurmountable barrier between Will and his love-objects. Significantly more at home in a hotel than in his house, he has, for most of his life, failed to connect with the rest of humankind.

THE DEEP SLEEP

In *The Deep Sleep*, Morris again presents a hero who has died, this time Judge Howard Porter. Porter's "witnesses" include the hired man Parson, who has worked for the Porter family for thirty years and loves the almost unlovable Mrs. Porter; the Judge's son-in-law Paul Webb, who gets to know him well just before the funeral, and the Judge's mother, who communicates by tapping her cane and never became acquainted with her son at all. Mrs. Porter had known her husband twice—once in the biblical sense, when their first child was conceived, and a second time just before the funeral, when she told their daughter Katherine that she missed him.

Paul Webb discovers that Mrs. Porter had not ruled her husband as iron-handedly as she had thought. Like Violet Ormsby's husband, the Judge had found a basement-toilet retreat where he stashed his whiskey. In addition, Paul discovers, Judge Porter had an attic hideout where he smoked cigars and admired his expensive Swiss watch, while he carried a cheap, loud, dollar watch in public. The artist Webb is objective enough to get a balanced picture of the Porter family as he studies the house, room by room. While his wife Katherine fears that he cannot show her mother the sympathy she deserves, the fact that the two finally arrive at the same conclusion about Judge and Mrs. Porter suggests that both are fair in their appraisal.

Like Gussie in *The Man Who Was There*, Webb takes on an additional characteristic of the dead man every time he gains a new insight. As Webb becomes the Judge's spiritual son, he reaches a better understanding of Mrs. Porter. The two watches become the artifacts that connect Webb and his mother-in-law, whose sense of order ("Never go to bed with dirty dishes in the house") leads to an understanding with daughter Katherine. Webb finds satisfaction in a compassionate act: He places the gold watch in the cabinet, where Mrs. Porter will have the pleasure of finding it herself.

David Madden explains that the novel's title refers to the deep sleep into which American males of the twentieth century have allowed themselves to fall. Like the sleep induced in Adam before God created Eve from his rib, it is so deep that the man never awakens. Woman is born; she dominates, and man sleeps on. That this is a twentieth century phenomenon is demonstrated in Morris's 1980 novel *Plains Song, for Female Voices*, whose character Cora carries out her wifely duties with such distaste that she bites herself on her wedding night. Her husband Emerson feels obliged to explain to the frontier doctor that Cora suffers from the bite of a horse; the uncomplaining Cora finds most of her life as a Nebraska farmwife distasteful, but rebellion never occurs to her.

THE HUGE SEASON

Another novel with a dead hero, *The Huge Season* is different because it is told from the single viewpoint of Peter Foley, a professor of classics in a small Pennsylvania college and himself a fully developed character. Foley attempts to escape the bondage of two experiences from the past. The first took place at Colton College in California: Foley shared a suite with several other young men, among them Charles Lawrence, a would-be great tennis player who has since committed suicide. The second experience was a single day spent in New York after one of his other suitemates, Jesse Proctor, testified before the Senate Committee on UnAmerican Activities.

Lawrence, the hero who affects all the other men, is another Midwesterner with an audacious grandfather. Lawrence himself tries to be audacious, both in the bullring and on the tennis court. He succeeds at tennis, not because he plays well, but because he wills himself to win. As is to be expected, the hero strongly influences the lives of his witnesses—three of them actually write books about him.

Foley finally frees himself from captivity by re-creating the past in his mind while wearing his hero's jacket around the house. As he achieves his own freedom, Foley at the same time understands more about America. The title of the novel refers to the past—the youth—that Foley realizes is over when he is released into the present. Lawrence, however, continues to live in the imagination of his witness, who has also acquired the tennis player's audacity.

LOVE AMONG THE CANNIBALS

The past, so important in *The Huge Season*, is missing in *Love Among the Cannibals*. Macgregor and Horter, two middle-aged Hollywood songwriters, take two girls to Acapulco, one a Memphis "chick" who reads Norman Vincent Peale, the other Eva the Greek. The story is about people who live to the tune of "What Next?," a song in progress when Horter and Eva meet. Their car, a fire-engine-red convertible with green leather upholstery, has a built-in record player. Macgregor, a true Hollywood cliché and composer of sentimental popular music, insists that what he is looking for in a woman is "the real thing." Horter, who writes clichéd lyrics because that is what Hollywood demands, persuades Billie, Eva, and Mac that they can write a Mexican musical if they have the proper setting. Mac and Billie find romance in Acapulco and swear to be true to each other, but Eva leaves with a ladybug-shaped biologist, Dr. Leggett.

The Hollywood beach with its suntan oil and portable radios symbolizes the artificial present with no traditions or values, the Mexican beach the real present, unspoiled, honest, and authentic. The two "artists" deal in clichés of the kind demanded by mass culture, but Horter recognizes that even clichés can be powerful. He is transformed in Mexico by the natural, physical powers of the Greek, who is unabashedly tanned all over. As he appreciates her vitality and audacity, he even considers returning to the life of a serious poet. He has been stripped to essentials and returned to a wholeness and a recognition of his past that bring with them a hope for the future.

THE FIELD OF VISION

Morris's critics generally agree that *The Field of Vision* and *Ceremony in Lone Tree*, both dealing with the same central characters, are his most successful novels. Both employ several narrators viewing the same events and interpreting them differently. The actions of the main character, Gordon Boyd, are witnessed by his best friend, Walter McKee. The two are in love with the same woman, but Lois chooses the more stable Walter.

In *The Field of Vision*, Nebraskans Gordon and Walter recall their experiences while attending a bullfight in Mexico. More than any Morris character, Gordon, a failed writer, is a prisoner of his past, formed by three pivotal events. As a boy, Gordon tries to walk on water but ends by trying to drag himself out in a feeble effort at convincing Walter he can at least swim. The second is Gordon's ripping the back pocket off Ty Cobb's pants during an exhibition baseball game in Omaha, yet another incident witnessed by Walter. When Walter introduces Lois, Gordon kisses her. They fall in love, but she marries Walter anyway, feeling constant guilt afterward. The passive, ineffectual Walter realizes how she feels but is unable to help her.

These events are repeated from several points of view until they take on almost mythic dimensions. The walk represents Gordon's penchant for audacity and accompanying failure. The pocket, which Gordon always carries with him, becomes a tattered emblem of his unattained dreams. The kiss suggests the characters' lack of romantic fulfillment, the kind of emotional austerity all too typical of the residents of Morris's Midwest. Gordon attempts an exorcism of sorts by tossing the imitation coonskin cap of McKee's young grandson into the bullring and lowering the boy, named Gordon, down to retrieve it.

CEREMONY IN LONE TREE

Ceremony in Lone Tree gathers four generations in a small Nebraska town, their birthday celebration for Lois's elderly father contrasting with a backdrop of contemporary violence. While an atomic bomb fails to go off at a Nevada testing site the day before, two other bombs have exploded: The nephew of one character runs down three bullies with his hot rod, killing two of them, and Charlie Munger murders ten people during a shooting spree in nearby Lincoln because he wants to be somebody. Morris's America seems capable of only two extremes of behavior: violence or enervating nostalgia. The protagonists have sunk into a stultifying slumber from which even irrational murder and the threat of nuclear annihilation cannot arouse them.

Gordon, accompanied by a tawdry young woman he calls Daughter, arrives to seek a final break with his past through dying a symbolic death. Walter, on the other hand, finally awakens from his deep sleep to stand up to his friend for the first time. Stirred to action by a subconscious recognition of her emotional paralysis, Lois fires her father's ancient six-shooter, the shot ironically causing the old man to drop dead on the morning of his ninetieth birthday. These acts seem to free the McKees from the past somewhat, though the novel, as is typical of Morris, ends ambiguously. *Ceremony in Lone Tree* is the most detailed of Morris's many explorations of the American need to free itself both from the tenacious hold of the past and the banality of the present so that the future can unfold without encumbrance.

PLAINS SONG, FOR FEMALE VOICES

After several decades of novels about women who dominated their men, lured them into sex, and left them, or married them and honeymooned shrouded in a sheet, Morris's *Plains Song, for Female Voices* should perhaps have redressed some grievances. Madge, however, the only happy wife in the novel, is content with being a bearer of children and smelling Fels-Naptha soap. Cora, a plain Ohio girl, who marries Emerson to move to Nebraska, becomes Madge's mother. Cora's world is Emerson's farm, and although she finds enjoyment only with her chickens and her garden, she never considers widening her horizon. Sharon Rose, Madge's cousin, is the modern woman and artist who shuns men altogether, finding her happiness in fleeing Nebraska for Chicago and music study. Sharon cannot understand her past and cannot understand why her relatives are content with their bleak lives, but she does attain a certain amount of self-knowledge.

Like so many of Morris's protagonists, Sharon tries to go home again. What startles her memory is not the paint scaling off Emerson's house but the absence of people. The dipper (a marvelous artifact) floats in a bucket of water, and Sharon smells

scorched ironing. Displeased that Madge's husband Ned refers to his car as a "good girl," Sharon becomes ill when Avery, who plans to be a veterinarian, chips tartar off the teeth of a Maltese cat with his thumbnail while she is at the dinner table. On the train on the way back to Chicago, however, Sharon is ashamed of disliking these friendly, decent people. She writes Madge's daughter to suggest that Blanche attend a private school for girls in Waukegan and spend her weekends in Chicago, because Sharon cannot bear the "thought of Blanche thick with child by some loutish youth."

When the pretty girl arrives, Sharon deliberately dresses her in a way to "emphasize her adolescence" so that the "idling males" will not be tempted to molest her. When she finds Blanche with a "beardless, oafish" young man, his arm about the girl's waist, she knows that her efforts to "citify" Blanche—actually to make her independent—have been in vain, and she allows her to return home to her daddy, whom she has missed a great deal.

Sharon finally teaches at Wellesley, more respected than liked by her students. On her last trip home for Cora's funeral, Madge's daughter Caroline assures Sharon that because of her example, the girls "don't get married anymore unless [they] want to." All that is left of her parents' farm is a pitted field of stumps. "There was nothing worth saving," says Caroline, who adds that she would never forgive Cora for her failure to complain about the hard farm life.

Funerals and eggs—an unlikely combination—continue to recur in Morris's fiction. Unlikely, until one realizes that, in a Morris novel, the dying will "connect" with and transform many characters, perhaps even achieving resurrection through them, and that eggs, important to Morris since his father sold them, represent not only a new and ongoing life but also the rural Midwest to which he returns again and again for his fictional world.

The wasteland motif, actually verbalized in some of the novels, is to be found in a society without imagination, as on the Los Angeles beach where women wear bathing caps that look like fake hair. The one who can deliver others from such a wasteland is a man or woman with a creative heart—an audacious artist who dares to transform the clichés of the past into the wonders of the present and future, who can convert the raw material of America into values that enable humanity to endure.

Sue L. Kimball, updated by Michael Adams

OTHER MAJOR WORKS

SHORT FICTION: *Green Grass, Blue Sky, White House*, 1970; *Here Is Einbaum*, 1973; *Real Losses, Imaginary Gains*, 1976; *Collected Stories: 1948-1986*, 1986.

NONFICTION: *The Inhabitants*, 1946; *The Territory Ahead*, 1958, 1963; *A Bill of Rites, a Bill of Wrongs, a Bill of Goods*, 1968; *God's Country and My People*, 1968; *Love Affair: A Venetian Journal*, 1972; *Wright Morris: Structures and Artifacts, Photographs, 1933-1954*, 1975; *About Fiction: Reverent Reflections on the Nature of Fiction with Irreverent Observations on Writers, Readers, and Other Abuses*, 1975; *Earthly Delights, Unearthly Adornments*, 1978; *Will's Boy*, 1981; *Photographs and Words*, 1982; *Picture America*, 1982; *Solo: An American Dreamer in Europe, 1933-1934*, 1983; *A Cloak of Light: Writing My Life*, 1985; *Time Pieces: Photographs, Writing, and Memory*, 1989.

MISCELLANEOUS: *Wright Morris: A Reader*, 1970.

BIBLIOGRAPHY

Bird, Roy K. *Wright Morris: Memory and Imagination*. New York: Peter Lang, 1985. Makes the case that the most rewarding elements of Morris's works are his authorial intrusions and meditations on the status and meaning of fiction. Draws extensively from Morris's critical and autobiographical writings to illustrate his creation of self-conscious narratives, especially in *The Fork River Space Project* and *Plains Song, for Female Voices*. This perceptive study includes a bibliography and an index.

Knoll, Robert E., ed. *Conversations with Wright Morris: Critical Views and Responses*. Lincoln: University of Nebraska Press, 1977. This excellent collection contains three analyses of Morris's work, four interviews with him, an essay by Morris, a selection of his photographs, the most exten-

sive bibliography available which includes reviews of his books, and an index.

Madden, David. *Wright Morris*. New York: Twayne, 1964. This first book-length analysis of Morris is still the best and lays the groundwork for all further study, examining his works through *Cause for Wonder*. Madden, who has written several later essays about Morris, believes him to be the most thoroughly American contemporary writer and shows how the brilliance of his style transforms the ordinary into art. Includes a lengthy annotated bibliography, a chronology, and an index.

Wydeven, Joseph J. "Images and Icons: The Fiction and Photography of Wright Morris." In *Under the Sun: Myth and Realism in Western American Literature*, edited by Barbara Howard Meldrum. Troy, N.Y.: Whitston, 1985. This lengthy essay is the best examination of the relation between Morris's photography and his fiction. Shows how he explores the complex relation between the reality and the myth of the American West. Six photographs are included.

_____. *Wright Morris Revisited*. New York: Twayne, 1998. A scholar who has written often about Morris updates Madden's study.

TONI MORRISON

Born: Lorain, Ohio; February 18, 1931

PRINCIPAL LONG FICTION

The Bluest Eye, 1970
Sula, 1973
Song of Solomon, 1977
Tar Baby, 1981
Beloved, 1987
Jazz, 1992
Paradise, 1998

OTHER LITERARY FORMS

Toni Morrison, primarily a novelist, edited *The Black Book* (1974), a collection of documents and articles on African American history compiled by Middleton Harris, and published a short story, "Big Box," in *Ms.* magazine (1980). Morrison's first play, *Dreaming Emmett* (1986), was commissioned by the New York State Writers Institute of the State University of New York. Morrison has written many essays, some of the most notable of which are "The Site of Memory" in *Inventing the Truth: The Art and Craft of Memoir*, edited by William Zinsser (1987), and "Unspeakable Things Unspoken: The Afro-American Presence in American Literature" (*Michigan Quarterly Review* 28 [Winter, 1989]: 1-34). "Honey and Rue," with lyrics by Toni Morrison and music by André Previn, was commissioned by Carnegie Hall for soprano Kathleen Battle and premiered in January, 1992. Another collection of essays, *Birth of a Nation'hood: Gaze, Script, and Spectacle in the O. J. Simpson Case*, was published in 1997.

ACHIEVEMENTS

Morrison is widely regarded as one of the most significant black American novelists to have emerged in the 1970's. Her novel *Sula* was nominated for the National Book Award in 1975. In 1977, *Song of Solomon* won the National Book Critics Circle Award. The former was a Book-of-the-Month Club alternate and the latter, a main selection. In 1988, *Beloved* was awarded the Pulitzer Prize, and in 1993, Morrison earned the Nobel Prize in Literature.

Morrison's fiction, especially *Song of Solomon*, has been compared to Ralph Ellison's *Invisible Man* (1952) for its mixture of the literal and the fantastic, the real and the surreal. Morrison has been praised for her use of language and for the sense of voice that emerges not only in her dialogue but also in the movement of her narratives. Morrison's novels are also remarkable for their sense of place, for the detailed, coherent physical worlds she creates. Finally, her fiction is noteworthy for its depiction of the deep psychic realities of women's experience.

(Maria Mulas)

BIOGRAPHY

Toni Morrison was the first black woman to receive the Nobel Prize in Literature. Morrison, whose father was a shipyard welder, was born the second of four children. In the first grade, she was the only black student and the only child able to read in her class. Her early literary influences included Leo Tolstoy, Gustave Flaubert, and Jane Austen. At Howard University, Morrison toured the South with the Howard University Players. She was married in 1958 and divorced in 1964. She has two children, Harold Ford and Slade Kevin.

Morrison received her B.A. in English and minored in classics. She taught at the State University of New York at Purchase as a professor of English from 1971 to 1972 and was the Albert

Schweitzer Chair in the Humanities at State University of New York at Albany from 1984 to 1989. Beginning in 1989, Morrison held the position of Robert F. Goheen Professor in the Council of the Humanities at Princeton University. Other positions include trustee of the National Humanities Center, cochair of the Schomberg Commission for the Preservation of Black Culture, and member of the American Academy and Institute of Arts, the American Academy of Arts and Sciences, the National Council on the Arts, the Authors Guild, and the Authors League of America. Morrison became a popular public lecturer, focusing on African American literature.

ANALYSIS

In all of her fiction, Toni Morrison explores the conflict between society and the individual. She shows how the individual who defies social pressures can forge a self by drawing on the resources of the natural world, on a sense of continuity within the family and within the history of a people, and on dreams and other unaccountable sources of psychic power.

THE BLUEST EYE

In *The Bluest Eye*, Morrison shows how society inflicts on its members an inappropriate standard of beauty and worth, a standard that mandates that to be loved one must meet the absolute "white" standard of blond hair and blue eyes. Morrison's narrator says that two of the most destructive ideas in history are the idea of romantic love (canceling both lust and caring) and the idea of an absolute, univocal standard of beauty.

In the novel, the most extreme victim of these destructive ideas is Pecola, who finds refuge in madness after she has been thoroughly convinced of her own ugliness (confirmed when she is raped by her own father, Cholly). Mrs. Breedlove, Pecola's mother, is another victim who gets her idea of an unvarying standard of beauty from romantic motion pictures which glorify white film stars. When she realizes the impassible gap between that ideal and her physical self (she has a deformed foot and two missing teeth), she also gives up any hope of maintaining a relationship with Cholly, her husband, except one

of complete antagonism and opposition. Mrs. Breedlove even comes to prefer the little white girl she takes care of at work to her own daughter, Pecola, whom she has always perceived as ugly.

The ideal of unattainable physical beauty is reinforced by the sugary, unattainable world of the family depicted in the school readers—of Mother and Father and Dick and Jane and their middle-class, suburban existence. The contrast between that false standard of life and the reality lived by the children makes them ashamed of their reality, of the physical intimacy of families in which the children have seen their fathers naked.

Although Pecola is thoroughly victimized, Freida and Claudia MacTeer, schoolmates of Pecola, do survive with some integrity and richness. Freida seems to accept Shirley Temple as the ideal of cuteness, but her sister Claudia, a center of consciousness in the novel, responds with anger and defiance, dismembering the hard, cold, smirking baby dolls she receives at Christmas. What Claudia really desires at Christmas is simply an experience of family closeness in the kitchen, an experience of flowers, fruit, and music, of security.

Claudia's anger at the white baby dolls springs from a conviction of her own reality and her own worth. In defense of her own individuality, Claudia rejects Shirley Temple and "Meringue Pie," the high yellow princess, Maureen Peal. It is that defense of her own reality that makes Claudia sympathize with Pecola and try to defend her, even to the point of sacrificing Freida's money and her own.

Claudia is especially puzzled and regretful that nobody says "poor baby" to the raped Pecola, that nobody wants to welcome her unborn baby into the world. It would be only natural, "human nature," it seems, for people to sympathize with a victim and rejoice at the creation of a human life. Instead, the springs of human sympathy have been dammed up by social disapproval. Suffering from the self-hatred they have absorbed from the society around them, the black community maintains inflexible social standards and achieves respectability by looking down on Pecola. The two MacTeer sisters appeal to nature to help Pecola and her unborn baby, but nature fails them just as prayer did: No marigolds sprout and grow that year. The earth is unyielding. The baby is stillborn. Eventually, even the two girls become distanced from Pecola, whose only friend is an imaginary one, a part of herself who can see the blue eyes she was promised. Pecola functions as a scapegoat for the society around her, and Claudia's sympathy later grows into an understanding of how the community used Pecola to protect themselves from scorn and insult. What finally flowers in Claudia is insight and a more conscious respect for her own reality.

SULA

Sula also explores the oppressive nature of white society, evident in the very name of the "Bottom," a hillside community which had its origin in the duplicitous white treatment of an emancipated black slave who was promised fertile "bottom land" along with his freedom. In a bitterly ironic twist, the whites take over the hillside again when they want suburban houses that will catch the breeze. In taking back the Bottom, they destroy a place, a community with its own identity. In turn, the black community, corrupted by white society, rejects Sula for her experimenting with her life, for trying to live free like a man instead of accepting the restrictions of the traditional female role.

Sula provokes the reader to question socially accepted concepts of good and evil. As Sula is dying, she asks her girlhood friend Nel, "How do you know that you were the good one?" Although considered morally loose and a witch by the townspeople, the unconventional Sula cannot believe herself to be an inferior individual. Contrasting the traditional role of mother and church woman that Nel has embraced, Sula's individuality is refreshing and intriguing. Despite her death, Sula maintains an independence that ultimately stands in proud opposition to the established network of relationships that exist within conventional society.

The novel shows that the Bottom society encompasses both good and evil. The people are accustomed to suffering and enduring evil. In varying degrees, they accept Eva's murder of her drug-addict son, Plum, and Hannah's seduction of their husbands, one after another. The community, nevertheless, can-

not encompass Sula, a woman who thinks for herself without conforming to their sensibilities. They have to turn her into a witch, so that they can mobilize themselves against her "evil" and cherish their goodness. Without the witch, their goodness grows faint again. Like Pecola, Sula is made a scapegoat.

Growing up in the Bottom, Sula creates an identity for herself, first from the reality of physical experience. When she sees her mother Hannah burning up in front of her eyes, she feels curiosity. Her curiosity is as honest as Hannah's admission that she loves her daughter Sula the way any mother would, but that she does not like her. Hearing her mother reject her individuality, Sula concludes that there is no one to count on except herself.

In forging a self, Sula also draws on sexual experience as a means of joy, as a means of feeling sadness, and as a means of feeling her own power. Sula does not substitute a romantic dream for the reality of that physical experience. She does finally desire a widening of that sexual experience into a continuing relationship with Ajax, but the role of nurturing and possession is fatal to her. Ajax leaves, and Sula sickens and dies.

A closeness to the elemental processes of nature gives a depth to the lives of the Bottom-dwellers, although nature does not act with benevolence or even with consistency. Plum and Hannah, two of Eva's children, die by fire, one sacrificed by Eva and one ignited by capricious accident. Chicken Little and several of those who follow Shadrack on National Suicide Day drown because acts of play go wrong and inexplicably lead to their destruction. Sula's supposed identity as a witch is connected to the plague of robins that coincides with her return to the Bottom. The people of the Bottom live within Nature and try to make some sense of it, even though their constructions are strained and self-serving.

On one level, Sula refuses any connection with history and family continuity. Her grandmother Eva says that Sula should get a man and make babies, but Sula says that she would rather make herself. On the other hand, Sula is a descendant of the independent women Eva and Hannah, both of whom did what they had to do. It is at least rumored that Eva let her leg be cut off by a train so that she could get insurance money to take care of her three children when BoyBoy, her husband, abandoned her. When her husband died, Hannah needed "manlove," and she got it from her neighbors' husbands, despite community disapproval. In their mold, Sula is independent enough to threaten Eva with fire and to assert her own right to live, even if her grandmother does not like Sula's way of living.

To flourish, Morrison suggests, conventional society needs an opposite pole. A richness comes from the opposition and the balance—from the difference—and an acceptance of that difference would make scapegoats unnecessary. The world of the Bottom is poorer with Sula dead and out of it.

SONG OF SOLOMON

In *Song of Solomon*, Morrison again traces the making of a self. The novel is a departure for Morrison in that the protagonist is not female, but a young man, Milkman Dead. Milkman grows up in a comfortable, insulated, middle-class family, the grandson of a doctor on his mother's side and the son of a businessman, whose father owned his own farm. Son of a doting mother, Milkman is nursed a long time, the reason for his nickname, and is sent to school in velvet knickers. Guitar Baines, a Southside black, becomes Milkman's friend and an ally against the other children's teasing.

As the novel progresses, though, and as Milkman discovers the reality of his family and friends as separate people with their own griefs and torments, Milkman comes to feel that everyone wants him dead. Ironically, Milkman's last name actually is "Dead," the result of a drunken clerk's error when Milkman's grandfather was registering with the Freedmen's Bureau.

Milkman learns that his mere existence is extraordinary, since even before his birth, his father tried to kill him. Milkman survived that threat through the intercession of his mother and, especially, of his aunt, Pilate, a woman with no navel. After having been conjured by Pilate into making love to his wife again, years after he had turned against her, Macon Dead wanted the resulting baby aborted. Ruth, the baby's mother, out of fear of her husband, took measures to bring about an abortion, but Pilate intervened again and helped Ruth to find the courage to save the child and bear him.

In the present action of the novel, Hagar, Milkman's cousin, his first love and his first lover, pursues him month after month with whatever weapon she can find to kill him. Hagar wants Milkman's living life, not his dead life, but Milkman has rejected her, out of boredom and fear that he will be maneuvered into marrying her. At this point, he does not want to be tied down: He wants freedom and escape.

Hagar, like Pecola of *The Bluest Eye*, feels unlovely and unloved, rejected because Milkman does not like her black, curly hair. Pilate says that Milkman cannot *not* love her hair without *not* loving himself because it is the same hair that grows from his own body. Hagar is another victim of an absolutely univocal standard of beauty, and she is a character who needs a supporting society, a chorus of aunts and cousins and sisters to surround her with advice and protection. Instead, she has only Pilate and Reba, grandmother and mother, two women so strong and independent that they do not understand her weakness. Unhinged by Milkman's rejection of her, Hagar chases Milkman with various weapons, is repeatedly disarmed, and finally dies in total discouragement.

Trying to find out about his family's past, Milkman travels to Virginia, to Shalimar, a black town, where the men in the general store challenge him to fight, and one attacks him with a knife. Milkman does not understand why these people want his life, but they think he has insulted and denied their masculinity with his powerful northern money and his brusque treatment of them, by not asking their names and not offering his own.

The most serious threat to Milkman's life, however, turns out to be Guitar, Milkman's friend and spiritual brother. When Guitar tries to kill Milkman, he is betraying the reality of their friendship for the idea of revenge against whites and compensation for the personal deprivation he has suffered. Guitar thinks that Milkman has a cache of gold that he is not sharing with him, so he decides to kill him. Guitar rationalizes his decision by saying that the money is for the cause, for the work of the Seven Days, a group of seven black men sworn to avenge the deaths of innocent blacks at the hands of the whites.

Milkman's being alive at all, then, is a triumph, a victory that he slowly comes to appreciate after coming out of his comfortable shell of self-involvement. Unwillingly, Milkman comes to know the suffering and griefs of his mother and father and even his sisters Magdelene and Corinthians. The decisive experience in his self-making, however, is the quest for Pilate's gold on which his father sets him. In the first stage, the men are convinced that Pilate's gold hangs in a green sack from the ceiling of her house, and Guitar and Milkman attempt to steal it. The two friends succeed in taking the sack because the women in the house are simply puzzled, wondering why the men want a sack which is really full of old bones. In leaving the house, though, the two men are arrested, and Pilate must rescue them and the bones by doing an Aunt Jemima act for the white policemen. Milkman's father, Macon, is convinced that the gold still exists somewhere, and Milkman sets out to find it by going back to Pennsylvania, where Macon and Pilate grew up, and later to Virginia, where the previous generation lived.

Milkman's making of a self includes many of the archetypal adventures of the heroes of legend and myth. Like other heroes of legend, Milkman limps, with one leg shorter than the other, a mark of his specialness. Like Oedipus's parents, his parents try to kill him early in his life. There is a wise old lady who gives him help and advice. He goes on a quest for a treasure, and he hopes for gold and the hand of a beautiful princess. He solves a puzzle or riddle to achieve his quest and confirm his identity. He has a transcendent experience and reaches heights of prowess (he can fly). When his people turn against him, he gives his life for them.

Like *Sula*, too, Milkman creates a self from the reality of physical experience, the processes of nature, a connection to history and family continuity, and springs of human possibility through myth, dreams, legends, and other sources of psychic power. Milkman reaches an understanding of physical experience and the processes of nature in a struggle against the physical environment. As a rich city boy, Milkman

was insulated from nature, but in his trip south to try to get the gold, he overcomes a series of physical obstacles to reach the cave where Macon and Pilate in their youth encountered white people and gold. Milkman gets there only after falling into the river and climbing up twenty feet of rock, splitting his shoes and the clothes that mark him as a city man. During the trip, Milkman loses his possessions—trunk, clothes, and whiskey—and he makes it on his own, in a place where his father's name and father's money do not protect him. Milkman succeeds in finding Circe, who years ago sheltered Pilate and Macon when their father was killed, and he reaches the cave where there is no longer any gold.

Milkman also encounters nature as an obstacle to be overcome when, after the knife fight in Shalimar, he is invited to go on a coon hunt into the woods with the older men of Shalimar. Again, Milkman undergoes a test, having to move through the woods in the dark, having to show the courage and physical endurance necessary to be one of the hunters. Milkman also experiences the music of the hunt, the communication between the men and the dogs, the language before language, of a time when people were so close to their physical reality that they were in harmony with all creatures.

Milkman also creates himself in searching for his origins. In searching for his fathers, he discovers himself; like the Telemachus of Greek mythology and James Joyce's Stephen Dedalus, Milkman must find the reality of his fathers to know his own potential. Milkman's original pursuit of the gold seems to be an impulse he gets from his father, the man of business, and even from his father's father, who was a lover of property. The quest, however, changes as Milkman pursues it, finding the thread of his family's history. Stopping in Pennsylvania, Milkman hears the stories of the men who knew his father and grandfather and who rejoice in their successes. The story of the Dead family dramatizes the dream and the failure of that dream for blacks in America. When the older Macon Dead was killed by white men for his flourishing farm, the possibilities of his neighbors were narrowed and their lives scarred. Seeing his father and grandfather through their former neighbor's eyes helps Milkman to understand better the pride that Macon had when he said that his father had let Macon work side by side with him and trusted him to share in his achievements.

In Shalimar, Milkman also learns about his great-grandfather by piecing together the memories of people there and by deciphering the children's game and song, a song about Solomon and Rynah that seems to be interspersed with nonsense words. Milkman matches this song to a song that he had heard Pilate sing about Sugarman. He solves the riddle of the song, and he even figures out what the ghost of Pilate's father meant when he said, "Sing," and when he told Pilate to go get the bones. Finally, he discovers that his grandmother was an American Indian, Singing Bird, and that his great-grandfather, Solomon, was one of the legendary flying Africans, the father of twenty-one sons, a slave who one day flew back to Africa. His grandfather Jake had fallen through the branches of a tree when Solomon dropped him, trying to take his last baby son back with him. Learning about that magic enables Milkman himself to fly when he surrenders to the air and lets himself be upheld.

Milkman creates a self so that he can share it and even sacrifice it for a friend. With Pilate, Milkman buries the bones of Jake, his grandfather, on Solomon's Leap. Guitar, who has continued to stalk Milkman, shoots and kills Pilate, but Milkman, saying to Guitar, "Do you want my life? Take it if it is any good to you," leaps into the air and flies. Guitar is free to kill his friend, but Milkman soars.

The ending of the novel shows the transcendence of the spirit, as the hero achieves his destiny. The satisfaction of the ending, which also soars into legend, comes from the triumph of the human spirit, the triumph that even death cannot destroy. *Song of Solomon* is a beautiful, serious, funny novel that moves beyond the social to the mythic.

TAR BABY

Tar Baby explores three kinds of relationships: the relationship between blacks and whites; the relationships within families, especially between parents and children; and the relationship between the American black man and black woman. In the epigraph to the novel, Saint Paul reproaches the Corinthians for allowing contentions to exist among their ranks; the quote serves to foreshadow the discord that abounds in the novel's relationships.

In *Tar Baby*, Morrison depicts not a self-contained black society, but an onstage interaction between blacks and whites. The novel juxtaposes two families, a white family of masters and a black family of servants. The white family includes a retired candymaker, Valerian Street, and his wife Margaret, once the "Principal Beauty of Maine," who is now in her fifties. The couple's only son Michael lives abroad; his arrival for Christmas is expected and denied by various characters.

The black family consists of the husband, Sidney Childs, who is Valerian's valet and butler, and the wife, Ondine, who serves as cook and housekeeper. They are childless, but their orphan niece Jadine plays the role of their daughter. (Valerian has acted as Jadine's patron, paying for her education at the Sorbonne.)

The pivotal character, however, who enters and changes the balance of power and the habitual responses of the families, is a black man who rises out of the sea. His true name is Son, although he has gone by other aliases. The veneer of politeness and familiarity between the characters is shaken by Son's abrupt appearance. Uncomfortable racial and personal assumptions are put into words and cannot be retracted. The Principal Beauty is convinced that Son has come to rape her: What else would a black man want? (Jadine is convinced that if Son wants to rape anyone, it is she, not Margaret.) Sidney finds Son a threat to his respectability as a Philadelphia black because when Son appears, the white people lump all blacks together. Ondine seems less threatened, but most of her energy goes into her running battle with the Principal Beauty. Jadine is apprehensive at Son's wild appearance, and later she is affronted by his direct sexual approach. Only Valerian welcomes Son. He sees him as a vision of his absent son Michael, and he invites him to sit down at the dining table and be a guest.

Son's coming is the catalyst that causes time-worn relationships to explode when Michael does not come for Christmas. His failure to appear leads to the revelation that the Principal Beauty abused her son as a child, pricking him with pins and burning him with cigarettes. Ondine, the black woman, finally hurls this accusation at Margaret, the white, and makes explicit what the two women have known mutually since the beginning. Valerian, who has been haunted by the memory of Michael as a lonely child who would hide under the sink and sing to himself, is hit with a reality much harsher than he has known or admitted.

Structured as it is in terms of families, the whole novel revolves around family responsibilities, especially between parents and children. Michael Street does not come home for Christmas, but the abuse he suffered as a child seems to justify his absence. Thus, the undutiful mother Margaret has thrown the whole family off balance. In the black family, later in the novel, attention is drawn to the undutiful daughter Jadine, although it seems implied that she has learned this undutifulness, partly at least, from whites, wanting her individual success to be separate from family ties and responsibilities.

This undutifulness also springs from a question of identity. In Paris, even before she comes to Valerian's island, Jadine feels affronted by a beautiful, proud, contemptuous African woman in yellow, who buys three eggs and carries them on her head. She is herself and embodies her tradition consummately, exhibiting balance and physical grace which symbolize spiritual poise. Jadine feels diminished and threatened by the African woman, who spits at her. The scorn sends Jadine back to her family, Sydney and Ondine.

Jadine is similarly disturbed by her dream of the women with breasts, the mothers, who reproach her for not joining that chain of mothers and daughters who become mothers with daughters. Although Jadine herself is an orphan, reared by Ondine and Sydney and owing much to their care, she refuses to take the self-sacrificing role of the woman who cares for her family. Jadine wants money and the power it brings in the white world. After a little more modeling, she wants to run her own business, perhaps a boutique. Also, she may choose a white husband, like the man who bought her a seductive sealskin coat.

Jadine is the Tar Baby of the novel, and Son is Brer Rabbit from the Uncle Remus stories. As the Tar Baby, Jadine acts as a possible trap for Son set by his enemies, white society. Jadine, who has absorbed many white values, wants money and success. Son wants something purer, something associated with nature (he is associated with the sea and the beauty of the savannahs) and with family tradition. Nature, direct physical experience, and family traditions that are integral to personal identity are all important values in Son's existence. Son has a home—the completely black town of Eloe—and there he abides by the ideas of respectability held by his father and his Aunt Rosa. (He asks Jadine to sleep at Aunt Rosa's, apart from him, and he comes to her secretly only when she threatens to leave if he does not.) To amuse herself in the traditional town, in which she is uncomfortable, Jadine takes photographs of the people and steals their souls, stealing their individual beauty and grace. In the photographs, they seem graceless, poor, and stupid, even to Son, who usually sees them with loving eyes.

Individually, Son and Jadine love each other, but they seem unable to find a world in which they can both thrive. Yet Son is an undaunted lover, unwilling to let Jadine go, even when she flees from him. Son tries to return to Isle de Chevaliers, Valerian's island, to get news of Jadine, but the only way he can get there seems to be through the help of Thérèse, the half-blind, fifty-year-old black woman who says that her breasts still give milk. Thérèse takes him by boat to the island of the horsemen. Son has said that he cannot give up Jadine, but Thérèse tells him to join the fabled black horsemen who see with the mind. At the end of the novel, Son is running toward his destiny, whether that be Jadine and some way to make her part of his world or the black horsemen who ride free through the hills. Readers do not know what Son's fate is to be; they only know that Son is running toward it, just as Brer Rabbit ran from his enemy Brer Fox and from the Tar Baby. Like Milkman Dead at the end of *Song of Solomon*, Son leaps into mythic possibility; like Brer Rabbit, Son, the black man, is a figure with the power to survive.

BELOVED

In editing *The Black Book*, a collection of African American historical memorabilia, Toni Morrison discovered an article that would serve as the foundation of her fifth novel. *Beloved* is based on a true account of a runaway slave mother who, rather than allowing her children to be taken back into slavery, murders three of the four. As the novel begins, Sethe's sons, Buglar and Howard, have already run away, while Denver, the youngest child, survived the murder attempt and still lives with her mother in a house beset by her murdered sister Beloved's spirit. Morrison deliberately disorients the reader as she delves into the "interior life" of slavery, creating an experience similar to that of slavery, as the narrative breaks apart, shifts, and confounds. The author personifies 124 Bluestone Road as a tormented being when Beloved returns, emerging from a lake, fully clothed, the same age she would have been had she survived the infanticide. What the spirit wants initially is unclear. Morrison uses metaphorical imagery with tremendous skill, for example when describing Sethe's back, a relief map of scars from savage beatings, as resembling the branches of a chokecherry tree. When Paul D, a former slave whom Sethe once knew, moves in, Beloved wreaks havoc. The spirit behaves like an enraged toddler, but the damage she does is that of a full-grown woman. As the ghost continues to threaten her mother and sister, the characters' thoughts intertwine until one cannot be certain which character is which.

JAZZ

Toni Morrison intended *Jazz*, another novel inspired by a news article, to follow *Beloved* as the second of a trilogy, although the narrative does not pick up where *Beloved* ends. Joe Trace, a married man and cosmetics salesman, shoots his teen lover, Dorcas, at a party. She dies refusing to reveal his name. At her funeral, Violet, Joe's wife, a hairdresser, defaces the girl's corpse. Set in 1926, *Jazz* begins after Violet has cut the dead girl's face, twenty years after she and Joe arrived in Harlem from the South, where they scraped out a living as sharecroppers. After Dorcas's funeral, Violet returns home and releases her caged parrot, the only creature in her life who says "I love you" anymore. The deep, unrealized passion for human contact in *Beloved* takes root in *Jazz*, but it too becomes messy, dangerous, and out of control. Violet's mind unravels, and, strangely, she turns to Alice Manfred, Dorcas's aunt, for comfort. *Beloved*'s theme of mother loss, profound and frustrated, continues in *Jazz*: Dorcas's mother burns to death in an intentionally set fire; Violet's mother throws herself down a well from despair over not providing for her children. Years later, Violet longs so achingly for a child she considers stealing one. It is only at the end of *Jazz*, when Violet and Joe reconcile and Violet buys a sick parrot that she nurses back to health by playing jazz for it, that there is some hope of a lasting human connection.

PARADISE

Paradise, Morrison's seventh novel, like her previous two, was inspired by a little-known event in African American history, this time the 1970's westward migration of former slaves set on establishing their own all-black utopia, known in the book as Ruby. Shifting back and forth across a century of time, *Paradise* begins in 1976, when a group of the settlers' male descendants attack a mansion-turned-convent of women, convinced it is the women's eschewing of male companionship and their questionable pasts that threaten the town's survival. Ruby is founded as a response not only to white racism but also to other African Americans who turned away settlers for having skin that was "too black." Twin brothers Deacon and Steward, the town's elders, are deeply committed to keeping Ruby as pristine and trouble-free as possible. Together, they symbolize Ruby's twin identity and conscience.

Initially, the town has no crime and therefore needs no police. There is no hunger; everyone assists those in need. However, such total isolation from the outside world proves to be the town's undoing, as the rebellion of the 1960's youth movement seeps into Ruby. A ragtag group of women, most escaping either abusive relationships or responsibilities of motherhood, settle outside Ruby. Among others, there is Consolata, the maternal leader; Seneca, abandoned as a child by her teen mother; and Pallas, a white woman fleeing from her wealthy but negligent parents. The violent confrontation between the men of Ruby and the self-exiled women is, in part, brought on by the black men's anger at women who have willfully chosen a life without them. *Paradise* is a significant addition to Morrison's body of work.

Kate Begnal, updated by Nika Hoffman

OTHER MAJOR WORKS

PLAY: *Dreaming Emmett*, pr. 1986.

NONFICTION: *Playing in the Dark: Whiteness and the Literary Imagination*, 1992; *Birth of a Nation'hood: Gaze, Script, and Spectacle in the O. J. Simpson Case*, 1997.

CHILDREN'S LITERATURE: *The Big Box*, 1999 (with Slade Morrison and Giselle Potter)

EDITED TEXTS: *The Black Book*, 1974; *Race-ing Justice, En-gendering Power: Essays on Anita Hill, Clarence Thomas, and the Construction of Social Reality*, 1992.

BIBLIOGRAPHY

Bloom, Harold, ed. *Toni Morrison: Modern Critical Views*. New York: Chelsea House, 1990. A fine selection of criticism on Morrison, with an excellent introduction by Bloom and an extensive bibliography. *Beloved* is discussed in three essays by Margaret Atwood, Margaret Sale, and M. S. Mobley. The real gem, however, is an essay by Morrison herself in which she argues for inclusion of black literature in the canon of American literature.

Bruck, Peter, and Wolfgange Karrer, eds. *The Afro-American Novel Since 1960*. Amsterdam: B. R. Gruener, 1982. This compilation of essays on black authors includes a chapter on Morrison by Bruck, entitled "Returning to One's Roots: The Motif of Searching and Flying in Toni Morrison's *Song of Solomon*" (originally printed in 1977).

Furman, Jan. *Toni Morrison's Fiction*. Columbia: University of South Carolina Press, 1996. Part of the Understanding Contemporary American Literature series, this book addresses such topics as black womanhood, male consciousness, and community and cultural identity in Morrison's novels. Includes bibliography and index.

Harris, Trudier. *Fiction and Folklore: The Novels of*
Toni Morrison. Knoxville: University of Tennessee Press, 1991. A collection of essays that examine Morrison's novels from an African and African American mythological and folkloric perspective and examine the archetypes and antiheroes that pervade her stories. An important scholarly guide to understanding the subtext of Morrison's work.

Holloway, Karen F. C., and Stephanie A. Demetrakopoulos. *New Dimensions of Spirituality: The Novels of Toni Morrison*. New York: Greenwood Press, 1987. In this study, each author contributes individually with a common theme of spiritual development in Morrison's first four novels. Demetrakopoulos has a Jungian background and examines the archetypal feminine images of Morrison's heroines. The notes are themselves excellent secondary resources. The chapter "A Critical Perspective" provides valuable views on the criticism available on Morrison.

Kubitschek, Missy Dehn. *Toni Morrison: A Critical Companion*. Westport, Conn.: Greenwood Press, 1998. An excellent source of literary criticism. Contains bibliography and index.

McKay, Nellie Y., ed. *Critical Essays on Toni Morrison*. Boston: G. K. Hall, 1988. This volume, which is part of a series on American literature, firmly places Morrison on the list as one of the "most important writers in America." A compilation of reprinted essays by various authors, nine of which are original and written specifically for this publication. Also includes reviews, interviews, and literary criticism of Morrison's first four novels. A diverse and comprehensive work on Morrison. No bibliography.

Middleton, David L. *Toni Morrison: An Annotated Bibliography*. New York: Garland, 1987. The articles and essays by Morrison and the interviews with her listed here are arranged chronologically to present clearly the evolution of her ideas. Includes critical reviews of her fiction and a listing of honors and awards. Subject index provided. An indispensable guide.

Otten, Terry. *The Crime of Innocence in the Fiction of Toni Morrison*. Columbia: University of Missouri Press, 1989. In this groundbreaking study of

Morrison's first five novels, Otten explores the mythic substance in her writings by tracing the motif of the biblical fall. Insightful readings and unflagging attention to the historical and literary backdrop. A valuable guide to the increasing scholarship on Morrison.

Peach, Linden, ed. *Toni Morrison*. New York: St. Martin's Press, 1998. Focuses on interpretation and criticism of Morrison's works and examines African American women in literature. Provides bibliography and index.

Samuels, Wilfred D., and Clenora Hudson-Weems. *Toni Morrison*. Boston: Twayne, 1990. This study analyzes five of Morrison's novels, including *Beloved*. The authors explore common themes such as black folklore and mysticism in Morrison's writings. Contains excerpts from interviews.

IRIS MURDOCH

Born: Dublin, Ireland; July 15, 1919
Died: Oxford, England; February 8, 1999

PRINCIPAL LONG FICTION

Under the Net, 1954
The Flight from the Enchanter, 1956
The Sandcastle, 1957
The Bell, 1958
A Severed Head, 1961
An Unofficial Rose, 1962
The Unicorn, 1963
The Italian Girl, 1964
The Red and the Green, 1965
The Time of the Angels, 1966
The Nice and the Good, 1968
Bruno's Dream, 1969
A Fairly Honourable Defeat, 1970
An Accidental Man, 1971
The Black Prince, 1973
The Sacred and Profane Love Machine, 1974
A Word Child, 1975
Henry and Cato, 1976

The Sea, the Sea, 1978
Nuns and Soldiers, 1980
The Philosopher's Pupil, 1983
The Good Apprentice, 1985
The Book and the Brotherhood, 1987
The Message to the Planet, 1989
The Green Knight, 1993
Jackson's Dilemma, 1995

OTHER LITERARY FORMS

Iris Murdoch produced a considerable amount of work in areas other than fiction, particularly in the areas of literary criticism, drama, and, most important, philosophy. Her first book, *Sartre: Romantic Rationalist* (1953), was a critique of Jean-Paul Sartre's philosophy as it appears in his novels. She wrote three plays for the theater and adapted several of her novels for the stage. *The Servants and the Snow* was first performed at the Greenwich Theatre in 1970, and *The Three Arrows* at the Arts Theatre, Cambridge, in 1972; the two plays were published together in 1973 as *The Three Arrows, and The Servants and the Snow: Two Plays*. Another play, *Art and Eros*, was performed at the National Theatre in 1980. Murdoch collaborated with J. B. Priestley to adapt her novel *A Severed Head* for the stage in 1963 (published in 1964), and with James Saunders to adapt *The Italian Girl* in 1967 (published in 1969). *The Black Prince* has also been adapted for the stage and was performed at the Aldwych Theatre in 1989.

Murdoch also produced books on the subject of philosophy: *The Sovereignty of Good* (1970), which consists of three essays on moral philosophy, "The Idea of Perfection," "On 'God' and 'Good,'" and "The Sovereignty of Good Over Other Concepts"; and *The Fire and the Sun: Why Plato Banished the Artists* (1977), a study of Plato's objections to art and artists. Murdoch added to her work on Plato in the form of two "platonic dialogues" entitled "Art and Eros: A Dialogue about Art" and "Above the Gods: A Dialogue about Religion," which she combined in a 1986 book entitled *Acastos: Two Platonic Dialogues*. *Metaphysics as a Guide to Morals* appeared in 1992, and a collection of essays entitled *Existentialists and Mystics: Writings on Philosophy and Literature* was

(Thomas Victor)

published in 1997. She also published several philosophical papers in the Proceedings of the Aristotelian Society and other important articles on philosophy and aesthetics, including "The Sublime and the Good" (*Chicago Review*) and "The Sublime and the Beautiful Revisited" (*Yale Review*). Her best-known essay, "Against Dryness: A Polemical Sketch," which appeared in the January, 1961, issue of *Encounter*, is a work of literary criticism that urges a return to the capacious realism of the great nineteenth century novelists.

ACHIEVEMENTS

Murdoch, who is universally acknowledged as one of the most important novelists of postwar Britain, combined a prolific output with a consistently high level of fictional achievement. From the beginning of her career as a novelist, she was a critical and popular success in both Great Britain and the United States. In general, Murdoch is thought of as a "philosophical novelist," and despite her objections to this description, she attempted a fusion of aesthetic and philosophical ideas in her fiction. Including her first novel, *Under the Net*, published in 1954, she published twenty-six novels and received a variety of literary awards and honors. In 1973, she was awarded the James Tait Black Memorial Prize for Fiction for *The Black Prince* and in 1974 received the Whitbread Literary Award for Fiction for *The Sacred and Profane Love Machine*. *The Sea, the Sea* won the Booker Prize for Fiction in 1978. Murdoch became a member of the Irish Academy in 1970, an honorary member of the American Academy of Arts and Letters in 1975, and was awarded the honorary title of Commander of the British Empire in 1976. She was made a Dame of the Order of the British Empire in 1987, and in 1990 she received the Medal of Honor for Literature from the National Arts Club in New York.

BIOGRAPHY

Jean Iris Murdoch was born in Dublin, Ireland, on July 15, 1919, to Anglo-Irish parents, Wills John Hughes Murdoch and Irene Alice Richardson. The family later moved to London, where Murdoch attended the Froebel Education Institute; she finished her secondary education at the Badminton School, Bristol, in 1937. From 1938 to 1942, she attended Somerville College at Oxford University, studying classical literature, ancient history, and philosophy. After obtaining a first-class honors degree, she worked from 1942 to 1944 as the assistant principal in the British Treasury, and from 1944 to 1946 served as an administrative officer with the United Nations Relief and Rehabilitation Administration in England, Austria, and Belgium.

After the war, an interest in existentialism led Murdoch to turn her attention to philosophy. She was unable to accept a scholarship to study in the United States because she had become a member of the Communist Party while an undergraduate at Oxford, and instead attended Newnham College at Cambridge University from 1947 to 1948 after receiving the Sarah Smithson Studentship in philosophy. In 1948, she was made a fellow of St. Anne's College, Oxford, where she lectured in philosophy until 1963, when she was named an honorary fellow of the college. In 1956, she married John Bayley, the author of many books of literary criticism and many book reviews. For many years Bayley was the Thomas Warton Professor of English Literature at Oxford. He has also written several novels, including *The Queer Captain* (1995).

From 1963 to 1967, Murdoch lectured at the Royal College of Art in London, after which she stopped teaching to devote all her time to writing fiction and philosophy. Her novels have won many awards, including the Book of the Year Award from the Yorkshire *Post* (1969), the James Tait Black Memorial Prize (1974), and the Booker Prize (1978). Murdoch became a Commander of the Order of the British Empire (CBE) in 1976 and a Dame of the same order

(DBE) in 1987. Oxford University awarded her an honorary D. Litt. in 1987; Cambridge University followed in 1993. In 1992, she published her major philosophical work, *Metaphysics as a Guide to Morals*, a brilliant and sometimes garrulous survey of her ideas about many more topics than its title indicates. In 1997, many of her writings on philosophy and literature were collected in *Existentialists and Mystics*.

At one time Murdoch maintained a London flat in the Earls Court area, but she and her husband always had their primary residence in or near Oxford. In the mid-1990's, Murdoch was diagnosed as suffering from Alzheimer's disease. Her husband described their life together, including how they coped with her mental condition, in *Iris: A Memoir* (1998), published in the United States as *An Elegy for Iris* in 1999, the year Murdoch died.

ANALYSIS

A knowledge of Iris Murdoch's philosophical and critical essays is invaluable for the reader wishing to understand her fiction. Her moral philosophy, which entails a rejection of existentialism, behaviorism, and linguistic empiricism, informs her fiction throughout and provides a basis for an interpretation of both the content and the form of her work. Although early influenced by Sartrean existentialism, she developed a radically different view of the human condition. The major disagreement she had with the existentialist position is its emphasis on choice, a belief Murdoch characterizes as "unrealistic, over-optimistic, romantic" because it fails to consider the true nature of human consciousness and what she called "a sort of continuous background with a life of its own." Existentialism, which she called "the last fling of liberal Romanticism in philosophy," presents humanity with "too grand" a conception of itself as isolated from its surroundings and capable of rational, free choice. She describes this picture of humankind as "Kantian man-gods" who are "free, independent, lonely, powerful, rational, responsible, and brave." Although Murdoch denied being a Freudian, Sigmund Freud's "realistic and detailed picture of the fallen man" is much closer to her own conception of human nature, and she agreed with what she called Freud's "thoroughly pessimistic view" in which the psyche is described as an "egocentric system of quasi-mechanical energy" determined by its individual history; the natural attachments of this psyche are "sexual, ambiguous, and hard for the subject to control." The most important dimension of this description of the individual is his lack of rational free will, and Murdoch's statement in "Against Dryness" that "we are not isolated free choosers, monarchs of all we survey, but benighted creatures sunk in a reality whose nature we are constantly and overwhelmingly tempted to deform by fantasy" is perhaps her tersest summary of the human condition.

Murdoch's philosophical position is the basis for her choice of prose fiction as the most realistic literary genre. The novelist's advantage is his "blessed freedom from rationalism," and she saw the novel as the literary form which, because of its lack of formal restrictions, could best portray the "open world, a world of absurdity and loose ends and ignorance." Although she had reservations about modern literature and believed that the twentieth century novel tends either to be "crystalline" (self-contained, mythic, sometimes allegorical, and frequently neurotic) or "journalistic" (semidocumentary, descriptive, and factual), the nineteenth century novel as written by Leo Tolstoy, Jane Austen, and George Eliot remains the best example of how fiction can create free, independent characters who are not "merely puppets in the exteriorization of some closely-locked psychological conflict" of the author. The nineteenth century novel, because it "throve upon a dynamic merging of the idea of person with the idea of class," was not simply a representation of the human condition but rather contained "real various individuals struggling in society"; in other words, it presented characters *and* the "continuous background with a life of its own."

Murdoch believed that the most important obligation for the novelist is the creation of particularized, unique, and ultimately indefinable human beings, characters who move outside the novelist's consciousness into an independent ontological status. This aesthetic theory has its corollary in Murdoch's moral philosophy, in which she stresses the need for the individual to recognize the "otherness" of other individuals. The great novelist, like the "good" person, has an "apprehension of the absurd irreducible uniqueness of people and of their relations with each other," an apprehension she castigates Sartre for lacking. Recognition of otherness is, to a degree, dependent upon the individual's ability to "attend" to other individuals, a concept Murdoch derives from the philosophy of Simone Weil. Murdoch describes attention as a "patient, loving regard, directed upon a person, a thing, a situation" and believes that we *"grow by looking"*; morality, both for the individual and the novelist who is attempting a realistic portrayal of human beings in the world, is an endless process of attending to a reality outside the individual consciousness. Attention is seeing, "a just and loving gaze directed upon an individual reality," and as such is an effort to counteract "states of illusion" brought about by selfish fantasy. For Murdoch, attention is also another name for love, and "the ability to direct attention is love." Imaginative prose literature, Murdoch believed, is the best medium in which to focus attention on the individual because it is *par excellence* the form of art most concerned with the existence of other persons."

In "The Sublime and the Good," Murdoch defines love as "the perception of individuals. Love is the extremely difficult realization that something other than oneself is real. Love, and so art and morals, is the discovery of reality." She has also said that the main subject of her fiction is love, and her novels usually depict the difficulties involved in recognizing the uniqueness and independence of other human beings. In *The Bell*, the Abbess tells Michael Meade that "all of our failures are ultimately failures in love," a statement that neatly describes Murdoch's fictional world. The enemy of love in her novels is the propensity of the individual to fantasize and to create false pictures of reality, particularly distorted conceptions of other people. As a result, her novels frequently present situations in which characters are forced to confront the "otherness" of those around them, situations which often involve a realization of the past or present sexual involvements of other persons. The comfort and safety of the "old world," as it is called by many Murdoch characters, is destroyed by a discovery about the past or by characters suddenly falling passionately in love with each other. *A Severed Head*, in which Martin Lynch-Gibbon is shocked by a series of revelations about his wife and friends and falls precipitately and unpredictably in love with Honor Klein, is one of the best examples of this recurring pattern in Murdoch's work.

Murdoch believed that the experience of art can serve to shock the individual into an awareness of a reality outside the personal psyche, and her novels contain several scenes in which characters who gaze upon paintings are able to escape temporarily from solipsistic fantasy. Dora Greenfield in *The Bell*, Harriet Gavender in *The Sacred and Profane Love Machine*, and Tim Reede in *Nuns and Soldiers* each experience what Murdoch calls "unselfing" and Harriet Gavender describes as "not being myself any more"; in fact, Dora Greenfield notes that paintings give her "something which her consciousness could not wretchedly devour. . . . The pictures were something real outside herself." Murdoch, in "The Sublime and the Beautiful Revisited," calls art "spiritual experience" because it can bring out this radical change in perception, and in *The Fire and the Sun: Why Plato Banished the Artists*, she claims that in an unreligious age good art provides people with "their clearest experience of something grasped as separate and precious and beneficial and held quietly and unpossessively in the attention."

Murdoch's ambivalent attitudes about the role of art and artists are present in both her fiction and her philosophy. In an interview with Michael Bellamy, in *Contemporary Literature* (1977), she described art as a "temptation to impose from where perhaps it isn't always appropriate," and in the same discussion noted that "morality has to do with not imposing form, except appropriately and cautiously and carefully and with attention to appropriate detail." Murdoch suggested to several interviewers that the basis of her novels is what she calls the conflict between "the saint and the artist," or the dichotomy between the "truthful, formless figure" and the "form-maker." She mentioned Tallis Browne and Julius King in *A*

Fairly Honourable Defeat, Ann and Randall Peronett in *An Unofficial Rose*, and Hugo Belfounder and Jake Donaghue in *Under the Net* as examples. She believes that Plato's life exemplifies this conflict: "We can see played out in that great spirit the peculiarly distressing struggle between the artist and the saint." The true or "good" artist must avoid the "ruthless subjection of characters" to his will and should use symbolism judiciously in a "natural, subordinate way" that attempts to be "perfectly realistic." In her fiction, Murdoch's artist-figures are often demonic individuals who manipulate people in real life without regard for their well-being or independence as persons. Her "saint" figures have a corresponding lack of form, or sense of self, and are frequently unable or unwilling to act in any way. Douglas Swann's comment in *An Unofficial Rose* that "nothing is more fatal to love than to want everything to have form" is also true of Murdoch's attitude toward art.

Many of Murdoch's characters attempt to find form in their own lives in order to explain the apparent chaos that surrounds them. In her essay "Vision and Choice in Morality," Murdoch talks about the need at times to stress "not the comprehensibility of the world but its incomprehensibility" and says that "there are even moments when understanding *ought* to be withheld." In *The Flight from the Enchanter*, John Rainborough experiences a moment of joy when he feels "how little I know, and how little it is possible to know," but this happiness in a lack of knowledge is rare in Murdoch's fiction. In the same novel, Rosa Keepe, a much more representative Murdoch character, listens to the sound of the machines in the factory, hoping to hear a "harmonious and repetitive pattern," just as Michael Meade in *The Bell* expects to find "the emergence in his life of patterns and signs." At the end of the novel, he regretfully concludes that the apparent pattern he had observed in his life was merely his own "romantic imagination. At the human level there was no pattern."

The search for rational, discernible causal relationships is the major structuring principle in *An Accidental Man*, a novel concerned with the discovery of, in Gracie Tisbourne's words, "a world . . . quite without order." In "The Sovereignty of Good Over Other Concepts," Murdoch says that "there are properly many patterns and purposes within life, but there is no general and as it were externally guaranteed pattern or purpose of the kind for which philosophers and theologians used to search," and she has also stated her desire to write novels that, because they contain more of the contingent, accidental dimensions of life, are more realistic than "patterned" fiction.

Murdoch's reservations about form in life and art are paralleled by her suspicions about language. A fervent defender of literature and language who said in "Salvation by Words" that "words constitute the ultimate texture and stuff of our moral being. . . . The fundamental distinctions can only be made in words" and in *The Fire and the Sun* that "the careful responsible skillful use of words is our highest instrument of thought and one of our highest modes of being," Murdoch also voiced suspicions about the ironic nature of language, its potential to distort the truth and to create false pictures of reality. This distrust of language is evident in her first novel, *Under the Net*, and continued to inform her fiction. In this respect, Murdoch was greatly influenced by Ludwig Wittgenstein; direct references and sly, sometimes ironic allusions to Wittgenstein appear repeatedly in her novels.

In spite of these reservations, however, Murdoch mounts one of the most eloquent defenses of art and literature in modern times in *The Sovereignty of Good* and *The Fire and the Sun*. She claims in "The Sovereignty of Good over Other Concepts" that art "can enlarge the sensibility of its consumer. It is a kind of goodness by proxy," and in "On 'God' and 'Good,'" she asserts that art, rather than being any kind of playful diversion for the human race, is "the place of its most fundamental insight." According to Murdoch, literature is the most important art because of its unique ability to shed light on the human condition: "The most essential and fundamental aspect of culture is the study of literature, since this is an education in how to picture and understand human situations." This statement in "The Idea of Perfection" obviously places an enormous burden on the novelist, a burden which Murdoch's prolific output, technical virtuosity, and moral vision appear to be capable of bearing.

UNDER THE NET

Jake Donaghue, the narrator-protagonist of *Under the Net*, informs the reader early in the novel that the story's central theme is his acquaintance with Hugo Belfounder. The relationship between the two men illustrates Murdoch's philosophical and aesthetic concerns, for the Hugo-Jake friendship represents the saint-artist dichotomy; this "philosophical novel" allows her to explore the problem of theoretical approaches to reality, the issue of contingency, the realization of the otherness of individuals, and the ambiguities of language and art.

The character of Hugo Belfounder is based in part on that of the enigmatic Elias Canetti, winner of the Nobel Prize for Literature in 1981; the Bulgarian-born Canetti, who has lived in England since 1939, appears in various guises in several of Murdoch's early novels. Hugo, some of whose precepts also suggest the influence of Wittgenstein, is Murdoch's first "saint" figure, and he embodies many of the qualities of the "good" characters who appear later in her fiction. Hugo's saintliness is a result of his truthfulness and his lack of desire for form or structure in life and art. Opposed to him is Jake, who, fearing that he may actually tell the truth to Mrs. Tinckham about being evicted by Madge, delays telling his story until he can present it in a "more dramatic way . . . as yet it lacked form." Form, as Jake tacitly admits, is a kind of lying, an imposition of structure that distorts reality. Hugo, on the other hand, is attracted by the ephermerality and formlessness of the firework displays he has created, and he abandons them when they receive the attention of art critics who begin to classify his work into styles. Hugo is also characterized by a selflessness that Jake finds astonishing: It does not occur to him that he is responsible for the concepts discussed in Jake's book *The Silencer*, or that Anna Quentin's mime theater is based upon her interpretation of his beliefs.

The difference between the two men is also evident in their attitude toward theory. After his conversations with Hugo, Jake concedes that his own ap-

Unlike Rupert, who believes that his duty is to love others, Julius's attitude toward human beings is one of contempt, an emotion the narrator describes as "the opposite extreme from love: the cynicism of a deliberate contemptuous diminution of another person." One of the major reasons for his low valuation of people is the very quality that makes them vulnerable to his manipulation—their malleability, or, as he phrases it, the easiness with which they are "beguiled." In a conversation with Tallis, Julius says that most individuals, motivated by fear and egotism, will cooperate in almost any deception. The most obvious examples of his theory in *A Fairly Honourable Defeat* are Morgan Browne and Simon Foster. Morgan, titillated by Julius's boast that he can "divide anybody from anybody," first encourages him in his plan to separate Simon and Axel and later unknowlingly becomes one of his victims; Simon, afraid that Julius will destroy his relationship with Axel, unwillingly allows Julius to "arrange" a relationship between Rupert and Morgan. In fact, Julius's claim that he is an "artist" and a "magician" depends upon the moral weaknesses of the characters whose lives he carefully "plots."

Both Leonard Browne and Julius King mount verbal assaults on the world; in some respects, their diatribes sound remarkably similar. Like Leonard, Julius believes that the human race is a "loathesome crew" who inhabit a "paltry planet"; he goes further than Leonard, however, in his statement that human beings "don't deserve to survive," and, more important, in his desire to see the reification of his ideas. Julius's theory that people are merely puppets who need to be educated becomes, in practice, a tragedy. Although, like Hugo Belfounder, he claims that philosophy is the subtlest "method of flight" from consciousness and that its attempted truths are "tissues of illusions." In *Theories*, he is entranced with his own theorizing as is Rupert. Good, he says, is dull, and what passes for human goodness is a "tiny phenomenon" that is "messy, limited, truncated." Evil, by comparison, "reaches far far away into the depths of the human spirit and is connected with the deepest springs of human vitality." Good, according to Julius, is not even a "coherent concept; it is

unimaginable for human beings, like certain things in physics."

One of Murdoch's saintlike characters, James Tayper Pace in *The Bell*, also discusses the difficulty of comprehending goodness while he emphasizes the need for the individual to seek the good beyond the confines of his own consciousness: "And where do we look for perfection? Not in some imaginary concoction out of our own idea of our own character—but in something so external and so remote that we can get only now and then a distant hint of it." In "The Sovereignty of Good Over Other Concepts," Murdoch talks about contemplating goodness, and, like James Tayper Pace, defines it as "an attempt to look right away from self towards a distant transcendent perfection, a source of uncontaminated energy, a source of *new* and quite undreamt-of virtue." Unlike Pace and Murdoch, Julius is unwilling to waste his energies in the contemplation of a concept so "remote" and "transcendent" and is instead beguiled by the immediacy and vitality of evil.

Tallis Browne, the "saint" of *A Fairly Honourable Defeat*, is one of the strangest characters in Murdoch's fiction. Early in the novel, his wife Morgan, talking about the human psyche, complains that "it stretches away and away to the ends of the world and it's soft and sticky and warm. There's nothing real, no hard parts, no centre." This description of human consciousness also explains Morgan's dissatisfaction with her husband, who is completely lacking in the qualities she so admires in Julius King: form and myth. With Tallis, says Morgan, "there were no forms and limits, things had no boundaries"; he lacks any kind of personal "myth," while she characterizes Julius as "almost all myth." Like Julius, Tallis does not believe in theories, and at one point he correctly accuses Morgan of being "theory-ridden" and chasing "empty abstractions"; unlike Julius, however, he has no theories about human nature or behavior, a fact that Julius acknowledges when he tells Tallis that Rupert probably feels that "theorizing would be quite out of place with you." While Julius manipulates the relationships of those around him according to his ideas about human weakness and Rupert writes a text on morality and goodness, Tallis nurses his dying father and helps to feed and shelter the poverty-stricken immigrants in his neighborhood.

The formlessness of Tallis's goodness causes him to have no desire to analyze the tragedy of Rupert's death or to assign reasons or blame. He grieves "blankly" over what appears to have been a "disastrous compound" of human failure, muddle, and sheer chance, and mourns Rupert by attempting to remember him simply with a kind of mindless pain. His reaction to the loss of his wife is similar. Rather than indulging in anger, grief, or speculations about their future relationship, he simply lets her "continue to occupy his heart." His unwillingness to impose any kind of form or to structure his surroundings in any way extends to his feelings for his father Leonard, who is dying of cancer. Tallis cannot find the appropriate moment to tell his father of his impending death because, as he tells Julius, "It seems so arbitrary, at any particular instant of time, to change the world to that degree." Rather than seeing human beings as puppets, as does Julius, Tallis has reached a crisis state in which he fears that any action may have a deleterious effect on those around him. Significantly, however, in spite of Tallis's passivity he is the only character in the novel who is capable of positive action. As Axel phrases it, he is "the only person about the place with really sound instincts." In the Chinese restaurant, he strikes the young man who is abusing the Jamaican, and later he forces Julius to telephone Hilda Foster to explain that it is Julius who has created the "affair" between Morgan and Rupert.

At the end of the novel, Tallis has abandoned the idea of prayer, which the narrator notes could only be a "superstition" for him at that point, and has instead become a completely passive and receptive consciousness. He catches hold of objects "not so as to perform any act himself, but so as to immobilize himself for a moment to be, if that were possible, perhaps acted upon, perhaps touched." The similarity of this statement to Simone Weil's definition of "attention" in *Waiting for God* (1951), where she describes the act of attention as "suspending our thought, leaving it detached, empty, and ready to be penetrated by the object . . . our thought should be empty, waiting, not seeking anything," is clear. Much

earlier in the novel, Morgan has grabbed an object, a green paperweight belonging to Rupert, in an attempt to escape from the formlessness of the psyche. Tallis, on the other hand, uses objects as a way to attend to reality, as a means of opening himself up to the world outside himself.

A Fairly Honourable Defeat ends with Tallis weeping over his father's approaching death and Julius, after contemplating his choices of Parisian restaurants, concluding that "life was good." The conversation between the two men which precedes this, however, is much more ambiguous. Julius, in an apparent attempt to win Tallis's approbation for his actions, reveals a great deal about himself personally and asks Tallis to agree that he is "an instrument of justice." Tallis's attitude toward Julius is one of detached tolerance, and his response to Julius's statement is merely to smile. A parallel to his calm acceptance of Julius's evil is his response to the "weird crawling things," apparently rats, mice, and insects, which inhabit his house; he feels for them "pity rather than disgust" and has advanced far beyond Rupert's claim to love "paving stones and leaves on trees." Tallis's acceptance of the world, which has grown to embrace even its most despicable and horrible elements, makes him the most saintlike character in Murdoch's fiction. He is her answer to Sartre's Roquentin in *Nausea*: Instead of becoming nauseated by the world's plethora of objects and the muddle of existence, as does Roquentin, Tallis, at the end of *A Fairly Honourable Defeat*, is capable of feeling only pity and acceptance for everything that surrounds him.

AN ACCIDENTAL MAN

In *An Accidental Man*, Murdoch presents a chaotic world of accident and unpredictability in which several of her characters search for—and fail to find—any kind of pattern or causal relationships in their lives. Perhaps Murdoch's fear that form in fiction can hinder the characters' development as complex and fully realized individuals and that intricately patterned fiction sometimes prevents the author from exploring "the contradictions or paradoxes or more painful aspects of the subject matter" led her to write a novel in which the narrative voice is almost completely absent: In *An Accidental Man*, the characters appear to have taken over the novel. In an interview with W. K. Rose, in *Shenandoah* (Winter, 1968), Murdoch expressed the desire to write a novel "made up entirely of peripheral characters, sort of accidental people like Dickens's people," and mentioned that the author "might go so far as starting to invent the novel and then abolishing the central characters." *An Accidental Man* is the result of these speculations about fiction, for it contains a Dickensian sweep of characters and lacks any kind of "protagonist." The inclusion of more "accident" in Murdoch's work is one aspect of her wish to write realistic fiction, for she believes that the novelist should portray the world as "aimless, chancy, and huge." *An Accidental Man*, a brittle comedy of manners which contains four deaths, two attempted suicides, and more than twenty characters, some of whom are suffering from mental retardation, schizophrenia, and brain damage, is Murdoch's vision of a contingent, random, and godless world.

Many characters in the novel share this vision. At the conclusion, Matthew Gibson Grey notes that Austin's appropriation of Mavis Argyll "has been, like so many other things in the story, accidental." Charlotte Ledgard, contemplating suicide, sees herself as "the slave of chance" and the world as being made up of "chaos upon which everything rested and out of which it was made." Ludwig Leferrier senses that "human life perches always on the brink of dissolution," and Gracie Tisbourne, who is usually not given to philosophical speculations, has "a sense of the world being quite without order and of other things looking through." The characters in *An Accidental Man* wander through mazes in which they lack important information about their own and others' lives, or they become the victims of "accidents" which radically transform their existence. London's labyrinthine streets become symbolic of their ignorance and blindness as they pass and miss one another, and, in the instance of Rosalind Monkley, symbolic of accidental death itself. Garth Gibson Grey, Matthew Gibson Grey, Ludwig Leferrier, and Mavis Argyll all hope to find some kind of logical order and rationality in the world, but are finally defeated by

the "absolute contradiction . . . at the heart of things," and instead encounter what Garth calls "the rhetoric of the casually absent god."

Although Murdoch is generally not interested in experimentation in form, *An Accidental Man* shows her moving beyond the traditional narrative form of her earlier work in search of new structures to embody the philosophical assumptions that underlie the novel. Conspicuously missing in this novel is an authoritative narrative voice; instead, one tenth of the book is in epistolary form and a significant portion consists of chapters of untagged dialogue. In *An Accidental Man*, Murdoch, who has stated her wish to expel herself from her fiction in order to avoid imposing "the form of one's own mind" on the characters, creates a work in which the narrator is frequently not privy to the inner thoughts or reactions of the characters and can only report their spoken and written words without comment or elucidation. The disappearance of the narrator in certain sections of the novel parallels the absence of god; Murdoch creates a novelistic world in which the reader must search for his own patterns and conclusions without the guiding presence of the authorial voice which was present in her earlier fiction. In addition, the narrator's refusal to pass judgments or give information about the thoughts of the characters, despite the fact that he has shown himself to be omniscient in certain situations, results in a coldly detached tone which refuses to grant a fundamental importance to any act.

Like the chapters of dialogue, the epistolary sections of the novel create a voyeuristic situation for the reader that parallels the voyeurism that takes place several times during the narrative. The reader is privileged to read correspondence and to overhear important conversations while being denied access to the characters' thoughts, just as the characters in *An Accidental Man* have a noticeable penchant for eavesdropping on one another's conversations and reading other people's letters. The epistolary sections also create comically ironic effects because the reader knows more about the entire situation than any of the individual letter-writers, and the ignorance, lies, and exaggerations of the writers are juxtaposed in ways that underscore the limited and fallacious viewpoint of each individual. These chapters also give Murdoch an opportunity to open up the novel, expanding its boundaries to encompass more and more territory—a narrative technique which corresponds to her desire to write fiction that depicts reality as "a rich receding background" with "a life of its own."

The widening framework of the novel creates a constantly changing perspective, for when the narrator withdraws from a direct presentation of events in order to present the reactions of peripheral or uninvolved characters, the importance of these events is reduced through distancing and in the process rendered comic. The same technique is used in the chapters of pure dialogue, where events which have been treated seriously in earlier episodes become the subject of comically trivial cocktail-party conversations. The dialogic and epistolary sections are central elements in the novel, for Murdoch uses them to advance the narrative through fragmentary bits of information which are often necessary for a complete understanding of what is happening; her belief that "reality is not given whole" is expressed in her narrative technique.

The self-acknowledged "accidental man" of the novel's title is Austin Gibson Grey. Neurotically obsessed with his older brother, Matthew, and unable to keep either his wife or his job, Austin is nevertheless a survivor who depends upon his own egotism for his continued well-being. One aspect of Austin's ability to survive is his refusal to allow the catastrophes of others to affect him. He observes that "a man can see himself becoming more callous to events because he has to survive," and his reaction to the death of Rosalind Monkley, whom he has killed in an automobile accident, is typical. He writes to his wife, Dorina, that "I will survive and recover, I have had worse blows than this"; he does not mention any guilt he may feel about the incident or the pain Rosalind's death may have caused her family. Similarly, after Dorina's accidental death, Austin tells Matthew that "Poor old Dorina was just a sort of half person really, a maimed creature, she had to die, like certain kinds of cripples have to. They can't last." In spite of Austin's selfishness, however, he is merely the most ex-

aggerated example of egotism in *An Accidental Man*. The statement by an unnamed character at the novel's conclusion that "Austin is like all of us only more so" is, unfortunately, correct.

Austin Gibson Grey resembles several other characters in Murdoch's fiction, all of whom show a talent for survival and an ability to turn unfortunate incidents to their account. In the same way, Austin's wife Dorina is representative of another character-type which recurs throughout Murdoch's novels: the individual who functions as a scapegoat or assumes the consequences of the sins of others. Frequently, through no fault of their own, such characters cannot cope with the events happening around them and either choose suicide or become the victims of an "accidental" death that appears to be inevitable. Traditionally, the scapegoat or *pharmakos* figure is an individual who must be expelled from society in order to maintain its continued existence and vitality. Dorina Gibson Grey is a *pharmakos* who manifests all of these characteristics. Early in the novel, she feels as if "something were closing in for the kill," and after her death, her sister Mavis voices the opinion that "she has died for me," telling Matthew that "she has somehow died for us, for you and me, taking herself away, clearing herself away, so that our world should be easier and simpler." Dorina's death enables Garth Gibson Grey to feel love once again for his father. Her death also rejuvenates her husband, as Matthew ironically observes: "Something or other had . . . done Austin good. Perhaps it was simply Dorina's death." Her death has an almost ritualistic dimension in *An Accidental Man*, and it ensures the rejuvenation of several of the characters.

The ending of *An Accidental Man* is one of the darkest in Murdoch's fiction, and very few of the defeats suffered in this novel can be termed "honourable." In fact, several characters, including Matthew Gibson Grey, Garth Gibson Grey, and Charlotte Ledgard, appear to have settled for what Julius King in *A Fairly Honourable Defeat* calls a "sensible acceptance of the second rate." Matthew, en route with Ludwig Leferrier to the United States, where Ludwig will receive a prison sentence for refusing to fight in Vietnam, realizes that "he would never be a hero. . . .

that the function of art is to reveal reality rather than to console its creator or consumer, portrays Charles as the "bad" artist who attempts to use art and the creative process for solace instead of revelation.

Just as Murdoch's characters often misuse art and their own creative impulses, they frequently fall in love suddenly and violently, an experience that produces a state of delusion and neurotic obsession. Although she says in *The Fire and the Sun* that the "lover" can be shocked into an awareness of "an entirely separate reality" during the experience of love, the lover's ego usually causes him to wish to "dominate and possess" the beloved. The lover, rather than wishing to "serve and adore," instead wants "to derealize the other, devour and absorb him, subject him to the mechanism of . . . fantasy." Charles Arrowby's "Quest of the Bearded Lady," as one character terms his pursuit of Hartley, exemplifies this dimension of falling in love; his feelings for her are typical of the obsessive, self-centered, fantasy-ridden love that Murdoch believes is antithetical to an objective, free apprehension of others. He admits that he is "like a madman" and compares himself to a "frenzied animal." Later, he says that "I was sane enough to know that I was in a state of total obsession and that I . . . *could only* run continually along the same rat-paths of fantasy and intent." Unlike his cousin James, who has cultivated the intellectual and spiritual detachment of Eastern philosophy combined with a concern for the well-being and "otherness" of individuals, Charles's passion for Hartley Fitch is, at bottom, an obsession with his own past and loss of innocence.

In two earlier novels, *An Accidental Man* and *The Black Prince*, Murdoch uses narrative devices such as epistolary and dialogic chapters and the addition of "postscripts" by other characters to alter the reader's perspective and interpretation of events. In *The Sea, the Sea*, she allows Charles Arrowby to add a "revision" to his novel that qualifies and contradicts much of his earlier narrative. At the end of the "History" section of *The Sea, the Sea*, he closes his story on a note of repentance and revelation, goes to sleep hearing "singing," and awakens to see the seals he had previously been unable to sight.

Murdoch believes that fiction should reflect the "muddle" of reality, and thus she adds a postscript by the narrator appropriately entitled "Life Goes On." Charles begins by mocking his "conclusion" and observing that life, unlike art, "has an irritating way of bumping and limping on, undoing conversions, casting doubt on solutions"; he then decides to continue his story a while longer, this time in the form of a "diary" in which he alters his own version of events and reveals that he has learned very little from them. In this way, Murdoch further reduces the stature of her "failed Prospero," and the picture of Charles that emerges in the postscript is that of a rapidly aging man with an incipient heart condition. Another addition to the group of "power figures" in Murdoch's fiction who believe that they can "invent" reality and manipulate other people for aesthetic purposes, Charles Arrowby represents Murdoch's belief in the final impossibility of one human being's controlling another. In *The Sea, the Sea*, the would-be director who thought himself a "god" or "king" is revealed as a relatively powerless individual over whom the formlessness and unpredictability of "transcendent reality" triumphs.

THE GOOD APPRENTICE

Murdoch's most critically acclaimed novel of the 1980's is *The Good Apprentice*, a novel that reflects her continuing desire to write fiction whose length and complexity embody her belief in a contingent, infinitely particularized universe in which goodness is easily discussed but achieved, if at all, with great difficulty and pain. The "good apprentice" can refer to either of two characters in the novel. Edward Baltram has recently been responsible for the death of his best friend and is attempting to deal with his resulting guilt and self-hatred; Stuart Cuno, his stepbrother, is, like many other Murdochian characters, seeking goodness and finding it a problematical goal.

Murdoch make Stuart Cuno the mouthpiece of some of her most cherished ideas about the nature of goodness. Like Murdoch, Stuart acknowledges that goodness is often an unimaginable concept that involves inaction rather than action, and several times in the story he is referred to as a "negative presence." Stuart has rejected the entire concept of God and instead attempts to meditate blankly, to empty his mind out in order to perceive clearly, what Murdoch calls "an instinctive craving for nothingness which was also a desire to be able to love and enjoy and 'touch' everything, to *help* everything." Psychoanalyst Thomas McCaskerville, who stands in direct opposition to Stuart's nontheoretical approach to goodness, catechizes the younger man at length in an important conversation that reveals Thomas's dependence on the cozy theories of psychoanalysis that Murdoch has mocked in her earlier novels. Thomas has a conceptual framework for almost any idea or event, and his discovery that his wife Midge has been having an affair with Stuart's father Harry Cuno only temporarily shocks him out of his comfortable mental and emotional world. His further realization that his supposedly psychotic patient Mr. Blinnet is actually quite sane and has been faking mental illness for years is another blow at Thomas's carefully constructed theoretical world.

It is the artist Jesse Baltram, Edward's father, who best represents one of the most enduring and interesting figures in Murdoch's fiction, the magician-artist power figure who mysteriously spellbinds those around him and functions as a catalyst for many important events. Edward goes to Seegard, Jesse's home, to be "healed" and "purified" of his friend's death. In the process he meets May Baltram, Jesse's wife, his two half sisters, and, finally, his father, who has been reduced by an unspecified illness to childlike behavior and incoherence. Jesse's difficulty in making rational conversation is another alternative in the novel to Stuart's "blankness" and "whiteness" and Thomas's frenziedly articulate philosophizing: It signifies that the logical ordering principle of language ultimately cannot describe or explain a reality that is always "boiling over" with energy and creativity. Jesse's description of the world and the relationship between good and evil, in which syntax and logic break down, is directly opposed to the other characters' slick facility with language. He tells Edward,

"What I knew once—about good and evil and those— all *those* things—people don't really have them, meet them—in their lives at all, most people don't—only a

few—want that—that fight, you know—think they want—good—have to have evil—not real, either—of course—all inside something else—it's a dance—you see—world needs power—always round and round— it's all power and—energy—which sometimes—rears up its beautiful head—like a dragon—that's the meaning of it all—I think—in the shadows now—can't remember—doesn't matter—what I need—is a long sleep—so as to dream it all—over again."

Jesse's connection with the supernatural and paranormal dimension of Edward's stay at Seegard reveals Murdoch again experimenting with the limits of realistic fiction. As in *The Sea, the Sea*, she is willing to force the reader to accept the unexplained and acknowledge the thin line between the natural and the supernatural, between distortion of perception and a glimpse into another world where the usual rational rules no longer apply. *The Good Apprentice* shows Murdoch at the height of her powers as a novelist, combining her "moral psychology" with her long-held aesthetic theories in a work that proves the undiminished fecundity of her imagination and intelligence.

THE BOOK AND THE BROTHERHOOD

In another important novel of the 1980's, *The Book and the Brotherhood*, Murdoch's power-figure is as charismatic as Jesse but is neither impotent nor incoherent. David Crimond is an intellectual of the far Left (the communists kicked him out for being too radical). Years ago at Oxford, a group of Crimond's friends pledged to support him while he wrote the volume of revolutionary economic and social philosophy they thought world needed. Years later, although Crimond's book remains unpublished, his intellectual, personal, and even sexual power over the group remains undiminished. The novel shows how the friends try to define their moderating political views in relation to Crimond's.

The novel also shows how the friends and *their* friends try to make peace with the world. Each yearns for fulfillment, though in widely different ways— some of them touching, some admirable, some reprehensible. Gerard, perhaps the novel's central character, yearns for a vague something (his yearning began with his affection for his pet parrot, as described in one of Murdoch's most brilliant passages). Rose, a passive woman, yearns for Gerard. Duncan yearns for his wife, who yearns for Crimond. Jenkins, a saintly schoolmaster, yearns for a perfect act. Other characters are less important but stranger. At the end of an Oxford party, Gulliver is awakened by a deer's kiss; later he has a paranormal experience in a London railway station. Other inexplicable forces are exerted by buried Roman roads and by Church rituals performed by an unbelieving priest.

The Book and the Brotherhood offers no certainties, for neither Crimond's ideas nor Gerard's refutations are convincing. It shows a wide spectrum of memorable characters yearning earnestly and sometimes comically toward some things they cannot fully define.

THE GREEN KNIGHT

Murdoch's last great novel, *The Green Knight*, is one of her most perplexing. The story is bizarre. It often resembles (but does not strictly parallel) that of the medieval narrative poem *Sir Gawain and the Green Knight*. In its central act, Murdoch once again pushes the bounds of realism. One dark night in a public park, Lucas Graffe, while attempting to kill his brother Clement with a baseball bat, hits a third man instead and kills him. Later, like the medieval Green Knight, the supposedly dead man reappears. His name is Peter Mir, and he is this novel's powerful magician; he is alive and demands justice. His demand is worked out in a way that also recalls *Sir Gawain and the Green Knight*. (Mir also is said to resemble Mr. Pickwick, Prospero, the Minotaur, and Mephistopheles.)

The stories of other characters encircle the central one. Clement hopelessly loves Louise Anderson, whose magical house contains three wonderful daughters about to begin life's journey. The most mysterious is Moy, who can move small stones at a distance. The Anderson's keep a dog named Anax, one of Murdoch's finest animal creations. His master, Bellamy, gave him away to embark on a spiritual quest for which he is ill suited. At one point Anax, who may embody the goodness of the flesh, escapes and tries to find his master in an anxious lope through the streets of London.

Murdoch's conclusion of this novel may not satisfy everyone, but the journey through the novel is exciting and rewarding. Her last novel, *Jackson's Dilemma*, has many high spots, but it is often confusing. By the time the reviews appeared, her Alzheimer's disease had progressed so far that she could not understand them.

Angela Hague, updated by George Soule

OTHER MAJOR WORKS

PLAYS: *A Severed Head*, pr. 1963 (with J. B. Priestley); *The Italian Girl*, pr. 1967 (with James Saunders); *The Servants and the Snow*, pr. 1970; *The Three Arrows*, pr. 1972; *The Three Arrows, and The Servants and the Snow: Plays*, pb. 1973; *Art and Eros*, pr. 1980; *The Black Prince*, pr. 1989; *Joanna Joanna*, pb. 1994; *The One Alone*, pb. 1995.

NONFICTION: *Sartre: Romantic Rationalist*, 1953; *The Sovereignty of Good*, 1970; *The Fire and the Sun: Why Plato Banished the Artists*, 1977; *Acastos: Two Platonic Dialogues*, 1986; *Metaphysics as a Guide to Morals*, 1992; *Existentialists and Mystics: Writings on Philosophy and Literature*, 1997 (edited by Peter Conradi).

BIBLIOGRAPHY

Bloom, Harold, ed. *Iris Murdoch*. New York: Chelsea House, 1986. Bloom's collection of essays, a representative selection of some of the best articles and book chapters on Murdoch, includes his introductory analysis of *The Good Apprentice* and Murdoch's essay "Against Dryness."

Bove, Cheryl K. *Understanding Iris Murdoch*. Columbia: University of South Carolina Press, 1993. A lucid and valuable handbook for college students. Early chapters summarize Murdoch's philosophical ideas.

Byatt, Antonia S. *Degrees of Freedom: The Novels of Iris Murdoch*. New York: Barnes & Noble Books, 1965; expanded edition, London: Vintage, 1994. This important study focuses on the degrees of freedom that characters have in Murdoch's early novels and notes Murdoch's failings. The expanded edition reprints the original edition and adds a foreword, the entire text of Byatt's pamphlet *Iris Murdoch* (1976), a review of Byatt's first book, and Byatt's own reviews of many of Murdoch's later novels.

Dipple, Elizabeth. *Iris Murdoch: Work for the Spirit.* Chicago: University of Chicago Press, 1982. A valuable and essential study of the aesthetic, moral, and philosophical dimensions of Murdoch's works through *Nuns and Soldiers.* Dipple discusses Murdoch's use of Plato's concept of the Good and perhaps overemphasizes the bleak Buddhist elements in the novels.

Gordon, David J. *Iris Murdoch's Fable's of Unselfing.* Columbia: University of Missouri Press, 1995. Gordon discusses many of Murdoch's ideas, especially those concerning power and human motives.

Heusel, Barbara. *Patterned Aimlessness: Iris Murdoch's Novels of the 1970's and 1980's.* Athens: University of Georgia Press, 1995. Heusel analyzes Murdoch's relation to many philosophers, Wittgenstein in particular. She uses Bakhtin's dialogic method to illuminate how Murdoch's character's interact.

Johnson, Deborah. *Iris Murdoch.* Bloomington: Indiana University Press, 1987. Johnson uses Anglo-American and French feminist theories to analyze Murdoch from a feminist perspective, focusing on Murdoch's male narrators, the issue of confinement, the symbol of the cave, and the problem of endings in the fiction.

Soule, George. *Four British Women Novelists: Anita Brookner, Margaret Drabble, Iris Murdoch, Barbara Pym—An Annotated and Critical Secondary Bibliography.* Lanham, Md.: Scarecrow Press, 1998. An analysis of most critical books and articles on this author through 1996, with evaluations.

Todd, Richard. *Iris Murdoch: The Shakespearian Interest.* New York: Barnes & Noble Books, 1979. Murdoch's frequently noted debt to Shakespeare is explored in this study, which pays particular attention to *The Black Prince, Bruno's Dream, A Word Child, The Nice and the Good*, and *A Fairly Honourable Defeat.*

N

VLADIMIR NABOKOV

Born: St. Petersburg, Russia; April 23, 1899
Died: Montreux, Switzerland; July 2, 1977

PRINCIPAL LONG FICTION

Mashenka, 1926 (*Mary*, 1970)
Korol', dama, valet, 1928 (*King, Queen, Knave,* 1968)
Zashchita Luzhina, 1929 (serial), 1930 (book; *The Defense*, 1964)
Podvig, 1932 (*Glory*, 1971)
Kamera obskura, 1932 (*Camera Obscura*, 1936 revised as *Laughter in the Dark*, 1938)
Otchayanie, 1934 (serial), 1936 (book; *Despair*, 1937 rev. 1966)
Dar, 1937-1938 (serial), 1952 (book; *The Gift*, 1963)
Priglashenie na kazn', 1935-1936 (serial), 1938 (book; *Invitation to a Beheading*, 1959)
The Real Life of Sebastian Knight, 1941
Bend Sinister, 1947
Lolita, 1955
Pnin, 1957
Pale Fire, 1962
Ada or Ardor: A Family Chronicle, 1969
Transparent Things, 1972
Look at the Harlequins!, 1974

OTHER LITERARY FORMS

Vladimir Nabokov began, as many novelists do, as a poet. As a youth, he published privately what now would be called a chapbook and a full book of poetry before emigrating from Russia. Throughout his life, he continued to publish poetry in periodicals and several book-length collections, including *Stikhotvorenia, 1929-1951* (1952), *Poems* (1959), and *Poems and Problems* (1970). Some critics even consider the long poem "Pale Fire" (an integral part of

the novel *Pale Fire*) a worthy neo-Romantic poem in itself. Nabokov also published a good deal of short fiction, first in a variety of short-lived émigré publications such as *Rul'*, *Sovremennye Zapiski*, and *Russkoe ekho*, and later in such prominent magazines as *The New Yorker, The Atlantic Monthly, Playboy, Harper's Bazaar,* and *Tri-Quarterly*. His stories were collected in *Vozrashchenie Chorba* (1930; the return of Chorb, which also included twenty-four poems), *Solgyadatay* (1938; the eye), *Nine Stories* (1947), and *Nabokov's Dozen* (1958), among others. His plays include: *Smert'* (1923; death); *Tragediya gospodina Morna* (1924; the tragedy of Mister Morn); *Chelovek iz SSSR* (1927; the man from the USSR); *Sobytiye* (1938; the event); and *Izobretenie Val'sa* (1938; *The Waltz Invention*, 1966). He also worked on a screenplay for the film version of *Lolita* (1962). Besides translating his own works from Russian to English (and vice versa, as well as occasionally from French to Russian to English), he often translated the works of other writers, including Lewis Carroll's 1865 *Alice's Adventures in Wonderland*, and poetry of Rupert Brooke, Alexander Pushkin, Arthur Rimbaud, William Shakespeare, and Alfred de Musset. In nonfiction prose, Nabokov's fascinating life is recalled in three volumes of memoirs, *Conclusive Evidence* (1951), *Drugie Berega* (1954; other shores), and *Speak, Memory* (1966, a revision and expansion of the earlier works). Throughout his life, his often idiosyncratic criticism was widely published, and the publication after his death of several volumes of his lectures on world literature provoked much discussion among literary scholars. As a lepidopterist, Nabokov published a number of scholarly articles in such journals as *The Entomologist, Journal of the New York Entomological Society, Psyche,* and *The Lepidopterists' News*.

ACHIEVEMENTS

An extraordinary individual, Nabokov's strength as a writer lay in his control and mastery of style. Writers are sometimes successful in a language other than their native language, but only a select few are capable of writing equally well in two languages, and Nabokov may be alone in his ability to master the insinuations of two extraordinarily different and subtle languages such as Russian and English. Under the pen name "V. Sirin," Nabokov was recognized as a noteworthy émigré novelist and poet in Berlin and Paris. After fleeing the rise of Nazism and settling in the United States, he became recognized as a major English-language author with the publication of *Lolita* in 1955. As was the case with Gustave Flaubert, James Joyce, and D. H. Lawrence, all of whose international sales were aided by the controversies surrounding their works, Nabokov received worldwide attention as critics debated the morality of *Lolita*, prompting the republication and translation of many of his earlier works. Few writers with such an uncompromising style achieve such popularity. Nabokov was often in financial difficulty before *Lolita*, yet he always remained the consummate craftsman. He has come to be regarded as one of the literary giants of his generation.

BIOGRAPHY

Vladimir Vladimirovich Nabokov was born to Vladimir Dmitrievich and Elena Rukavishnikov Nabokov in St. Petersburg, Russia, the eldest of five children. He grew up in comfortable circumstances, tracing his ancestry back to a Tartar prince of the 1380's and through a number of military men, statesmen, Siberian merchants, and the first president of the Russian Imperial Academy of Medicine. His father was a noted liberal who had helped found the Constitutional Democratic Party, was elected to the first Duma, and coedited the sole liberal newspaper in St. Petersburg. In his childhood, the young Nabokov was taken on trips to France, Italy, and Spain, and he summered on the country estate of Vyra, accumulating memories which would become woven into his later writings. His father, an Anglophile, provided governesses who taught the boy English at a very early age. He once remarked that he had learned to read English even before he had learned Russian. He was also taught French.

Entering puberty, Nabokov attended the liberal Prince Tenishev School, where he first developed a hatred of coercion but played soccer and chess, started collecting butterflies, and showed some artis-

tic talent. He began writing poetry, and a now lost brochure of a single poem "in a violet paper cover" was privately published in 1914. In 1916, he privately published a recollection that provoked his cousin to beg him to "never, never be a writer," and in 1918, he collaborated on a collection with Andrei Balashov. Nabokov inherited an estate and the equivalent of two million dollars when his Uncle Ruka died and seemed to be on his way to the comfortable life of a Russian bourgeois when history intervened. His father became part of the Provisional Government in the March Revolution of 1917, but in October, when the Bolsheviks displaced the Alexander Kerensky government, the Nabokov family fled, first to the Crimea and then, in 1919, into permanent exile in the West on an old Greek ship ironically named *Nadezhda* ("Hope").

Nabokov studied at Trinity College, Cambridge University, paying little attention to anything but soc-

(Library of Congress)

cer, tennis, and girls. He did, however, do many translations (of Rupert Brooke, Seumas O'Sullivan, W. B. Yeats, George Gordon, Lord Byron, and others) and came under the influence of English poetry. He also read and was influenced by James Joyce. Despite his claim that he never once visited the library, he was graduated with honors in French and Russian literature in 1923. This was shortly following his father's assassination in Berlin in March, 1922, as two reactionaries shot the elder Nabokov in error as he was introducing their intended victim. After Cambridge, the twenty-five-year-old Nabokov moved to Berlin, where, in 1925, he married Vera Evseevna Slonim, and a year later he published his first novel, *Mary*, under a pseudonym. He felt that his father had prior claim to the name "Vladimir Nabokov," and he wrote all of his early Russian works as "V. Sirin."

With very little money, Nabokov published poems, stories, and essays in Berlin's émigré newspapers, and later, as the Nazis grew in power (his wife was Jewish), in similar Parisian publications. He survived by teaching tennis, devising crossword puzzles in Russian, making up chess problems, teaching Russian, and translating. He sold the Russian translation of *Alice's Adventures in Wonderland* (*Anya v strane chudes*, 1923), for example, for the equivalent of five dollars. In 1934, his only son, Dmitri, was born, and four years later, Nabokov fled to Paris. As early as 1935, he decided to immigrate to the United States, probably recognizing that Europe was no longer safe. He was invited by the Soviet government during the 1930's to return to Russia several times, but he refused.

Nabokov's novels in Berlin and Paris had been relatively successful, and several had been translated into English with and without his assistance. He made the remarkable and difficult decision to abandon the language in which he had written so well. "My private tragedy," he later wrote, "which cannot, indeed should not, be anybody's concern, is that I had to abandon my natural idiom, my untrammeled, rich, and infinitely docile Russian tongue for a second-rate brand of English." Stanford University invited him to teach in the summer of 1940, and he set sail for America on the liner *Champlain* in May, just ahead

of the German invasion. He had already begun writing his first English novel, *The Real Life of Sebastian Knight*, while in Paris, and, in 1941, it was published in the United States after several friends helped him edit it. He taught Russian grammar and literature at Wellesley College from 1941 to 1948, also serving as a research fellow at the Museum of Comparative Zoology at Harvard University. He became a prominent lepidopterist, publishing many monographs, articles, and reviews. He spent summers roaming America searching for butterflies and discovered several species and subspecies, including "Nabokov's wood nymph." After seeing praise for his work on the Lycaeides genus in a field guide, Nabokov is said to have remarked, "That's real fame. That means more than anything a literary critic could say."

In 1944, Nabokov published a critical book on Nikolai Gogol, and in 1947, his first novel written in the United States, *Bend Sinister*, appeared. From 1948 to 1959, he taught at Cornell University, carefully writing out his lectures, combining his attacks on such intellectual touchstones as Karl Marx, Charles Darwin, and especially Sigmund Freud with dramatic classroom readings. Well before the publication of *Lolita*, he was recognized as a remarkable talent in certain quarters, as is indicated by his receipt of grants from the Guggenheim Foundation in 1943 and 1953 and by an award from the American Academy of Arts and Letters in 1953; students in his classes at Cornell, however, were often unaware that their teacher was also a writer, although he published stories and articles in *The New Yorker, The Atlantic Monthly, Hudson Review*, and others. *Lolita* changed all that. Rejected by several American publishers, it was brought out by publisher Maurice Girodias's Olympia Press in Paris in 1955. As one of the most controversial books ever published—banned for a while in France, debated in the British Parliament, and forbidden in many American libraries—it swept the best-seller lists and freed Nabokov from teaching. Besides the royalties, he received $150,000 and a percentage on the film rights and wrote a screenplay (which was later substantially changed) for Stanley Kubrick's 1962 film.

In 1960, Nabokov moved to Montreux, Switzerland, where he and his wife lived in a sixth-floor apartment in the Palace Hotel overlooking Lake Geneva, in order to be near their son Dmitri, who was having some success as an opera singer. In the wake of *Lolita*, Nabokov and his son translated many of his earlier novels into English and introduced several collections of his short stories to American readers. His novels *Pale Fire, Ada or Ardor, Transparent Things*, and *Look at the Harlequins!* were all published during this period. He was regularly discussed as a possible recipient of the Nobel Prize until his death of a viral infection in 1977.

ANALYSIS

In 1937, Vladeslav Khodasevich, an émigré poet and champion of "V. Sirin's" work, wrote, "Sirin [Nabokov] proves for the most part to be an artist of form, of the writer's device, and not only in that . . . sense of which . . . his writing is distinguished by exceptional diversity, complexity, brilliance, and novelty." Khodasevich went on to say that the key to all Sirin's work was his ability to put all his literary devices on display, with little or no attempt to conceal them, thus entertaining his readers more with the revelation of how the magician performs his tricks, than with the trick itself. "The life of the artist and the life of a device in the consciousness of an artist—this is Sirin's theme." Khodasevich, although he had not yet read *The Gift*—purported to be Vladimir Nabokov's greatest Russian novel—had discovered the most important element of Nabokov's fiction.

Throughout his entire life, although Nabokov underwent great changes in his circumstances, he was consistent, whether writing in Russian or English, in his unflagging delight in literary devices of all sorts, art for its own sake, and a contempt for mimetic conventions, simplistic psychological motivation, ordinary plot structure, and anything that inhibits the literary imagination. He can, in many respects, be called an aesthete, but his rejection of most schools of thought makes him difficult to classify. He strove for and achieved a uniqueness that runs as a thread throughout his oeuvre. Clarence Brown once commented in a critical essay that "for well over a quarter of a century now . . . [Nabokov] has been writing in

book after book about the same thing," and Nabokov is said to have admitted that Brown was probably correct.

MARY and KING, QUEEN, KNAVE

Nabokov's first novel, *Mary*, is rather sentimental and probably based on Nabokov's regret for a lost love, but it already contains two elements he would use repeatedly—the love triangle and uncertain identity. *King, Queen, Knave*, however, is an even more obvious reflection of the Nabokov canon. In it, a character named Franz Bubendorf, a country bumpkin on his way to the city, apparently to be corrupted by the bourgeois life, is, in fact, already corrupted by his distaste for his own class, which distorts his perception. As if to emphasize this distortion of perception, Franz steps on his glasses and Berlin becomes a blur. Again, there is a love triangle, and each of the participants is, in his or her own way, unable to perceive reality. The melodrama of a love triangle and a planned murder is handled with the authorial detachment that is one of Nabokov's hallmarks. The novel becomes a parody of traditional forms, and the characters become obvious contrivances of the author. Derived from a Hans Christian Andersen work of the same title, the novel consists of thirteen chapters, as there are thirteen cards in each suit in a deck of cards. The card metaphor is carried throughout the work, even in the description of clothes.

LAUGHTER IN THE DARK

Laughter in the Dark opens with a parody of the fairy tale revealing the entire plot, here a relatively conventional bourgeois love story that Nabokov typically manipulates. The main character, blinded by love, becomes literally blinded and trapped in a love triangle, which results in his murder (accomplished in a scene that is a parody of motion-picture melodrama). This type of parody, which partially represents Nabokov's delight in mocking inferior art, can also be seen as a parody of the reader's expectations. Nabokov constantly thwarts the reader who wants a nice, comfortable, conventional novel. The writer is always in control, always tugging the reader this way and that, never allowing a moment of certainty. Perceptions are distorted on all levels. The characters have distorted perceptions of one another. The

teristic of great romantic loves: Tristan and Isolde, Abélard and Héloise, Dante and Beatrice, Petrarch and Laura. Humbert often justifies his pedophilia by references to the courtly love tradition. There is also much reference to the story of Edgar Allan Poe's love for Virginia Clemm (Humbert's first teenage love was a girl named Annabel Leigh).

Although many critics attempted to justify *Lolita* as having an important moral message, Nabokov rebuked the notion by saying, "I am no messenger boy." His aesthetic philosophy would never have permitted him to subordinate his art to a moral. He once said that Lolita was about his love for the English language, but even that is an oversimplification of an immensely complex book. Among the various elements critics have noted are the *Doppelgänger* relation of Quilty to Humbert, chess metaphors, puns on names, the question of the masks of the narrator (the probably unreliable Humbert through the clinical Ray through the mischievous Nabokov), and the supposed immortality of Humbert's love, a love that becomes timeless through a work of art. It has even been argued that Nabokov's description of Lolita very much resembles his description of a certain species of butterfly in his scientific studies. While *Lolita*'s place in the canon of world literature is still debated, there is little doubt that it may be the finest example of the author's "game-playing" method of artistic creation.

PALE FIRE

In *Pale Fire*, readers were once again amused, perplexed, or horrified with Nabokov's ironic wit. This experimental novel inspired extremes of praise—such as Mary McCarthy's judgment that "it is one of the great works of art of this century"—and mockery. The novel is presented in the form of a scholarly edition of a poem entitled "Pale Fire" by John Shade, with commentary by Charles Kinbote. Both worked at Wordsmith University, where Kinbote seems to have believed that Shade was writing a poem about Kinbote's obsession with Charles Xavier Vseslav, "The Beloved," the King of Zembla who was forced to flee the revolution that replaced him. *Pale Fire* can be described as a series of Russian dolls, one enclosed within another. John Shade's poem (as edited

by Kinbote) is explained by Kinbote, who intends to give life to the extraordinary personality of Shade. He writes in the foreword, "without my notes Shade's text simply has no human reality at all," but the reader soon recognizes that Kinbote is a madman who either is, or imagines himself to be, the displaced King of Zembla, and whatever human reality Shade may have exists only through his colleague's warped interpretation of events. On another level, the reader finds some of Shade's "reality" in the text of his poem and reads much into and between Kinbote's lines as the madman gradually exposes his own madness. Yet, Nabokov never wants his reader to forget that all this invention is entirely of his making. Much more is intended than a mere parody of scholarly editions, scholars, and neo-Romantic poetry. Once more, Nabokov wittily develops his lifelong theme that reality exists only in the eyes of its interpreter.

J. Madison Davis

OTHER MAJOR WORKS

SHORT FICTION: *Vozrashchenie Chorba*, 1930; *Soglyadatay*, 1938; *Nine Stories*, 1947; *Vesna v Fialte i drugie rasskazy*, 1956; *Nabokov's Dozen: A Collection of Thirteen Stories*, 1958; *Nabokov's Quartet*, 1966; *A Russian Beauty and Other Stories*, 1973; *Tyrants Destroyed and Other Stories*, 1975; *Details of a Sunset and Other Stories*, 1976.

PLAYS: *Smert'*, pb. 1923; *Dedushka*, pb. 1923; *Polius*, pb. 1924; *Tragediya gospodina Morna*, pb. 1924; *Chelovek iz SSSR*, pb. 1927; *Sobytiye*, pr., pb. 1938; *Izobretenie Val'sa*, pb. 1938 (*The Waltz Invention*, 1966).

SCREENPLAY: *Lolita*, 1962.

POETRY: *Stikhi*, 1916; *Dva puti*, 1918; *Gorny put*, 1923; *Grozd'*, 1923; *Stikhotvorenia, 1929-1951*, 1952; *Poems*, 1959; *Poems and Problems*, 1970.

NONFICTION: *Nikolai Gogol*, 1944; *Conclusive Evidence: A Memoir*, 1951; *Drugie berega*, 1954; *Speak, Memory: An Autobiography Revisited*, 1966 (revision of *Conclusive Evidence* and *Drugie berega*); *Strong Opinions*, 1973; *The Nabokov-Wilson Letters, 1940-1971*, 1979; *Lectures on Literature: British, French, and German*, 1980; *Lectures on Russian Literature*, 1981; *Lectures on Don Quixote*,

1983; *Vladimir Nabokov: Selected Letters, 1940-1977*, 1989.

TRANSLATIONS: *Anya v strane chudes*, 1923 (of Lewis Carroll's novel *Alice's Adventures in Wonderland*); *Three Russian Poets: Translations of Pushkin, Lermontov, and Tiutchev*, 1944 (with Dmitri Nabokov); *A Hero of Our Time*, 1958 (of Mikhail Lermontov's novel; with Dmitri Nabokov); *The Song of Igor's Campaign*, 1960 (of the twelfth century epic *Slovo o polki Igoreve*); *Eugene Onegin*, 1964 (of Alexander Pushkin's novel).

BIBLIOGRAPHY

Appel, Alfred, Jr., and Charles Newman, eds. *Nabokov: Criticism, Reminiscences, Translations, Tributes*. Evanston, Ill.: Northwestern University Press, 1970. A good introduction to Nabokov's writing, including a varied sampling of material about the man, about the writer, and about his several unique works. Perhaps a hodgepodge, but an early collection that contrasts dramatically with later criticism, which suggested that Nabokov was a humanist if also a kind of verbal magician.

Bloom, Harold, ed. *Vladimir Nabokov.* New York: Chelsea House, 1987. Essays on Nabokov's handling of time, illusion and reality, and art. There are separate essays on each of his major novels, as well as an introduction, chronology, and bibliography.

Boyd, Brian. *Vladimir Nabokov: The Russian Years.* Princeton, N.J.: Princeton University Press, 1990. The first volume of the definitive biography, fully researched and written with the cooperation of Nabokov's family. Boyd has an extraordinary command of the origins of Nabokov's art. This volume includes a discussion of Nabokov's years in Europe after he left Russia.

_____. *Vladimir Nabokov: The American Years.* Princeton, N.J.: Princeton University Press, 1991. Boyd concludes his masterful biography. As with volume 1, his work is copiously illustrated with detailed notes and an invaluable index.

Field, Andrew. *Nabokov, His Life in Part.* New York: Viking Press, 1977. An intimate portrait written by an author who was often very close to Nabokov during the latter part of Nabokov's life. The book may also suggest to would-be biographers some of the difficulties of writing a biography while enjoying an intimate relationship with the subject. Follows Field's critical work, *Nabokov, His Life in Art: A Critical Narrative* (Boston: Little, Brown, 1967).

_____. *VN: The Life and Art of Vladimir Nabokov.* New York: Crown, 1986. Not as definitive as Boyd, but still a very important biographical/critical study of Nabokov. Field has been called the "father of Nabokovian studies. Includes illustrations, detailed notes, and index. The best one-volume biography of Nabokov.

Foster, John Burt. *Nabokov's Art of Memory and European Modernism.* Princeton, N.J.: Princeton University Press, 1993. Burt divides his study into three parts: Nabokov's early years in Russia, his period in Europe, and his prolonged period in America. This is a more specialized study for advanced students.

Pifer, Ellen. *Nabokov and the Novel.* Cambridge, Mass.: Harvard University Press, 1980. Uses as an epigraph Flannery O'Connor's "All novelists are fundamentally seekers and describers of the real, but the realism of each novelist will depend on his view of the ultimate reaches of reality" to develop a critical dialogue about Nabokov's technique, not surprisingly including realism. Ends in a discussion on Nabokov's humanism. Robert Alter called this book "poised and precise," and it is excellent for serious, critical readers of Nabokov.

V. S. NAIPAUL

Born: Chaguanas, Trinidad; August 17, 1932

PRINCIPAL LONG FICTION

The Mystic Masseur, 1957
The Suffrage of Elvira, 1958
Miguel Street, 1959
A House for Mr. Biswas, 1961
Mr. Stone and the Knights Companion, 1963

(Thomas Victor)

The Mimic Men, 1967
In a Free State, 1971
Guerrillas, 1975
A Bend in the River, 1979
The Enigma of Arrival, 1987
A Way in the World, 1994

OTHER LITERARY FORMS

V. S. Naipaul is a rarity among writers in that he enjoys equal recognition for his novels and for his works of nonfiction. Indeed, had Naipaul never published a novel, his works of nonfiction would in themselves be sufficient to assure his reputation as a major writer. As a writer of nonfiction, Naipaul has specialized in a distinctive blend of travelogue, reportage, and autobiography, offering penetrating accounts of regions as diverse as his native Trinidad, India (the home of his ancestors and the subject of several of his books), Africa, the Middle East, Southeast Asia, and the American South.

Naipaul is a prolific writer, and, as a journalist and fiction editor for the *New Statesman*, he wrote a considerable number of articles, book reviews, and short stories for a variety of magazines both in the United States and the United Kingdom. Most of these have not been collected in any form.

ACHIEVEMENTS

"He began to write in London in 1954. He has followed no other profession" is Naipaul's own crisp author's note to the Penguin editions of his books. In *Naipaul: An Introduction to His Work*, Paul Theroux points out that Naipaul had no other occupation, held no job other than being a full-time writer. He is a man completely dedicated to his art. It is interesting to note that the characters Ganesh (*The Mystic Masseur*), Biswas (*A House for Mr. Biswas*), Ralph Kirpal Singh (*The Mimic Men*), and Mr. Stone (*Mr. Stone and the Knights Companion*) are writers and that they participate in the "thrilling, tedious struggle with the agony and discouraging, exhilarating process of making a book." Naipaul looks upon his travels as essential to his writing, and he travels extensively. He considers such wanderings as essential to sustaining his life as a writer and to releasing his imagination from familiar, deadening scenes.

Starting his career as a comic interpreter of Trinidad society, Naipaul gradually moved to becoming an interpreter of global issues and convulsions of culture. *The Mystic Masseur*, his first novel, had a regional cast and flavor while *In a Free State*, written fourteen years later, has an international cast. His landscapes shifted from the alleys and lanes of Miguel Street to East Africa, French Africa, South America, and India. From the Dickensian comedy and irony of *A House for Mr. Biswas*, he moved to probing the heart of universal darkness in *Guerrillas* and *A Bend in the River*. This growth and development as a serious novelist involved with human concerns is one of Naipaul's major achievements.

Naipaul has received wide critical attention. He is the subject of a number of full-length critical studies and innumerable articles. His books have received front-page reviews; and Irving Howe has called him "the world's writer, a master of language and perception, our sardonic blessing." Writer Elizabeth Hardwick considers the sweep of Naipaul's imagination and the brilliant fictional frame it encompasses unique and without equal in contemporary literature. Writer Paul Theroux considers him superior to existentialist author Albert Camus in his treatment of the theme of displacement. Critic Michael Thorpe, in a brief study of Naipaul, calls him Joseph Conrad's heir as a political novelist. Critics and students of Naipaul place him in the company of such masters of fiction as Joseph Conrad—intensely admired by Naipaul—and Graham Greene. Moreover, even his critics praise his mastery of English prose. For example, Nobel laureate Derek Walcott, a Caribbean-born poet who rejects many of Naipaul's views, wrote in 1987 that Naipaul is "our finest writer of the English sentence."

In his nonfiction writing, Naipaul has proven himself adept at the scholar's meticulous research, and in his travelogues he displays the journalist's ability for brilliant reportage coupled with the novelist's ability for narrative skill and dramatization of human concerns. In all his work, Naipaul confirms his stature as a writer of uncompromising standards and values, of relentless inquiry and tough judgment, thereby establishing him as one of the foremost masters of contemporary fiction.

BIOGRAPHY

Vidiadhar Surajprasad Naipaul, a third generation West Indian of East Indian ancestry, was born in Lion House—which is reincarnated as Hanuman House in his fourth novel, *A House for Mr. Biswas*—into a Hindu Brahmin family in Chaguanas in Central Trinidad, on August 17, 1932.

Naipaul grew up in a large Indian joint family with a brother, five sisters, and more than fifty cousins. Such a family, according to Naipaul, was "a microcosm of the authoritarian state" where power was supreme and growing up in such an atmosphere provided the seamy aspects of human behavior.

Naipaul's father, Seepersad Naipaul, was a correspondent for *The Trinidad Guardian* and an avid reader of Charles Dickens. He was also the author of *Gurudeva and Other Indian Tales* (1943, 1946), a collection of short stories. Naipaul used this book as one of his models to discover "the trick of writing." He was very close to his father, and in the love story

of a father and son in his first major novel, *A House for Mr. Biswas*, he distills this affection and tenderness for his father. Even so, Naipaul, while talking about his childhood in Trinidad (*The Listener*, September 7, 1972), described his father as "a defeated man," who, like Mr. Biswas, felt alienated from the hierarchy of the family and solaced himself with "easy contempt."

Naipaul spent about two years at Chaguanas Government School. His father had attended the same school about twenty years earlier when it was the Canadian Mission School. In 1938, when his father was transferred to the capital city, Port of Spain, Naipaul transferred to Tranquillity Boys' School. He distinguished himself and won a free place at the prestigious Queens Royal College, where he studied for six years, specializing in French and English. The school features in three of his novels, and Naipaul wrote an article to the *Queens Royal College Chronicle* for 1948. It was a discussion of W. Somerset Maugham's first novel, *Liza of Lambeth* (1897), and it explores the origins of Maugham's skills as a novelist. Maugham's study of slum life in *Liza of Lambeth* fascinated Naipaul and in his third novel, *Miguel Street*, he explored the same theme.

Naipaul developed a great urge to get out of Trinidad, and in his book of travel essays about the West Indies, *The Middle Passage* (1962), he describes this passionate obsession to leave the tropical island of his birth. Even after he left, his biggest nightmare was the dream that he had returned to Trinidad. He left Trinidad when he was seventeen and entered University College, Oxford, in the middle of 1950, where, after four years, he took a degree in English. While he was at Oxford, his father died. After graduation in 1955, Naipaul married Patricia Ann Hale and settled in London.

Naipaul worked as editor of the B.B.C. *Caribbean Voices* program and served as fiction reviewer on the staff of the *New Statesman* until 1961. From May, 1950, to May, 1960, he reviewed as many as sixty-one novels. He does not think very highly of these reviews, and none has been included in *The Overcrowded Barracoon and Other Articles* (1972), in which he reflects negatively on his eight-year stay in London and fears that a continued London stay would lead to his own sterility.

To overcome this fear of sterility, Naipaul undertook travels, first to Trinidad for seven months, his first visit home, and then to India for a year to research his cultural heritage. The Trinidad visit resulted in *The Middle Passage* and the India visit produced *An Area of Darkness* (1964). It was also during his India travels, while in Kashmir, that Naipaul wrote his first novel about London, *Mr. Stone and the Knights Companion*, which won the Hawthornden Prize. Despite this literary productivity, the travels only fueled Naipaul's restlessness and intensified his sense of displacement and his difficulty in summoning a positive response to London. This mood of "being physically lost" is brilliantly articulated in Naipaul's next novel, *The Mimic Men*, which was completed in Uganda. The novel was awarded the W. H. Smith Prize.

Four years later, in 1971, Naipaul seemed to break out of his state of detachment by signing a petition in support of the birth of Bangladesh. This active commitment clearly marks a new trend in Naipaul's works, such as his nonfiction *The Loss of El Dorado* (1969). A historical study of Trinidad, meticulously researched, it was selected by *Time* magazine as one of the ten best nonfiction books of 1969.

In a Free State, Naipaul's next book, won England's highest literary award, the Booker Prize. Naipaul's realization that homelessness is not merely an Indian or West Indian trait but a universal feature of the modern world is eloquently expressed in the series of linked stories that make up the book. In *Guerrillas*, named by *The New York Times* as the best novel of 1975, and *A Bend in the River*, Naipaul attempts to portray "the ordeals and absurdities of living in the third world." Travels again took him out of London to visit Ayatollah Khomeini's Iran, General Zia's Pakistan and two other Muslim nations, Indonesia and Malaysia. The result of these seven months of travel was *Among the Believers* (1981), a journalistic report on the new Islamic energy sweeping these nations.

Following the death of his first wife, in 1996 Naipaul married Nadira Khannum Alvi, born in Kenya of Pakistani descent. They settled in London. In 1994 and 1995, Naipaul returned to the countries discussed in *Among the Believers*. In *Beyond Belief*, published in 1998, he again interviewed many of the people and places of the first book, tracing the development of Islam-dominated politics during the fifteen-year interval between the two books. Naipaul's studies of Third World countries inspired admiration and indignation in almost equal proportions. His writing is often praised in the United States and Great Britain but vilified in Middle Eastern, Asian, and Caribbean nations, where nationalists find his pro-Western orientation and contempt for postcolonial cultures to be elitist and even misanthropic. Naipaul is also a controversial figure in England because of his acerbic, unconventional remarks on politics and culture. Nevertheless, he has won every major literary prize offered in Great Britain, including the David Cohen Literature Prize in 1993 for lifetime achievement, and he has been nominated for the Nobel Prize several times. In 1990 he was knighted.

ANALYSIS

"The novel is my main delight," says V. S. Naipaul; in a brief prefatory note to *The Return of Eva Perón, with the Killings in Trinidad* (1980), however, he states that when a novel does not offer itself to him, he travels and turns to nonfiction. In *India: A Wounded Civilization* (1977), Naipaul calls the novel a form of social inquiry. In *An Area of Darkness*, Naipaul insists that the novel must be concerned with the conditions of humanity and respond to the here and now. To him, the novel in its finest form is indistinguishable from truth. It is important to keep these comments in mind when studying Naipaul's novels.

Naipaul grew up in the multiracial society of Trinidad, peopled by migrants from four continents. He was a part of a joint Hindu family with its rigid, clannish, and suffocating atmosphere. Naipaul was an alien in the midst of other aliens. He observed how the various migrant groups, including his own, attempted to maintain their own identity. They failed to do so because they were uncertain about what constituted their identity. They were either unaware of their cultural background or had a romantic fantasy about their past. When they were unable to latch on to their ethnic identity, they often rejected their past and attempted to adapt the identity of their colonial masters, acquiring in the process a hodgepodge of pseudo-Westernization. Ganesh in *The Mystic Masseur* is a classic example; East Indian by tradition, Trinidadian by birth, he sets out as a champion of Hinduism, but when that fails, he swings to the other extreme. He changes his name from Ganesh Ramsumair to G. Ramsay Muir, Esq., M.B.E., completely rejecting his past.

The pseudo-Westernization that Naipaul's characters pursue is in itself symtomatic of their rootlessness. This theme of displacement and the consequences of such displacement, comically absurd at first, later tragic, is a major theme in Naipaul's works. Naipaul himself desperately wanted to escape from Trinidad when he was young; yet, when he moved to London, he was a stranger in search of a tradition, feeling the burden of his double displacement from India and Trinidad. In order to resolve the dilemma and find a resting place for his imagination, Naipaul undertook a voyage of self-discovery to India. He journeyed to the very village from which his ancestors had migrated to Trinidad. Instead of clarifying the past, the trip thrust him into the heart of an area of darkness; the trip was a complete failure and broke his life in two. On his return to England, he had to confront his own emptiness, a sense of dark negation. Naipaul unflinchingly distills these personal experiences of his life into his novels. Possibly no other contemporary author, with the possible exception of Albert Camus, is so quintessentially the voice of exile and alienation.

Naipaul's three early novels, *The Mystic Masseur*, *The Suffrage of Elvira*, and *Miguel Street* belong to his apprentice years. The novels are comedies of Trinidadian manners, and Naipaul uses satire and irony in portraying the Trinidad of "crazy people." Ganesh Ramsumair "the great belcher" whose rise "from laughing-stock to success" with his political poster "A vote for Ganesh is a vote for God," in *The Mystic Masseur*, and Surujpat "Pat" Harbans, in *The Suffrage of Elvira*, with its political theme and setting in Elvira "the smallest, most isolated and most

neglected of the nine counties of Trinidad," and the colorful cannery-row-type Caribbean characters in *Miguel Street* all belong to the rootless, homeless, nomadic migrant world of Naipaul. In satirizing them, Naipaul reveals a Dickensian influence on his work.

Naipaul began writing as a satirist of his society, but to him the novel is a form of social inquiry as well. He is also a serious thinker; thus, in presenting his gallery of misfits and nomadic exiles, he also probes into the ethos of the half societies in which they drift. They are the debris from wounded civilizations. Trinidad, India, French Africa, and Latin America are not romantic lands of primitive innocence, but rather they are harsh and inhospitable, barbaric and cruel, and very different from the images of the slick travel brochures. Naipaul uncompromisingly portrays the "ordeals and absurdities of living in new 'third world' countries."

A HOUSE FOR MR. BISWAS

A House for Mr. Biswas is Naipaul's first serious work, the book in which he discovered "the trick of writing." Dickensian in approach, it meticulously and leisurely chronicles one man's obsession with establishing his identity. Mohun Biswas's desire to own a house in order to give himself a physical and spiritual home is a universal feeling. In *A House for Mr. Biswas*, Naipaul has moved from the regional character portraits of his early novels to a universal theme.

The novel's mood is serious and the comic tone is muted. Events are seen from Biswas's point of view as the reader follows his trials and tribulations within the Tulsi family and his attempts to be a writer. Biswas is modeled upon Seepersad Naipaul, Naipaul's father. Although Naipaul has protested that the work is not autobiographical, the love story between Biswas and his son at the heart of the novel echoes the affection Naipaul and his father had for each other.

Naipaul's narrative style parallels the story line: lyrical when describing the environment and short and crisp when expressing the frustrations and disappointments of Biswas. Social history, characterization, comedy, and the sense of tragedy all blend in the novel, making it that rare thing, "a novel indistinguishable from truth."

MR. STONE AND THE KNIGHTS COMPANION

Mr. Stone and the Knights Companion, written during Naipaul's visit to Kashmir, India, in the early 1960's, has a completely English setting. In the character of Mr. Stone, Naipaul again echoes his theme of rootlessness and the feeling of emptiness. Mr. Stone, a former colonial, has returned to England and faces an identity crisis. His immediate environment seems hostile to him and his colonial memories are second-hand. The novel is concerned with the three years before his mandatory retirement at sixty-five, when Mr. Stone is faced with a sense of insecurity and is apprehensive about the approaching emptiness of life, the "experience of nothingness, an experience of death." Mr. Stone's attempt to avoid this emptiness is the novel's central theme.

Mr. Stone decides to establish a commune for old men and thus is born the idea of the Knights companions. He wants to give old men like himself something to do. He perfects the idea by writing about it, and the act of writing gives him deep satisfaction. Passages describing Mr. Stone going to his study and wrestling with the challenge of writing with full concentration are some of the most forceful passages in the novel.

The project on which he works so devotedly is taken away by Bill Whymper, a colleague. Whymper has a knack for "licking things into shape." Insensitive to the human concern for old age, which had motivated Mr. Stone's proposal, he turns Stone's idea into a slick public relations project. Mr. Stone is heartbroken and inwardly rages with anger, yet, totally alienated, he is unable to share it with anyone. Gradually, Mr. Stone calms down and stoically takes consolation from merely having survived.

THE MIMIC MEN

The Mimic Men, in the form of fictional autobiography, is the story of Ranjit "Ralph" Kirpal Singh, a forty-year-old Indian from the West Indies. It is Naipaul's darkest novel, and Ralph Kirpal Singh expresses the unrelieved mood and feeling of emptiness even more intensely than Mr. Stone. *The Mimic Men* is also one of Naipaul's most complex novels; there is no real chronological sequence. Closeted in an old hotel in London, Kirpal Singh writes the story of his life, attempting to establish a sense of order of the four periods of his life, "student, householder, and man of affairs, recluse." His opinions and remembrance of events are episodic and constantly shifting, depending on the intensity of his feelings. He alternates between images of fantasy and reality as he moves from India to London and back to Isabella, the West Indian island where he grew up. Like Naipaul, Kirpal Singh also is drawn to London. In London, his marriage to Sandra, an English girl, does not succeed. He returns to Isabella where he is successful in real estate and runs for political office. All these "actions" are, he perceives, "roles" that he is playing, imitating others. He has become one of the mimic men. They are absurd; he is absurd and, he concludes, "shipwrecked." He wants to escape again, this time "to a place unknown, among people whose lives and even language" he need never enter. The best he could do is escape to an old hotel.

Kirpal Singh is *the* Naipaul man: educated, sophisticated, complex, forever conscious of his physical and spiritual rootlessness. He echoes Naipaul's own belief that one cannot return to an ordered harmony or hope for magical moments of tranquillity. One must accept what one has, since the pursuit of illusions is the absurd role of mimic men.

IN A FREE STATE

In a Free State, which contains a short novel—a series of interconnected stories—and two fragments of a travel diary, marks an important stage in Naipaul's career. After its publication, Naipaul described the novel as a "rather final statement" of the themes he had already exhausted.

In a Free State presents five different kinds of wandering, represented by a group of international characters. They are all in middle passage—in a free state—yet they are not truly free in that they do not belong in the countries they are in and are unable to belong in the countries from which they come. The very title is indicative of the aimless drift of contemporary aliens. The varied characters in the book include an Indian in America ("one out of many"); a displaced Indian from the West Indies ("tell me who to kill"); a West Indian in London; and an Englishman and Englishwoman in Africa ("In a free state").

The prologue ("The Tramp at Piraeus") and the epilogue ("The Circus at Luxor") of the work make an important statement about Naipaul himself. In the prologue, a tramp is harassed by a fat Egyptian student, an incident watched by Naipaul. In the epilogue, when a group of Arab beggar boys are whipped by another Arab boy for a group of Italians to photograph, Naipaul rebels and puts a stop to it. His action represents the quality missing in his characters in *In a Free State*; they have surrendered and resigned without any attempt at protest. The writer, however, must protest against injustice and remind the world of its responsibility to humanity.

GUERRILLAS

Guerrillas was written "in five months of controlled frenzy." *Guerrillas*, like *In a Free State* and *A Bend in the River*, realistically presents "the ordeals and absurdities of living in the third world." The title is ironic because none of the major characters in the novel engages in any revolutionary action. There is pretension to guerrilla activity, which results in a murder as a result of sexual shame. The words of "revolutionary" Jimmy Ahmed, "when everybody wants to fight there's nothing to fight for. Everybody wants to fight his own little war, everybody is a guerrilla," placed as epigraph to the novel, summarize the philosophic core of the book.

Jimmy Ahmed is another one of Naipaul's rootless heroes. He is half-black and half-Chinese, and even his name is assumed, an imitation of the black Muslims, and so he has no authentic identity whatsoever. Michael de Freitas, alias Michael X, the Trinidadian black power leader who was hanged for murder, is the inspiration for Jimmy Ahmed.

Jimmy Ahmed's fantasy is to be the true hero. He lives in an imaginary world, talking much about revolutionary guerrilla activity and thereby play acting in much the same way Kirpal Singh did in *The Mimic Men* and the various characters do in *In a Free State*. Jimmy, who has fled from England, where he had been involved in a rape case, has an army made up of slum rejects; his attempt at a peaceful commune is pathetic.

Peter Roche, a white South African who had been tortured and imprisoned because of his opposition to the apartheid regime, and Roche's girlfriend, Jane, one of those "liberals who come flashing their milk white thighs and think they're contributing to the cause," travel to Jimmy's commune to help him. All three are homeless, and yet none of them really trusts the other or is committed to any cause, but each of their pretensions to guerrilla activity gives them a needed escape, a façade.

The city of the emerging Caribbean island is bristling with political corruption and greedy men from multinational corporations. Naipaul is brilliant in evoking the locale, "a place at the end of the world, a place that had exhausted its possibilities." He captures the smell and substance of the third world with its irritations, bureaucracy, and nightmarish fantasies. The city reaches its breaking point, and when it snaps, anger and violence take over. The trio—Jimmy, Peter, and Jane—are jolted from their fantasy and what results is one of the harshest sexual violations in contemporary literature, followed by Jane's brutal murder.

In *Guerrillas*, Naipaul demonstrates how far he has traveled from the Dickensian irony and comedy of *The Mystic Masseur* and from the regionalism of Trinidad to the global universal tragedy of rootlessness.

A BEND IN THE RIVER

A Bend in the River is set in Africa, and the country could resemble either Zaire under General Mobutu Sese Seko or Uganda. It is an Africa with Colonial vestiges, the same terrain Conrad had explored in *Heart of Darkness* (1902). The story is told by Salim, a young Indian shopkeeper from the East Coast of Africa. Salim is an outsider, the quintessential Naipaul hero, an exile in a damaged land. Salim's ancestors came from Northern India, and Salim has traveled to the interior of the country, about a thousand miles from the capital, to set up a shop "at a bend in the great river," a place "where the future had come and gone." The novel describes approximately seven years in his life, during which time he carries on his modest trade in pencils, copybooks, toothbrushes, and pots and pans. He keeps to himself, limiting his wanderings to "flat, shop, club, bar, the river embankment at sunset."

Independence comes to the country, and it emerges from its own past. In spite of all the trappings of modern civilization—tall buildings, schools and universities, long radio broadcasts by the Big man who's now elected himself for life—the country has a hard time becoming a part of the contemporary world.

It is this absurd, violent, corrupt, twilight world that Naipaul sketches in *A Bend in the River*. The capital has the Big man with his army, sorcery, and terrorism, while in the bush lurk the guerrillas of the Liberation Army and the ghosts of an ancestral past. In Salim's town at the bend of the river are refugees, impoverished Africans, and corrupt officials, who are anxious and nervous about the bloodshed that preceded independence.

Each character in the novel contributes to the tension and the rage: Raymond, the French scholar who was once a close adviser to the Big man, "the Big man's white man"; Metty, "someone of mixed race," Salim's lifelong servant whose relations with Salim disintegrate because he no longer gets the traditional protection from his master; Father Huisman, the Belgian priest who collects African tribal masks which are decaying, reflecting the world from where they come; Yvette, Raymond's wife, who has an affair with Salim, which makes him say "I felt blessed and remade"; and Ferdinand, son of a woman from the bush, a student who vociferously repeats the Big man's sayings of national pride.

Salim's shop is confiscated as part of the Big man's radicalization and given to citizen Theotime, who hires Salim as his manager. Then Salim is arrested and imprisoned and released by Ferdinand, who sums up what is happening in this attempt to impress order on disorder: "We're all going to hell, and every man knows this in his bones. . . . Everyone wants to make his money and run away. But where?" He answers that question cryptically by saying, "The bush burns itself. But there is no place to go."

To make the darkness even more intense, Naipaul creates an incident in the novel where Salim visits his friend Nazruddin in London, before his decision to leave Africa. Nazruddin tells Salim that people are stampeding, everyone—Argentines, Chinese, blacks, Koreans—"All of them are on the run. They

are frightened of the fire. You musn't think it's only Africa people are running from." Thus, rootlessness and wandering become worldwide.

THE ENIGMA OF ARRIVAL

In 1987, Naipaul published *The Enigma of Arrival*, his first novel in almost a decade. In several ways this book marked a change of direction for Naipaul. Set primarily in Wiltshire, England, and spanning the period from 1950 to 1984, *The Enigma of Arrival* is by far Naipaul's most autobiographical novel. The protagonist, like Naipaul himself, is a middle-aged writer, a native of Trinidad who came to England on a scholarship to study at the University of Oxford. Like Naipaul, too, he has settled in the English countryside. Indeed, so close are the parallels between author and protagonist that some reviewers wondered why Naipaul had published the book as a novel. In its reflective tone and its relative lack of novelistic incident, *The Enigma of Arrival* could easily be mistaken for a memoir.

Nevertheless, Naipaul chose to treat his experience from a distance by casting it in the form of a novel. His reflections on his Wiltshire neighbors, his memories of his early years in England, and his account of a return to Trinidad for a memorial service after the death of his sister—these quietly developed scenes sound a note that is new in Naipaul's work: a sense of reconciliation, of serenity even, growing out of an awareness of the endless cycles of life and death. In the English countryside, it seems, Naipaul has found a vision which is central to the Indian heritage that he left behind.

A WAY IN THE WORLD

In 1994 Naipaul published his eleventh novel, *A Way in the World*. It is a difficult book to categorize: The publisher listed it as a novel, but critics demurred, finding it a mixture of short stories, history, and autobiography that does not fit established genres. In structure, the book resembles *In a Free State*. It comprises nine narratives, some clearly fictional and involving historical persons (English navigator Sir Walter Raleigh and Venezuelan dictator Francisco de Miranda) and some ostensibly factual, involving historical figures or people supposedly known by Naipaul (such as a novelist named Foster Morris), and reminiscences, which the reader is to assume are factual in spirit if not in every detail. Together, the narratives examine various types of cultural displacement—how the principal characters find their way in a world in which two cultures meet, clash, and mingle.

In the opening narrative Naipaul mulls his youth in the mixed society of Trinidad. He meets an ambitious black man, Blair, who represents the successful postcolonial Trinidadian. Whereas Naipaul leaves Trinidad to become an expatriate in England, Blair remains in Trinidad and becomes a successful politician. In the book's last section, the two meet again, decades later, in East Africa, where Blair is advising a fledgling government on economic policy. In the book's most touching scene, the two men, with mutual empathy, recognize the different sorts of alienation their careers have brought them, one as a writer and the other as an political consultant for the Third World. Soon afterward, Blair is brutally murdered. Although African in heritage, a Caribbean-born man, such as Blair, Naipaul intimates, cannot return to his ancestral roots.

The other narratives also show that returns are perilous, if not impossible, for the culturally displaced. Raleigh, for instance, finds that after staking his future on discovering gold in the Orinoco region of South America he cannot return to England without facing derision and execution because of his failure. By contrast, Francisco de Miranda, part revolutionary and part confidence man, devotes his life to freeing Venezuela, his homeland, from Spain, traveling through the United States and Europe gaining support for his cause, but when his chance finally comes, he too fails in his attempt to return home—he is even betrayed by his protégé, revolutionary Simón Bolívar—and is imprisoned in Spain.

A Way in the World shows how people who are adrift in the world make their ways by redefining themselves. The result is a psychological chimera, made up partly of inherited traits, which are often poorly understood; partly of acquired interests, as from education; and partly of experience from random incidents in foreign contexts. This plunges the book's culturally displaced characters into, at best, eventual irrelevance, and, at worst, disaster. The

book's tone is elegiac: The product of postcolonial displacement is often tragedy.

K. Bhaskara Rao, updated by Roger Smith

OTHER MAJOR WORKS

SHORT FICTION: *A Flag on the Island*, 1967.

NONFICTION: *The Middle Passage: Impressions of Five Societies—British, French, and Dutch—in the West Indies and South America*, 1962; *An Area of Darkness: An Experience of India*, 1964; *The Loss of El Dorado: A History*, 1969; *The Overcrowded Barracoon and Other Articles*, 1972; *India: A Wounded Civilization*, 1977; *The Return of Eva Perón, with the Killings in Trinidad*, 1980; *Among the Believers: An Islamic Journey*, 1981; *Finding the Center: Two Narratives*, 1984; *A Turn in the South*, 1989; *India: A Million Mutinies Now*, 1990; *Beyond Belief: Islamic Excursions Among the Converted Peoples*, 1998; *Between Father and Son: Family Letters: Selected Correspondence of V. S. Naipaul and His Family, 1949-1953*, 2000 (pb. in England as *Letters Between a Father and Son*, 1999).

BIBLIOGRAPHY

Cudjoe, Selwyn R. *V. S. Naipaul: A Materialist Reading*. Amherst: University of Massachusetts Press, 1988. A fellow Trinidadian but of black descent, Cudjoe understandably takes a negative stance with regard to Naipaul's work, attacking him for his racist views. He also employs psychoanalytical references to explain Naipaul's literary characters and the man himself. A strong counterpart to the praise given Naipaul by many British critics.

Gorra, Michael. *After Empire: Scott, Naipaul, Rushdie*. Chicago: University of Chicago Press, 1997. Like Paul Scott and Salman Rushdie, Naipaul is a novelist who explores his English education against the backdrop of a culturally blurred society left behind by British imperialism, according to Gorra. As such, Naipaul concerns himself with history, the nature of identity, and the mimicry inherent in postcolonial society.

King, Bruce. *V. S. Naipaul*. New York: St. Martin's Press, 1993. King finds a moral honesty in Naipaul's writing that, with his unusual Caribbean-

Indian-British background, brings freshness to his fiction, which deals with major social, psychological, political, and cultural changes of modern times. King analyzes Naipaul's fictional works in individual chapters. He also discusses Naipaul's nonfiction, and appendices concern Naipaul's family and experiences in Trinidad and Africa.

Morris, Robert K. *Paradoxes of Order: Some Perspectives on the Fiction of V. S. Naipaul.* Columbia: University of Missouri Press, 1975. A slim volume (105 pages) that gives particular emphasis to *The Mimic Men.* Offers some interesting religious background on Naipaul, and the influence of his Hindu upbringing on his work.

Mustafa, Fawzia. *V. S. Naipaul.* Cambridge, England: Cambridge University Press, 1995. Mustafa stresses the influence of Joseph Conrad, to whom, like Naipaul, English literature was a borrowed tradition. In six chapters dividing Naipaul's work into four decades, Mustafa examines the novelistic techniques Naipaul uses to understand the postcolonial condition of the Third World through his fiction and nonfiction.

Nightingale, Peggy. *Journey Through Darkness: The Writing of V. S. Naipaul.* New York: University of Queensland Press, 1987. A thorough examination of the major writings of Naipaul, covering his background and core themes in both his fiction and nonfiction. A scholarly work, yet quite readable. Includes an extensive bibliography until 1984.

Nixon, Rob. *London Calling: V. S. Naipaul, Postcolonial Mandarin.* New York: Oxford University Press, 1992. Nixon discusses the rhetorical character and political circumstances of Naipaul's travel books in order to understand their harsh portraits of developing countries, but he makes frequent reference to Naipaul's novels as well, and the comparisons illuminate the fictional themes.

Thorpe, Michael. *Writers and Their Work: V. S. Naipaul,* edited by Ian ScottKilvert. Essex, England: Longman, 1976. A slim volume relating the nonfiction to autobiographical elements in Naipaul's novels, eight of which are analyzed here. Selected bibliography.

Walsh, William. *V. S. Naipaul.* New York: Barnes & Noble, 1973. This small volume manages to analyze eleven works of Naipaul. Special emphasis is given to *A House for Mr. Biswas.* Includes quotes from Naipaul's novels and a bibliography. Contains a chapter on various critics' responses to Naipaul.

R. K. NARAYAN

Born: Madras, India; October 10, 1906

PRINCIPAL LONG FICTION

Swami and Friends, 1935
The Bachelor of Arts, 1937
The Dark Room, 1938
The English Teacher, 1945 (also known as *Grateful to Life and Death*, 1953)
Mr. Sampath, 1949 (also known as *The Printer of Malgudi*, 1957)
The Financial Expert, 1952
Waiting for the Mahatma, 1955
The Guide, 1958
The Man-Eater of Malgudi, 1961
The Sweet-Vendor, 1967 (also known as *The Vendor of Sweets*)
The Painter of Signs, 1976
A Tiger for Malgudi, 1983
Talkative Man: A Novel of Malgudi, 1987
The World of Nagaraj, 1990

OTHER LITERARY FORMS

In addition to his novels, R. K. Narayan published a number of volumes of short stories. The title of his first collection of short stories, *Malgudi Days* (1941), is also the title of a later collection, published by Viking in 1982. Other collections include *Dodu and Other Stories* (1943), *Cyclone and Other Stories* (1944), *Lawley Road: Thirty-two Short Stories* (1956), *A Horse and Two Goats and Other Stories* (1970), *Old and New* (1981), *Under the Banyan Tree and Other Stories* (1985), and *The Grandmother's*

Tale and Selected Stories (1994). Two autobiographical works are *My Days* (1974), which covers four decades of Narayan's career as a writer, and *My Dateless Diary* (1960), a journal of his travels through America. "Gods, Demons and Modern Times," a talk given at Columbia University in 1972, is collected together with tales from Indian mythology in *Gods, Demons, and Others* (1964). Narayan also published translations of *The Ramayana* (1972) and *The Mahabharata* (1978). During the war years, he edited *Indian Thought*, and his weekly newspaper "middles" were collected in *Next Sunday: Sketches and Essays* (1960). Harvey Breit's stage adaptation of *The Guide* only incurred Narayan's displeasure. Despite his attempt to withhold permission for production, *The Guide* opened on Broadway in March, 1968, and was subsequently made into a motion picture.

ACHIEVEMENTS

R. K. Narayan was inducted into the American Academy of Arts and Letters in 1982. He was also made a member of the Sahitya Academy (Literary Academy) in India.

BIOGRAPHY

Rasipuram Krishnaswami Narayan was born in Madras on October 10, 1906. During his early years he was reared by his grandmother in Madras. Very early in his autobiography, *My Days*, he records his dislike of education, of the mission schools, of the British colleges, and of his short-lived adventure as a schoolteacher. All these experiences permeate his writing and have become the subject matter of his fiction. His literary education was predominantly Victorian in flavor. Francis Palgrave's *Golden Treasury* (1861), Sir Walter Scott, and reading William Shakespeare aloud were its staples. In 1933, he fell in love with a woman named Rajam, whom he married only after great difficulties because their horoscopes would not match; she died of typhoid in 1939. The trauma of this loss, the inability to come to terms with his fate, and the effort to defy his destiny led to Narayan's interest in purported psychic communication with the dead and provided the inspiration for

The English Teacher. A feeling of helplessness in the face of destiny takes sometimes comic and sometimes tragic turns throughout Narayan's work.

Commissioned by the Dewan of Mysore, Narayan wrote a travel book on Mysore. After several years of writing for *The Hindu* and other journalistic experiences, Narayan began publishing *Indian Thought*, a quarterly of literature, philosophy, and culture. Not until October, 1956, did Narayan travel outside the boundaries of the three-city area of Madras, Mysore, and Coimbatore. He went to Berkeley, California, on a Rockefeller Foundation grant to write a novel, *The Guide*. Subsequently, he visited the United States several times, while continuing to live and write in Mysore and Madras. The death of his daughter Hema in the early 1990's caused him to become extremely reclusive.

(Library of Congress)

ANALYSIS

On January 18, 1982, Narayan was inducted into the American Academy of Arts and Letters. Though he received a similar honor in India from the Sahitya Academy (Literary Academy), it was not without debate. Could a South Indian writer who had never stirred outside his home region, who was writing in English rather than his mother tongue, whose fiction was not concerned with lofty nationalistic issues, actually be worthy of a literary prize? Indeed, it is toNarayan's credit that he continued to write in English. His writing is neither imitative nor experimental. Never feeling compelled to work within the boundaries of large literary or nationalistic trends, Narayan did not find it necessary to vary the English language or to describe moments of nationalistic history as a means of establishing his identity. Joycean word coinage, attempts to introduce the rhythms of various Indian languages in his English style, or the use of Indian-English dialect are not Narayan's tools. It is through character description and his characters' worldviews that Narayan expresses a distinctly Indian sensibility. For him, Standard English is the most effective medium for conveying this sensibility. To Narayan, English is so opaque that it can take on the "tint of any country."

Thus, Narayan's bilingual situation is not a handicap. It provided him with the means to know and use English while keeping him in touch with his own roots and cultural wisdom. It kept him aware of English literary history, yet his style does not show "the marks of a labored acquisition." On the contrary, it reflects the English language in its "process of transmutation," as Narayan described the adoption of English in India. Most of Narayan's characters speak and use the sort of Standard English Narayan himself would speak in India. Occasionally, an Indian-English idiom reflects a character's situation.

Narayan's consistent use of Standard English is, more often than not, appropriate to the circumstances of his fiction. Swami and his cricket-playing cohorts, reading the Messrs. Binn's catalog of cricket equipment, are not likely to be speaking in a native language, nor are the boys educated at Albert Mission college. In *The Guide*, Raju, providing instruction to Velan the villager, is not likely to be speaking English or Indian English, yet his Tamil is best translated into straightforward, crisp, Standard English. Thus, Narayan does not provide any superfluous Tamil lilt to the English prose of these passages. The characters and situations are more than sufficient expressions of Indianness.

Narayan gained much criticism for being immune to the stylistic experimentation other commonwealth writers seem to have found necessary. He was also criticized for the very sentence structure for which Ernest Hemingway was praised. In his *A Human Idiom* (1964), Professor William Walsh, while admiring Narayan's style for "its pure and easy flow," finds it lacking in the "adventitiously injected" energy that "marks the writing of the West Indians." A number of Indian critics objected that Narayan's prose seems oblivious to the tradition of English literary style. What they mean is that it lacks a "Macaulayan amplitude of phrase." Narayan's distance from the centers where the language is changing and developing is seen as yet another handicap to the development of his style.

Such criticism fails to recognize Narayan's supreme achievement as an Indian writer in English: his refusal to heed critical stereotypes and his development of an individual style based on his understanding of the process of the English language's transmutation in India. By his rejection both of an overt Indian idiom and of a self-conscious literary English, Narayan was able to maintain his unobtrusive authorial stance. His style is far from monotonous; it often changes pace to reflect action and character. Both in *The Guide* and in *The Painter of Signs*, it reflects the breathlessness with which the action takes place, but slows down as it reflects moments of repose in the consciousness of his characters.

By using simple sentence constructions, Narayan is known for bending the English language to describe suitably the languorous quality of South Indian life. Ironically, this effect is achieved with short, crisp, Hemingwayesque sentences with simple variations on the subject-object construction. While for Hemingway this technique would yield "sparse and muscular prose" which conveys the American character, in Narayan's prose it conveys the leisurely nature characteristic of the Indian's ordinary life and daily conversation.

In elevating ordinary life through style, character, and situation, Narayan's fiction is like a prism that reflects a many-colored Indianness. Ignoring the obvious means of providing his work with an Indian identity, Narayan focuses instead on quintessential situations in which Indian character develops. "Episode and escapade," "moment and mood," in their peculiarly Indian contexts of a belief in destiny, astrology, and arranged marriages, give Narayan's fictional locale, Malgudi, its own postage stamp that says, "In India we trust."

The common man in his passage toward self-knowledge, in his sometimes comic and sometimes tragic struggle against destiny, is the subject of Narayan's fiction. Narayan's recurring preoccupations are universal, but they are given form in an intensely particularized fictional world, as palpable and idiosyncratic as William Faulkner's Yoknapatawpha. The reality of Narayan's Malgudi is established in his first novel, *Swami and Friends*.

SWAMI AND FRIENDS

With *Swami and Friends*, the Malgudi town became reality. Lawley extension was laid out at a perfect distance from the Sarayu river, just enough distance to be comfortable for the Westernized Indian and the British Sahibs. The railway station made civilized connections possible, while an old trunk road wound through the forest. It is through following the trunk road and spending a night out in the cold that Swami comes to an understanding of himself. He makes the passage from innocence to experience, very much like Mark Twain's Huck Finn. British and Indian critics have compared him to Richmal Crompton's William and Jennings, both very young British school boys, who through several volumes fail to mature. It is the universal experience of childhood, the process of "growing up" that *Swami and Friends* captures and yet Swami's misadventures are played out in uniquely Indian settings. The cricket games and cricket bat catalogs are as Indian and real to the bicultural situation as grandmother, the monkey, and mango chutney.

THE BACHELOR OF ARTS

In another work, the teenage years become a time of learning and realization; and Chandran, in *The Bachelor of Arts*, learns about the importance of success and failure. Though this success and failure are centered around seemingly trivial issues—the passing of college examinations, the winning of college elections, and the gaining of attention from the opposite sex—these situations are tremendously important in the life of the Indian college student. At the same time, however, they are infused with the general human yearning for success at any cost, the debating of the ethics of such situations, and the human fear of failure. Each little question of conscience holds its own cathartic tragicomedy. Narayan's preeminence among Indian writers in English lies in his ability to capture moments in time, as much a part of his reader's life as they are of the life of his characters, and to depict both the comic and tragic aspects of those moments.

THE ENGLISH TEACHER

The English Teacher, or *Grateful to Life and Death*, describes the existential moments through which almost any individual faces the "eternal now." The Malgudi adolescent moves to the householder stage, yet cannot procure the woman whom he loves in marriage: The horoscopes do not match. The astrologers will not give their consent. The English teacher, however, is able to persuade the astrologer that the girl's horoscope has some adverse stars that might cancel out those in the boy's horoscope. He then triumphantly brings his wife home to an idyllic happiness, a happiness that reigns despite an unsuccessful teaching career and returned manuscripts.

Yet every individual must face the disparity between "man's hope" and "man's fate." The Karmic wheel turns, and the English teacher is helpless in the face of merciless fate, in this case, typhoid. Intensely personal, it is a private tragedy of the "felt experience"—the tragedy that no human being can fully accept. In his refusal of his destiny, the English teacher attempts to transcend his fate. His struggle against death and his eventual acceptance of it takes the form of efforts to communicate with the dead. While this second half of the novel seems melodramatic and

Appellations such as the "Indian Chekhov" and the "Indian Jane Austen" fall short of Narayan's achievement. He is *the* "Indian Narayan," as Indian as William Faulkner is American. His concern is the heroic quality of the ordinary Indian individual's struggle with his destiny, as it is portrayed through personal, seemingly trivial experiences. This is what makes Narayan's fiction "moral art."

Feroza Jussawalla, updated by Geralyn Strecker

OTHER MAJOR WORKS

SHORT FICTION: *Malgudi Days*, 1941, 1982; *Dodu and Other Stories*, 1943; *Cyclone and Other Stories*, 1944; *An Astrologer's Day and Other Stories*, 1947; *Lawley Road: Thirty-two Short Stories*, 1956; *Gods, Demons, and Others*, 1964; *A Horse and Two Goats and Other Stories*, 1970; *Old and New*, 1981; *Under the Banyan Tree and Other Stories*, 1985; *The Grandmother's Tale and Selected Stories*, 1994.

NONFICTION: *Mysore*, 1944; *My Dateless Diary*, 1960; *Next Sunday: Sketches and Essays*, 1960; *My Days*, 1974; *Reluctant Guru*, 1974; *A Writer's Nightmare: Selected Essays, 1958-1988*, 1988.

TRANSLATIONS: *The Ramayana: A Shortened Modern Prose Version of the Indian Epic*, 1972 (of Vālmīki); *The Mahabharata: A Shortened Prose Version of the Indian Epic*, 1978

BIBLIOGRAPHY

French, Warren. "R. K. Narayan." In *Contemporary Novelists*, edited by James Vinson. New York: St. Martin's Press, 1982. Reviews the success of Narayan in his tales of the imaginary community of Malgudi. According to French, the Malgudi stories can be read both as character studies and as an inner process from "fanaticism to serenity." A marvelous introduction to Narayan, albeit in contracted form; there is nothing extraneous here.

Kain, Geoffrey, ed. *R. K. Narayan: Contemporary Critical Perspectives*. East Lansing: Michigan State University, 1993. This volume encompasses a wide range of essays on areas such as plot, motif, and theme, as well as select essays influenced by contemporary cultural and postmodernist criticism. Features two essays that contradict the customary commendatory nature of Narayan criticism and a short essay on Narayan as a dramatist.

Raizada, Harish. *A Critical Study of R. K. Narayan*. New Delhi: Young Asia Publications, 1969. A standard-type critical study, chronicling Narayan's life and novels. The book is peppered with extracts from Narayan's writing, set off in denser type for easy reading. The most interesting chapter is the last in which Raizada explores Narayan's characteristics as a writer. Bibliography.

Ram, Atma, ed. *Perspectives on R. K. Narayan*. Indo-English Writers Series 3. Ghaziabad, India: Vimal Prakashan, 1981. A collection of essays on Narayan, all new except for one reprint. Preface by Warren French. Some interesting views on Narayan's writing, such as Lakshmi Holstrom's study of women characters in the novels and Rameshwar Gupta's "The Gandhi in Narayan." Select bibliography. A valuable resource on Narayan.

Ram, Susan, and N. Ram. *R. K. Narayan: The Early Years, 1906-1945*. New Delhi: Viking Press, 1996. Prepared with the cooperation of Narayan's family and friends, the Rams' biography of Narayan's early years is excellent.

Walsh, William. *R. K. Narayan: A Critical Appreciation*. London: William Heinemann, 1982. A thoughtful, comprehensive criticism of Narayan's writings, from his early novels to his mature works. A definitive work, thorough and accessible; the writing is a delight, the transitions smooth, and happily free from jargon. Select bibliography.

GLORIA NAYLOR

Born: New York, New York; January 25, 1950

PRINCIPAL LONG FICTION

The Women of Brewster Place: A Novel in Seven Stories, 1982
Linden Hills, 1985
Mama Day, 1988

Bailey's Café, 1992
The Men of Brewster Place, 1998

OTHER LITERARY FORMS

In 1986, Gloria Naylor wrote a column, *Hers*, for *The New York Times*. She is also the writer of a number of screenplays, short stories, and articles for various periodicals. She is known primarily, however, for her novels.

ACHIEVEMENTS

Enjoying both critical and popular acclaim, Naylor's work has reached a wide audience. *The Women of Brewster Place* won the 1983 American Book Award for best first novel and was later made into a television miniseries. Naylor's other awards include a National Endowment for the Arts Fellowship in 1985 and a Guggenheim Fellowship in 1988.

Surveying the range of black life in America, from poor ghetto to affluent suburb to Southern offshore island, Naylor's work examines questions of black identity and, in particular, celebrates black women. In the face of enormous problems and frequent victimization, black women are shown coping through their sense of community and their special powers. Male readers might find less to cheer about in Naylor's early works, as she writes from a feminist perspective. Later works, however, recognize the plight of black males, acknowledging their struggles and celebrating their achievements. Though Naylor's focus is the black experience, her depictions of courage, community, and cultural identity have universal appeal.

BIOGRAPHY

The oldest child of parents who had migrated from Mississippi, Gloria Naylor was born and reared in New York City, her parents having left the South the year before her birth. An avid reader as a child, Naylor seemed to have inherited her passion for reading from her mother, a woman who would go to great lengths to purchase books to which she was denied access in Mississippi libraries since blacks were not allowed inside. The year Naylor graduated from high school, Dr. Martin Luther King, Jr., was assassinated,

(Kimberly Dawson Kurnizki)

and the shock of this event caused Naylor to delay her college education. She chose instead to become a missionary for the Jehovah's Witnesses in New York, North Carolina, and Florida. She eventually found missionary life too strict, but her zeal apparently carried over into her later feminism. Although her writings are not religious, a fundamentalist pattern of thinking pervades them. She tends to separate her characters into the sheep and the goats (the latter mostly men), the saved and the damned, with one whole book, *Linden Hills*, being modeled after Dante Alighieri's *Inferno* (c. 1320).

In high school Naylor read widely in the nineteenth century British novelists, but later in a creative writing course at Brooklyn College she came across the book that influenced her most—*The Bluest Eye* (1970), by the black American novelist Toni Morrison. The example of Morrison inspired Naylor to write fiction and to focus on the lives of black women, who Naylor felt were underrepresented (if not ignored) in American literature. Naylor began work on *The Women of Brewster Place*, which was published the year after her graduation from Brooklyn College with a B.A. in English. By that time, Naylor was studying on a fellowship at Yale University, from which she received an M.A. in African American studies in 1983.

Naylor's background and literary achievements won for her numerous invitations for lectureships or other appointments in academia. She held visiting posts at George Washington University, the University of Pennsylvania, Princeton University, New York University, Boston University, Brandeis University, and Cornell University. Diverse in her pursuits, Naylor wrote a stage adaptation of *Bailey's Café*. She founded One Way Productions, an independent film company, and became involved in a literacy program in the Bronx. She settled in Brooklyn, New York.

ANALYSIS

White people do not appear often and are not featured in the work of Gloria Naylor. Yet their presence can be felt like a white background noise, or like the boulevard traffic on the other side of the wall from Brewster Place. White culture is simply another fact of life, like a nearby nuclear reactor or toxic waste dump, and the effects of racism and discrimination are omnipresent in Naylor's work. Against these stifling effects her characters live their lives and try to define their sense of black identity, from the ghetto dwellers of Brewster Place to the social climbers of Linden Hills to the denizens of Willow Springs, a pristine Southern island relatively untouched by slavery and segregation.

Naylor writes about these settings and characters in a romantic mode that sometimes verges on the melodramatic or gothic. The influence of her earlier reading—such authors as Charlotte and Emily Brontë, Charles Dickens, William Faulkner, and Morrison—is apparent. The settings have heavy but obvious symbolic meanings, some derived from literary references: Brewster Place is a dead-end street, Linden Hills is a modern version of Dante's Hell, and Willow Springs recalls the magical isle of William Shakespeare's *The Tempest* (1611). The weather and numerous details also carry symbolic freight, almost as much as they do for such an emblematic writer as Nathaniel Hawthorne. In addition to literary influences, the symbolism seems to draw on Hollywood, particularly Hollywood's gothic genre, horror films;

for example, in *Linden Hills* the character Norman Anderson suffers from attacks of "the pinks"—imaginary blobs of pink slime—while the rich undertaker Luther Nedeed locks his wife and child away in the basement.

These two examples also show, in an exaggerated fashion, how Naylor's characters fit into the Romantic mode. Her characters tend to go to extremes, to be emotional and obsessive, or to have a single trait or commit a single act that determines their whole life course. While rather one-dimensional and melodramatic, they nevertheless linger in the memory. Such is the case with Luther Nedeed, who represents Satan in *Linden Hills*, and with the old conjure woman Miranda "Mama" Day, who represents Satan's usual opposition in the scheme of things.

In Naylor, this scheme of things illustrates how she has transferred her former missionary fervor, along with the framework of religious thought, to her feminism. Luther Nedeed's behavior is only the most sensational example of men's cruelty to women in Naylor's work; he has a large following. On the other hand, the mystical ability of Mama Day, the Prospero of women's liberation, to command the forces of nature and the spirit world is only the most sensational example of women's special powers in Naylor's thinking. Even the women of Brewster Place demonstrate these powers through their mutual love and support, enabling them to triumph over devastating personal tragedies and demeaning circumstances.

Naylor's men are another story: If not outright demons or headed that way, they seem to lack some vital force. Even the best men are fatally flawed—they are subject to "the pinks," are addicted to wine, or have weak hearts. Failing at key moments, they are useful only as sacrifices to the feminine mystique. A prime example is the engineer George Andrews of *Mama Day*, who, for all his masculine rationality and New York smarts, does not know how to handle (significantly) a brooding hen. A close reading of Naylor's works reveals the men's victimization, along with the women's; however, Naylor is concerned with the women in her earlier novels. Naylor's later works indicate that she has expanded her vision to include men.

THE WOMEN OF BREWSTER PLACE

Naylor began fulfilling her commitment to make black women more prominent in American fiction with *The Women of Brewster Place*, subtitled *A Novel in Seven Stories*. The seven stories, featuring seven women, can be read separately, but they are connected by their setting of Brewster Place and by characters who appear, or are mentioned, in more than one story. The women arrive on the dead-end street by different routes that exhibit the variety of lives of black women, but on Brewster Place they unite into a community.

The middle-aged bastion of Brewster Street is Mattie Michael, who over the course of her life was betrayed by each of the three men she loved—her seducer, her father, and her son. She mothers Lucielia Louise Turner (whose grandmother once sheltered Mattie) when Ciel's abusive boyfriend destroys her life. In addition, Mattie welcomes her close friend Etta Mae Johnson, who also once gave Mattie refuge. Etta Mae is a fading beauty who has used men all of her life but is now herself used by a sleazy preacher for a one-night stand. The other women featured are the young unwed Cora Lee, a baby factory; Kiswana Browne, an aspiring social reformer who hails from the affluent suburb of Linden Hills; and Lorraine and Theresa, two lesbians seeking privacy for their love.

Few men are in evidence on Brewster Place, and these few inspire little confidence. C. C. Baker and his youth gang lurk about the alleyway and, in the novel's brutal climax, rape Lorraine. The crazed Lorraine in turn kills the wino Ben, the old janitor who earlier had befriended her. Yet Naylor acknowledges the plight of the men. In her description of the gang members, she says,

Born with the appendages of power, circumcised by a guillotine, and baptized with the steam of a million nonreflective mirrors, these young men wouldn't be called upon to thrust a bayonet into an Asian farmer, target a torpedo, scatter their iron seed from a B-52 into the wound of the earth, point a finger to move a nation, or stick a pole into the moon—and they knew it. They only had that three-hundred-foot alley to serve them as stateroom, armored tank, and executioner's chamber.

As these scenes suggest, Brewster Place is located in a ghetto plagued by social ills. The women must face these on a daily basis in addition to their personal tragedies and dislocations. Instead of being overcome by their sufferings, however, the women find within themselves a common fate and a basis for community. They gain strength and hope from their mutual caring and support. Besides their informal support system, they form a block association to address larger problems. The ability of women to unite in such a community inspires admiration for their courage and their special powers.

LINDEN HILLS

The community feelings of Brewster Place, from which the women gain a positive sense of identity, somehow make the ghetto's problems seem less awesome, paradoxically, than those of Linden Hills, an affluent suburb. If Brewster Place is a ghetto, Linden Hills is a hell. Naylor underlines this metaphor by deliberately modeling her novel *Linden Hills* after Dante's *Inferno*. Linden Hills is not a group of hills, but only a V-shaped area on a hillside intersected by eight streets. As one travels down the hill, the residents become richer but lower on the moral scale. Lester and Willie, two young unemployed poets who perform odd jobs for Christmas money (they are the modern counterparts of Vergil and Dante), take the reader on a guided tour.

The residents of Linden Hills have sold out for affluence: They suffer from a loss of black identity, or soul, as the result of adopting white attitudes, compromising their personal loyalties, and denying their kinship with other blacks. Lester's sister Roxanne deems black Africans in Zimbabwe unready for independence; one young executive, Maxwell Smyth, encourages another, Xavier Donnell, no longer to consider Roxanne as a prospective corporate bride; and Dr. Daniel Braithwaite has written the authorized twelve-volume history of Linden Hills without making a single moral judgment. Other sellouts are more personal: The young lawyer Winston Alcott leaves his homosexual lover to marry respectably, and Chester Parker is eager to bury his dead wife in order to remarry.

Significantly, Linden Hills is ruled by men. The

archfiend is Luther Nedeed, the local undertaker and real estate tycoon who occupies the lowest point in Linden Hills. Speaking against a low-income housing project planned for an adjacent poor black neighborhood, Nedeed urges outraged Linden Hills property owners to make common cause with the racist Wayne County Citizens Alliance. Most damning of all, however, is that Nedeed disowns his own wife and child and imprisons them in an old basement morgue; the child starves, but the wife climbs up to confront the archfiend on Christmas Eve.

MAMA DAY

It is clear that, while examining problems of middle-class black identity in *Linden Hills*, Naylor has not overlooked the plight of black women. In *Mama Day*, Naylor returns to a more celebratory mood on both subjects. The setting of *Mama Day* is a unique black American culture presided over by a woman with even more unique powers.

The coastal island of Willow Springs, located off South Carolina and Georgia but belonging to no state, has been largely bypassed by the tides of American history, particularly racism. The island was originally owned by a white man, Bascombe Wade, who also owned slaves. Bascombe married Sapphira, one of his slaves, however, who bore their seven sons. In 1823 Bascombe freed his other slaves and deeded the island to them, his sons, and their respective descendants in perpetuity (the land cannot be sold, only inherited). Bascombe was more or less assimilated, and a black culture grew up on the island that was closely tied to the land, to the culture's beginnings, and to African roots. In other words, Willow Springs is definitely a mythical island—a tiny but free black state flourishing unnoticed under the nose of the Confederacy. Naylor underlines the island's mythic qualities by drawing parallels between it and the magical isle of *The Tempest*.

If Prospero presides over Shakespeare's island, then Prospero's daughter, Miranda "Mama" Day (actually a great-granddaughter of the Wades), presides over Willow Springs. Known and respected locally as an old conjure woman, Mama Day is a repository and embodiment of the culture's wisdom. In particular, she is versed in herbs and other natural phenomena,

but she also speaks with the island's spirits. Mama Day uses her powers to heal and aid new life, but other island people who have similar powers are not so benevolent. One such person is Ruby, who stirs her knowledge with hoodoo to kill any woman who might take her man.

Unhappily, Mama Day's grandniece Cocoa, down from New York on a visit with her husband George, arouses Ruby's jealousy. By pretending to be friendly, Ruby is able to give Cocoa a deadly nightshade rinse, scalp massage, and hairdo. Just as a big hurricane hits the island, Cocoa begins to feel the effects of the poison. George, an engineer, native New Yorker, and football fan, works frantically to save Cocoa, but he is overmatched. With his urbanized, masculine rationality, he cannot conceive of what he is up against or how to oppose it. Suffering from exhaustion and a weak heart, he is eventually killed in an encounter with a brooding hen.

Meanwhile, Mama Day has been working her powers. She confronts Ruby in a conjuring match, good magic versus bad magic, just as in Mali's oral epic tradition of the thirteenth century ruler Sundjata and in other traditions of modern Africa. Ruby is destroyed by lightning strikes, and Cocoa is saved. It is too late for George the doubter, however, who learns about the mystical powers of women the hard way.

BAILEY'S CAFÉ

In each of Naylor's first three novels, clear links to the work that follow it are evident. The character Kiswana Browne in *The Women of Brewster Place* serves as the connection to *Linden Hills*, having moved from that bourgeois community to Brewster Place in order to stay in touch with the struggles of her people. Willa Prescott Nedeed, the imprisoned wife in *Linden Hills*, points the way to *Mama Day*, since she is grandniece to Mama Day and first cousin to Cocoa. It is George, Cocoa's husband, who provides the link to *Bailey's Café*, Naylor's fourth novel.

In perhaps her most ambitious work yet, Naylor moves her readers from the magical island of Willow Springs to an equally intriguing site, for Bailey's Café is both nowhere and everywhere. It is sitting at the edge of the world yet is found in every town. As the café's proprietor, Bailey (though that is not his real name), tells readers, "Even though this planet is round, there are just too many spots where you can find yourself hanging onto the edge . . . and unless there's some place, some space, to take a breather for a while, the edge of the world—frightening as it is—could be the end of the world." His café offers that breather, though some who enter the front door decide not to take it, instead going right through the café out the back door and dropping off into the void.

Like the inhabitants of Brewster Place, the customers in Bailey's Café are marginalized people. Their lives have taken them beyond the poverty and hard times of their urban sisters and brothers to the very edge of despair. However, for the women who people this extraordinary novel, Bailey's is simply a place to get directions to Eve's boardinghouse. Sweet Esther, abused to the point that she will receive visitors only in the dark; Peaches, whose effect on men drives her to mutilate her face with a can opener; Jesse, whose loss of marriage, child, and good name lead her to female lovers and heroin; and the pregnant virgin Mariam, ostracized from her village and bearing the effects of female circumcision—all find at Eve's a haven for their battered souls.

Throughout the individual stories of these women, Naylor uses unifying imagery: flower imagery, since each woman is associated with a particular bloom; musical imagery, jazz mostly, though the chords of the broken lives suggest the blues; religious imagery, figuring heavily in Eve and her garden, but most noticeably in the virgin birth at the end of the novel. This birth is where the connection to *Mama Day* is made clear. Explaining the circumstances of his birth to Cocoa, George told of being left as an infant outside Bailey's Café by his mother, who was later found drowned. The last few pages of *Bailey's Café* reveal George as the drowned Mariam's child, recursively pointing back to *Mama Day*.

Similar to Naylor's other novels in its concentration on the diverse lives of black people, *Bailey's Café* nonetheless marks a shift for Naylor. This shift is evident in her inclusion of Mariam, from Ethiopia, who broadens the depiction of the black experience by encompassing an African one. Mariam is also Jewish, a fact which links her to the Jewish shop-

keeper, Gabriel, in the novel. The coming together of the characters in celebration of the baby's birth—a celebration which intermixes different cultural and religious beliefs—brings a multicultural component to the novel absent in Naylor's other works.

Another notable change is Naylor's foregrounding of male characters. Bailey himself, the novel's narrator, is an example. His running commentary on the customers who find themselves in his establishment, his knowledge of the Negro Baseball Leagues, and his narration of his courtship of his wife Nadine make him a central and engaging figure throughout the book. Another example is Miss Maples, the cross-dressing male housekeeper at Eve's boardinghouse. His rather lengthy individual story is included with those of the women; it points to Naylor's intention to portray a different kind of male identity as well as her desire to cultivate a different relationship with her male characters. This shift links *Bailey's Café* to *The Men of Brewster Place*, Naylor's fifth novel.

THE MEN OF BREWSTER PLACE

Naylor's return to Brewster Place gives readers the opportunity to revisit the male characters introduced in the first book (generally portrayed negatively) and see them in a different light. No longer assuming background roles, they are up front, giving an account of their actions in the first book. In *The Women of Brewster Place*, Mattie's son Basil skipped town while awaiting sentencing, causing his mother to lose the property she had put up for his bail. Here Basil does return, check in hand, to repay his mother for her loss; however, she is dead, and his unfulfilled desire to make amends leads him into a detrimental relationship and a prison sentence. Eugene, absent from his daughter's funeral in the first book, is in fact on site. His grief compels him to undergo a harsh punishment, one that has much to do with the fact that he could never tell Ciel that he is gay. C. C. Baker, responsible for the vicious gang rape of Lorraine, executes another heinous crime in this book but gives the reader insight into his tragic character. When he squeezes the trigger to kill his brother, he does so with eyes closed, thanking God "for giving him the courage to do it. The courage to be a man."

In *The Men of Brewster Place*, Naylor seems to be acknowledging that there is after all more than one side to a story and that she is ready to let the whole story be known. Passages from the first book provide continuity between the two works, as does the resurrected voice of Ben, the janitor killed by Lorraine. Reminiscent of the character Bailey in *Bailey's Café*, Ben is both character and narrator.

However, Naylor brings some new voices to Brewster Place when she introduces Brother Jerome and Greasy. These characters link together the lives of the men living in Brewster Place. Brother Jerome is a retarded child with an ability to play the piano that speaks of genius. The blues that pour from his fingers speak of the lives of each man, rendering their conditions tangible. Greasy makes his brief but memorable appearance in the story called "The Barbershop," leaving the men to carry the burden of his self-inflicted demise. Naylor's portrayals of these two characters are perhaps the most moving of the book. These characterizations, along with the complexity of all the male characters, point to a Naylor who is taking a broader view. She had prefaced *The Women of Brewster Place* with a poem by Langston Hughes that asked the question, "What happens to a dream deferred?" In *The Men of Brewster Place*, she seems ready to acknowledge that deferred dreams are not only the province of women.

Harold Branam, updated by Jacquelyn Benton

BIBLIOGRAPHY

Braxton, Joanne M., and Andrée Nicola McLaughlin, eds. *Wild Women in the Whirlwind: Afro-American Culture and the Contemporary Literary Renaissance*. New Brunswick, N.J.: Rutgers University Press, 1990. This wide-ranging collection of critical articles brings the cultural history of black women's writing up to the 1980's. Barbara Smith's article "The Truth That Never Hurts: Black Lesbians in Fiction in the 1980's" discusses the section of *The Women of Brewster Place* entitled "The Two," but other articles also bear indirectly on important themes in Naylor.

Carby, Hazel V. *Reconstructing Womanhood: The Emergence of the Afro-American Woman Novelist.*

New York: Oxford University Press, 1987. While this book includes nothing on Naylor, it is good background reading. Tracing black women's writing from early slave narratives through the first two major black women novelists in the early twentieth century, it provides a cultural history that reveals the forces and assumptions that black women faced.

Kelley, Margot Anne, ed. *Gloria Naylor's Early Novels*. Gainesville: University Press of Florida, 1999. A good study of Naylor's early works. Includes bibliographical references and an index.

Montgomery, Maxine Lavon. "Authority, Multivocality, and the New World Order in Gloria Naylor's *Bailey's Café*." *African American Review* 29, no. 1 (Spring, 1995): 27. Montgomery discusses *Bailey's Café* as a woman-centered work that draws on black art forms and biblical allusions. Though she fails to recognize the true identity of Mariam's child (George of *Mama Day*), Montgomery otherwise provides a valid reading of *Bailey's Café*, commenting on the "more mature voice" with which Naylor addresses the concerns of her earlier novels.

Naylor, Gloria, and Toni Morrison. "A Conversation." *The Southern Review* 21 (Summer, 1985): 567-593. In this recorded conversation, Naylor visits her role model, Toni Morrison, whose novel *The Bluest Eye* (1970) had the deepest influence on her. Their conversation ranges over men, marriage, the inspiration for their various books, how they went about writing them, and the characters in them. Naylor says that she tried in *The Women of Brewster Place* not to depict men negatively and thought that she had succeeded.

Puhr, Kathleen M. "Healers in Gloria Naylor's fiction." *Twentieth Century Literature* 40, no. 4 (Winter, 1994): 518. Puhr discusses the healing powers of Naylor's female characters, principally Mattie Michael (*The Women of Brewster Place*), Willa Nedeed (*Linden Hills*), and Miranda (*Mama Day*), as well as Naylor's healing places, particularly the café and Eve's garden in *Bailey's Café*. She also discusses Naylor's works in terms of African American ancestry, generational conflicts, and broken dreams.

Rowell, Charles H. "An Interview with Gloria Naylor." *Callaloo* 20, no. 1 (Winter, 1997): 179-192. Charles H. Rowell discusses a range of topics with Naylor, including her educational background, her feelings about writing, the genesis of *The Women of Brewster Place* and *Bailey's Café*, and her feelings about the novel she is intending to write, which turns out to be *The Men of Brewster Place*.

Whitt, Margaret Earley. *Understanding Gloria Naylor*. Columbia: University of South Carolina Press, 1998. A thoughtful book of criticism of Naylor's novels.

NGUGI WA THIONG'O

Born: Kamiriithu village, near Limuru, Kenya; January 5, 1938

PRINCIPAL LONG FICTION

Weep Not, Child, 1964
The River Between, 1965
A Grain of Wheat, 1967
Secret Lives, 1974
Petals of Blood, 1977
Caitaani Mutharaba-Ini, 1980 (*Devil on the Cross*, 1982)
Matigari ma Njiruungi, 1986 (*Matigari*, 1989)

OTHER LITERARY FORMS

In addition to the above novels, Ngugi wa Thiong'o has published a collection of short stories, *Secret Lives and Other Stories* (1975). He has written numerous plays, including *The Black Hermit* (1962), *This Time Tomorrow: Three Plays* (1970; includes *The Rebels*, *The Wound in My Heart*, and *This Time Tomorrow*), *The Trial of Dedan Kimathi* (1974, with Micere Githae-Mugo), *Ngaahika Ndeenda* (1977, with Ngugi wa Mirii; *I Will Marry When I Want*, 1982), *Maitu Njugira* (1982, with Ngugi wa Mirii; *Mother, Sing for Me*, 1986).

Ngugi's commitment to his political responsibility as a writer has expressed itself in numerous works of literary, political, and social criticism including *Homecoming: Essays on African and Caribbean Literature, Culture, and Politics* (1972); *Writers in Politics* (1981), which was enlarged, revised, and subtitled *A Re-engagement with Issues of Literature and Society* in a 1997 edition; *Detained: A Writer's Prison Diary* (1981); *Barrel of a Pen: Resistance to Repression in Neo-Colonial Kenya* (1983); and *Decolonising the Mind: The Politics of Language in African Literature* (1986). In the 1980's he pursued his interest in African-based educational curricula by recasting stories of the Mau Mau resistance, many of which had appeared in his novels, as works for children, written first in his native Kikuyu and later translated into English. A collection of essays and talks between 1985 and 1990 appeared in *Moving the Centre: The Struggle for Cultural Freedoms* (1993).

ACHIEVEMENTS

With the publication of his first three novels, Ngugi quickly established himself as the major East African writer of the anglophone literary movement that began in Africa in the late 1950's and early 1960's. This anglophone literary school, which must be distinguished from the preceding romantic francophone movement called "Negritude" because of its different political assumptions and its stress on realism, coincided with the bitter political and at times military struggle and the eventual achievement of independence by most African countries under British colonial rule. Given the political situation, this literary movement was naturally preoccupied with assessing the impact of colonialism and defining independent and syncretic African cultures. With a handful of other African writers, Ngugi stands out as a literary pioneer in this movement. His systematic examination of the manner in which indigenous cultures were destroyed by colonialism has distinguished him from many of his colleagues, while his depiction of these cultures' attempts to reconstitute themselves has made him unique. His refusal to divorce literature from politics and his acerbic portrayal of corruption in independent Kenya—first

the closing of schools. Young Kikuyus were being exhorted to master Western knowledge and use it as a weapon of liberation, but the political and military crises blocked access to education and therefore to the possibility of leadership. This deprivation was rendered even more painful by the sustained messianic fervor which reemphasized the role of leadership. This, then, was the nexus of forces that composed the sociopolitical and religious ambience in which Ngugi reached maturity. Yet because he was so young when he began writing, his early fiction shows an imperfect understanding of his predicament. His first two novels graphically depict his entanglement in the peripeteia of values, whereas his third and fourth novels, written after a study of Frantz Fanon's psychopolitical analysis of colonialism, show a sudden and clearer understanding of the ambiguities and contradictions of colonial society.

WEEP NOT, CHILD

Set in Kenya in the 1940's and 1950's and ending in the midst of the Mau Mau war, *Weep Not, Child* is Ngugi's most autobiographical novel; Njoroge, its child protagonist, is about the same age as Ngugi would have been at that time. The novel is an anticlimactic, truncated *Bildungsroman* in that it follows the development of a child into adolescence but does not adequately resolve the question of what precisely has been learned by the hero.

The novel rapidly and cogently focuses on Njoroge's preoccupation with education and messianism. Ngotho, Njoroge's father, is confused and emasculated by his inability to comprehend and resist the appropriation of his land by an English settler named Howlands, so the family begins to disintegrate, reflecting in a microcosm the general social fragmentation. The family's burden passes to Njoroge, who is fortunate enough to be receiving a formal education (which annually consumes the wages of two brothers). When Njoroge graduates into secondary school, the entire village contributes to his tuition, and thus the hero is transformed from the "son of Ngotho to the son of the land." Thus he begins to feel that through his education he will become a great leader. Kenyatta's imprisonment further fuels his grandiose fantasies: He even envisions himself as the new mes-

siah. His self-image, however, remains insubstantial. His love of "education" is abstract: He does not care for particular subjects, nor does his vision encompass specific goals or projects. His messianic delusions are equally empty, and his egocentric world crumbles as soon as he is confronted with the reality of the war. When his father dies from severe torture and castration, when his brothers are either imprisoned or killed, and when he too is tortured in spite of his innocence, his illusions are shattered. Finally, the girl he loves rejects him, and he attempts suicide but is easily dissuaded by his mother. The novel ends with his recognition that he is a coward.

Ngotho's rapid descent from the height of self-importance to the nadir of self-negation is enacted against the backdrop of a society in violent turmoil, which Ngugi depicts in effective detail. The complex social entanglements and contradictions—the different political views and the conflict between generations within Ngotho's family, the enmity between Ngotho and Jacobo, whose loyalty to the British is rewarded with wealth and political power, the mixture of fear, hatred, and respect that Howlands harbors for Ngotho because he has occupied the latter's land, the Englishman's desire to torture and kill Ngotho which leads to the retaliatory murder of Howlands by Ngotho's son, Howlands's contempt for Jacobo's collaboration, Njoroge's love for Mwihaki, Jacobo's daughter, and his brief friendship with Howlands's son—as well as the descriptions of torture and summary executions by the British and the Mau Mau—create a powerful microcosmic picture of a whole society being ripped apart by economic and political conflict. The novel brilliantly depicts the trauma and the ambiguities of a revolution. Yet Njoroge's actual experience is not derived from active involvement in this upheaval; rather, he functions as a passive, reluctant witness. His experience is that of a highly suggestive and solitary adolescent who easily internalizes the hopes, frustrations, and anguish of his society and then soothes his own trauma with self-aggrandizing fantasies.

The violence and trauma to which Njoroge is subject only partially account for the oscillation of his self-image. The rest of the explanation lies in the abrupt change of values that engulfs the hero and the narrator. Njoroge's early subscription to English values includes a naïve belief in biblical messianic prophecies which supplement the Kikuyu myth. As a self-styled messiah, he attempts to soothe the fears of a *"weeping child."* Thus his attitude to others exactly parallels the narrator's depiction of Njoroge as the weeping child. This profound sympathy and parallelism between the narrator's and the hero's views underscore the complete absence of irony in Ngugi's portrayal of Njoroge.

The denouement of the novel also confirms this underlying problem. Without any justification, Njoroge assumes all the guilt of the trauma suffered by several families and accuses the girl he loves of betraying him before he tries to commit suicide. Thus, he is still following the model of Christ, of a messiah who assumed all human guilt, was betrayed, and was then turned into a scapegoat. By allowing his hero to transform his self-image from that of a savior to that of a scapegoat, Ngugi allows him to retain his original egocentricity. This essential continuity in Njoroge's characterization testifies to the powerful influence of Christianity on Ngugi himself. If Njoroge's fantasies are a product of the sociopolitical and religious factors in this specific colonial situation, then the ambiguity in the narrative attitude to Njoroge can be ascribed to the same forces. In the final analysis, it is Ngugi's inability to define adequately his stand toward these factors that is responsibile for the narrative ambiguity. The novel, then, can be seen simultaneously as a portrayal *and* a product of the changing values. The persistence of this confusion led Ngugi to a reworking of the same issues in his next novel.

THE RIVER BETWEEN

The plot of *The River Between*, set in the late 1920's and 1930's, is centered once more on a combination of education and messianism, while the subplot examines the clash of values through the emotionally and culturally charged controversy over female circumcision. The geographical setting is allegorical: The events take place in the "heart and soul" of Kikuyu land and culture among the communities on two ridges ranged on either side of the river Honia (which means "Regeneration" in Kikuyu). Both ridges, Kameno and Makuyu, claim to be the source of Kikuyu culture, but as the novel progresses, Kameno, home of the Kikuyu prophet Mugo wa Kibiro and his descendant Waiyaki, the novel's protagonist, becomes the base for those who want to retain the purity of Kikuyu culture, whereas Makuyu becomes the home of those who have converted to Christianity and have renounced various "evil" aspects of their original tradition. The ensuing conflict thus becomes emblematic of the problems of upheaval experienced by the entire culture. The stylized characterization reflects this antagonism between the desire for cultural purity and the desire to abrogate traditional values.

Among the older generation, which provides the secondary characters, the opposition is embodied in Chege and Joshua. Chege, Waiyaki's father, a minor prophet embittered by the people's disregard for his claims, is realistically aware of the specific cultural and technological superiority of European society and thus, in spite of inherent dangers, commands his son to attend the missionary school and master Western knowledge without absorbing its vices. He is simultaneously concerned with preserving Kikuyu purity and with ensuring its survival through the absorption of clearly efficacious aspects of Western culture. On the other hand, Joshua, a zealous convert who has become a self-righteous, puritanical minister, renounces Kikuyu culture as dirty, heathen, and evil. He has entirely dedicated himself to his own and other people's salvation through Christianity. Ngugi balances these static and absolute oppositions with the dynamic and relativistic attitudes of Waiyaki and Joshua's two daughters, Muthoni and Nyambura, who attempt in their different ways to synthesize the two cultures.

The subplot depicts Muthoni's disastrous attempt to combine what she considers to be the best aspects of both cultures. Even though her parents will not permit her to undergo circumcision because the Church has forbidden this rite of purification and rebirth in Kikuyu culture, Muthoni decides that she must be circumcised. By becoming a circumcised Christian she hopes to combine the two cultures within herself. Unfortunately, an infection contracted during the ceremony kills Muthoni. In addition to radicalizing the two factions, her apostasy and death reveal the more profound problems of cultural transition. The fact that her notion of womanhood is predicated on circumcision shows that peripeteia involves not only physical and social but ontological changes; specific modifications of a culture become meaningless unless the entire cultural gestalt is altered to accommodate particular infusions. Waiyaki sees Muthoni as a sacrifice to the clash of cultures, and when he falls in love with her uncircumcised sister, Nyambura, the subplot is deftly woven into the main plot—Waiyaki's attempt to become a messiah and an educator.

Unlike *Weep Not, Child*, where the messianic possibility is entirely confined to Njoroge's fantasies, *The River Between* presents it as an actual, unambiguous fact: While Waiyaki is still a child, his "mission" to master Western knowledge and unite the Kikuyus is revealed to him. When, along with many other students, he resigns from the Christian mission school, he gets his chance to fulfill his destiny. With the help of the people and his colleagues he establishes an independent Kikuyu school which flourishes and thus earns him the respect befitting a messiah; by successfully mediating between the English and Kikuyu cultures and by making the positive aspects of the former available to the latter, he seems to have fulfilled the prophecy. His success, however, is short-lived. Jealousy and political ambition spur a faction from Kemano to accuse him of treason and spiritual contamination because he loves an uncircumcised woman. Since he is unwilling to renounce Nyambura, Waiyaki is forced to relinquish his leadership, and his personal fate remains ominously ambiguous at the end of the novel.

The River Between is a better *Bildungsroman* than Ngugi's first novel because Waiyaki does realize that he is a product of shifting values and that cultural synthesis is an ambiguous, complex, and even dangerous undertaking. Yet, this education of the hero is not sufficient to save the novel from the confusion caused by a double narrative intention. Overtly, the narrator clearly intends to present Waiyaki as a man constantly concerned with communal welfare, yet the rhetoric of Waiyaki's contemplation demonstrates that he is entirely engrossed in his own messianic potentiality: All his dealings with people always revert to questions about his status and leadership. Furthermore, the divine source of his authority, by providing him with *transcendent* knowledge, severs him from the Kikuyu to the extent that his vision of the future, and actions based on that vision, need not rely on mundane familiarity with the people's social and political desires.

The major problem of the novel is that Ngugi seems unable to decide whether to treat his protagonist as a real messiah or whether to portray him as a character whose prophetic calling is a self-delusion: Waiyaki is simultaneously subjected to divine surety and human fallibility. At the end of the novel, Ngugi seems to sympathize with two incompatible feelings—with Waiyaki's decision to choose a personal relationship over communal obligation, a private cultural synthesis over a larger social synthesis, and with the people's decision to protect their culture by sacrificing a promising individual. The persistent ambiguity about Waiyaki and the final recourse to scapegoating, which resembles so closely the pattern of grandiose self-delusion and vindication through persecution in *Weep Not Child*, reveal once more that *The River Between* is a product of subjective anxiety. Waiyaki's insight into the anxiety caused by the peripeteia of values is applicable to the novel as a whole. According to him this anxiety can cause a person to cling fanatically to whatever promises security. For Waiyaki and Ngugi, messianism provides that security. If one considers Ngugi's predicament at the age of fifteen, when he internalized the social preoccupation with education, leadership, and messianism, one can see that the ambiguity and the ambivalence of *The River Between* are a literary transformation of his own traumatic experience.

A GRAIN OF WHEAT

Before writing his next novel, *A Grain of Wheat*, Ngugi studied Frantz Fanon's *The Wretched of the Earth* (1961), which unmistakably altered his understanding of the psychological and cultural changes that take place in the process of anticolonial revolutions. The view that education and messianism are panaceas is entirely displaced by a clear and deep comprehension of the way out of the psychological bind produced by colonial subjugation. In *A Grain of Wheat*, Ngugi is still concerned with the reintegration of Kikuyu society, but his method has changed drastically. Instead of focusing on a single protagonist Ngugi uses five major characters, Mugo, Karanja, Kihika, Gikonyo, and Mumbi, and a host of minor ones in order to contrast different kinds of personal isolation, love, and sympathy for others, and then he orchestrates a complex pattern wherein some characters move from isolation to community, some move in the opposite direction, while still others remain relatively static. By contrasting and interweaving these movements, Ngugi creates a polyphonic novel in which the experience of social regeneration and communal cohesiveness lies not in the awareness of any single character but in the interactions between various individuals and in the reader's experience of these interactions.

The novel's plot concerns an intriguing search for the traitor who betrayed Kihika, a leader of the Mau Mau guerrillas. The war is over, and, just prior to independence day, Kihika's comrades emerge from the forests in order to seek the traitor. The search, however, is really a vehicle for investigating various characters' motives and actions during the war that has destroyed the village of Thabai. The actual time encompassed by the novel is only six days, but through retrospection the reader is allowed to experience the whole Mau Mau revolution and even the prerevolutionary childhood of the protagonists as well as the mythic past of the Kikuyus. The multiplicity of viewpoints through which one is led to understand the characters conveys admirably Ngugi's notion that an organic community can be apprehended only through its historical and interpersonal interactions.

Ngugi's investigation of patterns of isolation and communality is focused on four males and one female. Two men, Mugo and Karanja, are motivated by an almost pathological desire for isolation and two, Kihika and Gikonyo, are deeply dependent on their different views of communality. Mugo, deprived of human warmth since childhood, attempts in vain to

avoid all involvement. His isolation is repeatedly shattered, first by Kihika, who is seeking shelter from the colonial soldiers and whom Mugo betrays, and then by the whole village of Thabai, which, having mistaken Mugo for a supporter of Kihika and a staunch patriot, ironically invites him to become the village chief on independence day. While Mugo gradually journeys from isolation to social integration, Karanja moves in the opposite direction. In order to remain with Mumbi, who had earlier rejected him for Gikonyo, Karanja joins the colonial police when Gikonyo is sent to a concentration camp. His collaboration with the British naturally earns him the enmity of the entire village, which expels him on independence day. While Karanja betrays the community as an abstract entity in order to remain with a specific woman, Kihika abandons his pregnant lover in order to become a guerrilla fighter and plays an important part in winning the freedom of his society. In contrast to Kihika, Gikonyo has always been dependent on concrete relationships with his mother and Mumbi. His personality and the very meaning of existence crumble when he is forcibly isolated from them. He confesses his involvement with the Mau Mau so that he can return to his village, only to find when he arrives that Mumbi has given birth to Karanja's child.

Ngugi explores these labyrinthine relationships with great skill. The retrospections, juxtapositions, and multiple interpretations of events, and the gradual, interrupted revelation of the truth represent in a concrete and poignant manner the actual reintegration of a community that has been destroyed. Ngugi's main objective, admirably realized, is to show that strength in one character can be a weakness in another and that what is constructive and desirable at one stage in a community's history is harmful at another—that all forms of fortitude and lapses are necessary for social cohesion. Even Mugo's betrayal performs a vital function in the end. His confession of the betrayal fits into the pattern of complementary wills which is essential for the cohesion of a community. Thus, where Kihika's callousness toward individuals may be undesirable in itself, its reverse, his concern for abstract humanity, proves invaluable

MATIGARI

In *Matigari* Ngugi continues to record Kenya's postcolonial struggle, but in this novel he moves away from realism and adopts a fluidity of time and space that is mythological in tone. At the outset, he warns the "Reader/Listener" that the narrative is purely imaginary in its action, character, and setting. It follows the adventures of the mythical Matigari, who embodies the virtues, values, and purity of the betrayed and abused people he sets out to arouse from their apathy. Whether Ngugi succeeded in mythologizing remains questionable, for the landscape, characters, circumstances, and historical events are obviously Kenyan. In fact, when the 1986 edition appeared in the original Kikuyu language, so many Kenyans were talking about Matigari that officials ordered his arrest. Once they discovered that the suspected rabble-rouser was fictional, they banned the book. A Kenyan edition became available in English translation in 1989.

Matigari denounces contemporary Kenya, where a privileged few in connection with representatives of overseas interests rule and exploit the masses, thereby reversing the hard-fought war of independence. Matigari ma Njiruungi, whose name means "he who survived the bullets," emerges from the forest, sets his weapons aside, and dons the belt of peace to move through the countryside to rediscover his true family—a free Kenyan people who live in a just society and who share its wealth. Along the way he meets the downtrodden and dispossessed, and he faces all the ills the contaminated society has produced: homeless children, dissidents harassed and murdered by the police, young women forced into prostitution, and much more. In opposition to the suffering masses stand the black politicians and their cronies, who have grown rich through collaboration with international business interests.

The novel also contains variations on familiar themes, such as the role of Christianity in oppression and the failure of Western education. At the same time, Ngugi subverts the Christian myth by turning Matigari into a modern Jesus, who moves among the people and faces rejection. The biblical allusions become especially evident in the prison scenes. For ex-

ample, his fellow detainees resemble Jesus' disciples; one even betrays Matigari. The novel also contains the Swiftian elements of satire that characterize *Devil on the Cross*. Yet *Matigari* finally emerges as a powerful account of the postcolonial state, an indictment not only against the corruption in Kenya but also against the conditions that prevail in numerous African nations.

Abdul R. JanMohamed, updated by Robert L. Ross

OTHER MAJOR WORKS

SHORT FICTION: *Secret Lives and Other Stories*, 1975.

PLAYS: *The Black Hermit*, pr. 1962; *This Time Tomorrow: Three Plays*, pb. 1970 (includes *The Rebels*, *The Wound in My Heart*, and *This Time Tomorrow*); *The Trial of Dedan Kimathi*, pr. 1974 (with Micere Githae-Mugo); *Ngaahika Ndeenda*, pr. 1977 (with Ngugi wa Mirii; *I Will Marry When I Want*, 1982); *Maitu Njugira*, pb. 1982 (with Ngugi wa Mirii; *Mother, Sing for Me*, 1986).

NONFICTION: *Homecoming: Essays on African and Caribbean Literature, Culture, and Politics*, 1972; *Writers in Politics*, 1981, revised 1997; *Detained: A Writer's Prison Diary*, 1981; *Barrel of a Pen: Resistance to Repression in Neo-Colonial Kenya*, 1983; *Decolonising the Mind: The Politics of Language in African Literature*, 1986; *Writing Against Neocolonialism*, 1986; *Moving the Centre: The Struggle for Cultural Freedoms*, 1993; *Penpoints, Gunpoints, and Dreams: Toward a Critical Theory of the Arts and the State in Africa*, 1998.

BIBLIOGRAPHY

Carter, Steven R. "Decolonization and Detective Fiction: Ngugi wa Thiong'o's *Petals of Blood*." *Clues: A Journal of Detection* 1 (Spring/Summer, 1987): 101-126. This analytic article tackles the issues of capitalism, neocolonialism, foreign narrative forms, and detective fiction in the novel. Includes notes.

Cook, David, and Michael Okenimkpe. *Ngugi wa Thiong'o: An Exploration of His Writings*. Portsmouth, N.H.: Heinemann, 1997. Part of the Studies in African Literature series, this volume offers insightful comments about Ngugi's work.

Killam, G. D. *An Introduction to the Writings of Ngugi*. London: Heinemann, 1980. A good starting point for the study of Ngugi, with a biographical outline, an introduction, individual chapters devoted to one title, a bibliography, and an index.

_____. "Ngugi wa Thiong'o." In *The Writing of East and Central Africa*. London: Heinemann, 1984. The three parts of this volume contain chapters surveying writing in six countries, chapters on genres, and chapters on individual authors. A useful study for those who wish to understand authors in these contexts. Includes an index.

Moore, Gerald. "Ngugi wa Thiong'o: Towards Uhuru." In *Twelve African Writers*. Bloomington: Indiana University Press, 1980. The introduction provides a quick overview of issues in studying African literature. The twelve authors, selected for their longevity as writers, are appraised individually and comparatively. Contains references, a bibliography of primary sources, a suggested reading list, and an index.

Palmer, Eustace. "Negritude Rediscovered: A Reading of the Recent Novels of Armah, Ngugi, and Soyinka." *The International Fiction Review* 8 (1981): 1-11. This discussion of the concept of Negritude pays particular attention to three works: Wole Soyinka's *Season of Anomy*, Ngugi's *Petals of Blood*, and Ayi Kwei Armah's *Two Thousand Seasons*. Includes notes.

Parker, Michael, and Roger Starkey, eds. *Postcolonial Literatures: Achebe, Ngugi, Desai, Walcott*. New York: St. Martin's Press, 1995. The works of Ngugi, Chinua Achebe, Anita Desai, and Derek Walcott are discussed in this thoughtful volume. Includes bibliographical references and an index.

Shyam, Jai. "Plights of Contemporary Life in Recent African Fiction." *The Arizona Quarterly* 42 (Autumn, 1986): 248-260. This scholarly article discusses the alienating results of Western individualism in African society as depicted in novels by four writers. Ngugi's *Petals of Blood* is discussed.

Sicherman, Carol. *Ngugi wa Thiong'o: A Bibliography of Primary and Secondary Sources, 1957-1987*. London: Hans Zell, 1989. A treasure for the scholar, with citations of Ngugi's works in the original languages, manuscripts and other unpublished material, translations, secondary sources, undated material, nonprint media, and indexes of authors, editors, translators, titles, interviews, and subjects. Includes a brief introduction and preface.

ANAÏS NIN

Born: Paris, France; February 21, 1903
Died: Los Angeles, California; January 14, 1977

PRINCIPAL LONG FICTION

House of Incest, 1936
Winter of Artifice, 1939
Winter of Artifice: Three Novelettes, 1945 (contains *Winter of Artifice*, "Stella," and "The Voice")
This Hunger, 1945
Cities of the Interior: A Continuous Novel, 1959 (contains *Ladders to Fire*, 1946; *Children of the Albatross*, 1947; *The Four-Chambered Heart*, 1950; *A Spy in the House of Love*, 1954; *Solar Barque*, 1958)
Seduction of the Minotaur, 1961
Collages, 1964

OTHER LITERARY FORMS

Anaïs Nin published numerous volumes of perceptive literary criticism. Highly acclaimed, her first book of nonfiction, *D. H. Lawrence: An Unprofessional Study*, appeared in 1932. In 1968, near the end of her career, she wrote *The Novel of the Future*, partly as an attempt to explain the literary philosophy that inspired her innovative fiction. In 1976, a collection of her essays appeared, entitled *In Favor of the Sensitive Man and Other Essays*. During the last decade of her life, Nin was extremely active as a public speaker; her lectures, seminars, and interviews have been edited by Evelyn J. Hinz and published as *A Woman Speaks* (1975).

(Christian Du Bois Larson)

Nin's published short stories, like her criticism, span her career. The most distinguished collection is *Under a Glass Bell and Other Stories* (1944). Her apprentice writing is available in another collection, *Waste of Timelessness and Other Early Stories* (1977), while two volumes of erotica were published after Nin's death: *Delta of Venus* (1977) and *Little Birds* (1979).

In addition to her works of fiction and criticism, Nin's extensive diary has been published. Edited from a vast manuscript, this autobiographical work has appeared in two series. The first series, entitled *The Diary of Anaïs Nin*, comprises seven volumes which appeared periodically since 1966. The second series contains two volumes, *Linotte: The Early Diary of Anaïs Nin, 1914-1920* (1978) and *The Early Diary of Anaïs Nin: Volume Two, 1920-1923* (1982).

ACHIEVEMENTS

Nin's achievement in literature is of two distinct kinds: artistic and sociological. Strongly influenced

by Arthur Rimbaud, Marcel Proust, and D. H. Lawrence, Nin conceived of and developed a uniquely personal approach to style and structure that places her within the modernist tradition as it evolved in the French literature of the early decades of the twentieth century. Nin persisted in articulating, refining, and extending an avowedly "feminine" ideal of the novel; this resulted in lyrical novels in which the imagistic manner of the poet is fused with the psychological penetration of the novelist. In her treatment of character, of time and of space, Nin belongs with such writers as Virginia Woolf, Djuna Barnes, and Anna Kavan.

Nin's sociological importance is related to her intention to create a specifically "feminine" novel in which the emphasis is on the evocation of feeling, and to portray as deeply and as honestly as possible an authentically female emotional experience. In this respect, her achievement may be compared with that of Woolf, Dorothy Richardson, Marguerite Duras, and a number of French writers, including Annie LeClerc, Hélène Cixous, Monique Witting, and Julia Kristeva.

The audience for Nin's novels is smaller than for either her diary or her collections of erotica. As the diary has increased Nin's audience, it has also brought her fiction to the attention of well-qualified critics and scholars, many of whom have been able to interpret it in ways that make it more accessible to a general readership accustomed to the conventions of realism. Considering the climate of growing respect for and interest in Nin's novels, it seems that her reputation as a literary artist is now securely established.

BIOGRAPHY

On February 21, 1903, Anaïs Nin was born in Paris, the oldest child of musicians Joaquin Nin and Rosa Culmell-Nin. Her parents' marriage was turbulent, and in 1913, Joaquin Nin deserted his family at Archachon, France. The following year, Rosa Culmell-Nin transported her daughter and two sons, Thorvald and Joaquin, to the United States. For some years, they lived in New York City and in Queens, actively participating in the lively Cuban community there, many of whose members were musicians. Nin has recorded this period of her life in *Linotte*. What stands out most poignantly is her inconsolable grief at the loss of her father and her intense worship of her mother. At this time, Nin's aspiration to become an artist of one sort or another strongly manifested itself, and her account of her adolescence is a rich study of the formative years of an artist.

In 1918, Nin left school in order to manage the household for her mother, who worked for Lord and Taylor as a special buyer for the Cuban clientele, and in 1923, Nin married Hugh P. Guiler (known as an engraver and filmmaker under the name of Ian Hugo). As a young married woman, Nin lived in France. Marriage caused her to experience intense conflicts which she has described and analyzed in her diary. During those years, as in adolescence, Nin continued to write, and in 1932, she published her first book, *D. H. Lawrence: An Unprofessional Study*. This work brought about the explosive friendship with Henry and June Miller which she describes in the first published diary. Nin and Miller maintained a relationship until Nin's death.

In Paris during the 1930's, Nin embarked upon a lifelong devotion to psychotherapy. Her therapeutic relationship with the renowned Viennese psychoanalyst Otto Rank is recounted in the first volume of *The Diary of Anaïs Nin*. An independent, original, and forceful thinker whose special area of interest was the artist, Rank was of great assistance to Nin in the fulfillment of her artistic aspirations. His influence on her was so persuasive that for a time she actually considered making a living as a lay psychoanalyst. For a few months in 1934, she lived in New York and assisted Rank with his practice. In 1935, however, she resumed her literary work and returned to France to rejoin her husband, but with the outbreak of World War II, she again returned to the United States. This move in 1939 was to become permanent. It was not easy for Nin to give up her "romantic life" in Paris, as she called it, and her difficulty understanding Americans' disdain for the arts is a recurrent theme of her diary in the 1940's and 1950's.

Throughout her life, Nin maintained many friendships with writers and other artists. Among her friends and acquaintances were Lawrence Durrell, Robert Duncan, James Merrill, and Kenneth Patchen;

performers Canada Lee, Josephine Premice, and Louise Rainer; Caresse Crosby, proprietor of the Black Sun Press; composer Edgard Varèse and his wife, translator Louise Varèse; collage artist Janko Varda; and the owner of the influential Gotham Book Mart, Frances Steloff. Even though Nin had widespread contacts among writers and artists in New York City and on the West Coast, she experienced continual frustration in the publishing world. On the whole, editors and critics were either hostile to her work or simply ignored it. The breakthrough of this period was the acceptance by Alan Swallow, founder of the famed Swallow Press then located in Denver, Colorado, of the five works that constitute *Cities of the Interior: A Continuous Novel*. For many years, Nin was an underground literary figure with a small but enthusiastic following.

In 1966, Nin's status changed suddenly; she had already published all her fiction, the last book, *Collages*, appearing in 1964. When Harcourt Brace and World, with The Swallow Press, brought out the first volume of *The Diary of Anaïs Nin*, Nin quickly became a public figure. Because the content of the work expressed the feelings of many women who were experiencing deep evolutionary changes in their own lives, Nin involuntarily became a spokesperson for the women's movement. She achieved the "dialogue with the world" for which she had longed since childhood.

During the remaining years of Nin's life, individual volumes of her diary continued to appear, and Nin, although viewed as controversial by leaders of the women's movement, received considerable public acclaim. Traveling throughout the United States, she gave hundreds of talks at colleges and universities and undertook trips to various countries, including Sweden and Bali. In 1970, she was awarded the French Prix Sévigné, and in 1974, she was elected to the National Institute of Arts and Letters. Nin's books have been translated into all the major Western languages as well as Serbo-Croatian and Japanese.

ANALYSIS

It was natural that Anaïs Nin should grow up desiring to be an artist. Her father was a friend of

narcissist, however, "Stella" is an insightful piece of work, and it is brilliantly expressed.

When evaluated exclusively as art, "The Voice" is one of Nin's most original and daring pieces. It is both an extended portrait of a kind and self-neglectful psychotherapist (perhaps suggested by Otto Rank), and an animated essay or exposition of ideas through a seemingly random selection of characters and incidents. "The Voice" is a virtuoso piece that spins off from contrasting motions: soaring, plummeting, floating, sinking, spiraling, rushing, and flowing; it is an excellent example of Nin's deft way of translating characters and incidents into imagery. The center of this active world is a psychoanalyst's office located in a skyscraper. Tortured New Yorkers, The Voice's patients include Djuna (who becomes one of the principals in *Cities of the Interior*), a young violinist who wishes to be released from lesbianism; Mischa, a cellist whose emotions are paralyzed; and Lilith, who suffers from frigidity. The Voice himself falls in love with Lilith, the only one of his patients who can see beyond her own needs to the hungers of the man whose voice is so comforting to the others. As in Nin's later books, Djuna plays the role of comforting confidante to both parties in this impossible dream of love between analyst and patient.

Winter of Artifice is perhaps the most "musical" of Nin's works; it is also among the most courageous in its subject: an adult daughter's flirtation and near-union with the handsome, seductive father who abandoned her when she was a child. The theme is "musique Ancienne," to quote Nin, the Oedipal temptation told from the point of view of the highly intelligent yet vulnerable daughter. *Winter of Artifice* was begun in 1933, when Nin started therapy with Rank, and was completed in 1939, the year of Rank's death.

The novelette is organized in thirteen "movements." A climax of emotional and erotic yearning occurs in the sixth, central movement. From this excruciating height of desire, the work subsides into a slower rhythm and a sadder tone. Eventually, *Winter of Artifice* becomes a solo for the daughter. When she sees her father's "feminine-looking" foot, she imagines that it is really her foot and that he has stolen it.

Now she understands that he would like to steal her youth and her capacity for action, her mobility. "Tired of his ballet dancing" (formal, traditional movements), the daughter symbolically reclaims her foot and, with it, her ability to flee from the dangers of the attraction: *"Music runs and I run with it."*

CITIES OF THE INTERIOR

The five novels found in the final version of *Cities of the Interior*, Nin's "continuous novel," are *Ladders to Fire, Children of the Albatross, The Four-Chambered Heart, A Spy in the House of Love*, and *Seduction of the Minotaur*. They were first published individually during the 1940's and 1950's. Entries in Nin's diary indicate that she began writing *Ladders to Fire* in 1937; she made substantial revisions as late as 1962. *Seduction of the Minotaur*, which was published individually in 1961, was begun in 1938 and expanded in 1958 to include *Solar Barque*. Alan Swallow, a pioneer among small-press publishers, brought out the five novels under their collective title in 1959. When it was first published, *Cities of the Interior* had been growing for twenty years. An extraordinary work, it displays a brilliance of conception, a mastery of image and metaphor, and a refinement of structural technique that make it the equal of many better-known modern masterpieces.

The title, *Cities of the Interior: A Continuous Novel*, suggests the timeless scope of this work. The "cities" are both ancient and modern. Nin set out to excavate the buried "cities" or the psychic worlds of her three main characters: Lillian, Djuna, and Sabina. The idea of "continuity," however, is more complex. It suggests that *Cities of the Interior* is an "open" work, like certain modern sculptures that extend into and penetrate the space which surrounds them, interacting with their setting.

This multifaceted work is not set apart from life, not carved out of it, not bounded by the conventions of classically written fiction with its concluding "resolution." "Cities of the Interior" remains "open" to the addition of new parts and to the rearrangement of its five basic novel units. The individual books are entirely self-contained. As Nin uses the word, "continuous" does not mean "to be continued." It does not refer to linear progressive time. There is no fixed starting point and no concluding point. The books have been bound—because books, seemingly, must be bound—in the order in which they were written.

A reader can begin with any one of the five volumes and move to the other four in any order, losing no essential connections. In short, the five novels of *Cities of the Interior* are interchangeable in the total composition, which can be viewed as a type of mobile, an innovation in fiction inspired by the example of modern sculpture. Nin's characters are totally immersed in the flow of internalized psychic time, in the patterns of their own growth. One of the main figures in *Collages* quotes the Qur'an, saying, "Nothing is ever finished." The French philosopher Henri Bergson, whose ideas influenced a number of modern novelists, including Proust, stated the concept of personal evolution succinctly and elegantly: "If matter appeared to us as a perpetual flowering, we should assign no termination to any of our actions." To Nin, life does indeed appear as a "perpetual flowering." In *Cities of the Interior*, she has selected and expressed significant relationships and states of feeling in the ever-changing, continuous process of growth. Life, as distinct from existence, is possible only for those who can accept mutability, knowing that while change promises growth, it also demands inevitable loss.

LADDERS TO FIRE

Lillian's development spans *Cities of the Interior*, opening and closing the work when it is read in conventional sequence. The first part of *Ladders to Fire* describes "This Hunger," Lillian's ravenous need for love. Spontaneous, impetuous, unsure of her physical attractiveness, and compulsively generous, she gives up her career as a pianist so that she can support her lover's ambition to paint, but this sacrifice does not bring her the loyalty and security she desires. Jay repays Lillian's devotion by having affairs with other women.

The most threatening of Lillian's rivals is Sabina. The relationship between these two women is the most compelling in the novel and a superb example of Nin's brilliance at unmasking psychological motivations. When Lillian attempts to stop Sabina's pursuit of Jay by overwhelming the other woman

with friendship, she discovers that she, too, is powerfully attracted to Sabina. For different reasons, both women are angry at Jay: Lillian because he has neglected her, Sabina because he would like to conquer her. The two women form an alliance against him. After dancing together in a working-class tavern, they go to Sabina's room to make love, but they discover that it is not sensuality they are seeking in each other so much as an exchange of feminine qualities. They both feel a "mysterious craving . . . to become each other."

During the dazzling party scene with which *Ladders to Fire* closes, Lillian commits "invisible hara-kiri" with an outburst of harmful self-criticism. It is clear to the reader that she has grown, that her anger at herself is partly an expression of this growth, and that she will soon end her unsatisfying relationship with Jay.

CHILDREN OF THE ALBATROSS

A delicate, playful book with an undercurrent of sadness, *Children of the Albatross* traces a theme that is familiar in French literature but something of a novelty in the United States: the initiation of a young man by an older woman. Djuna, in her late twenties, becomes involved with Paul, seventeen. The other "children" of the novel's title are their friends, young gay men who meet with Paul and Djuna in her "house of innocence and faith." Here, they dance, paint, and play, celebrating their love of freedom from responsibility. The young men and Djuna are drawn together by their mutual fear of tyrannical, authoritarian fathers. For Djuna, this figure is represented by the cruel and lecherous watchman who terrified her when she was a child living in an orphanage. The positive creative act of evoking a counterworld to erect against the conventional and materialistic values of the "fathers" ignites sympathy among the rebellious "children."

From the start of *Children of the Albatross*, it is clear that Djuna's affair with Paul will be brief and will provide her with little emotional sustenance. Predictably, Paul's family disapproves of her, not only because she is "older" but also because she is a dancer. A crucial dream, in which Djuna imagines herself as Ariadne, predicts that after she has guided

Paul safely through the passage from adolescence to early manhood, she will be abandoned. At the novel's end, Paul embarks upon an exciting journey to India, leaving Djuna behind. Feeling empty and dissatisfied, she searches the unexplored "cities" of her self. She begins to seek a fuller emotional life with a more mature partner.

THE FOUR-CHAMBERED HEART

In *The Four-Chambered Heart*, Nin explores the psychological complexity of a woman's involvement with a married man. Romantically ensconced in a houseboat on the Seine are Djuna and Rango, a tempestuous vagabond, so she imagines. Their relationship is initially enthralling but ultimately frustrating; both parties are weighed down by responsibilities to demanding hypochondriacs: he to his wife Zora, Djuna to her father. Heavy rains force the lovers to move their houseboat up and down the river. Like their relationship, the boat does not "go anywhere"; it merely plies its way back and forth over the same area.

Djuna and Rango's passion attains its height in the novel's first thirty pages. After that, there is conflict and threatened violence. Zora makes a bizarre attempt to kill Djuna. Rango comes to the boat very late one night and falls into a heavy depressed sleep. Djuna, desperate to initiate a change of some sort, rips up floorboards in a wild attempt to sink the boat. It is swept down the river; everyone survives, though not in the same form. A fisherman rescues a doll from the water with a joke about its having tried to commit suicide. The doll is a comment on Djuna's passivity with regard to her own life and to the image of conventional femininity that she has been struggling to maintain, at the expense of her "true" self. It is time for her to move beyond the static situation she experiences with Rango, to give up the illusion of her generosity toward Zora, and to recognize and accept the negative qualities she has been "acting out" through Rango. Djuna must grow.

A SPY IN THE HOUSE OF LOVE

In *A Spy in the House of Love*, Sabina is portrayed as a glamorous woman seeking to express herself as "Don Juana." Married to a fatherly, indulgent man, she is free to fulfill her desire for adventure, which she experiences through relationships with men. Each of Sabina's partners embodies an aura, a sense of place, an ambience that lies waiting for her exploration and participation. There is the opera star Philip; he represents "Vienna before the war." There is Mambo, a black musician transplanted to Greenwich Village from a Caribbean island. There is John, a former aviator who has been grounded because of uncontrollable anxiety. Finally, there is Donald, a gay man who returns Sabina's maternal love with an irresistibly flattering letter-portrait of her idealized self. This balances the grossly sexual and cruel portrait given to her by her former lover, Jay, a painter.

A Spy in the House of Love is a musical novel both in style and structure. There is a prelude in which Sabina invites the detection of her "crime" (experiencing sex without feeling) by phoning a "lie detector." There is a coda in which Djuna, Sabina's consoling friend, plays a late Beethoven quartet to soothe and heal the dejected Don Juana. The body of the novel is a series of variations on the central theme: Sabina's attempt to live through her relationships with men who—so she deludes herself into believing—have far more exciting lives than she herself has. Each man is associated with a particular type of music, while Igor Stravinsky's "Firebird" is said to be Sabina's "unerring musical autobiography."

SEDUCTION OF THE MINOTAUR

At once the most mature in theme and the most resplendent in imagery among Nin's novels, *Seduction of the Minotaur* takes up the story of Lillian. She has developed considerably since *Ladders to Fire*. Now a jazz performer instead of an interpreter of the classics, Lillian journeys to Mexico, imagining that she has finally freed herself from everything that imprisoned her in the past.

Traveling alone, Lillian meets a series of men, each of whom becomes a teacher or guide of sorts, revealing something of great significance in her own circuitous passage through the labyrinth of the self. The most engaging of these figures is Dr. Hernandez, a male version of Ariadne. He helps Lillian to see that she is not yet as free as she has imagined, wisely telling her that "we live by a series of repetitions until the experience is solved, understood, liquidated."

The monster Lillian confronts is a "masked woman," the part of herself that she has previously been unwilling to recognize.

In Lillian's journey to Mexico and her confrontation with herself, Nin creates a living dream simultaneously in the past, present, and future. The meaning of freedom is not flight, as Sabina imagines, but commitment. If a woman can discover and love the many aspects of one man, she can be fulfilled with a single love. Lillian learns to see her husband Larry, from whom she has been separated, as a complex, multidimensional person. This discovery brings a new excitement, a forgiveness, the grace of understanding to her feelings about him. Because she untangles the knots in her own past, Lillian rediscovers the love of her husband. Thus, there is reconciliation instead of separation.

COLLAGES

A more ambitious and a deeper book than its easy surface and gentle humor suggest, *Collages* is composed of nineteen short blocks of prose, showing once again Nin's preference for constructed rather than narrated fiction. *Collages* begins and ends with the same passage. Its circular structure encloses twenty-two characters portrayed in a wide variety of quickly sketched settings. The cement that binds these colorful elements into a composition is Renate, a woman artist who "makes her own patterns." She weaves in and out of the lives of the others, bringing inspiration not only to her paintings but also to her friends.

Collage art is shown to work magic transformations. In this book, Nin once again stresses the many ways in which dream and fantasy enrich life. There is an intense relationship, for example, between a young woman and a raven. An elderly man feels closer to seals than to human beings; he finally develops the courage to renounce people in order to live with the animals he loves. A gardener pretends to be a millionaire in order to fulfill his dream of financing a literary magazine. A woman whose husband has rejected her for a younger woman replaces him with an exotic phantom lover. In *Collages*, imagination is sovereign.

The healing power of genuine relationships is shown as complementary to that of creative fantasy.

Collages closes with the reluctant emergence of a woman writer from a bitter, self-imposed isolation. Elderly Judith Sands allows herself to be "courted" by Renate and an Israeli admirer, Dr. Mann. Made more trusting by their friendship, Sands actually shows the visitors one of her manuscripts. Its opening words are the same words with which *Collages* begins. This repetition helps endow *Collages* with its circular form and also underscores Nin's conviction that there is an unbroken connection from one person to another, from one imaginative writer to another, and that life is redeemed through the alchemical transformation of art. *Collages* is an assured and accomplished example of Nin's skill at adapting techniques from the nonverbal arts to literature; it is also the most imaginatively conceived of display of her convictions about the mutually nourishing exchange between art and life.

Sharon Spencer

OTHER MAJOR WORKS

SHORT FICTION: *Under a Glass Bell and Other Stories*, 1944; *Delta of Venus: Erotica*, 1977; *Waste of Timelessness and Other Early Stories*, 1977; *Little Birds: Erotica*, 1979.

NONFICTION: *D. H. Lawrence: An Unprofessional Study*, 1932; *Realism and Reality*, 1946; *On Writing*, 1947; *The Diary of Anaïs Nin: 1931-1934*, 1966; *The Diary of Anaïs Nin: 1934-1939*, 1967; *The Novel of the Future*, 1968; *The Diary of Anaïs Nin: 1939-1944*, 1969; *The Diary of Anaïs Nin: 1944-1947*, 1971; *Paris Revisited*, 1972; *The Diary of Anaïs Nin: 1947-1955*, 1974; *A Photographic Supplement to the Diary of Anaïs Nin*, 1974; *A Woman Speaks: The Lectures, Seminars, and Interviews of Anaïs Nin*, 1975; *The Diary of Anaïs Nin: 1955-1966*, 1976; *In Favor of the Sensitive Man and Other Essays*, 1976; *Linotte: The Early Diary of Anaïs Nin, 1914-1920*, 1978; *The Diary of Anaïs Nin: 1966-1974*, 1980; *The Early Diary of Anaïs Nin: Volume Two, 1920-1923*, 1982.

BIBLIOGRAPHY

Bair, Deirdre. *Anaïs Nin: A Biography*. New York: Putnam, 1995. A massive biography by a scholar steeped in the literature of the period and author of biographies of Samuel Beckett and Simone de Beauvoir. Supplements but does not supersede Fitch's shorter but also livelier biography.

Evans, Oliver. *Anaïs Nin*. Carbondale: Southern Illinois University Press, 1968. The result of a twenty-year study of the work and life of Nin. Through extensive research, reading, and lengthy personal interviews, Evans provides new and insightful interpretations of *House of Incest*, Nin's first two diaries, and other major fiction works, but omits Nin's nonfiction works. Nin is presented as a writer in the genre of her good friend Henry Miller. Also contains detailed end notes and an index.

Fitch, Noel Riley. *Anaïs: The Erotic Life of Anaïs Nin*. Boston: Little, Brown, 1993. As the subtitle suggests, Fitch is concerned with tracing Nin's erotic relationships and close friendships with male and female writers. A biographer of Sylvia Beach and an expert on Paris, Fitch writes with verve and expertise.

Franklin, Benjamin, and Duane Schneider. *Anaïs Nin: An Introduction*. Athens: Ohio University Press, 1979. A complete study of the canon of Nin's works, encompassing all of her early fiction works (*Under a Glass Bell and Other Stories* through *Collages*) and devoted to much discussion of the first six volumes of her diary (written between 1931 and 1966). A third section briefly covers Nin's criticism and her nonfiction and presents Nin as a feminist writer. Notes to every chapter are included, as well as an excellent selected bibliography (with an annotated list of secondary sources) and an index.

Hinz, Evelyn J. *The Mirror and the Garden: Realism and Reality in the Writings of Anaïs Nin*. 2d ed. New York: Harcourt Brace Jovanovich, 1973. Envisioned as a continuing study of a living writer, viewing Nin not only as a feminist writer but also as an American one. Her understanding and presentation of the psychological novel is examined at length in the context of her major fiction works. Nin's self-examination in her first four diaries and her critical methodology are also discussed. A

bibliography of works and secondary sources (including journal articles) is included with an index.

Jason, Philip K., ed. *The Critical Response to Anaïs Nin*. Westport, Conn.: Greenwood Press, 1996. A selection of essays examining Nin's works. Includes bibliographical references and an index.

Zaller, Robert, ed. *A Casebook on Anaïs Nin*. New York: New American Library, 1974. This collection of essays is useful as a chronological study of the emergence of Nin as a feminist and novelist. Focuses on her early novels, including *House of Incest*, and moves on quickly to *Cities of the Interior* and the first and fourth volumes of her diary.

FRANK NORRIS

Born: Chicago, Illinois; March 5, 1870
Died: San Francisco, California; October 25, 1902

PRINCIPAL LONG FICTION
Moran of the Lady Letty, 1898
McTeague, 1899
Blix, 1899
A Man's Woman, 1900
The Octopus, 1901
The Pit, 1903
Vandover and the Brute, 1914

OTHER LITERARY FORMS

Frank Norris's published work includes poems, short stories, essays, newspaper articles, novels, and literary criticism. Although he is best known today for his novels, Norris is also remembered for his popular short-story contributions to the San Francisco *Wave* and his insightful literary criticism, published in *The Responsibilities of the Novelist* (1903) and *The Literary Criticism of Frank Norris* (1964).

Norris's first published book, *Yvernelle: A Tale of Feudal France* (published in 1892 while Norris was still in college), was neither a short story nor a novel, but a medieval love poem written in the romantic verse style of Sir Walter Scott. Had it not been subsi-

(Library of Congress)

dized by Gertrude Norris (the author's mother), the book would probably never have been published. Today it is notable only for the high price it brings in the rare book trade.

Norris's success as a reporter was also minimal. His reports on the Boer War were published in the San Francisco *Chronicle*, but his later writings on the Spanish-American War were not published for some time afterward, and never by *McClure's Magazine*, which originally sent him there.

Norris was successful, however, as a short-story writer. Much of his early work first appeared in the San Francisco *Wave*, a weekly newspaper featuring mostly local literary talent. The stories he wrote for the newspaper were later collected in three volumes: *A Deal in Wheat and Other Stories of the New and Old West* (1903), *The Third Circle* (1909), and *Frank Norris of "The Wave"* (1931).

The majority of Norris's writings were collected in a ten-volume *Complete Edition*, published by Doubleday, Doran and Company in 1928. That same year, Doubleday also issued the Argonaut manuscript edition of Norris's works. Identical in content with

the *Complete Edition*, the Argonaut manuscript edition was finely bound and included a manuscript page from *McTeague*. In the late twentieth century, more Norris pieces were unearthed, including his Harvard student theses. The record of his brief literary career is almost complete. His major works are still in print in both hardcover and inexpensive paperbound editions.

ACHIEVEMENTS

Called by many (including himself) "the boy Zola" because his style was so reminiscent of that French author's writings, Norris spearheaded the naturalistic movement in American literature. Although Norris's contemporaries were, by and large, critical of his portrayal of the savage, seamy side of life, it is that very quality in his work which has helped to keep his fiction alive and readable. Even more than his challenge to the Victorian code of the turn of the century, Norris's capacity to portray corruption and its evil effects upon man and his ability to make scenes and characters seem vibrant and real, will rank him high among twentieth century writers.

Norris never achieved the immense popularity of some of the other writers of his day, such as Jack London. He did not even live to see his most successful novel, *The Pit*, become a best-seller. Indeed, it was not until publication of *The Octopus* that he was able to enjoy even a modest financial success. His readers were simply not able to accept his preoccupation with sordid realities, including his treatment of sex, which by Victorian standards was quite shocking. Because of his unsavory choice of subject matter, Norris was ignored by reviewers who understood only the elegant prose and fine writing of an earlier era. Today, Norris's pioneering work in American naturalism is universally acknowledged.

BIOGRAPHY

Frank Norris was the son of Benjamin Franklin Norris, a successful businessman specializing in wholesale jewelry, and Gertrude Doggett. Born in 1870, Norris's early years were spent in Chicago. Except for a trip to Europe when he was eight, Norris's childhood was rather uneventful.

At fourteen, Norris moved with his family to California. They settled first in Oakland and then moved to a large house on Sacramento Street in San Francisco. Benjamin Norris began a real estate development business, building cheap houses for working-class people to rent, and enjoyed financial success. His son would later write about these houses in his first novel.

Frank Norris found San Francisco stimulating. The family home was located only a block from fashionable Van Ness Avenue with its ongoing series of parades and pageants, and only a few blocks from the business section of Polk Street with its rich variety of small shops—there was even a dental parlor with a grotesque golden tooth sign hanging from the building. The scenes and settings were memorable, and Norris captured many of them for later use as local color in his novels.

In 1885, Norris was enrolled in the Belmont Academy. This marked the beginning of a long, largely unsuccessful attempt at formal schooling. Norris had neither the temperament nor the talent in mathematics for scholarship, and, after breaking his arm playing football scarcely one year after enrolling, he quit the Academy for a convalescence at home. It was during this period that he made up his mind to pursue a career as an artist.

After a short stint at Boy's High School, Norris convinced his parents to send him to the San Francisco Art Association School. His success there persuaded Benjamin Norris to send him to the finest art schools in Paris. While Norris did not learn how to paint in Paris, he did learn the fundamentals and principles of art and also the discipline which would later serve him well as a writer.

Convinced that his son was not spending his time painting, Norris's father called him home in 1889. Norris returned from France with a new interest in writing and, more important, a solid foundation upon which to build his writing career.

In the fall of 1890, Norris entered the University of California, determined to become a writer. Almost at once he found himself at odds with the English Department faculty over proper methods of composition. His academic progress in mathematics was abysmal. Norris turned to a more social life and joined Phi Gamma Delta fraternity. There he found a perfect outlet for his frustrations and a wealth of amusements to occupy his time. Although his academic career at Berkeley was undistinguished, Norris's fraternity pranks were memorable.

While Norris was gaining a reputation as a prankster, his family was quickly breaking apart, and Benjamin Norris left, alone, for Europe; while on the trip, he fell in love with another woman. Upon his return, he divorced Gertrude, married his new love, and moved to Chicago; Norris never saw his father again.

In 1894, Norris's marginal academic success caught up with him. Although he had done well in Joseph Le Conte's science classes, his failures in mathematics forced him to leave the university without a degree. Harvard appealed to him as the proper place to polish his writing talents, so he enrolled the following fall as a special student, taking courses in English and French. There he found success in the classes taught by Professor Lewis Gates. Under Gates's watchful eye, Norris began work on his first two novels: *Vandover and the Brute* and *McTeague*.

After a year at Harvard, Norris returned to San Francisco, taking a job with the *Chronicle* as a special correspondent. He convinced the paper to send him to South Africa, where he covered the beginnings of the Boer War. Norris's reports from the strife-torn land were not memorable, but the tropical fever he contracted would later contribute to his death.

Norris next joined the staff of the San Francisco *Wave*, then under the editorship of John O'Hara Cosgrave. As an assistant editor, Norris wrote short stories, reviewed books and art exhibits, and composed feature stories to fill the pages of the weekly newspaper. He found it impossible to work for extended periods of time, however, and interrupted his employment at least twice: once to journey to the Big Dipper Mine near Colfax, California, where he finished *McTeague*; another time to begin work on his third novel, *Moran of the Lady Letty*. He found no trouble selling the first installments of this new novel to the magazines, and as it was running, the story caught the eye of S. S. McClure, who invited Norris to join the staff of Doubleday as a reader. The position paid poorly and offered little status, but Norris took it anyway, perhaps because it allowed him time to finish *Moran of the Lady Letty* and begin other projects as well. After a time, however, Norris began to hate his self-imposed poverty and, at the outbreak of the Spanish-American War, begged McClure to send him to Cuba to cover the conflict as a correspondent for *McClure's Magazine*. McClure agreed; Norris went to Cuba, met Stephen Crane, suffered another attack of fever, and was forced to return to New York. *McClure's Magazine* did not publish any of Norris's war reports.

Never sure of his status with McClure, Norris left the firm in 1899 to join the newly founded firm of Doubleday, Page & Company, again as a part-time, poorly paid reader. He wrote *Blix* and *A Man's Woman* and began *The Octopus* during this time, and he also married Jeannette Black. His major contribution to the firm came when Theodore Dreiser's *Sister Carrie* (1900) was submitted; Norris read the novel in manuscript and insisted upon its publication. After a contract was signed, Doubleday raised objections to the novel and tried to cancel publication. Norris counseled Dreiser to stand firm and insist that his contract be upheld, whereupon Doubleday issued *Sister Carrie* in a limited edition and allowed it quickly to go out of print.

As Norris's royalties grew from the sale of his own novels, he found the financial independence to return to California, and he made plans to purchase a ranch in the southern range of the Santa Cruz mountains. He completed *The Pit*, the second book in his projected trilogy of wheat novels, and planned a journey to the tropics with his wife. That journey was interrupted, however, when Jeannette underwent surgery to remove an inflamed appendix. While she was recovering in the hospital, Norris, too, began suffering stomach pains. Thinking it only a minor ailment, he refused to go to a doctor until he became seriously ill. Suffering from peritonitis and weakened by fever, Norris entered Mt. Zion hospital in San Francisco and died there on October 25, 1902, at the age of thirty-two.

ANALYSIS

Frank Norris was one of a handful of writers at the turn of the century who applied the literary naturalism of Émile Zola to American subjects and themes. As a writer in this tradition, Norris treated his subject matter brutally but sincerely. His characters are but pawns, driven by outside forces over which they have no control. Devoid of souls, they are helpless creatures determined by their heredity and environment. In Norris's most successful novels, these naturalistic ideas are employed with great faithfulness, and his depiction of human beings following a slow but inevitable course toward destruction has an enduring power.

Norris's fiction underwent various stages of development. In *McTeague* and *Vandover and the Brute*, Norris focused his attentions on the naturalistic novel of character, where both McTeague and Vandover proceed slowly toward their inevitable destruction. In Norris's next three novels, *Moran of the Lady Letty, Blix*, and *A Man's Woman*, he bowed to social pressure: Moral values overwhelm deterministic forces in these inferior works. In Norris's last two novels, *The Octopus* and *The Pit*, he again returned to naturalistic themes, but in a broader, more worldly sense, showing greater compassion and involvement with his characters. The progression from *Vandover and the Brute*, a highly dispassionate view of one man's descent, to *The Pit*, which analyzes the social forces at work in the wheat industry, marks Norris's own maturation as both a writer and a man, and his increasingly complex worldview.

VANDOVER AND THE BRUTE

Written while Norris was still in college, *Vandover and the Brute* is concerned with moral weakness. It is the story of a wealthy man who, unable to sustain his ambition to become an artist, descends to a bestial level. As a study of moral and physical disintegration, the novel follows a characteristically didactic naturalistic course. Vandover's descent is governed by a series of chance events and hastened by his own flawed heredity. Because his position in society allows it, Vandover leads a life of pointless leisure. Unable to focus his desire to become an artist, he starts gambling, drinking, and leading a loose

wheat industry. In the first novel of the trilogy, *The Octopus*, Norris returned to naturalistic formulas. In *The Octopus*, the wheat is planted, grown, and harvested. In *The Pit*, the wheat is traded and taken to market. In *The Wolf*, the planned but never written conclusion to the trilogy, the wheat would be consumed by the hungry masses of Europe. Norris did not live to complete this third book. When he died in 1902, the second volume was only then being serialized.

The Octopus and *The Pit* both deal with the problems of society as a whole rather than with the individual. While Norris was successful in remaining true to his theme in *The Octopus*, the theme and naturalistic treatment is blurred somewhat in *The Pit* by a dual story: the trading of wheat in the Chicago Board of Trade and the love story featuring the protagonists of the novel, Curtis Jadwin and Laura Dearborn.

Jadwin, a weak, irresolute man, is a famous capitalist speculator. A taker of chances, he manages for a time to corner the wheat market and enjoy financial prosperity. His fortunes are wiped out, however, when the wheat crops of the West are harvested. Helpless in the face of vast economic forces that he cannot control—and helpless too in the face of his own heredity, which has forced upon him an uncontrollable urge to gamble—Jadwin is destroyed.

There is another story in *The Pit*, however, which runs concurrent to the story of Jadwin's business: the story of the love between Jadwin and Laura, his wife. Laura feels alone and deserted when Jadwin occupies himself in the pit, completely absorbed in the business of trading wheat, and so has an affair with Sheldon Corthell, a superficial artist. The collapse of Jadwin's fortune in wheat breaks him completely, and, with nowhere else to turn, he reasserts his love for Laura. The novel ends, anticlimactically, with Laura and Jadwin facing west, ready to begin life anew. Thus, although powerful in its conception, Norris's last novel is not equal to his best work. He largely neglects his theme (the wheat is rarely physically present in the novel), abandoning naturalistic forces in favor of a love story with autobiographical overtones.

At his best when objectively and dispassionately analyzing his characters and allowing them to be subjected, like pawns, to the naturalistic forces of the universe, Norris faltered when he became too closely involved with his subject. When as in *Blix, Moran of the Lady Letty*, and *The Pit*, romantic themes are allowed to gain paramount importance, Norris's naturalistic intentions and power are subverted. Norris was more, however, than a didactic sociologist in the guise of a novelist. His best work is characterized by a faithful reproduction of setting, by creative exuberance. Thus, one does not merely read about Polk Street in *McTeague*, or the San Joaquin Valley in *The Octopus*, or the Board of Trade in *The Pit*, but one also breathes the air of these places, smells their pungent smells. It is this fundamental sense of reality which gives Norris's fiction a lasting appeal.

David Mike Hamilton

OTHER MAJOR WORKS

SHORT FICTION: *A Deal in Wheat and Other Stories of the New and Old West*, 1903; *The Joyous Miracle*, 1906; *The Third Circle*, 1909; *Frank Norris of "The Wave,"* 1931 (Oscar Lewis, editor).

POETRY: *Yvernelle: A Tale of Feudal France*, 1892; *Two Poems and "Kim" Reviewed*, 1930.

NONFICTION: *The Responsibilities of the Novelist*, 1903; *The Surrender of Santiago*, 1917; *The Letters of Frank Norris*, 1956; *The Literary Criticism of Frank Norris*, 1964.

MISCELLANEOUS: *The Complete Edition of Frank Norris*, 1928.

BIBLIOGRAPHY

Boyd, Jennifer. *Frank Norris Spatial Form and Narrative Time*. New York: Peter Lang, 1993. Chapters on all of Norris's novels, with discussions of his pictorialism, his relationship to Zola and naturalism, and the structures of his longer fictional works. Includes notes and bibliography.

Graham, Don. *The Fiction of Frank Norris: The Aesthetic Context*. Columbia: University of Missouri Press, 1978. Following an apologia for writing about an author who some readers may not enjoy greatly, Graham analyzes the aesthetic aspects of

Norris's *Vandover and the Brute, McTeague, The Octopus*, and *The Pit*. An afterword highlights Norris's uniqueness. Supplemented by a good bibliography and an index.

Hankins, Barry. *God's Rascal: J. Frank Norris and the Beginnings of Southern Fundamentalism.* Lexington: University Press of Kentucky, 1996. Part of the Religion and the South series, this volume examines Norris's fundamentalist themes. With bibliographical references and an index.

McElrath, Joseph R. *Frank Norris Revisited.* New York: Twayne, 1992. An updating and rewriting of a volume that first appeared in 1962 under the authorship of Warren French. This introductory study includes a chapter on the "novelist in the making," followed by subsequent chapters that discuss each of Norris's novels. Includes a chronology, notes, and an annotated bibliography.

Marchand, Ernest. *Frank Norris: A Study.* New York: Octagon Books, 1964. Studies Norris in the context of the wider social, intellectual, and literary background of his period. Addresses his view of the novel, social ideas, and style and ends with a critical evaluation, a bibliography, and an index.

Pizer, Donald, ed. *The Literary Criticism of Frank Norris.* Austin: University of Texas Press, 1964. Attempts to correct deficiencies in a posthumous 1903 collection of Norris criticism. The collection is organized into five parts, each of which treats a relevant facet of criticism. Contains an introductory essay, a note on authorship, a bibliographical note, a checklist of literary criticism, and an index.

_____. *The Novels of Frank Norris.* Bloomington: Indiana University Press, 1966. Studies Norris's mind and art by examining his novels and ideas. Approaches the novels as "all of a piece," maintaining that they "arise out of a coherent conception of man, nature, and God." In addition to a preface and an introduction, includes notes, a selected bibliography, and an index.

prison. She frees herself from the world he is doomed to inhabit.

It is a world that is of his own design. After Arlene has joined Kasch, her former lover, Earl Tuller, returns to threaten and bully her. In a rage, Kasch kills him and seals his fate as a prisoner. He has dreamed of being a murderer, but now that his fantasy has been accidentally granted, he is unable to bear the results. He has been defeated by his own desires mixed with the mindless tide of the universe. The novel ends with Arlene musing over the turn their lives have taken. Laney returns to Kasch's mansion, but he will not answer the door. Imagining that she sees him behind a curtained window, she calls out. She feels she is strong enough, has changed enough from the girl that she was, to save him, and so in a flush of anticipation she waits for "a sign, a sign," but it never comes. Oates demonstrates in *Childwold* the tragic consequences of the conflict between humanity's ambitions and the machinations of the world.

BELLEFLEUR

In *Bellefleur*, Oates combines the gothic grotesque and a sense of realism to create a novel that, incredibly, has believable unhuman creatures. If this type of book seems out of character for her, it may be she wishes to warn her audience that what seems extraordinary may, upon examination, be simply ordinary. In one episode, a huge rodent runs screaming into the house; the next morning, it is nothing but a cat. On the other hand, normality might suddenly become monstrous.

Bellefleur traces the history of the Bellefleur family through several generations and as many psychological aberrations. There are psychics in the family, the gnome who serves Leah Bellefleur, and several ghosts. Jedediah Bellefleur is the manifestation in this novel of the character who forces himself to exist against the will of nature. He is a recurring character in Oates's novels, and in *Bellefleur*, Jedediah is delightfully crazy. In the end, he is persuaded to continue the Bellefleur line despite his (and the reader's) misgivings.

The novel is difficult to read, because it jumps back and forth from past to present. Another diffi-

culty stems from the fact that the main character of interest, the telepathic Germaine Bellefleur, ages only four years from her birth during the entire action of the novel, but her father ages two or three decades. The setting of the novel itself—the Adirondack mountain range—ages thousands of years. In addition, the mountains and the people shrink or grow spasmodically. The final chapters contain spiritual references that, at first, seem disjointed. After Gideon's transformation into the skeletal Angel of Death, however, a Native American appears to the ancestral Jedediah and tells him to embrace the world that he has abandoned. This is Oates's final message to the reader, that only in a full and relished life is there union with God's body. Thus, as in her first novel, Oates's characters do battle with their own existences, their own beings. They struggle, escape, and wander only to return to their initial resting places within themselves and within the confines of their destinies.

MYSTERIES OF WINTERTHURN

The characters in *Mysteries of Winterthurn*, however, appear to have relinquished their resting places for ghostly—and ghastly—forays among the living. This gothic mystery novel has been hailed as a feminist dissertation, a charge that has not been denied by Oates. Although the main character is male and the action in the novel is seen through his eyes, most of the victims are women and children, and it is to their plight that the narrator and the reader grow sympathetic. In *Mysteries of Winterthurn*, Oates discusses the existence of women in a male-dominated society, and a pitiable existence it is.

Even though Oates owes much of her presentation of the situation of nineteenth century women and children to several other popular authors, her interpretation is uniquely her own. Her victims are disposable pawns in a society that is more than willing to sacrifice them for its own (male) devices. Oates inserts the supernatural into the novel to allow her women a modicum of revenge upon these perpetrators. If this seems to be impossible (the unreal attacking the real), Oates insists that once something is thought to be real, it becomes so whether it should be real or not. Thus, the view of women as passive, thoughtless beings is true for the males in her novel, even though it is a false concept. The women victims in the novel are freed by this misconception to react violently to those who misuse them because they (the women) cannot have acted in such a manner within the male scheme of things.

To drive this point home, Oates repeats it three times during the novel. The first story, "The Virgin in the Rose-Bower," deals with a sadistic husband and father, Erasmus Kilgarven, who has a hand in the brutal deaths of his two wives and commits incest for several years with his daughter, Georgina, causing her to become pregnant several times. Georgina kills her infants but claims that they have been destroyed by angels painted on the ceiling of her bedroom. The narrator, young Xavier Kilgarven, sees one painted angel bleed, and this leads to the discovery of several other infant corpses, silent witnesses to Erasmus Kilgarven's hideous habit. By claiming supernatural murder (and rape), Georgina is able to evade guilt and exact a small amount of revenge on her father.

In the persona of Iphigenia, her pen name, Georgina is also able to free her female family members by publishing her poetry. The money she receives from this enterprise, until her father forbids it as unseemly, is later used to finance even more unfeminine exploits by the young Perdita. Perdita needs no spectral avenger; she takes matters into her own hands, although she is never seen as a murderer by anyone but the reader. The only people who are capable of violent acts in *Mysteries of Winterthurn* are male; the females are those upon whom these acts are perpetrated. Thus, an invisible shield is created around Perdita, enabling her to murder several people in order to achieve her goal, union with young Xavier.

The third sister, Thérèse, is able to profit from her sisters' cloaked deeds, and, indeed, there are indications that she may be involved in Perdita's violent crimes in a peripheral manner. This is only hinted at, however; outwardly, Thérèse appears to be a happy, modern woman. It is here that Oates's use of paradox—the woman who is both angel and demon, visible and invisible—culminates. All the women in the novel have been so seduced by the theory of their own guilt that they must violently oppose it in order to free themselves.

FOXFIRE

Another brilliantly innovative work encompassing Oates's feminist vision is *Foxfire: Confessions of a Girl Gang*. This novel, set in upstate New York in the 1950's, centers on five high school girls who seek and get revenge on the men who exploit them. By chronicling the exploits of the Foxfire gang, which comprises Legs Sadovsky, Goldie, Lana, Rita, and Maddy Wirtz, Oates reveals how male exploitation of females and class conflict consistently reinforce each other. Unlike the female characters in *Mysteries of Winterhurn*, the girl gang members are not paralyzed by their fear, guilt, or insecurity. Finding strength in solidarity, the girls, all from low-income families who daily feel the sting of poverty and the humiliation of male chauvinism, resolve not to suffer at the hands of their exploiters, villains they cast as upper-class white men. The girls, in a wild experiment of role reversal, aggressively seek out their own victims, men who have hurt one or all of them. They subsequently put these men on "trial," and all their victims are "sentenced" to some punishment. By inflicting physical pain or by causing irreversible damage to the men's reputations, the girls see to it that the guilty suffer for the psychic wounds they have caused. While Oates's sympathies clearly lie with the girls, she mitigates the gang's actions by providing them with an important insight. All the girls come to realize that evil is not strictly the province of males or the upperclass; their own acts of violence clearly reveal to them that, tragically, the propensity for harming others exists in all human beings.

WHAT I LIVED FOR

In *What I Lived For*, Jerome "Corky" Corcoran, the main character, makes a discovery similar to that of the Foxfire gang. As Corky bounces from one volatile situation to another throughout the dense, highly intricate plot of the novel, he becomes the principal figure in a modern tragedy. The narrative, an account of the three most intense days of Corky's life, related by the protagonist himself, reveals his participation in situations and relationships that, as they disintegrate before his eyes, challenge all of Corky's beliefs

Creighton explores the autobiographical elements, feminist subtexts, and realistic dimensions of the novels. Select bibliography.

Friedman, Ellen G. *Joyce Carol Oates.* New York: Frederick Ungar, 1980. This text gives very clear and concise criticisms of nine of Oates's novels, from *With Shuddering Fall* to *Son of the Morning.* After a first chapter that provides a biographical and environmental background for the longer works, each chapter is devoted solely to one novel. There are no comparisons that make researching one subject so annoying; these are included in the epilogue. Notes, a bibliography, and an index round out the book.

Grant, Mary Kathryn. *The Tragic Vision of Joyce Carol Oates.* Durham, N.C.: Duke University Press, 1978. As a study of the use of violence in Oates's fiction, this text delves into the early works (1963-1975) and examines the impact of inner-city danger on her themes and characters. The chapters are augmented by references to specific works, and the text itself includes a bibliography, notes, an appendix, and index.

Johnson, Greg. *Invisible Writer: A Biography of Joyce Carol Oates.* New York: Penguin Putnam, 1998. Johnson provides a thorough analysis of Oates's work and life in this full-length authorized biography. Draws on a variety of sources, including Oates's private letters and journals.

_____. *Joyce Carol Oates: A Study of the Short Fiction.* New York: Twayne, 1991. This study provides an in-depth analysis of several of Oates's most popular and enduring stories. The work is divided into three parts: The Short Fiction, The Writer, and The Critics. Essential to any student of Oates, also includes a lengthy bibliography.

Wesley, Marilyn. *Refusal and Transgression in Joyce Carol Oates's Fiction.* Westport, Conn.: Greenwood, 1993. A feminist analysis, this work focuses on the family as portrayed in Oates's fiction. Wesley contends that the young protagonists of many of Oates's stories and novels commit acts of transgression that serve as critiques of the American family. Wesley maintains that the acts indict the society that produces and supports

these unstable, dysfunctional, and often violent families.

EDNA O'BRIEN

Born: Tuamgraney, Ireland; December 15, 1930

PRINCIPAL LONG FICTION

The Country Girls, 1960
The Lonely Girl, 1962 (reprinted in 1964 as *Girl with Green Eyes*)
Girls in Their Married Bliss, 1964
August Is a Wicked Month, 1965
Casualties of Peace, 1966
A Pagan Place, 1970
Zee and Co.: A Novel, 1971
Night, 1972
Johnny I Hardly Knew You, 1977 (pb. in U.S. as *I Hardly Knew You*)
The Country Girls Trilogy and Epilogue, 1986
The High Road, 1988
Time and Tide, 1992
An Edna O'Brien Reader, 1994
House of Splendid Isolation, 1994
Down by the River, 1996
Wild Decembers, 1999

OTHER LITERARY FORMS

Edna O'Brien's short stories appear regularly in magazines such as *The New Yorker* and *The Atlantic Monthly*; some have been collected in *The Love Object* (1968), *A Scandalous Woman and Other Stories* (1974), and *Mrs. Reinhardt* (1978). O'Brien has written plays, including *A Cheap Bunch of Nice Flowers* (1962) and *Virginia* (1981); the screenplays *Girl with Green Eyes* (1964), *Time Lost and Time Remembered* (1966), *Three into Two Won't Go* (1968), and *X, Y and Zee* (1971); television plays, including *Mrs. Reinhardt* (1981); and nonfiction, including the autobiographical *Mother Ireland* (1976), a travel book, *Arabian Days* (1977), an anthology, *Some Irish Loving* (1979), and an essay on the Joyces, *James and Nora* (1981).

ACHIEVEMENTS

After moving to London from Dublin in 1959, O'Brien published at a furious pace, mining her early experiences in Ireland and then as a single parent with two sons to rear in England. There was something of a lull in her long fiction, however, from 1977 to 1986. Nearly always from a female narrator's point of view, O'Brien has brilliantly transmuted her personal experiences into art. Her recall and selection of the tiny details that make up the texture of life, particularly in her Irish scenes (*The Country Girls, The Lonely Girl, A Pagan Place*) are most dazzling. Impressive, too, is her evident love and savoring of words, sometimes clearly in a James Joyce fashion, for their own sake, and often in good dialogue. Perhaps because of the speed with which she works, the vivacity and brilliance of her prolific output is frequently marred by awkward grammar, punctuation, and syntax. Apparently, her editors have felt these stylistic lapses are all part of her Irish use of the language and have accordingly let them stand.

O'Brien was a feminist before the term became fashionable, but her works also affirm a wider humanistic sympathy for all people. Early, she took up the topics of women's attitudes toward their bodies, their sexuality, and their roles as mothers and daughters. In Ireland several of her books have been banned because of their often negative comments on the Roman Catholic Church, more common in her early work, and her frequent employment of graphic sexual terms and scenes. She has never received an Irish literary prize. Outside Ireland, her reputation as a writer of fiction seems assured, although reviewer Marianne Wiggins, writing in *The Nation*, rather tartly observed that "to the English [she is] a minor self-promoting legend." In 1970, O'Brien earned *The Yorkshire Post* Award for Novel of the Year for *A Pagan Place* and was given the *Los Angeles Times* Book Award in 1990 for her book of short stories *Lantern Slides*. Her acclaim will be even more certain when she can distance more effectively the bitterness she feels about her Irish upbringing, achieving the balance typical of the best of the many Irish writers in exile.

BIOGRAPHY

Edna O'Brien was born to Michael and Lena (Cleary) O'Brien in Tuamgraney, County Clare, Ireland, on December 15, 1930. She has one brother and two sisters. Her father was an impractical man who bred horses and squandered his wealth; her mother worked in the United States for eight years, returning to Ireland to marry. O'Brien characterizes her mother as an ambitious, frustrated woman who mistrusted books and was unsympathetic to her daughter's emerging literary interests. (Although O'Brien dedicated her first novel to her mother, she later found her mother's copy with the inscription page torn out and angry comments written throughout.) O'Brien first attended Scarriff National School in 1936, then boarded at the Convent of Mercy, Loughrea, County Galway, in 1941 before going off to the Pharmaceutical College of Ireland in Dublin in 1946, where she worked in a chemist's shop during the day and attended lectures at night. One of her first purchases in Dublin was a secondhand copy of *Introducing James Joyce* (1944), edited by T. S. Eliot, which first exposed her to the influence of that Irish literary giant. In 1948, she began to write short pieces for the *Irish Press*. In 1951,

(Terry O'Neill)

O'Brien married novelist Ernest Gebler and lived for a time in rural County Wicklow (the marriage ended in 1964). Two sons, Carlos and Sasha, were born, in 1952 and 1954. In 1959, the family moved to London, and O'Brien's career as a published writer was quickly launched. In three weeks, far from County Clare, she wrote *The Country Girls*, tracing the development of fourteen-year-old Caithleen Brady. The trilogy was continued in *The Lonely Girl* and *Girls in Their Married Bliss* and was appended with *Epilogue* in 1986. In 1959, O'Brien settled in London, frequently traveling abroad to Europe, the Middle East, and the Americas—for pleasure and profit, as a tourist, and as a reader-lecturer.

ANALYSIS

Edna O'Brien's early years in Ireland profoundly affected her view of the world, and particularly of women's relationships and their place in society. Being Irish, she says in *Mother Ireland*, gives one a unique view of pleasure and punishment, life and death. O'Brien's work is lyrical and lively. Her memory for people and places, for the minutiae of daily living, is prodigious; her zest for language is Joycean. She is frequently on the attack, but at her best, which is often, she transcends her immediate cause to encourage, with a grain of humor, those who still dream of love achieved through kindness and decency—common virtues still no more common than they ever were.

O'Brien's concerns are most readily accessible in her very eccentric travel/autobiography *Mother Ireland*. Her Irishness is something of which O'Brien is proud: "It's a state of mind." She is not, however, blind to Ireland's faults, appreciating that there must be something "secretly catastrophic" about a country that so many people leave. After an iconoclastic opening chapter on Irish history, with its uncanonized patron saint and its paunchy Firbolgs, follow six chapters in which are sketched O'Brien's dominant themes: loneliness; the longing for adventure (often sexual); the repressive Irish Roman Catholic Church; family ties (the martyred mother and the rollicking father); the courageous hopelessness with which life at best must be lived.

It would be a melancholy picture if it were not for O'Brien's saving, ironic sense of humor and the skill with which she roots her observations in the sensual details of the actual world. Her readers share vividly with her a world of wet batteries for radios, ink powder, walls with fragments of bottles embedded in their tops, Fox's (Glacier) Mints, orange-boxes, and lice fine-combed from a child's head onto a newspaper. O'Brien's recurring themes, her experiments with form, and the feeling she succeeds in communicating that this Irish microcosm has its universal significance are all clearly present in *Mother Ireland*.

THE COUNTRY GIRLS

From its detailed, evocative opening page, redolent of genteel poverty, *The Country Girls*, O'Brien's first novel, serves notice of an unusual voice. The shy and sensitive Caithleen tells her first-person story and shares the action with her alter ego, the volatile and malicious Baba. It is a world divided into two warring camps, male and female, where Caithleen's aspirations toward romantic love are doomed to failure. Mr. Gentleman is the first in a long line of rotters (the drunken, brutal father; Eugene Gaillard; Herod; Dr. Flaggler), far outnumbering the few men with decent inclinations (Hickey, Auro); in such a world women stand little chance, single, married in the usual sense, or brides of Christ.

The repressive effects of poverty and a patriarchal society are hardly alleviated by the Church and its proscriptions. Her mother drowned, Caithleen spends her mid-teen years boarding in a strict convent school from which Baba contrives their expulsion for writing a ribald note. In their late teens, joyously, they come up to Dublin, Baba to take a commercial course, Caithleen to work as a grocer's assistant until she can take the Civil Service examinations. Loneliness, however, follows them: Baba contracts tuberculosis; Caithleen's Mr. Gentleman lets her down. Yet with the resilience of youth her last line in this novel is, "I was almost certain that I wouldn't sleep that night."

THE LONELY GIRL

The Lonely Girl continues the saga two years later, with Baba healthy again. It is, however, largely Caithleen's story; again she is the narrator. The repressive effects of her family, her village community, and her convent education are again in evidence. O'Brien has her heroine involved romantically with Eugene Gaillard, whose face reminds her of a saint, and who is about the same height as her father; he is a cultivated snob, and in an often cold fashion he begins the further education of his naïve, prudish, "student," both in bed and in the salon. (In *Edna O'Brien*, 1974, Grace Eckley points out that Caithleen's stiff tutor and O'Brien's former husband, Ernest Gebler, share the same initials.) At the novel's conclusion, Caithleen, wild and debased "because of some damned man," is learning, is changing; she is, as she says, finding her feet, "and when I'm able to talk I imagine that I won't be alone." Still seeking their connection, she and Baba sail on the *Hibernia*, from Dublin to Liverpool and London.

GIRLS IN THEIR MARRIED BLISS

Girls in Their Married Bliss continues the story of the two in London, where, for the first time, Baba assumes the first-person narration, alternating with an omniscient voice distancing O'Brien and the reader from Caithleen's role—a process she will carry even further with her protagonist in *A Pagan Place*. The women, now about twenty-five years old, have not left their Irish baggage behind in Dublin; there is a splendid, blustery Celtic quality to the scapegrace Baba's style. Kate (as Caithleen is called), too, has her share of one-liners, word associations, epigrams, and zany metaphors: "Self-interest," she observes on one occasion, "was a common crime"; on another, at a party, she is amused by a girl wearing a strawberry punnet on her head to make herself taller.

In these early novels, O'Brien, like her leading characters, is learning and developing her skills. In *Girls in Their Married Bliss*, the topic is still the female search for love and connection. The novel is a precisely observed account of a marriage failing. People rub exquisitely on one another's nerves in the larger context of women's role in society; in the smaller context of bedroom politics, "Men are pure fools." Marriage, at least on the grounds on which the women enter it here, is evidently no end to the quest. Baba makes a calculated move for comfort; Kate sees that her interest in people is generated solely by her own needs. They have matured to the point where

they no longer believe much in romantic plans. Kate's answer to the biological unfairness of God's scheme for women, as Baba sees it, is to have herself sterilized; she will not make the same mistake again: No other child of hers will be abducted by its father; no further child of hers will in its turn become a parent.

The complete trilogy was reissued in 1986 in one volume, with a brief *Epilogue* in the form of a monologue delivered by Baba. Here the ebullient Baba brings the reader up to date: The despairing Kate is dead; she drowned, perhaps deliberately.

AUGUST IS A WICKED MONTH

In O'Brien's next, new, full-length novel, *August Is a Wicked Month*, an omniscient narrator describes the protagonist's abortive attempts at self-liberation, largely through sexual activity. Ellen is a Kate-like, superstitious, convent-bred, twenty-eight-year-old Irish magazine writer, formerly a nurse, living in London when the novel begins. She takes a trip to France when the husband from whom she is separated and their eight-year-old son, Mark, who lives with her, go on a camping holiday together. Her "pathetic struggles towards wickedness" involve rejecting the first sexual invitations she encounters. Eventually, however, when Ellen does become intimately involved with a high-living group, O'Brien subjects her to two catastrophic accidents: She receives a call from her husband, who tells her that her son has been killed by a car in a roadside accident, and she fears, wrongly as it turns out, that she has contracted a venereal disease. The guilt and the judgment are clear; perhaps they are too clear to make this novel an artistic success. Ellen finally finds an uneasy autumnal peace, unlike the women in O'Brien's next novel, who have a genuine joy ripped away from them.

CASUALTIES OF PEACE

In *Casualties of Peace*, Willa McCord, artist in glass, and her earthy domestic, Patsy Wiley, are the protagonists, exemplary victims of male violence. An omniscient narrator views the two unhappy women—Willa having escaped from a nightmarish marriage to the sadistic Herod, Patsy presently suffering her husband Tom's blows. Both have their dreams of happiness outside marriage shattered. There was a chance for peace for them, but accidents prevented them from knowing joy. Patsy blabs to Willa about leaving Tom rather than doing it immediately, as planned, and her lover, Ron, believes she has let him down. Willa, just when a loving connection with Auro seems possible, is murdered by Tom, who mistakes her for Patsy.

Casualties of Peace is, with the exception of *Night*, which it anticipates to some extent, O'Brien's most Joycean novel. Patsy's love letters to Ron are reminiscent of the earthiest of James Joyce and Nora Barnacle's correspondence; Patsy indeed is a kind of Molly Bloom figure (more clearly developed in *Night*). Willa's letters to Auro, delivered posthumously, share the same stream-of-consciousness qualities: Words pile up into lists; associations trigger other more graphic associations; "memory is the bugger." At times lyrical, at times humorous, O'Brien develops here the Celtic flair with words that is associated with Joyce or Dylan Thomas. Her theme is loneliness and its myriad causes; her characters search to alleviate their pain, to make connections, to overcome their feelings of guilt for being themselves.

A Pagan Place

A Pagan Place is a very odd novel; it is largely a sophisticated rewrite of *The Country Girls*, as O'Brien perhaps would have written that work had she had ten years more reading, writing, and living behind her at the time. Baba is dropped in favor of one unnamed, preadolescent girl whose sexual arousal when her father beats her accomplishes her move toward adolescence. Getting away from her Irish family and Irish community with their hereditary guilt will, it is suggested, take her yet a stage further. At the end of the novel she leaves to the accompaniment of an eerie Hibernian howl.

Throughout the work an omniscient narrator, who sometimes uses dialect forms, sometimes very erudite words, and who is clearly unreliable in matters of fact (putting an English "general" on Nelson's pillar), places the reader at the center of the action by using the second-person narrative. No one but "you," then, is at the center of the action; the narrator and the writer are similarly distanced from the action.

Perhaps in this novel O'Brien exorcised the worst of her Irishness; certainly, very violent feelings surface, all in the consciousness of a young girl. O'Brien, in contrast to her contemporaries among Irish writers of fiction, such as Brian Friel or Benedict Kiely, really seems to dislike her Celtic community. Here is a very bitter indictment of the Church, and perhaps its ultimate rejection in the priest's attempt to seduce "you," masturbating and ejaculating on "you." Here, too, is a savage, repressive, guilt-ridden world of so-called Christians, where unwed mothers receive no *caritas*, where legally wed mothers and fathers show no love either. It is a world where Holy Water is sprinkled on thoroughbred foals, where a black dog, chasing a frog that jumps out of the ashes at Della's wake, is seen as one and the same with the devil. All in all, it is, with few exceptions, a nightmarish community, especially for a child. For "you" as a child at the center of this world, deserted even by "your" mother at one period, a thing "you" thought would never happen, the only certainty is that "you" want to escape, whatever the burden of guilt "you" carry.

Zee & Co.

The theme of escape is continued in *Zee & Co.*, where O'Brien's heroines are back in London, and again a pair. Zee moves increasingly aggressively and ruthlessly to hold her man, Robert, while dominating Stella, her rival. She succeeds in both endeavors. As the war of the sexes heats up, Zee refuses to be a victim; she is no patsy. O'Brien's long preoccupation with the defensive role of women in society appears to be shifting to the offensive in her later works as her heroines themselves become less fragmented. A person needs to be integrated psychically to withstand not only sexual partners and spouses, but also all manifestations of phantoms, prejudice, repression, guilt, and loneliness. This new positive attitude is well illustrated in the rambunctious Mary Hooligan, whose nightlong monologue forms O'Brien's next work, *Night*.

Night

In form and style, *Night* is O'Brien's most Joycean novel. In a harangue from her bed in England, Mary Hooligan—Irish, abused, divorced—delivers herself of an aggressive, courageous, independent, first-person autobiographical statement. Beginning with an Anglo-Saxon monosyllable in the opening paragraph, the nonconciliatory tone of her monologue is established. "I am a woman," Mary affirms, and proceeds to weave, in time and place, the story of her connection with her father and mother, her former husband—"the original Prince of Darkness"—and her son. It is an exuberant linguistic spree: From a "trepidation" of gelatinlike dessert to the welcome "tap o' the mornin'," metaphors and apt words are savored and invented. The pervasive humor is wry; the aggressive tone and confident technique perfectly match the content of a work whose burden is rebellion against loveless unions and ignorance.

Mary Hooligan is another in O'Brien's procession of outsiders, an Irish woman in England, merely house-sitting so even less important in the community. O'Brien, however, establishes Mary as a force on her own: Mary rejects her friend, Madge (Mary needs no Kate-figure to complement her being); she is complete on her own. The theme under review remains the eternal search for love in its myriad manifestations; what is new here is the heroine's joyful attack as she continues her pilgrimage to "the higher shores of love." Family, community, and marriage settings are again explored. Many of the details are familiar: the vicious father, the ignoramuses who could not tell cheese from soap, the cold-fish husband. Constant and familiar in O'Brien is the warm regard for children, particularly the mothers' regard for their sons. This aspect of love leads her to flirt with incest in her most violent work, *I Hardly Knew You*, where the narrator has an affair with and then murders her son's friend.

I HARDLY KNEW YOU

Nora, the protagonist of *I Hardly Knew You*, tells her story in yet another night monologue, from her prison cell, as she awaits trial for the murder of Hart, her young lover. Again, O'Brien's narrator is an Irish exile in England, divorced from an overly frugal husband, with a son, and literally in prison, isolated from all society. Loneliness is at the core of her existence, as it is, she remarks, at the core of Celtic songs. Her monologue shuffles time and space more formally than Mary Hooligan's in *Night* and reveals a world

of increasing violence. Details and incidents from O'Brien's previous works, as far back even as *The Country Girls*, show up: the drunken father taking the cure; the abducted-child threat; the child scraping the toilet-seat paint; the kicking match engaged in by the brutish relatives. The world has become an increasingly violent place, and the response of O'Brien's narrator matches it. Like Mary's, Nora's personality is integrated, but toward the Kate side. She engages in an explicitly lesbian encounter, but she needs no other woman to complement her. Indeed, she acts increasingly like the worst stereotype of the sadistic male predator, who uses and abuses other people, particularly women and especially wives. This is a chilling picture of a person driven to violence, to kill without regret. Here is a woman who has lost her balance and whose sweeping indictment of men must surely be viewed as just as reprehensible as male chauvinism. "I am proud . . . to have killed one of the breed to whom I owe nothing but cruelty, deceit, and the asp's emission," she avers, ignoring absolutely O'Brien's often-stated support for "human decency" and kindness among people of whatever sex.

The graph of O'Brien's fictional, split personalities is by no means a straight line. A clearly differentiated pair in the early trilogy, each "Kate" and "Baba" is subsequently given an alternating fictional forum. The *Epilogue* may have seemed to clear the way for Baba and zesty Baba-types, but *The High Road*, which comes next, has readers once again seeing a sophisticated society through the moist eyes of a Kate-type.

THE HIGH ROAD

Anna, the narrator in *The High Road*, like many of the women in O'Brien's short stories as well, has come on Easter Sunday to a Mediterranean paradise to get over a London love doomed from its inception. In this exotic setting, she encounters eccentric members of the international set: the superannuated debutante, Portia; the grotesques who make up a German fashion-magazine staff on location; the fading jet-setter, Iris; the itinerant Irish painter, D'Arcy, with the Joycean language flair; and Catalina, the hotel chambermaid, with whom she has an affair.

It all ends in murder; D'Arcy, to buy some time, paints "Lesbos" on a multitude of walls, not merely on Catalina's gable, where the word first appeared, but to no avail. Clutching a scarf full of Catalina's blood-soaked hair, in what in its accumulation of similes seems at times a parody of the Gothic romance, Anna sets out, she says, for the last time, for home. Whether she has left behind her the purgatory of motherhood, in its various manifestations, remains to be read.

HOUSE OF SPLENDID ISOLATION

O'Brien returns to her native territory with a projected trilogy of novels set in Ireland. The first, *House of Splendid Isolation*, is a stunning book, quite different from her previous work. It reveals a microcosm of divided Ireland, embodied by the patriot-terrorist McGreevy and the widow Josie O'Meara. McGreevy, seeking to free Northern Ireland from British rule, has been sent to the complacent South to murder a prominent English visitor. He plans to hide in Josie's decaying mansion, which he believes is empty. Feared as a coldly efficient terrorist, McGreevy emerges as a surprisingly kind, ordinary man who has been honed to a thin edge by violence.

Josie, ill with pneumonia and high blood pressure, has just been released from a nursing home to her house of isolation. She seems pluckier than most O'Brien heroines, perhaps because she is elderly, although flashbacks illuminate the early life that formed her. The collision of the revolutionary and the antiterrorist, and their gradual sympathy and understanding, define the conflict of the novel and the hunt that follows. Josie can be seen as the *Shan Van Vocht*, the Poor Old Woman, a historical symbol of Ireland, exemplifying the domestic life of her people. McGreevy represents the bitter fruit of their troubled political history. The inevitable conclusion proceeds as well-meaning, patriotic volunteers from both factions struggle with duty, guilt, and grief.

Surprisingly, O'Brien avoids her usual male stereotypes; she presents imperfect men, both law-abiding and lawless, who are racked by ambivalence. She remains neutral, revealing with rueful detachment the human damage from centuries of conflict. This novel is a portrait of Ireland in all its complexity, its intense people, and its bloody and heartbreaking history.

DOWN BY THE RIVER

Down by the River is a less objective book, inspired by a controversial incident that took place in Ireland in 1992, when a pregnant fourteen-year-old girl fled to England for an abortion but was brought back and made a ward of the court. O'Brien has changed some details; in her version, Mary Mac-Namara is impulsively raped by her father as they are picking berries. Mary's dying mother and a female doctor suspect the truth, as do others, but no one acts. Mary becomes pregnant.

Here again is that familiar world of repression and guilt, in which people do not look directly at each other or say what needs to be said. In a tacit conspiracy of avoidance, everyone knows what is happening to Mary, but no one will confront it. Worse is the hypocrisy of those quick to judge without mercy. Self-righteous adulterers preen in anti-abortion meetings while a shrill speaker waves bloody photographs, even as a retired midwife recalls the dead babies she has found stuffed in drawers and toilets. Other folks are genuinely troubled, torn between religious conviction and pity for the girl. Although a sympathetic neighbor finally agrees to help Mary escape to London, the abortion is thwarted. People on both sides of the issue exploit her for their own purposes, and the ending is tense and melodramatic, though not entirely convincing.

Archibald E. Irwin, updated by Joanne McCarthy

OTHER MAJOR WORKS

SHORT FICTION: *The Love Object*, 1968; *A Scandalous Woman and Other Stories*, 1974; *Mrs. Reinhardt*, 1978 (pb. in U.S. as *A Rose in the Heart*, 1979); *Returning*, 1982; *A Fanatic Heart*, 1984; *Lantern Slides*, 1990.

PLAYS: *A Cheap Bunch of Nice Flowers*, pr. 1962; *A Pagan Place*, pr. 1972; *The Gathering*, pr. 1974; *Virginia*, pr. 1980.

SCREENPLAYS: *Girl with Green Eyes*, 1964; *Time Lost and Time Remembered*, 1966 (with Desmond Davis); *Three into Two Won't Go*, 1969; *X, Y, and Zee*, 1971.

TELEPLAYS: *The Wedding Dress*, 1963; *Nothing's Ever Over*, 1968; *Mrs. Reinhardt*, 1981.

POETRY: *On the Bone*, 1989.

NONFICTION: *Mother Ireland*, 1976; *Arabian Days*, 1977; *Some Irish Loving*, 1979 (edited); *James and Nora: A Portrait of Joyce's Marriage*, 1981; *Vanishing Ireland*, 1986; *James Joyce*, 1999.

CHILDREN'S LITERATURE: *The Dazzle*, 1981; *A Christmas Treat*, 1982; *The Expedition*, 1982; *The Rescue*, 1983; *Tales for the Telling: Irish Folk and Fairy Stories*, 1986.

BIBLIOGRAPHY

Eckley, Grace. *Edna O'Brien*. Lewisburg, Pa.: Bucknell University Press, 1974. The first book-length study of O'Brien. Eckley discusses individually, in a very sympathetic and perceptive fashion, O'Brien's longer works of fiction through *Night* (1972). This excellent starting place for a study of O'Brien needs to be brought up to date, however, in its primary and secondary sources. O'Brien's work generally is reviewed in the major dailies and weeklies; she grants many interviews but is largely ignored by the Academy.

Guppy, Shusha. "The Art of Fiction, LXXXII: Edna O'Brien." *Paris Review* 26 (Summer, 1984): 22-50. Presents a comprehensive interview with O'Brien.

Haule, James M. "Tough Luck: The Unfortunate Birth of Edna O'Brien." *Colby Library Quarterly* 23 (December, 1987): 216-224. Examines, particularly in the short story, "A Scandalous Woman," the potential difficulties of mothering in Ireland.

Irwin, Archibald E. "Give Us Baba." *Irish Literary Supplement*, Spring, 1987, 19. A review of *The Country Girls Trilogy and Epilogue*, highlighting the split personality of O'Brien's heroines.

L'Heureux, John. "The Terrorist and the Lady." *The New York Times Book Review*, June 26, 1994, 7. A mixed review remarking, perhaps too harshly, on O'Brien's use of symbolism and metaphoric language in *House of Splendid Isolation*. Although L'Heureux praises the novel, he considers much of Josie O'Meara's past life irrelevant to the central conflict with the terrorist McGreevy.

O'Brien, Edna. Interview by Molly McQuade. *Publishers Weekly*, May 18, 1992, 48-49. O'Brien throws further light on her tense and difficult relationship with her mother. She also speaks of her obsession with words and the ensuing repercussions in her own life.

O'Brien, Peggy. "The Silly and the Serious: An Assessment of Edna O'Brien." *The Massachusetts Review* 18 (Autumn, 1987): 474-488. A provocative psychological appraisal to account for the mixed responses to O'Brien's work. O'Brien's blurring of the boundaries between herself and her protagonists, and the evaluative doubts that result, are seen as a product of the author's unresolved parental influences.

Roth, Philip. "A Conversation with Edna O'Brien." *The New York Times Book Review*, November 18, 1984, 38-40. A perceptive, supportive interview, in which the importance of place in O'Brien's fiction is examined.

Woodward, Richard B. "Edna O'Brien: Reveling in Heartbreak." *The New York Times Magazine*, March 12, 1989, 42, 50, 51. An essentially snide, though revealing, look at O'Brien's ambivalences.

FLANN O'BRIEN
Brian O'Nolan

Born: Strabane, Ireland; October 5, 1911
Died: Dublin, Ireland; April 1, 1966

PRINCIPAL LONG FICTION

At Swim-Two-Birds, 1939
An Béal Bocht, 1941 (pb. in U.S. as *The Poor Mouth*, 1973)
The Hard Life, 1961
The Dalkey Archive, 1964
The Third Policeman, 1967

OTHER LITERARY FORMS

Flann O'Brien was the pen name used by Brian O'Nolan for the four novels he wrote in English, and so it is used here, although his work in other forms appeared under other names. He was a talented and prolific journalist as well as a novelist. He began to write satirical essays for student publications at University College, Dublin; a sampling of this student work was reprinted in the "Flann O'Brien Number" published by the *Journal of Irish Studies* in 1974. Although a civil servant by profession, O'Brien also wrote a famous column for *The Irish Times* under the name Myles na Gopaleen. This column continued to be printed on a regular basis for twenty-five years; selections were reprinted in *Cruiskeen Lawn* (1943), *The Best of Myles* (1968), and *The Various Lives of Keats and Chapman and the Brother* (1976). Throughout his career, O'Brien sporadically produced skits for theater, essays other than journalism, and short stories. These are most conveniently located in two posthumous collections. *Stories and Plays* (1973) reprints two dramatic skits, two short stories, an essay on James Joyce called "A Bash in the Tunnel," and the seven existing chapters of an unfinished novel called *Slattery's Sago Saga*. *A Flann O'Brien Reader* (1978) includes examples of his journalism, short fiction, and essays, along with excerpts from his five novels.

Achievements

O'Brien's contemporary reputation rests on the rediscovery of his first novel, *At Swim-Two-Birds*, an event that occurred about twenty years after the novel was published. The novel had received praise from James Joyce, Dylan Thomas, and Graham Greene, among others, but its possibilities for broad critical and popular success were thwarted by the onset of World War II. His next novel, *The Third Policeman*, could find no publisher until after his death, and his third novel, *The Poor Mouth*, was written in Gaelic and thus limited to an extremely small audience. These three novels are now considered to be O'Brien's most important works. About 1960, O'Brien's work was rediscovered by the American writers S. J. Perelman and William Saroyan. Their praise, principally of his journalism, led to a reissue of *At Swim-Two-Birds* and critical recognition of it as an important novel. In response to this renewal of interest in

his fiction, O'Brien wrote *The Hard Life* and *The Dalkey Archive*, but neither of these later novels is as interesting nor as important as his three earlier novels. O'Brien's journalism, in posthumous collections, is the source of most of his popular appeal today, particularly in Ireland. The focus of almost all critical interest in his work, however, is on his novels, especially *At Swim-Two-Birds* and *The Third Policeman*. O'Brien is now universally recognized as the most important Irish novelist of his generation.

Biography

The novelist known as Flann O'Brien was born Brian O'Nolan on October 5, 1911, in Strabane, County Tyrone, Ireland. He was the third of twelve children of Michael Victor O'Nolan, a customs officer, and Agnes Gormlet O'Nolan. O'Brien's family was frequently relocated in the course of his father's profession, and this postponed his early formal education. His family was extremely literate, however, and in the home O'Brien developed early fluency in Irish Gaelic as well as English and also some familiarity with Latin and Greek classics. It was only in 1923, when his father was transferred to Dublin, that O'Brien was enrolled, at the age of twelve, in the Synge Street School run by the Christian Brothers. In 1925, his father was appointed a revenue commissioner in Dublin Castle, and this advancement permitted the family to settle permanently in Blackrock, a southern suburb of Dublin, in 1927. In that year, O'Brien was enrolled in Blackrock College, a preparatory school. In 1929, he entered University College, Dublin.

At University College, O'Brien was a success in his studies and in extracurricular literary activities. In 1933, he earned his B.A. in English, Irish, and German; won the school's gold medal for debate; and was awarded a scholarship for study at the University of Cologne. After a year in Germany, he returned to University College and earned his M.A. in 1935 with a thesis on Irish poetry in Gaelic. The early intimations of his literary career, however, were more apparent in his nonscholarly activities. In 1931, he invented the persona "Brother Barnabas" for the student magazine *Comhthrom Féinne*.

A subsequent series of articles under this name was brought to a close in 1934 by a "posthumous" piece called "Scenes from a Novel" that anticipates the metafictional premise of *At Swim-Two-Birds*. In 1934, O'Brien also invented the persona "Count O'Blather" for his own short-lived magazine in English called *Blather.*

Following the conclusion of his graduate work, O'Brien joined the Irish Civil Service in 1935; he would continue in its employ until 1953. In 1935 he also began work on *At Swim-Two-Birds*, which was published in 1939 but commercially undone by the decimation of English book sales by World War II. By 1940, he had completed *The Third Policeman*, which was not published until after his death. In subsequent years, O'Brien told friends that he had lost this manuscript, but he nevertheless reworked it into the much more superficial novel *The Dalkey Archive* two decades later.

These discouraging setbacks were offset to some extent by the success of an outrageous literary scam. Under a series of fictitious names, O'Brien and Niall Sheridan began an attack on Dublin's presiding literary deities in the pages of *The Irish Times*, and, during the exchange of heated letters to the newspaper that followed, they began to attack their own original position under new fictitious names. When the scheme came to light, *The Irish Times* editor R. M. Smyllie had the goodwill and foresight to hire O'Brien to write a regular column. First in Irish and then in English, these columns of Myles na Gopaleen appeared at a rate of approximately three per week from October 4, 1940, until his final illness in 1966. As an outgrowth of his first columns in Irish, O'Brien wrote *The Poor Mouth* in Irish under the name Myles na Gopaleen in 1941.

O'Brien had thus completed his three important novels by the age of thirty; one was generally ignored, one remained in manuscript, and one was published in a language inaccessible even to most Irish citizens. A combination of cynicism and absorption in journalism effectively ended his career as a novelist at that point. By the time of the rediscovery of *At Swim-Two-Birds*, O'Brien was already suffering from the effects of lifelong heavy drinking. He managed to respond to interest in his past work with *The Hard Life* and *The Dalkey Archive*, but these works lack the textual complexities of his earlier and more important novels. It is a final, appropriate irony that Flann O'Brien, inventor of fictional disguises and elaborate literary conceits, died of alcohol-related maladies on April Fools' Day of 1966.

ANALYSIS

Flann O'Brien's first and most important novel, *At Swim-Two-Birds*, was published the year that William Butler Yeats died. The coincidence is notable because the novel was a parodistic melange of styles spawned by the Irish literary revival championed by Yeats and because all of O'Brien's important novels critique literary fabrications akin to those of the revival. The Irish literary revival was based on the rediscovery of the special identity of Ireland, especially as this was apparent in the literature of the Celtic legends. In popularizing these legends, the participants in the revival, many of whom—unlike O'Brien—had no fluency in the Gaelic language, were prone to literary extravagance and inflated notions of Celtic nobility. The literature of the revival was instrumental in arousing political energies that led to the creation of the Irish Free State, but after this goal of political independence had been realized, many of the revival's own literary excesses became apparent. Modern problems such as economic recession, entanglements of church and state, and the entrenched conservatism of an emerging middle class made the essential artifice of the inspiring revival literature especially visible for the first time.

O'Brien wrote none of the important fiction about the Irish Republic of his own day; instead, his major works look back to the earlier mythologizing of Celtic identity and modern Irish culture. *At Swim-Two-Birds*, *The Third Policeman*, and *The Poor Mouth* all ridicule the pretensions of literature by emphasizing its artificiality. O'Brien's work is satirical in effect because it implicitly corrects notions of literary authority, cultural privilege, and innate national aristocracy. Its primary mode is parody, adoption and exaggeration of a variety of recognizable literary styles to demonstrate their essential mandacity.

The salient quality of O'Brien's career is ambiguity concerning his name and identity. He took the pen name Flann O'Brien from Gerald Griffin's 1829 novel *The Collegians*, while the name Myles na Gopaleen came from Dion Boucicault's play *The Colleen Bawn* (1860), based on Griffin's novel. Both of these pseudonyms recall stage Irishmen, a stereotype of nineteenth century English fiction. In the revival, a new domestic stereotype of the Irish prevailed, one as falsely noble as the earlier English one was debased. Thus, these names attached to O'Brien's novels challenged the new literary identity of Ireland as a sheer fabrication.

O'Brien's first three novels are relentless in their scrutiny of fabricated literary identities; his later two novels are less successful because that scrutiny is limited, and because some assumptions about identity are allowed to stand unchallenged. Ultimately, his finest works have affinities with that strain of modern literature that asserts the reality of a metaphysical void, a senseless core of anonymity beneath the guises, literary and otherwise, protectively adopted to give life a semblance of meaning. This is especially true of *The Third Policeman*, which is freer of provincial references than O'Brien's other novels. The relish for parodying things Irish, most apparent in *At Swim-Two-Birds* and *The Poor Mouth*, however, suggests that the primary frame of reference for O'Brien's novels will always be the cultural history of early twentieth century Ireland.

At Swim-Two-Birds

At Swim-Two-Birds, O'Brien's first and most important novel, which takes its name from the literal translation of a Gaelic place-name, is the most complete critique in novel form of the excesses of the Irish literary revival. O'Brien was fluent in Gaelic and a talented parodist, and in this novel he exploits the essential artifice of revival literature by placing its various literary styles in collision with one another. Here Finn MacCool, evoked in all his epic splendor, meets the hack writer Dermot Trellis; the mad bard Sweeny, whose verses are included in hilarious literal translations into English, meets Jem Casey, poet of porter; the Good Fairy, taken from the most sentimental of Irish tourist literature, sits down

to cards with urban characters taken from the bleak world of James Joyce's *Dubliners* (1914). The product is a novel about the unreality of various kinds of fictions, an exercise in style whose only subject is the extravagance of the styles it exploits by parody.

At Swim-Two-Birds is a collection of brief fragments organized only by the desire to express the multiple contrasts of their incompatible styles. The thread that links these fragments is situational rather than narrative: A university student is attempting to write a novel whose three possible openings and four possible conclusions frame *At Swim-Two-Birds*; among the characters in his novel is Dermot Trellis, himself a novelist with a work in progress; the characters in Trellis's novel are dissatisfied with their treatment and so wreak revenge by writing their own novel about Trellis, whose authorial control lapses when he sleeps. This conceit allows O'Brien to include in his novel a plethora of styles from imaginary authors, especially rich in ironies for readers knowledgeable about Irish literature from the Celtic legends to modern writers such as Yeats.

As many of its commentators have pointed out, *At Swim-Two-Birds* has far more appeal and significance than most metafictional novels about a novel in progress. It is, above all else, exuberantly comic rather than pretentious. It also carries the possibilities of metafiction to a new extreme because of the intricacy and multiplicity of its narrative levels. The novel has a special significance in the history of modern Irish fiction because its sources and frames of reference are entirely local, unlike the more exotic allusions that control Joyce's *Ulysses* (1922) and Samuel Beckett's early novels: *At Swim-Two-Birds* is a critique of Ireland and Irish fictions written from within the Republic rather than from cosmopolitan France. One effect of this circumstance is that *At Swim-Two-Birds*, while it lacks the international literary ambitions of the comparable works by expatriate Irish writers, is more thoroughly imbued with the literary climate of Dublin and more convincing in its criticisms of local literary preoccupations.

The Third Policeman

Although it was not published until after O'Brien's death, *The Third Policeman* was written immediately after *At Swim-Two-Birds*, and it should be considered beside that novel, despite its publication date. Like *At Swim-Two-Birds*, it is a very modernist exercise in the novel as a self-contained and self-generating literary text. In this case, however, O'Brien is less concerned with the identifiable styles of the Irish revival than with the ways any style creates an identity in narrative fiction, the ways style is a source of authority and control in fiction. It is crucial to this novel that the narrator be nameless; without the identity provided by a name, he must create a persona for himself by appropriating styles of expression.

The novel opens with the robbery and murder of a businessman named Mathers by the narrator and his accomplice, John Diviney. The fantastic events that ensue concern the narrator's attempts to recover the stolen money and to hide his complicity in the crime from an omniscient but apparently uninterested pair of policemen. The appearance of Fox, the third policeman, seems to promise the release of the narrator from his predicament, but in fact it presages the realization that the narrator has been dead since the opening pages, betrayed and himself murdered by Diviney.

Released from even the faintest restraints of realism by setting his novel in the afterlife, O'Brien is free in *The Third Policeman* to allow language and rhetoric, rather than cause and effect, to determine the direction of his tale. The most prominent style and source of authority in the novel is an academic one related to the narrator's interest in a fictional philosopher named de Selby, whose works are evoked for the sake of clarification, summarized, and cited in scholarly footnotes throughout the novel. Elsewhere, *The Third Policeman* sporadically adopts the style of the modern murder mystery, a pretentious opera review, scientific analysis, Eastern myticism, and gothic romance. These intrusive styles color the events of the novel for the reader, much as the alien laws of the afterlife color the experiences of the narrator: They are oblique, intriguing, and ultimately baffling.

The Third Policeman lacks the dimension of cultural commentary provided by evocation of local literary styles in *At Swim-Two-Birds*. This same generalized environment, however, makes O'Brien's second novel an even richer contemplation on the nature of identity than his first, one that is capable of generalizations about definitions of self that rise above provincial contexts. It is also fully self-contained by a cyclic conclusion that returns the narrator, now accompanied by Diviney, to the earliest situations in the novel. It is precisely this degree of absorption in the interior logic of its own conceits that distinguishes *The Third Policeman* from O'Brien's later, less interesting reworking of these ideas in *The Dalkey Archive*.

THE POOR MOUTH

In a letter to Sean O'Casey quoted in *The Flann O'Brien Reader*, the author described *The Poor Mouth*, in its original Gaelic version, as "an honest attempt to get under the skin of a certain type of 'Gael,' which I find the most nauseating phenomena in Europe." This kind of Gael was in fact more a creation of the literary revival than a significant social group. *The Poor Mouth*, as translated by Patrick C. Power after O'Brien's death, is a parody of a literary genre rather than a parody of life in *Gaeltachts*, the remote Irish-speaking areas of Ireland that continue to erode in character despite well-intentioned government subsidies. The primary targets of the parody are the enormously popular autobiographies of *Gaeltacht* life such as *Twenty Years A-Growing* (1933) by Maurice O'Sullivan, but O'Brien's more general object of parody is all fictionalized versions of peasantry, from the folktales of Standish Hayes O'Grady to the plays of Lady Gregory and J. M. Synge.

The title of the novel evokes the idiom of "poor-mouthing," or inventing poverty for self-serving purposes, and *The Poor Mouth* is about the discovery by enthusiastic outsiders of a *Gaeltacht* in the midst of truly astonishing poverty. The wretched cohabitation of these peasants with their pigs in leaky shacks is a source of some tall-tale humor in the novel, although this poverty does have its darker side, as indicated by casual references to disease and death from starvation, alcoholism, and fighting. O'Brien's real focus here, however, is on the willful self-degradation of the peasants at the feet of their enlightened English-speaking visitors, who gauge the merit of Gaelic tales by the poverty of the teller and limit their own charity lest they spoil the purity of the peasants' profound misery.

The great irony of *The Poor Mouth*, and an essential component of its publication in Gaelic, is that these visitors are, rather than actual Englishmen, anglicized Irishmen enamored of the peasantry. The pure bile of the novel, which is well preserved in its English translation, derives from this image of Ireland foisting a factitious sterotype on itself, of romanticizing a peasantry in such rigid ways that all males in this *Gaeltacht* are called James O'Donnell. The use of this collective name is only the most obvious indication of the novel's relevance to O'Brien's governing interest in the theme of identity. Rather than a parody of multiple identities, however, *The Poor Mouth* is a portrait of surrender after limited resistance to a bleak and uniform identity. It has a special importance in O'Brien's work for this pessimism, for its publication in Gaelic, for his refusal to permit a translation, and for the fact that he would not write another novel until twenty years later.

THE HARD LIFE

The Hard Life lacks the literary frames of reference that give O'Brien's first three novels their focus and energy. Published in the wake of the rediscovery of *At Swim-Two-Birds*, it is a charming rather than derisory treatment of characteristically Irish forms of naïveté and provinciality, one that panders to audience expectations about Irish writing that were ridiculed by the ironies of O'Brien's earlier novels. It is harsh in its criticisms of the Jesuit Father Kurt Fahrt, the misguided Dubliner Mr. Collopy, and his slatternly daughter Annie. These satirical elements, however, are rendered benign by the time frame of the novel, written in 1961 but set in the years preceding 1910. The most attractive qualities of the novel—its digressive narration, bitter account of lower-class Dublin propriety, and the extravagantly misinformed conversations of Father Fahrt and Collopy—are facile if skillful entertainments never qualified by the shrewd ironies surrounding such mannerisms in O'Brien's earlier novels.

In all of O'Brien's novels, narrative structure is incidental to stylistic preoccupations, but in *The Hard Life* there is no literary focus to compensate for the lack of narrative structure. The comedy of the Fahrt-Collopy conversations and of several of the improbable events in the novel is brilliant, but the lack of an informing literary prespective renders them isolated exercises in caricature, resembling in tone and length the best of O'Brien's newspaper columns.

THE DALKEY ARCHIVE

In reworking some of the central conceits, notably the de Selby material, from *The Third Policeman*, O'Brien made *The Dalkey Archive* his only novel narrated in the third person. This alteration eliminates many of the ambiguities and complications found in his earlier novels because of their limited narrators. In other respects, too, *The Dalkey Archive* turns away from the most imaginative conceits of O'Brien's earlier work. As such, it represents a distinctly regressive coda in the works of O'Brien.

The novel individually treats the imaginative constructions of three personages. St. Augustine appears and reveals that neither his youthful sins nor his religious conversion were as complete as have been supposed. Sergeant Fottrell reveals his theory that the molecules of men and bicycles mix during riding, with predictable results. Finally, James Joyce, discovered living in retirement in the seaside resort called the Skerries, denounces *Ulysses* as a scam perpetrated by Parisian intellectuals and reveals that his true vocation is writing pamphlets for the Catholic Truth Society. These three are joined by their shared intellectual pride, a characteristic that the novel condemns even as it luxuriates in the pleasures of intricate shams.

O'Brien's first three novels were entirely enclosed within their literary conceits. In *The Dalkey Archive*, however, the elaborate shams and crazed logic are dispersed and corrected by the omniscient narrator on surprisingly moralistic grounds. In O'Brien's first three novels, no assumptions about identity were exempt from scrutiny, but *The Dalkey Archive* ends with an extremely complacent announcement of betrothal by its lackluster central characters Mick and Mary. With this gesture, O'Brien's last novel relinquishes the imaginative explorations of self and the elaborate metafictional elements of his finest novels.

Brian O'Nolan adopted the pseudonyms Flann O'Brien and Myles na Gopaleen with a characteristically ironic purpose: He would, under the names of one literary fabrication about Ireland and the Irish, expose the fabulous nature of a later image of the country and the people. At the end of his life, he wrote two novels, *The Hard Life* and *The Dalkey Archive*, deficient in the ironic intent of his important novels. It was as if at this point in his career he actually became Flann O'Brien, the stage Irishman, content with the identity foisted upon him. In *At Swim-Two-Birds, The Third Policeman,* and *The Poor Mouth*, however, the ironies surrounding his choice of pseudonyms were in full operation. The complexities and opacities of those novels represent a break from the mainstream of modern Irish literature and the most probing examination of the new national literature's roots in the mythologies of the Irish literary revival.

John P. Harrington

OTHER MAJOR WORKS

NONFICTION: *Cruiskeen Lawn*, 1943; *The Best of Myles*, 1968; *The Various Lives of Keats and Chapman and the Brother*, 1976; *Myles Away from Dublin*, 1985 (selected essays from journal columns).

MISCELLANEOUS: *Stories and Plays*, 1973; *A Flann O'Brien Reader*, 1978.

BIBLIOGRAPHY

Asbee, Sue. *Flann O'Brien*. Boston: Twayne, 1991. Following the format of the Twayne series, this volume includes a chapter of biography followed by solid discussion of O'Brien's major prose fiction. Includes chronology, notes, and an annotated bibliography.

Clissmann, Anne. *Flann O'Brien: A Critical Introduction to His Writings*. New York: Barnes & Noble Books, 1975. An exhaustive discussion of all the author's writings in English, with lengthy chapters on the major novels. Very useful for its discussion of O'Brien's student writings and for its review of the end of his career, including his attempts to write for television. Contains a bibliography.

Clissmann, Anne, and David Powell, eds. "A Flann O'Brien-Myles na Gopaleen Number." *Journal of Irish Studies* 3 (January, 1974). A special issue devoted to O'Brien's work. Contains juvenilia, stories, critical essays on O'Brien, and the texts of two of his short plays, including his version of Karel Capek's *The Insect Play*. Also includes a selection of O'Brien's letters and a valuable checklist of his publications.

Clune, Anne, and Tess Hurson, eds. *Conjuring Complexities: Essays on Flann O'Brien*. Belfast: Institute of Irish Studies, The Queen's University of Belfast, 1997. A solid volume of critical essays on O'Brien's work. Includes bibliographical references and an index.

Cronin, Anthony. *No Laughing Matter*. London: Grafton, 1989. As close as there is likely to be to a conventional biography of the complex and somewhat reclusive O'Brien. Written by a poet, novelist, and man of letters who was acquainted with O'Brien and his Dublin. The focus is on the man, rather than on the work, and some little-known personal details illustrate the narrative. A thorough treatment of a difficult subject.

Imhof, Rudiger, ed. *Alive, Alive O! Flann O'Brien's "At Swim-Two-Birds."* Dublin: Wolfhound Press, 1985. A compilation of key contemporary reviews, critical articles and background readings on one of the author's masterpieces. Valuable as a research tool, containing a comprehensive bibliography.

O'Keeffe, Timothy, ed. *Myles: Portraits of Brian O'Nolan*. London: Martin Brian & O'Keeffe, 1973. An invaluable source of biographical information and critical commentary on O'Brien. Contains reminiscences by friends, colleagues, and one of the author's brothers. Among the critical commentaries, the essay by J. C. C. Mays, "Flann O'Brien: Literalist of the Imagination," must be singled out.

Ryan, John. *Remembering How We Stood: Bohemian Dublin at Mid-Century*. New York: Taplinger, 1975. An attractive and informative memoir of the social and cultural milieu to which O'Brien belonged, structured as an overview followed by a presentation of individual participants in the scene. Devotes a chapter to O'Brien called "The Incomparable Myles" and also contains a number of inimitable glimpses of him. Illustrated.

Shea, Thomas F. *Flann O'Brien's Exorbitant Novels.* Lewisburg: Bucknell University Press, 1992. A chapter on early experiments followed by discussions of O'Brien's major fiction. Includes notes and bibliography.

KATE O'BRIEN

Born: Limerick, Ireland; December 3, 1897
Died: Canterbury, England; August 13, 1974

PRINCIPAL LONG FICTION

Without My Cloak, 1931
The Anteroom, 1934
Mary Lavelle, 1936
Pray for the Wanderer, 1938
The Land of Spices, 1941
The Last of Summer, 1943
That Lady, 1946 (also known as *For One Sweet Grape*)
The Flower of May, 1953
As Music and Splendour, 1958

OTHER LITERARY FORMS

Kate O'Brien's first success was a play, *Distinguished Villa*, which had a three-month run in London's West End in 1926. She successfully dramatized her novel *That Lady* for a Broadway production (1949) in which Katherine Cornell played the title role. O'Brien was also the author of two travel books, *Farewell, Spain* (1937) and *My Ireland* (1962). Her *English Diaries and Journals* was published in 1943 and a biography, *Teresa of Avila*, in 1951. Her last major published work was a book of reminiscences, *Presentation Parlour* (1963).

ACHIEVEMENTS

While her first novel, *Without My Cloak*, received two of the English literary establishment's most pres-

(Library of Congress)

tigious awards, the Hawthornden Prize and the James Tait Black Memorial Prize, Kate O'Brien's most notable achievement may best be assessed in the context of contemporary Irish literature. In this context, she remains—together with, though in a much more culturally significant manner than, her perhaps better-known contemporary Elizabeth Bowen—an exemplary representative not only of women's writing but also, through her works and career, of women's potential, broadly considered. Partial recognition of her achievement came in 1947 with her election to the Irish Academy of Letters.

BIOGRAPHY

Kate O'Brien was born in the city of Limerick, Ireland, on December 3, 1897, to a comfortable, middle-class family. Educated at a local convent, she went on to attend University College, Dublin, at a time when Ireland's capital was witnessing the consolidation of the Irish Literary Revival, though the cultural enthusiasm of the time left little or no mark either on O'Brien's student days or on her writing.

The years immediately following graduation seem to have been marked by a degree of uncertainty. She worked at first in England as a journalist for the (then) *Manchester Guardian* and as a teacher. A brief period in Washington, D.C., as a diplomatic aide was followed by a sojourn in Bilbao, Spain, as a governess. Returning to London in 1924, she married Gustav Renier; the marriage was not a success. Spain soon became her second home, though for more than ten years after the completion of her World War II service at the Ministry of Information in London she was refused admission to the country, her depiction of King Philip II in *That Lady* having rendered her *persona non grata*. By this time, O'Brien was no stranger to controversy arising out of her fiction: Her 1941 novel, *The Land of Spices*, was notoriously banned by the Irish Censorship Board for alleged sexual impropriety. In 1950 she took up residence again in Ireland and lived there until 1961, when she returned to England. She died on August 13, 1974.

ANALYSIS

Kate O'Brien's career emerged and developed during a difficult time for Irish writing; indeed, models of Irish women novelists who might have provided her with beneficial influence and nurturing were virtually nonexistent. Despite these unpromising cultural origins, and despite the obvious struggle O'Brien experienced in order to express herself and command a responsive and sustaining audience, her career can be seen in historical retrospect to be marked with notable integrity, independence of mind and action, and devotion to her art. In a literary culture where women have not always received sufficient critical attention and have not had their works readily incorporated into the canon of a given generation's achievements, critical responses to O'Brien's life and work have belatedly been seen as manifestations of unwarranted narrowness. The belatedness of this view is perhaps a result of the author's long years of exile, along with the fact that her one major popular success, *That Lady*, published when a fresh audience was ready for her work, is a historical romance

rather than another in her sequence of novels about Irish family life. Yet the republication of many of her works during the 1980's not only facilitated a reappraisal of her literary achievements but also had the effect of redrawing the map of Irish literary culture at a crucial period in its development.

The generation of Irish writers to which O'Brien belongs had the unenviable task of following in the path-breaking footsteps of the principal artists of the Irish Literary Revival—the novelist George Moore, the poet William Butler Yeats, and the playwright John Millington Synge. O'Brien's generation was as different in background and outlook from these three illustrious avatars as it is possible to be. Provincial in upbringing, nationalist in politics, unexperimental in art, and Catholic in cultural formation, this generation had at once a greater intimacy with the actual life of its fellow citizens and a more actively critical perception of the society in whose name it had elected to speak. It also had the not inconsiderable disadvantage of attempting to assert its cultural and artistic validity and viability while the star of the Revival had not yet entirely waned, and while Yeats, for example, was willing to co-opt new voices to articulate the agenda of his cultural politics.

The most important writers of this generation—those who went on to establish a somewhat more populist orientation for Irish literature, or at least a more populist role for the Irish writer—have long been considered to be Seán O'Faoláin, Frank O'Connor, and Liam O'Flaherty. The different orientation that they represent may be initially discerned in the fact that they each espoused a form largely neglected by the Revival—namely prose fiction, in particular the short story—and implicitly rejected the formal and ideological explorations of their more modernist forbears. O'Brien is a member of this generation not merely by virtue of her provincial background and conventional education but also because her works reflect this generation's concerns, a reflection that receives added point and importance from the fact of its feminist—or, to be historically accurate, protofeminist—perspectives. The disillusion and disorientation that emerge as a resonant theme in Irish fiction during the 1930's, the problematized

rendering of the independence that the country secured in the late twentieth century in juridical and
political terms, and the conflicts between tradition
and individuality as the culture seeks not merely aesthetic but moral renewal, far from being neglected by
O'Brien, are all the more authentically present in her
work through being presented from the standpoint
of already marginalized female protagonists. (With
the exception of *Pray for the Wanderer*, with its protagonist Matt Costello, all of O'Brien's works feature
female protagonists.)

WITHOUT MY CLOAK

O'Brien's first novel, *Without My Cloak*, re-
hearses a number of the problems that arise from her
heritage and anticipates the most important of her fiction's preoccupations. A family saga, it brings to
awareness, through the use of an essentially nineteenth century model, the social and psychological
forces that gave cultural and moral legitimacy to
O'Brien's own class and ideological background.
The novel traces the development of the Considine
family through three generations from the late eighteenth century, plausibly detailing its establishment
in an urban, mercantile setting, for which the author
uses her native Limerick. A major motif in the work
is the question of security. The Considine ethos consists of a sublimation of development in consolidation, and the emotional claustrophobia that results
from this mode of behavior within the family circle is
memorably detailed. The security motif is tensely related to its obverse, a quest for independence; the dy-
namics of the novel enact the struggle familiar from
nineteenth century fiction between individual and society, between the assertion of selfhood and institutional constraints, with the emphasis in this instance
falling on the power of institutions.

In particular, the social and moral function of the
Catholic church receives special attention in *Without
My Cloak* and retains a particularly important place
throughout O'Brien's fiction. Because of its status in
her first novel, it is possible to refer to the Considine
family as embodying an ethos, since the church operates as a source of moral and social identity, and alternative sources of such security and self-awareness
are nowhere to be found. The power of the Church to

authorize selfhood as a tissue of constraints makes
of it a second, larger, more absolute family, and the
matter of the effect of its power on the individual
conscience and consciousness, rather than being resolved in *Without My Cloak*, becomes an increasingly emphatic preoccupation in O'Brien's fiction prior to the publication of *That Lady*. (The fact
that O'Brien herself seems to have considered the
conflicts of her first novel unresolved may be in-
ferred from their reenactment in condensed and more
artistically disciplined form in her next work, *The
Anteroom*.) The role and power of the church is so
central to her work that O'Brien has frequently been
thought of as a Catholic, more than as an Irish, novelist. Like most Irish writers, however, she is concerned with the culture of Catholicism, its social,
personal, and interpersonal influence, and its significance as a generator of a politics of the spirit rather
than as a spiritual convalescent home. Indeed, one
of her most fundamental fictional preoccupations is
with the difficulty of dealing with impersonal authority, whether conceived as institutional or, as in the
portrait of Philip II in *That Lady*, monarchical.

MARY LAVELLE

The fact that O'Brien perceived her preoccupations as continuing difficulty rather than as eventual
solution is suggested by the regularity with which her
protagonists, for all the author's sympathetic dramatization of their intensity of their struggles, typically
fail to attain the independence they desire. An exception to this general outcome is the eponymous heroine of *Mary Lavelle*. This novel, which draws more
directly on immediate personal experience than does
Without My Cloak, tells of a young Irish woman
working as a governess for a bourgeois Spanish
family. In some sense an account of an innocent
abroad—Mary seems to be innocence itself—the
novel is also a narrative of conflicting loyalties. The
heroine is in many respects an ideal employee, fitting
into the Areavaga family with the ease of somebody
familiar with a culture in which people know their
places. It is Mary's very compliance, however, that is
responsible for the novel's central drama. She involuntarily falls for Juanito, the married son of the
house, a state of affairs that brings her into conflict

not only with the outlook in which she had been rigorously brought up in Ireland but also with its powerfully reinforced presence in Doña Consuelo, the commanding head of the household. The conflict between duty and freedom, between individual desire and ethical obligation, in addition to the novelist's welcome transposition of her concerns to a non-Irish locale and the development of a sexual dimension to Mary's struggle for authentic womanhood, contributes to an impressive sense of the novelist's development. Nevertheless, it is not clear what the overall effect of Mary's experiences has been, whether she accepts or rejects the conflict-laden nature of her experiences. "Anguish and anger for everyone and only one little, fantastic, impossible hope," read the closing lines of *Mary Lavelle*, "was the fruit of her journey to Spain." An unexpected fruit of the publication of *Mary Lavelle*, however, was its banning by the Irish Censorship of Publications Board, an act that may be read now as an unintended tribute to O'Brien's insightful presentation of her heroine's moral authenticity but that, at the time, deepened the alienation from her background that her works articulated with increasing conviction.

THE LAND OF SPICES

This alienation reached its highest level when her next novel, *The Land of Spices*, met with a similar fate to that of *Mary Lavelle* at the hands of the censors, as a result of which the novel achieved unjust notoriety—and subsequently, when censorship was relaxed in the early 1970's, a certain amount of popular success. The banning of *The Land of Spices* proved instrumental in calling the censorship board's procedures into question and led indirectly to a revision of its mode of operation. It might be argued that the board's very existence was in itself strongly illustrative of the cultural conflicts and repressions that, from a broader, nonbureaucratic, social perspective, form the core of O'Brien's fictional concerns. The pretext for banning *The Land of Spices* was so slender—consisting of a mere handful of words with potentially homosexual implications—that it came to be seen as a paradigm of the narrow-minded, prurient, and often antifeminist orientation of the official guardians of Irish literary culture.

The Land of Spices can be read as a redeployment and intensification of the mother-and-governess relationship in *Mary Lavelle*, a relationship that is emblematic of relationships conceived throughout O'Brien's work as exercises in power. On this occasion, foreignness of setting and the enclosed nature of the immediate environment are combined to attain a new level of intensity: The action takes place within an Irish convent of a French order of nuns. In addition, this work's animating relationship now has the intimacy of teacher, Mère Marie-Hélène Archer, and pupil, Anna Murphy, with all of its reverberations of nurturing and mastery, the source of which is the overarching presence of Mother Church. The pressures Mary Lavelle felt with regard to her moral development and sense of autonomy are here articulated more dramatically, given how much more difficult it is to escape them, and the sexual component of *Mary Lavelle* is similarly intensified.

Yet the novel has a more meditative than critical tone. Taking its title from the English metaphysical poet George Herbert's "Prayer (1)" ("Church bells beyond the stars heard, the soul's blood,/ The land of spices, something understood"), the emphasis falls on the ritualistic and selfless aspects of the vocational life, on the complexities of agape rather than the challenge of eros, on the willingness to serve rather than the urge to escape, while at the same time remaining crucially sensitive to the urgent presence of humanity and its needs. *The Land of Spices* will seem to many O'Brien's most satisfying production, in which she attains more objective possession of her psychological and spiritual preoccupations without running the risk of compromising them.

THAT LADY

O'Brien's characterization of a woman's fate in the context of power relationships receives its most lavish treatment in her greatest popular success, *That Lady*; as well as being adapted for the stage, *That Lady* was filmed with Olivia de Havilland in the title role in 1955. Set in sixteenth century Spain, the novel tells the story of Ana de Mendoza y de la Cerda, Princess of Eboli and Duchess of Pastrana; clearly, despite O'Brien's strong Spanish interests, it is an entirely new departure for her as a novelist. Instead of concentrating on the various stages of Ana's life as a woman in an attempt to reconstruct a novel of historical verisimilitude, O'Brien concentrates instead on the years of Ana's unlikely liberation into an experience of womanhood that had hitherto been hidden from her. The reader is explicitly informed in a foreword that this "is not a historical novel"; instead, the imaginative treatment of the material dwells centrally on a dramatization of the psychological and emotional conflicts of the case. Thus, despite a certain amount of costumery, inevitable under the circumstances, *That Lady* achieves an internal consistency with O'Brien's other novels.

That Lady covers the years spent by Ana, now widowed, in state service. To some extent, her work for the Spanish Crown during this brief period recapitulates her early years, when by virtue of her noble birth and excellent marriage she became intimate with affairs of state. Together with the old intimacy, however, there now comes a new, and this development of an additional dimension in Ana's life is at once enhancing and destructive, enriching her personal existence while risking a scandal that would entail the king's serious displeasure. Because of the character of the prevailing power structure, the most significant experience in Ana's personal life—the affair with Don Antonio Pérez—becomes the occasion of her banishment and confinement. The novel's heightened courtly context accentuates rather than dilutes its emphasis on tensions familiar from O'Brien's earlier novels—between passion and form, between desire and responsibility, between a woman's external role and her internal needs. To these tensions and conflicts her work returns again and again, and it is in her identification and negotiation of them that O'Brien's fiction is worthy of the critical attention that, beginning in the late 1980's, it has at length come to receive.

O'Brien's work is noteworthy on two levels. In the first place, it represents significant additions to the history of anglophone women's writing in the period between the two world wars. Her location of her female protagonists in conditions of moral difficulty, emotional complexity, cultural unfamiliarity, and even geographical estrangement provides a comprehensive method of dramatizing women's experience as problematic and unamenable to tidying away by the powers that be. O'Brien's own willingness to live a life as autonomous as that sought by her protagonists testifies to her steadfastness, courage, and integrity. The fact that so much of her writing life was spent in exile is a tribute to both her singularity and her perseverance.

In addition, however, her accomplishments become all the more significant when seen in an Irish context. While her novels do not articulate the concerns of her generation as explicitly as the critiques of nationalism and assumption of embattled cultural and ideological positions favored by many of her contemporaries, her work belongs with theirs as part of a concerted effort to render more authentically— that is, with greater respect for individuality and its internal realities—the life of her time. Kate O'Brien's original contributions to this effort make her the first important woman writer of independent Ireland.

George O'Brien

OTHER MAJOR WORKS

PLAYS: *Distinguished Villa*, pr. 1926; *The Bridge*, pr. 1927; *The Schoolroom Window*, pr. 1937; *That Lady*, pr. 1949.

NONFICTION: *Farewell, Spain*, 1937; *English Diaries and Journals*, 1943; *Teresa of Avila*, 1951; *My Ireland*, 1962 (travel); *Presentation Parlour*, 1963 (reminiscence).

BIBLIOGRAPHY

Boland, Eavan. "That Lady: A Profile of Kate O'Brien." *The Critic* 34 (Winter, 1975): 16-25. An insightful assessment of O'Brien's contribution to Irish women's writing by the best-known contemporary Irish woman poet.

Dalsimer, Adele. *Kate O'Brien: A Critical Study.* Dublin: Gill and Macmillan, 1990. The first comprehensive study of Kate O'Brien's entire literary output. The emphasis is on her works' feminist dimension, and a critical case is made for the significance of her generally neglected later works. O'Brien's attainment is set in its larger biographical, cultural, and political contexts. A useful bibliography is included.

O'Brien, Kate. "The Art of Writing." *University Review* 3 (1965): 6-14. An article that provides valuable insights into the author's thoughts about writing.

Reynolds, Lorna. *Kate O'Brien: A Literary Portrait.* Totowa, N.J.: Barnes & Noble Books, 1987. A succinct portrait by an academic who knew Kate O'Brien. The study is divided into two parts, the first dealing with the major fiction in chronological order and the second surveying O'Brien's treatment of various major themes. Also contains a valuable treatment of O'Brien's family background.

Stony Thursday Book 7 (1981). This Kate O'Brien issue of the periodical contains much important material, including an extract from a final, unfinished novel, "Constancy"; a review of *The Land of Spices* by O'Brien's noteworthy contemporary, the poet Austin Clarke; and critiques of O'Brien by such leading authorities on her achievement as Eavan Boland and Benedict Kiely.

Walshe, Eibhear, ed. *Ordinary People Dancing: Essays on Kate O'Brien.* Cork, Ireland: Cork University Press, 1993. This selection of critical essays examines O'Brien's heritage and feminism.

(AP/Wide World Photos)

TIM O'BRIEN

Born: Austin, Minnesota; October 1, 1946

PRINCIPAL LONG FICTION
Northern Lights, 1975
Going After Cacciato, 1978
The Nuclear Age, 1981 (limited ed.), 1985
In the Lake of the Woods, 1994
Tomcat in Love, 1998

OTHER LITERARY FORMS

Tim O'Brien wrote magazine and newspaper articles about the Vietnam War while he was a soldier. He published articles on American politics as a re-

porter for the *Washington Post* in the mid-1970's. Popular magazines and literary quarterlies also published his short stories and essays. *If I Die in a Combat Zone, Box Me Up and Ship Me Home* (1973, revised 1979) contains partially fictionalized memoirs, and *The Things They Carried* (1990) collects short stories that are also closely based upon his tour of duty in Vietnam. Some critics consider these books loosely organized, episodic novels.

ACHIEVEMENTS

O'Brien won accolades from war veterans and literary critics for his fiction and memoirs concerning the Vietnam War. In 1976 and 1978 he received the O. Henry Memorial Award for chapters of *Going After Cacciato*, which also earned for him the National Book Award in 1979. He won the Vietnam Veterans of America Award in 1987 and, the same year, the National Magazine Award in Fiction for the short story "The Things They Carried." In 1990, he was awarded the Heartland Prize from the *Chicago Tri-*

bune, and in 1991 he was nominated for both the National Book Critics Circle's Melcher Book Award and the Pulitzer Prize for *The Things They Carried*. He also received France's Prix du Meilleur Livre Étranger for that book and the James Fenimore Cooper Prize of the Society of American Historians for *In the Lake of the Woods*. O'Brien held fellowships from the National Academy of Arts, Breadloaf Writers' Conference, the American Academy of Arts and Letters, and the Guggenheim Foundation.

BIOGRAPHY

William Timothy O'Brien, Jr., was born in Austin, Minnesota, in 1946, placing him among the baby-boom generation, which would become eligible for the draft during the Vietnam War (1964-1973). His father was an insurance salesman and a World War II combat veteran; his mother, Ava Schultz O'Brien, was an elementary school teacher. When O'Brien was nine years old, the family, which included a younger sister and brother, moved to Worthington, near the Minnesota-Iowa border, and he grew up there. His childhood, by his own account, was lonely. He played baseball and golf but occupied himself mainly with magic and reading.

After high school, O'Brien attended Macalester College and majored in political science. He participated in protests against the Vietnam War, wrote antiwar editorials for the college newspaper, and canvassed in support of Senator Eugene McCarthy's presidential campaign in 1968. He was elected student-body president his senior year. Immediately after graduating with a bachelor's degree, summa cum laude, he was drafted into the army. Despite his hatred for the war, he quelled the urge to flee to Canada and was trained as an infantryman.

In February, 1969, he arrived at an advanced firebase in Quang Ngai Province, Republic of Vietnam. Nearby was My Lai, a hamlet where troops from O'Brien's division had murdered as many as five hundred civilians in one day. O'Brien, like most Americans, did not learn about the massacre there until one year later. For most of every month his company patrolled a deadly combat zone, battling the Viet Cong and constantly terrified of land mines, dis-

ease, and the prospect of appearing cowardly. He saw many wounds and deaths. In fact, he was wounded by shrapnel from a grenade, and his best friend died in a skirmish, two events that deeply affected him. Even before leaving the country, he published accounts of his experience in Minnesota newspapers and *Playboy* magazine.

After his discharge in 1970, O'Brien studied at the Harvard School of Government. In 1973 he published *If I Die in a Combat Zone, Box Me Up and Ship Me Home*, and he joined the staff of the *Washington Post*, reporting on national affairs. He married Ann Elizabeth Weller, an editorial assistant; they divorced eighteen years later. After a year at the *Post*, he returned to his studies at Harvard but left before completing a degree, in order to become a writer. In the meantime he had published his first novel.

After finishing his fourth novel, *In the Lake of the Woods*, in 1994, O'Brien stopped writing, complaining that he was "burned out." With his girlfriend and a *New York Times* photographer, he returned to Vietnam. It was an emotional visit, during which he searched for the Quang Ngai firebase of his infantry company, spoke with Vietnamese veterans, and interviewed survivors of the My Lai massacre. In a famous *New York Times Magazine* article, "The Vietnam in Me" (1994), he told how the experience brought him close to suicide but finally helped him purge some of his anxious obsession with the war. Living in an apartment near Harvard, he resumed writing, in 1998 publishing *Tomcat in Love*. Although the Vietnam War influences the plot, it does so far less than in his previous fiction.

ANALYSIS

O'Brien draws material for his novels from his own experience. He uses imagination and fiction to find meaning in these experiences, and because he was part of defining events of the post-World War II generation, the passions and ideas in his novels appeal to American readers with broad differences in political allegiance and social background. Having fought in Vietnam, O'Brien can create fictional soldiers so realistic in attitude, speech, and behavior that readers who are veterans of the war readily identify with them. An activist in the antiwar movement of the 1960's, O'Brien likewise draws faithful imitations of the political rebels of the times. A former graduate student in political science and a campaign worker, O'Brien offers fictional politicians convincingly lifelike enough to appeal to the American passion for political scandal. Moreover, coming from a small town in the Midwest, O'Brien (and some of his characters) appears to fulfill a particularly American literary convention: the small-town kid who does well for himself in the outside world. His characters include a university professor, a wealthy geologist, and a lieutenant governor.

Some critics complain that the distinction between historical or personal facts and fiction is blurred in O'Brien's work. Indeed, the "Tim O'Brien" who narrates his two volumes of memoirs is a fictionalized construct, as the author admitted. Similarly, he incorporates historical records, apparently quoted verbatim, in the novel *In the Lake of the Woods*. This mixing of fact and fiction, as well as of memory and fantasy, underlies O'Brien's thematic interests, all of which concern his characters' emotional struggle during events, more than the verisimilitude or logic of the events themselves. The novels are intimately personal, psychological, and exploratory. Among the major themes are the relation between storytelling and truth, father-son relationships, true courage, the psychological effect of war, loneliness, magic, and obsession.

To develop such themes, O'Brien uses narrative techniques that give readers access to the minds of characters, in order to portray their reactions to events in the plot. *Northern Lights*, *Going After Cacciato*, and *In the Lake of the Woods* are told from the third-person point of view either of an unnamed narrator or of a narrator whom readers are encouraged to identify with the author. This narrator recounts the thoughts and emotions of characters so that readers may empathize with their confusion and obsessions. *The Nuclear Age* and *Tomcat in Love* both employ the first-person point of view of the main character. Some episodes are told in the present tense and some in the past tense, as the characters reminisce. These techniques enable O'Brien to place the reader even

more intimately in the minds of characters and display the tricky, often self-deluding action of memory. Moreover, rapid changes from past to present, changes from one story line to another within a novel's plot, intricate wordplay, and dreamlike sequences immerse readers in the mental states of the principal characters.

O'Brien told interviewers that he was obsessed with American writer Ernest Hemingway as a youth. Hemingway's influence is apparent. O'Brien writes in short, crisp sentences that often derive their power from vivid verbs. He relies on extensive dialogue and uses description more to reflect the impressions of his main characters than to construct a visually detailed setting. Unlike Hemingway, O'Brien frequently uses fragmentary sentences and questions to imitate the thought processes of characters, especially when they are under stress. Cumulatively, his style establishes an energetic narrative pace.

GOING AFTER CACCIATO

Going After Cacciato, O'Brien's second published novel, was his first critical and popular success. A best-seller, it quickly earned notice as one of the first serious literary treatments of the Vietnam War, winning the National Book Award in 1979, and it remained a classic statement of the war's bewildering effects on the young Americans drafted to fight there. Paul Berlin, the point-of-view character, is a member of an infantry platoon. With his platoon he chases one of their number who has deserted, Cacciato ("the hunted" in Italian). Cacciato has vowed to escape the war and walk all the way to Paris, a crazy idea that nevertheless earns him admiration among the other soldiers. They catch Cacciato near the Laotian border, and the literal plot is over. While on guard duty, however, Berlin fantasizes. He imagines that Cacciato constantly manages to evade them, and the platoon must pursue him to Paris. He dreams up grotesque adventures in countries along the route, some hilarious escapades, some adolescent sexual fantasies, and some chilling encounters. His fantasies interrupt and blend into the literal story of the chase, giving the narrative a nightmarish quality. Berlin and his fellow soldiers are innocents trapped in a corrupt, bizarre world, but the only character who seems truly courageous in the story is Cacciato. Even though his desertion is a nonsensical gesture, it frees him from the compromises to which the others cling: acceding to the draft, fighting a war that few believe in, conforming so as to not endure shame and disapproval.

IN THE LAKE OF THE WOODS

In the Lake of the Woods is O'Brien's most disturbing novel. It is an attempt, he contends, to understand evil. The story opens at the Lake of the Woods in northern Minnesota. John and Kathy Wade are on vacation, trying to knit together an unraveling marriage and lives in disarray. Lieutenant governor of the state, Wade has just lost the primary election for the U.S. Senate because news stories have revealed that he took part in the My Lai massacre in Vietnam. As a soldier, Wade was known as Wizard, a nickname he earned for his magic tricks, but the importance of deception and illusion is deep in his psyche, and he manages to erase most records of his involvement in the massacre, escape court-martial, and keep the secret even from his wife. As the story of his war experience, political career, and family life unfolds, the distinction between truth and the illusions he creates blur in his mind—and in the reader's. However, interrupting the narrative are sections called "Evidence," which contain transcripts of actual court-martial testimony and quotations from history books. These brief sections give the story historical perspective and keep it from turning completely into Wade's illusion.

The war haunts Wade; his failure to maintain protective illusions drives him toward madness. When his wife disappears from their cabin, Wade cooperates with the authorities in searching for her, but it becomes gradually apparent that Wade himself has murdered her. What is not clear, however, is whether he understands what he has done, so lost is he in self-delusions about his past. The end of the book is ambiguous. As the authorities increasingly suspect him of murder, Wade takes a speed boat out onto the lake, and his purpose seems to be to find his wife, escape the law, and commit suicide at the same time. Since this muddled behavior resulted from a lonely childhood and the My Lai massacre, Vietnam is cast as a pervasive, mysterious, malign burden on Wade and his generation.

TOMCAT IN LOVE

Tomcat in Love is a comic novel in texture but a serious work in intent; it reexamines the themes of love and disaster, storytelling and truth, and obsession. Thomas H. Chippering is a tenured professor of linguistics whose wife has divorced him. Told in flashbacks, the novel is a record of their relationship, beginning in childhood and continuing with marriage, her departure, and his desperate crusade to win her back and to punish her family for causing the divorce. Chippering is pompous, vindictive, pedantic, obsessed with words, and bent on trying to seduce every woman he encounters. He is also blind to his own faults and to the feelings of those around him, while constantly interpreting himself in a suave, heroic light. He has even fabricated a record as a hero in Vietnam to impress others. (Although the war does not dominate the story as it does in O'Brien's previous novel, it does figure in the plot.) Much of the situational humor originates from Chippering's obvious self-delusions and the ridiculous mistakes he makes about others. His ex-wife spurns him, he loses his faculty position because of student complaints of sexual harassment, he becomes engaged to a woman whose first name he cannot bring himself to use, his ex-brother-in-law publicly humiliates him, and he eventually discovers that his ex-wife, contrary to what he had always believed, is even crazier than he is. Chippering has a few redeeming features that rescue the story from simple farce. His obsession is with the human heart, and he pursues the ambiguities of love with unflagging persistence, much as Miguel de Cervantes' Don Quixote pursued chivalry. In the end, he transcends his obsession and grows spiritually, learning to treat others, women especially, as human beings rather than as objects to manipulate or adore.

Roger Smith

OTHER MAJOR WORKS

SHORT FICTION: *The Things They Carried*, 1990.

NONFICTION: *If I Die in a Combat Zone, Box Me Up and Ship Me Home*, 1973, rev. 1979; "The Vietnam in Me," 1994.

BIBLIOGRAPHY

Beidler, Philip D. *American Literature and the Experience of Vietnam*. Athens: University of Georgia Press, 1982. Beidler devotes chapters to *If I Die in a Combat Zone, Box Me Up and Ship Me Home* and *Going After Cacciato*. He treats both as O'Brien's attempt to solidify some meaning from the nightmare of combat in a war with an unclear purpose.

Herzog, Tobey C. *Tim O'Brien*. New York: Twayne, 1997. Herzog explains the autobiographical elements in O'Brien's novels and the role of imagination in understanding their meaning. Chapters concern O'Brien's background, writing style, portrayal of soldiering, treatment of love, and the anti-Vietnam War movement. Herzog emphasizes that mystery and ambiguity are fundamental characteristics of O'Brien's fiction. A chronology and bibliography accompany the discussions.

Kaplan, Steven. *Understanding Tim O'Brien*. Columbia: University of South Carolina Press, 1994. In the introductory chapter, Kaplan stresses the importance of storytelling, memory, and imagination in O'Brien's life and fiction. Subsequent chapters explicate O'Brien's first five books, particularly their theme of courage. Generous bibliography. A concise, lucid introduction to O'Brien's work.

Myers, Thomas Robert. *Walking Point: American Narratives of Vietnam*. New York: Oxford University Press, 1988. Myers surveys the American literary reaction to Vietnam, discussing *If I Die in a Combat Zone, Box Me Up and Ship Me Home* in the context of personal narratives about the war. As well as explaining the theme of courage, the book provides critical background for readers interested in comparing O'Brien's contribution with those of his contemporaries.

FLANNERY O'CONNOR

Born: Savannah, Georgia; March 25, 1925
Died: Milledgeville, Georgia; August 3, 1964

PRINCIPAL LONG FICTION

Wise Blood, 1952
The Violent Bear It Away, 1960

OTHER LITERARY FORMS

Flannery O'Connor, most renowned as a writer of short fiction, published the short-story collection *A Good Man Is Hard to Find* in 1955; her canon also includes two posthumous collections, *Everything That Rises Must Converge* (1965) and *The Complete Stories* (1971). Three posthumous nonfiction works provide insight into her craft and thought: *Mystery and Manners* (1969), a collection of her occasional lectures and essays on literary art; *The Habit of Being: Letters* (1979), which consists of letters compiled by her literary executor, Sally Fitzgerald; and *The Presence of Grace* (1983), a collection of her book reviews.

ACHIEVEMENTS

O'Connor's art was best suited to the medium of the short story, where her sharp, shocking, and grotesque characterizations could have full impact on the reader. Nevertheless, her depiction of the Christ-haunted Hazel Motes in *Wise Blood* ranks as the most memorable and piercing postmodern delineation of Western society's anxiety over God's absence. O'Connor's ability to create supernatural tension, to provoke the potentially hostile reader into considering the possibility of divine invasion of the human sphere, is unparalleled by any postwar writer. Seeing "by the light of Christian orthodoxy," O'Connor refused to chisel away or compromise her convictions to make them more congenial to her readers. She knew that it is difficult to place the Christian faith in front of the contemporary reader with any credibility, but her resolve was firm. She understood, in the words of the late John Gardner (*On Moral Fiction*, 1978), that "art which tries to tell the truth unretouched is difficult and often offensive," since it "violates our canons of politeness and humane compromise." O'Connor succeeded not in making Christianity more palatable but in making its claims unavoidable.

O'Connor was committed not only to telling the "truth unretouched" but also to telling a good story.

This meant rejecting predetermined morals—homilies tacked onto stories and processed uncritically by her readers: "When you can state the theme of a story, when you can separate it from the story itself, then you can be sure the story is not a very good one." Instead of literary proselytizing, she offered a literature of evangelism, of incarnation, a fusing of literary form with authorial vision. Her evangelistic mode was not proselytizing, but *proclaiming*, the ancient and more honorable practice of declaring news, of heralding its goodness to a usually indifferent, sometimes hostile audience. O'Connor had a keen perception of her audience's mindset and cultural milieu; her proclamation was calculated to subvert the habitualization of faith and to make such notions as redemption, resurrection, and eternal life seem new and strange to a Western society that had reduced them to commonplaces empty of significance. Readers and critics continue to respond to O'Connor's clear spiritual vision and piercing narrative style, a style uncluttered by a false pluralism or sectarian debate. O'Connor, the devout Catholic, neither preached nor compelled; she simply proclaimed.

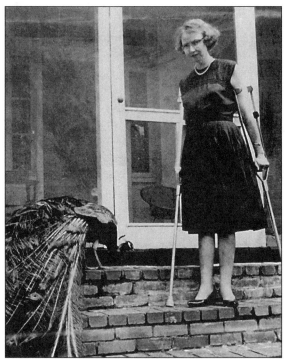

(Joe McTyre)

BIOGRAPHY

Mary Flannery O'Connor was born in Savannah, Georgia, in 1925 and moved with her mother to Milledgeville, Georgia, in 1938. She took her B.A. degree from Women's College of Georgia in 1945 and received an M.F.A. degree from the State University of Iowa in 1947. She published her first short story, "The Geranium" (*Accent*, 1946), during her years in Iowa. In 1947, she won the Rinehart-Iowa fiction award for a first novel with a portion of *Wise Blood*.

On the strength of this award and her promise as a writer, O'Connor was offered a fellowship by the Yaddo Foundation. She accepted and spent several months at Saratoga Springs, New York, but eventually returned to Milledgeville. A few months later, O'Connor moved in with the Robert Fitzgerald family in Connecticut to complete *Wise Blood*. A serious illness, lupus erythematosus, redirected her life back to Milledgeville in 1951; there she would do the rest of her writing, and there she would die in 1964. From Milledgeville, she carried on a lively correspondence with friends, readers, critics, and her editors at Farrar and Giroux. When health permitted, she made trips to colleges and universities, many of them Catholic schools, to discuss her work and literary art.

O'Connor won a Kenyon Review fellowship in fiction in 1953, a National Institute of Arts and Letters grant in 1957, and an O. Henry first prize in short fiction in 1957. She also was granted honorary degrees from St. Mary's College (1962) and Smith College (1963). She spent the last months of her life completing the stories eventually published in her posthumous collection *Everything That Rises Must Converge*. *The Complete Stories* won the National Book Award for Fiction in 1971.

ANALYSIS

Few postmodern writers have spoken as articulately and as compellingly about their craft and the relationship of their fiction to its perceived audience as did Flannery O'Connor. In her occasional prose, in her letters, and in her book reviews, O'Connor evinced an uncommonly perceptive grasp of her readers and the society in which they lived. Addressing the children of a demythologized and desacralized century, she confronted boldly the rancor and apathy with which modern culture meets the religious and the supernatural. To shake and sharpen the sensibilities of a culture made lethargic by the heritage of American civil religion, she turned to shock, to the literally awful and the grotesque, to proclaim her gospel: "To the hard of hearing you shout, and for the almost-blind you draw large and startling figures."

The underlying premise which informs all of O'Connor's fiction, and especially her two novels, *Wise Blood* and *The Violent Bear It Away*, is that men and women, as they are, are not *whole*. This "wholeness," lost in Eden, is now embodied and supplied to humans freely in the person of the incarnate Son of God. In order to make this now familiar theme "seeable" and creditable to her readers, O'Connor was led to herald a Christ who bore little resemblance to the "gentle Jesus, meek and mild" of childhood hymnody. Her Christ is a tiger who disturbs and terrorizes. One thinks especially of Hazel Motes, evangelist of the "Church of Christ without Christ" in *Wise Blood*, who fights ferociously to avoid that Jesus "in the back of his mind, a wild, ragged figure motioning to him to turn around and come off into the dark where he was not sure of his footing, where he might be walking on water and not know it and suddenly know it and drown."

Motes is a child of the fundamentalist South, but in O'Connor's economy, he is also Everyman; those who refuse Christ's offer to help them, force Him to haunt them. O'Connor used sudden death, disease, or trauma to depict the devastating encounter with Christ which must occur before one can be truly alive in this world. Worse things than mere death can befall a person made in God's image; her characters more often than not must be brought to the brink of crisis or death to see themselves as they are: in dire need of repentance and grace. In O'Connor's view, humankind did not accidentally stumble into rebellion against God; each man or woman deliberately chooses to do so. Consequently, she records with merciless precision the rationalizations of her protagonists, stripping them bare of their pretensions of goodness and innocence. She endeavored to confront

her readers with the full scandal of Christianity. Those O'Connor characters who attempt to redeem themselves with arrant scientism or sheer intellectualism meet a savage Savior—manifested in a bull, a haunting prophecy, or a terrifying vision—who will not release them until they confess Him or utterly denounce Him.

For O'Connor, there was no middle ground, no neutral corner; all who are not with Him are against Him. Her narrative voice had little room for authorial compassion or tenderness. Relentlessly exposing human pride, avarice, and weakness, she agreed with writer C. S. Lewis that all things that are not eternal are eternally out of date. Western culture was already too sentimental, too complacent about Christ and Christianity; her mission was to pound on the table, to cast the moneychangers—sacred or secular—out of the literary temple.

One must ask how O'Connor avoided mere tractarianism, as her continuing popularity among critics and ubiquity in college literature anthologies attest she did. Part of the answer is that she frankly confronted the tenuous relationships which exist among audience, medium, story, and craft. It was her genius to lead her readers through and from the seemingly mundane and ordinary to a vision of reality as sacramental, as always pointing to a divine presence in human activity. "When I write a novel in which the central action is baptism, I am aware that for a majority of my readers, baptism is a meaningless rite . . . so I have to see that this baptism carries enough awe and mystery to jar the reader into some kind of emotional recognition of its significance." Her fiction strips away the jaded images of the faith, forcing a dynamic confrontation with the gospel as it is played out in the lives of professed believers and as it is rejected by the worldly wise. As the reader follows Hazel Motes or Francis Marion Tarwater on his journey to belief, he is confronted with grace—a grace that enlarges his perception of the world, enabling him to see both the natural and the supernatural anew, to both discover and retrieve deeper images of the *real*. As O'Connor states it, this journey frequently entails "an action in which the devil has been the unwilling instrument of grace. This is not a piece of knowledge that I consciously put into my stories; it is a discovery that I get out of them." It is this "awful rowing toward God" that is chronicled in O'Connor's two novels, *Wise Blood* and *The Violent Bear It Away.*

WISE BLOOD

Hazel Motes, the protagonist of *Wise Blood*, is, O'Connor says, a "Christian *malgré lui*," a believer in spite of himself, a harried wayfarer who has been displaced from Eastrod, Tennessee, and from the religious life of the South. That religious life is distinctively Protestant, the religion of a South of beleaguered prophets and street-corner preachers, a South haunted by Jesus and by a theological definition of man's identity and destiny. Motes is determined to escape salvation and anything that smacks of supernatural origin. Like Francis Marion Tarwater in *The Violent Bear It Away*, Motes's story is a reverse *Bildungsroman*, a novel of an antiquest in which the protagonist tries to *avoid*, rather than *seek*, his destiny.

O'Connor maintained that *Wise Blood* is a "comic novel," and nonetheless so because it deals with "matters of life and death." Though many readers try to locate the integrity of Motes in his vigorous struggle to escape that "ragged figure moving from tree to tree in the back of his mind," O'Connor avers: "His integrity lies in his not being able to [escape] it." His attempted flight from Jesus begins on the train to Taulkinham. Discharged from military service, Motes parries with a Mrs. Hitchcock, challenging her claim to redemption. "If you've been redeemed," Motes snaps, "I wouldn't want to be." Later, he exclaims to no one in particular, "Do you think I believe in Jesus? . . . Well, I wouldn't even if He existed. Even if He was on this train." Motes has determined that the way to avoid Jesus is to avoid sin; one who is not a sinner needs no redemption—he is already "clean"—if he is free from transgression. This "freedom," however, does not mean that Motes can avoid becoming a preacher. When he first reaches the city and decides to look up Miss Leora Watts—who owns the "Friendliest Bed in Town"—both she and the cabdriver who brings him there accuse him of being a preacher; he simply looks the part.

Very soon, Motes encounters some potential dis-

ciples: Enoch Emery, who wants to help him find a "new jesus," and Sabbath Lily Hawks, the lustful daughter of a street preacher who feigns blindness. Following Sabbath and her father in order to ridicule their shallow evangelism, Motes declares that he will start a new church, a church *without* Christ. "I don't need Jesus," he tells the crowd gathering about him, "I got Leora Watts." Motes's obsession with the Hawks duo leads him to drive around the city in his beat-up Essex. His desperate flight from belief compels him to hound Asa Hawks, confronting him with the strange fact of his blindness—if Jesus is real, then why does He not heal His servants? Motes is tortured by his lack of a theodicy, a defense of God's absence; his only solace is to throw himself into his own "ministry": street-side preaching of the "Church of Christ without Christ" from the hood of his Essex.

His nightly forays into sermonizing yield only one "convert," a would-be Aaron to Motes's Moses, Onnie Jay Holy—a slick packager of religion and faith who knows a money-making scam when he sees it. Crediting Motes-the-prophet with changing his life, Holy drowns out the frustrated antipreacher, who learns to speak the truth in spite of himself: "Listen!" Motes screams. "It don't cost you any money to know the truth!" It is at this point that O'Connor's protagonist has begun his inexorable trek toward recognizing his true state and the call of God. When Enoch Emery answers Motes's call for a "new jesus" by stealing a mummified pygmy from a local museum and delivering it to the now domesticated Sabbath Lily Hawks, the reader is introduced to what Caroline Gordon called "the unholy family." Slinking into Motes's room, Sabbath introduces the mummy as their child. Sensing the blasphemy of the moment, Motes seizes the mummy and crushes it against the wall. The prophet must now leave this desecrated place and search for a new city in which he can begin his ministry afresh. Before he can leave, however, he must confront a false prophet—hired by Hoover Shoats, née Onnie Jay Holy—who has supplanted him on the streets of Taulkinham. Following him out onto a lonely road, Motes first knocks his car into the ditch and then runs over his counterpart, killing him and thus carrying out the Old

Testament vengeance against false prophets.

From here, Motes inevitably heads for his own Calvary, his own "death unto life": The words of Jesus in Matthew 5:29, "And if thy right eye offend thee, pluck it out," are taken literally. Motes blinds himself so that he can see with a spiritual vision which bogus believers such as Asa Hawks and Hoover Shoats can never attain. He is fully focused now; there is no intent to escape or flee. His landlady, Mrs. Flood, represents the kind of "Christian" O'Connor loved to contrast with her dramatic, utterly committed antisaints such as Hazel Motes, the Misfit in "A Good Man Is Hard to Find," and Manley Pointer in "Good Country People." She cannot fathom Motes's sudden devotion—which extended to the bearing of the marks of Christ on his body: "I'm as good, Mr. Motes, not believing in Jesus as many a one that does," she boastfully proclaims. When she sees the barbed wire wrapped around his chest, she exclaims, "There's no reason for it. People have quit doing it." His reply, anthem and testimony for all latter-day believers, seals his fate: "They ain't quit doing it as long as I'm doing it." Motes's death is as anticlimactic as Christ's; the policemen who discover him in the drainage ditch, like the soldiers at the foot of the cross who bargain for Christ's robe, mouth inanities and treat Motes as a troublesome derelict, quite worthy of being put out of his misery.

The story of Hazel Motes is the tale of one of God's creatures and his struggle with the fundamental choice to serve God or deny Him. O'Connor's avowed purpose was to "deepen the mystery of free will," which is not the war between one will and another but of "many wills conflicting in one man." In *Wise Blood*, whose title comes from Enoch Emery's claim to "know things" because of his ancestral blood, O'Connor has created a parable of twentieth century man's inner debate over God's existence and presence in the modern world. It is ironic, although not too surprising, that O'Connor's Christian readers sometimes responded less enthusiastically to her achievement than did her nonreligious readers. Such a response was simply a corroboration of O'Connor's perceptions regarding the state of belief in postwar America.

THE VIOLENT BEAR IT AWAY

In her second novel, *The Violent Bear It Away*, written some ten years after she had originally begun *Wise Blood*, O'Connor once again returned to the theme of the antiquest, this time with a protagonist who tries to escape the daunting prophecy of his great-uncle. The title comes from an ambiguous passage found in Matthew 11:12: "From the days of John the Baptist until now, the kingdom of heaven suffereth violence and the violent bear it away." It is the dual message of this scripture which, in part, gives the novel its underlying power as still another O'Connor portrayal of the conflict of wills within man, a conflict of reason tempered with godly knowledge and an uncritical, gullible trust in the scientific method. The passage suggests, first, that with the coming of the promised Messiah, humankind can receive the kingdom of God; second, it suggests that there remain calloused and unprincipled unbelievers who will seek to bar the faithful from entering that hallowed ground. These two opposing forces are focused in the protagonist and antagonist of the novel: Francis Marion Tarwater and Rayber the schoolteacher.

Mason Tarwater had reared his nephew, Francis, to be "more than a Christian, a prophet." His prophetic task consisted of two matters: First, he was to make sure that the elder Tarwater had a proper burial, his gravesite marked by a cross; second, he was to baptize Bishop, the "dimwitted child" of Rayber. Mason had earlier tried to rear Rayber as a prophet, too, but he encountered a resistance which eventually turned into a vigorously antireligious posture. Mason Tarwater had finally broken off all relations with Rayber after the latter wrote a psychoanalysis of Tarwater for a "schoolteacher's magazine" which mocked his beliefs. Francis Tarwater, also, does not come easily to his prophetic office. At his great-uncle's death, he abandons the old man and burns down his house, balking at his obsession with Jesus; the choice is not between "Jesus and the devil," he resolves—"it's Jesus or me." Francis, like Hazel Motes, is nevertheless haunted by the presence of Jesus: "Jesus? He felt a terrible disappointment in that conclusion, a dread that it was true." He can no more escape his destiny than Motes could; it is "hidden in the blood."

Rayber is a familiar O'Connor character type, the rationalist who attempts to explain away religion as illusion or delusion. He will have no part of the Tarwaters' prophetic ministry. Just as the sense of sight was a potent symbol in *Wise Blood*, O'Connor here uses the sense of hearing, Rayber's need for a hearing aid, to underscore his spiritual ignorance: "Do you think in the box," Francis Tarwater ridiculed, "or do you think in your head?" The religious people of Rayber's acquaintance—the Tarwaters, the Carmody family—have all been "exploited" people, bilked by the foolish rhetoric of insane cadgers and shysters. Yet Rayber's will is not powerful enough to withstand the force of a prophet of God. True to his call, Francis must drown Bishop in baptism, the enduring Christian symbol of new life from death.

O'Connor organized the events of this novel into three distinct parts. Part 1 reveals the eccentric life of the prophet; as Elijah the Old Testament prophet gave his mantle to the younger Elisha, so Mason Tarwater passes his own "burden" to his charge. Part 2 depicts Francis Tarwater's struggle to free himself, like a latter-day Jonah, from the burden laid upon him; here the city is emblematic of all the distractions and temptations that might deter him from his task. Part 3 relates the purification and cleansing of the prophet who encounters his burning bush and receives his commission to "warn the children of God of the terrible speed of mercy" in the "dark city" beyond him.

The Violent Bear It Away more fully develops themes O'Connor explored in such short stories as "The Enduring Chill," "The Artificial Nigger," "Good Country People," and "The Lame Shall Enter First." Her consistent focus is placed upon the human will tortured by indecision, clouded by technology, and rendered impotent by its flight from knowledge of God. The only remedy offered is the laying down of weapons and the complete surrender of the soul. Francis Tarwater and Hazel Motes both discover that their only rest from this ordeal is acquiescence to the will of God.

Throughout her fiction, O'Connor defamiliarized the all-too-familiar concepts of conversion and discipleship and articulated the shallow view of Christ lurking behind modern faith. She wanted her readers to escape the jaundiced vision of their own time. In *Mystery and Manners*, she paralleled her task with that of St. Cyril of Jerusalem, who, in instructing catechumens, warned them of passing by the dragon on their way to the Father of Souls:

No matter what form the dragon may take, it is of this mysterious passage past him, or into his jaws, that stories of any depth will always be concerned to tell, and this being the case, it requires considerable courage at any time, in any country, not to turn away from the storyteller.

O'Connor refused to turn away from the dragon or the storyteller, and she asked of her readers the same courage.

Bruce L. Edwards, Jr.

OTHER MAJOR WORKS

SHORT FICTION: *A Good Man Is Hard to Find*, 1955; *Everything That Rises Must Converge*, 1965; *The Complete Stories*, 1971.

NONFICTION: *Mystery and Manners*, 1969; *The Habit of Being: Letters*, 1979; *The Presence of Grace*, 1983; *The Correspondence of Flannery O'Connor and Brainard Cheneys*, 1986.

MISCELLANEOUS: *Collected Works*, 1988.

BIBLIOGRAPHY

Asals, Frederick. *Flannery O'Connor: The Imagination of Extremity*. Athens: University of Georgia Press, 1982. Asals's stated intention in this volume is to point out thematic patterns which he believes are consistent throughout all of O'Connor's fiction. As a result, this study is comprehensive, dealing with lesser-known works as fully as with those usually treated. Includes an introduction containing a useful analysis of O'Connor criticism, a full bibliography, and an index.

Desmond, John F. *Risen Sons: Flannery O'Connor's Vision of History*. Athens: University of Georgia Press, 1987. Traces O'Connor's artistic development in the context of her spiritual development. Desmond's assumption is that O'Connor's Christianity, and particularly her growing understanding of the principle of redemption, dominates her fiction. A complete bibliography and an index are provided.

Enjolras, Laurence. *Flannery O'Connor's Characters*. Lanham, MD: University Press of America, 1998. Chapters on O'Connor's descriptions of the body, of wicked children, of "conceited, self-righteous Christians," of "intellectuals and would-be artists." Includes notes and bibliography.

Orvell, Miles. *Flannery O'Connor: An Introduction*. Jackson: University Press of Mississippi, 1991. Chapters on the novels as well as explorations of O'Connor's treatment of the South, of belief, of art, of the American romance tradition, of prophets and failed prophets, and of comedy. Appendices include a chronological list of the fiction, book reviews by Flannery O'Connor, notes, and bibliography.

Paulson, Suzanne Morrow. *Flannery O'Connor: A Study of the Short Fiction*. Boston: Twayne, 1988. In addition to an excellent critical analysis of O'Connor's short stories, Paulson's volume contains relevant comments by O'Connor, her friends and acquaintances, and her editors. Concludes with a collection of excerpts from various critics, a bibliography, and an index.

Rath, Sura P., and Mary Neff Shaw, eds. *Flannery O'Connor: New Perspectives*. Athens: University of Georgia Press, 1996. Essays on the development and reception of O'Connor's career, her treatment of gender, race, and religion. Includes a bibliography.

Stephens, Martha. *The Question of Flannery O'Connor*. Baton Rouge: Louisiana State University Press, 1973. Stephens explores what she sees as an ambiguity in tone which is evident throughout O'Connor's fiction: on the one hand, the assertion of faith in Christianity, and on the other hand, a pervading pessimism, which suggests the improbability of redemption. Includes a useful annotated bibliography, a full list of sources, and an index.

KENZABURŌ ŌE

Born: Ōse, Shikoku, Japan; January 31, 1935

PRINCIPAL LONG FICTION

Memushiri kouchi, 1958 (*Nip the Buds, Shoot the Kids*, 1995)
Warera no jidai, 1959
Yoru yo yuruyaka ni ayume, 1959
Seinenno omei, 1960
Okurete kita seinen, 1962
Sakebigoe, 1963
Nichyoseikatsu no boken, 1964
Kojinteki na taiken, 1964 (*A Personal Matter*, 1968)
Man'en gannen no futtoboru, 1967 (*The Silent Cry*, 1974)
Nichijo seikatsu no boken, 1971
Kōzui wa waga tamashii ni oyobi, 1973
Pinchi rannā chōsho, 1976 (*The Pinch Runner Memorandum*, 1994)
Dōjidai gemu, 1979
Atarashii hito yo mezameyo, 1983
Natsukashii toshi e no tegami, 1987
Jinsei no shinseki, 1989 (*An Echo of Heaven*, 1996)
Chiryōtō, 1990
Shizuka na seikatsu, 1990 (*A Quiet Life*, 1996)
Chiryōtō wakusei, 1991
Moeagaru midori no ki, 1993-1995 (includes "*Sukuinushi*" *ga nagurareru made*, 1993; *Yureugoku* "*vashireshon*," 1994; *Ōinaru hi ni*, 1995)

OTHER LITERARY FORMS

Kenzaburō Ōe's short stories have been collected in *Warera no kyoki o ikinobiru michi o oshieyo* (1969, 1975; *Teach Us to Outgrow Our Madness*, 1977). Ōe has also been a major writer of essays, speeches, and a personal memoir of his family's life, *Kaifuku suru kazoku* (1995; *A Healing Family*, 1996). Much of his nonfiction work, which includes the texts of many of his speeches, has been collected in *Aimai na Nihon no watashi* (1995; *Japan, the Ambiguous, and My-*

self, 1995). In Japanese, there exist two multivolume editions of Ōe's collected works by the publishers Shinchosa and Iwanami. The twelve-volume work by Shinchosha was updated and revised in 1994, and it contains Ōe's novels, principal short fiction, and nonfiction up to that date.

ACHIEVEMENTS

Winning the Nobel Prize in Literature in 1994 was a joyful surprise for Kenzaburō Ōe, who was the second Japanese writer in history to win this award. In his acceptance speech in Stockholm on December 7, 1994, Ōe ironically pointed at the great gulf between his unconventional, politically charged writing and the beautiful texts which had earned his predecessor, Yasunari Kawabata, the award in 1968. Ōe's Stockholm speech, in which he claimed the prize in part on behalf of other dissident Asian writers, indirectly explained why the author had immediately declined Japan's Imperial Order of Culture, which he earned days after the Nobel Prize. Rejecting what he perceived as a symbol of a still-existent, antidemocratic cult of the emperor, Ōe antagonized many Japanese who could not understand this action.

Yet Kenzaburō Ōe has always occupied an ambiguous position in the literary world of Japan. His conscious attempts to forge a new Japanese literary language, his focus on alienation and suffering, and his unbending political opposition to nuclear weapons and to the emperor have earned him both admiration and puzzled rejection. In spite of this split in the Japanese reception of his works, Ōe's writings have earned him prestigious national and international awards from the beginning of his career. One of his first short stories, "Kimyo na shigoto" (1957; a strange job), about a student paid to kill dogs, won the Tokyo University May Festival Prize in 1957. One year later, Ōe's short story "Shiiku" (1958; "The Catch," 1966; "Prize Stock," 1977), describing the friendship between a Japanese boy and a black American pilot shot down over Japan, earned for Ōe Japan's prestigious Akutagawa Prize for 1958. In 1964, *A Personal Matter*, one of Ōe's most widely read novels about a youthful rebel, received the important Shinchosa Literary Prize. *The Silent Cry* was

(The Nobel Foundation)

recognized with the Tanizaki Jun'ichirō Prize in 1967.

As his novels continued to win major Japanese literary awards, such as the Noma Literary Prize in 1973, the Yomiuri Prize in 1982, and the Ito Sei Literary Prize in 1990, Ōe's reputation as a major contemporary Japanese writer solidified at home and began to attract international attention. His nonfiction work was awarded the Osaragi Jiro Prize in 1983. Overseas, the European Community awarded Ōe the Europelia Prize in 1989. Winning the Italian Mondelosso Prize in 1993 signaled his high standing in international literature, which was crowned by the Nobel Prize in 1994.

Ōe, as a member of the postwar generation, recognizes the human problems peculiar to the twentieth century, the century of nuclear explosions. This age of anxiety and its problems are internationally popular themes in literature as well as in the other arts. In that sense, the "antitraditional Ōe" has helped make Japanese literature a part of world literature. Ōe successfully created in Japanese literature a new tradition more closely related and integral to modern world literature than the traditional canons of ancient and medieval Japan.

Biography

Kenzaburō Ōe was born in the small town of Ōse in the prefecture of Ehime, on Shikoku Island, Japan, on January 31, 1935. The first important chain of events in his life, in terms of the literary tendencies he later developed, began with Japan's defeat in World War II, the subsequent declaration of the Emperor's change of status from divine to human, and the taking over of Japan by the United States Army. These drastic changes resulted in an unimaginable chaos of values in postwar Japan.

In 1954, Ōe became a student at Tokyo University, majoring in French literature. He began writing short stories while devouring such authors as Blaise Pascal, Albert Camus, Jean-Paul Sartre, Norman Mailer, William Faulkner, and Saul Bellow. His first novel, *Nip the Buds, Shoot the Kids*, was published in the same year. One year after his graduation from the university in 1959, he was married to Yukari Itami, the daughter of film director Mansaku Itami. He participated in organizing various protests in an attempt to cut off Japan from the nuclear umbrella of the United States, but became disillusioned and finally discontinued his efforts when he found that left-wing organizations did not condemn nuclear tests conducted by Communist countries.

In 1963, Ōe's first child, a son whom his parents named Hikari, meaning "light" in English, had to undergo a series of operations shortly after birth because of defective bone structure in the head. The field trip that Ōe made to Hiroshima in the following summer as a reporter revealed the incredible hardships of the atomic-bomb victims, which he associated with his personal ordeal. In combination, these two experiences produced a novel, *A Personal Matter*, in 1964. After this novel, the motif of physical deformity became pervasive in his novels and short stories.

Ōe traveled widely. In 1960, as a member of the Japanese literature delegation, he went to China, where he met Mao Tse-tung. In 1961, he stayed in Europe for four months at the invitation of Bulgaria and Poland. He also visited, on this occasion, the Soviet Union, England, and France, where he interviewed Sartre. Ōe also visited Australia, Mexico, and the United States. A collection of essays entitled *Sekai no wakamonotachi* (the youth of the world), published in 1962, reflects his experiences abroad.

In 1976, Ōe decided on a long stay in Mexico after finishing a semester as lecturer at the Collegio de Mexico. This brought him in touch with writers such as the Colombian Gabriel García Márquez, for whose works Ōe developed a deep affinity. Returning to Japan, Ōe published *Shosetsu no hoho* (1978), in which he promoted the Western literary theory of structuralism to revive Japanese writing. Many of Ōe's next novels reveal his fascination with structuralism and marginal existence, which also brought him in touch with Western literary critics and authors. Traveling frequently to Europe after 1980, in 1982 Ōe visited to gather material on the Western European antinuclear movement. His never-ending involvement in political issues brought him to the former Soviet Union, where he attended a 1987 Conference on Peace in Moscow.

Becoming familiar with the contemporary European literary world and beginning to earn European literary prizes, Ōe publicly debated authors such as the German Günter Grass in 1990 and the French Michel Tournier in 1991. In 1994 Ōe won the Nobel Prize in Literature and swiftly renounced his award of Japan's Imperial Order of Culture. He also told a stunned public that he would stop writing novels because his mentally handicapped son Hikari had become a successful composer of music.

Hikari has always been central to Ōe's work, as evidenced by the story of their family's life together in *A Healing Family*, a text illustrated by Yukari Ōe's watercolors. While proclaiming his end to novelwriting, Ōe continued his political involvement, participating in protests against French nuclear testing in the Pacific in 1997. Although he settled in Tokyo with his wife and family, Ōe would give literary lectures around the world.

ANALYSIS

Madness and despair are the recurring themes in the novels of Kenzaburo Ōe. His main characters are usually trapped physically, psychologically, or metaphorically. They realize their entrapment when they find themselves suddenly alienated from the major part of society to which they thought they belonged. The harder the victims try to escape from their trap, the more impossible it becomes. Madness and despair then start to develop and reverberate in the characters' lonely confinement. They become somewhat disoriented and therefore become social misfits. The conflict between the ostracized (minority) and the authoritarian (majority) is presented in Ōe's fiction in various forms: adults versus children; teachers versus juvenile delinquents; the successful versus the dropouts; police versus criminals; organizations versus individuals. The resolution usually comes in one of two ways: Either the ostracized character destroys himself, or he accepts everything in an existential way.

The notion of disorientation in Ōe may be a reflection of his experiences of the drastic changes that took place after Japan's defeat in World War II. As a young boy, Ōe had been educated at school and elsewhere to become a brave soldier and to die in the war for the sake of the Emperor. Suddenly on August 15, 1945, this great cause was taken away and the Emperor declared that he was a fellow human instead of a god for whom Ōe should be willing to die. The humiliation of being a defeated nation was combined with the fear of a possible massacre and mass rape by the soldiers of the occupying army.

After his visit to Hiroshima in 1963, Ōe published a work of nonfiction entitled *Hiroshima nōto* (1965; *Hiroshima Notes*, 1981), in which he expressed deep sympathy for the people suffering from the effects of nuclear radiation. In the essay, Ōe criticizes the inadequate governmental assistance and the irresponsible and sometimes inhumane treatment his people have received. Ōe warns the reader never to forget Hiroshima. In *A Personal Matter*, Ōe deals with a man's struggle against becoming entrapped by a son, whose deformity may have been caused by nuclear radiation. Later, the theme of the agonies of the nuclear

age becomes more and more pervasive in works such as *Kōzui wa waga tamashii ni oyobi* (the flood unto my soul) and *The Pinch Runner Memorandum*. Here, Ōe's themes of entrapment, madness, and despair are far more intense, because the situation of the main characters is totally impossible: It has become a global problem. Ōe seems to suggest an analogy with Noah's Ark, in *Sakebigoe* (outcries) or in *Kōzui wa waga tamashii ni oyobi*, as archetypal of escape, but in both, the escape fails, and "departure," Ōe's favorite term, is never achieved.

Ōe presents his theme of madness and despair through the literary technique of the grotesque. One of the classic devices of the grotesque is the animalization of human beings. Some of Ōe's characters—especially those in later works such as *A Personal Matter*, *The Silent Cry*, and *Kōzui wa waga tamashii ni oyobi*—are named after animals. They are often reduced to a biological level. Physical deformity, another important ingredient in the grotesque, is no rarity among the inhabitants of Ōe's imaginative world. The best example of this is the two-headed monster baby in *A Personal Matter*; other monstrous or deformed characters include a one-eyed doctor in *A Personal Matter*, an extremely obese woman who eats continuously in *The Silent Cry*, and even a shrinking man in *Kōzui wa waga tamashii ni oyobi*. Sexual behavior is described animalistically, totally lacking in romantic-erotic connotations. Actions are atrocious, and imagery—often related to human waste—is shocking and repulsive. All these grotesque elements create a violent and sometimes ludicrous effect and an incredibly maddening atmosphere—an atmosphere derived from confinement (estrangement) and from the dread of uncertainty in life.

Ōe's novels can be loosely categorized into different groups. The first group consists of six earlier works in which the treatment of the nuclear age and its agonies is not yet in the forefront, and in which Ōe's use of the grotesque is still not fully developed. Of these six novels, *Okuretekita seinen* (the youth who arrived late) may be the most important, because it embodies all the themes with which Ōe had been dealing in the other novels as well as in his short stories: disorientation, estrangement, distrust of adults, confinement, departure only to be trapped in another impossible situation, violent tortures, humiliation, and the final and undignified acceptance of the situation by the hero. The work is the longest of the six, second only to the longest of all, *Kōzui wa waga tamashii ni oyobi.*

OKURETEKITA SEINEN

Okuretekita seinen consists of two parts: The first deals with the struggle of the protagonist, the first-person narrator, against his surroundings in a small village, and the second part, with the adventures and frustrations of the hero in Tokyo. A small village in part 1 can probably be identified as the author's native town on the island of Shikoku. The hero is a sixth-grader, and the story begins on the very day that Japan surrenders. The narrator's awareness of being born too late for everything, especially for the war, is intense; in his difficulty in accepting the fact of Japan's defeat followed by the Emperor's change of status, it seems to him that the whole world has turned upside down. The villagers make quick adjustments and wear sycophantic smiles for the incoming army. In order to live at peace with the occupation forces, the villagers make scapegoats of the minority groups (Koreans and native Shikokuans, called "Highlanders"). These shameless incidents estrange the narrator, make him rebellious and lead to his affinity for a Korean boy, Kō, with whom the narrator remains friendly all the way through the novel. Kō and the narrator escape from the village, or "depart" as Ōe likes to put it, in order to join a group of Japanese soldiers who refuse to admit Japan's defeat. Ironically, this departure leads the narrator to an even more strict confinement—in a correctional institution.

NIP THE BUDS, SHOOT THE KIDS

The fear of confinement in an isolated village is also the theme of Ōe's first novel, *Nip the Buds, Shoot the Kids.* In this novel, the theme is presented in a clearcut fashion: Certain inmates, children who had been transferred from an urban correctional institution in an attempt to avoid air raids, find themselves imprisoned in a village where there is a heap of dead animals that have died in an epidemic. The

villagers, having evacuated the village, shoot at the children as they try to escape. In *Warera no jidai* (our age), the notion of confinement is more metaphorical. A university student, Yasuo Minami, like Ōe, majoring in French literature, is fed up with a decadent life with an oversexed prostitute but cannot escape from her, since she provides the major part of his living expenses. Later, he almost leaves Japan, and his decadent life, to accept an invitation from French authorities who wish to reward him for his prizewinning essay. In the end, this invitation is canceled, since Minami is found to be involved in underground revolutionary activities. Thus, he has only one place to return—to the prostitute's house.

By contrast, the narrator in *Okuretekita seinen* successfully finishes his term in a correctional institution, passes the entrance examination for Tokyo University, and departs for Tokyo, where he finds only another trap. The narrator hates successful people so much that he is determined to become one himself in order to take his revenge. His target is an influential conservative politician whose daughter he tutors in French and plans to seduce. Ironically, he is too late. The daughter is pregnant by another man. The narrator claims to be the baby's father in order to attract the politician's attention and receive money from him for an abortion. The money, however, makes him a target for sadistic left-wing students—the violence described here is mostly related to sex. The narrator uses these experiences to approach the politician and succeeds to some extent in gaining his favor. This part of the plot, it is hinted, is inspired by the ambition-driven Julien Sorel in Stendhal's *Le Rouge et le noir* (1830; *The Red and the Black,* 1898). Ōe's protagonist declines rapidly, as his past as a juvenile delinquent is revealed. In the end, he realizes that his sole option is to accept whatever is offered to him. Unlike his French counterpart, who detroys himself, Ōe's protagonist here is anti-heroic, grossly diminished, and reduced to a mere biological, rather than fully human, existence. He realizes after so many experiences of humiliation and frustration that his dignity as a human being is completely gone. He no longer has even the dignity of madness, since madness is the manifestation of sanity in an insane society. Ōe's narrator, in his calm and yet profound despair, chooses to live. Death can no longer be tragic, since he was born too late for the war, in which a heroic death was possible. Only one who dies a heroic death can live eternally in glory.

A PERSONAL MATTER and NICHYOSEIKATSU NO BOKEN

A nightmarish city life is the setting for *A Personal Matter*. At the start of the novel, the twenty-seven-year-old protagonist, Bird, nicknamed for his birdlike facial features, tries to escape to Africa from a city life laden with responsibilities. Africa, in Ōe's imaginative world, seems to have a deceptive ambiguity: It looks like ultimate freedom, the antithesis of city life, yet it actually is an ominous image associated with death. Bird looks at a map of Africa and thinks the shape of the continent resembles that of a skull. In *Nichyoseikatsu no boken* (adventures in everyday life), written before *A Personal Matter*, Africa presents the same ambiguity. The hero, Saikichi (*Sai* means "rhinoceros"), does go to Africa: This trip suggests a return home (a rhinoceros goes to Africa), but he kills himself in a hotel room there. Bird's wish to flee to Africa, then, represents an unconscious desire for a world of adventure, like the world of war, where he might be able to put an end to his life. The motif of Africa reappears in *The Silent Cry*. Interestingly enough, Africa is one of the continents which Ōe has never visited. For that matter, he has not gone to war either.

Another conspicuous correlation between *Nichyoseikatsu no boken* and *A Personal Matter* is the existence of a woman called Himiko. Himiko in *Nichyoseikatsu no boken* is the first wife of Saikichi. Her name is presented with the same characters as those of Queen Himiko of the legendary Yamatai Kingdom of the second century. According to the legend, Queen Himiko committed incest with her younger brother in order to continue her line. She eventually was killed by the wrath of God, immediately after giving birth to a baby boy. In *Nichyoseikatsu no boken*, Himiko liberates Saikichi with her uninhibited attitude toward sex. Similarly, Himiko in *A Personal Matter* (the name has the same sounds but is written with different characters) cures Bird's impo-

tence by offering him anal intercourse. Sex in Ōe's world is often used to break psychological confinement and is stripped to the bare facts of desire and anatomy.

Bird's awareness of psychological confinement intensifies when his wife gives birth to a baby whose head seems twice as big as that of a normal baby. He tries to kill the deformed baby. After desperately struggling with himself, however, he finally realizes that the baby is nothing but an extension of his life, an existential realization that life has to be continued whether it seems meaningful or not. Ōe's technique here is the literary grotesque, a distortion of reality. He creates an unfeeling, apathetic urban society. It is populated with such monstrous characters as a doctor who is interested only in the baby's autopsy, even though it is still alive, and Bird's girlfriend, Himiko, who leads an active life only during the night hours and sleeps during the day. This deformed reality strongly suggests a loss in human qualities. It is vaguely hinted that the deformity of the baby might be a result of the fallout in the rain caused by nuclear experiments. Bird had participated as a student in protest rallies and street demonstrations against those experiments. Now the problem comes to Bird in a much more concrete form—it is a personal matter indeed.

The seemingly optimistic ending of *A Personal Matter*, one of Ōe's most popular novels, is not in harmony with the pessimistic tone of the novel as a whole. In the last two pages, Bird emerges with his family into the sun from the darkness of the hospital. The baby, now in its mother's arms, has undergone surgery, which reveals a benign tumor instead of a fatal brain hernia. This ending is anticlimactic, unlike, for example, the ending of *Kōzui wa waga tamashii ni oyobi*, which concludes with the symbolic death of the protagonist, or that of *The Pinch Runner Memorandum*, whose last scene describes a spectacular bonfire into which the protagonist plunges headlong. If the theory of the grotesque is extended to this work, then the ending suggests madness in people who are not, in terms of characterization, mad. Bird has ceased to behave like a madman, indicating his madness; his father-in-law has given him a bottle of whiskey knowing that Bird was once an alcoholic; and his mother-in-law has wished for the baby's death. The overwhelming optimism at the end comes from the fact that the baby is saved, but nothing has changed for Bird. He has to give up his dream of Africa and is more deeply trapped than ever, without hope.

THE SILENT CRY

In *The Silent Cry*, Ōe deals with the two brothers who return from city life to their native village—an action that reverses that of *Okuretekita seinen*. In the journey, planned as a quest for identity, they trace their origin symbolically to the mother's womb. The womb is the village, located in a valley, and is called Ōkubo, which means "a large hollow." The valley is surrounded by almost impenetrable, dense forests. The brothers not only find themselves confined spatially in this isolated area on the island of Shikoku, but gradually they also recognize their temporal confinement.

The older brother, Mitsusaburo, often abbreviated to Mitsu, is the pensive narrator. His wife has become an alcoholic since their deformed baby was put in an institution. The narrator's younger brother, formerly active on the streets as a student radical, is named Takashi, or simply Taka (Hawk), and therefore is more a man of action. Their last name is Nedokoro, meaning "the place where there is the root." The Nedokoro brothers' immediate purpose in visiting the native village is to sell the family estate to a new supermarket chain. The other purpose, just as important, is to investigate what actually happened to their great-grandfather and his younger brother, who were involved in a peasants' rebellion in the first year of the Manen era, one hundred years before the narrative present.

Unconsciously, Taka and Mitsu try to identify themselves with their ancestors. There are many intricate parallels between these pairs of brothers. Mitsu and Taka experience what their great-grandfather and great-uncle experienced a hundred years before. Taka, the younger brother, organizes the villagers and starts a rebellion against the ever-expanding influence of the supermarket on the village, just as the ancestral younger brother had organized the peasants

against the overwhelming power of governmental authority. When the historical rebellion failed, the organizer disappeared; what had become of him is not revealed until the end of the novel. Taka commits suicide by shooting himself in the face with a shotgun, not because of the failure of the rebellion but because of his own madness—madness resulting from his guilt centering on the death of his younger sister, with whom he had had an incestuous relationship. The parallelism between these two incidents, only temporally separated but spatially overlapped, is a literary technique that might be called "simultaneity." It helps create a sense of helpless confinement not only in space but also in time.

At the start of the novel, a good friend of the narrator commits suicide in a most grotesque way—he hangs himself naked, his head painted vermilion, with a cucumber in his anus. This episode clearly establishes overtones of madness. The madness innate in Taka as well as in Mitsu is symbolized by the womblike or tomblike hollow in the ground where the narrator wakes up in the morning at the beginning of the novel. At the end of the novel, evidence is found that the organizer of the historical rebellion had been kept in confinement for the rest of his life in the secret basement of the Nedokoro mansion. This is another subterranean manifestation of the fate of posterity. Mitsu's wife is now pregnant not by her husband but by his insane dead brother, but the husband and wife wish to start a new life with the children—one an idiot and the other yet to be born. Mitsusaburo looks forward to setting off for Africa, the continent of ominous ambiguity.

There are several symbolically deformed characters. The narrator had lost one eye some time before and has designated his hollow eyesocket as the eye for looking inside himself. Jin, who used to be the wet nurse for the narrator, is now an extremely obese woman living in the Nedokoro estate. She is famous for her obesity but continues to eat obsessively. When the Nedokoro mansion is demolished, she suddenly stops eating and starts to die. Another of these characters is a diminutive man who had hidden himself in a dense forest in order to avoid the draft in wartime. This man, called Gii the Hermit, has a head so small it looks like a shrunken, mummified head.

Grotesquerie is ubiquitous and pervasive in this novel. The eldest brother of the Nedokoros, for example, was killed in the war, and his diary records all kinds of wartime atrocities—such as a graphic description of captives being beheaded. The second brother, known only as "Brother S," had come back from the war, but later was beaten to death by a group of Koreans as retribution for the ransacking of their village by the Japanese. His brain seeps out of his cracked skull. Taka, before committing suicide, insists that he killed a village girl in an attempted rape and describes how he smashed her head against a huge rock after she had bitten off his fingertips. Combining these repulsive scenes with evocations of eerie masked dances and music peculiar to this region's festival, Ōe builds up an atmosphere of intense madness and despair which leads to the theme of the final and inescapable horror—the deracination of human beings by a nuclear war in the next two novels.

KŌZUI WA WAGA TAMASHII NI OYOBI

The main character in *Kōzui wa waga tamashii ni oyobi*, Isana Ōki (Big Trees-Whales), lives in a nuclear shelter with his five-year-old mentally handicapped son, Jin. Isana has separated from his wife and settled down in the shelter in order to provide a quiet life for his autistic son, who can respond only to birds' chirping. The father believes himself able to communicate with the spirits of whales and trees. A group of five or six social dropouts called the Free Navigators intrude upon the life of the father and son. The Free Navigators live together, learn how to operate a schooner, steal cars, and practice combat drills. Their purpose is to escape from Japan as soon as a natural or nuclear disaster hits. Later, they steal firearms and explosives from an army camp and lynch a fellow member, the "Shrinking Man." The final scene is a shoot-out with the police at the shelter in which Isana and another fanatic are hiding. In the end, Isana drowns himself in the water which the police have poured in.

Kōzui wa waga tamashii ni oyobi includes many of Ōe's familiar motifs. For example, Isana is a son-in-law of a hideous politician who is dying of cancer. This is the family situation that the narrator in

Okuretekita seinen had to accept. Isana's son is no doubt an extension of the monster baby in *A Personal Matter*. The trio—that is, the monstrous enigmatic politician, the disoriented father, and his mentally handicapped son—are also used as main characters in the next novel, *The Pinch Runner Memorandum*. The name Jin is immediately associated with the Jin in *The Silent Cry*. Right after he is born, the baby refuses to eat, as if he wished to commit suicide, but later, he slowly gains weight.

A total social misfit, Isana tries to save his son from autism by developing an affinity with nature. He calls himself the representative of trees and whales, hence his name. Ironically, however, his name indicates the exact opposite of what he represents. Whales are large and mobile; Isana is insignificant and immobile in his trap. Trees reach toward the sky and symbolize life; his psyche is directed downward and he is to die. His longing for nature is symbolized by a hole in the concrete floor of his nuclear shelter in which he can put his bare feet directly on the soil. His situation is another image used to present "madness." Ironically, the water that kills Isana gushes into the shelter through this hole, the only opening in the walls.

The Free Navigators are actually outlaws, but their plan for a seaborne enterprise clearly reflects the motif of escape based on the biblical episode of Noah's Ark treated in *Sakebigoe*. The plan fails as it did before, and Isana, trapped and drowning in the whalelike shelter, resembles Jonah, who is swallowed by a whale as a result of his disobeying the Word of God. No final salvation comes to Isana.

The sense of estrangement that Isana experiences during the course of the novel results from the change that takes place in the mind of his son Jin. When the Free Navigators step into their life, Jin gradually starts to open his mind, especially to a young girl called Inako. The Navigators are violent criminals. Some of them are extremely sadomasochistic, yet they are not nearly as depraved as the monstrous politician, whose sexual preference is for young boys. As Jin begins to have simple conversations with the intruders, Isana realizes that he has suddenly lost his *raison d'être*.

Of the members of the Free Navigators, Inako is the most sensible and humane character, even though she is naturally promiscuous and uninhibited. The most grotesque character of them all is the Shrinking Man. He is a professional photographer who once won a prize for the pictures he took of children suffering from muscular dystrophy. It is not clear if his "shrinking" is metaphorical or physical, but he claims that since his thirty-fifth birthday, he has started to shrink. As his body shrinks, his sexual organ becomes bigger. He calls this phenomenon "implosion" instead of "explosion." The Shrinking Man takes pictures of the group's secret combat drills and sells them to a weekly magazine; this betrayal provokes the group to lynch him. The lynching takes a most atrocious and repulsive form: He dies, his naked body skewered through the rectum. The scene is all the more shocking because Ōe creates a ludicrous atmosphere—the lynchers constantly laugh and giggle as if they are enjoying some kind of game.

The death of Isana at the conclusion of the novel is symbolic of the fate of human beings who have discovered nuclear fission, perhaps against the will of God. It also represents the meaninglessness of survival in the case of a nuclear disaster. As it is meaningless to die in a nuclear shelter in peacetime, so is it meaningless to survive a nuclear war. Thus, the notion of doomsday deepens Ōe's despair, and a world of madness and absurdity unfolds itself in the novel.

THE PINCH RUNNER MEMORANDUM

The mentally handicapped son in *The Pinch Runner Memorandum*, aged eight, is named Mori. The name has a double meaning: "forest" in Japanese and "death" in Latin. "Forest" suggests the mythical power that dominates human existence in *Nip the Buds, Shoot the Kids* as well as in *The Silent Cry*. Death is the major motif throughout Ōe's fiction. Mori's thirty-eight-year-old father has no name of his own and is identified only as "Mori/father." He is supposed to be contaminated by plutonium, and he and his wife believe that their son's idiocy comes from radioactivity. One morning, the father and son find themselves transformed: The father is reduced to an eighteen-year-old boy, and the son is now a mature man of twenty-eight. The father thinks that this

"switch" has been brought about by some kind of extraterrestrial power called "The Will of the Universe." The father, now a teenager, becomes involved in a violent conflict between two militant factions in the student movement over the issue of which student group should manufacture an atomic bomb. As the novel progresses, it gradually becomes clear that both factions are manipulated by one political and financial magnate called Mr. A. In the meantime, Mori attacks Mr. A, again guided by the will of the universe, but succeeds only in wounding him in the head. When hospitalized, Mr. A is found to be dying of cancer, not of the wound in the head. Mr. A's plan is to create social chaos, first by providing funds for the militant student factions to produce nuclear bombs and then by helping the government annihilate them to save Tokyo, and thereby to die as a savior. Mori finally succeeds in stopping Mr. A by smashing his head with an iron bar; then, Mori commits suicide by jumping into a gigantic bonfire made by the masqueraders from Mr. A's native village in order to exorcize the evil spirit called "cancer."

The novel is a fantasy-farce, based on the notion that every creature on earth is nothing but a make-believe shadow created by a huge slide projector delivered by an unidentified flying object (UFO). No character has a realistic name; no character is a character from the viewpoint of the realistic novel. The narrator's wife, for example, is an alcoholic lunatic who brandishes a razor and cuts the husband's cheek so deeply that he can stick his tongue out of the cut. The wound disappears, however, as soon as the "switch" takes place, since the narrator has reversed the flow of time. The hijackers who attack a truck carrying radioactive waste look like so many tin men from L. Frank Baum's *Wonderful Wizard of Oz* (1900). A man known as the "Righteous Man," who comes from the island of Shikoku to participate in a protest rally only to be killed in the battle between the student factions, uses his denture as a weapon. Mori, the protagonist, never speaks except for occasional groans, even though he communicates with his father by telepathy.

The work is highly satiric, caricaturing world politics concerning nuclear weaponry and the student protest movements in Japan as well. It seems that the novel, published in 1976, foreshadows the renewed hysteria over nuclear competition between the world powers in the early 1980's. *The Pinch Runner Memorandum* is also alarming; the foundation of its farcical plot is the fact that an individual with a certain amount of knowledge about nuclear physics could produce a nuclear bomb if funds were provided. This is no longer merely a possibility, but is a constant danger. Mr. A, with his long involvement in Japanese economic expansion into Asian countries, is presented as a reactionary figure intending to restore political power to the Emperor.

In order to achieve his tragicomic ambiguity, Ōe uses a peculiar style which might be called "vulgar colloquialism"—loosely worded, seemingly unending and undirected sentences, including slang and coarse expressions uncommon in contemporary Japanese literature. It is a conversational style commonly used among modern Japanese students, vaguely recalling the particular terminology of the late 1960's student activists. The style is in harmony with the absurd content and heightens the horror of this seemingly fantastic yet unnervingly realistic novel.

DŌJIDAI GEMU

Upon his return from Mexico, Ōe began to experiment with structuralism in his next novel, *Dōjidai gemu* (the game of contemporaneity). Its sometimes surrealistic plot centers on a band of exiled warriors who fight the Japanese Imperial Army to a standstill in a remote forest during World War II. They surrender only when the army threatens to burn the forest, thereby saving nature rather than themselves. With this resolution, the novel has been interpreted as Ōe's fictional response to Yukio Mishima's dramatic suicide by *seppuku* in 1970. Thus, Mishima's action, which sought to revive a traditional warrior cult, is replaced by Ōe's deep appeal to humanism.

AN ECHO OF HEAVEN

Ōe's texts constantly revisit familiar terrain, and *Dōjidai gemu*'s remote forest of Shikoku, where Ōe was born, features prominently in many of his next novels. *An Echo of Heaven*, however, moves from Japan to Mexico. Here, Marie Kuraki finds a spiritual refuge after the suicide of her two handicapped sons

in Japan. The novel hauntingly combines Ōe's earlier themes of physically deformed children with a reflection of Marie's encounter with Mexican Magical Realism, as peasants begin to venerate her as a new saint in the tradition of the Dark Virgin of Guadalupe. The remote village of Shikoku has been transported by Ōe to Mexico and functions again as a microcosm where agonies and aspirations of human existence play themselves out against a backdrop of myth and grotesque realism. Ōe's interest in structuralism continues as he deliberately fragments the narrative of his novel, refusing to pursue a more convential approach to storytelling.

A QUIET LIFE

After writing two postapocalyptic science-fiction novels, Ōe's *A Quiet Life* returns to the present. As her parents leave for a university in California, the twenty-year-old narrator is left behind in Japan to complete her graduation thesis and look after her two brothers. The handicapped older one, Eeyore, quickly becomes the novel's true protagonist, again reflecting some traces of Ōe's real-life son Hiraki. The gentle love among the family members reaffirms Ōe's belief in human dignity and compassion; typically, there are political allusions to topical events, such as social unrest in Poland in 1989.

MOEAGARU MIDORI NO KI

Ōe's magnificent "flaming green tree" trilogy was completed in 1995 and, according to its author, represents Ōe's final novelistic work. The three volumes feature two central characters, a young male who undergoes a sex change operation to become a woman and an intelligent savior figure known as Elder Brother Gii. Fighting to save their village from a hostile outer world, the characters are part of a work fused with Ōe's trademark grotesque realism. Ōe's occasionally bitter humor shines throughout the trilogy, as does the author's insistence on human compassion in the face of private and political madness and disaster. Thus, a mythic tree's connection to the ground becomes a symbolic safeguard for the continuation of generation after generation of humans, who may be able to escape nuclear self-immolation.

From the beginning of his literary career, confinement and estrangement have been Ōe's recurring themes. Increasingly, madness, despair, and failure to escape have dominated his works. At the same time, his use of the grotesque has expanded—perhaps suggesting that contemporary life can be expressed only by extreme distortion as nuclear annihilation appears probable. Ōe is Japan's major contemporary writer; his themes and techniques are directly in tune with those of Western modernism. He is one of the few major Japanese writers to use the unique Japanese experience of Hiroshima and Nagasaki for literary analysis of global concerns, and he searches constantly for more adequate verbal expression of human existence toward the end of the twentieth century.

Sanroku Yoshida, updated by R. C. Lutz

OTHER MAJOR WORKS

SHORT FICTION: "Kimyo na shigoto," 1957; "Shisha no ogori," 1957 ("Lavish the Dead," 1965); "Shiiku," 1958 ("The Catch," 1966; "Prize Stock," 1977); *Miru mae ni tobe,* 1958; *Kodoku na seinen no kyuka,* 1960; "Sebuntin," ("Seventeen," 1996), 1961; "Seiji shonen shisu," 1961; *Seiteki ningen,* 1963; *Warera no kyōki o ikinobiru michi o oshieyo,* 1969, 1975 (*Teach Us to Outgrow Our Madness: Four Short Novels,* 1977); *Gendai denikshu,* 1980; "*Ame no ki" o kiku onnatachi,* 1982; "*Rein tsurī" o kiku onnatachi,* 1982; *Ika ni ki o korosu ka,* 1984; *Kaba ni kamareru,* 1985; *Boku ga hontō ni wakakatta koro,* 1992.

NONFICTION: *Sekai no wakamonotachi,* 1962; *Genshuku na tsunawatari,* 1965; *Hiroshima nōto,* 1965 (*Hiroshima Notes,* 1981); *Jisokusuru kokorozashi,* 1968; *Kowaremoto to shite no ningen,* 1970; *Okinawa nōto,* 1970; *Kakujidai no sōzōryoku,* 1970; *Dōjidai to shite no sengo,* 1973; *Bungaku noto,* 1974; *Jōkyō e,* 1974; *Kotoba ni yotte,* 1976; *Shōsetsu no hōhō,* 1978; *Ōe Kenzaburō dojidaironshu,* 1981; *Sengo bungakusha,* 1981; *Kaku no taika to "ningen" no koe,* 1982; *Atarashii bungaku no tame ni,* 1988; *Bungaku sainyūmon,* 1992; *Aimai na Nihon no watakushi,* 1995 (*Japan, the Ambiguous, and Myself,* 1995); *Kaifuku suru kazoku,* 1995 (*A Healing Family,* 1996).

BIBLIOGRAPHY

Cameron, Lindsley. *The Music of Light: The Extraordinary Story of Hikari and Kenzaburō Ōe.* New York: Free Press, 1998. Discusses the lives of Ōe and his son. Includes bibliography and index.

Napier, Susan J. *Escape from the Wasteland: Romanticism and Realism in the Fiction of Mishima Yukio and Ōe Kenzaburō.* Cambridge, Mass.: Harvard University Press, 1991. An excellent, indepth comparative analysis of key texts by both writers. The book provides great insight into the literary imagination of these two important, yet very different, writers.

_____. "Marginal Arcadias: Ōe Kenzaburō's Pastoral and Antipastoral." *Review of Japanese Culture and Society* 5 (December, 1993): 48-58. An intelligent critical study of the treatment of nature in Ōe's works. Relates Ōe's often fantastic and grotesque description of rural life to the author's childhood at the remote margins of Japanese society. Successfully analyzes Ōe's connection to the traditions of Western pastoralism.

Wilson, Michiko Niikuni. "Kenzaburō Ōe: An Imaginative Anarchist with a Heart." *The Georgia Review* 49, no. 1 (Spring, 1995): 334-350. Combines a good overview of Ōe's life with a sophisticated interpretation of his literary output. Argues convincingly that the outstanding features of Ōe's fiction are a complete rejection of evil, a tenderness for all humans, and a biting irony. Wilson's insistence that Ōe's writing, as well his politics, still remain something of a mystery for his Japanese audience is well supported.

_____. *The Marginal World of Ōe Kenzaburō: A Study in Themes and Techniques.* Armonk, N.Y.: M. E. Sharpe, 1986. An authoritative, book-length study of Ōe in English. For Wilson, Ōe's texts are very different from traditional Japanese literary works. Provides a very useful introduction to Ōe's imaginative world.

Yamanouchi, Hisaaki. *Ōe Kenzaburō and Contemporary Japanese Literature.* Oxford, England: Nissan Institute of Japanese Studies, 1986. Discusses Ōe's oeuvre in regard to other Japanese writers of the time.

Yoshida, Sanroku. "The Burning Tree: The Spatialized World of Kenzaburō Ōe." *World Literature Today* 69, no. 1 (Winter, 1995): 10-16. Connects Ōe's fiction to the grotesque realism favored by French author François Rabelais, whose influence Ōe acknowledged in his acceptance speech for the Nobel Prize. While offering a compelling literary analysis of the key motifs of trees and birds throughout Ōe's fiction, the article also stresses Ōe's never-ending radical political commitment, which has alienated him from more conservative Japanese readers.

JOHN O'HARA

Born: Pottsville, Pennsylvania; January 31, 1905
Died: Princeton, New Jersey; April 11, 1970

PRINCIPAL LONG FICTION

Appointment in Samarra, 1934
Butterfield 8, 1935
A Rage to Live, 1949
The Farmer's Hotel, 1951
Ten North Frederick, 1955
A Family Party, 1956
From the Terrace, 1958
Ourselves to Know, 1960
Sermons and Soda Water, 1960
The Big Laugh, 1962
Elizabeth Appleton, 1963
The Lockwood Concern, 1965
The Instrument, 1967
Lovey Childs: A Philadelphian's Story, 1969
The Ewings, 1972

OTHER LITERARY FORMS

John O'Hara was a prolific writer of short stories, and eleven volumes of stories were published during his lifetime. After O'Hara's death, Random House, his publisher since 1947, brought out two additional collections: *The Time Element and Other Stories* (1972) and *Good Samaritan and Other Stories* (1974).

Scattered throughout the short-story collections are most of O'Hara's works in the novella form; the only novellas to be separately published are the three in *Sermons and Soda Water*. The play version of the story "Pal Joey" was published in 1952, and in 1961 it was reissued with four others in *Five Plays*. O'Hara's last complete play, *Far from Heaven* (1962), was first published posthumously in 1979, along with an unproduced original screenplay, *The Man Who Could Not Lose* (1959), under the title *Two by O'Hara*. Like many other writers of his period, O'Hara wrote and collaborated on film scripts from the 1930's through the 1950's, and several of his novels were made into films during his lifetime. O'Hara began his writing career as a journalist, and he was several times a newspaper columnist. Two collections of his columns were published: *Sweet and Sour* (1954)—columns written for the Trenton *Sunday Times-Advertiser*—and *My Turn* (1966), a series of syndicated columns written for *Newsday*. A collection of O'Hara's speeches, essays, and interviews, entitled *An Artist Is His Own Fault*, was edited by Matthew J. Bruccoli in 1977.

ACHIEVEMENTS

Often dismissed as a popular novelist with tendencies toward sensationalism, or as a "social historian," O'Hara nevertheless secured a faithful following among many literary critics for his skill at storytelling and his evocation of times, places, and manners in American society in the first half of the twentieth century. O'Hara himself was equivocal about the label "social historian." In a speech in 1961, he said, "I deny that I am a social historian"; yet he went on to say that "before deciding to write a novel, I consider what opportunities a story offers for my comments on my times." Matthew J. Bruccoli is probably most accurate in calling O'Hara a "novelist of manners," in the sense that he was primarily concerned with the accurate depiction of a social matrix and its effect on human behavior and potential. Like William Faulkner and other twentieth century American novelists, O'Hara turned the realities of his hometown experience into a fictional world; unlike Faulkner, he probed this milieu with a dedication to social realism rather than elevating it to mythic status. In addition to his native eastern Pennsylvania, O'Hara used New York and Hollywood as frequent settings for his fiction. Although he lived and worked in both places, he is most clearly identified with the "Region" of Pennsylvania, on which he could bring to bear an insider's perceptions.

The fact that O'Hara was a realistic storyteller rather than an "experimental" novelist was detrimental to his critical reputation during his lifetime. Ironically, the explicit sexuality in much of his work (though restrained by today's standards), which was partially responsible for creating wide popular interest in his novels and which caused *Ten North Frederick* to be suppressed in several cities, overshadowed the depth of his concern with societal mores and pressures. Although he emphasized the role of fate and chance, O'Hara is usually considered a realist rather than a naturalist, largely because he allowed the possibility of moral choice. His long, detailed novels characteristically show people of a privileged socioeconomic level struggling with the realities of social class, personal worth, and complex human relationships.

O'Hara's treatment of his women characters has been overlooked by most critics, yet it may help to account for his enormous contemporary popularity. Long before it was fashionable or even allowable to do so, O'Hara realistically portrayed women as sexual human beings and even dealt openly with lesbianism in some of his novels and stories. Though several of his major female characters (such as Edith Chapin in *Ten North Frederick* and the title character of *Elizabeth Appleton*) are stereotypically manipulative, they are believable, complex people whose motivations are clearly the result of cultural pressures. It would be inaccurate to call O'Hara a feminist novelist, but he acknowledged women's power and their problems in ways that set him apart from most novelists of his period.

Whatever the eventual critical evaluation of O'Hara as a twentieth century American novelist, it is certain that his work will be used as a valuable resource for information about customs, manners, and attitudes in America from the 1920's through the

(Library of Congress)

1950's, much as one consults the work of Theodore Dreiser, Sinclair Lewis, or John Updike. The ear for dialogue, the eye for detail, and the perception of human nature that made him a popular novelist will also ensure his continued importance.

BIOGRAPHY

John Henry O'Hara was born on January 31, 1905, in Pottsville, Pennsylvania. The town of Pottsville became the "Gibbsville" of his fiction, and the surrounding eastern Pennsylvania anthracite coal-mining area, known to residents as the "Region," was the locale of his major novels and stories. The author's father, Patrick O'Hara, was a doctor whose father had settled in the area during the Civil War, and his mother, Katharine Delaney O'Hara, was the daughter of a prosperous businessman in nearby Lykens, which became O'Hara's fictional "Lyons." Dr. Patrick O'Hara was a respected surgeon, necessarily specializing in injuries resulting from mining accidents, and he was seriously disappointed at his firstborn son's refusal to study medicine. Rather than inspiring a dedication to the medical profession, O'Hara's travels with his father to the scenes of medical emergencies provided him with regional lore which found its way into his writing.

Living on Pottsville's "best" street, Mahantongo ("Lantenengo" in the fictional Gibbsville), was a sign of the O'Hara family's relative affluence and provided O'Hara with an awareness of the rigid economic and ethnic stratification of the town. Until his father's early death in 1925, O'Hara led a fairly privileged existence, and his dream of attending Yale was thwarted less by lack of funds than by O'Hara's dismissals from three preparatory schools for low grades and disregard of discipline. The alternative to college was a job as a reporter on the Pottsville *Journal* in 1924, which effectively launched O'Hara's career as a writer.

In 1928, O'Hara left Pottsville for New York, where he worked briefly for the *Herald-Tribune* and *Time* and began to contribute stories to *The New Yorker*, which eventually published more than two hundred of his short stories; accordingly, some have attributed to O'Hara the creation of that subgenre, the "*New Yorker* story." During these early years in New York, O'Hara established friendships with Franklin P. Adams (F. P. A.)—to whose New York *World* column "The Conning Tower" he sometimes contributed—Robert Benchley, Dorothy Parker, and F. Scott Fitzgerald. In 1931, he married Helen Ritchie Petit ("Pet"), but his heavy drinking and frequent unemployment led to a divorce in 1933.

Appointment in Samarra, the first of O'Hara's fifteen novels, was published in 1934, and his first collection of short stories, *The Doctor's Son and Other Stories*, appeared the following year. Although he was not financially secure for some time, O'Hara's reputation as a fiction writer grew steadily, and for the next twenty years, he lived alternately on the East Coast and in Hollywood, where he wrote film scripts. Although he intermittently aspired to be a playwright, O'Hara's only successful play was *Pal Joey*, based on a series of stories in *The New Yorker*, which ran on Broadway between 1940 and 1941. It was made into a film, starring Frank Sinatra and Rita

Hayworth, in 1957. In 1956, O'Hara was given the National Book Award for *Ten North Frederick*, and in 1957 he was inducted into the National Institute of Arts and Letters, from which he resigned in 1961 because he had not been nominated for its Gold Medal for fiction.

In 1937, O'Hara was married for the second time, to Belle Mulford Wylie, the mother of his only child, Wylie Delaney O'Hara, born in 1945. The O'Haras moved to Princeton, New Jersey, in 1949, and in 1953, a serious ulcer condition prompted O'Hara to quit drinking permanently. Following Belle's death in 1954, O'Hara married Katharine Barnes Bryan ("Sister") in 1955, and the family moved two years later to Linebrook, a home in Princeton that O'Hara and Sister had designed. O'Hara died at Linebrook April 11, 1970, while working on a sequel to *The Ewings*, his last published novel.

ANALYSIS

In the spring of 1960, John O'Hara wrote as part of his preface to *Sermons and Soda Water*: "The Twenties, the Thirties, and the Forties are already history, but I cannot be content to leave their story in the hands of the historians and the editors of picture books. I want to record the way people talked and thought and felt." Despite his frequent rejection of the seemingly derogatory critical label of "social historian," which seemed to separate him in the minds of critics from more "serious" novelists, O'Hara was committed throughout his career to providing accurate records of the decades and places in which he lived. The novels and novellas that resulted from this commitment are uneven in quality as examples of the art of fiction, but they provide an unmatched portrait of segments of American society in the first half of the century. The central characters of much of his fiction are wealthy, prominent people, whether they are the leading citizens of Gibbsville, Pennsylvania, or Hollywood film stars, yet O'Hara frequently illuminates their circumstances by juxtaposing them with members of other socioeconomic groups: servants, tradesmen, laborers. The result is a panoramic social canvas, consonant with O'Hara's conception of the traditional novel form. Occasionally, as in *From the Terrace*, the realist's attempt at panoramic vision overwhelms artistic control; as Sheldon Grebstein remarks in *John O'Hara* (1966), "the *tranche de vie . . .* has been cut too thick to be digestible." At his best, however, O'Hara's work reflects the rich diversity of American society, as in his counterpointing of the savvy political boss Mike Slattery and the wealthy, naïve, would-be politician Joe Chapin in *Ten North Frederick*.

As the example of politics suggests, one of O'Hara's major themes is power—not only the power of money, though that is a central metaphor, but also the power inherent in talent, morality, and sexuality. O'Hara shared with F. Scott Fitzgerald a fascination with wealth and social prestige, but his treatment of their influence is far more analytical. His novels typically trace the establishment of a family dynasty, as in *The Lockwood Concern*, or the progress of an individual's aspirations for himself or herself, as in *Ten North Frederick*, and *Elizabeth Appleton*—always within the constraints of a social web rendered palpable by realistic settings and dialogue. O'Hara is concerned particularly with showing the limits of human power, not in the face of an overwhelming fate, but as the result of miscalculation, error, or simple human frailty. When Julian English throws a drink in the face of Harry Reilly in *Appointment in Samarra*, or when George Lockwood, in *The Lockwood Concern*, builds a wall around his mansion, neither can foresee the fatal consequences, but both have made choices that dictate inevitable results.

As money is a metaphor for power in O'Hara's fiction, sexuality is an ambivalent metaphor for love. Though he was accused of sensationalism and bad taste in his relatively explicit depiction of sexual relationships, O'Hara was primarily interested in showing the potential for manipulation in the human sexual relationship. Women as well as men are portrayed as captive to sexual desire, and both sexes frequently mistake love for possession, or sex for love. From Grace Caldwell Tate's injudicious couplings in *A Rage to Live* to the tender relationship between Jim Malloy and Charlotte Sears in *The Girl on the Baggage Truck* (from *Sermons and Soda Water*), the possibility of true romantic love seems remote in O'Hara's fiction. His realistic approach assumes a basic human egotism and desire for power which renders such love rare.

The structures of O'Hara's novels and novellas reinforce the sense of inevitability of consequence. His novels frequently begin with an apparently small but significant event or action which spins out in mystery-story fashion to create the web that catches the characters and demonstrates their ultimate powerlessness. Yet he avoids the predictability of formulaic fiction by using multiple points of view and a wealth of complex, believable characters to play out the drama. In the novellas, the structure is frequently circular, the story beginning at a moment of culmination and then tracing the events which have brought the characters to that point. Common too, especially in the novellas, is O'Hara's use of a narrator, usually Jim Malloy, a journalist whose background and attitudes resemble those of O'Hara. Although these structural devices were not original with O'Hara, he used them skillfully to suit his fictional purposes.

Character is of supreme importance in O'Hara's fiction, and the achievement of adequate characterization determined the form he used. As he said in one of his Rider College lectures, "before I have finished two pages of manuscript my author's instinct has told me how much I want to tell about this character, and thus the length of the story is dictated." The majority of O'Hara's characters inhabit the Pennsylvania "Region" in which he spent his youth, and the fictional canon provides a vivid picture of relationships among people of various social levels over time. The reappearance of certain characters in many works reinforces the sense of a coherent world wherein the codes of morality and propriety dictate the shape of both society and individual human lives.

In its settings, characters, and incidents, O'Hara's fiction is strongly autobiographical, a circumstance which is a natural outgrowth of his desire to be a recorder of his times. Though he did not live in Pottsville, Pennsylvania, after 1930, the town and its people continued to serve as a microcosm of the American culture he dissected throughout his career. Like his autobiographical narrator Jim Malloy, O'Hara returned to Pottsville "only long enough to stand at a grave, to toast a bride, to spend a few minutes beside a sickbed," but the years he spent there left an indelible impression. From his vantage point as the doctor's son, O'Hara observed both the leading citizens and the transients, and later he explored, in his novels and novellas, the lives he imagined to exist behind the placid exterior of the American small town. Part of the autobiographical content of the fiction, however, comes from O'Hara's unfulfilled aspirations rather than from his actual experience. Although his dream of attending an Ivy League college was thwarted by his checkered prep school record and the death of his father, O'Hara's upperclass male characters typically attend prestigious universities and benefit from larger family fortunes than O'Hara's family ever enjoyed. His fiction, like that of Fitzgerald, thus conveys an ambivalent attitude toward the privileged: the wistfulness of the outsider and the realist's desire to reduce them to understandable human terms.

The span of O'Hara's career, from 1934 to 1970, coincided with a period of intense experimentation in literary forms. The fiction of James Joyce and William Faulkner, among others, tested the limits of the novel, and critical opinion during these years favored attempts to break the mold of traditional fiction, to push beyond the bounds of realistic documentation of recognizable human events. Thus, O'Hara's accurate rendition of dialogue lost place to stream of consciousness as an acclaimed technique, and the chronicling of successive generations was less favored than novels spanning a single day, controlled by a single consciousness. O'Hara's novels continue to be appreciated more for their documentary usefulness than for their creative force, yet within the limits of the traditional novel form, O'Hara was a master craftsman who captured and conveyed the human drama and social fabric of a complex period in American life.

APPOINTMENT IN SAMARRA

In 1961, O'Hara referred to *Appointment in Samarra* as "a live novel twenty-five years after first publication." O'Hara's first novel would continue to "live," in several senses. It is obviously the work of a professional writer; O'Hara's powers of observation

and skill in plot construction are already highly developed in this short novel. Also, *Appointment in Samarra* is set in the "Region" of eastern Pennsylvania, the setting of much of his long fiction throughout his career, and it has strong autobiographical elements. Finally, the novel deals starkly and dramatically with the themes of power and fate and demonstrates O'Hara's understanding of individual human destiny as a delicate balance between necessity and accident. The novel's title derives from a quotation from W. Somerset Maugham; the "appointment in Samarra" is an inescapable appointment with death, yet Julian English, O'Hara's main character, is doomed by his own actions—his tragedy is of his own making.

The story of Julian English is set against a richly detailed social and geographical background. O'Hara takes pains to provide the reader with the flavor of the early Depression years: the names of popular songs, the intricacies of the bootlegger's profession, and the subdued desperation of both rich and poor. To tie the novel even further to an era, there are topical references; Julian English mentions having recently read Ernest Hemingway's *A Farewell to Arms* (1929), and Irma Fleigler counts on President Herbert Hoover's promise that next year will be better for everyone, so that she and her husband can join the country club to which the Englishes belong. The club, and the town and region of which it is the social pinnacle, are treated with the same careful detail. O'Hara devotes several pages to the peculiarities of the anthracite coal region and the social hierarchy of Gibbsville, making clear that no person or action is independent of the social context. Despite the anxieties of what was called in 1930 a "slump," Gibbsville and its inhabitants are filled with self-importance, and none more so than Julian English, the doctor's son.

English and O'Hara share several biographical similarities. Julian, like O'Hara, has refused to adopt his doctor-father's profession, and his refusal has caused a serious rift in the father-son relationship. Julian English admires Franklin P. Adams (F. P. A.), to whom O'Hara dedicated *Appointment in Samarra*, and when a priest asks him whether he is a "frustrated literary man," Julian answers, "I'm not anything. I guess I should have been a doctor." The most important similarity between English and his creator is the sense of insecurity betrayed by this remark, an insecurity which leads both men to heavy drinking and defensive belligerence. The significant difference is that Julian English does not survive his own nature.

To dramatize his perception that the individual is inextricably bound up in his social context, O'Hara deftly shifts the point of view in the novel from interior to exterior views of Julian English, emphasizing the extent to which one person becomes the object of others' scrutiny. The novel covers the last three days of Julian's life, from the moment he throws a drink in Harry Reilly's face at the country club Christmas party until he commits suicide by carbon monoxide poisoning, yet the narrative begins and ends with the observations of Luther and Irma Fleigler, a middle-class couple whose solid respectability and loving relationship contrast sharply with the weakness and manipulation of the far wealthier Julian and Caroline English. Julian's action is, in itself, insignificant—a social error from which all parties could have recovered in time—but it becomes symbolic of Julian's misperception of his own strength and power. With the inevitability of Greek tragedy, social ostracism follows Julian's throwing of the drink; he becomes an outsider to his own group, and he fails in all his efforts to pick up the pieces of his life.

O'Hara presents, one by one, the sources of comfort to which twentieth century men turn in times of personal trouble and shows them all to be ineffective. Family, sex, work, drink, religion, even a simple apology—none provides solace to Julian, who is the isolated twentieth century man, left with nothing in which to believe. If Julian does not understand the motivation for his action, neither does anyone else around him, and neither his father, Dr. English, nor his wife can respond adequately to his anguish. Work fails as an escape because, as the president of a Cadillac dealership, Julian is dependent upon precisely the good will of potential customers, which his action has temporarily denied him, and drink leads to either self-pity or further belligerence. Monsignor Creedon, to whom Julian, a Protestant, feels obscurely drawn, confesses that he has sometimes wished he had chosen a different life's work; lacking a true vocation, he cannot provide a spiritual solution to Julian's guilt and loneliness.

Although the major conflict in the novel is that between Julian's personal responsibility for his own actions and fate and the effect of his social surroundings on that fate, O'Hara introduces a third element: heredity. Conscious of his own family heritage, and especially of his forebears' struggle through generations for greater status and respectability in the "Region," O'Hara places great importance on a sense of heritage. His characters are typically aware of where they come from, who their ancestors are, and to what this background entitles them on the social scale. Julian English's grandfather had committed suicide after embezzling money from a bank, and after Julian's suicide, Dr. English consoles himself regarding his own reputation by assuming that people "would see how the suicide strain has skipped one generation to come out in the next."

Dr. English reappears in several of O'Hara's later works, as do several other characters introduced. Jim Malloy, mentioned previously, becomes the narrator of the novellas in *Sermons and Soda Water*, and the relationship between Whit Hofman, here a minor character, and Pat Collins is the basis of the novella *Pat Collins*. In short, *Appointment in Samarra* established O'Hara's major locale, characters, and themes, and much of his fictional canon enlarged upon what was set forth in this novel.

The critical reception of O'Hara's first novel was generally favorable, though some reviewers were disturbed by its relatively explicit sexuality. This reaction was intensified by his next two major novels, *Butterfield 8* and *A Rage to Live*, both of which sold well in part because of the furor, and his collections of short stories were consistently well received. *Appointment in Samarra* had launched its author on a successful career.

TEN NORTH FREDERICK

Although many of the short stories O'Hara published in the five collections between 1935 and 1947 were set in the "Region," *Ten North Frederick* was the first novel after *Appointment in Samarra* to deal with that locale. *Ten North Frederick* marked the beginning of the major phase of O'Hara's work as well as a new stage in his life. Two years before its publication, he had suffered the bleeding ulcer which convinced him to give up alcohol permanently, and a few months before, he had married Katharine Barnes Bryan, whom he referred to as "Sister." For the next fifteen years until his death, O'Hara would live a more settled, productive life than ever before. The timing of the novel's publication also began a tradition that continued for the rest of his career. Because O'Hara, always sensitive to reviews, wanted the task of reviewing *Ten North Frederick* to fall to a particular writer for *The New York Times*, the novel was issued on a Thursday in late November. The day was Thanksgiving, and the publication of an O'Hara novel or collection became an annual Thanksgiving event.

Butterfield 8 had been a *roman à clef*, based on the sensational and tragic story of Starr Faithfull, but despite certain resemblances between the lives of Joe Chapin and Franklin Delano Roosevelt, *Ten North Frederick* is not. Rather, as Matthew Bruccoli suggests, the novel is a "what-if study: what if Roosevelt had been a Gibbsville Republican?" O'Hara undoubtedly had Roosevelt in mind as he created Joe Chapin, and he used some elements of Roosevelt's life—the strong mother with ambitions for her son and a physical crippling in midlife—but his intention was not, as it was in *Butterfield 8*, to write a fictional account of a well-known person. Indeed, whereas Roosevelt's story is one of triumph over personal adversity, *Ten North Frederick* chronicles the failure of Joe Chapin's ambitions.

Those ambitions are far from modest. Joe Chapin wants nothing less than to leave each of his children a million dollars upon his death and to become president of the United States. That he achieves neither goal is in part the result of circumstances (the Depression reduces his financial assets) and in part of errors in judgment, such as his attempting to circumvent the local political system managed by Mike Slattery. Despite the magnitude of his hopes, Chapin is neither grasping nor overwhelmingly egotistical.

Although he makes some ill-considered decisions about the lives of others—notably his daughter's abortion and the dissolution of her marriage to an Italian musician—he is not a power-hungry schemer. Instead, he is unaware that his own power has limits. Reared to believe in the privileges of wealth and status and trained in the proprieties of social forms, Chapin is merely inflexible. Rules and forms have taken precedence over human responsiveness, and his one extramarital affair, late in his life, seems to be the only spontaneous action of which he is capable.

Joe Chapin's life thus has an opaque surface which prevents even his closest Gibbsville associates from knowing him well. At Chapin's funeral, one of his cousins remarks, "I could never figure Joe out," to which Mike Slattery replies, "We knew exactly what Joe wanted us to know. And believe me, that wasn't much." Coming at the beginning of the novel, this exchange might have foreshadowed the revelation of a secret life that Chapin had hidden carefully from his friends, but O'Hara's intention instead is to show that the reality of Chapin's life is one with its facade. Behind the mask of respectability is a life that is just as sterile as the mask would suggest. With the exception of minor scandals, such as his daughter's elopement and pregnancy, Chapin's experience has been one of single-minded devotion to the accumulation of wealth and status.

Beginning *Ten North Frederick* with the funeral of his main character, O'Hara employed a structural device that attested to his development as a novelist. Both *Appointment in Samarra* and *Ten North Frederick* begin with a moment of crisis or transition, but whereas in *Appointment in Samarra* the rest of the novel traces the inevitable results of that moment, *Ten North Frederick* begins with the conclusion—the death of Joe Chapin—and then proceeds to explore the life that has ended. The fact that the major threads of that life are introduced in the conversations at Chapin's funeral and are later developed in all their complexity has caused Sheldon Grebstein to call this a "tapestry novel." Having revealed the significant facts about Joe Chapin's life early in the novel, O'Hara must compel the reader to continue by means other than suspense.

The major strength of *Ten North Frederick*, as of most of O'Hara's fiction, is its characterization. The novel deals with three generations of the Chapin family, beginning with Joe Chapin's parents, though instead of a straight chronological narrative O'Hara uses a flashback technique, weaving past and present together to emphasize the effect of family— especially women—on the formation of character and ambition. Both Joe's mother, Charlotte, and his wife, Edith, have plans for his life; both are women for whom love means power and ownership, and for whom sex is a form of manipulation. Edith Chapin articulates this persistent theme of O'Hara's novels as she thinks, on her wedding night, "It was not Love; Love might easily have very little to do with it; but it was as strong a desire as Love or Hate and it was going to be her life, the owning of this man." As clearly as anywhere in his fiction, O'Hara here portrays women who, because they are denied most masculine forms of power, participate vicariously by requiring their men to succeed in their stead.

Yet Joe Chapin is a failure. If there is a "secret" in his life, it is the depth of his desire for high political office. On the surface a personable, respected pillar of Gibbsville, highly regarded by most of its leading citizens, Chapin nurses the ambition for which his mother has groomed him, but he is not willing to play the political games required to gain the backing of Mike Slattery's organization, nor can money buy him the office he seeks. After he is forced to withdraw from the political arena, only his brief affair with his daughter's friend Kate Drummond gives his life meaning, and when that ends he slowly begins to commit suicide by drinking heavily.

Many of O'Hara's own feelings about accomplishment and aging informed his creation of Joe Chapin. O'Hara was fifty when the novel was completed. Like Chapin, he had gained the respect of many of his contemporaries, but certain measures of "success" had eluded him: in particular, recognition as a first-rate novelist. Both O'Hara and his character had suffered frightening indications of poor health; Chapin ignored the warning that alcohol was killing him, but O'Hara did not. Time had become precious to him, and he reflects on this in the final paragraph of *Ten North Frederick*: "There is always enough to do while the heart keeps pumping. There is never, never enough time to do it all." O'Hara was rewarded for his persistence when *Ten North Frederick* received the National Book Award for 1955. The award citation read in part: "Tough-minded as usual, Mr. O'Hara has written a novel of emotional depth and moral conviction."

SERMONS AND SODA WATER

The swift passing of time to which O'Hara referred in *Ten North Frederick* was one of the reasons he turned to the novella form in the three pieces that comprise *Sermons and Soda Water*. The novella took, he said, "a minimum of research," as compared to the "big novel" he was working on simultaneously (probably *The Lockwood Concern*). He wrote these novellas to "get it all down on paper while I can"; "at fifty-five I have no right to waste time." The novella, in other words, could be written quickly, from memory, rather than requiring years of research and writing. This distinction between the novel and the novella suggests that the material for the latter was more likely to be autobiographical, and his use of Jim Malloy as narrator in these three novellas adds to the impression that these are personal narratives.

Although O'Hara never fully defined the terms "novella" and "novelette" as he used them, he suggested in 1968 that the important consideration was character. The form, he said, "tells all that you need to know about certain people in certain circumstances so that those people become figures in the reader's personal library." He had first experimented with a form midway in length between the short story and the novel in the title story of *The Doctor's Son and Other Stories*, his first collection of short stories, but during the last decade of his career, beginning with *Sermons and Soda Water*, he developed the novella form as a means of disentangling one thread from the usual complex tapestry of his novels. The novella as O'Hara conceived of it has an episodic structure. It follows one conflict, relationship, or problem through a lengthy time span, isolating for dramatic attention only the crucial periods, and briefly summarizing intervening months or years. There are no subplots, and minor characters are functional rather than centers of interest in their own right.

The use of a first-person narrator with a limited consciousness, rather than the omniscient point of view O'Hara employed in most of his novels, helps to ensure the sharp focus required for the novella. Jim Malloy, the narrator of *Sermons and Soda Water*, tells the reader about the people he has known in his hometown of Gibbsville or those he meets as a journalist in New York. He is a thin mask for O'Hara in the early days of the author's career: the young man from the coal region who begins his career in New York, encounters the wealthy and famous, and keeps up with a few of the people back home. Yet, Malloy has the mature vision of O'Hara at fifty-five, and his perspective on the characters' lives is that of a concerned friend rather than an impressionable young man. Malloy, like O'Hara, is a shrewd observer of human nature, one who finds patterns in life. In *We're Friends Again*, the third novella in *Sermons and Soda Water*, he comments on this ability: "The way things tie up, one with another, is likely to go unnoticed until a lawyer or a writer calls our attention to it." Malloy's function in these novellas is to demonstrate how "things tie up" while remaining more or less removed from the central stories.

In this ultimate detachment from the lives of the characters he describes, Malloy underscores the central theme of *Sermons and Soda Water*: human loneliness and isolation. At the end of *We're Friends Again*, Malloy calls loneliness "the final condition of us all," and O'Hara shows that it affects people at all levels of society—from Charlotte Sears, the film star in *The Girl on the Baggage Truck*, to Pete and Bobbie McCrea of Gibbsville in *Imagine Kissing Pete*. The solution to loneliness is love, but, as O'Hara so often suggests, love is elusive, and one often settles for approximations: attraction, sex, power. As Charlotte Sears says about her relationship with the wealthy, reclusive Thomas Hunterden, "There ought to be another word for love, for people like Hunterden and me." It is left to Malloy, as the controlling consciousness, to find meaning in the lives he relates, and that meaning resides ultimately in his capacity as a writer to discern patterns of inevitability in human life.

THE LOCKWOOD CONCERN

Of the novels written during O'Hara's last decade, *The Lockwood Concern* is particularly interesting as a culmination of many aspects of his career. During this period he used a variety of settings for his fiction—Hollywood in *The Big Laugh*, Philadelphia in *Lovey Childs*—but in *The Lockwood Concern* he returned to the "Region," to the characters and situations that he handled with ease and familiarity. Throughout the early 1960's, O'Hara referred to a "big" novel on which he was working, and at one point he projected that it would be a two-volume work. *The Lockwood Concern* is in fact a one-volume work of average length, but its scope justifies O'Hara's adjective: It is a multigenerational novel, a "century-spanning saga," as the jacket blurb proclaimed.

The theme of *The Lockwood Concern* is consistent with much of O'Hara's other work, and reaches back to *Appointment in Samarra*: the ultimate powerlessness of the individual against the force of circumstance, particularly the folly of attempting to control the destinies of others. The attempts of Abraham and George Lockwood, the second and third generations of the Lockwood family of Swedish Haven (actually Schuylkill Haven, near Pottsville), to establish a family dynasty break down in the fourth generation when George Lockwood's son and daughter reject the town and the family and adopt ways of life antithetical to dynastic responsibilities. The "concern" of the title is a Quaker concept, denoting an overwhelming sense of mission. Abraham Lockwood, in the late nineteenth century, has secularized this religious concept and translated it into a vision of generations of Lockwoods enjoying increasing wealth and prestige, including entrance to the clubs and other bastions of gentility denied him by the uncouth background and behavior of his own father, Moses Lockwood.

The central figure of *The Lockwood Concern* is George Lockwood, who has adopted Abraham's dream and brought it to the point of realization. George Lockwood's children will be the first generation to enjoy full acceptance by elite society, and as an emblem of this progress he has built a family mansion near Swedish Haven. The high, spiked wall around the house testifies to George's sense of exclusivity; it is also the cause of the death of a neighboring farm boy, who becomes impaled while attempting to climb the fence before the house is completed. This tragedy, which George Lockwood hastens to keep quiet, opens the novel, a signal of the crumbling of the erstwhile dynasty. From this point, George struggles to maintain the "concern" against increasing evidence of its demise until he finally falls to his death down a secret staircase he has had built in the still-uninhabited mansion.

O'Hara here used the circular structure which he had perfected in both long and short fiction throughout his career. The novel begins and ends in the mid-1920's, but ranges back to the mid-nineteenth century as O'Hara details the history of the "Lockwood concern." It opens with the death of the unnamed farm boy and closes with the death of George Lockwood and, by implication, of the "concern." Simultaneously, the novel has the linear thrust of the historical novel. From the canny, vigorous survival of Moses Lockwood to the effete California existence of George's son Bing, the generations move through historical and cultural change, reflecting shifting values in American society. The novel argues that such change is inevitable, and that George Lockwood's attempt at consolidation and stasis is doomed from the start. Social flux is mirrored even in the names of the male Lockwoods over time, from the tradition and authority of "Moses" and "Abraham" to the frivolity of "Bing." Even with such change, however, basic human nature does not alter; George and Bing Lockwood are, in different ways, as conniving and self-interested as their ancestors, though protected by wealth and attorneys against open public disapproval.

The Lockwood Concern is a summation of much that O'Hara had tried and accomplished during thirty years of writing. Though not his best novel, it is one of his most ambitious in subject matter and scope. It provides a history of the "Region" from the time of O'Hara's ancestors until the time when he left it for New York, and it shows the growth of the region from a backwoods settlement to a thriving coal-mining and farming area that sent its sons to Prince-

ton and Harvard. Thematically, the novel shows that O'Hara had come to some conclusions about the interplay of destiny and choice. He had shown in *Appointment in Samarra* that an individual's power over his own life was limited by the influence of society and the intervention of chance. In *Ten North Frederick*, he added great wealth and ambition to the equation and demonstrated their ineffectuality. By the time he wrote *The Lockwood Concern*, O'Hara saw the limits to human power as determined not only by conflicting wills and accidents of fate, but also by the very sweep of time and change. Human aspiration pales before the only human certainty—death—which is described as a "secret" known only to those who have experienced it.

By entitling his biography of the author *The O'Hara Concern* (1975), Matthew J. Bruccoli suggests that O'Hara felt a sense of mission similar to that of the Lockwoods. If so, O'Hara's "concern" was not related to a family dynasty but instead to establishing himself among the first rank of American novelists. His lifelong war with literary critics and reviewers over the value of his contribution is evidence that he was never secure in his own reputation. Although he rejected the terms "social realist" and "social historian," these are appropriate characterizations of his best work. O'Hara's sense of history, his precise rendering of detail and dialogue, and his command of narrative technique make him one of the most significant chroniclers of American life in the first half of the twentieth century. The fact that he was a popular novelist during his career, in part because of the more sensational aspects of his work, has detracted from his critical reputation, but his position as an important novelist of manners seems secure.

Nancy Walker

OTHER MAJOR WORKS

SHORT FICTION: *The Doctor's Son and Other Stories*, 1935; *Hope of Heaven*, 1938; *Files on Parade*, 1939; *Pal Joey*, 1940; *Pipe Night*, 1945; *Hellbox*, 1947; *Assembly*, 1961; *The Cape Code Lighter*, 1962; *The Hat on the Bed*, 1963; *The Horse Knows the Way*, 1964; *Waiting for Winter*, 1966; *And Other*

Stories, 1968; *The O'Hara Generation*, 1969; *The Time Element and Other Stories*, 1972; *Good Samaritan and Other Stories*, 1974.

PLAYS: *Five Plays*, pb. 1961; *Two by O'Hara*, pb. 1979 (includes *Far from Heaven*, 1962, and the screenplay *The Man Who Could Not Lose*, 1959).

NONFICTION: *Sweet and Sour*, 1954; *My Turn*, 1966; *A Cub Tells His Story*, 1974; *An Artist Is His Own Fault*, 1977.

BIBLIOGRAPHY

Bruccoli, Matthew. *John O'Hara: A Descriptive Bibliography*. Pittsburgh: University of Pittsburgh Press, 1978. A thorough, scholarly bibliography on all aspects of O'Hara's work. A must for the serious student.

_____. *The O'Hara Concern: A Biography of John O'Hara*. New York: Random House, 1975. The expertise of Bruccoli is evident here in this comprehensive biography of O'Hara. Contains valuable background, critical references to his works, and a useful bibliography.

Eppard, Philip B., ed. *Critical Essays on John O'Hara*. New York: G. K. Hall, 1994. Divided into sections on reviews and essays. All of O'Hara's major fiction is discussed, as well as his relationship to naturalism, his view of society, his short stories, and his view of politics, the family, and small towns. Includes a comprehensive introductory chapter on O'Hara's career and the reception of his novels, but no bibliography.

Grebstein, Sheldon Norman. *John O'Hara*. New York: Twayne, 1966. This critical study both interprets and assesses O'Hara's work. Grebstein is mostly sympathetic toward O'Hara, but has some reservations about his writings. Also assesses other criticism on O'Hara.

MacShane, Frank. *The Life of John O'Hara*. New York: E. P. Dutton, 1980. Looks at O'Hara's life through his work. A thorough study well worth reading for its valuable insights.

Shannon, William V. *The American Irish*. New York: Macmillan, 1963. Deals with O'Hara's work from the point of view of his Irish ancestry and his desire to escape from it.

MICHAEL ONDAATJE

Born: Colombo, Ceylon (now Sri Lanka); September 12, 1943

PRINCIPAL LONG FICTION

The Collected Works of Billy the Kid, 1970
Coming Through Slaughter, 1976
In the Skin of a Lion, 1987
The English Patient, 1992
Anil's Ghost, 2000

OTHER LITERARY FORMS

Michael Ondaatje has published several volumes of poetry, including *The Dainty Monsters* (1967) and *There's a Trick with a Knife I'm Learning to Do: Poems, 1963-1978* (1979). He has also edited collections of short fiction by Canadian authors.

ACHIEVEMENTS

Ondaatje received Canada's Governor-General's Award in 1971 for *The Collected Works of Billy the Kid*, in 1980 for *There's a Trick with a Knife I'm Learning to Do*, and in 1992 for *The English Patient*. In 1973, *Billy the Kid* was a finalist for the Chalmer's Award. *Coming Through Slaughter* received *Books in Canada*'s First Novel Award in 1976, and *In the Skin of a Lion* received the 1988 City of Toronto Book Award and the Trillium Book Award. Ondaatje received the Order of Canada in 1988 and in 1992 became the first Canadian to win the Booker Prize, for *The English Patient*.

BIOGRAPHY

Born in Colombo, Ceylon (now Sri Lanka), Michael Ondaatje seldom referenced his upbringing in print until his 1982 "fictional memoir," *Running in the Family*. Ondaatje describes his early days as a "great childhood," although his parents divorced when he was two and he had little contact with his father. As an adult he completely lost contact with his father.

After moving with his mother and siblings to London at age eleven, Ondaatje completed school at Dulwich College. His writing career began with his move to Canada in 1962 at age nineteen, where he attended Bishop's College in Quebec. The teachings of Professor Arthur Moyter inspired Ondaatje's love for literature. In 1964, he married thirty-four-year-old artist Kim Jones, originally the wife of one of his professors, and they had two children. For years, they would spend their summers at Blue Roof Farm near Kingston, entertaining critics, artists, family, and friends. Ondaatje's sense of humor and fondness for practical jokes became legendary. The couple legally separated in 1980. Ondaatje then began a relationship with Linda Spalding, whom he met in Hawaii; they subsequently shared a home in Toronto with her two children.

By 1965, Ondaatje had received the Ralph Gustafson Poetry Award, and by 1966 his poems were included in *New Wave Canada*. He received a B.A. from the University of Toronto (1968) and an M.A. from Queen's University. While teaching at the University of Western Ontario, he won the President's Medal for his poem "Paris," wrote *The Dainty Monsters*, and staged a dramatic performance of *the man with seven toes* (1969) in Vancouver. In 1971, Ondaatje was fired for not seeking a Ph.D. Within days of his dismissal, he received the first of three Governor General's awards. He pursued a love of film by writing and producing the first of several short movies, *Sons of Captain Poetry*, which focused on the works of a Canadian poet.

In 1971 Ondaatje became an editor at Coach House Press, known for its postmodern publications, and he began teaching in the English department at Toronto's Glendon College, York University. He continued writing and publishing poetry and, in 1976, received the *Books in Canada* First Novel Award for *Coming Through Slaughter*. His novel *In the Skin of a Lion* made him a 1987 semifinalist, along with South African novelist Nadine Gordimer and American novelist Toni Morrison, for the fifty-thousand-dollar Ritz Hemingway Literary Prize (no prize was awarded). He donated the 7,500-dollar cash portion of the Wang International Festival Prize, an award memorializing his friend Nichol, to a fund supporting new writers. In 1991, he published *The Cinnamon Peeler: Selected Poems*, and he coedited *The Brick*

Reader with Linda Spalding. *The English Patient* made Ondaatje famous outside Canada, but he continued to write as a Canadian resident.

ANALYSIS

Canadian writer Margaret Atwood labeled Michael Ondaatje "vital and imaginative," while American writer Annie Dillard wrote of Ondaatje's language, it "is clean and energetic, with the pop of bullets." His early works have been aligned with those of modernist poet Wallace Stevens, due to his sharp imagery and lyric voice. The later longer works place him, writes critic Douglas Barbour, firmly within the tradition of poet Ezra Pound, with a jostled imagery that some critics have labeled incoherent. Others categorize such "incoherency" as a legitimate postmodern approach to writing, most specifically displayed in Ondaatje's extension and mixing of genres. This "collage" approach allows him to combine fragmented documentary information with narrative and lyric, as in *the man with seven toes* and *The Collected Works of Billy the Kid*, permitting a separation from lyric

(AP/Wide World Photos)

subjectivity through the blending of several points of view. Ondaatje investigates the modernist romantic figure of the artist as self-destructive, without becoming self-destructive himself. Barbour also mentions the poet's move toward postcolonialism with works such as *In the Skin of a Lion*, even though Ondaatje declared himself uninterested in public politics.

THE COLLECTED WORKS OF BILLY THE KID

In *The Collected Works of Billy the Kid*, Ondaatje synthesizes fact with legend in a fictional "journey into the mind" of the notorious historical figure William Bonney, known as Billy the Kid. The work's style may confuse readers accustomed to the traditional linear storytelling approach. A familiarity with the common postmodern use of collage, or a mixing of times and narratives, will aid readers in adjusting to the nontraditional writing. Ondaatje moves in and out of time, leaving gaps in his narrative, revising the traditional Western while rewriting the Old West and Billy's character. Eventually the work makes obvious the crucial nature of these narrative gaps. William Bonney's biography is so well known that Ondaatje remains confident of his readers' capability to fill in any breaks in his particular retelling of the historical "facts." Whatever readers make of the book, it remains one of the most frequently interpreted Canadian works.

Most critics take a thematic approach to the work, focusing on the opposition between Billy the Kid and Sheriff Pat Garrett. Seen as dichotomous figures, they may represent life versus death, chaos versus order, creation versus destruction. However, these figures should not be reduced to a simple binary opposition of good and evil, although their contradictory relationship may be seen as the cause of Billy's self-destructive behavior. Also, the work remains too complicated to be classified in mythic terms of the hero's, or, in this case, the antihero's, quest for identity through pursuit of a father figure. While the traditional hero often metaphorically "kills" his father in order to be "born" his own person, in Ondaatje's (and history's) ironic twist on that myth, the father-figure (Pat Garrett) kills the son, literally shooting Billy dead. Some might see that act as the only manner by which the dichotomy represented by Billy's

life can be resolved. The almost immediate surfacing of a theme of detachment offers readers a focal point for Billy and his bizarre conceptions of violence and the grotesque. To the gunslinger, killing remains a profession; he detaches himself by viewing violence in a poetic manner. According to some, Billy represents the dual aspects of outlaw and artist inherent in Ondaatje himself.

Using a 1926 account by Walter Noble Burns, *The Saga of Billy the Kid*, on which to base the documentary aspects of his book, Ondaatje also adopts Burns's approach toward Billy as more hero than outlaw. Ondaatje begins with his hero's death as preliminary to the creating of his life, suggesting an existence resembling a phoenix rising from the ashes for a man whose legend began with the bullet that ended his life. Billy's narrative voice hints at the difficult task that awaits the reader when he refers early on to his story as a "maze." The widely varying classifications of the work's form as poem, docudrama, fiction, and prose poem demonstrate the reader's implication in the text. Each individual brings an interpretation to a story already well known, an interpretation that revolves more on the manner of the story's telling than on the matter of the story itself. Thus, Ondaatje involves his audience in the creation of the work.

Readers must pay equal attention to the two storytellers present here—Billy and Ondaatje. Though Billy tells of a relationship with Miss Angela Dickinson of Tucson, no such person exists in historical accounts. However, one of Ondaatje's favorite actresses bears that name. The act of acting may be emphasized simply to keep readers focused on the dramatic license all writers assume. Angela represents the sexual "bad girl," versus the work's other female figure, Sallie Chisum, a true historical figure, the "good girl" of Ondaatje's version. In this manner the author supplies the balance to his story that readers desire, while he subverts the truth readers may demand from his saga.

The book opens with an empty space that is labeled a photo, suggesting that Billy the Kid cannot be fixed in space and time. That Billy gives an account of himself *following* his announced death, when he no longer exists as a corporeal reality, suggests the difficulty readers encounter in trying to affix to him a certain identity. As Barbour points out, the character questions the accounts of his life and death, particularly pertaining to the violence in which he engages. When Billy asks the question of his readers, "Was there a source for all this?," his language insists that readers view at least two meanings for the term "source." First, "source" refers to that within Billy that supports his actions; second, it refers to that account on which the reader depends for the judgments that he or she, and history, will pass on Billy. Billy's question promotes the postmodern interrogation of history as truth versus storytelling that remains contingent on circumstance and subjectivity. The book's final scene remains true to the entire account, offering gruesome and gripping imagery of life and death (Billy's) but no explanation of either. The only thing of which readers remain confident is Billy's departure from a body that defies identification.

THE ENGLISH PATIENT

The English Patient offers readers a collection of fragmented tales interwoven to form a narrative at once richly artistic and representational. Reflecting Ondaatje's lifelong fascination with history, the novel focuses on the end of World War II, a conflict solved by a hydrogen bomb, called by Ondaatje a *deus ex machina* for his generation and a major turning point for humanity. Two of the novel's four main characters—Hana, the nurse, and Caravaggio, a thief-turned-spy—are Canadians whom Ondaatje carries over from his previous novel *In the Skin of a Lion*. The other two characters are Hana's badly burned patient, a pilot named Almasy who Caravaggio feels might be responsible for the loss of parts of both of Caravaggio's hands in a war mission, and a young Sikh soldier in the British Army, Kirpal Singh (Kip). The four come together in a deserted Italian villa that serves as an army hospital.

Despite the time and geographic complexity of its setting—from 1930's desert exploration to 1940's wartime, and from India to Arabia, England, Italy, and Canada—this novel remains highly accessible. Ondaatje creates characters who are familiar yet defy rational explanation. As Barbour notes, they hold onto their secretive natures, with only the resultant emotional outbursts as evidence of their existence before the villa and the war. Their intertwining relationships offer readers studies in irony and frustration, foreshadowing the lack of a comfortable plot resolution. All four characters remained obsessed—Hana with keeping her obviously terminal patient alive, the patient with relating a story of which he himself remains unsure, Kip with defusing the terror represented by hidden bombs, and Caravaggio with discovering the patient's identity. Caravaggio's obsession becomes the reader's, as the patient's story is revealed only in fragments of his own narration.

The truth in this novel becomes a confused and, at times, moot issue, its elusive quality symbolized by the illusion of heroism and justice on which war's betrayal is based. Ondaatje focuses on betrayal in general as a theme, using his familiar topic of the adulterous, destructive love affair to frame the patient's frustrated relationship with the unattainable wife of a young pilot. Ondaatje's other characters also suffer betrayal from a war ideology that destroys elements of each of their lives. Hana's love for Kip, however strong, cannot survive beyond the war that nurtures it; Kip, having risked his life multiple times to defuse explosives, becomes enraged when the Allies drop the ultimate explosives on Hiroshima; Caravaggio is betrayed by his desire to seek revenge on the patient for his torture, only to discover he feels a kinship with his perceived enemy in the end.

The novel is filled with the strong images for which its author is famous: Kip lifting a friend into the air on a rope rig so that he might inspect the fabulous mosaics of a church ceiling, the black-charred body of the once-handsome Almasy, Hana's playing of a piano that might at any moment detonate hidden explosives, Caravaggio's sneaking naked into a room where two lovers lie. However, the images project a momentary existence that quickly fades. Ondaatje's fragmented glimpses into his characters' lives are of the most intimate, and the most fragile, nature. While Hana achieves some redemption, the novel's ending will leave some readers agreeing with one critic's description of the work as a "journey without maps," a road leading nowhere.

Virginia Brackett

OTHER MAJOR WORKS

POETRY: *The Dainty Monsters*, 1967; *the man with seven toes*, 1969; *Rat Jelly*, 1973; *There's a Trick with a Knife I'm Learning to Do: Poems, 1963-1978*, 1979; *The Cinnamon Peeler: Selected Poems*, 1991; *Handwriting*, 2000.

NONFICTION: *Running in the Family*, 1982.

EDITED TEXTS: *The Long Poem Anthology*, 1979; *The Faber Book of Contemporary Canadian Short Stories*, 1990; *From Ink Lake: Canadian Stories*, 1990.

BIBLIOGRAPHY

Barbour, Douglas. *Michael Ondaatje*. New York: Twayne, 1993. Barbour discusses each of Ondaatje's works, up to *The English Patient*, illuminating the works' influences. Ondaatje's penchant for the application of brilliant postmodern effects to what otherwise might be simply documentary becomes a focus for Barbour, as do Ondaatje's early works produced in the late-modernist tradition. Selected bibliography and chronology of Odaatje's life and accomplishments are included.

Clarke, George Elliott. "Michael Ondaatje and the Production of Myth." *Studies in Canadian Literature* 16, no. 1 (1991): 1-21. Clarke offers an interpretation of the idea of myth that he then applies to Ondaatje's works from *The Dainty Monsters* to *Secular Love*.

Jewinski, Ed. *Michael Ondaatje: Express Yourself Beautifully*. Toronto: ECW Press, 1994. Depending for a good part of his information on interviews with Ondaatje's ex-wife, Kim, and the writings of his brother, Christopher, Jewinski liberally peppers his biography with photographs and personal anecdotes. He believes Ondaatje's elusiveness is based on a desire to maintain privacy.

Mundwiler, Leslie. *Michael Ondaatje: Word, Image, Imagination*. Vancouver: Talonbooks, 1984. Mundwiler considers Ondaatje's works through *Running in the Family* as applying a phenomenological and political framework. A helpful seven-point definition of modernism is included.

Solecki, Sam, ed. *Spider Blues: Essays on Michael Ondaatje*. Montreal: Vehicule Press, 1985. This collection of essays from the 1970's and the 1980's includes, among others, Susan Glickman's consideration of the romantic code in Ondaatje's writings, Linda Hutcheon's focus on postmodern issues in Ondaatje's longer works, Travis Lane's psychoanalytic reading of *the man with seven toes*, and Sheila Watson's consideration of Ondaatje's use of violence in relation to precepts of modernist art.

GEORGE ORWELL
Eric Arthur Blair

Born: Motihari, India; June 25, 1903
Died: London, England; January 21, 1950

PRINCIPAL LONG FICTION

Burmese Days, 1934
A Clergyman's Daughter, 1935
Keep the Aspidistra Flying, 1936
Coming Up for Air, 1939
Animal Farm, 1945
Nineteen Eighty-Four, 1949

OTHER LITERARY FORMS

Since the mid-1940's, George Orwell has been considered one of the world's premier essayists. Combining reportage, the polemical essay, fictional techniques, and refracted autobiographical detail, his works defy precise generic definition. Orwell's numerous nonfiction works have been compiled in *The Collected Essays, Journalism, and Letters of George Orwell* (1968), edited by Sonia Orwell and Ian Angus.

ACHIEVEMENTS

Although Orwell is widely recognized as one of the best essayists of the twentieth century, his reputation as a novelist rests almost entirely on two works: the political allegory *Animal Farm* and the dystopian *Nineteen Eighty-Four*. Both have been translated into so many other languages and have been so widely read that the adjective "Orwellian" has international currency, synonymous with the "ghastly political future," as Bernard Crick has pointed out (*George Orwell: A Life*, 1980). Indeed, Jeffrey Meyers is convinced that Orwell, the writer of essays, political tracts, and fiction, "is more widely read than perhaps any other serious writer of the twentieth-century" (*A Reader's Guide to George Orwell*, 1975).

BIOGRAPHY

George Orwell was born Eric Arthur Blair, the son of Richard Walmesley Blair and Ida (Limouzin) Blair. Orwell was born in India and lived there for four years, until his father moved the family back to England, to a small house named "Nutshell" in Henley-on-Thames. After a short leave, Orwell's father returned alone to India, leaving his wife and children in England and rejoining them later, upon his retirement. With his father's return, Orwell, like most male members of the upper middle class, was sent away to boarding school, St. Cyprian's, located at Eastbourne on the Sussex Coast. After several miserable years, as Orwell described them in his autobiographical *Such, Such Were the Joys* (1953), he won a scholarship to Eton, the public school that would forever set him apart from the working classes about which he was so concerned during most of his adult life.

Considered rather unacademic at Eton, Orwell was graduated in December, 1921, and, after a decision not to attend the university, he applied to the India Office for the position of Imperial Police Officer. Five years in Burma, from 1922 to 1927, shaped the impressionable young man so as to make him forever sympathetic to individuals victimized by governmental bureaucracy and imperialistic power. Orwell left Burma in the summer of 1927, ostensibly on sick leave (he suffered from a lung condition most of his life). At some point early in his leave, Orwell wrote a letter of resignation to the India Office and explained to his skeptical parents that all he really wanted was to write.

In 1928, Orwell commenced a long, five-year apprenticeship as a writer, time spent as a tramp in both Paris and London, and in the writing and rewriting of

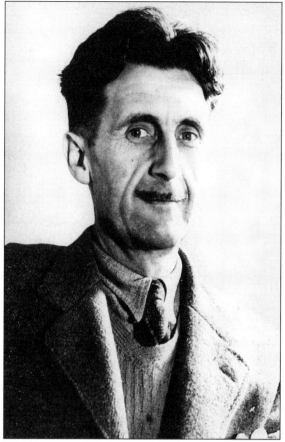

(Library of Congress)

countless manuscripts. By 1933, he had assumed the name by which he is known and had produced, in addition to at least two destroyed novels, the nonfictional *Down and Out in Paris and London* (1933) and his first novel, *Burmese Days*, published one year later.

From 1933 to 1937, Orwell continued to develop his literary talents, producing two more novels, a book about his experiences with poverty-stricken coal miners in Wigan (*The Road to Wigan Pier*, 1937), and several essays, occasional pieces, and book reviews. By the end of this period, he had also married, for the first time, and, within a year or so of that, gone to Spain. Perhaps the most singular experience of his life to date, the Spanish Civil War found Orwell on the front lines, a member of a *Partido Obrero de Unificación Marxista* (a Marxist worker's party) brigade; henceforth, Orwell passionately declared himself a fighter for "democratic Socialism" and, in that context, wrote his most famous nonfictional work, *Homage to Catalonia* (1938). After being wounded (and nearly imprisoned), Orwell escaped Spain with the help of his wife, returned to England, and continued his literary career. Within another year, his lungs still causing problems, Orwell moved to the dry climate of Morocco, where he wrote much of *Coming Up for Air.*

His fourth novel was buried under mounting war concerns and preparations. Orwell, unable to join the military because of health, became a spokesman for the British Broadcasting Corporation. During the last years of the war, Orwell finished writing *Animal Farm*, only to see it rejected by almost every major publisher in England and America. Finally brought out in August, 1945, during the last days of the Pacific War, *Animal Farm* was a work of near-perfection, making Orwell's name internationally known, so that when *Nineteen Eighty-Four* was published four years later, the world came to realize that both works would henceforth be considered literary classics, satires ranking with Thomas More's *Utopia* (1516) and Jonathan Swift's *A Tale of a Tub* (1704). Orwell's death in 1950 at the age of forty-six was a tragic loss to the world of letters and to the larger world with which he always kept in touch.

ANALYSIS

Excepting *Animal Farm*, most critics view George Orwell's fictions as aesthetically flawed creations, the work of a political thinker whose artistry was subordinate to his intensely didactic, partisan passions. This reaction to Orwell's novels was generally promoted posthumously, since his fiction in the 1930's was often ignored by the larger reading public and panned by those reviewers who did pick up one of his books. The early academic critics—up to the late 1960's—were often Orwell's personal friends or acquaintances, who tended to see his early novels as conventionally realistic and strongly autobiographical. Even his masterpieces, *Animal Farm* and *Nineteen Eighty-Four*, were viewed as formally undistinguished, however powerful their message. It was not until the second generation of critics began looking

at Orwell's fiction that a more balanced assessment was possible.

BURMESE DAYS

Orwell's first published novel, *Burmese Days*, concerns the life of John Flory, an English policeman in Burma during the early 1920's. The plot is fairly straightforward. After a lengthy introduction to Flory's personality and daily life, Orwell dramatizes him as a man blemished with a physical stigma, a birthmark, and puzzled by moral dilemma—how to deal with the increasingly rebellious natives, to whom he is secretly sympathetic but against whom he must wield the club of imperialistic authority. In the middle of this dilemma, Elizabeth arrives, a young English woman who is fresh faced but decidedly a traditional "burra memsahib." Flory attempts to win both her heart and mind—much to the dismay of his Burmese mistress, Ma Hla May—and succeeds in doing neither, even though he manages to half-succeed in proposing marriage during an earthquake. With a mind too closed to anything not properly British, and a heart only to be won by someone very English, Elizabeth forgets Flory's attentions with the arrival of Verrall, an English military policeman, who will in turn reject her after his billet is completed. A humble Flory waits for Elizabeth, and after Verrall has left takes her to church services, confident that he has outlasted his rival. Unfortunately, Flory is humiliated by Ma Hla May, is repulsed yet again by Elizabeth, and, in a mood of despair, commits suicide, killing both his dog and himself.

Burmese Days is interesting for its accurate psychological portrayal of a man trapped between two worlds: loving England, yet hating English imperialistic politics; loving and hating the subject people, the Burmese, yet fascinated by their culture and the beauty of their environment. Flory is strangely sympathetic to their struggle for independence while doing everything possible to keep it in check.

In such a world, Flory is emphatically not meant to be a sympathetic character, but rather a victim of the very political order he has sworn to uphold. In effect, Orwell has laid a trap for the unwary reader. Too close an identification with Flory, too intense a desire to have him succeed in marrying Elizabeth—an unholy alliance of imperialistic Englishwoman and revolutionary, thinking pariah—will prevent the reader from recognizing the irreconcilable contradictions inherent in the British presence in Burma.

COMING UP FOR AIR

Orwell's fourth published novel, *Coming Up for Air*, was written in Marrakesh, Morocco, shortly after he had recovered from yet another bout with tubercular lesions of the lungs. Although the novel sold moderately well for the time (a first printing, according to Bernard Crick, of two thousand copies and a second printing of one thousand), many critics were vaguely condescending toward the hero, George Bowling, a middle-class insurance salesman who longs for the golden country of the past while simultaneously dreading the horrors of a second world war, then only months away. Many of the themes more fully developed in *Nineteen Eighty-Four* find their initial expression in Orwell's last conventional novel, set before the outbreak of the devastation that the next six years would bring.

Coming Up for Air is set in London during the late 1930's; Orwell employs a first-person narrative to describe the life of George Bowling, a middle-aged, middle-class salesman, whose first set of false teeth marks a major milestone in his life. Musing in front of a mirror while he prepares for work one morning, George's mind wanders back to the past, the golden England of thirty years earlier when he was growing up. As he goes about his day, disgusted with all the evidence of modern life in front of him—the casual brutalities, the tasteless food, the bombers overhead—George forms a plan to return to Lower Binfield, his childhood home, and, by extension, the simple life he had once led. Unfortunately, his return only confirms the all-pervasive slovenliness of the modern world: Lower Binfield has been swallowed by a sprawling suburb, his adolescent sweetheart has become a frowsy old married woman (she is all of two years older than he), and the fishing hole (once filled with huge finny dreams) has been emptied of water and filled with trash. Shocked and completely disenchanted, Bowling makes plans to get at least a relaxing few days from the trip when a bomber accidentally drops a bomb close by, killing and wounding

several people. In thorough disgust, Bowling packs, leaves, and returns home to face his wife, who has somehow found out where he has gone, although his motives for going will be forever incomprehensible to her.

A plot summary of the novel fails to do justice to the subtle tonal shifts and complicated psychological changes Orwell employs in presenting his portrait of the average man waiting for the apocalypse. Orwell has used the ancient theme of the double (or *Doppelgänger*) to illustrate the self-fragmentation of European man prior to the outbreak of the war. George Bowling is divided into two "selves." Tubby is the outwardly fat, insensitive insurance tout who is able to function successfully in a fast-paced, competitive world that would eat up less hardened personalities, but his character can only survive at the cost of any sort of satisfying inner life. Georgie, on the other hand, would be lost in the modern rat race and so is protected by Tubby; nevertheless, Georgie can give expression to the memories, the sensitivities, the love for natural pleasures that Tubby (and George Bowling) would have to forgo to remain functional. Thus, George Bowling devised a strategy for living both materially successfully and psychologically well in the modern world, doing so by splitting his identity into Tubby and Georgie. *Coming Up for Air* details the ongoing dialogue between these two "selves"—a conversation which reflects the strains of modern living as well as any other novelist has done in the twentieth century.

Furthermore, Orwell has modified the literary conventions of the *Doppelgänger* to suit his own needs. Whereas the death of one-half of the double usually means the destruction, ultimately, of both, Orwell has Tubby live on after Georgie is symbolically destroyed by the bombing plane. The tonal change at this point, rather like the tonal change in Joseph Heller's *Catch-22* (1961) with the death of Kid Sampson, shows the reader the world that Orwell envisioned between 1938 and 1939, one horrible enough to prevent total escape even by death. It is, however, typically Orwellian that however horrible human bondage can make the cultural world, nature, of which humankind is a part, has enough ebullient energy to wait out any social mess—

a wait without immediate hope, without idols, but also without hopeless despair. George Bowling leaves Lower Binfield, returning to his scold of a wife, Hilda; to the everlasting round of bills, worries, war clouds on the horizon, and a death-in-life without Georgie; but, as the novel's epigraph states, "He's dead, but he won't lie down."

ANIMAL FARM

Animal Farm is one of those rare books before which the critic lays down his pen. As a self-contained "fairy story," the book can be read and understood by children not old enough to pronounce most of the words in an average junior high school history text. As a political satire, *Animal Farm* can be highly appreciated by those who actually lived through the terrible days of World War II. As an allegory concerned with the limitations and abuses of political power, the novel has been pored over eagerly by several generations of readers.

The novel is built around historical events in the Soviet Union, from before the October Revolution to the end of World War II; it does this by using the frame of reference of animals in a farmyard, the Manor Farm, owned by a Mr. Jones. Drunk most of the time and, like Czar Nicholas of Russia in the second decade of the twentieth century, out of touch with the governed, Jones neglects his farm (allegorically representing the Soviet Union, or by extension, almost any oppressed country), causing much discontent and resentment among his animals. One day, after Jones does his nightly rounds, Major, an imposing pig (V. I. Lenin), tells the other animals of a dream he has had concerning theories about the way they have been living. Animals have been exploited by Mr. Jones and humankind generally, but Major has dreamed of a time when they will throw over their yokes and live free, sharing equally both the profits and the hazards of their work. Major teaches the animals the words to a song, "Beasts of England" (The Internationale), and tells them to look to the future and the betterment of all animals; three days later he dies.

The smartest of the animals, the pigs, are aroused by his speech and by the song; they secretly learn to read and write, developing a philosophical system called animalism (Communism, Bolshevism) whose principles are taught to all the animals. When Jones forgets one day to feed them (as Russians starved near the end of their involvement in World War I), the animals revolt spontaneously, driving out Jones, his wife (Russian nobility), and Moses, the raven (the Russian Orthodox Church). The animals rejoice, feeling a sense of camaraderie and *esprit de corps*, and set about to build a new life.

The pigs, however, by taking on the responsibility of organization, also take over certain decision-making processes—as well as all the milk and apples; in fact, Orwell has himself stated that the first sign of corruption, the taking of the cow's milk, led to the inevitable destruction of everything else. Two pigs in particular, Snowball (Leon Trotsky) and Napoleon (Joseph Stalin), argue constantly, while a third, Squealer (*Pravda*, Tass) appears more than happy to endorse any course of action with his adroit use of language and his physical habit of skipping from side to side as he speaks. After changing the name from Manor Farm to Animal Farm, the pigs paint on the the side of the barn the seven commandments of animalism, the most important being: "All animals are equal." Meanwhile, Napoleon has been privately raising puppies born on the farm after the overthrow of Jones, puppies that develop into savage attack dogs (secret police, People's Commissariat of Internal Affairs [NKVD]); with these, he will one day drive off the farm all of his personal enemies, especially the brilliant theoretician, Snowball. Also soon to be lost to Animal Farm is Mollie (the bourgeoisie), who shows up at Pilkingtons (the West, England).

At this point, the work becomes more difficult, the pigs assume practical control, and the arguments become more intense. Even though Benjamin, the donkey (Tolstoyan intellectuals), remains cynical about the supposed heaven on earth, Boxer, the horse (the peasantry), vows to work harder; nevertheless, the animals continue to lose their spirit and cohesiveness until attacked by Farmer Jones, who tries to regain the Farm. Because of Snowball's brilliant strategy, Jones is driven off in what is thereafter called the Battle of the Cowshed (the Civil War).

Following the victory celebration, Snowball and Napoleon move toward a decisive parting: The former wants to move full speed ahead with the building of the windmill (permanent revolution), while the latter thinks the most important task immediately ahead is the increase in food production (develop socialism in Russia first). After much debate and just before what could be an affirmative vote for Snowball's policies, Napoleon unleashes his secretly kept dogs on his rival, chasing him out of Animal Farm forever. Henceforth, the unchallenged leader abolishes Sunday meetings, increasingly changes rules at will, and even announces that the building of the windmill was his idea.

The animals continue to work hard, still believing that they are working for themselves. The changes Napoleon institutes, however, are so at variance with the initial rules of Animal Farm, and life gets to be so much drudgery, that no one has the memory to recall the ideals of the past, nor the energy to change the present—even if memories were sound.

Very soon, life at Animal Farm seems indistinguishable from the life the animals led at Manor Farm. Orwell is not so much ultimately pessimistic as he is realistically moral: Institutionalized hierarchy begets privilege, which begets corruption of power. The first mistake of the animals was to give over their right to decide who got the the milk and apples. Lord Action's famous statement could not be more appropriate: "Power tends to corrupt; absolute power corrupts absolutely."

NINETEEN EIGHTY-FOUR

Nineteen Eighty-Four is Orwell's most famous work. As a fantasy set in the future, the novel has terrified readers for more than thirty years—frightened them into facing the prospect of the ultimate tyranny: mind control. As a parody of conditions in postwar England, it is, as Anthony Burgess has argued in *1985* (1978), a droll, rather Swiftean exaggeration of then current trends straining the social and political fabric of British culture. As a critique of the way in which human beings construct their social reality, the novel has so affected the modern world that much of its language (like that of its predecessor, *Animal Farm*) has entered into the everyday language of English-speaking peoples everywhere: *doublethink, newspeak, thoughtcrime,* and *Big Brother.* Bernard Crick argues that the novel is intimately related to *Animal Farm*—more so than most critics have hitherto acknowledged—and that both works convey Orwell's most important message: Liberty means telling people what they do not want to hear. If the vehicle for the telling gets corrupted, then the message itself will always be corrupted, garbled; finally, the very thoughts which led to the utterances in the first place will be shackled, constrained not only from the outside but also from the inside. To think clearly, to speak openly and precisely, was a heritage Englishmen received from their glorious past; it was a legacy so easily lost that it needed to be guarded fiercely, lest those who promulgated ideologies of right or left took away what had been won with such difficulty. That was where the danger lay, with those who practiced the "smelly little orthodoxies" that are still "contending for our souls."

The story begins with a man named Winston Smith who is hurrying home on a cold, windy April day as the clocks are striking thirteen. With this ominous beginning, the reader is quickly plunged into a gritty, decaying world where the political order so dominates everyday life that independent thought is a crime, love is forbidden, and language seems to say the opposite of what one has normally come to expect. As Winston's daily life unfolds, the reader quickly learns that the whole world has been divided into three geographical areas: Oceania, Eurasia, and Eastasia. All are engaged in perpetual warfare with one or both of the others, not for territorial or religious reasons but primarily for social control. At some point, atomic warfare had made total war unthinkable, yet it suits the political leaders of Oceania (the same is also true of the other two political areas) to keep the population in a general state of anxiety about foreign attack. Under the guise of national concern, Oceania's leaders keep the population under their collective thumb by the use of propaganda (from the Ministry of Truth), by outright, brutally applied force (from the Ministry of Love), by eternally short rations (Ministry of Plenty), and by the waging of perpetual war (Ministry of Peace). The ruling elite, called the Inner Party, makes up only two percent of the population; the Outer Party, the next thirteen percent. The remainder, some eighty-five percent of the population, are called Proles, the oppressed masses.

Winston, a member of the Outer Party, has been disturbed by strange thoughts of late, and one day he purchases a small, bound volume of blank paper, a diary where he can record his most private thoughts without being observed by the omnipresent telescreen, manned by members of the Thought Police. In his diary, he records his first thought: "Down with Big Brother!" To compound such a heinous thoughtcrime, he begins a liaison with a pretty young woman, a member of the Anti-Sex League, named Julia. After their affair has progressed for some time, they are contacted by a man named O'Brien, who enlists their aid in combating Big Brother by joining a group called the Brotherhood. O'Brien gives Winston a book, written by a man named Emannuel Goldstein, called *The Theory and Practice of Oligarchical Collectivism*. Having made love to Julia in a room rented from an old Prole (secretly a member of the Thought Police), Winston begins reading to her from Goldstein's book, actually an exposition of the theory that Orwell has used to construct *Nineteen Eighty-Four*.

Although Winston is fascinated, Julia, a rebel from the waist down only, falls asleep, and, after a while, so does Winston. They awake many hours later, are captured by the Thought Police, who apparently knew of their hideaway from the first, and are taken to rooms in the Ministry of Love. There, they find that O'Brien is in reality a member of the Thought Police; he alternately tortures and debates with Winston, trying to convince him that he must love Big Brother.

When torture fails, Winston is taken to Room 101, where he will be subjected to that which he fears most—in his case, rats. He gives in, begs them to "do it to Julia," and is ultimately convinced that he loves Big Brother. The novel ends as Winston, having exchanged mutual conversations of betrayal with Julia, sits at the Chestnut Café, drinking Victory Gin, completely brainwashed and committed to Big Brother.

Much has been said about the ultimate pessimism of *Nineteen Eighty-Four* being related to Orwell's fatal illness, which he fought unsuccessfully during the composition of the novel. If, however, one thinks of Orwell's fiction less in biographical terms and more in relation to artistic intention, then such a conclusion could be subject to argument. Although the novel ends with Winston in what Northrop Frye calls the sixth level of irony, unrelieved bondage, one should draw a distinction, as Orwell does in his other writings (most notably in the essay "A Good Word for the Vicar of Bray"), between man's actions as a cultural being and his activities as a creature of planet Earth, a natural being.

As a political creature, man and his purely cultural institutions could, Orwell believes, develop a world such as the one portrayed in *Nineteen Eighty-Four*. As a biological resident of the planet Earth, however, this would be impossible. Humankind never displays his hubris more graphically than does O'Brien in his speech about the party's supposed control of nature. In Orwell's view, man will never fully control nature, because man is only a part of that which he wishes to control. The great chestnut tree blossoming over Winston and his degeneration as a free being is Orwell's symbol indicating that the natural world can outlast man's cultural and political aberrations. "The planting of a tree," says Orwell, "if [it] takes root . . . will far outlive the visible effect of any of your other actions, good or evil." If there is hope for Oceania in the Proles, perhaps it is because they are instinctively closer to the natural world symbolized by the chestnut tree. Nevertheless, whether one thinks there is any hope for the people of that world or not, their existence has served as a warning to the larger world: The price of the right to tell people what they do not want to hear is never too high to pay.

John V. Knapp

OTHER MAJOR WORKS

NONFICTION: *Down and Out in Paris and London*, 1933; *The Road to Wigan Pier*, 1937; *Homage to Catalonia*, 1938; *Inside the Whale and Other Essays*, 1940; *The Lion and the Unicorn*, 1941; *Critical Es-*

says, 1946 (published in the U.S. as *Dickens, Dali, and Others*); *Shooting an Elephant and Other Essays*, 1950; *Such, Such Were the Joys*, 1953; *The Collected Essays, Journalism, and Letters of George Orwell*, 1968 (4 volumes; Sonia Orwell and Ian Angus, editors); *Orwell: The War Commentaries*, 1986.

MISCELLANEOUS: *Orwell: The Lost Writings*, 1985.

BIBLIOGRAPHY

Bloom, Harold, ed. *George Orwell*. New York: Chelsea House, 1987. This compilation includes thirteen articles from leading critics and scholars which deal for the most part with major themes and well-known novels. A short bibliography and chronology are also included.

Crick, Bernard. *George Orwell: A Life*. Boston: Little, Brown, 1980. The most important full-scale effort so far, considering all phases of Orwell's career and pointing out some odd contrasts and anomalies that lay beneath what was outwardly very much a private life. The first biography to benefit from unlimited rights of quotation from Orwell's works held under copyright. Based upon extensive use of the writer's archives and other manuscript sources, as well as numerous publications.

Davison, Peter. *George Orwell: A Literary Life*. New York: St. Martin's Press, 1996. This book follows the course of Orwell's career as a writer. Although it does contain background chapters explaining his origins, it is chiefly concerned with his literary influences and relationships, including those with his publishers and editors. Davison served as the editor of *The Complete Works of George Orwell*, an experience that makes him particularly suited to the task of writing a literary biography that is something other than the usual "life and works."

Gardner, Averil. *George Orwell*. Boston: Twayne, 1987. This interesting and sensible summary treatment of Orwell's career and literary contributions takes note of areas where interpretive controversies have arisen. The chronology and the annotated selected bibliography are also useful.

Holderness, Graham, Bryan Loughrey, Nahem Yousaf, eds. *George Orwell*. New York: St. Martin's Press, 1998. Essays on Orwell's novels; his use of allegory; his politics; his handling of form, character, and theme; and his view of England. Includes a bibliography.

Reilly, Patrick. *"Nineteen Eighty-Four": Past, Present, and Future*. Boston: Twayne, 1989. This spirited defense of Orwell's last novel upholds his conceptions against the claims of modern detractors. Contains a detailed chronology and an annotated bibliography. Reilly also wrote an earlier critical study of Orwell's fiction, *George Orwell: The Age's Adversary* (New York: St. Martin's Press, 1986).

Rodden, John. *The Politics of Literary Reputation: The Making and Claiming of "St. George" Orwell*. New York: Oxford University Press, 1989. Essentially a study of publications about Orwell rather than of the writer himself. Points to the seemingly ubiquitous impact of phrases and concepts associated with his ideas, many of which have been used in recent contexts that Orwell himself scarcely could have foreseen. The breadth of Rodden's research, in more obscure newspapers and journals, is impressive.

Sandison, Alan. *George Orwell After "Nineteen Eighty-Four."* London: Macmillan, 1986. This interpretive effort, based on an earlier work, regards Orwell's writings as a reflection of a long intellectual tradition of religious and philosophical individualism. A lengthy postscript presents Sandison's views on other works about Orwell.

Sheldon, Michael. *Orwell: The Authorized Biography*. New York: HarperCollins, 1991. A major biography, with extensive notes and bibliography.

Slater, Ian. *Orwell: The Road to Airstrip One*. New York: W. W. Norton, 1985. This attempt to trace the events of Orwell's life by way of his major works becomes slightly awkward in places but also reaches some interesting conclusions on matters of politics and literature.

Stansky, Peter, and William Abrahams. *Orwell: The Transformation*. London: Constable, 1979. Deals with Orwell's work through his period of combat service in the Spanish Civil War, discussing the origins of five early works. Concludes that Or-

middle of the country, far from coasts and foreign dangers.

His idol becomes the "Dual Curriculum," a mixture of Jewish and non-Jewish culture that finds a small, fashionable following but which to Ozick represents assimilation killing the roots of culture: "[W]hen a Jew becomes a secular person he is no longer a Jew." Brill's escape into dullness continues for years, but it is finally interrupted by the introduction of Hesther Lilt, a brilliant and aggressive intellectual. She is a self-described "imagistic linguistic logician" who enters her daughter, Beulah, in his school. Hesther fascinates Brill and reminds him of his many compromises. He is particularly obsessed with the relationship between mother and daughter.

Beulah is an ordinary child without any of the spark shown by her mother. How disappointed the mother must be, Brill thinks. In a central conversation, he accuses Hesther of failing her daughter because she lacks a maternal instinct. In return, she tells him that she is "nothing but maternal" and that he has stopped too soon in maintaining his hope for Beulah. Her obsession with Beulah's development is in fact her idol, and it finally cannibalizes her as Brill's idol has cannibalized him.

Brill, freed from his obsession with Hesther, marries another woman, fathers a son, and sinks into a stupor of boredom and frustration. One day years later he sees Beulah being interviewed on television. In a startling switch of personality, she has become a fashionable avant-garde artist. She publicly demeans her mother and ridicules her education at his school as meaningless. Hesther has accomplished the creation of her idol at the cost of destroying her relationship with her daughter. Brill's son, Nephali, meanwhile, seems enormously talented, a prodigy, everything Brill's idol-worshipping heart could have wished. As he develops into manhood, however, he becomes a mediocrity, "a business major at the University of Miami," showing none of his early promise. The end of Brill's life is a coma of boredom, his having failed to meet life in its immediacy.

THE MESSIAH OF STOCKHOLM

The Messiah of Stockholm further examines these themes in an entirely different background. Lars An-

demening, a Polish refugee who has taken a Swedish name and who supports himself as a once-a-week book reviewer, believes himself to be the son of Bruno Schulz, a Polish Jewish writer and victim of the Holocaust with a phantasmagorical and prophetic style. Lars has no proof whatsoever of his identity, only his dreams and conjectures from Schulz's work. He seizes upon rumors of a lost manuscript by Schulz, *The Messiah*, and devotes his life to finding it. His quest leads him to Heidi, the proprietor of a bookstore, and Dr. Eklund, her shadowy husband, who is "an authority on texts." They too are refugees with an uncertain background, and it is uncertain why they should they bother with the penniless and apparently deluded Lars. The mystery deepens when Adela, a woman representing herself as Schulz's daughter, appears with a manuscript she claims to be that of the *The Messiah* in Schulz's own hand.

Dr. Eklund pronounces the text authentic, and Lars is confronted with a reality that lays waste the fragile structure of his fantasies. The text itself is a dreamscape of Schulz's hometown of Drohobycz, now emptied of people and dominated only by idols who have no one left to worship them. Finally the idols themselves are destroyed by a small bird carrying a bit of hay from the synagogue which had been slept on by a saintly Jew. The text, therefore, declares the fallacy of the idolatry of which Lars has been guilty.

Dr. Eklund urges Lars to use his newspaper column to introduce this literary discovery. Lars, however, denied his illusions and his special status in respect to Schulz, accuses Eklund and Adela of attempting a literary hoax—the actual truth about the manuscript hangs rather ambiguously. Lars burns the manuscript, figuratively burning the idolatrous dream out of his life. No longer does he see his father's eye peering down on him in his sleep. As did Joseph Brill before him, he sinks into a mediocrity without vision. His newspaper column, now devoted to popular writers instead of middle European visionaries, becomes a huge success. On a direct level, the novel seems to illustrate the truth of the Second Commandment. However, questions remain—notably, has Lars fared better or worse without his illusions?

THE PUTTERMESSER PAPERS

The Puttermesser Papers was developed into a novel from two stories about Ruth Puttermesser (her name means *butter knife*) from Ozick's *Levitations: Five Fictions*. Though the supernatural and the improbable have been common elements in her fiction, Ozick now ventures freely into the fantastic, using material from the *Kabbala*, Jewish mystical writings dating back to the middle ages. The novel's formlessness, improbability, and swift changes of direction show an increasingly greater distance from the ideals of Henry James.

In a manner that suggests Kafka, the novel takes readers through Ruth Puttermesser's entire adult life. Initially she is a repressed, bookish woman, a lawyer and a bureaucrat in New York City's Department of Receipts and Disbursements, still living in the Bronx apartment in which she was brought up. She yearns for a Jewish identity, which her assimilated parents did not give her. She fantasizes a relationship with an imaginary Uncle Zindel and immerses herself in Hebrew and arcane Jewish lore. When she is forty-six, Ruth's regulated life is smashed into pieces. She loses her job in an unfair political maneuver; her married lover, Morris Rappoport, walks out on her; and she loses her beloved apartment to the arsonists of a changing neighborhood. Even her gums are giving way to periodontal disease.

Then a miracle happens. From the earth and water of her flower pots, combined with the sacred name of God, Ruth inadvertently creates a golem, a being whose creation ritual is described in ancient Jewish writings. The golem insists on being called Xanthippe, after the shrewish wife of Socrates, and wants to be regarded as Ruth's daughter. The story becomes wildly comic. Through the golem's power, Ruth becomes mayor of New York. The city is magically transformed into something close to paradise on earth: Gangs disappear, graffiti is erased, and civility rules the streets. Xanthippe's powers turn to rebellion, however—the created idol, wanting to be human, demands more and more from Ruth—and the city once more decays. Ruth is compelled to return the golem to its original elements.

A major episode again illustrates the idolatry of art.

Ruth, a fervent admirer of English novelist George Eliot (the pen name of Mary Ann Evans), wishes to find a mate similar to George Lewes, Eliot's married lover, with whom Eliot had a fabled romance of powerful mutual interests. She lures Rupert Rabeeno, who reproduces the paintings of masters on postcards (a thoroughly noncreative activity) into a fascination with Eliot and Lewes. Rupert, the unimaginative duplicator, focuses instead on Johnny Cross, the man who tried to imitate Lewes after his death. Once again, Ruth's idolatrous attempts to incorporate meaning into her life lead to personal disaster. Rupert leaves her on their honeymoon in Venice—as Cross had left Eliot in the same city.

The novel ends with Ruth in heaven. She had looked forward to a time when she could live entirely in her imagination, with all eternity to seek out the pleasures that had fascinated her. However, heaven itself is a disappointment. Though everything is available, nothing sustains itself. Ruth should have relied on the texture of life being lived. Idolatry and the uninterpreted life caused her suffering despite her good will.

Bruce Olsen

OTHER MAJOR WORKS

SHORT FICTION: *The Pagan Rabbi and Other Stories*, 1971; *Bloodshed and Three Novellas*, 1976; *Levitation: Five Fictions*, 1982; *The Shawl*, 1989.

PLAY: *Blue Light*, pr. 1994 (based on *The Shawl*).

POETRY: *Epodes: First Poems*, 1992.

NONFICTION: *Art and Ardor*, 1983; *Metaphor and Memory: Essays*, 1989; *What Henry James Knew, and Other Essays on Writers*, 1993; *Portrait of the Artist as a Bad Character: and Other Essays on Writing*, 1996; *Fame and Folly: Essays*, 1996.

BIBLIOGRAPHY

Bloom, Harold, ed. *Cynthia Ozick.* New York: Chelsea House, 1986. A collection that includes several fine essays on Ozick's work; contains essays on individual works and on the Jewish nature of her writing.

Cohen, Sarah Blacher. *Cynthia Ozick's Comic Art.* Bloomington: Indiana University Press, 1995.

Though it is unintentionally comic, Cohen says, Ozick's fiction gives its readers "wry jokes on reality."

Friedman, Lawrence S. *Understanding Cynthia Ozick*. Columbia: University of South Carolina Press, 1991. Well-written, concise, and informed. Friedman's analysis is a good place to start in exploring Ozick's themes.

Kauvar, Elaine M. *Cynthia Ozick's Fiction*. Bloomington: Indiana University Press, 1993. Covers Ozick's work by examining such aspects as "The Struggle for 'Exactitude'" and "The Uses of Fantasy."

Lowin, Joseph. *Cynthia Ozick*. Boston: Twayne, 1988. Contains a biography and a good general introduction to her work.

Strandberg, Victor. *Greek Mind/Jewish Soul*. Madison: University of Wisconsin Press, 1994. A scholarly work that attempts to elucidate the matrix of Ozick's thought and art.

P

BORIS PASTERNAK

Born: Moscow, Russia; February 10, 1890
Died: Peredelkino, U.S.S.R.; May 30, 1960

PRINCIPAL LONG FICTION
Doktor Zhivago, 1957 (*Doctor Zhivago*, 1958)

OTHER LITERARY FORMS

Boris Pasternak's only novel, *Doctor Zhivago*, was the final product of a creative life devoted largely to poetry. Pasternak was initially recognized as a lyric poet who synthesized Symbolist musicality and Futurist colloquialism, but after the 1917 Revolution, as he indicated in his address to the First Congress of the Union of Soviet Writers in 1934, he came to believe that poetry was in fact "pure prose in its pristine intensity." During the Stalinist purges of the 1930's and through World War II, Pasternak took refuge in the long and distinguished Russian tradition of poetic translation, and he produced outstanding versions of many classic Western dramas. Pasternak also wrote epic poems on revolutionary themes; two prose autobiographies, *Okhrannaya gramota* (1931; *A Safe-Conduct*, 1945) and *Avtobiograficheskiy ocherk* (1958; *I Remember: Sketch for an Autobiography*, 1959); short fiction, of which several sketches are early studies for his novel; and an unfinished play, *Slepaya krasavitsa* (1969; *The Blind Beauty*, 1969), which he intended as a nineteenth century prologue to *Doctor Zhivago*. By incorporating "The Poems of Yuri Zhivago" into the fabric of the novel *Doctor Zhivago*, Pasternak returned to the lyricism of his youth.

ACHIEVEMENTS

Doctor Zhivago was the first major Russian work not to be first published in the former Soviet Union. By 1959, it had already appeared in twenty-three other languages, but even though Pasternak had been chosen to receive the Nobel Prize in Literature in 1958, Soviet governmental pressure forced him to refuse it. For the brief remainder of his life, as he observed in his pain-filled lyric "The Nobel Prize," he was "caught like a beast at bay" in his homeland, one of the most tragic figures of modern literature.

Literature, particularly poetry, plays in Russian life a role almost inconceivable to Westerners. To Russians, art, politics, and morality have always been inseparable. From their ancient oral folk epics, the *byliny*, to twentieth century verse recitals and the explosion of *samizdat* (self-published) works, poetry has helped shape the Russians' responses to social and political issues. In the vein of Russia's greatest poets, Alexander Pushkin and Mikhail Lermontov, Pasternak's famous public reading in 1948 intensified both his listeners' love of poetry and their desperate yearning to witness a Russian poet challenging unreasonable governmental oppression. Pasternak's early poetry, somewhat resembling T. S. Eliot's diffi-

(CORBIS/Bettmann)

in 1944, were sympathetic renderings of dramas of doomed love that strangely foreshadowed events in Pasternak's own life. His translation in 1945 of Shakespeare's *Othello* (1604), a parable of betrayal, paralleled the unfavorable reception the official critics gave Pasternak's war poetry volume, *Zemnoy prostor* (1945; *The Vastness of Earth*, 1964).

The figure of Lara, to become the heart of *Doctor Zhivago*, appeared almost casually to Pasternak at the offices of the literary journal *Novy mir* in 1946, the year Soviet authorities undertook a massive campaign, the *zhdanovshchina* (Zhdanov era), against "decadent cosmopolitanism" in art and literature. At a meeting which Pasternak did not attend, claiming illness, Anna Akhmatova and Mikhail Zoshchenko were condemned and expelled from the Writers' Union. After meeting Olga Ivinskaya in October, Pasternak began to see her daily, and the following spring they declared their love.

The joy Pasternak and Ivinskaya shared became paradoxically their worst torment. At first, Pasternak's financial burden was eased somewhat by a contract to translate Goethe's *Faust* (1808, 1833), that archetypal vision of human striving, and after Andrei Zhdanov's death, in 1948, Pasternak received wide popular support for his public poetry readings and his translation of Shakespeare's *Henry IV* (1597-1598), a denunciation of the political principle that "might makes right." In 1949, however, he suffered the first of a long series of heart attacks, and in a government ploy to force Pasternak's recantation of positions unfavorable to the regime, Ivinskaya was arrested, held for more than one year in the Lyubyanka Prison, and sent to a Siberian labor camp because she refused to incriminate him. Appropriately enough at this time of misery, Pasternak was translating Shakespeare's *King Lear* (1605-1606).

Upon the death of Stalin in 1953 and the ensuing general amnesty, Ivinskaya was released, and Pasternak took up residence with her in Moscow. Despite his worsening physical condition, he was supporting both of their families. In 1954, the periodical *Znamia* published ten poems from *Doctor Zhivago*, and Pasternak finished the novel in the fall of 1955. He then started on *I Remember: Sketch for an Autobiography*,

which he hoped would be a preface for his collected work.

Pasternak also naïvely expected that *Doctor Zhivago* might appear in *Novy mir*, but after a complicated series of events during which the novel was rejected in the Soviet Union, it appeared in Italian in 1957. Pasternak began to translate again in 1959 after being forced to refuse the Nobel Prize, choosing Schiller's *Maria Stuart* (1800), a woman's tragedy of epic proportion. A combination of cancer, heart disease, and emotional prostration overcame him at last, and he died at Peredelkino on May 30, 1960. Less than three months later, Ivinskaya and her daughter were sentenced to a Siberian labor camp again. To this day, as Hedrick Smith noted in *The Russians* (1976), on the anniversary of Pasternak's death "scores of Muscovites . . . quietly . . . [lay] their unpretentious bouquets on his white tombstone . . . all the more meaningful an occasion because it [has] been forgotten by the state and remembered by private individuals."

ANALYSIS

Boris Pasternak worked on *Doctor Zhivago* between 1938 and 1956, when the savage circumstances within the Soviet Union permitted, but the evidence of his short fiction indicates that all of his creative life went into *Doctor Zhivago*. Incidents, characterizations, and the style of his other stories strongly resemble elements of the novel, and Ivinskaya saw in Zhenia Luvers "the Lara of the future," a sensitive portrayal of the sad lot of women, one of Pasternak's recurring themes. Nadezhda Mandelstam, the wife of Osip Mandelstam, observed that Pasternak could not proceed with the novel until the war provided "a momentarily restored sense of community" impossible during the purges of the 1930's. Pasternak's fruitless defense of Osip Mandelstam, who died in a transit camp en route to the mines of Kalyma, may also have strengthened his resolve to produce a chronicle of Russia's intelligentsia, the "children of Russia's terrible years," as they are called in *Doctor Zhivago*. It became nothing less than his sacred duty.

By 1950, when he had survived physical and emotional blows that were only the beginning of his anguish, Pasternak observed to one of his many correspondents that "love of people and gratitude to the past for its brilliance . . . a concern for repaying it with the same kind of beauty and warmth" were for him "spiritual values . . . at the foundation of taste." He gladly accepted the heavy price for his artistic and humanistic convictions: "If there is suffering anywhere, why should not my art suffer and myself with it? I am speaking of the most artistic in the artist . . . of the sacrifice without which art becomes unnecessary."

Beyond the practical sacrifices of Pasternak's own restricted life, for which political compromise might have meant considerable but soulless comfort, and even beyond the emotional sacrifice of watching friends endure hardships he could not share, Pasternak, in creating *Doctor Zhivago*, had to be reborn into a new form of artistic expression entirely new to him and to Russian literature. The technical innovations of *Doctor Zhivago*, often ignored or misunderstood, are Pasternak's chief means of voicing his major themes, art as sacrifice and its resulting spiritual redemption. In his shift from the lyric to the epic mode, in his departure from the form of the great Russian nineteenth century novels, and in his impressionistic use of symbolic coincidence, Pasternak implemented an effective new medium of fictional expression.

DOCTOR ZHIVAGO

For *Doctor Zhivago*, Pasternak deliberately abandoned the first-person narrative he had used in his earlier prose sketches for the less subjective third person, a vital transposition of emphasis by which he could develop the character of Yuri Zhivago in important directions hinted at in his laconic description of the hero, which appeared prefatory to the ten poems published in *Znamia:* "a physician, a thinking man in search [of truth], with a creative and artistic bent." Pasternak's main character, his evocation of the cultured Russian intellectual at the mercy of historical forces beyond human control, is first a physician, his title significantly used by Pasternak in the novel's name to emphasize the duty as healer and teacher that Zhivago fulfills through his personal sacrifice. "Zhivago" itself derives from the Russian verb "to live," lending irony to the opening scene of the novel, the funeral of Zhivago's mother: "'Who's being buried?'—'Zhivago' [the living one]." The name also has a wealth of religious connotations stemming from the risen Christ's question in the Orthodox Easter liturgy, "Why seek you the living [*zhivago*] among the dead?" In his search for truth, the thinking man Yuri Zhivago at first naïvely embraces revolution as the natural result of the czarist repression of the people, only gradually realizing that enforced collectivization under the Soviets means the spiritual slavery of the very souls it falsely purported to free. The truth at which Yuri Zhivago at last arrives, after his long journey through the revolutions of 1905 and 1917, the savagery of World War I and the Civil War, and the struggle for survival that faced his people during the 1920's, is the old truth of humanity's youth—that an individual can be fulfilled only by free choice in pursuing his own creativity, his own love, unhampered by political or social stricture. By viewing Zhivago through many different eyes in the major section of the novel, Pasternak can reflect with stunning accuracy the myriad beams and shadows cast by the flickering light that is a human soul.

At first glance, *Doctor Zhivago* appears to resemble the traditional Russian novel, spread over nearboundless time and space and probing uncannily into the recesses of human suffering. Its structure, however, is not panoramic but multigeneric, presenting the life of Yuri Zhivago in three discrete treatments like the movements of a great literary sonata: the discursive past, a personalized and omniscient narrative incorporating many motifs throughout the first fifteen chapters of the book, spanning the years from 1905 to 1929, and dominated by the great duet between the masculine theme of Zhivago and its feminine counterpart of Lara; the brief melodic and retrospective epilogue, chapter 16, hymning Zhivago's blessing on the future of his "holy city" and the world, his song of "the freedom of the soul" embodied in his illegitimate daughter Tania; and "The Poems of Yuri Zhivago," a lyric cycle of love and redemption in an eternal now gained by heroic self-sacrifice joined to the divine sacrifice of Christ. The musical metaphor for the novel is suggested by Pasternak's lifelong love of Frédéric Chopin, not only for his monumental music, in which Pasternak said Chopin "regarded his own life as a means of apprehending every life in the world," but also for Chopin's "wider significance," as seen in the *Études*, which teach "a theory of childhood," "an introduction to death," and "history, the *structure* [Pasternak's italics] of the universe and whatever is more remote and general than playing the piano." Pasternak especially acclaimed Chopin's ability to "utter his new statement in the old language, without examining whether it was old or new."

The gains Pasternak realized by this tripartite structure are more felt in *Doctor Zhivago* than understood, in part because of the spirit of shared suffering that Virginia Woolf claimed in "The Russian Point of View" to produce the "sense of brotherhood" that permeates all Russian literature. In *Doctor Zhivago*, however, Pasternak advanced materially beyond the nineteenth century, employing a strange and lovely novelistic structure to merge past and present and future into a timeless moment of sacrifice and renewal.

Pasternak willingly gave *Doctor Zhivago* priority over the poetry to which he had devoted so many years. Ivinskaya records his assertion, "All my life I have wanted to write prose . . . writing poetry is easier!" Pasternak's reliance in the novel on coincidence, often criticized as violating the bounds of literary verisimilitude, is an impressionistic poetic technique, assembling apparently contradictory elements into a system of symbolism so intricate that each human name, each smallest detail of nature, possesses an amazingly complex signification unfortunately closed to most English-speaking readers. The enigmatic Evgraf, for example, Zhivago's mysterious half brother, appears at crucial episodes in the novel's first section to save Yuri first from physical disaster and at last from spiritual sterility. Evgraf's name is taken from the Greek words for "well written"; he is a youth with slanted Kirghiz eyes and a Siberian reindeer garment, a shamanistic figure who may represent Zhivago's "twin in the clouds," his heaven-sent poetic creativity, not the least of whose talents enabled Zhivago to survive in spirit through his writing.

Balancing the supernatural role of Evgraf is the contrapuntal role of Lara, who has been described as "the most poeticized woman in Russian literature." Lara, brutalized in her adolescence by the pragmatic survival specialist Komarovsky, surely represents Russia at least in part, demeaned by materialism under the Romanov czars, forced into shamelessness by the revolutionaries, eventually perishing no one knows where in the Far North, yet through everything a genuinely human figure inspiring such a love in Zhivago that he can create the writings which "confirm and encourage" the feeling of "tenderness and peace" that sustains Zhivago's old friends as they read the novel's epilogue.

Lara's husband, Pasha Antipov, clearly represents the spirit of revolution, a slum boy who idealizes Marxism and becomes the killer Strelnikov, a Red commander who typifies all that is dangerously nonhuman in the new regime: "'He needs a heart in addition to his principles,' said Yuri later, 'if he is to do good.'" In one of the climactic coincidences of the novel, Zhivago "the living one" and Strelnikov "the shooter" pass a night at Varykino talking of the Lara they both love. In the morning, Zhivago finds Strelnikov's body in the snow, a suicide, with frozen drops of blood recalling the rowanberries that symbolize Lara, a folk image from ancient tradition: "I shall see you, my perfect beauty, my rowan princess, drop of my very blood." In the final symbolic meeting of Zhivago and Antipov/Strelnikov, Evgraf conducts Yuri, ill and aging, to write and die in the Moscow room where Antipov began his life with Lara, as Zhivago, outside, glimpsed through a glass darkly the candle of love that he was never to forget.

Pasternak employed "the simple everyday words of sturdy unceremonious talk" that Lara praised in her lament over Yuri's body throughout the twenty-five poems which form the last chapter of his novel, recognizing with his mighty predecessor Lermontov that "There are words whose sense is obscure or trivial—yet one cannot listen to them without a tremor." This last movement of the sonata-novel that is *Doctor Zhivago* is a cycle praising the eternal rhythms of nature so closely bound to the Russian soul and echoing the religious cycle of the Savior's death and Resurrection presented in the liturgical year. Beginning with "Hamlet," which Pasternak's friend Aleksandr Gladkov recalled hearing him recite in an epiphany impossible to repeat, the poetic cycle opens, like the church year, with the agony of a Gethsemane: "For the present, release me from the cast," the poet begs. Through the Passion of Holy Week, over "Bad Roads in Spring" and after "Summer in Town," the poet bids farewell in "August" to "the image of the world through words made manifest/ And to creativity, and to working wonders" as Russia settles into a "Winter Night." "It snowed and snowed, the whole world over," and only "a candle burned," a small flame of hope that eventually blossoms for the poet into the "Star of the Nativity," "gazing on the Maid," for Pasternak, like Zhivago, believed that all conceptions were immaculate. The poems close upon another Holy Week, the "Evil Days" of a return to the "holy city" on Palm Sunday, in which the "dark forces of the Temple/ Gave Him up to be judged by the off-scourings," and upon the vision of Mary Magdalene, perhaps modeled upon Ivinskaya (in whose presence Pasternak rewrote many of these poems, originally composed in 1946), who learns "to embrace/ The squared beam of the cross." The last of Yuri Zhivago's poems, "Garden of Gethsemane," returns the cycle to its opening, with the agony of abandonment and betrayal that culminates in the vision of the third day, when

> Even as rafts float down a river,
> So shall the centuries drift, trailing like a caravan,
> Coming for judgment, out of the dark, to me.

Although Pasternak insisted that *Doctor Zhivago* "must not be judged along theological lines," and his prime intention was always to depict the fate of the Russian intelligentsia in the first decades of the twentieth century, the mythic dimension of *Doctor Zhivago* exemplifies the endurance which the religious historian Mircea Eliade believes is humanity's only support through "the catastrophes and horrors of history." These cannot be tolerated, Eliade says, if they are at worst only the result of the liberties taken by a minority "on the stage of universal history," precisely the stage upon which Pasternak

played his vital role. In reacting against the liberties imposed by the Communist minority upon the helpless Russian people by writing *Doctor Zhivago*, Pasternak exercised what the Trappist monk and poet Thomas Merton called "the problematical quality" of his Christianity, "that it is reduced to the barest and most elementary essentials: intense awareness of all cosmic and human reality as 'life in Christ,' and the consequent plunge into love as the only dynamic and creative force which really honors this 'Life' by creating itself anew in Life's—Christ's—image." In the glorious healing lesson of *Doctor Zhivago*, that modern man's renewal lies in identification of his sufferings with those of his Savior, undistracted by selfish materialistic desire, the poet of *Doctor Zhivago* thus is "the living one" against whom godless history cannot prevail. In this remarkable novel, as Pasternak said of all art, "The man is silent, and the image speaks."

Mitzi M. Brunsdale

OTHER MAJOR WORKS

SHORT FICTION: *Rasskazy*, 1925; *Sochineniya*, 1961 (*Collected Short Prose*, 1977).

PLAY: *Slepaya krasavitsa*, pb. 1969 (*The Blind Beauty*, 1969).

POETRY: *Bliznets v tuchakh*, 1914; *Poverkh barierov*, 1917 (*Above the Barriers*, 1959); *Sestra moia zhizn'*, 1922 (*My Sister, Life*, 1964); *Temy i variatsii*, 1923 (*Themes and Variations*, 1964); *Vysokaya bolezn'*, 1924 (*High Malady*, 1958); *Carousel: Verse for Children*, 1925; *Devyatsot pyaty god*, 1926 (*The Year 1905*, 1989); *Lyutenant Shmidt*, 1927 (*Lieutenant Schmidt*, 1992); *Spektorsky*, 1931; *Vtoroye rozhdeniye*, 1932 (*Second Birth*, 1964); *Na rannikh poezdakh*, 1943 (*On Early Trains*, 1964); *Zemnoy prostor*, 1945 (*The Vastness of Earth*, 1964); *Kogda razgulyayetsa*, 1959 (*When the Skies Clear*, 1964); *The Poetry of Boris Pasternak, 1914-1960*, 1959; *The Poetry of Boris Pasternak, 1917-1959*, 1959; *Poems*, 1959; *Poems, 1955-1959*, 1960; *In the Interlude: Poems, 1945-1960*, 1962; *Fifty Poems*, 1963; *The Poems of Doctor Zhivago*, 1965; *Stikhotvoreniya i poemy*, 1965, 1976; *The Poetry of Boris Pasternak*, 1969; *Selected Poems*, 1983.

NONFICTION: *Pis'ma k gruzinskim*, n.d. (*Letters to Georgian Friends by Boris Pasternak*, 1968); *Okhrannaya gramota*, 1931 (autobiography; *A Safe-Conduct*, 1945); *Avtobiograficheskiy ocherk*, 1958 (*I Remember: Sketch for an Autobiography*, 1959); *An Essay in Autobiography*, 1959; *Essays*, 1976; *The Correspondence of Boris Pasternak and Olga Freidenberg, 1910-1954*, 1981; *Pasternak on Art and Creativity*, 1985.

DRAMA TRANSLATIONS: *Hamlet*, 1941 (of William Shakespeare); *Romeo i Juliet*, 1943 (of Shakespeare); *Antony i Cleopatra*, 1944 (of Shakespeare); *Othello*, 1945 (of Shakespeare); *King Lear*, 1949 (of Shakespeare); *Faust*, 1953 (of Johann Wolfgang von Goethe); *Maria Stuart*, 1957 (of Friedrich Schiller).

MISCELLANEOUS: *Safe Conduct: An Early Autobiography and Other Works by Boris Pasternak*, 1949; *Sochinenii*, 1961; *Vozdushnye puti: Proza raz nykh let*, 1982; *The Voice of Prose*, 1986.

BIBLIOGRAPHY

Barnes, Christopher. *Boris Pasternak: A Literary Biography, Volume One: 1890-1928*. New York: Cambridge University Press, 1990. A comprehensive biography, scholarly but also accessible.

Bowra, C. M. *The Creative Experiment*. London: Macmillan, 1949. Contains one of the classic essays on Pasternak. While Bowra concentrates on Pasternak's poetry, he provides considerable insight into the sensibility that informs Pasternak's fiction as well.

Chiaromonte, Nicola. *The Paradox of History: Stendhal, Pasternak, and Others*. London: Weidenfeld and Nicolson, 1970. A deft exploration of Pasternak's understanding of history and his handling of the theme of human freedom. Chiaromonte, one of the twentieth century's great intellectuals, provides analysis of specific scenes in *Doctor Zhivago*.

Erlich, Victor, ed. *Pasternak: A Collection of Critical Essays*. Englewood Cliffs, N.J.: Prentice Hall, 1978. Contains three essays devoted exclusively to *Doctor Zhivago*. See Erlich's introduction for an informed discussion of Pasternak's life and writing career. Includes a chronology and bibliography.

Muchnic, Helen. *Russian Writers Notes and Essays*. New York: Random House, 1971. Provides a succinct introductory essay on Pasternak's life and fiction.

Poggioli, Renato. *The Poets of Russia: 1890-1930*. Cambridge, Mass.: Harvard University Press, 1960. In spite of his book's title, Poggioli gives a detailed discussion of *Doctor Zhivago* and its place in Pasternak's career.

Rudova, Larissa. *Understanding Boris Pasternak*. Columbia, S.C.: University of South Carolina Press, 1997. A general introduction to Pasternak's work, including both his early poetry and prose and his later work; provides analyses of individual novels and stories.

Wain, John. *A House for the Truth: Critical Essays*. New York: Viking, 1972. Contains one of the classic essays on Doctor Zhivago by one of England's finest poets and critics.

WALTER PATER

Born: London, England; August 4, 1839
Died: Oxford, England; July 30, 1894

PRINCIPAL LONG FICTION

Marius the Epicurean: His Sensations and Ideas, 1885 (two volumes)
Gaston de Latour: An Unfinished Romance, 1896

OTHER LITERARY FORMS

Walter Pater is principally remembered as a critic. His most influential work, *Studies in the History of the Renaissance* (1873; revised as *The Renaissance: Studies in Art and Poetry*, 1877, 1888, 1893), decisively changed the Victorian conception of art as a vehicle for the expression of uplifting sentiments or edifying ideals. Pater, whose unnamed antagonist was John Ruskin, argued that art is preeminently concerned with the dextrous elaboration of its own sensuous ingredients. Form, color, balance, and tone: These are the elements of which art is constituted.

Hence, the imposition of a moral upon a painting, a poem, or a musical composition subverts the integrity of the work and distorts the function of criticism. The genuine critic begins with an analysis of the impression which a painting or a poem communicates and then endeavors to trace that impression to the structural elements of which the work is composed. Ultimately, as the notorious conclusion to *The Renaissance* makes clear, art is chiefly to be cherished as a means of enhancing, expanding, and enlarging the faculties of sensuous apprehension and as a catalyst in the pursuit of more varied, exquisite, and complex sensations. In the last analysis, Pater was inclined to evaluate and judge life itself as an aesthetic phenomenon.

Pater qualified this position in his later works, however, and since *Marius the Epicurean*—his one completed novel—was expressly written to revise and reevaluate the conclusion of *The Renaissance*, it is necessary to acquire some preliminary understanding of Pater's earlier and less complex point of view.

By way of preparation for *Marius the Epicurean*, Pater composed a series of stories that foreshadow the mature techniques of his novel. The best of these stories, "The Child in the House," traces the influence of a child's environment upon the formation of his sensibility and character. Here, in a statement which may be regarded as a keynote to the author's subsequent utterances, Pater expresses through the character of Florian Deleal the distinguishing quality that informs not only his own sensibility but also the sensibility of Marius and, indeed, of all his protagonists: "For with the desire of physical beauty," observes Pater of Florian, "mingled itself early the fear of death—the fear of death intensified by the desire of beauty."

Before examining the implications of this sentiment in the context of *Marius the Epicurean*, it is interesting to note that virtually all of Pater's other works—in both criticism and fiction—are meditations on the propinquity of beauty and death and on the desire that this meditation engenders in Pater to conceive of an absolute which defines itself in and gives broader significance to the sensuous flux of existence. As Pater observes in his study of Plato, "to

(Library of Congress)

realize unity in variety, to discover *cosmos*—an order that shall satisfy one's reasonable soul—below and within apparent chaos: is from first to last the continuous purpose of what we call philosophy."

In addition to *The Renaissance*, then, Pater's other works are briefly these: *Imaginary Portraits* (1887), a collection of stories that prefigure *Marius the Epicurean* in their emphasis on the aesthetic quality and philosophical repercussions of experience upon a sensitive and circumspect temperament rather than with the dramatization of experience itself; *Appreciations* (1889), a heterogeneous collection of literary criticisms that apply the principles adduced in *The Renaissance* to the examination of English and French literary figures; *Plato and Platonism* (1893), the philosophical and theoretical counterpart to *Marius the Epicurean*, which examines the respective relations between the temporal and the eternal, the relative and the absolute, the ideal and the real in the works of Plato; *Greek Studies* (1895), an examination of the myths of Dionysus and Persephone and their symbolic relation to the spirit of art; and *Miscellaneous Studies* (1895), a grouping of Pater's most important writings on figures of literary, religious, and artistic significance. Of special interest in the latter is the short essay "Diaphaneité," wherein Pater delineates those attributes that go into the making of an ideal and yet realizable humanity. Finally, *Essays from the "Guardian"* (1896) is a collection of Pater's reviews on the writers of his day.

ACHIEVEMENTS

Pater's achievement as a novelist and a critic is central to the modern vision of art. Though he was not always edified by the scandalous manner in which his disciples interpreted his message, nor gratified by the distortion of his ideas by an entire generation of aesthetes and decadents, Pater, when he is fully understood, emerges as a figure of incalculable importance in the evolution of twentieth century literature. In the first place, he did away with much of the fustian that obscured the appreciation of art in his own day, and he left a critical legacy, which extended into the present century in the works of Bernard Berenson and Roger Fry. Moreover, as Harold Bloom observes of Pater's most memorable character, "Marius, more than any fictional character of our age, is the representative modern poet as well as the representative man of literary culture who remains the only audience for that poet." As a stylist, too, Pater was wonderfully suggestive and original. Adapting the rich and ornate cadences of Ruskin to his more subtle purpose, Pater evolved a style that is the last word in delicacy, refinement, and understated eloquence. His sentences are characterized by elaborate parentheses, delicately wrought rhythms, and mannered circumlocutions—annoying to some readers—and his malleable prose matches with minute accuracy the uncertainties, doubts, and deliberations of a mind in debate with itself, a mind fastidiously alive to the full complexity of human experience and scrupulously intent upon a verbal music that, in its hesitant rhythms, remains faithful to that experience. In this regard, he clearly anticipates Marcel Proust.

It is not, however, on the level of style alone that Pater's influence has been indelible. *Marius the Epicurean*, in the role which it assigns to memory, its tone of melancholy retrospect, its analysis of a highly developed sensibility enamored of perfection yet resigned to uncertainty, anticipates, to a remarkable degree, the structural, tonal, and thematic underpinnings of Proust's novels. When one adds to this Pater's lasting influence on Oscar Wilde, James Joyce, André Gide, and William Butler Yeats—(the last of whom claimed that *Marius the Epicurean* is "the only great prose in modern English")—one is compelled to admit that Pater was one of the first major sensibilities of the modern age.

BIOGRAPHY

For a writer who was to become the subject of numerous debates and controversies regarding the tendency of his works, the quality of his influence, and the dubiety of his doctrines, Walter Horatio Pater's life seems, at first glance, a singularly colorless affair. The youngest son of a dedicated physician who died prematurely, Pater was reared in a household dominated by his sisters, his mother, and his godmother. He remained, throughout childhood, indifferent to the activities or sports of his peers, preferring to imagine a world of ceremonious gallantry and hieratic ritual. He manifested a deep attachment to the solemn devotions and sumptuous worship of the Anglican Church. A need to remain true to the irrepressible skepticism and intellectual scrupulousness of his own nature prevented him, at the last, from acting upon his early impulses and taking orders. With a temperament more than commonly inclined to self-analysis and introspection, Pater, following his matriculation at Queens College, Oxford, chose to pursue an academic career. He was elected a junior fellow at Brasenose College in 1864.

From the first, the young don was regarded with certain suspicions, "having acquired," as Humphry Ward observed, "a new and daring philosophy of his own, and a wonderful gift of style." Benjamin Jowett, the famous translator of Plato, was acutely displeased with the seemingly subversive conclusion to *The Renaissance* and successfully hindered Pater's advancement at Oxford. In defiance, however, of Jowett's reprobations, Pater continued to enjoy a steady advance in influence and reputation. Ultimately, his increased fame warranted the taking of additional rooms in London, and there, in the company of sisters and friends, Pater enjoyed the sympathy and civility which were sometimes denied him at Oxford. Modest, retiring, elusive, and enigmatic: These are the epithets that most frequently occur in contemporary portraits of Pater. It was doubtless these qualities that won him the admiration of his most famous pupil: Gerard Manley Hopkins. It is interesting to note (and much to Pater's credit) that, in the surcharged evangelical atmosphere of Oxford, where professors more often strove to win converts than to foster independence of mind, Pater was the single instructor who continued to be loyal to Hopkins after his embrace of Catholicism. Indeed, Pater's elasticity and insouciance, his careful cultivation of what John Keats called "negative capability," were as characteristic of the man as they were of the artist. Pater died as a result of a heart attack in 1894.

ANALYSIS

Walter Pater's *Marius the Epicurean* is the culminating expression of a fictional genre that began in the 1830's and continued until the turn of the century. This genre, a peculiar mixture of religious speculation and personal confession, developed almost synchronously with the assault of science against traditional Christianity, beginning with the publication, in 1832, of Sir Charles Lyell's *Principles of Geology*. Lyell's book, which exploded the biblical account of creation, was the first of several—the most famous being Charles Darwin's—that shook Western culture to its foundations. The passage of the Reform Bill, the theories of Darwin and Karl Marx, the development of the so-called "higher" criticism in the exegesis of biblical texts, the rise in population, and the spread of revolution, were but a few events that challenged the inherited certainties of Victorian England. Men were forced to reevaluate old beliefs, to doubt discredited traditions, to revise social policies, to change moral valuations. It is not surprising that the confessional novel, the novel of doubt and faith, should acquire an unprecedented significance during such a period. The absence of reliable guideposts

threw men back upon themselves and obliged them to search for unity, purpose, and direction in the kaleidoscopic sequence of their own lives.

MARIUS THE EPICUREAN

Marius the Epicurean is one of the finest offshoots of a literary tradition inaugurated by Thomas Carlyle's *Sartor Resartus* (1835) and sustained in such works as John Henry Newman's *Loss and Gain* (1848), William Hale White's *The Autobiography of Mark Rutherford* (1885), and Mrs. Humphry Ward's *Robert Elsmere* (1888). Pater chose to set his search for meaning and purpose amid the disintegrating spectacle of Antonine Rome, but its bearing on the condition of late Victorian England is emphatically underlined: "Let the reader pardon me if here and there I seem to be passing from Marius to his modern representatives—from Rome, to Paris or London," Pater interpolates at one point. Marius is clearly meant to be prototypical: He dramatizes a quest for religious values that satisfies the demands of modern consciousness and reflects the ambiguity of a shattered world.

This is not to say that his growth is haphazard or random; on the contrary, Pater implies an underlying teleology in Marius's development: However dim and faint the sense of a superintending providence, his life is oriented toward the climactic moment of self-sacrifice with which the novel ends. Marius does not, however, fully resolve the conflicting calls of conscience and sensation, beauty and duty, engagement and withdrawal, in the fulfillment of that end. Though Pater evidently sees Marius's entire existence as an elaborate preparation for the revelatory moment in which his moral and spiritual being are ultimately defined, critics have generally judged that this is accomplished, if at all, without dramatic conviction.

Marius's youth is characterized, as was Pater's, by a more than common susceptibility to sensuous impressions. His home, "White Nights," a villa with adjacent farm, contributes to these susceptibilities. The note of grave beauty, of life lived under the conditions of animal sacrifice and seasonal change, develops in the boy a wistful reverence and wonder, which deepen with the passage of years. The Wordsworthian element in all this is not fortuitous, for Marius is destined to enact precisely that pattern of spiritual growth enunciated in "Lines Composed a Few Miles Above Tintern Abbey" and "Ode: Intimations of Immortality"—a pattern that involves a gradual conversion from the sensory to the spiritual planes of existence, a slow but steady ascension from the "aching joys" and "dizzy raptures" of his first impulsive response to beauty to the sober steadfastness of a mind that recognizes "a sense sublime of something far more deeply interfused." This conversion, if such it may be called, does not, for Marius, issue in the renunciation of his former pleasures, but rather a deepening awareness of their ultimate origin and tendency. In brief, Marius comes to dwell consciously in the presence of a spirit which is implied in his first naïve responses to nature and beauty. Hence, the pagan ceremonies, which solicit Marius's devotion and awe, already foreshadow "certain heavy demands" that will not become apparent to the lad until he acquires the mature self-consciousness of adulthood. It is then, on the level of discursive thought, that he will begin to recognize "some ampler vision, which should take up into itself and explain this world's delightful shows." "White Nights" is, therefore, as Pater suggests, not only a domestic dwelling place but also a state of mind peculiar to youth and prior to the self-dedication that maturity exacts.

In any event, it is not long before Marius is obliged to abandon the "world's delightful shows" in the pursuit of a more bracing conception of beauty. To cure a childhood illness, Marius is sent to the Temple of Aesculapius. The process of healing is complemented by meditations on Platonic texts. While these constitute a cherishable legacy for Marius, the boy reacts against a world of abstract essences. The impalpable ideas of Plato attract him only insofar as they fuse with the world of spatio-temporal objects, "green fields, for instance, or children's faces." Here, Pater is clearly attempting to revise the "impressionism" of his youth, itself a recrudescence of the Heraclitean theory of perpetual flux, with a Symbolist theory of correspondences. Beauty will no longer be an end in itself but "an outward imagery identifying itself with unseen morali-

ties." While Marius does not achieve such an identification at once or without great difficulty, Pater clearly intends that the boy's unthinking empiricism should be shaken and unsettled. In a word, the exhortation "to burn with a hard gem-like flame," which Pater formerly enunciated in *The Renaissance*, is now being duly qualified by an obligation "to discriminate, ever more and more fastidiously, select form and colour in things from what was less select." Pater is avid to demonstrate, through his hero Marius, the correct application of the aesthetic theory to life, an application that requires a transvaluation of the concept "Beauty" to include "not pleasure, but fulness of life, and insight as conducting to that fulness . . . whatever form of human life, in short, might be heroic, impassioned, ideal." Marius's stay at the temple initiates an intellectual or moral awakening, a search for a hieratic order of conduct and beauty that is truly serviceable to that ideal. Dissatisfied with the abstractness of the Platonic method, Marius rejects the world of ideal forms in the pursuit of its equivalent in a living community, a veritable body of fellow aspirants. His search for this community determines the subsequent shape of the novel.

Immediately prior to his departure from the temple, Marius is vouchsafed a distant view of a city which appears to be an earthly incarnation of the Platonic archetype he is seeking. This first glimpse of Rome kindles in Marius the illusion that it, perhaps, is that "new city coming down 'like a bride out of heaven,'" of which Plato discoursed so eloquently. Accordingly, Marius takes practical steps to bring him closer to "the most religious city in the world." He moves next to Pisa, preparing for his future obligations as secretary to the Emperor Aurelius. He is soon befriended by an aspiring youth of literary ambitions by the name of Flavian—a character who clearly represents one aspect of Marius's own divided consciousness.

Flavian's function in the novel is to bear involuntary witness to the limitations of aesthetic hedonism. Pater clearly intends through this subordinate character to disabuse his devotees of the notion that burning with a hard, gemlike flame is equivalent to self-indulgent dissipation. Beneath "the perfection of form" that Flavian achieves in his bearing and his poetry, Marius recognizes "a depth of corruption," which compels him to follow his friend only so far. Pater anticipates, here, to a remarkable degree the theme of Thomas Mann's *Death in Venice* (1912): the awareness that an exclusive preoccupation with artistic form may have the effect of neutralizing both good and evil by reducing them to complementary colors, lights, and shades in a composition. Nevertheless, Flavian performs a vital role in the drama of Marius's development: It is he who introduces Marius to the "golden book" of Apuleius.

At this point, Pater reproduces in full Apuleius's tale of Cupid and Psyche. Through subtle and strategic modifications of the original, Pater conceives of the tale as a presentiment of Marius's spiritual development. Evoking the solemn harmonies of the King James version of the Bible and softening the racy idiom of Apuleius, Pater endows the story of Cupid and Psyche with a "gentle idealism" and facilitates its interpretation as an allegory. Just as Psyche, symbol of the human soul, is redeemed from death by the intervention of Cupid, so Marius—bewildered, distracted, and divided by the contradictory sects and philosophical schools of decadent Rome—is presumably redeemed from despair by the appearance of a community that claims to satisfy the deepest needs of the human spirit. The road to that community is, however, difficult, uncertain, and devious.

Flavian's life is prematurely ended by an outbreak of plague. Marius, who remains, as ever, faithful to the evidence of his senses, is convinced of "nothing less than the soul's extinction." It may be parenthetically observed that despite his later sympathy with the Christian response to suffering, Marius never fully abandons those scruples "which can make no sincere claim to have apprehended anything beyond the veil of immediate experience." With his departure for Rome, he remains in a state of suspended judgment with regard to the ultimate destiny appointed for the human soul.

The actual journey to the capital of the ancient world includes a number of incidents that undermine the philosophic detachment of the young Marius. Notwithstanding the glory of the Roman *campagna*,

the many idyllic details of which Marius, with his habitual eye for the concrete, discerns with "a fresh, primeval poetry," he is plunged, following a scarcely averted accident, into further uncomfortable wrestling with the eternal questions. This accident— a loosened boulder falls from a wall beside the path Marius is following—has the effect of shaking him into a recognition that "his elaborate philosophy had not put beneath his feet the terror of mere bodily evil." The force, however, that is destined to correct the deficiencies in Marius's scheme of existence is not far away. Stopping at an inn to revive his spirits, Marius orders a glass of wine and muses vacantly over the "ring of delicate foam" that sparkles in his cup. Presently, his attention is arrested by a voice— "a youthful voice, with a reassuring clearness of note, which completes his cure." As he will soon learn, it is the voice of Cornelius, a young Roman soldier whose influence is destined to supersede that of Flavian's. It is not, however, until much later in his pilgrimage that Marius discovers that the origin of Cornelius's gracious alacrity of spirit is traceable to "some new knighthood or chivalry, just then coming into the world."

Marius, however, is not yet in a position to be irresistibly won over to that knighthood. He must first extend his philosophical hypotheses beyond the immediate circle of his own sensations; the role of Marcus Aurelius in the novel is to facilitate this extension. Unlike Flavian and Cornelius, the philosophical emperor of Rome is more than merely a shadowy personification of Marius's fractured ego: Aurelius is a figure of vital warmth and sympathy who encourages Marius to enlarge his spiritual perspective and to discover that an exclusive preoccupation with the passing moment may actually narrow the range of experience, curtail the development of character, and inhibit the acquisition of wisdom. The upshot of Aurelius's teachings is to reinforce Marius's search for a "comely order . . . to which, as to all other beautiful phenomena in life, he must, for his own peace, adjust himself."

While his influence is certainly salutary, Aurelius remains, in the final analysis, incapable of reconciling his devotion to that "comely order" with the debased reality of Antonine Rome. It is not long before Marius discovers a number of serious shortcomings in Aurelius's view of existence. To be sure, Marius accepts the merits of a philosophical scheme that posits a universal reason, or *logos*, a point of rest and a center of calm from which to withstand the vertiginous whirl of feelings and events, the traumatic blows of fate and destiny. Unfortunately, such a scheme, as Marius equally recognizes, may easily devolve into a pretext for neglecting one's peers in the present, for averting one's eyes from the plenitude and plurality of the living world. While freely granting the efficacy of believing in a "universal commonwealth of mind"—the sense of expanded horizons, the freedom from petty vexations, the glimpse of imperishable ideals that it allows—Marius rejects the concomitant calm and serenity that Aurelius, for example, maintains in the midst of human misery.

Two episodes in particular underline the deficiencies of the Stoical system. The first of these occurs during a performance at the Colosseum over which Aurelius, notwithstanding his own aversion to the gladiatorial games, presides with an air of tolerance. This indifference to the unspeakable butchery of men and animals, a consequence of the Stoic divorce of reason from reality, provokes Marius "to mark Aurelius as his inferior, now and for ever, on the question of righteousness." When it comes, however, to the suffering and death of his son, Lucius Verus, Aurelius is presented in a more sympathetic light. This episode, too, leaves an indelible mark in Marius's consciousness. The disparity between the imperturbable calm of the professed Stoic and the irrepressible grief of the stricken parent is poignantly dramatized when the boy, after an operation of surpassing agony, lapses into a coma from which he never recovers.

The chapter that immediately follows this episode signals the direction that Marius henceforth will take. An epigraph from the Psalms—"My heart is ready, O God, a ready heart is mine"—clearly enunciates the imminence of that spiritual crisis toward which his whole life has been moving. It would be a mistake, however, to construe this crisis as a sudden shattering encounter with the divine. On the contrary, nothing in the sense of a clear dramatic conversion

may be said to happen. The epiphany that Marius is vouchsafed has all the character of a Wordsworthian "spot of time." In one of his vagrant wanderings on the outskirts of Rome, Marius pauses at an outdoor inn to gaze at the extensive Roman *compagna*. His attention is divided among a number of apparently trivial and unrelated details—"a bird came and sang among the wattled hedge-roses: an animal feeding crept nearer: the child who kept it was gazing quietly"—when, suddenly, the entire scene presents itself as the outward and tangible emblem of "that . . . Ideal, to which the Old Testament gives the name of Creator, which for the philosophers of Greece is the Eternal Reason, and in the New Testament the Father of Men." The mundane world is transfigured and transvalued in a moment of privileged perception: no less and no more. The departure of this mood is as quiet and unobtrusive as its inception, but it leaves Marius with the firm conviction that the remainder of his life must be "a search for the equivalent of that Ideal . . . a gathering together of every trace and token of it, which his actual experience might present." The event is clearly something of a watershed.

At this juncture, Marius is given the opportunity to visit a pair of houses that represent two opposing visions of reality. The first house represents the finest flowering of classical antiquity. It is here that Marius meets his former idol, the poet Apuleius; enjoys the refined pleasures and urbane conversation of the Roman intelligentsia; and delights in the delectations of a banquet replete with music, dance, and fine condiments. The whole proceedings, however, are tainted by a certain foppish connoisseurism, a pampered elegance, a "facility" and "self-complacency" in the exchange of ideas. Marius departs with a nagging sense of weariness and disillusion.

The second house, to which he is introduced by Cornelius, is that of the Christian saint, Cecilia. It is characteristic that Pater should choose the canonized patroness of music as the agent of Marius's contact with Christianity. Presumably, if art can obscure the moral being of man, as in the case of Flavian, it can also reveal that moral being. The grave, refined, and simple dignity of the Christian community—its air of domestic and filial piety, its comely rectitude of spirit, its solicitude for the departed, care for the living, and faith in things to come—stands in favorable contrast to the enervating amusements and facile wit of the Roman upper crust. Yet it is important to note that the early Church, as Pater presents it, has nothing of that apocalyptic fervor that looks forward to the end of the world and the last things. On the contrary, "the contrast between the church and the world" Pater tells us, "was becoming less pronounced." By far the largest part of Marius's attraction to this community derives from his contemplation of "the beautiful house of Cecilia, its lights and flowers, of Cecilia herself, moving among the lilies, with an enchanted grace."

The fact is that Marius remains ultimately indifferent to the dogmatic foundations of Christianity. To be sure, he returns to his childhood home and supervises the reburial of his ancestors according to the usages of the early Church. Furthermore, he willingly intercedes on Cornelius's behalf following an officially sanctioned purge of the growing Christian community. There is, however, a considerable degree of ambiguity involved in Marius's position vis-à-vis the Christian faith. Marius is arrested along with Cornelius for being present at a community act of worship. An outbreak of plague shatters the fragile tolerance extended to the Church and initiates widespread persecution of the Christians. On the strength of his relations with Aurelius, Marius contrives to have Cornelius released. He is compelled, however, to give a deposition on his friend's behalf and to join the other prisoners in the long and arduous journey to Rome. This generosity of spirit on the part of Marius is prompted by a mistaken notion that Cornelius is Cecilia's intended: The latter's vows of chastity entirely elude Marius's understanding. Traveling to Rome in company with the other captives, Marius is stricken with plague and abandoned at a neighboring farm which, as it turns out, is the dwelling of some recent converts. Lying in a state of semidelirium for several days, he finds consolation, during the lucid intervals allowed him, in "the scent of newmown hay . . . and the sounds of cattle . . . from the green places around." The occupants, erroneously assuming that he is a Christian, administer

to the dying Marius the last rites of their faith.

Is Marius, then, a Christian? This question has been the subject of critical debate since the novel's appearance. For Paul Elmer More, *Marius the Epicurean* is "only another manifestation of that aestheticism which Pater sucked from the Romantic school of his century and disguised in the phraseology of ancient faith." He further adds, "to write thus was to betray Christianity with a kiss." T. S. Eliot has no hesitation in asserting that "of the essence of the Christian Faith . . . Pater knew almost nothing." Arthur Benson is equally forthright in claiming that "the very peace which Marius discerns in Christianity is the old philosophical peace over again." The point is that Marius fails to grasp and remains largely indifferent to the theoretical foundations of Christianity. "Our creeds," as Pater observes, "are but the brief abstract of our prayer and song." Inasmuch as Christianity invests that song with a deeper pathos, frees the mind from its empirical trammels, and endows existence with a warmer hope, it is clearly a serviceable hypothesis for the questing human spirit. Its dogmatic underpinnings, however, are of secondary importance.

Some might claim that Pater's enterprise in *Marius the Epicurean* is fundamentally affiliated with the Christian existentialism of Søren Kierkegaard. There is, however, one signal and important difference. Unlike Kierkegaard, who posits a leap of faith in which reason is virtually annihilated, Pater viewed all such leaps as a source of potential fanaticism. Christianity, for Pater, is clearly a stage in the development of human potential, but he would jealously protect that potential from any claim that might threaten its autonomy. The Church of Cecilia is, at bottom, a fictive structure in which there is "no forced opposition between soul and body, the world and the spirit." It is even identified, at one point, with that "half-humorous placidity of soul, of a kind illustrated later very effectively by Montaigne." Just as modern-day theologians who attempt to gerrymander Christianity into the camps of Marx, Sigmund Freud, Friedrich Nietzsche, or Ludwig Feuerbach, Pater has created a church of his own making—distinctly unrecognizable to the average believer. From the perspective of

Christ's statement, "He who is not with me is against me," Marius is most certainly not a Christian; on the other hand, if one considers the earlier phrasing of this statement in the gospel of Mark, "He who is not against us is for us," then the question of Marius's death as "a kind of sacrament with plenary grace" remains open.

GASTON DE LATOUR

Moreover, as Pater was to recognize in *Gaston de Latour*, institutional Christianity, insofar as it defines itself in what a man professes rather than in what he is, is as prodigal of sectarian bigotry and bloodshed as the worst excesses of pagan Rome. Like *Marius the Epicurean, Gaston de Latour* examines the situation of faith in an "age of transition . . . when the problem of man's destiny and his relations to the unseen was undergoing a new solution." Though Pater never lived to complete the novel—it remains, at best, a series of discontinuous meditations on the religious and political ferment of the Reformation—its essential outlines are as follows. Born in the midst of growing strife between Huguenots and Catholics, Gaston comes of age in "the cornlands of France," in close proximity to the cathedral of Chartres and amid the luxuries of his rustic manor house. He becomes acquainted with King Charles the Ninth, joins the "episcopal household of Chartres as a page," and falls under the influence of the poetry of Pierre de Ronsard. Like Marius, in a different context, he becomes the votary of a great philosopher: in this instance, Michel de Montaigne. He eventually travels to Paris and takes up with a spirited Huguenot girl; under the pressure of her brothers, he marries her in a Protestant ceremony which exerts no real claim upon him: "The transaction seemed to have but that transitoriness as also the guilt of a vagrant love." Miscalculating the forces of destruction gathered on the eve of St. Bartholomew, Gaston returns to his homestead at Deux-manoirs, "his wife left behind there in Paris." He later learns of the death of his wife "while the stairways of the Louvre, the streets, the trap-doors of Paris, run blood." Following the banishment of King Charles, Gaston returns to Paris and falls under the influence of the heterodox monk Giordano Bruno. Here the novel abruptly ends.

What is clearly significant about this work is its relation to *Marius the Epicurean*. Just as Marius qualifies the hedonism of *The Renaissance*, so *Gaston de Latour* qualifies the Christianity of *Marius the Epicurean*. Indeed, of Gaston himself the reader is told that "the very genius of qualification followed him through his keen, constant, changeful consideration of men and things."

Pater's attitude is obvious. He clearly distrusts the external machinery of a church that absorbs the individual conscience and resolves all doubts in cozy conformity, irresponsible anonymity, and superstitious fear. Pater rejects dogmatic formulations and ideologies of any kind, especially insofar as these inhibit the cultivation of human sympathy or the development of individual character. "The man who never alters his opinion is like standing water, and breeds reptiles of the mind," wrote William Blake, and Pater would have most certainly agreed. Indeed, the true saint of the Reformation, for Pater, is Montaigne, and the legitimate attitude in all matters speculative and religious is not the intransigence of the doctrinaire but the suspended judgment of a humanist. "It was something to have been," writes Pater of Montaigne, "in the matter of religious tolerance, as in so many other matters of justice and gentleness, the solitary conscience of the age."

In the final analysis, the question of whether Pater's protagonists are ultimately Christian pales before the question of whether they are comprehensively human. Thoughtful, but without energy; sensitive, but without resolve; scrupulous, but without conviction; both Marius and Gaston remain imprisoned, each in his own consciousness and incapable of genuine community with others. The essentially selfish conviction that informs these novels and that may be taken as a motto for Pater's life and work is perhaps stated most succinctly in one of the Pythian Odes of the Latin poet Pindar: "O my soul, do not aspire to immortal life, but exhaust the limits of the possible." Pater once remarked of Marius that his was a philosophy that at least guaranteed its possessor of living a life without harm to others. The question remains, however, whether such a philosophy is adequate to the full range of human experience. In the absence of more solid and substantial convictions than those which Pater demonstrates in his writings, this question remains a point of legitimate concern in any final estimate of his achievement.

Stephen I. Gurney

OTHER MAJOR WORKS

SHORT FICTION: *Imaginary Portraits*, 1887.

NONFICTION: *Studies in the History of the Renaissance*, 1873 (rev. as *The Renaissance: Studies in Art and Poetry*, 1877, 1888, 1893); *Appreciations: With an Essay on Style*, 1889; *Plato and Platonism: A Series of Lectures*, 1893; *Greek Studies: A Series of Essays*, 1895; *Miscellaneous Studies*, 1895; *Essays from the "Guardian,"* 1896.

BIBLIOGRAPHY

Bloom, Harold, ed. *Modern Critical Views: Walter Pater*. New York: Chelsea House, 1985. Bloom has compiled what he considers some of the best criticism available on Pater. The introduction by Bloom provides a useful overview of Pater's work and contains much insight. Also includes a reprint of an unabridged pamphlet on Pater by Ian Fletcher, a highly respected critic of Pater. A valuable and well-rounded study.

Brake, Laurel, and Ian Small, eds. *Pater in the 1990's*. Greensboro, N.C.: ELT Press, 1991. This collection of fifteen critical essays was culled from papers offered at a 1988 Pater conference at Oxford University. The editors note that while half of the essays they include reflect the older New Criticism approach to literature, the other half demonstrate the shift in Pater criticism toward consideration of his works in historical and biographical contexts. Topics range from editing Pater to his friends and literary influences to his own lasting influence on writers such as James Joyce.

Buckler, William E. *Walter Pater: The Critic as Artist of Ideas*. New York: New York University Press, 1987. This scholarly study examines the breadth and depth of Pater's prose and poetry, as well as his role as a critic, acknowledging him as a major but underrated writer. The work focuses on Pater's aestheticism in his work, and chapter 8 examines Pater's *Plato and Platonism*, which has been generally ignored by critics.

Court, Franklin E. *Walter Pater: An Annotated Bibliography of Writings About Him*. De Kalb: Northern Illinois Press, 1980. This volume includes a checklist of a representative body of criticism on Pater from 1871 through 1973. Contains abstracts of critical articles, reminiscences, biographies, and letters to editors. A rich source of bibliographical information for the Pater scholar.

Levey, Michael. *The Case of Walter Pater*. London: Thames and Hudson, 1978. An appreciative study of Pater, largely biographical and executed with thoroughness. Levey promotes Pater's case but alludes to the difficulty in placing Pater's writing because he moved so fluidly from fiction to fact.

Moliterno, Frank. *The Dialectics of Sense and Spirit in Pater and Joyce*. Greensboro: ELT Press, University of North Carolina at Greensboro, 1998. Compares themes and aesthetics in Pater and James Joyce. With bibliographical references and an index.

Monsman, Gerald. *Walter Pater*. Boston: Twayne, 1977. A chronological look at Pater's work and life. Examines the heroes in his works, in particular the hero in *Marius the Epicurean*. A useful study for the beginning reader of Pater. A selected bibliography is provided.

Shuter, William. *Rereading Walter Pater*. New York: Cambridge University Press, 1997. Part of the Cambridge Studies in Nineteenth Century Literature series, this volume examines Pater's works with a critical eye.

ALAN PATON

Born: Pietermaritzburg, Natal, South Africa; January 11, 1903

Died: Botha's Hill, Natal, South Africa; April 12, 1988

PRINCIPAL LONG FICTION

Cry, the Beloved Country, 1948
Too Late the Phalarope, 1953
Ah, but Your Land Is Beautiful, 1981

OTHER LITERARY FORMS

Before his first two novels, Paton wrote only juvenile poems and a play, while at college. A collection of his short stories, *Tales from a Troubled Land*, published in 1961, was republished that same year as *Debbie Go Home*. He produced two plays, *Lost in the Stars* (1950) with Maxwell Anderson, and *Sponono* (1964) with Krishna Shah. His major biography is *Hofmeyr* (1964), better known in its abridged American version, *South African Tragedy: The Life and Times of Jan Hofmeyr* (1965). Paton's autobiographies include *Towards the Mountain* (1980) and *Journey Continued* (1988).

(Library of Congress)

ACHIEVEMENTS

Paton burst upon the international literary scene with his novel *Cry, the Beloved Country*. Seldom has a first work had such immediate and yet such long-lasting impact. This first novel, published when its author was already forty-five years of age, sold fifteen million copies by the time of Paton's death in 1988, forty years later. The persistence of the book's popularity can also be seen in its having been made into films in 1951 and 1995. In addition to popular acclaim, Paton has been awarded considerable critical respect, receiving both British and American awards within a year of the publication of *Cry, the Beloved Country*.

His accomplishments as an author are impressively paradoxical. His novels are set concretely in the landscape of South Africa, based specifically on the social conditions of that country, incorporating actual political events into their plots. Yet from those localized elements emerges not the narrow regionalism that might be expected, but rather cosmic concern with shared humanity. Deeply concerned with issues of political justice, Paton seldom degenerates into preaching or sentimentality. Carefully crafted as his lyrical style is, it is mostly admired not for its aesthetic competence but rather for its simplicity and naturalness.

BIOGRAPHY

Much that matters in his writing stems from the fact that Alan Paton was born in 1903 in Pietermaritzburg in Natal, South Africa. He loved that local land as much as he loved books. Both passions, which figure prominently in his writings, were learned from his father, James Paton, immigrant from Scotland, and his mother, Eunice Warder James Paton, the daughter of English immigrants. His father was a deeply religious Christian and a strict authoritarian, so strict his disciplinary practices provoked Alan to resist authoritarianism in any form.

Paton married Doris (Dorrie) Olive Francis in 1928, and they had two sons, David and Jonathan. Following Dorrie's death in 1967 he married Anne Hopkins. After teaching chemistry and mathematics in high school and college, Paton worked as principal of the Diepkloof reformatory from 1935 until the publication of *Cry, the Beloved Country*, his first novel, written from the homesick perspective gained during a three-month tour of prisons in England and the United States.

Among the earliest voices for racial equality in South Africa, Paton helped create and vigorously promoted the Liberal Party during the 1950's, actively opposing his country's policy of apartheid. That opposition resulted in confiscation of his passport, eventual dissolution of the party, and governmental banning of his beloved Defence and Aid Fund, which had provided legal fees for oppressed blacks. By the time of his death at age eighty-five Paton had been honored throughout the world with international awards for his humanitarian work and honorary degrees in recognition of his writing from such prestigious universities as Harvard, Yale, and Edinburgh.

ANALYSIS

Paton's novels are much admired for their lyrical language, their closeness to the land, and their heartfelt moral purpose. Though some readers have felt he falters in his attempt to integrate native and English elements into an archaic prose, most readers enjoy the lyrical quality of Paton's style. His ear for the rhythms and nuances of spoken South African English is as sensitive as writer Mark Twain's for Americanisms. As a result of that linguistic giftedness we hear in his writing an impressive chorus of voices: the clamoring voices of South Africa, the sonorous voice of the Old Testament, the still, sad voice of humanity, and, integrating all those, the earnestly reforming voice of Alan Paton.

Paton's second literary virtue is the realism of his fiction. Precise awareness of his South African home pervades every page of his fiction, and his narrative is illuminated by his honesty of perspective. Paton sees with a clear eye the complex urban degeneracies of Johannesburg and the tragedies of modern life. He is perhaps at his best viewing the simple natural glories of the Natal countryside. The plot of *Too Late the Phalarope*, for instance, hinges upon his hero's awareness of the phalarope, a little-known bird of his

homeland, a creature Pieter and his father understand better than the outland expert who writes the definitive book on Natal birds. Critic Edward Callan compares Paton's sensitivity to the natural life of South Africa to poet Robert Frost's keen awareness of the landscape of New England.

For most readers the most profound power of Alan Paton's fiction is generated by his moral earnestness. Some have worried that the directness of his moral purpose verges on melodrama, even propaganda. Consensus assessment of Paton's fiction agrees, however, that his insistence on the value of individual human dignity and worth "plumbs deep into human suffering and punishment" without "moralizing or . . . maudlin sentimentality." Fierce passion for reform without the downside of preaching is a rare literary achievement. Paton wrote *Cry, the Beloved Country* after reading American author John Steinbeck's classic novel of social protest, *The Grapes of Wrath* (1939). It may be, as critic F. Charles Rooney suggests, that Paton captures in his writing "all Steinbeck's heart, plus *soul.*"

CRY, THE BELOVED COUNTRY

Paton's first novel is also his best. Written from his personal experience with issues of freedom in his native South Africa, it is a lament for conditions that imprison the human spirit, a cry for freedom. Old Stephen Kumalo, pastor of the church in his Zulu village, ventures into sophisticated Johannesburg in search of his sister Gertrude, his brother John, and his son Absalom. He finds there a parable of the erosion of tribal society under the storm of white culture. He discovers Absalom in jail, the confessed murderer of a gentle and generous white man. In ironic confirmation of the relatedness of all humanity, the murdered man turns out to be the son of the plantation owner in Kumalo's home valley. Kumalo's sister, unable to find the husband who has deserted her, has become a prostitute. Kumalo's brother John has sold out totally to urban temptations of materialistic politics.

Yet Kumalo also finds amid the corruptions of Johannesburg the generosity of fellow priest Msimangu, whose Christian compassion reaches so far as to cause him to worry even about whites, "that one day when they turn to loving, they will find we are turned to hating." Kumalo finds along with the sin in this modern Sodom the determined social restructurings of the reformatory teacher, a man strikingly reminiscent of Paton himself. The weary old Zulu returns home to the father of the man his son has killed to tell him he is sorry, and they share across the abyss of race their mutual grief.

Kumalo's quest for his family ends in the worst of disasters. Fictional Johannesburg swallows the villagers who venture there as destructively as Western culture sapped the tribal values in mid-twentieth century South Africa. Yet Paton's humanitarian ideals somehow prevail. When "that dawn will come, of our emancipation, from the fear of bondage and the bondage of fear" we cannot know. Yet we can see even through the "clouded eyes" of those two bereaved fathers looking toward a dawn that signals end to the wasted life of Absalom Kumalo, the hope of that "faint steady lightening in the east."

The magnificent simplicity of the sad but hopeful plot is reflected in Paton's expression. The author has a gift for capturing in naturally lyrical prose the rhythms of Zulu, of Afrikaans, and of his King James Bible-steeped central characters. "Quietly, my child, there is a lovely valley where you were born. The water sings over the stones, and the wind cools you. The cattle come down to the river, they stand there under the trees. Quietly my child." The style, at its best, is reminiscent of the lean profundity of the book of Genesis and functions to much the same purpose—Paton's heartfelt expression makes *Cry, the Beloved Country* a psalm, a cry to repentance, and a prophecy.

TOO LATE THE PHALAROPE

Paton's first novel documents the destructiveness of racist attitudes on the world of black South Africans. His second book shifts focus to look at the havoc wrought by racism among whites. The fall of Pieter van Vlaanderen is tragic. Pieter is a white man drawn to black women, trapped in a society that views racial mixing as the ultimate sin. This good man is crushed by the racism of such Afrikaaners as his rigid father Jakob, a man who understands justice better than he comprehends mercy, so convinced of his racist perspective he can write his son out of the family Bible when he learns of his adultery with

a black woman. Those fierce social attitudes are as realistic as the economic evils of Johannesburg painted in *Cry, the Beloved Country*. Harsh as it may seem, Paton wrote, in *Toward the Mountain*, as late as twenty years after the publication of *Too Late the Phalarope*, "three white men have committed suicide in the last few weeks rather than face trial."

As in *Cry, the Beloved Country*, redemptive forces temper the destructiveness of the racist attitudes. Pieter's Jewish friend Kappie talks him out of suicide. His wife Nella, steeped as strictly in South African racism as Pieter, stands by him at the trial. Thoughtful Captain Massingham decides that the worst human offense may not be racial mixing but what is being done to Pieter, "to punish and not to restore, that is the greatest of all offences . . . the sin against the Holy Ghost."

Too Late the Phalarope is a fine novel, a haunting examination of a man's conscience. At its best the narrative is reminiscent of the soul-searching novels of religious inner torment of English writer Graham Greene. However, the book suffers from the usual problem of sequels, diminution from the power of the original. Perhaps because of the European rather than native viewpoint, *Too Late the Phalarope* does not reach for most readers the profound levels of compassion tapped by *Cry, the Beloved Country*.

AH, BUT YOUR LAND IS BEAUTIFUL

The title of Paton's final novel is based on comments from foreign visitors, who wonder how such a lovely landscape can tolerate, let alone produce, such intense racial hatreds as those that scar South African attitudes. The land is so beautiful that outsiders are surprised such ugly attitudes can inhabit the souls of its inhabitants. Prem Bodasingh, heroine of the novel, is an eighteen-year-old South African equivalent of Rosa Parks, the African American who sparked the Montgomery, Alabama, bus boycott in 1955 by refusing to give up her seat to a white passenger. This graceful Native African teenager, a model student, quietly rebels against apartheid by sitting down in the Durban Library to read, a position forbidden to her as a nonwhite by South African laws against racial intermixing in places such as libraries (and, as we discover later, at funerals).

In counterpoint to Prem's personal resistance to the evil political system of her country, the novel traces the public resistance to apartheid, mainly through the genesis of the Liberal Party, which Paton presided over from 1958 to 1968. It is a tribute to Paton's competence as a writer that he focuses always on the immediate human dilemma rather than the larger political forces. Yet his conviction of the moral significance of every person's experience makes the action of the novel take on cosmic significance—Paton believes deeply, and from our perspective it appears almost prophetically, that things can be better in South Africa.

This is not only a competent but a heartfelt novel. However, *Ah, but Your Land Is Beautiful* continues the diminishment of his writing from the high-water mark of *Cry, the Beloved Country*. Perhaps that evaporation of Paton's literary force was inevitable. His first novel looks at the brutalities of racism from the perspective of blacks, for whom it was a matter of life and death. *Too Late the Phalarope* approaches racist issues from the viewpoint of whites, for whom racism is personal tragedy. *Ah, but Your Land Is Beautiful* broaches Paton's inevitable subject from a less involved viewpoint, that of relative South African outsiders, such as Indians and Jews, for whom racist political policy is more a matter of economics than the issue of moral urgency it is for whites, let alone the matter of life and death it is for blacks. Whatever the reason for its neglect, *Ah, but Your Land Is Beautiful* is the least read of Paton's novels and the least discussed by critics.

Steven C. Walker

OTHER MAJOR WORKS

SHORT FICTION: *Tales from a Troubled Land*, 1961 (pb. in England as *Debbie Go Home*).

PLAYS: *Lost in the Stars*, pr. 1950 (with Maxwell Anderson); *Sponono*, pr. 1964 (with Krishna Shah).

NONFICTION: *The Land and People of South Africa*, 1955; *South Africa in Transition*, 1956 (with Dan Weiner); *Hofmeyr*, 1964 (abridged as *South African Tragedy: The Life and Times of Jan Hofmeyr*, 1965); *Instrument of Thy Peace*, 1968 (meditations); *For You Departed*, 1969 (meditations; pb. in England as *Kontakion for You Departed*, 1969); *Apartheid and the Archbishop: The Life and Times of Geoffrey Clayton, Archbishop of Cape Town*, 1973; *Towards the Mountain*, 1980 (autobiography); *Journey Continued*, 1988 (autobiography).

BIBLIOGRAPHY

Alexander, Peter F. *Alan Paton: A Biography*. New York: Oxford University Press, 1994. A thorough, vast study of Paton's life, this volume is as engagingly written as it is well documented. Background on the major novels is particularly helpful.

Baker, Sheridan. *Paton's "Cry, the Beloved Country": The Novel, the Critics, the Setting*. New York: Charles Scribner's Sons, 1968. This useful collection of criticism of the novel includes Baker's own classic, "Paton's Beloved Country and the Morality of Geography."

Callan, Edward. *Alan Paton*. Rev. ed. Boston: Twayne, 1982. Callan sets critical assessment of Paton's writings within a general background of his life. This study was helpfully supplemented in 1991 by an eight-chapter study of *Cry, the Beloved Country*.

_____. *"Cry, the Beloved Country": A Novel of South Africa—A Study*. Boston: Twayne, 1991. Part of Twayne's Masterwork Studies, this volume discusses race relations, apartheid, and South African culture in relation to Paton's seminal work.

Fuller, Edmund. *Books with the Men Behind Them*. New York: Oxford University Press, 1959. Fuller assesses the tragic elements of Paton's major novels, admiring on these grounds *Too Late the Phalarope* even more than *Cry, the Beloved Country*.

Gardiner, Harold C. "Paton's Literary Achievement," *Reality* 20, no. 4 (1988): 8-11. Gardiner appraises *Cry, the Beloved Country* as a profound glimpse into human suffering, and he praises *Too Late the Phalarope* even more.

Paton, Jonathan. "Comfort in Desolation." In *International Literature in English: Essays on the Major Writers*, edited by Robert L. Ross. New York: Garland, 1991. Paton's youngest son describes the Christian call for comfort that underlies his father's first novel.

Rooney, F. Charles. "The Message of Alan Paton." *The Catholic World* 194, no. 1160 (November, 1961): 92-98. Rooney defends Paton from charges of propagandizing.

CESARE PAVESE

Born: Santo Stefano Belbo, Italy; September 9, 1908
Died: Turin, Italy; August 27, 1950

PRINCIPAL LONG FICTION

Paesi tuoi, 1941 (*The Harvesters*, 1961)
La spiaggia, 1942 (*The Beach*, 1963)
Il compagno, 1947 (*The Comrade*, 1959)
Il carcere, 1949 (*The Political Prisoner*, 1959)
La casa in collina, 1949 (*The House on the Hill*, 1956)
Prima che il gallo canti, 1949 (includes the two previous novels)
Il diavolo sulle colline, 1949 (*The Devil in the Hills*, 1954)
Tra donne sole, 1949 (*Among Women Only*, 1953)
La bella estate, 1949 (includes the two previous novels, *The Beautiful Summer*, 1959)
La luna e i falò, 1950 (*The Moon and the Bonfire*, 1952)
Fuoco grande, 1959 (with Bianca Garufi *A Great Fire*, 1963)
The Selected Works of Cesare Pavese, 1968

OTHER LITERARY FORMS

Though Cesare Pavese is best known as a novelist, his oeuvre includes work in a number of other literary forms. Like many novelists, he began as a poet and continued to return to that genre throughout his career. His poems are collected in *Lavorare stanca* (1936, 1943; *Hard Labor*, 1976) and in *Verra la morte e avra i tuoi occhi* (1951). Pavese's poetry is now available in a comprehensive edition, *Poesie edite e inedite* (1962), which also includes previously uncollected work. Pavese also published a number of short stories, collected in *Feria d'agosto* (1946; *Summer*

Storm and Other Stories, 1966) and *Notte di festa* (1953; *Festival Night and Other Stories*, 1964); these stories, as well as previously uncollected ones, are also available in *Racconti* (1960). The remainder of Pavese's work consists of *Dialoghi con Leucò* (1947; *Dialogues with Leucò*, 1966), *La letteratura americana e altri saggi* (1951; *American Literature: Essays and Opinions*, 1970), *Il mestiere di vivere: Diario, 1935-1950* (1952; *The Burning Brand: Diaries, 1935-1950*, 1961), and *Lettere* (1966; partial translation, *Selected Letters, 1924-1950*, 1969).

ACHIEVEMENTS

Pavese's fiction, which contributed significantly to the development of the modern Italian novel, reflects his intense, lifelong interest in American literature, in which he found the elements of local color, psychological and social realism, and cultural symbolism that he strove to incorporate into his own works. He employed these elements to construct an alternative to the convention-bound Hermetic tradition of his Italian predecessors, whose excessive, abstract formalism isolated art from life. Pavese became for many readers the greatest of all the Italian neorealists—that group of writers and filmmakers including such major figures as Ignazio Silone, Alberto Moravia, and Vittorio De Sica.

Pavese's personal contribution to modern Italian literature is not limited to the aesthetic formulated in his own work, however, for he also conveyed the shift in literary values that neorealism represented through his translations of, and critical essays on, major American novelists and poets from whom—in Pavese's case at least—these aesthetic values and precedents were in part derived. Pavese's first translation, and undoubtedly his most important contribution in terms of its effect on his contemporaries, was of Herman Melville's *Moby Dick* (1851), appearing in 1932. The intense and monumental effort Pavese devoted to this work is apparent in the numerous letters he exchanged with an Italian American friend, Antonio Chiuminatto, during the period in which he was working on this project. The translation of *Moby Dick* was followed by translations of other works by Melville, as well as of novels by such important modern authors as Sinclair Lewis, Sherwood Anderson, John Dos Passos, Gertrude Stein, and John Steinbeck, and critical essays not only on these authors but also on Edgar Lee Masters, O. Henry, Theodore Dreiser, Walt Whitman, and Richard Wright.

Pavese's second important contribution to neorealism was his abandonment of the detached, omniscient perspective of the refined narrator speaking in the standard *lingua pura* dialect of literary Italian—as was conventional in novels—for the first-person narrator speaking a region vernacular. The vernacular of Pavese's unlettered narrators was Piedmontese, which he was accustomed to hearing in the vicinity of Turin, where he lived.

Pavese was not the only neorealist to eschew the worn-out diction of literary Italian; his contemporary Moravia frequently employed working-class narra-

(Kimberly Dawson Kurnizki)

tors speaking the modern Roman vernacular. These two writers occupy a position of importance in the history of Italian literature somewhat analogous to that of William Wordsworth and Samuel Taylor Coleridge in England and Mark Twain and the southwestern humorists in the United States: They revolutionized the literary language of their time.

Finally, Pavese's novels are important as a response to Fascism and, in a larger sense, to totalitarianism, the disease of the twentieth century. Pavese himself was only fourteen when ruler Benito Mussolini came to power, and he lived under the shadow of fascist repression for more than twenty years. In fact, one might claim, as some critics have done, that Pavese's sense of social and national commitment as a writer, as well as his hesitant engagement with the Communist Party, was largely a defensive reaction to the destructive effects of totalitarianism upon the modern Italian consciousness.

It is upon these elements that Pavese's reputation as an important modern novelist rests. Taken singly, each element is a great accomplishment; taken together, they place Pavese with Silone and Moravia as one of the greatest twentieth century Italian novelists.

BIOGRAPHY

Cesare Pavese was born on September 9, 1908, in Santo Stefano Belbo, a small rural community in the hilly Langhe district of Piedmont, a province in northwestern Italy. His father, who was a minor official in the municipal court of Turin, died in 1914, when Pavese was six. His mother, whom Pavese described as strict and authoritarian in bearing, rarely showed either himself or his sister, Maria, who was six years older, any parental affection or support. Despite this fact, Pavese seems to have been strongly attached to her, and he continued living with her in the family home, remaining unmarried. Following her death in 1930, he moved to his sister's home, where he lived for the remainder of his life, entertaining friends and callers in the single room that served him as bedroom, study, and parlor.

Though Pavese's family belonged to the middle class, after the death of his father, the family had to sell the few assets it had to maintain this position.

Nevertheless, Pavese received an excellent education. During his early years, he attended school in Turin, spending every summer in the country at the family's farm in Santo Stefano Belbo, where he had been born. By 1918, however, only four years after the death of his father, the family could no longer afford the privilege of a second home, and the farm was sold, ending what Pavese saw as a vital part of his childhood experience. With the loss of the farm, his direct, personal contact with the simple peasants of the region and the renewing forces of the natural environment, which were so entwined with their agricultural lifestyle, was severed.

In 1923, Pavese entered a Turin *liceo*, or secondary school, where he received the classical education that was to form him into that special type of scholar, the humanistic intellectual. In 1927, he entered the University of Turin, from which he took his degree in letters in 1930 with a dissertation on Walt Whitman. The interest Pavese developed in American literature during this period had an important effect upon his later development as a writer. This interest in American literature, which was not well known in Italy at the time, seems to have been stimulated in part by his friendship with Antonio Chiuminatto, a young Italian American who came to study at the University of Turin in the summer of 1929. In any event, Pavese's interest in American literature and culture is clearly evident in his choice of Walt Whitman for his dissertation topic—against the counsel of his advisers.

Following his graduation, Pavese remained in Turin, making his living by teaching and tutoring. Because of the increasing power of the Fascist Party—which, by the time he was graduated, was in complete control of all levels of government bureaucracy—Pavese joined in 1932, as did everyone who wished to secure or maintain any position controlled by the government. That this action was a matter of convenience, not conviction, is attested by the fact that Pavese was one of the first contributors to the leftist journal *La cultura*, which was produced by the newly formed Einaudi publishing house, founded in 1933 by one of Pavese's university friends. During the next two years, Pavese became increasingly involved with *La cultura* and its publisher, Einaudi, as

well as with those who shared its leftist, and therefore anti-Fascist, sympathies.

In 1934, Pavese took charge of *La cultura* after its previous editor, Leone Ginzburg, was arrested by the Fascist authorities. Pavese must have realized the danger in which he was placing himself, for the authorities were becoming more and more openly intolerant of dissent. Moreover, by 1935, Pavese had become romantically involved with a young woman named Tina, who was an active member of the clandestine Communist resistance and who used his address to receive communications from other Party members.

In May of 1935, the Fascist authorities entered and searched Pavese's room, finding in Tina's letters what they believed was incriminating evidence. Besides, they reasoned, was not Pavese himself the editor of *La cultura*—a magazine that openly sympathized with such views? Pavese was arrested and sentenced to three years of political confinement, though this sentence was later reduced to ten months. He served the first two months of his sentence in jails at Turin and Rome and then was sent to serve the remainder of his confinement in the small village of Brancaleone, in remote southern Calabria, where he was isolated under police supervision.

It was there, in the later months of his confinement, that Pavese began the journal he kept from 1935 until his death. This work, posthumously published in 1952 as *The Burning Brand: Diaries, 1935-1950*, has brought Pavese nearly as much fame as his novels and has led critics to see in his work a strong autobiographical element, as well as a resigned philosophical orientation that links him to the existentialists Albert Camus and Jean-Paul Sartre.

When Pavese returned from his Calabrian exile early in 1936, he arrived in Turin to discover that Tina, the woman for whom he had been imprisoned, had married someone else the day before. This was the first, and undoubtedly the most intense, of the many disappointments in love he suffered from this time on. In 1936, Pavese's first collection of poetry, *Hard Labor*, appeared, and he resumed his association with Einaudi. In 1941, he published his novel *The Harvesters*, a work which revealed Pavese's renewed interest in the nonintellectual, primal world of the rural poor who live in direct contact with the creative and destructive forces of nature. Late in 1943, Pavese again left Turin to escape the German occupation of the city, moving to Serralanga di Crea in Monferrato, where he lived with his sister's family for nearly two years. Following the Allied liberation of northern Italy from German occupation in April, 1945, Pavese returned to Turin, and in the same year he was named editor in chief at Einaudi and became an official member of the Italian Communist Party.

The period that followed World War II was the final and most productive phase of Pavese's career as a writer. Seven of his ten novels were published between 1946 and 1950, as well as a collection of short stories, *Summer Storm*, and *Dialogues with Leucò*. In 1950, Pavese was awarded the prestigious Strega Prize for his novel *Among Women Only*. Yet, however much Pavese the author was successful, the man himself was plagued by a strong sense of frustration— particularly in his inability to commit himself effectively to political and social action. Moreover, his sense of failure in romantic endeavors still continued to torment him. One of Pavese's closest friends, Natalia Ginzburg, described Pavese's dilemma at this time in a moving tribute to the novelist published after his death: "He devised for himself over the years a system of ideas and principles, so entangled and severe as to bar him from the simplest decisions of everyday life." As Pavese himself implied in the revealing foreword to *Dialogues with Leucò*, the imaginary philosophical debates he constructed in that volume treat, in projected and universalized form, the personal dilemmas of existence with which he struggled in his own life: "Had it been possible, I would have gladly done without all this mythology. . . . When we retell an old myth . . . we are expressing . . . a general and comprehensive fact, a core of reality . . . an entire conceptual complex."

In 1950, Pavese formed another of the hopeless, unrequited romantic attachments that he had suffered repeatedly since his first tragic experience in 1935. This time, the woman was an American actress, Constance Dowling, and when she lost interest in Pavese upon her return home, he experienced again the deep depression and bitter resignation to his fate that played a significant part in his despairing assessment of man's absurd existence in a world stripped of meaning.

On the evening of August 26, 1950, Pavese left his sister's home, presumably to wander through the city, as he often did at night, visiting little bars and cafés. This time, however, he had in mind a more permanent remedy to his lifelong feelings of frustration and loneliness. He checked into a hotel near the main railroad station, where he was not known, and made a few calls to friends. On the morning of August 27, 1950, at the age of forty-one, he was found dead from an overdose of sleeping pills.

ANALYSIS

Of the many elements that characterize Cesare Pavese's novels, those that have received most attention from critics are his preference for local color and the vernacular speaker, his affinity for unusual narrative perspectives, his use of lyric elements in discursive prose, his method of developing (or not developing) characters and plot conflicts, and his treatment of recurring symbols and themes. Each of these elements contributes in its own way to the artistic complexity of Pavese's work; taken together, they form his particular version of the neorealist aesthetic.

THE POLITICAL PRISONER

Although not published until shortly before his death, *The Political Prisoner* was the first novel Pavese wrote. It was written very quickly, between November, 1938, and April, 1939. Chronologically, it falls between his return from Calabria in 1936 and the publication of *The Harvesters*, which was the first of Pavese's novels to be published.

The Political Prisoner, as the title suggests, draws upon Pavese's own political confinement, from which he had been only recently released, and thus seems autobiographical to a degree. Whatever his reasons for not publishing it at the time of its composition— whether because of its painful autobiographical disclosure, its technical immaturity, or the threat of Fascist censorship—the subject it treated was obviously an important one to Pavese. This novel, like the story from which the plot is partly derived—"Terra d'esilio" ("Land of Exile"), Pavese's first attempt at fiction—treats the isolating, alienating effects of totalitarian politics upon human relations.

The technical shortcomings of *The Political Prisoner* are readily apparent: the melodramatic shallowness of every character except the protagonist, the inadequate exposition of the protagonist's past and the way this flaw impinges upon his present motivation, the inadequate distancing of the protagonist as character from the author's own experience, and the mistaken choice of a limited omniscient point of view, which serves not to disguise but rather to compound the author's lack of narrative objectivity in the novel. Despite these technical defects, the novel is not the miserable failure some have claimed. Seen in the light of Pavese's mature novels, it constitutes the most powerful thematic expression of his fundamental alienation from the world, even if that expression is not always accomplished in an elegant, aesthetically pleasing way.

The Political Prisoner tells the story of a young northerner named Stefano who is sentenced to a period of isolation in a remote southern village because of his political activities. In this respect, the protagonist is like Pavese. There the resemblances end, however, for Stefano is an engineer, not a writer, and his experiences in the novel are based upon his developing awareness of the contrast between the urban life led by the working classes in the north—where the economy is based upon factory labor, capital investment, and wages—and the agrarian routine and grinding poverty of the rural inhabitants of the undeveloped, economically primitive south. For Stefano, this awareness of the influence of economic factors upon social conduct is the beginning of his feeling of alienation from the simple people around him. He receives with indifference small gifts and food from Concia and Elena, the two women with whom he becomes acquainted in the village although he is unable to establish any authentic relationship with either of them—or with Giannino, another political prisoner, who tries to communicate with him from a nearby village. For Stefano, these people remain wholly other, having no relationship to himself. His political isolation has become an ontological exile: Con-

fronted with the primary facts of totalitarian repression and the loss of his own freedom, he comes to see the situation of the individual in the modern world as a sort of absurd, metaphysical imprisonment into which man is thrust by accident and from which the isolated, reflecting self cannot escape. In this respect, Pavese's novel closely resembles such works as Camus's *The Stranger* (1942) and Sartre's play *No Exit* (1944).

THE HARVESTERS

In *The Harvesters*, one finds Pavese's first attempt to use the vernacular narrator that was to become such an important element of his mature work. Naturally, Berto, the unemployed mechanic who narrates the story, employs the Piedmontese dialect with which Pavese himself was so familiar, yet the language of this novel is not entirely vernacular, but rather a careful mixture of Piedmontese with the *lingua pura* (the standard literary language), which Pavese called "naturalistic impressionism." No doubt he learned this technique from his studies of American literature, in which this impressionistic use of the vernacular has been popular since the time of Mark Twain, though Pavese was probably familiar with it through his translation of works by Anderson and Steinbeck. *The Harvesters* marked an important turning point in Pavese's development as a neorealist, for the narrative strategy he worked out in this novel came to maturity in *Among Women Only* and *The Moon and the Bonfire*, which were based upon his experiences among the peasants of Serralunga.

The Harvesters was composed even more rapidly than Pavese's first novel, being completed in about ten weeks between June and August of 1939. When published, in 1941, the novel was criticized on two counts: for the use of an uneducated narrator and for the sensational nature of the subject matter. The first of these objections can be summarily dismissed; the second objection, however, is a much more serious one and does point to a shortcoming of the novel. The plot of *The Harvesters* focuses on the actions of the narrator, Berto, and his friend Talino. When the story begins, they have just been released from prison and have decided to escape the life of frustration and poverty they have known in the city by returning to Talino's home, the little Piedmontese hamlet of Monticello. When they arrive, however, they find not a carefree life of pastoral bliss but a round of ceaseless, backbreaking agrarian labor, which Berto gradually learns to accept with satisfaction. Talino, however, seems incorrigible, and the hostile impulses that led him to commit arson in the city are soon revealed to be part of a long history of senseless aggression—which is aggravated and intensified both by his return home and by Berto's growing romantic involvement with Talino's sister, Gisella. As the tension builds between the two men, additional facts are revealed that make a tragic and violent outcome seem inevitable: Talino's incestuous desire for his sister, which culminates in her rape and subsequent abortion, and her betrayal of his arson to the authorities to exact revenge. Talino murders Gisella during the harvest in a moment of blind rage, and the villagers avenge her death. *The Harvesters* is strongly reminiscent of William Faulkner's novels of violence and revenge, such as *The Sound and the Fury* (1929), *Sanctuary* (1931), *Light in August*, (1932), and *Absalom, Absalom!* (1936). Perhaps it is no accident that Pavese's translation of Faulkner's *The Hamlet* (1940, *Il borgo*)—which tells the story of the Snopes family, whose violent, perverse history resembles that of Talino and Gisella's family in striking ways—came out in 1942, the year following the publication of *The Harvesters*.

This impression of borrowing from Faulkner is not limited to the plot. The quality for which Pavese most admired Faulkner was the latter's skillful blending of mythic and symbolic elements with psychological and historical realism. The attempt to achieve this blending is apparent in *The Harvesters*—which, as critics such as Sergio Pacifici have pointed out, is heavily laden with suggestive imagery and symbolism. This new style of figurative associations mixed with narrative objectivity, however inconsistently and clumsily it is used in *The Harvesters*, came to fruition in *Among Women Only* and *The Moon and the Bonfire*, in which Pavese mastered this powerful stylistic technique.

THE BEACH

Pavese's shortest novel, *The Beach*, was written between November of 1940 and January of the fol-

lowing year. It was the only one of Pavese's novels to be serialized, appearing in the journal *Lettere d'oggi* in 1941 and, the following year, in a limited edition issued by the same journal. Though Pavese himself was dissatisfied with the novel and the conditions under which it was produced, *The Beach* illuminates an important portion of his work. Like his later novel *The Devil in the Hills* and like many of his mature short stories, *The Beach* neither employs a vernacular speaker nor focuses on portraying agrarian life; rather, it portrays the life of leisure led by the affluent middle class and employs a cultured, intellectual narrator.

The unnamed speaker of *The Beach* is a thirty-five-year-old *liceo* professor who, like Pavese himself, proudly asserts that he has managed to retain his youthful freedom from responsibility by remaining a bachelor. The story he tells recounts the summer vacation he spent at the beach with his boyhood friend Doro and Doro's wife, Clelia, who describes herself as "a spoiled child who doesn't know how to do anything." The main part of the action is set at Doro's villa on the Italian Riviera, and the narrator's intense, lyric evocation of summer life on the Ligurian coast illustrates the imagistic, poetic quality of Pavese's prose at its best.

The lyric prose style of *The Beach*, along with the novel's portrayal of the idle activities of the affluent, reminds one of the novels of F. Scott Fitzgerald, for which Pavese had such great admiration that he refused to translate them, fearing Fitzgerald's influence upon his own work would become too strong. The reader's impression of Fitzgerald's influence upon *The Beach* is reinforced by the unusual narrative strategy Pavese chose to employ in this novel. The unnamed narrator, much like Nick in Fitzgerald's *The Great Gatsby* (1925), is a detached observer of other people's actions—a character to whom little or nothing happens during the course of the novel. That, at least, is the way the narrator of *The Beach* sees himself as he tells the story of his summer with Doro and Clelia. Unlike Fitzgerald, however, Pavese makes the narrator himself—in his egotistical, Olympian detachment from the lives and concerns of those around him—the butt of the novel's irony. Fitzgerald's Nick calmly but compassionately reports the tragic downfall of his friend Jay Gatsby, while the tragedy of *The Beach* lies in the failure of the isolated, selfish narrator to establish any meaningful contact with those around him.

The irony implicit in the contrast between the reality of the characters' situation and the narrator's uncomprehending report of it is linked to Pavese's concept of characterization in the modern novel, which he explains in his diary: "The art of the nineteenth century was centered on the development of situations . . . the art of the twentieth, on static essentials. In the first, the hero was not the same at the beginning of the story as he was at the end; now he remains the same." Though uncomprehending critics have sometimes accused Pavese of creating nothing but static characters, this is not really true, for it is only the heroes of his novels who are static. The dynamism of Pavese's novels resides not within the hero himself but in the conflict that arises from his intransigence in the face of a world that demands growth, adaptation, and change. In this type of plot, the recognition takes place within the reader, not within the characters of the fiction. It is the failure to realize this intention that has prevented many readers from seeing the degree to which *The Beach* is an outstanding example of Pavese's methods of novelistic construction.

THE HOUSE ON THE HILL

The House on the Hill is perhaps the most balanced representative of Pavese's later novels, because it successfully combines all the important themes and qualities of his work as a novelist: the competing claims of self and society; the contrast between agrarian and urban life; the use of first-person narrative; the conflict between static and dynamic characters; and the mingling of the material, objective nature of reality with a mythic, symbolic dimension.

Corrado, the unmarried professor at a Turin *liceo* from whose perspective the story is told, is another one of those detached, egotistical narrators one so often finds in Pavese's fiction. Corrado is more aware of his disengagement from others than is the anonymous narrator of *The Beach*, however, as the former's reflections often make clear. Of the effects of war

upon human relations, at least, he has a clear understanding: "The war had made it legitimate to turn in on oneself and live from day to day without regretting lost opportunities."

This novel, which was written between September, 1947, and February, 1948, clearly draws on Pavese's experiences during the long period from 1943 to 1945 he spent at Serralunga. After the war, he frequently commented on his sense of guilt in retreating to the safety of the hills while many of his friends remained in Turin, joining the armed resistance to German occupation and braving the frequent Allied bombing attacks on the city. Indeed, some critics have suggested that Pavese's espousal of allegiance to the Communist Party following the war was an attempt to assuage this sense of guilt. *Prima che il gallo canti* (before the cock crows), the title of the volume in which *The House on the Hill* was first published together with *The Political Prisoner*, makes apparent, in its clear allusion to the biblical story of Saint Peter's cowardly denial of Christ, the central theme of commitment and betrayal that the novels share.

When the novel opens, Corrado describes his situation simply and directly, without any sense of guilt about his actions: "A whole class of people, the lucky, the top drawer, were going, or had gone, to their villas in the mountains or by the sea. There they lived pretty much as usual. . . . The war raged away, methodical and futile." Yet into the secure, complacent life of this static protagonist comes a disturbing catalyst named Cate—an old lover who is now actively engaged in the anti-Fascist Resistance in Turin, returning to the countryside only to avoid capture. In reflecting upon the differences between himself and Cate, Corrado reveals many of the egotistical weaknesses of Pavese's other static heroes. He says, for example, "I was happy not to have in my days any real affection or encumbrance, to be alone, not tied to anyone." This is especially true of his thoughts about love, as when he reflects upon his affair with Cate eight years before, and the possibility that her son, Dino, might well be his own unacknowledged offspring: "Once in a while I bought her a lipstick that filled her with joy, and then I began to see that you could maintain a woman, educate her, bring her to life, but if you know what her elegance is made out of, it loses its savor."

Yet the outcome of this novel establishes a new, more satisfying pattern of development that is entirely absent from *The Beach*. In *The House on the Hill*, the hero overcomes his alienation from life, developing some measure of compassion for humankind by the end of the novel. When Cate is eventually captured by the Fascists, Corrado, fearful that he will meet the same fate, takes refuge in a seminary where—in posing as a teacher—he encounters Dino, who soon afterward runs away to join the beleaguered partisans. Corrado, becoming fearful that the Fascists have discovered his priestly masquerade, flees even farther from the city. He returns to the hills where he was born and joins his family in hiding. Yet even there, Corrado cannot hide from the reality of the war; on his journey home, he witnesses the murder of a Fascist patrol by partisans lying in ambush. Of the dead soldiers, whose physical reality he cannot escape, he says: "It is they who have awakened me. . . . They are no longer somebody else's business, you don't feel that you have stumbled upon them by accident." He is now prepared for a recognition, and he remembers what Cate has told him earlier: "Whoever lets things go and is satisfied is already a fascist." Corrado, unwilling to accept the consequences of his secure isolation, ends his experience by sitting down to tell his tale, which—he is now finally able to admit—is the "story of a long illusion."

Cesare Pavese was more than another literary suicide, for—whatever the failures of his personal life—in the nine novels he published before his death, he succeeded in creating a body of fiction that has won international acclaim. He is one of the leading figures of Italian neorealism, equaled only by Silone and Moravia. In his short life, he made wide-ranging contributions to the development of the modern Italian novel: the vernacular narrator he first developed in *The Harvesters*, the existential perspective on modern life portrayed in *The Political Prisoner*, the alienation of the static character trapped in a dynamic world in *The Beach*, and the complex mingling of realism with symbolism in *The House on the Hill*. It is

for these reasons that Pavese is, and will continue to be, considered one of the greatest Italian novelists of the twentieth century.

Steven E. Colburn

OTHER MAJOR WORKS

SHORT FICTION: *Feria d'agosto*, 1946 (*Summer Storm and Other Stories*, 1966); *Notte di festa*, 1953 (*Festival Night and Other Stories*, 1964); *Racconti*, 1960; *Cesare Pavese: Racconti*, 1968; *Told in Confidence and Other Stories*, 1971; *The Leather Jacket: Stories*, 1980; *Stories*, 1987.

POETRY: *Lavorare stanca*, 1936, 1943 (*Hard Labor*, 1976); *La terra e la morte*, 1947; *Verra la morte e avra i tuoi occhi*, 1951; *Poesie edite e inedite*, 1962; *A Mania for Solitude: Selected Poems, 1930-1950*, 1969.

NONFICTION: *Dialoghi con Leucò*, 1947 (*Dialogues with Leucò*, 1966); *La letteratura americana e altri saggi*, 1951 (*American Literature: Essays and Opinions*, 1970); *Il mestiere di vivere: Diario, 1935-1950*, 1952 (*The Burning Brand: Diaries, 1935-1950*, 1961; also known as *The Business of Living*); *Lettere*, 1966 (partial trans, *Selected Letters, 1924-1950*, 1969).

TRANSLATIONS: *Il nostro signor Wrenn*, 1931 (of Sinclair Lewis's *Our Mr. Wrenn*); *Moby-Dick*, 1932 (of Herman Melville); *Riso nero*, 1932 (of Sherwood Anderson's *Dark Laughter*); *Il 42 parallelo*, 1935 (of John Dos Passos's *Forty-second Parallel*); *U omini e topi*, 1938 (of John Steinbeck's *Of Mice and Men*); *Tre esistenze*, 1940 (of Gertrude Stein's *Three Lives*); *Il borgo*, 1942 (of William Faulkner's *The Hamlet*).

BIBLIOGRAPHY

Biasin, Gian-Paolo. *The Smile of the Gods: A Thematic Study of Cesare Pavese's Works*. Ithaca, N.Y.: Cornell University Press, 1968. As Biasin's subtitle suggests, he is exploring a consistent motif in Pavese's work, notably the search for an absolute. See the introduction, which sets Pavese's work in its period and outlines the critic's desire to establish Pavese's continuing relevance. Includes detailed notes and bibliography.

Fiedler, Leslie. "Introducing Cesare Pavese." *Kenyon Review* 16 (1954): 536-553. The first essay on Pavese in English and still cited as a classic.

Lajolo, Davide. *An Absurd Vice: A Biography of Cesare Pavese.* New York: New Directions, 1983. A sound, well-researched work by a biographer from Pavese's region. With brief notes, illustrations, and bibliography.

O'Healy, Aine. *Cesare Pavese.* Boston: Twayne, 1988. A good introductory study, with an opening chapter on Pavese's life, followed by chapters on his poetry, narrative technique, evolution of symbolic imagery, articulation of the poetics of myth, exploration of myth and history, and the search for destiny. A concluding chapter discusses Pavese and his critics. Includes chronology, notes, and an annotated bibliography.

Sontag, Susan. *Against Interpretation.* New York: Farrar, Straus & Giroux, 1966. Although Sontag focuses on Pavese's diary, her theme of the "artist as exemplary sufferer" illuminates a good deal of his fiction.

Thompson, Doug. *Cesare Pavese: A Study of the Major Novels and Poems.* Cambridge, England: Cambridge University Press, 1982. A very comprehensive study. See especially the first chapter, "The World of Cesare Pavese." Includes notes and bibliography.

THOMAS LOVE PEACOCK

Born: Weymouth, England; October 18, 1785
Died: Halliford, England; January 23, 1866

PRINCIPAL LONG FICTION

Headlong Hall, 1816
Melincourt, 1817
Nightmare Abbey, 1818
Maid Marian, 1822
The Misfortunes of Elphin, 1829
Crotchet Castle, 1831
Gryll Grange, 1860

OTHER LITERARY FORMS

Before turning his talents to the satirical novel, Thomas Love Peacock wrote poetry. His early works include *Palmyra and Other Poems* (1806), *The Genius of the Thames* (1810), *The Philosophy of Melancholy* (1812), and *Sir Proteus: A Satirical Ballad* (1814). When his principal efforts turned to prose, Peacock continued to produce the occasional elegant lyric or rousing song, many of them incorporated into his novels. His long narrative poem *Rhododaphne* (1818), "a nympholeptic tale," attracted considerable contemporary attention and has retained a measure of continued critical esteem; his satirical *Paper Money Lyrics* (1837), topical and crotchety, is largely ignored. Early in his literary career Peacock also wrote two farces, *The Dilettanti* and *The Three Doctors,* both of which were unpublished. Throughout his life, and particularly during the periods when his responsibilities at the East India Company precluded sustained literary projects, Peacock wrote essays and reviews, the most famous being his unfinished but incisive "Essay on Fashionable Literature," in *The Four Ages of Poetry* (1820), the satirical critique of contemporary poetry's debasement that provoked Percy Bysshe Shelley's *A Defense of Poetry* (1840) and Peacock's four-part *Memoirs of Percy Bysshe Shelley* (1858-1862), which the reserved and fastidious Peacock, who deplored the publication of private matters, wrote grudgingly, as a corrective to the muddled enthusiasms and posthumous scandal-retailing that admirers and acquaintances of Shelley were offering as literary biography.

ACHIEVEMENTS

From the beginning of his career as a satirical novelist, Peacock always had an attentive audience, but never a wide one. His career in several ways has invited comparison with that of his contemporary, Jane Austen. Each writer set out to please himself or herself, uninfluenced by desire for fame or gold. Each swam against the Romantic mainstream. Each produced a slim shelf of novels distinguished by elegance, irony, and—detractors might add—limited scope. Whereas Austen limited herself to matters suitable to the notice of a lady, Peacock restricted himself yet more narrowly. Except for *Maid Marian* and *The Misfortunes of Elphin*, respectively set in the picturesque past of "Merrie England" and Arthurian Wales, Peacock's novels take place in an idyllic country-house world where conversation, varied by singing, dining, drinking, flirtation, and sightseeing, is the chief activity. Even so, in this Pavonian realm, the reader who is able to read the signs aright can find, as critic Marilyn Butler reveals, serious and well-grounded discussion of moral, political, aesthetic, economic, and scientific concerns.

The dense if oblique topicality of these conversations is something of an obstacle for the twentieth century reader. Another hurdle for the general public in any age is Peacock's learning: Only those who share Peacock's passion for the past, especially classical antiquity, can enjoy the novels' esoterica and allusions, and only readers nurtured in Greek and Latin (or possessing editions whose annotations compensate for such deficiency) can smile at the puns and scholarly jokes Peacock presents in the names and adventures of his characters. Writing for a few congenial spirits, Peacock attained in his own time the respect of Shelley, George Gordon, Lord Byron, and John Cam Hobhouse. He has retained the appreciative but limited audience Shelley's lines from *Letter to Maria Gisbourne* (1820) seem to prophesy: "his fine wit/ Makes such a wound, the knife is lost in it;/ A strain too learned for a shallow age,/ Too wise for selfish bigots."

BIOGRAPHY

Thomas Love Peacock was born at Weymouth in Dorset, England, in 1785. His father, Samuel, was a London merchant, his mother, Sarah, a woman of Devonshire. He attended a private school at Englefield Green until he was thirteen. After leaving school, he served for some time as a clerk at a mercantile house and as a private secretary. In his youth, Peacock found employment uncongenial, however, and his private resources, although insufficient to send him to a university, did preclude his having to work. Peacock used his leisure well. An apt and diligent student, he became a sound classicist through his independent reading. In 1812, Peacock met Percy

Bysshe Shelley through the agency of a mutual friend, Thomas Hookham. For the next few years he was often a part of the Shelley circle. Closely involved in Shelley's tangled domestic affairs, Peacock attempted to be true to his friend, fair to the poet's wife, Harriet, and civil to Shelley's new love, Mary Godwin. When Shelley went abroad, Peacock corresponded with him and transacted business for him. When Shelley died, Peacock, along with Byron, was named executor of the estate.

In 1819, Peacock was appointed assistant to the examiner in the East India Office. The salary he derived from his position enabled him to marry Jane Gryffydh, a rector's daughter whom he had last seen in 1811, when he had been on a walking tour of Wales. The Peacock marriage was not a particularly happy one; the professional appointment proved rather more auspicious. In 1837, on the retirement of James Mill, Peacock became examiner at East India House. He capably held this important administrative post until his retirement in 1856.

The pleasures of Peacock's maturity were those he ascribes to various characters (most of them urbane clergymen) in his novels: good wine, good dinners, hours in the garden or in his study with the classics, rural walks from his house at Halliford in the Thames valley. One of the few new friends Peacock made during the latter half of his life was John Cam Hobhouse, Lord Broughton. Peacock's peaceful old age was saddened by the unhappiness of his favorite daughter, the talented Mary Ellen, who had imprudently married the novelist George Meredith, and by her death in 1861. Peacock died at Halliford in 1866.

ANALYSIS

A writer with strong intelligence but weak invention is not likely to become a novelist. His talents would seem to be most serviceable elsewhere in the literary realm. Even so, the example of Peacock suggests that such a deficiency need not be fatal to a writer of fiction. True, his plots are often insignificant or implausible, and his characters tend to be sketches rather than rounded likenesses or, if three-dimensional, to have more opinions than emotions. His novels are nevertheless readable and re-readable, for he excels in anatomizing the follies, philosophies, and fashions that the age presents to his satirical eye. It is not enough for Peacock to make clear the inconsistencies and absurdities of pre-Reform Toryism, Byronic misanthropy, or the modern educational system: His talent for phrase-making ensures that even the bores and halfwits he creates spout golden epigrams.

Clear thinking and stylish writing are not the rarest of Peacock's gifts, though. Perhaps his distinctive excellence is his ability to embrace limitation without accepting diminution. He revels in ideas and delights in the good things of the world. A thoroughgoing classicist in his own views, he accurately understands most of the contemporary opinions and ideas he attacks (Samuel Taylor Coleridge's transcendentalism is a notable exception). He is opinionated without being ill humored. His erudition does not preclude strong practicality. The narrow range of emotions he articulates is the result of a positive rather than a negative quality, of brave stoicism rather than heartlessness. Although Peacock's novels are for the most part slender, they never seem the productions of a small mind.

HEADLONG HALL

Headlong Hall, Peacock's first novel, is far from being his finest piece, but it is a mature work in which the characteristic devices of Peacock's career are effectively, if not perfectly, deployed. One finds charming description of picturesque countryside, in this case Wales, where Peacock had happily traveled in 1809. One finds a rich rural lover of good conversation, Squire Headlong of the Hall, who, to gratify his taste, assembles a diverse set of wise and foolish talkers. Most important, one finds the talkers themselves.

In this novel, as in several of the later ones, Peacock's satire is general; his own perspective is not to be precisely identified with that of any one character. The principal way of grouping the speakers at Squire Headlong's symposium is to distinguish the philosphers, who genuinely seek to discover truth via Socratic dialogue, from the cranks, who find in conversation a chance to ride forth on their particular intellectual hobbyhorses, and who would rather lecture

than learn. When Peacock wrote *Headlong Hall* in 1815, he was in daily contact with the Percy Bysshe Shelley circle, and the novel's three philosophers reason from stances Shelley, Peacock, and their friend Thomas Jefferson Hogg adopted in their intellectual discussions. Peacock's naming of the three characters indicates their respective positions. Foster the perfectabilian (φωστηρ, "one who guards a flame") articulates a position that Shelley sometimes took, that the human race is improving largely through technological advances. At the other pole is Escot the deteriorationist (εs σκοτοr, "one looking on the dark side"), who takes the Rousseau-derived view that man has fallen from his pristine excellence largely because, as Shelley's friend J. F. Newton argued, he eats meat. Balancing these opposites is Jenkinson, the embracer of the status quo (αιεr εs ιοωr, "one who from equal measures can produce arguments on both sides"), who gives voice to Hogg's skepticism.

To fan the flames of intellectual discourse, Peacock provides an assortment of windy enthusiasts and eccentrics, none so finely drawn as later incarnations were to be, but none failing to amuse. The Reverend Mr. Gaster begins Peacock's series of gourmandizing clergymen; Panscope is his first and thinnest burlesque of Coleridge's transcendentalism. Marmaduke Milestone speaks for the Reptonian school of picturesque gardening, a taste Peacock deplored. The phrenologist Mr. Cranium leads off the series of freakish scientists that continues down through *Gryll Grange*. Representing literary enterprises, if not strictly speaking literature, are the poets Nightshade and Maclaurel, the reviewers Gall and Treacle, and Miss Philomela Poppyseed, a writer of feminine novels and one of the few stupid women in Peacock's gallery. Lest the fine arts be neglected, Peacock supplies Sir Patrick O'Prism, a painting dilettante, and Cornelius Chromatic, an amateur violinist.

The characters feast, drink, talk, sing. Having served their host's (and their author's) purposes, they are paired in the ordering dance of marriage, an inevitable conclusion according to the systems of both Foster and Escot, and an empirical state in which one suspects the two philosophers' theories will prove of precisely equal value.

MELINCOURT

Peacock's second and longest novel, *Melincourt*, is generally considered his weakest. At the time of its composition, Peacock's principal association was with Shelley, and in this novel Peacock drops the objectivity of the "laughing philosopher" and presents political views he shared with the poet, who was even then giving them poetic form in what was to be Shelley's *The Revolt of Islam* (1818). Melincourt sincerely satirizes the Tory government and, as Lord Byron's *The Vision of Judgment* (1822) would later do, former liberals such as the Lake Poets—Robert Southey, William Wordsworth, and Coleridge (Featherernest, Paperstamp, and Mystic in the novel)—who had grown less critical of the establishment as their places in that order grew more comfortable. Certain episodes in *Melincourt* are memorable. The election at Onevote presents a marvelous empirical case for parliamentary reform, and the Anti-Saccharine Fête celebrates Peacock's belief that sugar, because its production permitted the West Indian slave trade to prosper, was a morally and politically abominable commodity to be abjured by all true philanthropists "till it were sent them by freemen." For the most part, though, this sort of candor makes *Melincourt* shrill rather than forceful.

The romantic thread on which the beads of satiric incident are strung is likewise not among Peacock's strongest. The heroine of the piece and owner of its principal location is Anthelia Melincourt, "at the age of 21, mistress of herself and of ten thousand a year, and of a very ancient and venerable castle in one of the wildest valleys of Westmoreland." More than one critic has noticed that the assets mentioned and the rhetoric employed in this, *Melincourt's* opening passage, call to mind the famous first sentence of Jane Austen's *Emma*, published two years earlier in 1815. Unlike Austen's charming and self-deluded Miss Woodhouse, Miss Melincourt is an earnest and judicious lady, a fit match for Mr. Sylvan Forester, the second Peacock hero to embody Shelley's intellectual idealism.

These two young people, so obviously suited for each other, lose no time in discovering their mutual regard. The novel's complications and the lovers'

tribulations must come from without: Anthelia is abducted to Alga Castle by the enamoured Lord Anophel Achthar. Having lost his bride-to-be, Forester, ostensibly seeking her, wanders about England's Lake District and calls on poets and reviewers at Mainchance Villa and Cimmerian Lodge. His dilatory pursuit gives Lord Anophel time to tire of waiting for Anthelia to yield to his repeated proposals. He threatens to compromise her, and, even though the lady is too strong minded to think that his wickedness will be her disgrace, she is nevertheless grateful enough to be rescued from a test of her theory by Forester and his companion Sir Oran Hautton, who is barely prevented from administering "natural justice" by throwing Lord Anophel out the window.

The fierce, faithful, mute Sir Oran is, most readers agree, the book's chief delight, curious though it might seem for a speechless character to be the chief excellence in a book by a writer noted largely for his characters' conversations. In Sir Oran, who plays the flute, goes out in society, and gains a parliamentary seat, Peacock presents with only slight exaggerations a theory of the Scottish jurist Lord Monboddo that the orangutan is a "noble savage" distinguished from the rest of the human race only by its inability to speak. In the world of literature at least, Monboddo's argument may have more validity than readers might expect: A literary Darwin examining popular fiction might well be tempted to see in the still thriving breed of strong, silent, active heroes Sir Oran's not-too-distant descendants.

NIGHTMARE ABBEY

Peacock began writing his third novel, *Nightmare Abbey*, after Shelley and Mary Godwin departed England for Italy in March of 1818. The book is arguably his finest, certainly his best-focused and plotted, and easily his most controversial. In this novel, Peacock, one of the great English admirers of Aristophanes, lays himself open to the same sort of unfair criticisms that have been heaped on the Greek dramatist for his comedy *The Clouds* (423 B.C.E.). Just as Aristophanes was censured by various critics, from Plato on, for inaccurately and irresponsibly portraying Socrates, so Peacock has been condemned for faithlessness and poor taste by readers who consider

Nightmare Abbey an unseemly depiction of one of the less commendable interludes in Shelley's life—his period of wanting to have Mary Godwin without giving up his wife Harriet.

There are indeed resemblances between Shelley and the novelist's protagonist Scythrop—part romantic idealist, part misanthrope, part would-be reformer. Marionetta O'Carroll, the sprightly coquettish cousin Scythrop professes to love, is like Harriet Shelley in spirit and appearance. Scythrop's other love, the heiress Celinda Toobad (known to him as Stella) is tall and raven-haired, the physical opposite of Mary Godwin, but very like Peacock's impression of that grave lady in her passion for philosophical speculation, political discussion, and transcendental romantic literature. Invention of detail was at no time Peacock's strong suit; he was obliged to borrow from real life.

Yet, despite having drawn certain details of his novel from Shelley's situation in 1814, Peacock was neither so tasteless nor so unkind as to write a book centering on his friend's romantic and domestic difficulties. The surest sign of Peacock's goodwill is Shelley's own admiration of the novel: "I am delighted with *Nightmare Abbey*," he wrote from Italy. "I think Scythrop a character admirably conceived and executed; and I know not how to praise sufficiently the lightness, chastity, and strength of the language of the whole." Rather than personalities, Peacock's targets were the dark gloom of modern literature, Byron's *Childe Harold's Pilgrimage* (1812-1818), and such other determinedly dismal works, and the black bile and blue devils introduced by this literature into the lives of its readers.

Nightmare Abbey is the only Peacock novel to take place at one scene only, namely the dreary and semidilapidated seat of Christopher Glowry, a gentleman "naturally of an atrabilarious temperament, and much troubled with those phantoms of indigestion which are commonly called *blue devils*." Disappointed in love and marriage, the gloomy squire of the Abbey surrounds himself with owls, ivy, water weeds, and servants with the most dismal names: Raven, Crow, Graves, Deathshead. His son Scythrop, a reader of gothic novels and transcendental philosophies, stalks the Abbey like a grand inquisitor. The

young man is ruled by two passions: reforming the world by repairing the "crazy fabric of human nature" and drinking Madeira. These preoccupations alter materially when Mr. Glowry's sister and brother-in-law, their niece and ward Marionetta, and a host of other guests arrive for an extended taste of what hospitality the Abbey can afford. Among the house-guests are a particularly fine array of representative embodiments of morbid romanticism. The Honorable Mr. Listless, who spends whole days on a sofa, has perfected ennui. Mr. Flosky, who "plunged into the central opacity of Kantian metaphysics, and lay *perdu* several years in transcendental darkness, till the common daylight of common sense became intolerable to his eyes," is one of Peacock's more successful sketches of Coleridge. Mr. Toobad is a Manichaean Millenarian, the Byronic Mr. Cypress, a poet who, having quarreled with his wife, feels absolved from all duty and is about to set off on his travels.

Finely drawn though the gentlemen may be, as Marilyn Butler has noted in her treatment of *Nightmare Abbey*, Scythrop's two ladies divide the book between themselves. Scythrop's attraction to the volatile Marionetta, who playfully spurns him when he seems devoted and charms him when he seems distant, dominates the first half of the book, while his fascination for the mysterious and brilliant Stella, a creature of veils and conspiracies, overshadows lesser matters in the second half of the story. Scythrop can bring himself to dispense with neither lady: "I am doomed to be the victim of eternal disappointment," he laments in the tone of German high tragedy, "and I have no resource but a pistol." The two unrenounceable ladies, however, find it possible to renounce their suitor. Wishing Scythrop joy of Miss O'Carroll, Celinda/Stella turns to the metaphysical Mr. Flosky. Wishing him all happiness with Miss Toobad, Marionetta engages herself to Mr. Listless. His disappointment validated, his misanthropy doubly confirmed, Scythrop thinks himself unlikely to make a figure in the world. His story ends not with a gunshot but with a sound more familiar in the Peacock world: "Bring some Madeira."

Peacock's next two novels, *Maid Marian* and *The Misfortunes of Elphin*, depart from the prevailing "country-house conversation" pattern. Both works are generally labeled "satirical romances," being set in the picturesque past but laying out oblique observations on present-day situations.

MAID MARIAN

The first of these romances is perhaps Peacock's most widely known story, primarily because it forms the basis for a popular operetta by J. R. Planché, *Maid Marian: Or, The Huntress of Arlingford* (1822). Peacock was sometimes considered to have borrowed portions of his novel from Sir Walter Scott's *Ivanhoe* (1819), but actually Scott and Peacock, who wrote most of his novel in 1818, shared their primary source: Joseph Ritson's *Robin Hood*, a collection of ancient poems, songs, and ballads about that hero. Like Scott's work, Peacock's novel is no plausible portrait of medieval life. Robin Hood is not a responsible steward of the wealth he commandeers; his superiority lies in being less hypocritical than his adversaries, the sheriff and Prince John. Friar Tuck is one in Peacock's long gallery of wine-loving clergymen; Maid Marian, whose swordsmanship and archery are commendable, and who decides in liberated fashion at the novel's end to retain her virginal title "though the appellation was then as much a misnomer as that of Little John," is one of Peacock's admirably independent heroines. The satiric object of the forest idyll? To mock the repressive and reactionary Holy Alliance, on which Byron, too, was then turning his sights in his *Don Juan* (1819-1824).

THE MISFORTUNES OF ELPHIN

As a perennial wandering woodsman, particularly in Windsor Forest, which had recently been enclosed, Peacock might have grown up with an interest in the Robin Hood material. His interest in the legendary past presented in *The Misfortunes of Elphin* dates to a more specific series of events. In 1820, Peacock married Jane Gryffydh, a young woman he had met on his travels in Wales ten years before, and her fluency in Welsh reawakened his interest in the Celtic legends of Elphin, Taliesin, and Arthur on which his story is based. Peacock's pastiche of Welsh myths is notable for its rousing songs and its depiction of the splendidly amoral inebriate Seithenyn. Its political satire is particularly effective. The crumbling of the ruinous seawall and castle administered by the drunken Seithenyn could be an apt allegory for any self-indulgent, backward-looking ruling class blind to imminent revolution and indifferent to public responsibility. The situation and the speeches of Seithenyn, however, superbly transmuted from those of the nineteenth century politican George Canning, are particularly relevant to an England on the brink of parliamentary reform.

CROTCHET CASTLE

Crotchet Castle, written two years after *The Misfortunes of Elphin*, returns to the Pavonian mainstream. Here the mansion is a glorified villa; the owner, a rich and recently retired Scottish stockbroker; the target, progressive hypocrisy, represented in real life by Henry Brougham and in the novel by the "March of Mind." The novel divides into three parts. A house party at Crotchet Castle, carefully designed by its host to pit "the sentimental against the rational, the intuitive against the inductive, the ornamental against the useful, the intense against the tranquil, the romantic against the classical," is followed by a floating caravan proceeding up the Thames to the rural depths of Wales; the novel concludes with a Christmas gathering, more than a little Pickwickian, at the quasimedieval residence of Mr. Chainmail, a sturdy but sensitive anachronist patterned, as critic David Garnett has observed, after Sir Edward Strachey.

This tale of past and present—that is, the past as it should have been and the future that the present shows all too much promise of becoming—sets Mr. Chainmail and the Reverend Dr. Folliot, one of Peacock's fiercer Tory clergymen, against the liberal utilitarians of the "March of Mind" school, preeminent among them one Mr. MacQuedy ("*Mac Q.E.D.*, son of a demonstration," as Peacock annotates his own pun). Two pairs of lovers require proper pairing as well. Mr. Chainmail, by story's end, overcomes his excessive regard for old names and blood and marries Susannah Touchandgo, a financier's daughter once engaged to the prospering speculator Crochet, Jr. Having lost her fiancé when her father lost his fortune and decamped for America, Miss Touchandgo has withdrawn to a salubrious Welsh seclusion of music, country cream, fresh air, and exercise, in which charming situation Mr. Chainmail comes upon her.

If old names must be foresworn, so must new money; in the romance dovetailed with the Chainmail-Touchandgo one, Lady Clarinda Bossnowl, generally acclaimed as the most delectable of Peacock's exceptionally pleasing heroines, breaks her engagement to young Crotchet and commits herself to the poor, pedigreed, and talented Captain Fitzchrome. Perhaps the best philosopher in the Crotchet Castle party, Lady Clarinda begins by playing at utilitarianism, intent on not giving her heart away when she can sell it. The journey from the stockbroker's villa to romantic Wales, however, gives her judgment time to concur with what her feelings long have suggested: that love in a cottage—and not even a *cottage ornée*—with the Captain is better than comfort at the Castle. Lady Clarinda's raillery, Folliot's prejudices, and Chainmail's enthusiasms make the novel's conversation particularly fine, and the climax, a spirited defense of Chainmail Hall against "Captain Swing" and that "coming race," the mob, is perhaps Peacock's most active.

GRYLL GRANGE

Peacock, preoccupied with official duties and family concerns, did not write another novel for thirty years, but *Gryll Grange*, his last one, is of a vintage worth waiting for. Few readers would suspect that the author of this suave and mellow production was well acquainted with sorrow and disappointment. The satire here is less incisive and the development of character richer than in the earlier books—in part because the people portrayed have feelings as well as opinions, in part because Peacock's wit plays not on the characters but on the world outside Gryll Grange, the modern England of scientific advance, technological development, competitive examinations, and spiritualism—a society mocked by the Gryll Grange houseparty in their own satirical comedy "Aristophanes in London."

For the plot of *Gryll Grange*, Peacock harks back to the situation of *Melincourt*. Morgana, the niece and heiress of Gregory Gryll (the family, we learn, is descended from that Gryllus who alone among Ulysses' crewmen declined being released from the spell

by which Circe has turned him into a pig), needs a fit husband who will take her name. Squire Gryll's friend the Reverend Dr. Opimian, a hearty man much like Peacock in his relish for "a good library, a good dinner, a pleasant garden, and rural walks," finds just such a suitor in Mr. Falconer, the new resident of a nearby tower significantly called the "Duke's Folly" by the neighborhood. Falconer, the last of Peacock's fictional projections of the young Shelley, is an idealistic recluse who lives a comfortable, scholarly life with seven beautiful sisters who manage his household and make his music. Once juxtaposed by the well-tried divine machine of a thunderstorm, Miss Gryll and Falconer are mutually attracted: The subsequent story in large measure centers on the hero's vacillations. Should he renounce his monastic retreat and the seven maidens who have been his companions since childhood, or should he forswear the social world so fetchingly represented by Gryll Grange and the one lady he loves?

Also staying at the Grange are Lord Curryfin, a lively, inventive, and engagingly ridiculous fellow, and the serenely beautiful Miss Niphet. Their presence further complicates the romantic dilemma. Lord Curryfin, at first drawn to Miss Gryll, finds himself increasingly enamoured of the other charmer and knows not where to offer his heart and title. Miss Niphet, a good friend to Morgana, loves the young lord but hesitates to bag a bird on whom she believes her friend's sights to be trained. Miss Gryll, who knows she loves Falconer but doubts whether she can get him, believes she can get Lord Curryfin but wonders whether she could truly love him. This tangled web of love, honor, and jealousy, so mild that it never becomes a vice, is straightened out by an event yet more providential than the convenient thunderstorm: the appearance and acceptance of seven stalwart rustics who want to marry the maidens of the tower and who thereby free Falconer from his reservations. The novel ends with all the lovers properly betrothed, a multiple wedding, and, as is fitting in the Peacock world, a vinuous salute. Addressing the wedding party, Dr. Opimian concludes, "Let all the corks, when I give the signal, be discharged simultaneously; and we will receive it as a peal of Bacchic ordnance, in honor of the Power of the Joyful Event, whom we may assume to be presiding on this auspicious occasion."

Peter W. Graham

OTHER MAJOR WORKS

POETRY: *The Monks of St. Mark*, 1804; *Palmyra and Other Poems*, 1806; *The Genius of the Thames*, 1810; *The Philosophy of Melancholy*, 1812; *Sir Proteus: A Satirical Ballad*, 1814; *Rhododaphne*, 1818; *Paper Money Lyrics*, 1837.

NONFICTION: *The Four Ages of Poetry*, 1820; *Memoirs of Percy Bysshe Shelley*, 1858-1862.

BIBLIOGRAPHY

Burns, Bryan. *The Novels of Thomas Love Peacock*. London: Croom Helm, 1985. Focuses on Peacock's novels, providing a close reading and analysis for each. The introduction traces his intellectual debts, especially to classical authors. The novels are read with a primarily textual approach, discussing language, characterization, syntax, and irony and suggesting that they are "dialectical" in nature. Burns does not offer much interpretation of Peacock's novels, but does a good job of looking at their style, emphasizing their similarities but also insisting on their diversity. The bibliography is selective but includes important works, and the index is thorough.

Butler, Marilyn. *Peacock Displayed: A Satirist in His Context*. London: Routledge & Kegan Paul, 1979. A first-rate study of Peacock which focuses not only on him as an individual but also on the society in which he lived and worked. Discusses the relationship between Peacock and Percy Bysshe Shelley, contending that they derived mutual intellectual benefit from their friendship which is revealed in their work. Butler emphasizes Peacock's satiric abilities, attempting to explain that he does not debunk everything—a common charge against him—but instead is highly skeptical of systems. Includes a detailed reading of each of his major novels, plus an examination of Peacock as a critic. The introduction sets him in his literary, social, and biographical context.

Dawson, Carl. *His Fine Wit: A Study of Thomas Love Peacock*. Berkeley: University of California Press, 1970. Discusses most of Peacock's work in detail, including his poetry, essays, and music criticism. Does a very good job with his works and provides an alternative view, but is somewhat outdated. The chapter on Peacock's *The Four Ages of Poetry* provides illuminating background on the book and also on Percy Bysshe Shelley's response to it, which culminated in his famous *A Defense of Poetry*. Even so, Dawson does not treat Peacock as a minor writer or as a disciple of Shelley, as many critics do; in fact, he paints Shelley as something of a hypocrite. The index and chronology are not strong, and there is no bibliography; the book does include notes which could serve as a substitute.

McKay, Margaret. *Peacock's Progress: Aspects of Artistic Development in the Novels of Thomas Love Peacock*. Stockholm: Almqvist & Wiksell, 1992. Chapters on Peacock's poems and plays as well as on his novels. Peacock's major characters also receive considerable discussion. McKay provides good background information on the literary figures and movements Peacock satirized. Includes extensive bibliography.

Mulvihill, James. *Thomas Love Peacock*. Boston: Twayne, 1987. An excellent short sourcebook on Peacock, providing biographical background and sound context for each of his major works from his poetry to his novels (*Headlong Hall, Melincourt, Nightmare Abbey, Crotchet Castle, Gryll Grange, Maid Marian, The Misfortunes of Elphin*), as well as his essays and reviews. Attempts to place each work into its appropriate literary and historical background and provide a detailed, interesting, although fairly standard reading. A good starting place for work on Peacock because of its brevity. The bibliography and good chronology are helpful, as Peacock is such a little noticed author.

Prance, Claude A. *The Characters in the Novels of Thomas Love Peacock (1785-1866): With Bibliographical Lists*. Lewiston, N.Y.: E. Mellen Press, 1992. An excellent dictionary of characters in

Peacock's works. Indispensable for the student of Peacock.

Tomkinson, Neil. *The Christian Faith and Practice of Samuel Johnson, Thomas De Quincey, and Thomas Love Peacock.* Lewiston, N.Y.: E. Mellen Press, 1992. Examines the religious literature of Peacock, Johnson, and De Quincey. Includes bibliographical references and an index.

WALKER PERCY

Born: Birmingham, Alabama; May 28, 1916
Died: Covington, Louisiana; May 10, 1990

PRINCIPAL LONG FICTION

The Moviegoer, 1961
The Last Gentleman, 1966
Love in the Ruins: The Adventures of a Bad Catholic at a Time Near the End of the World, 1971
Lancelot, 1977
The Second Coming, 1980
The Thanatos Syndrome, 1987

OTHER LITERARY FORMS

As a writer of imaginative literature, Walker Percy devoted himself exclusively to the novel. However, he also wrote more than fifty reviews and essays on many of the same topics that inform his novels: existential philosophy, language theory, modern scientific method, contemporary American culture, the South, and literature. With one or two exceptions, the most important of these essays are collected in *The Message in the Bottle* (1975), which has as its peculiarly Percyean subtitle *How Queer Man Is, How Queer Language Is, and What One Has to Do with the Other.* An indispensable book, *The Message in the Bottle* not only clarifies the author's major concerns as well as his commitment to that most basic philosophical question, "What is man?," but also details the formidable intellectual foundation upon which his fiction so unpretentiously rests. That unpretentiousness is especially evident in *Lost in the*

Cosmos (1983), ironically subtitled *The Last Self-Help Book,* in which Percy employs satire and semiotics in an effort to clarify the human being's social and more especially spiritual predicament as a uniquely "lost" creature needing the good news of the gospels but all too often willing to settle for the insights of scientists and talk-show hosts.

ACHIEVEMENTS

Walker Percy is perhaps most easily described as a Catholic-existentialist-American-southern novelist, a baggy phrase that at least has the virtue of identifying the various currents which are blended together in his distinctive works. In Percy's fiction, Mark Twain's Huck Finn from the novel *The Adventures of Huckleberry Finn* (1884) and Jean-Paul Sartre's Antoine Roquentin from the play *Nausea* (1938) meet in a single character adrift in a world where, despite the formless sprawl of mass society, the possibility of grace still exists. Percy's fiction is readily identifiable by its distinctive narrative voice. That voice—laconic yet disarmingly honest and filled with wonder—gained for Percy both critical respect and a dedicated readership. Percy received the National Book Award for *The Moviegoer,* the *Los Angeles Times* Book Award for *The Second Coming,* and the St. Louis Literary Award for *Lost in the Cosmos.* Among his other literary honors were memberships in the National Institute of Arts and Letters and the American Academy of Arts and Sciences.

BIOGRAPHY

Walker Percy was born in Birmingham, Alabama, on May 28, 1916. When his father, lawyer Leroy Percy, committed suicide in 1929, the widow and her three sons moved to Greenville, Mississippi, where they lived with Leroy's bachelor cousin, William Alexander Percy, who adopted the boys in 1931, following their mother's death in an automobile accident. The Greenville home served as something of a local cultural center; the uncle, the author of several works, including an autobiographical memoir of the South entitled *Lanterns on the Levee* (1941), entertained such houseguests as William Faulkner, Carl Sandburg, Langston Hughes, David Cohn, and

Harry Stack Sullivan. In the early 1930's, Percy attended Greenville High School, where he wrote a gossip column and became the close friend of Shelby Foote, who was by then already committed to a literary career. At the University of North Carolina, which was noted for its school of behaviorism, Percy majored in chemistry and received a B.S. degree in 1937. He then enrolled in Columbia's College of Physicians and Surgeons (M.D., 1941), where, in addition to his studies, Percy underwent psychoanalysis and became a frequent filmgoer. The turning point in his life came in early 1942 when, as a resident at Bellevue Hospital in New York, Percy contracted tuberculosis. During his two-year convalescence at Saranac Lake, he began reading extensively in philosophy and literature (Sartre, Albert Camus, Søren Kierkegaard, Gabriel Marcel, Fyodor Dostoevski, Nikolai Gogol, Leo Tolstoy, Franz Kafka). What he discovered was that as a medical doctor he knew much about people but had no idea what a human really is.

Following a relapse and further convalescence in 1944, Percy seemed sure of only two things: He was a doctor who did not wish to practice medicine; he was literally as well as existentially homeless (his uncle having died in 1942). In 1945, he traveled with Shelby Foote to New Mexico and then stayed on alone for a time. On November 7, 1946, he married Mary Bernice Townsend, and less than a year later they both converted to Catholicism. (The decision to convert was, Percy said, in large measure the result of their reading of Kierkegaard's essay, "The Difference Between a Genius and an Apostle.") Soon after, the Percys moved from Sewanee, Tennessee, to New Orleans, Louisiana, where Percy contin-

(Nancy Crampton)

ued his contemplative life, financially secure—thanks to his uncle's estate—and intellectually rich—his landlord, Julius Friend, a professor of philosophy, introduced him to the writings of Charles Saunders Peirce, whose triadic theory of language formed the basis of Percy's own linguistic speculations. (Percy's interest in language had another and more personal source: The younger of his two daughters was born deaf.) In 1950, the Percys moved to Covington, Louisiana, "a pleasant non-place," Percy said, where it is possible to live as a stranger in one's own land; it is neither the "anyplace" that characterizes mass society nor the "someplace" of New Orleans or a Richmond, where the past haunts the present.

In the 1950's, Percy began publishing essays in such journals as *Thought, Commonweal*, and *Philosophy and Phenomenological Research*. After discarding two early novels, he began writing *The Moviegoer* in 1959, revising it four times before its publication two years later. Until his death on May 10, 1990, Percy lived quietly in Covington, Louisiana, a serious and meditative novelist who was also a Catholic, an existentialist, and a southerner, pondering the world in thought, fiction, and an occasional essay.

ANALYSIS

Walker Percy acknowledged that Søren Kierkegaard's writings provided him with "a theoretical frame of reference," and one of the most important ideas which he adapted from this frame is Kierkegaard's rejection of Hegelian rationalism in favor of a subjective and intensely passionate commitment on the part of the individual. In Percy's view, modern science in general and the social sciences in particular have mistakenly and indiscriminately adopted the behaviorist, or biological, method and have consequently defined the human being reductively and abstractly. Existentialism, including the existential novel, on the other hand, presents an alternative to behaviorism: a "concrete" phenomenological approach whose aim is the recovery of humankind's uniqueness. Percy admits that the behaviorist method is valid to a point; ultimately, however, it must fail, because, in classifying the human as a biological organism acting in accordance with rules applicable to all biological organisms, it fails to deal with what is distinctly human, the nonbiological goals. Concerned solely with sameness, the scientific method cannot account for Fyodor Dostoevski's underground man except as a deviation from the norm. Existentialism, Percy believes, does account for this, as does Christianity, which acknowledges the Fall of Man and his distance from God, and defines existence as "the journey of a wayfarer along life's way." Denying the Fall, modern science makes the Gnostic mistake; it

attempts to build Eden, the secular city, where human guilt and anxiety are conditioned away, where all biological needs are met, and where existence is certified by experts.

Percy rejects this "brave new world" and calls instead for a "radical anthropology" that can account for the ontological as well as the biological aspects of human existence. Guilt and anxiety, he points out, are not symptoms of maladjustment to be gotten rid of so that the individual (as human organism) can live the life of the satisfied consumer; rather, these signs of estrangement serve to summon a person not to self-fulfillment but to authentic existence. Humanity is on earth not to have needs met, Percy says, not to surrender sovereignty to the theories of experts (a view raised again by Christopher Lasch in his controversial book, *The Culture of Narcissism*, 1979), but to be saved, and that necessitates consciousness of the human situation.

It is important to realize that Percy's sovereign wayfarer, or castaway, is not entirely identifiable with Kierkegaard's knight of faith. In place of Kierkegaard's extreme subjectivity, Percy posits the intersubjectivity of Gabriel Marcel, a Christian existentialist whose *we are* stands in stark contrast with both Kierkegaard's *I choose* and René Descartes's *I think*. We know we exist, Marcel says, by participating in the world. He does not think of being as experience, however, but as a presence within experience which is to be understood as simultaneously transcendent *and* immanent. To separate the two components of being is to pervert them and to transmogrify the individual as sovereign wayfarer into either angel—the abstract knower, the objective consciousness—or beast—a culture organism satisfying its needs. (The terms are Percy's, borrowed from Blaise Pascal.)

Marcel's quest for being, which is the quest for salvation as well, manifests itself in Percy's theory of language as intersubjective communication, where *we name* implies the same religious affirmation as Marcel's *we are* and Martin Buber's *I-Thou*. Percy originally turned to language theory in order to answer the question "What is man?" because the answer provided by the behaviorist method was reductive and because the old theological view, along with the words in which it was couched, has been rendered ineffective by the general acceptance of the scientific method, which predisposed modern humanity to view itself as the behaviorists had defined it. Percy then set himself the task of finding "the delta factor": that which makes the human what it is and not something else. According to the old theological view, humankind's singularity is its "soul," a meaningless word in a scientific age that demands empirical proof. For soul, Percy substitutes language, which he defines not as a sign system (the behaviorist position) but as the uniquely human process of symbolization. At the heart of language (and therefore at the heart of humanity as well) is something mysterious (compare Marcel's "mystery of being"). The mystery is explained by what Percy calls the "coupling process," the intersubjective human context by which people name, or symbolize, the world and in this way come both to know it and to share it. Language is, therefore, an attempt to bridge the gap between self and other, or, considered in the religious context of the Fall of Man, between self and God. What complicates the situation is the fact that in the late twentieth century, Percy believed, language became as meaningless, as clichéd, as the old theology. Before there can be intersubjective communication, humankind must again learn how to speak.

To learn to name and therefore to know and share that knowledge with another is the basic plot of a Percy novel. As Robert Coles has pointed out, Percy's novels trace the protagonist's movement from lofty observation to active participation in the openness of life—its possibilities and the necessity of making choices. Each of his major characters feels estranged "from being, from his own being, from the being of other creatures in the world, from the transcendent being. He has lost something, but what he does not know; he only knows that he is sick to death with the loss of it." Since this quest for being is a quest for God, it involves the hero's progress through Kierkegaard's three stages: the aesthetic (the pursuit of pleasure; the self becomes an uncommitted ironic spectator detached from himself and from others); the ethical (living within a general human code, such as marriage); the religious (requiring an entirely personal and—Kierkegaard would say—absurd leap of faith). The hero's search for being begins only when he or she becomes conscious of his or her despair and tries either to understand it or to alleviate it in one of two ways: rotation or repetition. Rotation—the quest for new experiences to offset "everydayness"—makes up the comic substance of Percy's novels. Repetition—the return to the past—may be rendered comically, but more often it serves a darker purpose, for Percy's heroes are, like William Faulkner's, haunted by the past; as a result, they do not live fully in the present. Only when they confront the past directly and become conscious of it can they break its spell and become sovereign wayfarers.

Frequently, Percy equates the past with the Southern stoicism his uncle espoused, which, in Percy's judgment, leads only to pessimism, obsession with death, and "the wintry kingdom of self"; in short, it is the very antithesis of Percy's Christian existentialism. Rotation and repetition provide only temporary relief from the malaise that prevails within the aesthetic stage. The only escape from "aesthetic damnation" is through ordeal, especially the death of a loved one. Ordeal brings heroes face to face with mortality and enables them to see their world and themselves as if for the first time. The search they then begin is in effect a rejection of the absurdist position of aesthetic existentialists such as Albert Camus and Jean-Paul Sartre. The world is not absurd; it is a world to be named, known, and shared by the authentic self and the other in a mode of existence that is not so much religious *or* ethical as a synthesis of the two.

There are analogues for Walker Percy's religious-phenomenological conception of the human search for being in his method of composition and in his prose style. The author's search for narrative form parallels the hero's search for being. Beginning with a situation rather than a plot or set of characters, Percy wrote with no fixed purpose or end in mind. As he explained, the writing, while not "haphazard," involved "many false starts, many blind detours, many blind passages, many goings ahead and backing up. . . ." Stylistically, his elegantly and precisely written novels suggest wonder, humor, and forbearance rather than the ponderous solemnity of other existential novelists such as Sartre. Moreover, his prose is richly and sensuously detailed; like two other converts to Catholicism, Marcel and even more particularly Gerard Manley Hopkins, he took pleasure in a natural and human world that is, although marred by evil, essentially sacramental.

THE MOVIEGOER

John Bickerson Bolling—"Binx"—is the narrator and main character of *The Moviegoer* and the first of Percy's spiritually "sick" protagonists. At age twenty-nine, he is a successful broker in a modern world where the church has been replaced by the brokerage house. Although financially secure, Binx feels uneasy; although adept at planning his client's futures, he has trouble living his own life from day to day, fearful that he may at any moment succumb to that worst of all plagues, the malaise of "everydayness." To counter its effects, Binx becomes a moviegoer, partly because films project a "heightened . . . resplendent reality," albeit temporarily, and partly because films provide Binx with accepted role-models: thus his impersonations of such canonized figures as Gregory Peck, Clark Gable, Dana Andrews, and Rory Calhoun (who also serves as his confidant). The impersonation can never fully satisfy the moviegoer, however, who must eventually face the fact that the reality of his own life can never attain the heightened illusion of the star's gestural perfection. Moviegoing serves Binx in two additional ways: It enables him to view his world through the perspective of the films he has seen and, more important, to observe the world as if it were itself a film and he the passive audience.

Binx's detachment is both a virtue and a vice. As the detached spectator, he observes those around him closely and accurately, thus exposing the roles they have unknowingly adopted. Appropriately, the novel's temporal setting is the week before Mardi Gras, the period of rehearsals for New Orleans' city-wide impersonation. Instead of recognizing their situation as castaways, these others feel serenely at home in the world, whereas in fact they are, as Binx understands, "dead." Neither virtuous nor sinful, they are merely "nice"; they speak, but in clichés; they

ask questions, but neither expect nor desire answers. Binx, who fears becoming invisible—losing his identity—is right to keep his distance from these shadowy others. At the same time, however, he longs to be like them, to have his identity certified for him by such spurious means as films, identity cards, *Consumer Reports*, newspaper advice columns, and radio shows such as "This I Believe," which broadcasts the meaningless affirmations of abstracted religionists to a half-believing, half-skeptical Binx.

If it is his ironic detachment that saves Binx from the unreflective life of mass humanity, then it is his "search" that most clearly characterizes his longing for authenticity and being. "To become aware of the possibility of the search is to be onto something," Binx says. "Not to be onto something is to be in despair." Binx distinguishes two kinds of search. The "vertical" leads to abstraction: theories that explain the world but fail to explain what humankind is. (One alternative to such abstraction is the romanticism that killed Binx's father and that the son wisely rejects.) The other is the "horizontal" or phenomenological search that Percy himself counsels in *The Message in the Bottle*. While Binx is indeed "onto something," his search is different from Percy's; it constitutes a "debased" form of the religious search because, as Percy explained, Binx, like Sartre, "has already ruled God out." His search takes a purely aesthetic form. To ease "the pain of loss," he pursues money and women, but the pursuit leads only to boredom and depression because the novelty of his possessions quickly wears off and everydayness inevitably returns to remind him of his inauthenticity and his position as a castaway. Fortunately, Binx's yearning has a deeper current. As a college student, he found himself "lost in the mystery of being alive at such a time and place"; upon his return from the Korean War, he began his eight-year "exile" in the New Orleans suburb of Gentilly, which, like Covington, is a "non-place"; as a broker he has taken to reading *Arabia Deserta*, by the self-styled "God's pilgrim," Charles Montagu Doughty, concealed inside a Standard & Poor binder.

Binx's search begins with the fact of his own "invincible apathy" and eventually leads, after many wrong turns, to authenticity and intersubjective relationships with his fourteen-year-old half-brother, Lonnie Smith, and his twenty-five-year-old cousin Kate Cutrer. There exists a "complicity" between Binx and the dying Lonnie, who faces life with true serenity because he understands it religiously. Like the other dying children in Percy's novels, Lonnie represents the paradox of unmerited suffering in a world ruled by a supposedly benevolent God, a paradox Percy resolves by depicting their spiritual victory in a "world full of God's grace where sorrow and death do not have the final word." Binx attends to the "good news" that Lonnie embodies because, in part, Lonnie's monotonous way of talking makes his words fresh and therefore meaningful, "like a code tapped through a wall."

Kate, unlike Lonnie, lives in pure anxiety, swinging wildly between various extremes, especially the longing to be free and the desire "to be an anyone who is anywhere." Although she lacks Binx's degree of awareness as well as his ironic detachment and is more prone to impersonation than he, Kate, like Binx, is aware of her disease, which others can only understand in psychological terms. (Thus, the novel's epigraph, taken from Kierkegaard: "the specific character of despair is precisely this: it is unaware of being despair.") Binx and Kate neatly complement each other: His childlike "simplemindedness" allows her to feel secure enough to speak honestly, while she correctly points out that in his search Binx may be overlooking something "obvious." Her request that Binx be her God—by which she means he is to tell her what to do—is not at all absurd given Marcel's brand of Christian existentialism. Significantly, her other suitors play the part of intersubjective God rather badly: One wants to send her to a high-priced psychoanalyst; the other promises an interminable vista of "niceness" and everydayness.

Binx's leap from nominal Catholic existing in despair to sovereign wayfarer and authentic being occurs very late in the novel and is effected by what, in a parallel context, Percy calls "some dim dazzling trick of grace." In fact, only a few pages from the end Binx laments that, having but one gift, "a good nose for merde," the only course for him to follow is "to

fall prey to desire." There is even some justice to his Aunt Emily's judgment of him: in crucial situations, Binx invariably chooses to "default," to "exit." Yet, in the final pages, it is clear that Binx will do so no longer. Neither, however, will he play the part his aunt has chosen for him—Southern stoic. He will go to medical school, not because she wants him to but because now he knows what to do: to observe *and* to serve others. Binx's leap is reflected in the very texture of Percy's prose. Until the epilogue, which takes place one year later, Binx has narrated his tale chiefly in what may be termed his detached, matter-of-fact, moviegoer style, against which the very few lyrical passages, used to underscore Binx's wonder and the gracefulness of his world, stand in vivid contrast. In the epilogue, Binx drops the moviegoer style (and the references to films) entirely; instead, he speaks easily, authentically, authoritatively. The man who earlier had been cousin, half-brother, and ironic impersonator, now is husband, brother, and sovereign wayfarer.

THE LAST GENTLEMAN

The protagonist of Percy's second novel, *The Last Gentleman*, "Williston Bibb Barrett or Billy Barrett," is a modern-day version of Dostoevski's Prince Myshkin in *The Idiot* (1868). Although far less ironic than Binx Bolling, Barrett is far more disturbed, as his periodic fugue states and bouts of amnesia and déjà vu attest. Existing in a state of pure possibility, he is incapable of making any one decisive act or choice. He has tried and failed both to live the therapeutic life and to "engineer" his own destiny. Knowing something is missing in his life, Barrett seeks to recover reality and find his being in the "gap" between self and other. Specifically, these others are the members of the Vaught family, and his search is a spiritual odyssey, modeled on Mark Twain's *Adventures of Huckleberry Finn* (1884), that takes him from New York to his native Ithaca, then on to Mississippi, and finally to Santa Fe (Holy Faith), New Mexico, and the Sangre de Cristo (Blood of Christ) mountains.

The search begins when Barrett accidentally discovers Kitty Vaught and her sister-in-law, Rita, in Central Park. Rita, a secular humanist and advocate of self-fulfillment, quickly realizes she will not be able either to control or to convert Barrett and tries unsuccessfully to get rid of him. Barrett, however, has already fallen in love with Kitty, a rather pale version of Kate Cutrer—less anxiety-ridden, more successful in her impersonations. Barrett's love affair is both furthered and complicated by Kitty's younger brother, Jamie, whose traveling companion he becomes. The fact that Jamie is dying establishes definite limits to the pure possibility of his and Barrett's lives and causes Barrett to consider his search more profoundly when he meets another sister, Val, and brother, Sutter, the two "absentee experts" (as Barrett calls them) who force him to make his existential choice. Val, a convert to Catholicism and a nun, has dedicated herself to teaching mute children to speak and to believe the Catholic religion. (All people are like her children, she claims; they are waiting to be told what to do.) Whereas she is hopeful and apostolic, Sutter, a diagnostician and pathologist, is suicidal and ironically quixotic. He rejects her belief in the human as wayfarer, claiming "We are doomed to the transcendence of abstraction and I choose the only reentry into the world which remains to us": "lewdness," cynicism, and detachment.

Sutter's mistake, as Barrett well understands, is the positing of extreme alternatives such as God or no God, transcendence or immanence. Moreover, Sutter's concern for Jamie betrays his basically religious nature, and it is this, more than his medical expertise, that has led Barrett to look to him for answers. At Jamie's baptism, it is Sutter who comprehends what is happening. Barrett, although he acts as interpreter between Jamie and the priest, misses the religious significance. He does understand that something has happened, however, and to discover what that something is he tracks down Sutter, who has decided to commit suicide. Barrett's search for an answer is, as Percy noted, a search for a father, ultimately for the Father, God; his own father, Barrett finally realizes, had looked for his answer in all the wrong places—solitude, "old sad poetry," and the music of Johannes Brahms. The son's "wait" did not keep the father from killing himself, but it does save

Sutter, who appears in the final tableau less as an oracle than as Barrett's self-chosen—and therefore sovereign—responsibility.

LOVE IN THE RUINS

Subtitled *The Adventures of a Bad Catholic at a Time Near the End of the World, Love in the Ruins* is a broad satire on the state of the modern world—in particular, its behaviorist assumptions and political absurdities. The novel may be flawed, as some reviewers have contended, by the author's insistent and at times rather heavy-handed social criticism; there is, however, a comic vitality in this novel that seems to offset such reservations about it as literary art. This comic vitality, quite unlike the irony and understatement that characterize Percy's earlier novels, is appropriate to a work that has the topics of community and reconciliation as two of its major concerns. As Percy explained in an essay entitled "Notes for a Novel about the End of the World," the apocalyptic novelist serves two purposes: As prophet, or canary in the coal mine, he cries out in order to avert disaster, and as coupling agent, he connects humankind with reality. It is by means of the coupling process that disaster is averted, as Percy quietly suggests in the novel's closing image of a couple "twined about each other as the ivy twineth," in which what has been a sign of ruin (the ivy) is transformed into a symbol of intersubjective love.

The story, which is spoken into a pocket tape recorder by the hero, Tom More, as he keeps watch for snipers, follows a five-part structure (July Fourth, First, Second, Third, Fourth) that progressively becomes more chaotic until, in the epilogue ("Five Years Later"), peace and order are restored. The time of the novel is a not too distant future that bears a clear, if comically exaggerated, resemblance to the American 1960's: The fifteen-year war in Ecuador continues, racial tensions and Bantu uprisings are increasing, and the Catholic Church has split into three factions. In short, "the center did not hold." The physical setting is just as perverse as the social-political: Paradise Estates, home of the well-to-do and the spiritually impoverished; Fedville, a sprawling compound which includes a Masters and Johnson Love Clinic, where ex-priest Kev Kevin reads *Commonweal* and presides over the vaginal console; Honey Island Swamp, a counterculture retreat; and the golf course, where a banner proclaims "Jesus Christ, the Greatest Pro of Them All."

Percy's hero is as troubled as his society but in a different way. Forty-five years old and a collateral descendent of Sir/Saint Thomas, he is at once a doctor and a mental patient, a diagnostician but also a metaphysician in a world of behaviorists ready and willing to condition away any remaining feelings of guilt he may have. Loving, in descending order of importance, women, music, science, God, and, "hardly at all," his fellow human, he is the type of what Kierkegaard termed aesthetic damnation. He has lost that thread in the world-labyrinth which, until the death of his daughter Samantha, made the world seem sensible and holy. His faith gone, More has his own messianic ambition, a plan to "save" America with More's Qualitative Quantitative Ontological Lapsometer. His invention—"the stethoscope of the spirit . . . the first caliper of the soul"—is designed to measure the "gap" between the outer, social self and true, inner being; he hopes to modify the lapsometer so that it can cure as well as diagnose humankind's "fall" from being, to put together what Descartes tore apart. Like Percy and, to a degree, like Sutter Vaught, More is troubled by the modern world's indifference to being and people's willingness to define themselves in half-measures: the angel that, falling prey to abstraction, is unable to "reenter the lovely ordinary world," or the beast that adapts to its environment and so becomes the organism behaviorists say the human is.

Art Immelmann (Mephistopheles to More's Faust) tempts him with spurious "good news": a multimillion dollar development grant and the Nobel Prize. The price is, of course, More's soul—his being, his sense of personal responsibility. More resists the devil and so escapes aesthetic damnation; by not committing the unpardonable sin (refusing God's grace), he puts an end to the "feasting on death" that has preoccupied him since the onset of his daughter's illness and begins to live in the "lovely ordinary world" once again. Instead of an apocalypse, the novel ends with a new beginning, a Christmas morn-

ing. Reborn, Tom More no longer loves abstractly or bestially; he has married his former nurse, Ellen Oglethorpe, a Georgia Presbyterian, whose belief takes the form of charity. Equally important, More now knows what it is he wants: not prizes or women, but "just to figure out what I've hit on. Some day a man will walk into my office as ghost or beast or ghost-beast and walk out as a man, which is to say sovereign wayfarer, lordly exile, worker and waiter and watcher."

LANCELOT

Percy's fourth novel, *Lancelot*, is by far his most troubling. Structurally, it follows the odd dialogue form of Camus's *The Fall* (1956); until the last two pages, only the voice of the protagonist is heard, addressing a "you" whose responses are not given. More disturbing is the fact that, as Joyce Carol Oates has pointed out, the views of the main character, a self-righteous and unrepentant murderer, are strikingly similar to those of the author. Readers must recognize, as Percy surely does, the nature of the protagonist's grotesque mistake—the sources from which it derives and the ends to which it leads.

Lancelot Andrewes Lamar speaks his Poe-like tale from the Center for Aberrant Behavior in New Orleans, where he has been confined for one year. Although in the course of his apologia/confession Lance identifies his wife Margot's infidelity as the immediate cause of his murdering her and the members of the film company with whom she was involved, the actual causes go much further back and have less to do with Margot than with his own wasted life and his position as the last in a fallen line of Southern aristocrats. As a Lamar, Lance has inherited not only the family homestead, Belle Isle, but also a way of judging humankind in absolute terms. His first wife, Lucy, was (or so Lance remembers her) an angel, whereas Margot, who for a time he turned into a goddess, became beast or devil. Dividing his life into two parts—before he discovered his wife's adultery and after—he proclaims that the past is "absolutely dead" and the future will be "absolutely new." This penchant for absolutes suggests Lance's inability or unwillingness to confront the ambiguity and mystery of human existence and is related to the way the Lamars view human life in terms of individual, historically significant events. Thus, Lance's life is reduced to his 110-yard touchdown run against Alabama and his destruction of Belle Isle and everyone in it. Lance does understand that performing such feats is actually less difficult than living an ordinary life, but when he turns Margot's infidelity into a quest for the "unholy grail," he in effect sidesteps the ordinary life which is far "more complicated and ambiguous" than either the historical events venerated by the Lamars or the clichéd films of Margot and her friends.

Like their film, Lance's quest is superficial and derivative (it is cast in the mold of the Raymond Chandler detective novels he has been reading). Moreover, it leads Lance, as Cleanth Brooks has demonstrated, to commit a modern version of the Gnostic heresy. Claiming that the original sin was something God did to man and judging Christianity as much a failure as Southern stoicism, Lance determines to destroy the present age, which he cannot tolerate, and start over in a new Eden with his new Eve, Anna, a fellow patient who, he believes, as the victim of a brutal gang rape, has been restored to innocence. Lance is wrong about Anna, however; she never lost her innocence. He is also wrong about Christianity, if one distinguishes, as Kierkegaard did, between Christianity (as embodied in Percival, Lance's listener to whom the novel is spoken) and Christendom, which Lance is right to reject as a viable alternative to his intolerable age.

Lance's confession, as well as his predicament, brings his friend Percival's spiritual ambivalence into sharp focus; Percival, the "Prince Hal" of their early manhood who has since been ordained Father John, is torn between two roles—priest and psychiatrist— and two approaches to human existence—the religious and the behavioral. It is Percival's fellow psychiatrists who certify Lance as sane, even though both Lance and Percival know there is still something wrong, something missing. As a psychiatrist, Percival cannot help Lance, whose problem is ontological and spiritual rather than psychological, and whose self-righteous ranting masks his deeper uncertainty and longing. When, at the very end of the novel,

Lance asks, "Is there anything I can do for you before I leave?," Percival's *"Yes"* identifies him as the apostolic Father John, the bearer of the good news for which Lance has been waiting. Against such grand gestures as blowing up Belle Isle, Percy offers the power of a small, ordinary word freshly heard.

THE SECOND COMING

The Second Coming was, as Percy noted, his "first unalienated novel." Instead of the ambiguity that characterizes the endings of his earlier novels, here the author celebrates the unequivocal victory of love over death. While such a conclusion did not please all reviewers, many of whom found it unconvincing or even sentimental, it is consistent with Percy's religious vision and his flexible aesthetic with its various tones and broad range of narrative structures: the novelist's version of God's plenty.

The novel picks up the life of Will Barrett some twenty years after *The Last Gentleman*. At age forty-three, Will is a retired lawyer, a wealthy widower living in Linwood, North Carolina, and recent recipient of the Rotary's man-of-the-year award; yet, he is still a sick man, subject to dizzy spells and tricks of memory. What troubles Will is not the loss of his wife Marion but the sudden realization that he has wasted his life and been "only technically alive." At the brink of the abyss, he sees himself as a total stranger; only two percent of himself, he sets out to find the missing ninety-eight percent. His search takes him in a number of directions. One is back to his father, or more specifically to the only "event" in his life. This is a hunting accident that he comes to realize was no accident at all but instead the father's attempt to kill his son and then himself and so free them both from lives not worth living.

Like his father, Will rejects the "death in life" that characterizes modern believers as well as unbelievers; Will also rejects his father's solution, suicide, because it proves nothing. Instead, he devises the "ultimate scientific experiment" which will, he believes, provide conclusive proof of either God's existence or His nonexistence/noninvolvement. As the narrator points out, Will is mad; moreover, his plan (to starve himself and so force God either to save or abandon him) is badly flawed in two important ways. The language Will uses to define his experiment (actually more a "covenant") betrays his egotism as well as his legalistic frame of reference; to his "huge" bequest (his life), he attaches a "huge" condition (God's appearing to him). Not until much later in the novel does he learn "the economy of giving and getting" and the superiority of ordinary existence to his own ultimate experiments or his father's extraordinary "events." In addition, Will is looking for God in the wrong place. While waiting in the cave for "a clear yes [or] no," he misses the unambiguous beauty of Indian summer; and while he assails God's "unavailability," his own "fade outs," such as the cave experiment, preclude the very intersubjective relationships through which God manifests Himself to humankind. The sign he does receive, a toothache, is "a muddy maybe" that cuts short the experiment and sends Will howling in pain out of the wilderness of self and into a world that, while not physically new, can be seen in an original way.

The person who changes Will's angle of vision is Allison Huger (Kitty Vaught's daughter), who has just escaped her own cave, a mental hospital, and begun a new life in an abandoned greenhouse. She resembles Will in that she feels uncomfortable around other people, as well she should, for the Allison they see is the mentally disturbed organism for whom they can imagine nothing better than "the best-structured environment money can buy." Although she wants to live an entirely self-reliant life, each afternoon about four o'clock she experiences a sense of loss or emptiness. What she feels is identical to one of the symptoms of Will's disease (Hausmann's syndrome), which the doctors call "inappropriate longing." There is a pill to control Will's disease, but there is only one way to satisfy the longing, and that is by loving Allison, by finding his being in her just as she finds hers in him. As Allison explains in her characteristically melodic way, "Our lapses are not due to synapses." Percy's love story is not, therefore, simply romantic; rather, it is religious in the Christian existential sense. Their love is, to quote Allison again, "be-all" but not "end-all." When, in the novel's concluding scene, Will Barrett confronts Father Weatherbee, an old priest,

his heart leapt with joy. What is it I want from her and him, he wondered, not only want but must have? Is she a gift and therefore a sign of the giver? Could it be that the Lord is here, masquerading behind this simple holy face? Am I crazy to want both, her and Him? No, not want, must have. And will have.

Here, as in the four earlier novels, one finds what Sartre called humanity's "useless passion," but for Percy this passionate longing is not useless at all because the world is not absurd. Percy's search is not one of Sartre's purely arbitrary "projects"; rather it is a thoroughly modern and, for many readers, an entirely convincing rendition of John Bunyan's *The Pilgrim's Progress* (1678, 1684) in an age mired in the slough of behaviorism and unbelief.

THE THANATOS SYNDROME

The Thanatos Syndrome, Percy's sixth and last novel, ends a bit differently, which is to say less insistently. Narrator-protagonist Dr. Tom More's "well well well" befits the "smaller scale" of his latter-day desires, yet this fit proves ironic, given the novel's overgrand, at times messianic ambitions (of the kind More himself had in *Love in the Ruins*). Similarities between the two novels are obvious (they share a number of the same characters and the same Futurist-fantasy approach), but both the strengths and the weaknesses of *The Thanatos Syndrome* owe far more to *Lost in the Cosmos* than to *Love in the Ruins*: the satirizing of contemporary absurdities (inauthenticity in some of its craziest manifestations) and, unfortunately, the hardening of that spiritual need, which characterizes Will Barrett and Binx Bolling, into religious dogma. What was a translation of Christian belief into psychological, cultural, and semiotic terms in the earlier novels has begun to sound here like a propounding of conservative Catholic teachings, which undermines a novel that otherwise effectively mixes Sir Thomas More's 1516 *Utopia*, medieval romance, Fyodor Dostoevski, and Robin Cook.

The novel picks up the life and times of Tom More in the mid-1990's, a short while after his release from federal prison, where he has served a two-year term for illegally selling drugs. A brilliant diagnostician, More describes himself as "a psyche-iatrist, an old-fashioned physician of the soul" who believes that it is better, psychologically and spiritually speaking, to be sick (anxious, even terrified) than well, for disease is prolapsarian man's natural state. Many of the people around him are, he realizes, anything but anxious. They are, instead, content: without inhibitions, without anxiety, without anything more than rudimentary language skills, and, most important, without a sense of self. With the help of his epidemiologist cousin Lucy Lipscomb, More discovers "Blue Boy," a clandestinely funded pilot project which involves introducing heavy sodium into the local water supply in order to stem the tide of social deterioration (crime, teenage pregnancy, even acquired immunodeficiency syndrome).

Director of Blue Boy and indeed of the entire "Fedville" complex (including an "Equalitarian Center" with facilities for "pedeuthanasia" and "gereuthanasia" and a propensity for obfuscating acronyms) is the ironically "graceful" Bob Comeaux (née Robert D'Angelo Como), who calls Blue Boy "our Manhattan Project." He tries to cajole, seduce, bribe, and threaten More into complicity, all to no avail. Although he remains a lapsed Catholic throughout, the doctor nevertheless sides with the enigmatic, certainly depressed, previously alcoholic, perhaps mad Father Simon (as in Simeon Stylites and Simon Peter) Smith, who spends all of his time up in a fire tower silently triangulating the positions of forest fires, atoning for his sins, and on one notable occasion claiming that all tenderness inevitably leads to the gas chamber (or to the Equalitarian Center, which may be the same thing in a different, more socially acceptable, guise). Comeaux would make everyone happy, at the cost of his or her freedom as well as awareness of himself or herself as a distinctly human being: a creature caught in the malaise, lost in the cosmos, in need of something other than heavy sodium, self-help, or Phil Donahue. Like Saul Bellow's *The Dean's December* (1982), *The Thanatos Syndrome* expresses More's faith (in there being "more" than Comeaux allows) in the form of a doubt concerning the modern belief that the causes and cures of humankind's problems are invariably physical. To the extent that *The Thanatos Syndrome* articulates

this doubt, it, like Percy's other novels, succeeds extraordinarily well. To the extent that it propounds Catholic dogma in response to a host of topical issues (abortion, "quality of life," sexual "freedom," child abuse, bio- and behavioral engineering, among others), it fails according to the very terms that Percy himself adopted at the time of his conversion, turning the triadic mystery of Søren Kierkegaard's apostle into dyadic pronouncement, sign into signal, spiritual "predicament" into position paper.

Robert A. Morace

OTHER MAJOR WORKS

NONFICTION: *The Message in the Bottle*, 1975; *Lost in the Cosmos: The Last Self-Help Book*, 1983; *Conversations with Walker Percy*, 1985; *Signposts in a Strange Land*, 1991 (Patrick Samway, editor).

BIBLIOGRAPHY

Allen, William Rodney. *Walker Percy: A Southern Wayfarer.* Jackson: University Press of Mississippi, 1986. Allen reads Percy as a distinctly American, particularly Southern writer, claiming that the formative event in Percy's life was his father's suicide, not his reading of existentialist writers or conversion to Roman Catholicism. Allen's readings of individual novels emphasize the presence of weak fathers and rejection of the Southern stoic heritage on the part of Percy's protagonists.

Coles, Robert. *Walker Percy: An American Search.* Boston: Little, Brown, 1978. An early but always intelligent and certainly sensitive reading of Percy's essays and novels by a leading psychiatrist whose main contention is that Percy's work speaks directly to modern humanity. In Coles's words, Percy "has balanced a contemporary Christian existentialism with the pragmatism and empiricism of an American physician."

Desmond, John F. *At the Crossroads: Ethical and Religious Themes in the Writings of Walker Percy.* Troy, N.Y.: Whitston, 1997. Chapters on Percy and T. S. Eliot; on Percy's treatment of suicide; on Percy and Flannery O'Connor; on his treatment of myth, history, and religion; and his philosophical debt to pragmatism and Charles Sanders Pierce. A useful, accessible introduction to Percy's background in theology and philosophy.

Dupuy, Edward J. *Autobiography in Walker Percy: Repetition, Recovery, and Redemption*. Baton Rouge: Louisiana State University Press, 1996. Discusses Percy's autobiographical novels as psychological fiction. Includes bibliographical references and an index.

Hardy, John Edward. *The Fiction of Walker Percy*. Urbana: University of Illinois Press, 1987. The originality of this book, comprising an introduction and six chapters (one for each of the novels, including *The Thanatos Syndrome*), derives from Hardy's choosing to read the novels in terms of internal formal matters rather than (as is usually the case) Percy's essays, existentialism, Catholicism, or southern background. Hardy sees Percy as a novelist, not a prophet.

Lawson, Lewis A. *Following Percy: Essays on Walker Percy's Work*. Troy, N.Y.: Whitston, 1988. Collects essays originally published between 1969 and 1984 by one of Percy's most dedicated, prolific, and knowledgeable commentators. Discussions of *The Moviegoer* and *Lancelot* predominate.

Percy, Walker. *Conversations with Walker Percy*, edited by Lewis A. Lawson, and Victor A. Kramer. Jackson: University Press of Mississippi, 1985. This indispensable volume collects all the most important interviews with Percy, including one (with the editors) previously unpublished. The volume is especially important for biographical background, influences, discussion of writing habits, and the author's comments on individual works through *Lost in the Cosmos*.

Quinlan, Kieran. *Walker Percy: The Last Catholic Novelist*. Baton Rouge: Louisiana State University Press, 1996. Chapters on Percy as novelist and philosopher, existentialist, explorer of modern science. Recommended for the advanced student who has already read Desmond. Includes notes and bibliography.

Tharpe, Jac. *Walker Percy*. Boston: Twayne, 1983. Reading Percy as a Roman Catholic novelist concerned chiefly with eschatological matters,

Tharpe divides his study into ten chapters: "Biography, Background, and Influences," "Theory of Art," "Christendom," "Techniques," one chapter on each of the five novels through *The Second Coming*, and "Conclusion." The annotated secondary bibliography is especially good.

_____, ed. *Walker Percy: Art and Ethics*. Jackson: University Press of Mississippi, 1980. Ten essays by diverse hands, plus a bibliography. The essays focus on settings, existential sources, Martin Heidegger, Percy's theory of language, the semiotician Charles Saunders Peirce, Percy's politics, and *Lancelot* (in terms of his essays, Roman Catholicism, medieval sources, and semiotics).

BENITO PÉREZ GALDÓS

Born: Las Palmas, Canary Islands; May 10, 1843
Died: Madrid, Spain; January 4, 1920

PRINCIPAL LONG FICTION

La fontana de oro, 1868
El audaz, 1871
La sombra, 1871 (*The Shadow*, 1980)
Episodios nacionales, 1873-1912 (46 historical novellas written in 5 series, many of which were also published separately and are included in this list)
La corte de Carlos IV, 1873 (*The Court of Charles IV: A Romance of the Escorial*, 1888)
Trafalgar, 1873 (English translation, 1884)
Zaragoza, 1874 (*Saragossa: A Story of Spanish Valor*, 1899)
La batalla de los Arapiles, 1875 (*The Battle of Salamanca: A Tale of the Napoleonic War*, 1895)
Doña Perfecta, 1876 (English translation, 1880)
Gloria, 1876-1877 (English translation, 1879)
La familia de León Roch, 1878 (*The Family of León Roch*, 1888; also as *León Roch: A Romance*, 1888)

Marianela, 1878 (English translation, 1883)

La desheredada, 1881 (*The Disinherited Lady*, 1957)

El amigo Manso, 1882

El doctor Centeno, 1883

La de Bringas, 1884 (*The Spendthrifts*, 1951)

Tormento, 1884 (*Torment*, 1952)

Lo prohibido, 1884-1885

Fortunata y Jacinta, 1886-1887 (*Fortunata and Jacinta: Two Stories of Married Women*, 1973)

Miau, 1888 (English translation, 1963)

La incógnita, 1889

Realidad, 1889

Torquemada en la hoguera, 1889 (*Torquemada in the Flames*, 1956)

Ángel Guerra, 1890-1891

La loca de la casa, 1892

Tristana, 1892 (English translation, 1961)

Torquemada en la cruz, 1893 (*Torquemada's Cross*, 1973)

Torquemada en el purgatorio, 1894

Halma, 1895

Nazarín, 1895

Torquemada y San Pedro, 1895

El abuelo, 1897

Misericordia, 1897 (*Compassion*, 1962)

Casandra, 1905

Prim, 1906 (English translation, 1944)

El caballero encantado, 1909

La razón de la sinrazón, 1915

(Library of Congress)

OTHER LITERARY FORMS

Benito Pérez Galdós's works in other literary forms can be divided into three groups: twenty-two plays, including six dramatizations of previous novels: *Realidad* (1892), *La loca de la casa* (1893), *Gerona* (1893), *Doña Perfecta* (1896), *El abuelo* (1904; *The Grandfather*, 1910), and *Casandra* (1910); nonfiction works, such as *Discursos académicos* (1897), *Memoranda* (1906), *Fisonomías sociales* (1923), *Arte y crítica* (1923), *Política española* (1923), *Nuestro teatro* (1923), *Cronicón* (1924), *Toledo* (1924), *Viajes y fantasías* (1928), *Memorias* (1930), *Cronica de Madrid* (1933), *Cartas a Mesonero Romanos* (1943), *Crónica de la Quincena* (1948), and *Madrid* (1956); and hundreds of newspaper articles, many unsigned.

ACHIEVEMENTS

The Spanish Romantics of the middle decades of the nineteenth century sought to re-create the local color of the past or the fantasy of exotic surroundings, while the *costumbristas* (regionalists) described the peculiar atmosphere of particular Spanish regions and customs. It remained for the realists of the last part of the century to transcend the picturesque sketches and emotional excesses of their predecessors. The realists directed their attention to the multiplicity and variety of observable reality in an attempt to enhance the verisimilitude of their productions. At first, they concentrated on the surface elements of this multiple panorama, while presenting psychological portraits that displayed only a few dominant and usually harmonious traits.

For more than half a century, the novel had viewed people as conforming to general social patterns, and individual character was seen as constant and without development. A descriptive delineation of a person's dominant motives or reactions to particular situations was the novelist's goal. The change from this strictly social viewpoint to a preoccupation with distinct individuals became possible when people were given the role of persistent striving, when personality itself was seen as subject to psychological and environmental influences. These new novelistic perspectives were partly the result of the rise of the theory of evolution. Also contributing to the birth of the realistic novel was the development of new ideas concerning society (a rising middle class represented a new sector of reading public which looked for a literature depicting individual citizens amid a recognizable environment), history (seen now in relation to the ordinary person), and science (the growth of which stimulated the desire for more acute observation and documentation). Some critics view the rise of realism in the Spanish novel as a result of the intellectual ferment caused by the Revolution of 1868, which overthrew Queen Isabella II. During this period, writers began to place equal emphasis on plot and environment, with the two elements functioning within a unified, verisimilar whole.

Benito Pérez Galdós belonged to the mature stage of the realistic movement. He rejected the portrayal of static elements of human nature and turned instead to the description of the varying relationships between the individual personality and the environment. Next to Miguel de Cervantes, Pérez Galdós is perhaps the most important novelist that Spain has produced; he is the only Spaniard of his age who can

be compared to Honoré de Balzac, Charles Dickens, Leo Tolstoy, or Fyodor Dostoevski. In the course of his long career, he alone succeeded in reconciling the traditional and the liberal ideological currents then prevalent in Spain, demonstrating the significance of both past events and recent developments. In spite of the fact that most of his works were set in Madrid, he alone was able to transcend the regionalism of the Spanish realistic novel. Although his works represent a historical, social, and literary synthesis of his era, he was able to penetrate and develop themes of truly universal significance—ideas concerning charity and spiritual values, problems of modern science and of materialism, the yearning for social justice, the necessity of tolerance and of personal liberty, and the notion of human equality achieved through love.

Pérez Galdós was clearly a realistic writer. His choice of verisimilar subject matter, his convincing psychological portraits, the minimization of overt didacticism (in later novels), his basically objective organizational techniques, and the naturalness, descriptive immediacy, and dialogic emphasis of his style all attest this fact. Yet there are other factors unique to Pérez Galdós which suggest a transcendence of mere nineteenth century realism: symbolic representations, the inclusion of seemingly fantastic elements, and impressionistic descriptions, among others.

This particular combination of realistic and "idealistic" elements was one of the traits which Pérez Galdós seems to have inherited from Cervantes. A basic goodness, a positive, conciliatory spirit, a special kind of ironic humor also came from the master. Like Cervantes, Pérez Galdós was able to penetrate beneath the psychological façades of his characters. He exposed the consistently contradictory nature of his fellow man, revealing wisdom in the insane, a sense of honor in the humble, charity among beggars, and the anguish for salvation in the person of a miserly moneylender.

Pérez Galdós was also one of the few Spanish writers of his time to recognize the importance and the greatness of contemporary literature of other countries. Indeed, the realistic movement can be said to have developed first and most completely in France with writers such as Balzac, Gustave Flaubert, and

Émile Zola. It was Pérez Galdós who first incorporated these foreign elements into a truly Spanish creation.

Above all, Pérez Galdós's realism was a *social* one, centered not on the delineation of regionalistic characters and landscape, not on the psychological investigation of isolated personalities, but rather on the complicated interaction between individual perspectives and aspirations and the social, usually urban milieu within which these viewpoints and desires are expressed. In short, Pérez Galdós's realism was a *human* one, focusing on the physical, psychic, and emotional effects that people have on one another and showing how these elements function within, against, or in line with the pressures of society. With *The Disinherited Lady*, Pérez Galdós recognized that an individual's personal characteristics are partly the result of social and cultural forces; conversely, societies and cultures gain a particular flavor from the individuals who constitute them. He was able to strengthen his picture of both levels (individual and social) by virtue of his perception of their interdependence and interplay.

Yet the individual-society conflict is not merely social or psychological. When the characters suffer from the extreme discrepancy between dream (illusions, romance) and reality, the conflict becomes a metaphysical one, reflecting the Hegelian dialectic implicit in the theories of realism proposed by such critics as Harry Levin, Arnold Hauser, José Ortega y Gasset, and Georg Lukács. In Pérez Galdós's mature novels, this dialectic operates in the individual's growth toward self-consciousness through his relationships with others, in the conflict between (and eventual integration of) social classes, and in the opposition and interplay of different elements within a character.

In part, the historical importance of Pérez Galdós's novels is that of having united and perfected the prevailing literary tendencies of the times: the interest in history and the past, initiated by the Romantics (whose sentimentality and imaginative excesses he avoided); the didactic or "thesis" approach, offered now without the sacrifice of psychological verisimilitude or artistic balance; and the emphasis on *cos-*

tumbrismo, extended from a local, regional level to a broader, national perspective in order to analyze and interpret the life and character of the entire Spanish community. For Pérez Galdós, these three aims were combined toward achieving a constant objective: to help his countrymen become conscious of their reality as a people, searching in the recent past for the explanation of current conditions, for a sense of direction which would work toward a future ideal of "trabajo y educación" (work and education), an ideal which would encourage an atmosphere of tolerance instead of constant civil strife.

BIOGRAPHY

Benito Pérez Galdós was born in Las Palmas on May 10, 1843, the last of ten children. Some critics feel that his place of birth, geographically and socially separate from the mainstream of Spanish life, contributed to his subsequent ability to view national events with relative candor and objectivity. Benito's father, Sebastián Pérez, sixteen years older than his wife and more a grandfather than a father to his younger children, had inherited sufficient property to maintain his family in comfort and had ample leisure time to regale his youngest offspring with tales of his military exploits, events which were to become part of *Episodios nacionales* (national episodes). It was Benito's mother, however, Doña Dolores, who was to dominate the family. Her rigid, puritanical religiosity, intolerance, strength of will, and constant need for order were to be reflected in several of Pérez Galdós's characters, most particularly Doña Perfecta. From his mother, Pérez Galdós seems to have inherited a Basque physique, stubbornness, and the ability to adhere to an unswerving, ordered routine.

Although interested in painting and music, the young Pérez Galdós found little to enjoy in his childhood schooling, usually appearing bored and absentminded. In 1862, he was sent to Madrid by Doña Dolores to study law, a course which, despite poor grades, irregular class attendance, and extensive extracurricular writing, he finished in 1869. His real interest during these years was the Ateneo, a literary and artistic club in Madrid which housed a remarkably good library and sponsored lectures and discussion groups. Here, Pérez Galdós developed the progressive, liberal spirit which would dominate his first novels, became exposed to the Krausist perspective of tolerance toward opposing views, and discovered the works of such European writers as Balzac, whose eighty volumes he himself collected.

It was during these years that Pérez Galdós began to write for such newspapers as *La nación, Las cortes*, and *El debate*. Later, in 1872 and 1873, he himself was the general director of the prestigious *Revista de España*. He traveled widely and in 1866 witnessed the uprising of "los sargentos de San Gil," a historical event which perhaps stimulated him to initiate the first series of *Episodios nacionales*. The composition of these works, which he undertook in 1873 and continued intermittently until his death, reflected a conception of history as a slow but inevitable development toward the establishment of a just and equitable society, one in which the growing bourgeoisie would absorb a decadent aristocracy and a well-meaning but ignorant lower class. The series was instantly popular, perhaps because of its stress on the importance of everyday events in the lives of common citizens. At first, the *Episodios nacionales* gave him the economic stability that he needed; later, however, even the resounding financial success of his play *Electra* (1901; English translation, 1911) was not enough to liquidate the debts which were to plague him sporadically throughout his life.

In 1886, Pérez Galdós entered politics, and in 1889, he accepted the governmentally rigged election results which made him a deputy for Puerto Rico; he served in Congress until 1890. While he did little to improve the well-being of his constituents across the ocean, he did subsequently devote considerable energy to liberal causes and eventually expended much of his meager financial resources on Republican politics.

It was also in 1889 that Pérez Galdós traveled to the Rhine Valley, where he met and had a brief affair with the Galician novelist Emilia Pardo Bazán. Despite her wish to continue the relationship, however, Pérez Galdós soon broke it off when he became involved with Lorenza Cobián, the woman who was to be the mother of his daughter María, born January 12, 1891. After Lorenza became insane and committed suicide in 1906, the novelist took charge of María's education and made her his legal beneficiary.

In 1889, Pérez Galdós was elected to the Royal Spanish Academy, but he did not take his seat until 1897. This, says Walter Pattison, was "owing in part to his timidity about making a public speech and perhaps partly to his resentment at having been passed over on the first vote."

In later years, Pérez Galdós served further Republican terms in Congress—in 1907 and 1910—but his health deteriorated rapidly. To the problem of arteriosclerosis was added a hemiplegic stroke in 1905. Several operations on his eyes were not enough to prevent blindness. These events, coupled with the disdain of the reactionaries and the indifference of the young *generación del 98*, left him bitter and resentful. The failure of his proponents to gain for him the Nobel Prize and the continued financial insecurity that came from his mismanagement of money matters added to the aging novelist's despair. Pérez Galdós had outlived his literary career. When his statue in Madrid's Retiro Park was unveiled in 1919, few prominent figures were present. Death came from uremia on January 4, 1920.

In his prime, Pérez Galdós had been reported as "tall and somewhat roughhewn in body and features, as if carved of stone. . . . His eyes were small and timid, his face not very expressive, his manner of speaking brief, fragmentary, and low-pitched; in short, he did not give . . . that impression of genius that we imagine in great men." He was shy, withdrawn, given to stage fright (he refused once to come to a large banquet in his honor, until friends pursued him and brought him back from Toledo). He preferred to listen and observe, rather than talk. Yet on the printed page, he could fight stubbornly and valiantly for his ideals. His outward simplicity was so great, said one friend, "that at times it bordered on commonness." The *generación del 98* called him "Don Benito el garbancero" (Mister Benito the grocer). Nevertheless, his remarkably exact and detailed descriptions attest his acute observational powers, and his fecundity and creativity amply demonstrate his remarkable imaginative capabilities.

He was thought to have had few close personal relationships, even within his own family; but his letters have now revealed a profound involvement with his relatives and with a broad circle of intimate acquaintances, all of whom he treated with sensitivity and charity, and with whom he was an entertaining and witty conversationalist. The tender care he offered to Lorenza Cobián and their daughter—another reason for his later impoverishment—reveals that he was indeed a warm and loving person.

Also erroneous is the notion that he was an obsessive womanizer. It is true that he had an affair with Pardo Bazán, produced an illegitimate daughter with Lorenza, and in his old age nurtured a close relationship with a refined lady named Teodosia Gandarias, but his interest in women was far from licentious or "pathological," as early critics have claimed. Perhaps a desire for individual freedom lay behind his reluctance to marry.

Despite his anticlerical activities and his hatred for the ritual and beliefs of the neo-Catholics, Pérez Galdós developed a deeply spiritual and religious orientation, related to a profound love of nature and to a Krausist upbringing which stressed tolerance, everyday ethics, and the basic goodness and harmony of human faculties. This orientation was particularly pronounced during the third phase of his literary career.

ANALYSIS

Through more than fifty years of literary creation, Benito Pérez Galdós's work underwent an evolution, a process of growth that both reflected and harmonized with broader European novelistic movements. In general, these shifts suggest a change from didacticism to more thorough, realistic documentary and later to a kind of symbolic spiritualism.

Pérez Galdós's initial orientation, however, was mostly historical. The Romantics had turned to the study of history in a desire to embrace the phenomenon of human temporality, but they had focused primarily on an atmosphere of the past—poetic, distant, and vague. Pérez Galdós and the realists inherited this historical sense, but utilized it primarily in an effort to understand the present. Pérez Galdós's first two novels, *La fontana de oro* and *El audaz*, reflect such a historical orientation.

It was also during these early years that Pérez Galdós began the *Episodios nacionales*. These works, forty-six in all, were written throughout his long literary career. They narrate the then-recent history of Spain, from the Battle of Trafalgar (1805) against Napoleon Bonaparte through the Restoration in 1874. Again, the author's aim was to guide his fellow Spaniards toward a greater understanding of contemporary psychological and social circumstances. His artistic formula was that of combining novelistic fiction—the continuing story of certain literary characters, which gives a loose unity to each series—with the graphic presentation of historical events. Aside from their literary merits, these works represent in their totality the most vivid and most complete documentary of nineteenth century history that has yet been compiled.

Aside from Pérez Galdós's almost unbroken historical preoccupations, his novelistic output can be divided into four general periods. Between the years 1876 and 1879, many of Pérez Galdós's so-called *novelas de la primera época* (novels of the first epoch) appeared. Three *novelas de tesis* (thesis novels) respresented a pronounced didactic intention, promulgating a liberal and *progresista* (progressive) spirit, opposed to religious and clerical intolerance and traditional absolutism. These novels expressed a youthful rebelliousness, a distinctly iconoclastic fervor. Indeed, the abstract, often symbolic level on which the young writer constructed such an ideological rebellion was in many respects distant from the objective immediacy of the contemporary European realists. *Doña Perfecta* describes the struggle of liberalism against outdated moral codes and religious bigotry, *Gloria* the mutual intolerance between Catholics and Jews, and *The Family of León Roch* a marriage that is the product of Catholic dogmatism.

In his second period, between 1881 and 1888, Pérez Galdós initiated the *novelas españolas contemporáneas* (contemporary Spanish novels). In these years, the author clearly settled into conformity with accepted European realistic techniques and attempted to offer something positive to replace those codes which he had tried to destroy during his early rebelliousness. *The Disinherited Lady* marks the change. A wholehearted adaptation of the use of background detail, a more complete treatment of central characters, increasing firsthand studies of his novels' milieus, a "biographical" method for exploring the interrelationships between the individual and society, and a constant attention to the ordinary circumstances of daily life—these factors suggest a stricter adherence to nineteenth century realistic practices and the influence of French naturalism. During these years also, a significant anomaly developed in Pérez Galdós's use of authorial perspective: Whereas the author appeared frequently as a minor character to enhance the effects of realism and autonomy, he allowed himself, at the same time, abundant revelations of a character's hidden thoughts, thus betraying authorial control.

Many of these novels attempted to depict Madrid society as representing a synthesis of national life. Among these works were some of Pérez Galdós's most important productions: *El amigo Manso, The Spendthrifts, Miau*, the first of the Torquemada novels, and the four-volume masterpiece *Fortunata and Jacinta*.

If the novels of Pérez Galdós's second period placed greater emphasis on the individual and his complicated relationships with the broad scope of society, those written between 1889 and 1897 presented the spiritual and philosphical aspects of that individual's predicament. An increasing tendency toward the theme of tolerance and compromise, along with a stronger emphasis on the values of love, compassion, self-discipline, and individual creativity characterized this phase. Pérez Galdós's realistic techniques were continued and refined, while a more profound sense of universality was added to an already deep patriotic sentiment. The author no longer attempted to define morality in absolute terms; his spiritualist hero struggles to purify himself rather than to find the ultimate meaning of existence. He accepts the reality of the life around him, a reality marked by pain but suggesting an abiding hope in the future. The priest in *Nazarín* and the beggar woman of *Compassion* practice Christian charity and come to ennoble the miserable surroundings in which they live. This last novel in particular seems to represent a synthesis of Galdosian techniques: Its theme, realistic—even naturalistic—documentation, and spiritualistic emphasis are united in a harmonious whole. Here, Pérez Galdós demonstrated that, while fiction is an illusion created by the imagination, life itself is also unreal—an illusion created by the senses as one encounters the external world.

In the works of his fourth and final period, beginning in 1898, Pérez Galdós revealed a profound change in artistic perspective. His seminaturalistic objectivism gave way to a kind of subjective impressionism. The third series of *Episodios nacionales* and novels such as *Casandra* and *El caballero encantado* marked the mellowness of old age, an increase in fantasy and symbolism, and, to a certain extent, a diminishing of artistic excellence. It was during this period that Pérez Galdós turned to the theater, adapting some previous "dialogue novels" to the stage (novels such as *Realidad* and *El abuelo*) and presenting such thesis plays as *Electra*, based on a condemnation of clerical intolerance and malpractice. Pérez Galdós, however, lacked true dramatic ability. Many of his plays were weighed down by psychological abstraction and slow-moving plots.

The first three stages of Pérez Galdós's literary production, then, reflect variations of general European realistic techniques of the nineteenth century. His youthful rebelliousness and abstractionism were an expression of the controversial atmosphere and ideological emphasis of the 1870's. Novels such as *The Disinherited Lady* and *Lo prohibido* reflect the moderate propagation of naturalistic ideas in Spain during the 1880's, as the author attempted a more detailed study of the individual and his environment. Pérez Galdós's interest in transcending spiritual values in turn suggests a similar reaction throughout Europe during the 1890's.

To summarize those factors relating to the author's choice of subject matter, one may say that his realism grew out of the careful exercise of his powers of observation; it was supported by verisimilitude; its guiding concern was with society, and, more specifically, the individual's complex relationships with that society; it dwelt, in proportion to their numbers, on authentic treatment of the various social classes, breaking new ground in its inclusion of the middle class, and possibly showing some preference, in later years, for the humbler members of the social order. Pérez Galdós's version of realism reflected the organic, evolutionary quality of society. It incorporated, at least superficially, some vestiges of the costumbristic tradition, from which the author attempted to liberate himself during the latter part of his career. Finally, it assimilated historical materials, to the degree that they could shed light on contemporary social circumstances.

With respect to authorial point of view, Pérez Galdós was a realist in the humoristic tradition. He recognized that irony is implicit in realism because it exposes the often odious comparison between actuality and what one desires of life. A fundamentally comic vision came most clearly into play when he ironically deflated pretentious aspirations, or when he exposed human extravagance and self-deception. Another target of his humor was the delusion that the merely relative is the absolute. His novels offer a vast comic panorama in which moments of tragedy seem to eclipse the fundamental spiritual truth. Consonant with Miguel de Cervantes' notions of the interplay of fiction and reality and of the ambiguity of truth, then, Pérez Galdós came to accept the view that finite truth changes. Any particular instance of human experience is only partially "true"; the total interrelation of these momentary revelations constitutes ultimate truth. Just as the multiplicity of realities remained a mystery to Pérez Galdós, so his characters fail to grasp absolute truth because they are permitted only glimpses of relative "realities."

Pérez Galdós's narrative point of view is a multiple one, suggesting the Cervantine idea that any person's view of reality is relative. These varied viewpoints include strictly impartial, omniscient commentary; total immersion within one character (made most striking by the use of *estilo indirecto libre* (free indirect style) and the *monólogo interior* (interior monologue); slanted (as opposed to neutral) omniscient perspectives; appearances of Pérez Galdós as omniscient author, speaking directly to his readers; moments in which Pérez Galdós appears as

one of the characters, himself ignorant of facts and circumstances because of his limited personal vision (striking examples of this can be found in *The Spendthrifts* and *El amigo Manso*); and total lack of direct authorial presence or intrusion, as manifested in the *novelas dialogadas*.

Thus, Pérez Galdós's attempts to describe all facets of contemporary Spanish society: his frequently lengthy, often unemotional descriptions, his basically impartial selectivity and means of organization, his shifting points of view—all of these contribute to a relative objectivity. At the same time, his didacticism or irony, his occasional failures to maintain authorial autonomy, and a strong, sympathetic identification with some of his characters serve to limit that very objective approach. His creations have life; they demonstrate verisimilitude, balance, and an almost infinite variety; but they come from the heart, and not the sociologist's notebook.

Pérez Galdós's characters are usually realistic in the sense that they are distinct individuals. At the same time, they are symbols: They are combinations of abstract types and concrete, humanized personalities. Torquemada, for example, symbolizes the coarse materialism of the rising Spanish middle class, but takes on a personal dimension in the emotionalism that erupts when his son dies, in his criticism at the banquet of businessmen like himself, his helplessness before the implacable Cruz, his comic attempts at verbal refinement, and his "transactions" with the Almighty. All of these factors particularize his predicament and suggest some measure of potential "roundness." Pérez Galdós's protagonists move within a double reality, reflecting the Cervantine notion that the human condition exists divided between secret, inner personality and acted, overt experience. Indeed, the constructs of the mind often seem more real than ordinary physical reality.

Despite Pérez Galdós's double emphasis upon social and individual characteristics, he does not attempt to explore the complexities and incongruities of personality in the manner of Dostoevski or some modern novelists. Often his characters are, by comparison, somewhat less complicated creatures, dominated generally by a limited number of motives (such as ambition, guilty conscience, charity, greed, and, above all, love).

With respect to style, Pérez Galdós was committed to painting even the smallest, seemingly least significant elements of reality. He was firmly convinced that the least noticeable facets of human existence and the least conspicuous details of a historical milieu are as important as the items which blaze from newspaper headlines. (Miguel de Unamuno y Jugo would later term this sphere of reality an *intrahistoria*.) Quite often, these small details are worked into descriptions of surprising length, and the *generación del 98* was quick to condemn the author's extraordinary descriptive elaboration. This trait is most noticeable in the novels of the 1880's, especially *Fortunata and Jacinta*. While it is true that this abundance occasionally tires the reader, one can still detect in it Pérez Galdós's larger motives: to picture the total sweep of contemporary Spanish life, to imply its actual magnitude and multiplicity.

The relative absence of natural settings is a well-known characteristic of Pérez Galdós's novels. The reason behind this is not hard to discern: Above all, Pérez Galdós was interested in people, and portraits of nature were subordinated to character treatment. Only rarely does one find lyric descriptions of landscape which are designed to capture the poetic nuances of the setting itself. As might be expected, such elaborations are important only for their symbolic or psychological enhancement of the people involved. Thus, the delightful description of an evening in the countryside in *Torquemada en el purgatorio* is contrasted ironically with Torquemada's imperviousness to its beauty.

Other stylistic features of Pérez Galdós's novels are especially pertinent to a discussion of realistic technique. One such feature is the naturalness of his vocabulary and phrasing: Despite its remarkable richness and variety, Pérez Galdós's language is unaffected, often colloquial. His imagery, though based on ordinary, concrete, even prosaic elements, is remarkably rich and vivid. Similes appear frequently, since they are found so often in common speech. Frequent dialogue functions as a means of actualizing his material; in one way, it helps to typify characters (to identify them as representatives of a social or vocational class), and, on the other hand, it helps to individualize them (by the use of distinguishing speech "tags"). Finally, Pérez Galdós frequently employs interior monologues; although such passages differ from the arbitrary, "free-association" techniques of the twentieth century, the novelist certainly anticipated the formulation of the "stream of consciousness" method.

DOÑA PERFECTA

Doña Perfecta best exemplifies Pérez Galdós's thesis novels, the type of writing produced during the more militant, aggressive years of his youth. It illustrates graphically Pérez Galdós's reaction to the intolerance expressed in the Constitution of 1876, which was widely discussed during the weeks when the work was appearing in installments in the *Revista de España*. The plot centers on Pepe Rey, a progressive, modern young engineer whose visit to the home of his aunt results in his sudden, tragic death. The author's main purpose is to depict the young man's struggle against the enemies of contemporary, liberal thought: bigotry, hypocrisy, reactionism, provincialism, and the weight of dead tradition.

At the suggestion of his father, Pepe goes to the remote cathedral town of Orbajosa (city of garlic), in order to survey the region for mining and irrigation projects, with the idea of meeting and possibly marrying his cousin Rosario. As the novel progresses, the conflict slowly develops between reactionary traditionalism (his aunt Doña Perfecta, the priest Inocencio, and the latter's niece María Remedios, who wants to marry her son Jacinto to Rosario) and modern thought (Pepe Rey, with the help of an army officer whose company is sent to Orbajosa to quell any possible uprisings of guerrilla bands). Finally, as Pepe tries to elope with Rosario, Doña Perfecta orders his execution. Afterward, Rosario becomes insane and is confined to an asylum, and Doña Perfecta continues her religious activities.

Thematically, then, Pérez Galdós condemns hypocrisy, fanatical religiosity, intolerance, and provincialism. On a slightly deeper level, however, he is also expressing his disdain for extremism of any kind, that passion which allows reason to be clouded by emotion. Spaniards, he says, must cast off a blind local patriotism rooted in ignorance, as well as the intolerance of many modern progressives (for Pepe's dogmatism and tactless inflexibility are also criticized). When violence engenders violence, when an oversimplified polarization of "them" and "us," of *moros* (Moors) and *cristianos* (Christians), takes place, there is no significant difference between the progressive and the reactionary perspectives. On the other hand, honesty, clearness of vision, restraint, charitable tolerance, and, above all, love are held up as factors which may unite the country and offer hope for the future. The lesson of the novel is ultimately a moral one which transcends the immediate political message about Spain of the 1870's.

Doña Perfecta, then, aptly demonstrates the Krausist justification of literature as an instrument of reform and education, as well as exemplifying the movement's belief that the moral and intellectual regeneration of the individual is the only path to the moral and intellectual reform of society. The Krausists' quest for "racial harmony," their recognition of the relationships between the whole and the part, relate directly to the technique in which biography and history are blended—the framework for this novel as well as for all the novellas in *Episodios nacionales*. Hence, Pepe's clash with his aunt, for example, is mirrored by the arrival of the troops from Madrid.

The artistic weakness of the novel lies primarily in its blatant didacticism and in the relative superficiality of its characterizations. Doña Perfecta, Pepe, Inocencio, Rosario, and María Remedios are what Stephen Gilman calls "rounded archetypes," symbolic representations of ideological viewpoints or human characteristics or passions (mostly negative).

Pepe himself is a kind of modern Don Quixote. His inevitable death, furthermore, is foreshadowed repeatedly by dramatic parallels and references to the Passion of Christ. He is individualized only by his flaws (inflexibility, tactlessness) and by his development from a straightforward, friendly, rational human being to a very intemperate, precipitous, even unethical conspirator. Generally, however, he remains a symbol.

Doña Perfecta, while more a symbolic type (almost a caricature) than a unique personality, is nevertheless also individualized somewhat and made understandable by aspects of her family background, her sincerity, and her own measure of development in the course of the novel. Rosario, whose main role is as a catalyst to the action, is nevertheless the most interesting of the characters, and Pérez Galdós's study of her conflicts, her dreams, and her neuroses is a superb precursor of the more profound pathological portraits which were to appear in later novels.

The author's style also points to later techniques. It is natural, direct, and at times even colloquial. A tone of irony predominates throughout the novel, usually expressed through dramatic contrast (Orbajosa's glorious past versus modern banditry; the symbolic dawn with which the novel opens versus the subsequent ineffectiveness of Pepe's actions; and so on). Theatrical elements abound, from the frequent use of dialogue to the descriptions of gestures and the author's "stage directions." Particular to this novel are the stress on animal imagery, classical references (as a means of revealing the ironic discrepancy between name and reality), and the symbolic use of sounds (such as the opening train whistle, the cockcrow, bugles, and the creaking of the cathedral weathercock).

The compact structure of the novel has been analyzed by two leading critics. Sherman H. Eoff has demonstrated that the movement of the plot is based on three decisive, progressively more intense moments of peripeteia: Pepe's "vehement defense of science at the end of chapter 8," his announcement of his intention to marry Rosario, and Doña Perfecta's ordering of his assassination. Stephen Gilman has suggested a number of parallels between the structure of the novel and that of neoclassical tragedy, in which "perfection" passes to "imperfection" through Pepe's tragic flaw and by way of a series of theatrically presented "acts." Indeed, the overt nature of the conflict (far different from the aim of synthesis and reconciliation evident in later works) made it an easy task to adapt the novel to the stage.

Doña Perfecta is far from a great work, and its tremendous popularity is probably undeserved. It is too schematized and melodramatic and lacks the warmth and humor, the feeling of movement, the depth of characterization, and the panorama of realistic detail that were to typify Pérez Galdós's best creations. Yet the skillful use of irony, the suggestion of pathological analysis (Rosario), and the start of a relativistic perspective in which a situation is viewed from several perspectives point to the more mature works which followed.

THE DISINHERITED LADY

The Disinherited Lady heralded a new phase in Pérez Galdós's career. The author no longer concentrated on examining merely the social implications of certain ideologies; rather, *The Disinherited Lady* reveals Pérez Galdós's forceful attempt to incorporate into the novel the world of external appearances, to accumulate innumerable, detailed images of outward, as well as inward, reality. Here, one finds the faithful representation of environment, daily customs, psychological motivation, and the formation of the new middle class—in short, the creation of an "accurate mirror of the society in which we live." This was now the author's central purpose, and the core of his subsequent realistic aspirations. Pérez Galdós now went to work on a broader canvas, including naturalistic suggestions of hereditary and environmental influence; he introduced "collective" characters (*manicomio, fábrica, taller, asilo, barrio bajo*, and so on) and the theme that people must face reality; he initiated the idea that the real world and the world of fiction interact and are mutually dependent. Finally, *The Disinherited Lady* represents a closer joining of the two narrative paths expressed previously in a more separate form: the *episodio* of contemporary history (here the abdication of Amadeo, the floundering of the First Republic, and the advent of the Restoration) and the didactic representation of society seen in the early *novelas contemporáneas*.

The plot deals with the life of a woman, Isidora Rufete, who tries in vain to prove her claims of nobility. As Isidora clings to the illusion of noble birth, which is her major standard of personal worth, she comes to live with, first, a man of aristocratic family and, later, one whose money can satisfy her desire for luxury. Only two episodes suggest actual nar-

rative "movement"—the heroine's visit to the Marquesa whose kinship she has claimed, and her eventual imprisonment for having supposedly falsified the documents that could prove her relation to the Marquesa's family. Isidora, says Eoff, thus "subordinates her wholesome inclinations of friendliness, sympathy, and honesty as she tries to prove her nobility; . . . she is increasingly tyrannized by the love of wealth and luxury; and . . . her integrity dissolves completely after the final disillusionment following her imprisonment." At the end, her illusions irreparably shattered, she descends to a life of prostitution.

Although Pérez Galdós's attitude and beliefs are less prominent here than in his earlier thesis novels, the tone of the work is far from objective. Most important is its pervasive air of indulgent, yet pointed, Cervantine irony; this is evident from the beginning, when Pérez Galdós draws a contrast between the beauty of nature and the frenzied self-occupation of the asylum inmates. It is seen also in the use of caricature (as in the descriptions of Isidora's friend Don José and of such minor characters as Tomás Rufete, Botín, and Juan Bou), in euphemism and in self-deception (in the moments of *estilo indirecto libre*, when self-deception is most conspicuous), and in the way in which the reader himself is deceived into identifying with the heroine.

Thematically, Pérez Galdós is saying that one must face reality as it is and reject false values and the worship of appearances; he condemns the attitude of "*quiero pero no puedo* (I want to but cannot)," supports the need for better educational facilities and opportunities (for the sake of children such as Pecado, Isidora's brother), and criticizes social parasites (such as her lover Joaquín). There are specific commentaries about the Spanish propensity for civil war (symbolized in the children's battle), the Church ("Entreacto en la iglesia"), nepotism, *caciquismo*, politics, and mental institutions. Only in his more mature novels was Pérez Galdós able to incorporate his desire to teach into a more completely artistic framework.

Many critics who have dealt with *The Disinherited Lady* have been specifically interested in the novel's naturalistic content. Most of them have concluded that this is one of Pérez Galdós's most naturalistic novels (and one which probably demonstrates stronger naturalistic influence than any other Spanish novel of its time), but they agree that it still offers no evidence of Pérez Galdós's complete adherence to the philosophical and linguistic tenets of Zola. Elements which suggest naturalistic influence include the force of heredity, some measure of environmental determinism, the topic of the *bestia humana* (man driven by his own mechanistic or animalistic impulses), and occasional frankness of language. Nowhere, however, does one find the morbidity of many of Zola's works. Despite the author's detail, he consciously avoided presenting the seamier aspects of Isidora's love affairs. There is no true fatalistic determinism. Above all, the novel is a moral work which acknowledges the power and possibilities open to the human will. Finally, Pérez Galdós avoided the cold, objective tone of the naturalists. Zola's rigor is neutralized here by "*la risa cervantina* (Cervantine humor)."

With respect to style, the growing force of realism in Pérez Galdós's new manner reveals itself most dramatically in the increased use of colloquial speech and in the descriptive atmosphere of the novel. The author "takes possession" of Madrid as the broad stage which was to form the background for so many of his works, leading the reader into all corners of the city and illuminating the contradictory, often oppressive aspects of the modern nineteenth century metropolis. Costumbristic scenes abound. Other linguistic techniques include theatrical elements, the fuller use of the *estilo indirecto libre*, the adaptation of language to circumstances and characters, and descriptions with an occasional impressionistic flavor. The last characteristic is evident, for example, at those moments when the author blurs the boundary between waking reality and reverie: "*insomnio número cinquenta y tantos*" and so on. The chapters entitled "Beethoven" and "Sigue Beethoven" are deliberate linguistic tours de force; here Pérez Galdós uses the modernistic techniques of triple and quadruple adjectival construction, *sinestesia*, and musical elements to produce two moods analogous to major and minor keys.

In *The Disinherited Lady*, Pérez Galdós thus subordinated moralistic militancy to a relative stress on character delineation for its own sake. He continued to base his personages on one or two central attitudes or passions, but this focal impulse now became more personal. The real interest of the work lies in the evolution of the heroine. Only this progression gives the novel's structure continuity. The psychological movement of the story shows how Isidora subordinates her instincts of honesty, friendliness, and sympathy to her tyrannical obsession with her noble beginnings and her hunger for wealth and luxury. Ultimately, her integrity dissolves completely, in the final disillusionment that follows her imprisonment.

Through Isidora, one sees Pérez Galdós's first real venture into a further extension of "environment," what may be termed the world of "fiction," as opposed to that of immediate, physical circumstance. The intangible realm of the heroine's thoughts and beliefs is as real as the visible reality around her, although contrasting with it. The reader is left uncertain about the reality of Isidora's situation until her climactic conversation with the Marquesa de Aransis at the end of the first part. Pérez Galdós makes full use of the idea that men and women depend on their dreams. Isidora "dies" when her illusions are smashed, having declared that "*mejor es soñar que ver* (it is better to dream than to see)." The author demonstrates how critically trauma or psychic shock can function in the sphere of nominal sanity. As in Pérez Galdós's later novels, dreams serve two basic functions in *The Disinherited Lady*: as a means of characterization (Isidora's obsession, Don José's feelings toward the heroine) and as foreshadowing (Isidora's premonitions in jail concerning her lawyer's failure). The fact that almost all the major characters are prone to dreams and illusions echoes the Cervantine ambiguity of reality, with its intimation that "real" existence is a complicated blend of exterior and interior perceptions.

Certainly, Isidora is in part symbolic, representing aspects of the Spanish people as a whole. Yet, more important, she is a unique case of semi-insanity, individualized both by her faults (her aristocratic obsession, her fear of vulgarity, egotistical pride, financial ineptness, extreme nervousness, and so on) and by her virtues (in particular, her generosity).

Don José, probably one of Pérez Galdós's finest and most poignant psychological creations, serves primarily to dramatize the heroine's downfall with his own incidental destruction. Like Isidora, he is both a type-character (a kind of pathetic Don Quixote whose Dulcinea is the protagonist) and a peculiar blend of self-sacrificing, Platonic generosity and senile sexual illusions. The minor characters in the novel contribute in an essentially static fashion to Isidora's negative development.

The work's structure is not a tight one. In a way, the plot starts and ends *in medias res*. At times, one feels that Pérez Galdós is improvising, guided only by a plan to study the process of Isidora's psychological degeneration. Nevertheless, there is considerable evidence in the novel of careful structural techniques: the framework of two parts, each with its *suicidio*, each with a criminal act by Pecado, and so on (the first part contains the confirmation of Isidora's illusions and the second the gradual destruction of those hopes when the world of reality gains mastery); the careful social progression of the heroine's lovers in part 2; and finally, a series of parallels and correspondences: the two key events (the meeting with the Marquesa, Isidora's imprisonment), Pecado's world versus Isidora's interior world, the parallel scenes involving both Isidora and Joaquín, the two "Beethoven" chapters, the crimes of Pecado, the *cordelería* versus Bou's shop, the manner in which Pecado and his playmate Majito are eventually united after separate, but related descriptions, and so on.

The Disinherited Lady, then, was an experiment, and as such a turning point for Pérez Galdós. The novel retains at least something of the argumentative quality and abstractness of his thesis novels, yet points ahead to the greater psychological depth of such later characters as Fortunata and Benina. The work, viewed as a whole, adds in two ways to Pérez Galdós's maturing realistic technique: His details now fill in the canvas of external reality, and his insights take the reader deeper into the labyrinth of human psychology.

FORTUNATA AND JACINTA

Fortunata and Jacinta is Pérez Galdós's most complex creation and can be considered his masterpiece, probably one of the three greatest novels in Spanish literature. The framework for the action is a broad, detailed social record of Madrid life in the 1870's, with a veritable encyclopedia of customs, national types, and topographical minutiae. Above all, the work is an extraordinary study of the mutual influence of individual personalities and an exhibition of how one person's freedom can vanquish the potentially lethal effects of an immensely materialistic and erotic collectivity. The naturalistic semideterminism of *The Disinherited Lady* has passed to a Cervantine open-ended quest for rehabilitating values.

In broadest outline, the story concerns the fortunes of two women, linked by Juanito Santa Cruz, an idle, pampered bourgeois. In the first half of the book, Juanito marries his cousin Jacinta, a woman obsessed with the idea of bearing a child, and Fortunata, a beautiful woman of the *pueblo* and Juanito's lover, marries the sickly Maximiliano Rubín. As the novel progresses, Juanito vacillates between the security and conformity of his upper-middle-class marriage to Jacinta and the spontaneous vitality of society's lower rank (Fortunata). Eventually, Fortunata, the real protagonist of the work, gravitates toward her refined rival, whom she comes to see as a victim of Juanito, as she is. In the end, Fortunata gives birth to Juanito's son and, in a final gesture of understanding and self-expression, gives the child over to Jacinta. Around these personalities, Pérez Galdós weaves a web of interrelating stories, events, and minor characters that is astounding in its richness and complexity.

Pérez Galdós's novelistic techniques had matured considerably since the publication of *The Disinherited Lady*, clearly visible in characterization, theme, and style. Although the two heroines are meant to symbolize the clash between natural and social law, they are above all extremely complex individuals. There are no exclusively malevolent or benevolent figures in the novel. Fortunata, purposely presented first without background description, makes a slow and intricate voyage through self-consciousness toward self-discovery. By the end, she has surpassed jealousy, emulation, and fear of inferiority. While maintaining her original straightforward sincerity, emotional temperament, compassion, and disregard for social convention, she undergoes the "civilizing" influence of Maxi's widowed aunt, Doña Lupe, the elderly bachelor, Evaristo Feijóo, the social conventionalism of the charity worker, Guillermina Pacheco, and, above all, the model of Jacinta. In comparison to the psychological penetration Pérez Galdós offered in *The Disinherited Lady* in his portrayal of the insomniac Isidora, whose consciousness is marked by the relentless ticking of the clock, the study of Fortunata allows for a kind of autonomous interior time in which development occurs more slowly, more hesitatingly, and more meaningfully. This psychological trajectory is the very essence of the novel and gives the work its structure.

Jacinta hides her feelings, at least most of the time, under a veneer of social propriety. She is dominated throughout the novel by her obsession with children. She is gentle and affectionate rather than passionate and volatile by nature. Her evolution is marked by a lessening of sentimentality, an increase in independence, and, later, by a deepening maturity as she clashes with and then is drawn to Fortunata. Juanito functions as a catalyst in the plot and is more a type-character: the idle, well-off, essentially superficial *señorito* (young master). The diminutive which is inevitably applied to his name suggests the apron strings to which he has been tied. While not a despicable Joaquín Pez (of *The Disinherited Lady*), he is frivolous, pedantic, selfishly unremorseful, and vain, calculating, and insatiable in his search for novelty. In general, his personality is too shallow to allow room for subtlety or surprise.

The character of Maximiliano is, in Geoffrey Ribbans's words, "second only to Don Quixote as a highly sympathetic study of madness in Spanish literature." One of Pérez Galdós's supreme examples of the dreamer given over to imagination, he conceives the romantic mission of redeeming Fortunata; Maxi's "madness" actually allows him to see her true worth. His development, marked by vacillations between outward anger and inward anguish, reveals the

writer's most original techniques of characterization. The minor figures serve primarily as links between or foils for the major characters, but many of their own individualized personalities demonstrate a marked tendency to evolve.

Thematically, *Fortunata and Jacinta* is less a study of the evils of Madrileñan society (although ample evidence of injustice, immorality, and ignorance is presented) than a demonstration that good cannot be neatly separated from evil and that, within the shifting relationships between the individual and his community, one person's expression of freedom, one act of giving, can, in Gilman's words, "be considered a final, self-justifying epic deed, an autonomous affirmation of humanity in the very teeth of history." While not complacent or overly optimistic, the author is hopeful, calling on the untapped potential for human progress.

In *Fortunata and Jacinta*, Pérez Galdós achieves an almost obsessive probing of the limits of daily speech, staged within a specificity of setting and topographical detail never before seen in the Spanish novel. Nowhere, with the possible exception of Leopoldo Alas's *La regenta* (1884), could readers find such richness, such fullness of descriptive elaboration. Particularly original to this work is the consistent bird imagery (for the purposes of characterization and structural development of the plot), the remarkable "proto-Freudian" use of dreams, and the increasingly complicated manipulations of point of view: authorial narrative, dialogue, *estilo indirecto libre*, and direct interior monologue (the recording of unspoken dialogue). Pérez Galdós's more frequent use of the unreliable narrator and the omnipresence of situational and verbal irony add to the ambiguities of the major characterizations and of the theme.

Fortunata and Jacinta presents a world of profound, interacting psychological portraits amidst an incredibly detailed material setting; in its denouement, it reveals the end of Pérez Galdós's naturalistic phase and the beginning of a spiritual emphasis which was to dominate many later works.

COMPASSION

Written during a time of great financial and legal difficulties for Pérez Galdós, *Compassion* nevertheless demonstrates a spirit of understanding, a philosophical serenity, and a proclamation of profound optimism for humankind. The novel represents the fullest and most artistic expression of Pérez Galdós' "spiritual" phase. The setting—the misery and poverty of the beggars' world in old Madrid—is portrayed with the same seminaturalistic verisimilitude seen in earlier works, but the unresolved struggle between good and evil seen in *Fortunata and Jacinta* gives way to a deeper humanization of outlook in which love, charity, and basic Christian values indicate the clear potential of final triumph for all human beings.

In contrast to *Fortunata and Jacinta, Compassion* presents a world of reduced dimensions. Although the technique of detailed examination is similar, the author has been more selective, more attuned to the proportion of microcosm, rather than macrocosm. Further, out of the process of increasing interiorization manifested in earlier works came a profound evolutionary step: the inclusion of fantasy and illusion as integral components in the creation of actual, physical, living entities.

Benina, the elderly protagonist, begs to provide the daily bread for her spendthrift mistress Doña Paca, telling her that this income is wages from work in the house of a fictitious priest, Don Romualdo. As the story develops, Benina's charity extends to Paca's daughter Obdulia, the pretentious Frasquito Ponte, and an increasingly broad circle of dependents. When she and her blind companion Almudena are arrested for begging in a prohibited area, she is taken to the poorhouse of Misericordia (compassion). During her absence, Paca, Paca's children, and Ponte are redeemed from poverty by an inheritance delivered to them by a priest named Romualdo Cedrón, whom they take to be Benina's Don Romualdo. Paca's domineering daughter-in-law Juliana comes forward to manage the new wealth, and when Benina finally returns, she is turned away. Her devotion to Paca has spawned only ingratitude.

Ironically, the inheritance leads only to misery. The dismissal of Benina and the lack of energy needed to fulfill their own pretentious visions lead the family to a life of spiritual emptiness. Benina

goes with Almudena to live in a hut near the outskirts of Madrid, where she is eventually visited by Juliana. Like Saint Paul, the latter has experienced a sudden conversion and begs Benina to bless her and assure her of her children's future well-being.

The novel is constructed on a series of thematic, structural, and psychological dualities. With respect to characterization, Benina (based perhaps on Pérez Galdós's family nurse in Las Palmas) is particularized by her *sisa* (pilfering from her "earnings"), her superstition, and occasional naïveté. Yet she stands as the personification of charity and is presented symbolically as a Christ figure who suffers and accepts sacrifice (parallels to the life and words of Jesus abound in the novel). In addition, she bears more than a little resemblance to traditional type-figures of Spanish literature (Lazarillo, Don Quixote). Her development consists of an expansion and intensification of her charitable ways toward a point of increased confidence and adjustability, in which charity and self-sacrifice are actually essential to her being. Through contact with others, she evolves toward a conscious recognition of the morality inherent in what originally were purely spontaneous acts of compassion.

Ponte is likewise a "dual" character. Born of costumbristic satire, he is the *proto-cursi* who attempts to relive the past; yet, when a fall from a horse leads to madness, he (like Maxi Rubín) is able to perceive the more profound truths concerning others. Almudena, one of Pérez Galdós's unique and most memorable creations, symbolizes the Moors and Jews who have been rejected and expelled from Spain and represents also the mystic exaltation of fantasy. His vices (egotism, jealousy, and so on) and his particular mixture of emotions toward Benina serve to individualize him. Paca embodies selfishness and irresponsibility, and the minor characters act as foils, parallels, or contrasts to Benina.

With respect to theme, the need to face reality is demonstrated, but (as the other side of the coin) certain kinds of fantasy or illusion (those with proper motives) are exalted as powerful, creative factors. The apparently "supernatural" appearance of Don Romualdo—which Benina herself feels may be the result of her own imagination—is the single most striking *point* of the novel and is meant to demonstrate this concept. A second general theme (the primary message) concerns the nature and importance of true charity. As a very significant link between the two main thematic statements, charity is seen to be the motive behind Benina's creature of fantasy, Don Romualdo. An additional bridge between the two messages lies in the thought that true charity provides a way of facing the hardships of reality.

Many elements of technique, tone, and style have been refined in *Compassion* but relate closely to those of Pérez Galdós's earlier works: expressive force, colloquial naturalness, frequent dialogue, naturalistic precision, costumbristic description, Cervantine irony, humor, the use of dreams, and so on. The gently ironic force of free indirect style is gradually abandoned in the later chapters, as Pérez Galdós identifies more closely with Benina, while allowing the heroine and others to testify more on their own behalf. The dualities of appearance and reality, seen throughout the author's career, are omnipresent here: Hunger becomes beneficial, blindness means vision, madness is wisdom, the servant is the leader, defeat equals victory.

The structure, based generally on Benina's development, reveals a dual or two-part organization. The first section (a week long, suggesting the Passion of Christ) is seen through Benina's eyes and presents the physical and temporal details of the beggars' lives and the heroine's expanding role; the second is a more generalized narration while Benina is in the poorhouse, leading to Paca's climactic rejection and the protagonist's final victory. Despite the relative haste with which Pérez Galdós composed the novel, the plot line is constructed with extraordinary care, exemplified by the steps leading to the meeting of Benina and the miserly Don Carlos at the start and by the careful stages in preparation for Don Romualdo's astonishing appearance with the news of the inheritance.

Compassion, then, is representative of Pérez Galdós's most mature creations. Within a framework of "spiritual" intentions, the work stands as the most artistic rendering of nineteenth century Cervantine dualities, seen from the two "faces" of the San Sebastián church, on the first page, through the seemingly contradictory reconciliations of charity and *la sisa* (Benina), Judaism/Mohammedanism and Christianity (Almudena), fantasy and truth (Don Romualdo), matter and spirit, naturalism and idealistic humanism. At the same time, one sees here the real culmination of Pérez Galdós's development as a novelist. At this stage, he was able to anticipate the twentieth century's expansion of the "realistic" approach; he recognized that one must go beyond the perceptible elements of physical surroundings to fill out a "realistic" perspective. The writer must also integrate into his picture qualities of transcendent, universal, or symbolic significance. The nineteenth century realistic novel did generally move in this direction; although it looked critically at the inclusion of imaginary events, it sometimes ended by absorbing the stuff of the imagination. A dose of "poetic substance" entered realistic transcription; myth was simultaneously destroyed and assimilated into the "real." Influenced by the Cervantine interplay of diverse "fictions" and "realities," Pérez Galdós demonstrated that "fiction" and "reality" are not dichotomous; rather, they are interacting components of the substance of human existence.

Jeremy T. Medina

OTHER MAJOR WORKS

PLAYS: *El hombre fuerte*, wr. 1864-1868, pb. 1902; *Un joven de provecho*, wr. 1867, pb. 1935; *Realidad*, pr., pb. 1892; *La loca de la casa*, pr., pb. 1893; *Gerona*, pr. 1893; *La de San Quintín*, pr., pb. 1894 (*The Duchess of San Quintín*, 1917); *Los condenados*, pr. 1894; *Voluntad*, pr. 1895; *Doña Perfecta*, pr., pb. 1896 (based on his novel); *La fiera*, pr. 1896; *Electra*, pr., pb. 1901 (English translation, 1911); *Alma y vida*, pr., pb. 1902; *Mariucha*, pr., pb. 1903; *El abuelo*, pr., pb. 1904 (*The Grandfather*, 1910); *Bárbara*, pr., pb. 1905; *Amor y ciencia*, pr., pb. 1905; *Pedro Minio*, pr. 1908; *Zaragoza*, pr., pb. 1908 (music by Arturo Lapuerto); *Casandra*, pr., pb. 1910 (based on his novel); *Celia en los infiernos*, pr., pb. 1913; *Alceste*, pr., pb. 1914; *Sor Simona*, pr., pb. 1915; *El tacaño Salomón*, pr., pb. 1916; *Santa Juana de Castilla*, pr., pb. 1918; *Antón Caballero*, pr. 1921 (completed by Serafín and Joaquín Álvarez Quintero).

NONFICTION: *Discursos académicos*, 1897; *Memoranda*, 1906; *Arte y crítica*, 1923; *Fisonomías sociales*, 1923; *Nuestro teatro*, 1923; *Política española*, 1923; *Cronicón*, 1924; *Toledo*, 1924; *Viajes y fantasías*, 1928; *Memorias*, 1930; *Crónica de Madrid*, 1933; *Cartas a Mesoneros Romanos*, 1943; *Crónica de la Quincena*, 1948; *Madrid*, 1956.

BIBLIOGRAPHY

Gilman, Stephen. *Galdós and the Art of the European Novel, 1867-1887*. Princeton, N.J.: Princeton University Press, 1981. Divided into one part on the historical novelist and two parts on *Fortunata and Jacinta*. A perceptive work of scholarship that provides an important context for understanding the novels. Includes an appendix on classical references in *Doña Perfecta*.

Gold, Hazel. *The Reframing of Realism: Galdós and the Discourses of the Nineteenth-Century Spanish Novel*. Durham, N.C.: Duke University Press, 1993. Divided into three sections, "Narrative Frames," "Cultural Frames," and "Critical Frames." Excellent discussions of individual novels as well a concluding chapter on the novelist's place in his native tradition. Includes an appendix on the political intertext in *Torquemada in the Flames*. Recommended for advanced students.

Pattison, Walter T. *Benito Pérez Galdós*. Boston: Twayne, 1975. A very helpful introduction, with a chapter on the novelist's life, his journalism and early novels, his first contemporary novels, his naturalistic style, and the end of his career. Includes chronology, detailed notes, and bibliography.

Percival, Anthony. *Galdós and His Critics*. Toronto: University of Toronto Press, 1985. Chapters on the biographical approach, literary history, literature and ideas, individual novels, and other writings. Includes detailed notes and bibliography, as well as an index of Galdósian works and characters cited.

Turner, Harriet S. *Benito Pérez Galdós, Fortunata and Jacinta*. Cambridge, England: Cambridge University Press, 1992. A painstaking study of this masterpiece, with a chronology of the novel's main events; genealogical tables; a biographical introduction to the author; and chapters on the social and historical contexts, the characters, and the novel's metaphors; and a guide to further reading.

Zlotchew, Clark M. *Libido into Literature: The "Primera Época" of Benito Pérez Galdós*. Edited by Daryl F. Mallett. San Bernardino, Calif.: Borgo Press, 1993. A good study of the life and works.

LUIGI PIRANDELLO

Born: Girgenti (now Agrigento), Italy; June 28, 1867
Died: Rome, Italy; December 10, 1936

PRINCIPAL LONG FICTION

L'esclusa, 1901 (*The Outcast*, 1925)
Il turno, 1902 (*The Merry-Go-Round of Love*, 1964)
Il fu Mattia Pascal, 1904 (*The Late Mattia Pascal*, 1923)
Suo marito, 1911
I vecchi e i giovani, 1913 (*The Old and the Young*, 1928)
Si gira . . ., 1916 (*Shoot! The Notebooks of Serafino Gubbio, Cinematograph Operator*, 1926)
Uno nessuno, centomila, 1925 (*One, None and a Hundred Thousand*, 1933)
Tutti i romanzi, 1941 (collected novels)

OTHER LITERARY FORMS

Luigi Pirandello was an exceptionally prolific writer. In addition to seven novels, he produced numerous volumes of short stories later collected in a series entitled *Novelle per un anno* (1922; two volumes), thus named because there is a tale for nearly every day of the year; several collections of poetry; more than forty plays; and a considerable number of essays, reviews, and journalistic pieces. The author produced most of his poetry between 1889 and 1912, in the earlier part of his career. It is as a poet that Pirandello is least remembered. His lyrics are relatively traditional, although they do mirror the writer's inner restlessness. The first compositions recall the strong moral fiber and tones of Giosuè Carducci, the most influential late nineteenth century Italian poet, as well as some of the darkly pessimistic character of critic Arturo Graf's lyrics, whereas the later collections were somewhat influenced by the melancholy and distressed quality of the Crepuscular poets.

The short stories are more interesting because they not only contain a number of Pirandellian motifs, narrative devices, and ideas, but also continue to intrigue the author as a genre. Pirandello produced his first short story as an adolescent; the last appeared the day before his death, although the majority of his stories were penned at the same time as his longer fiction. Pirandello's early stories reflect the influence of Verism; like his literary mentors, Luigi Capuana and Giovanni Verga, Pirandello drew a pessimistic portrait of lives stifled by social conventions and imbued with a tragic fatalism. Unlike his fellow Sicilians, however, Pirandello added elements of irony and paradox which were to become standard ingredients of his fiction. The irrational pervades these narratives; characters fall prey to chance as the unexpected intrudes upon them, all attempts at controlling life being futile; the bizarre and the grotesque are also staples of the Pirandellian diet, distinguishing him from other *veristi*.

This same universe houses the plays. Pirandello is unquestionably Italy's greatest modern playwright, yet his theater is closely allied in theme and thought to his prose fiction. The critic E. Allen McCormick has pointed out this artistic fraternity, suggesting that novel, short story, and drama "derive their peculiar Pirandellian shape through the interplay of plot and commentary on plot" or, in other terms, the fusion of "action and exposition of action." Nor is it incidental that more than twenty of Pirandello's plays were based on novellas or sections of novels. One example is *Liolà* (1916; English translation, 1952), a lighthearted version of an episode taken from the first part of *The Late Mattia Pascal*, which presents a similar plot with a darker sense of humor and a moralizing constituent.

Significantly, Pirandello's serious involvement in theater corresponded to his abandonment of the novel: Only *One, None and a Hundred Thousand* was published after his first great dra-

(CORBIS/Bettmann)

matic success, and that book had been fifteen years in the making. While Pirandello did change genres, he did not radically alter his vision. The author's perceptions of the relativity of reality, the multiplicity of the individual, and the chaos of life recur throughout his fiction and his plays. It is the message of *Così è (se vi pare)* (1917; *Right You Are [If You Think So]*, 1922), in which an entire town persecutes an unusual family triangle—husband, wife, and mother-in-law—in order to discover the "facts" surrounding their relationship. Is Mrs. Ponza the first or second wife? Is Mrs. Frola her mother or a sweet madwoman? Who is really crazy, the old woman or her son-in-law? Facts in Pirandello are not solutions: The documents which might answer these questions are unattainable. Thus the truth is irretrievable, as it often is for this writer. The holder of the key is Mrs. Ponza—first or second?—who enters the final scene veiled, only to declare to the assembled busybodies who are destroying her family's precarious emotional equilibrium: "As for myself, I am whoever you believe me to be." Lamberto Laudisi ends the play with his ironic laugh, a final statement on the impossibility of being known.

Laudisi is the playwright's spokesman, a cerebral protagonist who challenges friends and family to define him or themselves, noting that each person sees others differently, thus creating a series of diverse selves, every one distinguishable from another. The individual himself cannot totally know or control these different selves he contains, as symbolized by the utilization of the mirror—a common prop in both drama and fiction—which reflects the individual but also distorts reality: The image of ourselves is inevitably a perversion. This psychological lacuna is a source of pain as well as tragedy in the Pirandellian universe.

A number of the author's characters soothe their existential suffering by rationalizing or by evading their relative selves, or both, as in Henry IV's feigned madness, in Pirandello's *Enrico IV* (1922; *Henry IV*, 1923), which allows him to live within the fixed confines of medieval history as an emperor—but at the expense of his original identity and of human fellowship. To be aware is to be alone in this fictional universe where communication is blocked because of people's inherent inability to express themselves to others. Pirandello suitably termed his plays *maschere nude* (naked masks), for on the stage his characters uncover their painful humanity to themselves and to the public.

The playwright's themes and technical innovations are illustrated in his best-known work, *Sei personaggi in cerca d'autore* (1921; *Six Characters in Search of an Author*, 1922), in which the contrast between the fluidity of existence and the stability of form (in this case, art) is embodied in the protagonists. On the one hand, there are the six who come to a theater proposing to "be" the subject for a writer; they are unfulfilled characters, conceived but never written down, seeking the eternal life of art. On the other hand, the actors and directors who encounter them offer the flux and change of life. The two groups inevitably clash; the actors who mimic the words and gestures to the characters can only deform them, to the pained realization of the six that they can never be copied but only approximated at best. Art and life, form and flux, remain separate. Within this principal action, the "melo-drama" of the characters' "story" reiterates other Pirandellian motifs: human misunderstanding; the lack of love; the impossibility of communicating one's vision of one's self to others; the multiple aspects of the human personality and the roles deriving from it, which are both social and private; the tragedy of the disintegration of ties; and the need to express rationally passion and suffering. It is the dilemma of the characters that they can neither change their past—for it is Form and thus fixed—nor find absolute realization at the hands of a new writer or within the imitation of themselves offered by the thespians.

Just as *Six Characters in Search of an Author* defied traditional notions of subject matter or content, so too it challenged expectations concerning dramatic form. Indeed, this play marked the end of the traditional stage. In it, the action overflows into the main floor and behind the scenes; acts are abolished in favor of "accidental" divisions, such as the sudden drop of a curtain; there are no sets or backdrops, the stage is bare; characters come and go naturally, utilizing the entire theater. The action unfolds spontaneously, similar to the creative process at work. A character, Madame Pace, is necessary for the continuation of the story; she appears from nowhere, ready to take on her role. The demarcation between art and life disappears: The six relive their story; the actors re-create them, becoming characters. Illusion is made concrete for the audience, causing considerable intellectual and psychological discomfort. The technique of the play within a play is repeated later in *Ciascuno a suo modo* (1924; *Each in His Own Way*, 1924) and *Questa sera si recita a soggetto* (1930; *Tonight We Improvise*, 1932), in which reality and illusion are intertwined so completely as to befuddle audience and protagonists alike.

In his later years, Pirandello produced a series of three theatrical myths which encompass his final thoughts on people and art. *La nuova colonia* (1928; *The New Colony*, 1958) proposes the social myth of creating a new world, or, at least, a new social order. A group of misfits and undesirables bands together on an island to start their own utopia, only to have their formal social behavior reassert itself, exploding into violence and destruction. *Lazzaro* (1929; *Lazarus*, 1952) contrasts the inadequacy of dogmatic (and bigoted) religion and the instinctive faith of the natural woman Sara and her simple and sage mate. The last play of the trilogy is Pirandello's final, if incomplete, work.

I giganti della montagna (1931, 1934, 1937; *The Mountain Giants*, 1958) celebrates the mystery and magic of the imagination. Fantasies come to life, dreams materialize, and reality is suspended in this myth of art, but it is a delicate balance. The death of the main protagonist, an actress obsessed with her mission of bringing the masterpiece of a dead playwright to the world, is often interpreted as the allegory of the impossibility of art to survive in a materialistic world—the realm of the Giants. Unaware of the value of her gift, the brutish henchmen of the Giants kill the actress; they seek entertainment, not art. Crotone, the master of the realm of fantasy, warns that the creative imagination can only prosper in his small space, being doomed in the outside world. It is an appropriately ambiguous conclusion for a writer

who states that a feeling for the incongruity of things is an apt basis for literature. *The Mountain Giants* is both an affirmation of the power of art and its mystery and a declaration of its fragility.

ACHIEVEMENTS

Pirandello was one of the first writers to give voice to the dilemma of modern people. From the outset of his literary career, he exhibited what Carlo Salinari justly terms "the awareness of crisis," a feeling for the inherent absurdity of life and a sense of the anguish people experience when faced with chaos and nothingness. Pirandello challenged the postulates of Western civilization by subverting their very existence. Denying the possibility of an objective reality, declaring people's fundamental unknowability and multiplicity, and stressing the inherent fluidity of truth and the power of chance, this writer created a tragic vision of the human condition which would influence future generations of thinkers and artists, from the existentialists to Bertolt Brecht, from Eugène Ionesco to Samuel Beckett to Edward Albee.

Signaling the end of a belief in a structured and well-ordered universe, Pirandello opened the doors to anarchy and angst; his works are a death knell for nineteenth century optimism, with its faith in the human ability to shape reality and mold life. His protagonists are caught in uncertainties, trapped in their social masks, unable to forge some measure of meaning in their existence. The Pirandellian character is often disoriented and anxious, struggling in his attempt to establish a fragile inner balance to counteract the chaos and limitations around him. These attempts are illusory but necessary for survival. Often the protagonist who is aware seeks to control this inner turmoil by rationalizing it, by using logic to signify the irrational. For this reason, Pirandello has often been considered a cerebral writer, a philosopher of sorts, whose spokesmen are his heroes, eloquently arguing their points, in a continuous dialectic with themselves, society, their audience, and life itself.

Having declared the relativity of truth and the inconsistency of the human personality in his uniquely ironic manner, Pirandello poses some of the major themes of twentieth century literature in his own works: the individual's fractured sense of identity, the oppressive nature of society, the inability of words to communicate and reach others, the insufficiency of reason, the conflict between appearances and reality, the pain of living, the difficulty if not impossibility of finding authenticity, the categorizing of the individual into socially determined roles, the fruitless search for absolutes, the existence of unconscious motivations, the condemnation of traditional institutions as instruments of coercion. Pirandello's greatness may well derive from his ability to give these ideas human form and individual names—life—as the characters of dramatic fiction and stirring theater.

BIOGRAPHY

Luigi Pirandello was born a few years after the achievement of Italian unification, into a prosperous middle-class Sicilian family. Stefano Pirandello and Caterina Ricci-Gramitto had initially come together because of their shared patriotic zeal, an enthusiasm whose ashes their son was to depict in his historical novel, *The Old and the Young*. Following an early interest in literature, Pirandello studied classics and humanities at the University of Palermo, then at Rome, and finally at Bonn. During these student years, the fledgling writer experienced his first sentimental attachments and briefly flirted with Socialist ideas.

Upon finishing his thesis in linguistics on the dialect of his native Agrigento, Pirandello began his teaching career as a professor of Italian, first in Germany as a university lecturer and later at a women's teaching college in Rome. It was in the Italian capital that the young intellectual developed his first enduring friendships with some of the nation's leading literary figures, notably his fellow Sicilian Luigi Capuana, the father of Verism. It was the beginning of a prolific writing career which was to include numerous articles and reviews, hundreds of short stories, and seven novels, as well as more than forty theatrical works.

In 1894, Pirandello agreed to an arranged marriage to the daughter of a business associate of his father. Maria Antonietta Portulano was a typical Southern Italian of limited education, and Pirandello set out to mold her into his ideal woman. The naïve

Pygmalion soon discovered that his wife did not share his intellectual interests; indeed, she resented his literary associations and chose to center her life on marital and maternal duties. The marriage was not unhappy, however, and the couple had three children and a comfortable life financed by the family mining business in Sicily.

By 1903, the dilettante author had to his name two novels, three poetry collections, a literary journal, and a play. The collapse of the family's sulfur mine in that year, however, permanently altered the lives of Pirandello and his wife; financial ruin was soon followed by Antonietta's nervous collapse. Pirandello was forced to publish, tutor, and teach to survive. His work for some of the established national periodicals and the appearance of *The Late Mattia Pascal*—critically regarded as his most successful novel—opened the doors to Treves, Italy's most prestigious publishing house. These were years of intense activity but also years of living with a depressed, morbidly jealous wife whose paranoia served to foster his ideas on the multiplicity of the human personality. Antonietta's health deteriorated, as did her mental state, until Pirandello was forced to have her institutionalized in 1919, adding to his distress over his children: Both sons had enlisted in World War I, the elder spending considerable time as a prisoner of war, while his daughter attempted suicide—because of the stress of the family situation.

From narrative prose, Pirandello turned to the theater, his first successes coming with Angelo Musco's productions of two plays in Sicilian dialect. The stage became the center of the author's life. Play followed play, more than forty in all. The first typically Pirandellian drama was *Right You Are (If You Think So)*. Like the proverbial prophet, the playwright was not recognized in his own land; Pirandello's first major successes and international fame came from abroad, most notably with *Six Characters in Search of an Author*, whose Roman premiere was a fiasco—the dramatist and his daughter were mobbed by the crowd and had to be rescued. Acclaim came in Paris, London, and New York. As early as 1923, Manhattan's Fulton Theater created a "Pirandello Season" with the author in attendance. Pirandello's plays gradually entered the standard repertory of European companies. With fame, the writer was able to give up teaching and dedicate himself to his work and to constant international travel. Hoping to create a national theater, Pirandello became the artistic director of the Teatro d'Arte di Roma (1925-1928). The company drew some of Italy's finest acting talent, including Marta Abba, the young first lady who was to become Pirandello's friend, confidante, and inspiration. The now famous dramatist also wrote his last novel in 1925: *One, None and a Hundred Thousand*.

Pirandello's final years were no less intense: more plays, more travel, cinematic screenplays, constant acclaim. In 1929, he was named to the Italian Academy; the Nobel Prize for Literature followed in 1934. At the time of his death, in 1936, he was an institution, but he went to his final resting place as he desired: Naked, wrapped in a shroud, on a pauper's hearse, without ceremony or accompaniment, Luigi Pirandello was cremated.

ANALYSIS

Luigi Pirandello's first narratives were greatly influenced by the theories and stylistic attitudes of Verism: objective presentations, careful and detailed description, and an impersonal narrator, composing a "photograph" of a specific environment—generally that of the petite bourgeoisie or the proletariat in a regional setting. At first glance, *The Outcast*, composed in 1893, appears as an ideal companion to the novels of the major Sicilian naturalists: Verga's *I Malavoglia* (1881; *The House by the Medlar Tree*, 1964) and *Mastrodon Gesualdo* (1889; English translation, 1923), Capuana's *Il Marchese di Roccaverdina* (1901), and Federico De Roberto's *I Vicere* (1894; *The Viceroys*, 1962). In point of fact, the plot of Pirandello's novel is very similar to the story line of his friend Capuana's *Ribrezzo* (1885; revulsion): An attractive wife is mistakenly accused of adultery by her husband, is spurned by her father, becomes a social outcast, only to find herself actually committing the act for which she was unjustly blamed, almost as justification for her social leprosy. In naturalistic terms, it seems a stock plot, intended to criticize the prejudices and tyranny of a closed provincial

environment which smothers the individual with its notions of propriety, honor, and male supremacy. In *The Outcast*, however, such social commentary gives way to a Pirandellian twist: The punished but innocent wife demonstrates great self-awareness and independence, regaining a measure of her self-respect in her work, only to return to her contrite husband *after* having consummated the adulterous affair which caused so much pain and degradation to her and her entire family. It is a paradoxical, totally unexpected conclusion which clearly points to the novelist's fundamental sense of irony. The innocent victim is rejected while the guilty party is embraced.

THE MERRY-GO-ROUND OF LOVE

In a scholarly essay entitled *L'umorismo* (1908, revised 1920; partial translation, *On Humour*, 1966; complete translation, 1974), Pirandello defines his own inherently ironic voice while proposing a general psycho-artistic frame of mind based on a "feeling for the incongruous," which generates literary works that, in turn, create a similar feeling in their audience. His second novel captures just such humor, or irony, in a comic vein. The location is once again the Sicily of small towns and little minds in which *The Merry-Go-Round of Love* is initiated by a well-meaning father who decides to marry off his pretty daughter to an elderly four-time widower who should soon leave her well-to-do and free to follow her heart. In typically Pirandellian fashion, chance intervenes. Unwilling to wait, her lovesick young admirer calls on an influential relative to help him dissolve the girl's abhorrent union; the aggressive lawyer, in turn, falls in love with her, has the marriage annulled, whisks her off to a convent, convinces her of the inevitability of their meeting, and weds her himself in place of the young swain. Soon, however, the possessive and bilious groom dies suddenly; it can be assumed that it will finally be the turn of the patient youth. In this tale of succeeding husbands, unpredictable events accompany the plot to its unanticipated resolution, while the lively old widower contemplates a new bride.

THE OLD AND THE YOUNG

In a far different temper, *The Old and the Young* returns to the Sicily of the earlier novels to present a sweeping picture of the political and social events which dominated the island in the 1890's. In this historical novel, various factual occurrences are depicted—the rise of the middle class, the development of the Socialist Party, the atmosphere of social agitation leading to the proclamation of a state of siege and military repression, and the Banca Romana financial scandal which shook the peninsula—from the author's pessimistic viewpoint, painting a tableau of collective and personal failures, ranging from the betrayal of the Romantic ideals of the Italian struggle for unification to the fall of Southern socialism, from moral and financial bankruptcy to madness and murder. Numerous characters weave in and out of a complex narrative of social and private ambitions, class conflict, personal corruption, doomed loves, and human loss. The old are responsible for the demise of patriotic and social ideals and for the state of current ills; the young are caught in the crystallized social structures which suffocate them. It is a bitter vision, without any moderating illusions. Individuals fall under forces greater than themselves in a world full of misfits and alienated souls. In this novel, individual turmoil flows uneasily into historical chaos. The failed illusions of Pirandello's only historical novel are basically social—liberty, justice, equality, patriotism—but they evoke a similar defeat at the personal level. The novelist's best-known and most appreciated works are told by narrators/protagonists who concurrently expose their inner selves and comment on the world about them: Mattia Pascal, Serafino Gubbio, and Vitangelo Moscarda.

THE LATE MATTIA PASCAL

In *The Late Mattia Pascal*, Pascal's life story is quintessential Pirandello. After a happy and reckless childhood, Mattia is thrust into adulthood by his marriage to the lovely and pregnant Romilda, who comes to resent their poverty and becomes quite the shrew. Unhappily married, losing both his gentle mother and beloved baby, the hero runs off to Monte Carlo for a temporary reprieve. There he has some unusual encounters and wins a tidy sum at the casino. On the way back to Romilda (and his difficulties), Mattia reads about his own death, having been mistakenly recognized in the deformed body of a drowned sui-

cide. This unexpected turn of events offers him a great opportunity to be free, or so he believes. Taking on a new identity, a new presence, and a new lifestyle, Mattia becomes Adriano Meis, wanderer. After a lengthy period of travel, Adriano decides to settle in Rome awhile, becoming one of the pensioners in the Paleari family. Gradually, inevitably, Meis involves himself in society and in the lives of others, particularly interested in the delicate and sensitive Adriana Paleari. It is through these relationships and because of a series of casual events, such as the theft of some money, that the new man realizes he has no valid identity, lacking any documents and thus, any legal right to exist. Without social credentials, Adriano Meis cannot marry, own a dog, file a police report. Without a past, without human ties, his life and freedom become meaningless. Having sought authenticity, Mattia Pascal has become a shadow man instead. In order to exist once more, Adriano fakes a suicide and returns home as Mattia, only to find his wife contentedly remarried with a baby. The only solution is to remain dead, legally nonexistent but at least equipped with a social identity. The sign of this existential absurdity is the narrator's visits to the grave of the late Mattia Pascal.

Setting aside the naturalist emphasis on objective narration, Pirandello dives headlong into modernism. *The Late Mattia Pascal* is fictional autobiography and private confession, a work that is declaratively subjective. The novel is also a parable on people's relationship to the social environment; it is, in some ways, an ironic and modernized version of the Prodigal Son returning to a bitter homecoming. Caught in the prison of tradition and conventions, Pascal is a victim. He is not yet aware that his social roles define him and compose his connection to the world of others. Such awareness comes through his alter-ego, Adriano Meis. Having believed in his escape into freedom, the dual hero, Adriano/Mattia, must come face to face with the price of such presumed liberty: rootlessness and solitude. More important, he comes to the realization that liberty from one's self is impossible. Having become free of his past, he has become the spectator of life but can no longer be a participant. He is truly an outlaw, outside of the law's reach and also its security, excluded from all emotional fellowship and totally self-dependent and alone.

From an understandable impulse to escape, Mattia progresses to a meditative understanding of the absurdity of an anchorless existence, preferring subordination to the social ties and conventions which bind the individual but also define him. Pascal is one of Pirandello's first self-conscious protagonists, a type defined within the text by Anselmo Paleari, Adriano's philosophical landlord who has developed an ontological system called "lanternosophy" that speaks to modern man's sad privilege of "seeing himself live," which Paleari compares to a marionette, Orestes. Intent on his passionate thoughts of revenge (that is, "living"), Orestes suddenly perceives a rip in the paper sky of his puppet stage; action becomes contemplation. Aware of himself, Orestes stops, unable to act. He has been transformed into Hamlet, the embodiment of existential incongruity and psychological impotence. Modern man is this absurdly aware puppet of life.

Notwithstanding these themes of alienation and inescapability, the tone of *The Late Mattia Pascal* is not tragic, but humorous, as befits a narrator who has developed "a taste for laughing at all my misfortunes and at my every torment" and is well aware of "our infinite smallness." Naturally, it is the ironic lightness proposed in Pirandello's essay *On Humour*, with its emphasis on the incongruous. Much of the comedy in the novel is offered by the minor characters, for it is peopled with amusing, funny, and grotesque *macchiette*—character studies—that moderate the book's serious elements. Even death is presented for its mystery, unpredictability, and absurdity in much of the plot: Mattia wins at Monte Carlo using his mother's funeral money; it is the unknown suicide that allows him to become Adriano Meis, and it is a second suicide, planned and false, that permits him to resurrect Mattia; there is even Max, an obliging ghost, in attendance at Anselmo Paleari's séances. The unknown and the unexpected rule this fictional universe, appropriately symbolized by the roulette game, godmother of Pascal's transformation, wheel of fortune, goddess of chance. In a "Notice on the Scruples of Imagination" which accompanies this novel, Pirandello justifies the use of fantasy in its

plot and in art in general, stating that there is no need to defend such absurdities "that have no need to appear probable, for they are true."

SHOOT! THE NOTEBOOKS OF SERAFINO GUBBIO, CINEMATOGRAPH OPERATOR

Shoot! The Notebooks of Serafino Gubbio, Cinematograph Operator is a far less whimsical work. Set in the Roman world of silent filmmaking, its tale is unfolded in the pages of a diary or journal kept by Serafino Gubbio, cameraman by accident, as he observes and comments upon what he sees. "Seeing" is Gubbio's peculiar characteristic; his watching is really study, an attempt to glimpse in others what he lacks, namely "the certainty that they understand what they're doing" in the midst of their frenetic lives. Seeing is also part of his job: He is the eyes of his camera. Gubbio's is the most modern of Pirandellian alienations: people at the service of machines, seeking to become machinelike themselves, that is, to acquire a similar imperturbability—having already determined they had no need of a soul. Gubbio allows himself to grow depersonalized as a protective measure against the pain of living, hoping to become as desensitized to his surroundings as the camera he holds. If Mattia Pascal tries for an impossible authenticity, Gubbio prefers to escape his humanity altogether, watching everything, including himself, from a distance.

One of the objects of his visual study is the actress Varia Nestoroff, a Russian femme fatale, whose shady past has also touched the cameraman's former life. A young and gifted painter had loved her purely and completely; unable to bear his devotion, the woman proceeded to seduce his sister's fiancé, Aldo Nuti. Gubbio had known the family of the painter well, and they had formed the one idyllic memory of his existence until it was destroyed by the foreign beauty. Nestoroff is tortured by her inner demons and the weight of her secret guilt. Gubbio soon notes that the woman's acting is an externalization of her inner being: violent, dramatic, sensual, and overpowering.

For a brief period, the protagonist allows himself to be sucked into life. He feels compassion for Nestoroff, his landlord, a caged tiger, a vagabond musician, and the tormented Aldo Nuti, who also joins the film company. He also falls hopelessly in love with sweet little Luisetta who, in turn, is equally and hopelessly fond of Nuti, who still loves the memory of his former lost fiancée and hates the woman who seduced him. The past swarms into Gubbio's memory as well, filling him with nostalgic regret and pity for the tragic family he had loved. Nudged out of his impassiveness, Gubbio soon realizes the futility of his emotional expenditures. Thus, he returns behind the glass eye of his "black spider": It is a desire for oblivion. In front of him, the imitation of life with all of its frantic manifestations—the film scenes— plays on as he mechanically turns the handle. Arcangelo Leone De Castris suggests that shooting pictures is a way of portraying one's own absence from life, and it is to the state of nonbeing that Gubbio moves, distraught by his recently renewed connections to society and existence. The camera functions as a barrier between him and others. In this identity as a passive, mechanical spectator, Serafino Gubbio becomes totally enclosed in his "thing's silence" in the final pages of his notebooks. Shooting the last scene of an important adventure film, the cameraman is caught in the tragedy of Aldo Nuti and Varia Nestoroff. Instead of killing the tiger, Nuti turns his gun on his former mistress and is then torn to pieces by the cat. The perfect machine, Gubbio obeys the call of the camera, automatically registering it all, glued to the handle, and shocked into muteness, forever a willing thing in its silence.

Somewhat experimental stylistically, *Shoot! The Notebooks of Serafino Gubbio, Cinematograph Operator* is, however, an inconsistent work, accused of actually being three novels in one by critic Umberto Bosco, who catalogs it as a story of the destructive mechanization of modern life, an idyll in the nostalgic recovery of Gubbio's past memories, and a book about the early years of the cinema and its odd denizens. The novel is held together by the coexistence of all three threads in the single consciousness of its protagonist narrator.

ONE, NONE AND A HUNDRED THOUSAND

One, None and a Hundred Thousand takes introspective narration one step further. *The Late Mattia Pascal*'s protagonist tells the story of his life factu-

ally and chronologically, interspersing it with personal commentaries and insights; Serafino Gubbio presents a diary, notebooks which recount the inner man as well as external episodes; Vitangelo Moscarda's tale is the story of a spiritual journey. Pirandello was absorbed by *One, None and a Hundred Thousand*, working on it for more than a decade. Its themes are not new but evoke those contained in his earlier books. If Mattia Pascal attempts a new identity and Serafino Gubbio chooses "thing"-hood, Vitangelo Moscarda opts for madness.

Moscarda is thrown into self-awareness and self-analysis by his nose or, more exactly, by his wife Dida's banal remark on the tilt of his nose. Discovering that he is unfamiliar with his body, Moscarda quickly progresses to the realization that he is even more unfamiliar with his inner self. The next step in his road to insight is the perception that others do not know him as he knows himself but have their own images of him, which they firmly believe to be the true man. Like the Orestes/Hamlet puppet, Vitangelo Moscarda catches himself in the act of living, forcing him to contemplate his identity. At first it is the stranger reflected in a window or mirror that concerns him, but it soon becomes the stranger in himself that obsesses the young man. He analyzes his social roles, against which he quickly rebels, unwilling to be the idiotic "Gengè" his wife sees and loves, the "usurer" the town believes him to be, or any of a number of his other multiple selves. Moscarda makes a supreme effort to see himself from the outside, as others see him, as he cannot see himself, and soon intuits that the belief in a unified personality is a mirage. The novel's title is exegetical: People believe in their wholeness but are actually numerous persons, chameleons who adapt to their changing environments and audience; being the object of so many differing views, there are a hundred thousand "I"s and actually no *one* self.

Aware of being the daily construction of himself and others, Moscarda is driven by his discovery, feeling imprisoned in his body, his name(s), his house, his reputation, his town, his roles, and his very historical situation. Desperate to be for others what he wishes to be for himself, he challenges "normal" behavior. For example, to prove he is not a usurer, he first evicts a poor tenant and then gives him an attractive new home, thus obtaining the collective appellation of "madman." In a frenzy to take control of his own existence, Moscarda initially determines to stop the regular flow of his life by a series of abnormal acts that reflect his recognition of the relativity of all and challenge the world about him to reassess and redefine him as he himself has already done. Instead, the others react in disbelief, for they do not recognize "their" Vitangelo Moscarda(s). His wife leaves him, and his business managers view him as an idiot, particularly when he expresses a desire to give away all of his possessions because they do not come from "him," but rather are inherited. Lacking common (collective) sense, searching for self-determination free of all encumbrances, and frightfully aware of the innate solitude of every person—since no one can ever truly know another—Moscarda chooses spiritual liberation in the only way open to him: apart, one with nature, poor, and mad. Pirandello's novel concludes on this paradoxical note also sounded by his first novel: to be someone, the (anti-)hero must resolve to live as no one, dying and being reborn at every moment, "alive and whole, no longer in myself, but in every thing outside myself."

Fiora A. Bassanese

OTHER MAJOR WORKS

SHORT FICTION: *Amori senza amore*, 1894; *Beffe della morte e della vita*, 1902; *Quando'ero matto . . .*, 1902; *Bianche e nere*, 1904; *Erma bifronte*, 1906; *La vita nuda*, 1910; *Terzetti*, 1912; *Le due maschere*, 1914; *Erba del nostro orto*, 1915; *La trappola*, 1915; *E domani, lunedì*, 1917; *Un cavallo nella luna*, 1918; *Berecche e la guerra*, 1919; *Il carnevale dei morti*, 1919; *A Horse in the Moon and Twelve Short Stories*, 1932; *Better Think Twice About It! and Twelve Other Stories*, 1933; *The Naked Truth and Eleven Other Stories*, 1934; *Four Tales*, 1939; *The Medals and Other Stories*, 1939; *Short Stories*, 1959; *The Merry-Go-Round of Love and Selected Stories*, 1964; *Selected Stories*, 1964; *Short Stories*, 1964.

PLAYS: *La morsa*, pb. as *L'epilogo*, 1898, pr. 1910 (*The Vise*, 1928); *Scamandro*, pb. 1909; *Lumìe di*

Sicilia, pr. 1910 (*Sicilian Limes*, 1921); *Il dovere del medico*, pb. 1912 (*The Doctor's Duty*, 1928); *Se non così . . .*, pr. 1915; *All'uscita*, pr. 1916 (*At the Gate*, 1928); *Liolà*, pr. 1916 (English translation, 1952); *Pensaci, Giacomino!*, pr. 1916; *Il berretto a sonagli*, pr. 1917 (*Cap and Bells*, 1957); *Così è (se vi pare)*, pr. 1917 (*Right You Are (If You Think So)*, 1922); *La giara*, pr. 1917 (*The Jar*, 1928); *Il piacere dell'onestà*, pr. 1917 (*The Pleasure of Honesty*, 1923); *Il giuoco delle parti*, pr. 1918 (*The Rules of the Game*, 1959); *Ma non è una cosa seria*, pr. 1918; *La patente*, pb. 1918 (*The License*, 1964); *L'innesto*, pr. 1919; *L'uomo, la bestia, e la virtù*, pr., pb. 1919; *Maschere nude*, pb. 1919-1922 (4 volumes), pb. 1920-1928 (24 volumes), 1920-1929, 1929-1937 (second edition, 31 volumes), 1933-1938; *Come prima, meglio di prima*, pr. 1920; *La Signora Morli, una e due*, pr. 1920; *Tutto per bene*, pr., pb. 1920 (*All for the Best*, 1960); *Sei personaggi in cerca d'autore*, pr., pb. 1921 (*Six Characters in Search of an Author*, 1922); *Enrico IV*, pr., pb. 1922 (*Henry IV*, 1923); *L'imbecille*, pr. 1922 (*The Imbecile*, 1928); *Vestire gli ignudi*, pr. 1922 (*Naked*, 1924); *Three Plays (If You Think So)*, pb. 1922; *L'altro figlio*, pr. 1923 (*The House with the Column*, 1928); *L'uomo dal fiore in bocca*, pr. 1923 (*The Man with the Flower in His Mouth*, 1928); *La vita che ti diedi*, pr. 1923 (*The Life I Gave You*, 1959); *Each in His Own Way and Two Other Plays*, pb. 1923 (includes title play; *The Pleasure of Honesty; Naked*); *Ciascuno a suo modo*, pb. 1923 (*Each in His Own Way*, 1923); *Sagra del Signore della nave*, pb. 1924 (*Our Lord of the Ship*, 1928); *Diana e la Tuda*, Swiss pr. 1926, pr., pb. 1927 (*Diana and Tudo*, 1950); *L'amica della mogli*, pr., pb. 1927 (*The Wives' Friend*, 1949); *Bellavita*, pr. 1927 (English translation, 1964); *La nuova colonia*, pr., pb. 1928 (*The New Colony*, 1958); *The One-Act Plays of Luigi Pirandello*, pb. 1928; *Lazzaro*, pr., pb. 1929 (*Lazarus*, 1952); *O di uno o di nessuno*, pr., pb. 1929; *Sogno (ma forse no)*, pb. 1929 (*I'm Dreaming, But Am I?*, 1964); *Come tu mi vuoi*, pr., pb. 1930 (*As You Desire Me*, 1931); *Questa sera si recita a soggetto*, pr., pb. 1930 (*Tonight We Improvise*, 1932); *I giganti della montagna*, act 1 pb. 1931, act 2 pb. 1934, act 3 pr. 1937 (*The Mountain Giants*, 1958);

Trovarsi, pr., pb. 1932 (*To Find Oneself*, 1943); *Quando si è qualcuno*, pr. 1933 (*When Someone Is Somebody*, 1958); *La favola del figlio cambiato*, pr., pb. 1934; *Non si sa come*, pr. 1934 (*No One Knows How*, 1960); *Naked Masks: Five Plays*, pb. 1952.

POETRY: *Mal giocondo*, 1889; *Pasqua di Gea*, 1891; *Pier Gudrò*, 1894; *Elegie renane*, 1895; *Elegie romane*, 1896 (translation of Johann von Goethe's *Römische Elegien*); *Scamandro*, 1909 (dramatic poem); *Fuori de chiave*, 1912.

NONFICTION: *Arte e scienze*, 1908; *L'umorismo*, 1908, revised 1920 (partial translation, *On Humour*, 1966; complete translation, 1974); *Saggi*, 1939.

MISCELLANEOUS: *Opere*, 1966.

BIBLIOGRAPHY

Bassanese, Fiora A. *Understanding Luigi Pirandello*. Columbia: University of South Carolina Press, 1997. An introduction to Pirandello's work, focusing largely on his thought and the relationship of his life to his work. Examines the novels, myths, and plays.

Biasin, Gian-Paolo, and Manuela Gieri, eds. *Luigi Pirandello: Contemporary Perspectives*. Toronto: University of Toronto Press, 1999. Part of the Major Italian Authors series, this work offers thoughtful critiques of Pirandello's writing.

Budel, Oscar. *Pirandello*. New York: Hillary House, 1969. Chapters on the man and the writer, on the relativist, his use of humor, and his place in modern drama. Includes a list of biographical dates and a bibliography. A short, useful, introductory study.

Caesar, Ann. *Characters and Authors in Luigi Pirandello*. New York: Clarendon Press, 1998. A good study focusing on Pirandello's characters. Includes bibliographical references and an index.

Cambon, Glauco, ed. *Pirandello: A Collection of Critical Studies*. Englewood Cliffs, N.J.: Prentice-Hall, 1967. Essays on the major drama and fiction, with an introduction by a noted scholar. Includes chronology and bibliography.

DiGaetani, John Louis, ed. *A Companion to Pirandello Studies*. New York: Greenwood Press, 1991. A comprehensive volume, twenty-seven essays on

Pirandello's biography and work, with an excellent introduction and several appendices, including production histories and an extensive bibliography.

Matthaei, Renate. *Luigi Pirandello*. New York: Ungar, 1973. Divided into sections on Pirandello's life and work, with a separation discussion section on nine plays. A good short introduction, with a chronology and bibliography.

Ragusa, Olga. *Luigi Pirandello*. New York: Columbia University Press, 1968. A long introductory essay-pamphlet on Pirandello's life and work, perhaps the best of its kind for a quick introduction.

DAVID PLANTE

Born: Providence, Rhode Island; March 4, 1940

PRINCIPAL LONG FICTION
The Ghost of Henry James, 1970
Slides, 1971
Relatives, 1972
The Darkness of the Body, 1974
Figures in Bright Air, 1976
The Family, 1978
The Country, 1981
The Woods, 1982
The Francoeur Novels, 1983 (includes the preceding 3 novels)
The Foreigner, 1984
The Catholic, 1985
The Native, 1987
The Accident, 1991
Annunciation, 1994
The Age of Terror, 1999

OTHER LITERARY FORMS

David Plante was a frequent contributor of short fiction to *The New Yorker* magazine, including stories such as "Mr. Bonito" (July 7, 1980), "Work" (September 21, 1981), "The Accident" (August 9,

1982), and "A House of Women" (April 28, 1986). Plante also published one book of nonfiction, *Difficult Women: A Memoir of Three* (1983), an account of his relationships with Sonia Orwell, George Orwell's widow, and writers Jean Rhys and Germaine Greer. Plante also served as a reviewer and features writer for *The New York Times Book Review* and contributed essays and introductions to works such as *Wrestling with the Angel: Faith and Religion in the Lives of Gay Men* (1995).

ACHIEVEMENTS

While Plante never enjoyed a large readership, he achieved considerable recognition among his peers, winning the acclaim of Philip Roth and other prominent contemporaries. Plante began his career with several self-consciously artistic novels, but in his later works he fashioned a spare, radically simplified style with a deceptive look of artlessness. In contrast to the minimalist writers to whose works his fiction bears a superficial resemblance, Plante uses this pared-down style as a vehicle to explore the consciousness of his protagonists, which he presents in a manner that differs sharply from the involuted style of most novels of consciousness. This is Plante's distinctive achievement in contemporary American fiction.

Plante's sixth novel, *The Family*, was nominated for the National Book Award in 1979. In 1983, while teaching writing at the University of Tulsa, in Tulsa, Oklahoma, Plante received a Guggenheim grant, and in the same year he won the Prize for Artistic Merit from the American Academy and Institute of Arts and Letters. He also received an award from the British Arts Council Bursary.

BIOGRAPHY

David Plante was born in Providence, Rhode Island, on March 4, 1940, the son of Anaclet Joseph Adolph and Albina (Bison) Plante. From 1959 to

(Camera Press Ltd./Archive Photos)

1960, he attended the University of Louvain in Belgium, and in 1961 he was graduated with a B.A. from Boston College. After graduation, Plante taught at the English School in Rome, Italy, at the Boston School of Modern Languages, and at St. John's Preparatory School. He also worked for two years (1962-1964) as a researcher for *Hart's Guide to New York* in New York City. He settled in England in 1966. Plante was a writer-in-residence at the University of Tulsa (1979-1983) and at King's College, Cambridge (1984-1985). The first westerner allowed to teach at the Gorky Institute of Literature in Moscow, Plante also served as writer-in-residence at the University of East Anglia (1977-1978), Adelphi University (1980-1989), and L'Université du Quebec à Montreal (1990). In 1998, he was named Professor of Writing at Columbia University.

ANALYSIS

David Plante's work is significant primarily for its contribution to the genre of the modernist novel of consciousness. His early experimental novels, although static and highly derivative, adumbrate the techniques Plante would later refine in novels which artfully explore the self-consciousness of the individual as he strives to understand his relationship with the external world. Plante succeeds in creating, through an often masterful command of language, a powerful synesthesia, blending paintings of the mind with the art of storytelling.

The dominant themes in the novels of David Plante concern the nature of relationships and the efforts of the individual to break out of his own self-consciousness in order to participate in these relationships. He explores the forces which unite people, whether family members, friends, or lovers, and the ability of these forces to bind as well as alienate, create as well as destroy. His method of narration in his early works reveals unconventional techniques which he later incorporated into his more traditional novels. In his earliest works, such as *The Ghost of Henry James*, *Slides*, *Relatives*, *The Darkness of the Body*, and *Figures in Bright Air*, Plante experiments with an almost plotless structure with an emphasis on language and the expression of consciousness, echoing Henry James, Nathaniel Hawthorne, James Joyce, and Gertrude Stein. Instead of a narrative of progression and movement within a defined space and time, these novels present random associations from constantly changing perspectives. Plante often creates snapshots of consciousness in the form of numerous brief narrative sections which flash in front of the reader, revealing not concrete images but glimpses of various characters' impressions, perceptions, and emotions. Through this technique, Plante attempts to use a character's consciousness to define and describe meaning, leading many critics to observe that these early novels are not novels at all but rather collections of psychological fragments which, though often powerful, ultimately confuse and disappoint the reader.

THE FRANCOEUR NOVELS

With the publication of his largely autobiographical trilogy, *The Francoeur Novels*, in 1983 (which includes *The Family*, *The Country*, and *The Woods*), Plante continued to develop his theme of relationships between family members through the perspective of subjective consciousness and fragmented images, but he integrated these experimental techniques into a more traditionally defined narrative. The first book of the trilogy, *The Family*, introduces Daniel Francoeur, Plante's autobiographical counterpart in the trilogy, and his six brothers born to a Catholic, working-class, French-Canadian couple, Jim and Reena Francoeur. The novel is set primarily in Providence, Rhode Island, at the Francoeurs' newly acquired lake home. Plante traces the emotional struggle of the nine family members to remain unified, communicative, and productive in the face of internal tension and external threat. Because of their ethnic background and unsophisticated social orientation, the family members feel alienated from the Providence community, and when the father loses his job through union pressure, the internal problems within the family are magnified at the same time that the bonds of love and dependency between individual members are tested. Though most of the narrative is seen and evaluated through Daniel's consciousness, the focus of the novel is not on him or any one character but rather on the Francoeur family as a single living organism trying to support and nurture all of its parts for the survival of the whole. The dependency of each family member on the others' well-being is exemplified by the hysterical disintegration of the family unit when the mother experiences a recurrence of an emotional illness.

Plante develops Reena's character more fully than he does the others in *The Family*, and he examines her closely through Daniel's eyes, making her the touchstone for the novel's major theme: the fragility of the seemingly indestructible. Reena possesses the objectivity to see quite clearly the flaws in each son's character while simultaneously loving each totally; she is unable, however, to acknowledge her husband's inability to cope with his unemployment. Her failure to deal with her husband as a fallible human being forces her sons to take sides against their father and ultimately to question their familial duties. Despite her strength and authority as the Francoeur matriarch, Reena remains a child-wife, puzzled and victimized by an uncommunicative, brooding husband. She confides frequently in Daniel, who comes to see his mother's position in the family as isolated and vulnerable. The only woman in a world full of men, an interloper in a fraternity house environment, Reena has tried to remain as unobtrusive as possible in her husband's and sons' world, from avoiding flowers and lacy decorations which might intrude upon their male starkness to suppressing her fears and anger. She has created, literally, seven times over, a world which she can never enter. When her emotional breakdown occurs and Jim resists medical help for her, afraid she would come back from the sanatorium as something other than his submissive wife, the family organism suffers a shock and responds with violence: sons against father, mother against sons, brothers against brothers. The novel concludes with a semblance of unity, but the organism has been damaged.

The damage is subtly revealed in the second (although last written) book of the trilogy, *The Woods*. Peace has returned to the Francoeur home, but only because Jim and Reena have surrendered to a self-imposed isolation and stagnant existence. They appear only peripherally in the novel, and the focus remains on Daniel, who visits his parents' home during a vacation from college. An extremely self-conscious adolescent, Daniel finds himself facing terrifying indecision and overwhelming freedom. Though little action takes place in the novel's three brief chapters, Plante conveys in simple yet intense language Daniel's need to belong, to anchor himself somewhere, to overcome his apathy and lack of ambition. Daniel's first sexual experience brings him no closer to what he wants as he becomes increasingly obsessed with the maleness of his own body. His decision to file with the draft board as a conscientious objector, despite the influence of his older brother Albert, a life-long military man, role model, and major source of

financial support for the Francoeurs, does give Daniel a sense of definition, though mixed with shame. In *The Woods*, Plante creates in Daniel a representation of the time in adolescence when passivity is the safest action, when any other action seems too great a risk, and when even one's own body appears strange and threatening.

This period in Daniel's life has long passed when *The Country* opens. Once again Daniel, now a writer living in London, returns to his parents' home in Providence, where he joins his six brothers, not for any holiday or family celebration but as a response to the final assault on the family unit: the slow, degrading physical and mental deterioration of Reena and Jim Francoeur. Now in their eighties, they are weakened to the point of partial immobility and senility. The sons, some with wives and children, gather to take care of their parents' basic needs as well as attempt, in quiet desperation, to restore the bonds of familial understanding and love. Reena's mental problems have intensified with age, and Daniel listens, as always, to her frightened and often bitter ramblings about her sacrifices to her husband and family. In more tender moments, however, Reena shows her devotion to her dying husband, frequently enveloping his withered body in her arms, grasping his hands in silence, and kissing his cheek. Reena is also still able to express love toward her sons, sharing their secrets and laughing at the jokes whispered to her in French.

The Country does not, however, use Reena as a symbol for the state of the Francoeur family as the first novel did. Except for a brief flashback to twenty years earlier at a tense family gathering at the lake house, the last book of the Francoeur trilogy explores the character of Jim, who, in the earlier works, received uneven and ambiguous treatment. Through a first-person narrative, Daniel attempts to understand the complexities of a man who once seemed so simple. In moments of lucidity, Jim expresses to Daniel his doubts about having been a good father, husband, and worker, and Daniel realizes that, despite his father's domination over his mother and the unrelenting sense of social and familial duties imposed on his sons, Jim loved his family in every way that his old-world cultural background permitted, limited greatly by an inability to express his emotions. As Daniel witnesses the pathetic deterioration of his once hearty and active father, he frantically tries to reestablish communication and a sense of tradition. In response, his father awkwardly attempts to understand his son's life as a writer in a foreign country. Ultimately, the father, drifting in and out of the present in a cloudy mind, leaves his son the only wisdom he knows: "Work hard. . . . And be a good boy." When his father dies, Daniel is able to grieve honestly for a man who, he now realizes, "could not think of himself, but had to think of his duty to the outside world." Reena, after an initial feeling of emancipation from her husband's authority, reacts to his death by retreating into incessant speech and fearful imaginings, once again alone among the men she created.

In *The Country*, the strongest work in the trilogy, Plante achieved what he had been working toward since his first novels: the subordination of plot with an emphasis on emotion and perception. The only significant action in *The Country* is the observation of time and death, but the helplessness of every member of the Francoeur family is a haunting and consistent echo throughout the novel. This echo gives *The Country* a power never realized in the earlier works.

In the two novels succeeding the Francoeur trilogy, Plante's protagonist continues to narrate in the first person, though he is never mentioned by name in the earlier work, *The Foreigner*; only through allusions to the hero's family background does the author identify him as a member of the Francoeur family, probably Daniel once again. Adam Mars-Jones suggests in his review of *The Foreigner* in the *The Times Literary Supplement* that the narrator may be Daniel's older brother Andre, noting that at the end of *The Family* the Francoeurs receive a postcard from Andre, who is in Europe, the same postcard which is mentioned in *The Foreigner*. This connection does exist, but the narrator of *The Foreigner* undeniably possesses the same history, voice, and sensibility as the protagonist of *The Francoeur Novels*, whatever name the reader gives him.

THE FOREIGNER

The Foreigner does not relate to the trilogy in any other way, nor does it follow the previous work chro-

nologically. In this novel, the hero is twenty and leaving his Rhode Island home in 1959 to travel to Europe, hoping to shed his "Americanisms" and experience the expatriate lifestyle in the fashion of Ernest Hemingway, whose epigraph, "In Spain you could not tell anything," introduces the book. Instead of the romance and rebirth he expected, the narrator discovers loneliness and alienation from the environment and the people, even his American college friends who meet him in France. Wanting to get as far away as possible from what these friends represent, he is grateful to find a mysterious black woman he met previously on his crossing from America. From the moment he links himself with Angela Johnson and her emotionally disturbed lover Vincent, the strangeness and danger he craved are never far from him, though never fully defined. Angela and Vincent demand all of their new friend's money, leaving him totally dependent upon them by the time he realizes that they are possibly involved in illegal activities. The narrator's odd relationship with Angela and Vincent is revealed in the Hemingway style of terse dialogue and matter-of-fact description blended with Plante's characteristically fragmented narrative and vivid images of consciousness. *The Foreigner* is a unique work for Plante, however, in that it does make some attempt, though sporadic and uneven, to provide a climactic scene, the street-dance suicide of Vincent. No other Plante novel uses this traditional narrative element. Yet the circumstances which lead up to the story's climax remain subordinate to Plante's interest in the objective correlatives of his protagonist's consciousness, the means of representing his thoughts and emotions as concrete objects or communicable expressions. Many of these thoughts reflect the narrator's voyeuristic, homosexual obsession with Vincent and the total sense of alienation brought about by this attraction.

THE CATHOLIC

Daniel's homosexuality, only implied in *The Francoeur Novels*, is made explicit in *The Foreigner* and becomes the major focus of *The Catholic*. Early in the Francoeur trilogy, Daniel became obsessed with the figure of the nude, crucified Christ, a ubiquitous presence in his Catholic home. As he grew older,

Daniel developed strange correlations between the body of Christ and the power of male sexuality. In *The Catholic*, Daniel decides that the only way for him to overcome his intense self-consciousness and escape from his body's prison is to surrender himself physically and spiritually to another man. Women, in Daniel's perception, have no spirituality: They are fixed, concrete, earthbound objects and therefore can only give him back to himself as a mirror does, thus increasing his awareness of himself. Although Daniel turns to women as confidantes and advisers, sexually they cannot provide the transcendental experience he seeks. When Daniel falls in love with Henry, he mistakes sexual obsession with heightened consciousness. They spend only one night together, and Daniel immediately realizes that Henry wants to maintain his autonomy and selfhood as desperately as Daniel wants to lose his. The novel becomes little more than an explication of Daniel's frightening sexual compulsions and the aftermath of grief and guilt. *The Catholic* does not develop the narrative structures attempted in *The Francoeur Novels* and *The Foreigner* and resembles more closely the earlier novels in its extremely obscure language and disturbing images.

ANNUNCIATION

Plante's thirteenth novel, *Annunciation*, represents a culmination of many of the themes and images of the earlier novels, as well as something of a departure from their terseness and almost plotless structure. Intertwining the tale of art historian Claire O'Connel and her teenage daughter Rachel with that of art editor Claude Ricard, Plante examines the darkness that envelopes and threatens to overwhelm the characters. Attempting to shelter her daughter from the truth of her husband's suicide, Claire brings Rachel to England, where she is raped and becomes pregnant. The already tenuous relationship of the mother, sensual and with a survival instinct, and the daughter, ethereal and painfully like her father, is strained even more when Claire becomes engaged. Ironically, Claire's fascination with the subject of her thesis, Baroque artist Pietro Testa, and her quest to find a previously uncatalogued painting entitled, once again ironically, *Annunciation* eventually brings mother and daughter together.

Along the way other characters are able to touch the enigmatic Rachel in a way her mother has not been able to, including Belorussian Maurice Kurigan and Claude Ricard, a young art editor of Russian descent. Still stinging from a physical but unfulfilling relationship with an Englishwoman and the suicide of a distant cousin, Claude's depression and rage abate when he and Maurice throw themselves into helping Claire. To do so they travel to Moscow, where Maurice's contacts, the Poliakoffs, are unhelpful, Maurice dies, and Claude is stricken with fever before Claire's arrival. In a climactic scene, Rachel, even more determined than her mother to find the painting, walks away from her mother, who has finally told her of her father's suicide. Overwrought, Claire, led to the ailing Claude by Poliakoff, asks him to take her to the picture, which he had previously discovered. Stricken by the purity of the angel and the Virgin, Claire falls to her knees, overwhelmed with tears. In the final scene the Americans are together in the Poliakoff apartment as the Russians try to imagine the West. The novel ends with Claude's reverie on God: "No, I don't believe in God, but I can imagine him. . . . That vast dark space behind the image of a sunlit glass of water is the only way I can imagine God," an ending which brings the novel a redemptive full circle from the eight-word opening chapter: "A glass of water in a dark room—."

THE AGE OF TERROR

More experimental in form than *Annunciation*, and set almost exclusively in the Soviet Union, this novel traces a spiritual journey of sorts for twenty-three-year-old Joe, which begins after seeing a picture of Russian partisan Zoya Kosmodemyanskaya, who had been hanged and mutilated by Chancellor Adolf Hitler's Nazi troops. Impotent, without faith, and searching for the elusive, Joe encounters a modern Zoya, a former KGB operative now engaged in a joint venture with the American Gerald in selling people into prostitution under the guise of helping them flee the country. Interspersed with the modern scenes are vignettes of the Russian past, all of which prophesy a "different world," one beyond imagination which will replace this "terrible" world.

In the meantime, however, many cruelties exist, and Joe seems to simultaneously abhor and beckon them. Joe's ambivalence is counterpointed by Gerald's certainty: "The truth, which makes men of boys, is that no one will be saved, that we're all bad." No matter how much one wants to feel "something beyond the age of terror," there is nothing. Joe eventually buys into Gerald's philosophy, betraying the existence of Yura, Zoya's son, to Gerald, which leads to Yura's disappearance. Hallucinating and in a fever he accompanies the grieving Zoya into the midst of a snow-covered forest, the forest he had once worshipped in in his dreams. He follows her into a snow-drift and sees the vision of the brown clapboard house that is home. The final vision of *The Age of Terror* is thus, as is true of the body of Plante's work, one of redemption—difficult and even momentarily rejected, but redemption nonetheless.

Penelope A. LeFew,
updated by Jaquelyn W. Walsh

OTHER MAJOR WORK

NONFICTION: *Difficult Women: A Memoir of Three*, 1983.

BIBLIOGRAPHY

Dukes, Thomas. "David Plante." In *Contemporary Gay American Novelists: A Bio-Bibliographical Sourcebook*, edited by Emmanuel S. Nelson. Westport, Conn.: Greenwood Press, 1993. Gives a brief biography of Plante then moves to a discussion of Plante's major works and themes.

Ferraro, Thomas J., ed. *Catholic Lives, Contemporary America*. Durham, N.C.: Duke University Press, 1997. Contains fourteen essays concerning Catholicism, including Plante's "My Parents, My Religion, and My Writing."

Gablik, Suzi. *Conversations Before the End of Time*. New York: Thames and Hudson, 1995. This book of interviews includes one with Plante, "Creating the Space for a Miracle."

Gunton, Sharon R., and Jean C. Stine, eds. *Contemporary Literary Criticism*. Vol. 23. Detroit: Gale Research, 1983. Contains excerpts of reviews of Plante's work from 1970 to 1982, including reviews from *The Times Literary Supplement*, *The New York Times Book Review*, and *The Village Voice*. Most reviewers acknowledge that Plante finds his voice only with the trilogy *The Francoeur Novels*. Despite concerns that his first few novels, in particular *The Ghost of Henry James*, are derivative, Plante receives recognition—both favorable and unfavorable—for his experimental, minimalist writing.

Plante, David. Interview by John F. Baker. *Publishers Weekly* 222 (December 24, 1982): 12-13. This interview was conducted just prior to the publication of *Difficult Women*, a study of Germaine Greer, Jean Rhys, and Sonia Orwell, which has been dubbed a "deadpan literary memoir." Plante gives an overview of his development as a writer.

_____. "Seeing Through a Glass, Darkly: David Plante." Interview by Paul Baumann. *Commonweal* 121 (August 19, 1994): 14, 21-22. In this interview, Plante discusses the significance of religious themes in his work, the influence of Ernest Hemingway, and his French Blackfoot Indian heritage to his style, his fears about the lack of redemption in masterpieces of American literature, and his belief that writing can lead one outside oneself.

KATHERINE ANNE PORTER

Born: Indian Creek, Texas; May 15, 1890
Died: Silver Spring, Maryland; September 18, 1980

PRINCIPAL LONG FICTION

Pale Horse, Pale Rider: Three Short Novels, 1939 (includes *Old Mortality*, *Noon Wine*, and *Pale Horse, Pale Rider*)
Ship of Fools, 1962

OTHER LITERARY FORMS

Katherine Anne Porter is best known for her short fiction. Her stories appear in *Flowering Judas and Other Stories* (1930), *The Leaning Tower and Other*

Stories (1944), and *The Old Order* (1944) and were gathered in *The Collected Stories of Katherine Anne Porter* (1965). Criticism, essays, and poems were collected in *The Days Before* (1952) and *The Collected Essays and Occasional Writings* (1970).

ACHIEVEMENTS

Porter's solid and lasting reputation as a writer is based on a very small output of published work: one novel, a handful of novellas, and fewer than two dozen stories. This slender output, however, represents only a small portion of the fiction she wrote during her lifetime. Exacting and self-critical, she discarded many more stories than she published. By the time her first story appeared in print, she had al-

ready developed her fictional techniques to near perfection, and the maturity and craft of her style in *Flowering Judas and Other Stories*, her first published collection, never was surpassed by her later fiction.

Porter early established her reputation with literary critics and only later became widely known and read. In 1931, one year after the publication of her first volume, she was granted a Guggenheim Fellowship, an award she received again in 1938. The Society of Libraries of New York University awarded her its first annual gold medal for literature in 1940 upon the publication of *Pale Horse, Pale Rider*. A Modern Library edition of *Flowering Judas and Other Stories* appeared that same year. In 1943, she was elected a member of the National Institute of Arts and Letters, and in 1949, she accepted her first appointment as writer-in-residence and guest lecturer at Stanford University. In later years, she held similar positions in many other colleges and universities, including the University of Chicago, the University of Michigan, Washington and Lee University, the University of Liège, and the University of Virginia.

By the time she published *Ship of Fools* in 1962, Porter had received three more honors: a Ford Foundation grant in 1959, and in 1962, the O. Henry Memorial Award for her story "Holiday" and the Emerson-Thoreau Bronze medal of the American Academy of Arts and Sciences. *Ship of Fools* became a Book-of-the-Month-Club selection and an immediate best-seller. In the face of its overwhelming popular success, some critics charged that Porter had forsaken her artistic standards in favor of writing a book that would appeal to a large audience. *Ship of Fools* also was criticized for its pessimism and for its failure to conform neatly to the structure of a novel, a supposed

(Washington Star Collection, D.C. Public Library)

flaw especially irksome to those who had admired the formal perfection of Porter's earlier works. Porter herself was surprised by the book's popularity. She had abandoned the form of her earlier work—with its tight plots centered on the fate of a single character—but she had moved deliberately on to something else. She was still writing "honest," she said, a quality that characterized all her fiction. First and last, she was still an artist, a label she applied to herself unhesitatingly.

Though Porter published no new fiction after *Ship of Fools*, her critical and public acclaim grew. It reached its peak when she received both the Pulitzer Prize and the National Book Award for Fiction in 1966.

BIOGRAPHY

Katherine Anne Porter was born Collie Russell Porter in Indian Creek, Texas, on May 15, 1890. She was the third of five children born to Harrison and Mary Alice Jones Porter. When her mother died in 1892, she and her brothers and sisters moved to Kyle, Texas, where they were cared for by their paternal grandmother, Catherine Anne Porter. When Mrs. Porter senior died in 1901, Harrison Porter sold the farm in Kyle and moved with his family to San Antonio.

Facts about Porter's early life and education have been difficult to substantiate, partly because Porter's own accounts were evasive or inconsistent. Although her family apparently was Methodist, Porter attended convent schools, possibly for a time in New Orleans, which may be why later researchers have reported that she was a Catholic from birth. Porter denied this allegation when it appeared in a biographical sketch published by the University of Minnesota series on American writers. Precocious as a child and rebellious as a teenager, she ran away from school at age sixteen to marry. The name of her first husband is not known, although the marriage lasted three years.

After the divorce, Porter moved to Chicago, already cherishing the ambition of becoming a professional writer. She worked as a reporter on a Chicago newspaper for a time and signed on as an extra with a motion-picture company for a few months. Passing up the opportunity to travel to Hollywood with the film company, she returned to Texas, where she reported that she made a living as a traveling enter-

tainer, singing Scottish ballads, dressed in a costume she made herself. Thereafter, she wrote drama criticism and society gossip for a Fort Worth weekly, *The Critic*. One year later, she moved to Denver, Colorado, and became a reporter for the *Rocky Mountain News*. In Denver, during the influenza epidemic of 1918, she became severely ill and almost died. This experience, which she fictionalized in *Pale Horse, Pale Rider*, affected her profoundly. "I really had participated in death," she said years later in an interview with Barbara Thompson of the *Paris Review*. She had had "what the Christians call the 'beatific vision'"; she was no longer "like other people."

In 1919 she moved to New York City, where for a brief time she worked as a hack and ghostwriter. The following year she went to study in Mexico. Again she stayed only a short time, but for the next ten years Mexico was to be the center of her intellectual and imaginative life. Returning to Fort Worth, she began to write the stories based on her experiences there. During the next decade she traveled extensively, reviewed books for leading national magazines and newspapers, and worked and reworked the stories that were published in 1930 in *Flowering Judas and Other Stories*.

Supported by a Guggenheim Fellowship granted that year, she returned to Mexico. In 1931, she sailed aboard a German ship from Veracruz to Bremerhaven. This voyage gave her the setting for *Ship of Fools*, which was not to be published for another thirty years. She lived until the mid-1930's in Paris, marrying and later divorcing Eugene Pressly, a member of the American Foreign Service, and working on her fiction. After her divorce from Pressly, she married Albert Erskine, Jr., of the Louisiana State University faculty. Until her divorce from Erskine in 1942, she lived in Baton Rouge. During this time, she continued to work on her short fiction, but not until the late 1950's did she begin sustained effort on her only full-length novel, *Ship of Fools*. Although by that time many of her acquaintances believed she never would finish it, fragments of the novel appeared in magazines, and, in 1962, *Ship of Fools* was published. Porter wrote no more new fiction after that, although *The Collected Essays and Occasional*

Writings appeared in 1970. On September 18, 1980, at age of ninety, Katherine Anne Porter died in Silver Spring, Maryland.

ANALYSIS

Katherine Anne Porter once suggested that when she sat down to write about her life as accurately as possible, it turned into fiction; indeed, she knew no other way to write fiction. Whether this anecdote is true, it is certain that capturing the past with great detail was an important ingredient in her writing. In a number of the short stories, and in two of the best short novels, Miranda, the central character, is very close to being Porter herself. These stories follow Miranda's life from infancy in her grandmother's house in South Texas, to her scrape with death from influenza in Colorado at the age of twenty-four—her first major step toward maturity.

Concerning the time of her illness, Porter has said that it was as though a line were drawn through her life, separating everything that came before from everything that came after. She had been given up and then had survived, and in some ways all her time after that was borrowed. Perhaps that is why her overtly autobiographical stories deal with the time before that line, the time when she was "alive" and therefore had a life to record. The stories that take place after that incident present her, if at all, as an observer, as someone slightly distant and alienated from life. (It is a question of degree: Miranda is also, of course, an acute observer in the stories in which she takes part. Her name, in fact, means "observer" in Spanish.) Porter was in real life a passenger on the ship about which her novel *Ship of Fools* was written, but she speaks of herself as purely an observer, who scarcely spoke a word on the entire voyage. She does not appear directly as a character in the novel.

OLD MORTALITY

The girl, Miranda, in the short novel *Old Mortality*, runs away from school to get married, in part to escape from her family, so suffocatingly steeped in its own past. At the conclusion of the novella, she is determined to free herself once and for all from that past, so that she can begin to consider her own future; but she determines this, the reader is told in the ironic concluding lines, "in her hopefulness, her ignorance." The irony is that Miranda/Porter herself became so obsessed with that past that much of her best work is devoted to it. The explanation for Porter's obsession with the past can perhaps be guessed from the conclusion of *Pale Horse, Pale Rider*. Everything of importance to Miranda has died; only her ravaged body, her spark of a soul somehow survives. She finds that she has no future, only the slow progression to death once again. The past, then, is all she has, yet the past is finally intangible, as the girl in *Old Mortality* discovers as she sifts through all the evidence. At last no truth can be discovered, no objectivity, only the combined and contradictory subjectives: The only truth, once again, is the truth of fiction.

Porter said that in her fiction she is not interested in actions so much as she is interested in the various and subtle results of actions. Certainly, of all her works, *Old Mortality* deals directly with the ramifications of past actions. This short novel spans ten years in the life of the protagonist, Miranda, from the age of eight to the age of eighteen. In that time, the reader learns little of Miranda's life, except that she is bad tempered and that, unlike many of the young women in her widely extended family, she is not going to be a "beauty." She is, rather, the recording center of the novel: The events are brought to her and have their effect on the person she is becoming.

The crucial actions have occurred in the preceding generation. Miranda's family is obsessed by a past event. Miranda's aunt Amy was a great beauty, the measure, in fact, against which all the current crop of beauties are found wanting. She was glamorous, racy, even though tubercular, and for a long time spurned Gabriel's devoted courtship. Gabriel was himself wild, ran a string of racehorses, and was heir to the fortune. Only when he was disinherited and Amy found herself in the terminal stage of her illness did she consent to marry him. The couple went to New Orleans on their honeymoon, and almost immediately Amy died. Miranda tries to sift out the truth of the story. She looks at the photograph of Amy and does not find her so impossibly beautiful and indeed thinks she looks silly in her out-of-fashion dress.

Later, she is introduced to Gabriel, and instead of the dashing young man who had once challenged a rival to a duel over Amy, she finds him fat and drunken, down on his luck; the woman whom he married after Amy is bitter and depressed from living with a ne'er-do-well who has spent their whole married life talking about Amy. Later still, Miranda meets Eva, a homely spinster cousin from Gabriel's generation, and Eva says the real truth is that Amy was a lewd woman, who married only because someone else got her pregnant, and took her own life with an overdose of drugs.

After a moment of shock, Miranda realizes that Eva's version, in its negative way, is just as romantic as the others. Miranda does not want to know where the truth lies. By this time, she has left school and has run off to get married. Her father is cool with her, thinking she has deserted the family; indeed she has, and deliberately. She refuses to be trapped in the past, represented by this unknowable woman whose brief life still haunts the family. She wants instead to discover who she—Miranda—is; she wants her own life to exist in the present and future. This is what she determines—in the novel's ironic final line—"in her hopefulness, her ignorance."

In her ignorance, Miranda-Porter learns that her past is what she is, the result of those past actions. She has been touched by Amy even more than the others, for she has become Amy, the Amy who refused to live by the others' rules, and at last ran off, married, and never returned—just as Miranda has done. In so doing, Amy and Miranda become separated from the rest of the family, freezing its members in their moment of history just as Porter herself became separated from her family so that she could re-create them forever in her stories.

NOON WINE

Noon Wine is set in the rural turn-of-the-century southern Texas of Porter's childhood but does not deal with her family. The characters in this short novel are poor and uneducated farmers, but this does not stop the story from being an intricate and subtle moral allegory. The lingering effect of past actions is not the central theme, as it was in *Old Mortality*, but a sense of the cumulative force of a man's actions gives

the story a tragic inevitability. Mr. Thompson is a proud man, and as a result he marries above himself. Instead of a strong woman to help him in the strenuous operation of his farm, he marries a delicate and genteel woman who quickly becomes a near invalid. Further, she insists that they have a dairy, a bit higher class than an ordinary row-crop farm. In the end, Thompson is left with a wife who cannot help him and a kind of farmwork that he does not feel is masculine, and which he therefore shirks. The farm is deteriorating, and the couple are about to go under entirely, when a strange taciturn Swede from North Dakota arrives, asking for work. Instantly there is a revolution. The Swede fixes, paints, repairs everything, and shortly the failing farm becomes productive. As the years go by, the couple are able to buy such luxuries as an icebox, and Mr. Thompson is able to sit on the porch while the work is being done. One day Hatch arrives, a thoroughly evil man. He is a bounty hunter; the Swede, it is revealed, is an escaped homicidal maniac who in a berserk fury stabbed his own brother to death. Thompson refuses to give up the Swede. There is a scuffle; the Swede suddenly appears and steps between them; Thompson believing he sees Hatch stabbing the Swede in the stomach, smashes Hatch's skull with an ax.

The confrontation is remarkably complex. Hatch, as he is presented in the story, seems a pure manifestation of evil, and so perhaps he should be killed, but ironically he has in fact done nothing. The Swede is a primal murderer, a brother-killer like Cain, and is a threat to murder again. Thompson believes Hatch has stabbed the Swede and acts to defend him, but after he has killed Hatch, the Swede does not have a mark on him, not even, perhaps, the mark of Cain, which has been transferred to Thompson.

Thompson is easily acquitted of the crime in court, but his fundamentalist neighbors in the close-knit community look on him as a murderer. Most important, he must examine his own motives. Was he defending the Swede, or was he defending the success of his farm, which, he must have guiltily realized, was not the result of his work, but of the work of another, a sinner, a primal murderer? With his mark of Cain, Thompson goes the rounds of his neighbors, trying to tell his side of the story, believing it less each time himself, until he kills himself, the final consequence of his original pride.

PALE HORSE, PALE RIDER

Porter has called sleep "that little truce of God between living and dying." If dreams, therefore, take place in a landscape somewhere between life and death, it is appropriate that *Pale Horse, Pale Rider* begins with one of Miranda's many dreams to be recorded. Although the story is set during World War I in a small town in Colorado where Miranda is working for a newspaper, symbolically the story takes place in the dreamlike zone between life and death. In that initial dream, Death rides alongside Miranda, but she tells him to ride on ahead; she is not quite ready to go with him. She wakes up only to be reminded of the war, which is poisoning the lives of many people, who are full of despair because of their inability to control their destinies. The streets are filled with funerals, as the influenza epidemic kills people like a medieval plague. Miranda's work on the paper is hateful, and her only release is when, after work, she meets Adam. Adam, as his name suggests, is the man who should be her companion, her mate in life. He is a soldier, however, on his way to war and committed wholly to death, and so Miranda struggles to withhold her love from him.

The war and the plague, as presented in the novel, are symbols of the struggle of life and its vulnerability. Miranda and Adam differ from others in being existentially aware; all that exists for them is the present tense of their lives. They dance together in a cheap café, knowing that it is all they will ever have. Because they have so little—a brief moment of troubled life, and then death—the integrity of their actions becomes their only value. Miranda tells Adam that he is stupid to fight in a war in which old men send young men to die. He agrees, saying, however, that if he does not go, he can no longer face himself. Miranda has her own costly sense of integrity: As a reporter for the paper, she witnesses a pathetic scandal, and when the victims beg her not to write the story, she does not. The rival papers do, however, and her editor is furious; her colleagues think she is senseless. She is demoted to writing entertainment

reviews. Even there, when she writes an unfavorable review of a vaudeville act, she is confronted by the old, broken, has-been actor, and her subsequent compassion struggles against her dedication to her job. Her colleagues counsel her to fake the reviews and make everyone happy, but writing honest reviews is an important value to her.

Miranda gets the flu, and in a long delirious dream comes to the point of death and has a beatific vision. The doctor and nurse fighting to preserve her, working with their own existential integrity, bring her back, but it is so painful being taken away from her vision and back to life, that when life-giving drugs are injected into her, she feels them like "a current of agony."

Miranda had fought, with her tiny spark of consciousness, to survive, to survive for Adam. Then she learns that Adam, perhaps having caught flu from her, has himself died. Her dream of heaven had been so brilliant that the real world seems to her a monochrome, a bleak field in which, with Adam gone, she has nothing. The reader, however, can see beyond this point. Earlier, Miranda and Adam had sung an old spiritual together, of a pale horse with a pale rider, who takes a girl's lover away, leaving her behind to mourn. Miranda is the singer who is left behind to mourn and to record the story for the rest of the world.

SHIP OF FOOLS

Porter has described her fiction as an investigation of the "terrible failure of the life of man in the Western World." Her one full-length novel, *Ship of Fools*, is a bleak cross section of modern civilization. It follows the lives of literally dozens of characters, from all levels of the particular society it is observing. More than forty characters of various nationalities are presented in some detail: American, Spanish, Mexican, Cuban, German, Swiss, Swedish. The time is 1931, and chaos is spreading. Soon Adolf Hitler will be in power, the extermination camps will be in operation, and another world war will be under way. The title *Ship of Fools* is a translation of Sebastian Brant's medieval moral allegory, *Das Narrenschiff* (1494). The ship is the world; the time of the journey is the lifetime of the characters. They, of course, do not see it that way. They think of it as a temporary voyage. The lies they tell, the treacheries they enact, the hopeless relationships they form, are only temporary, have nothing to do with the course of their real lives, with the objectives they mean to obtain, the moral codes by which they mean to live.

The ship, the *Vera* (truth), leaves Veracruz, Mexico, for the nearly monthlong journey to Bremerhaven. It is a German ship, and the German passengers sit at the captain's table. From the pompous and second-rate captain on down, they are comic grotesques, guzzling their food swinishly and looking suspiciously at everyone who does not eat pork, or who has a slightly large nose, as potentially Jewish. The only seemingly human Germans are Wilhelm Freytag, concealing as long as he can the fact that he has a Jewish wife, and Dr. Schumann, the ship's doctor, the novel's most sympathetic character, urbane, gentle, wise—who, to his own horror, commits perhaps the basest act of anyone on board. The American characters are only slightly less grotesque. William Denny the Texan is pure caricature: To him everyone but a white Texan is a "nigger," "spick," "wop," or "damyankee." He devotes all his time to pursuing sexual pleasure but is fearful that he will be cheated into paying too much for it. The comic result is that he pays out everything and gets nothing in return but a severe drubbing. Mrs. Treadwell, a forty-five-year-old divorcee, is utterly selfish, yet she wonders why she gets nothing from life. David Scott and Jenny Brown, living together, fighting constantly, are, with Dr. Schumann and Wilhelm Freytag, the novel's main characters. David Scott is tied up within himself and will give up nothing to another. Jenny Brown sporadically gives up everything to mere acquaintances yet seems to have nothing of her own within.

One character after another debates humanity's nature: Are all people basically good; are all people naturally depraved; are the pure races good and the mongrel races evil? The characters seem intent on acting out all these possibilities. The most disciplined of them regularly lapse into helpless sentimentality. Freytag thinks that each woman he meets is the beautiful love of his life. One of these women is a Jew, whom he married during a period of extreme romanticism, and now he is déclassé among his German compatriots and cannot admit to himself how regretful he is. David and Jenny, needing everything from each other, have only gone as far as learning each other's weaknesses, of which they take full advantage to lacerate each other. They continue to cling together, always saying they will separate at some later time. Most painful is the folly of the sympathetic Dr. Schumann. He convinces himself that he is in love with a neurotic Spanish countess (he has a wife at home), and under pretense of caring for her as her doctor, he turns her into a hopeless and helpless drug addict in order to keep his power over her.

The most purely evil characters on the ship are the shoddy Spanish dance troupe. Through herculean efforts they almost take control of the ship and certainly take control of the lives of the characters, bringing out their deepest and worst traits, but at the end they sit listless and exhausted, as though the effort were immensely greater than any return they have had from it. This troupe of carnival performers cheats, steals, blackmails, and even kills right before the others, who remark on it, but do nothing to stop them, each character feeling it is not his place to do anything. At length, the troupe is sitting confidently at the captain's table, having rearranged everyone's position on the ship. In a kind of Walpurgis Night, they bring the many characters to some sort of climax in an eruption of drunken violence. It is Porter's vision of how World War II began: low thugs and gangsters taking power with the casual, half-intentional connivance of the world.

In the midst of this bleak and pessimistic picture of the Western world, there is one possibility of redemption. The rare positive moments in the novel are when the characters suddenly, often to their own surprise, come together in the act of sex—Porter emphasizing the sensuality of the contact rather than any spiritual qualities. Perhaps Porter is saying that in their fallen state human beings must start at the bottom, with earthly sensuality, in order to slowly acquire a knowledge of spiritual beauty.

Norman Lavers

vative rabbi in 1954, attracted by doctrines more liberal than those of strict Jewish Orthodoxy, Potok continued his struggle to reconcile fundamental Judaism with the findings of science (as historiography and textual criticism shed new light on ancient traditions). *The Chosen* inaugurated his public search for a voice with which to speak to his heritage as well as to the larger world.

In the early 1960's, Potok taught at the Jewish Theological Seminary in New York, edited *Conservative Judaism*, and in 1965 became editor-in-chief with the Jewish Publication Society of Philadelphia. In 1975 he became special projects editor. He was married to Adena Mosevitzky in 1958, and they took up residence in Merion, Pennsylvania. The Potoks had three children: Rena, Naama, and Akiva. Potok served as a visiting professor at the University of Pennsylvania, Bryn Mawr College, and The Johns Hopkins University.

ANALYSIS

In his novels, Chaim Potok returns again and again to the story of a young protagonist coming of age in a culture (usually Jewish) at once mysterious, beautiful, sad, and somehow inadequate. Usually told in the first person, Potok's stories surround the reader with forebodings of the larger, evil world (news of pogroms in Europe, the Holocaust, the first atom bomb) into which his characters are plunged. Potok creates a microcosm of feeling and reaction to events that shake the world. His sentences are simple and reportorial, at times almost a parody of the staccato style of Ernest Hemingway. The stories develop chronologically, though they are frequently invaded by dreams, visions, or voices from the "Other Side."

In each of his stories, Potok sets for himself a question to be answered and reworks his own experiences until he is satisfied with at least a provisional resolution. Controlling metaphors help shape the questions. In *The Chosen*, the baseball game symbolizes the competition between two Jewish cultures, the very strict Hasidic and the more openly assimilationist. What happens to those caught in between those two traditions? The vision of pups being born in *The Book of Lights* represents the entrance of fer-

tile Cabala mysticism into a world of strict Jewish law. How can Jewish mysticism enrich Orthodoxy? Asher Lev's dreams of his mythical ancestor foreshadow the young artist's confrontation with his own culture. What happens when art brings great hurt? The sound of a little door harp symbolizes the transforming power of the imagination for Ilana Davita Chandal (Potok's first female protagonist) of *Davita's Harp*. What is the place of the imagination in Jewish Orthodoxy? What is the place of women?

THE CHOSEN

The Chosen recounts the story of Danny Saunders, brilliant son of a Hasidic rabbi, chosen by tradition to one day succeed his father as leader of the fundamentalist community in Brooklyn, New York. Yet Danny is less interested in studying the Talmud (Jewish law) than in probing the works of Sigmund Freud and other secular psychologists. The story closes with the inevitable confrontation between Danny and his father, which is mediated by Danny's friend Reuvan Malter. In the climactic scene in Reb Saunders's office, the old rabbi turns to his son and addresses him as a father for the first time. (For years, Danny had been reared in silence, except for times of Talmud study.) With fatherly tears, Reb Saunders explains that the years of silence created a soul of compassion within his brilliant son. Though he may well leave the Hasidic community for secular studies, Danny will always carry with him the legacy of Jewish suffering. That legacy will provide the moral force to change the world.

Reuvan, son of a Talmud scholar of the new school of textual criticism, chooses to become a rabbi. The choices, for Reuvan and for Danny, do not, however, come easily. Reuvan faces ostracism by the Hasidic community for suggesting that some Talmudic texts were of inferior quality and subject to misinterpretation. Danny must seemingly turn against his father if he is to pursue secular studies and abandon his leadership obligations.

The novel is structured almost as a diary, with pages of detailed descriptions of schoolwork in the Jewish high school, visits to the local synagogue, and the ebb and flow of Reuvan's life. Though at times tedious, the very innocence of the language contributes to a certain dramatic intensity. The conflict in the novel is mirrored in the frequent news reports of World War II and in the ensuing controversy over the creation of a Jewish state, Israel, in 1949. The Hasidic community is content to wait for the Messiah to create such a state; Reuvan's father calls for an immediate political settlement. Political questions are present in each of Potok's novels and are of central interest in *Davita's Harp*.

THE PROMISE

Silence is again present in Potok's second novel, *The Promise*, which continues the story of Danny Saunders and Reuvan Malter as they enter their professional lives. The novel begins with shouts of rage from young Michael Gordon, the son of Professor Abraham Gordon, a controversial Jewish philosopher. Michael has been cheated at a carnival booth by an old Jewish man, and both Reuvan and his date, Rachel Gordon, Michael's cousin, stare in horror as Michael angrily denounces Orthodoxy. Michael's father had questioned the supernatural accounts in the Hebrew Bible and, as a result, was excommunicated from the Orthodox community; now Michael is releasing his hate on those who persecuted Professor Gordon. Subsequently, Michael is taken to Danny Saunders, now a psychologist at a residential treatment center. When the boy refuses to speak, Danny isolates him. The agonizing silence breaks Michael's will and he reveals the hate he feels for his father and his writings, writings that have brought condemnation to them both. Eventually, Michael is finally able to accept his own feelings and reconcile with his parents, and Danny and Rachel are married, the powerful coupling of the brilliant Hasid with the cosmopolitan daughter of a secularist philosopher.

The Promise continues the exploration of Reuvan's choice to receive his rabbinate from an Orthodox seminary and his refusal to become a secular Jew, as Professor Gordon has done. Yet Reuvan is uneasy with the traditional method of Talmud study advanced by Rav Kalman, one of his teachers. If the Talmud is the sacred oral tradition of the Jews in written form, contradictory commentaries from rabbis down through the centuries must always be reconciled by newer interpretations, so as not to call

God's Word into question. For Reuvan, there is another possibility; a corrupt text could be the source of confusion. Any correction, however, would mean violence to sacred scripture. Reuvan will become a rabbi so that he might debate Rav Kalman and the others from within a common tradition.

Reuvan's father, David Malter, is the voice of quiet wisdom throughout both books. Though a proponent of the new Talmud studies, he is sympathetic toward those whose tightly knit culture is being threatened. As he tells Reuvan in *The Promise*, "We cannot ignore the truth. At the same time, we cannot quite sing and dance as they do. . . . That is the dilemma of our time, Reuvan. I do not know what the answer is." Earlier, Reuvan's father had challenged his son to make his own meaning in the world. Those who had committed themselves to the Hasidic traditions had kept the faith alive through incomprehensible persecution. Now Reuvan must also choose with the greatest seriousness and fervency, for he, too, must make a mark on the world and endure hardship of his own.

MY NAME IS ASHER LEV

Potok picks up this theme in his third novel, *My Name Is Asher Lev*. Covering the period of the late 1940's through the late 1960's, the book is an apologia for the artist. The Orthodox Jewish surroundings are familiar, but this time the controversy is not over textual criticism but rather representational art. Painting is not strictly forbidden to the Orthodox Jew, but it is regarded as useless, as foolishness, as a waste of time better devoted to the study of the Torah, the five books of Moses. Moreover, certain pictures could come close to violating the commandment forbidding graven images. Asher Lev is a born painter, however, and throughout the novel, as he develops his talent, he is increasingly isolated from his family and culture. Asher is born in Crown Heights in Brooklyn in 1943. His father travels extensively for the local Rebbe in an effort to establish Ladover Hasid communities throughout Europe and to aid families immigrating to the United States. Asher's mother must stay with her son in New York because Asher refuses to leave his familiar streets to join his father in Europe. There are long nights of loneliness, waiting

tive, tracing the childhood of Ilana Davita Chandal, his first female lead character. She is the daughter of a nonbelieving Jewish mother and a nonbelieving Christian father. Spanning the years from the mid-1930's to 1942, the novel speaks with a new voice yet recapitulates some familiar themes. Davita grows up in the New York area; she remembers frequent moves, strange people coming and going, and the constant singing of the door harp. Her parents are involved in the Communist Party, attempting to fight Fascism in Spain and in the United States. Davita is precocious and inquisitive and her mother intelligent and cool, forever supplying Davita with the meaning of new words: proletariat, strike, idea, magic, war. Davita is spurred in her imaginative development by Aunt Sarah, a devout Episcopalian nurse, who tells her Bible stories, and by Jakob Daw, an Austrian writer, now suffering from having been gassed in World War I, who had loved Davita's mother when they were both in Vienna. Daw is sheltered for a time by Davita's parents and spins odd stories for her. There is the story of the little bird, flying to find the source of a beautiful music that soothes the world from the horrors of war. Only if the bird could stop the deceitful music would the world wake to its pain.

Davita's father, Michael Chandal, a journalist with *New Masses*, is killed during the bombing of Guernica during the Spanish Civil War. Soon after, both Jakob Daw and Davita's mother, Channah, become disillusioned with the Stalinists because the Communists, too, have committed atrocities. Davita has taken to attending a Jewish high school and becomes an outstanding student. Jakob Daw returns to Europe, where he dies, though his stories live in Davita's heart. Not long afterward, Ezra Dinn, an Orthodox Jew who had loved Davita's mother years before, marries Channah. Slowly, Davita's mother regains her sense of place.

Davita's time of innocence is over. Before Jakob Daw left for Europe, he finished his strange story of the bird. The bird, he said, gave up searching for the music of the world and became very small to fit inside the door harp. There, said Daw, the music was not deceitful but full of innocence. Now, however, Davita encounters something sinister in her adopted

tradition. She is the most brilliant student at her yeshiva but she is passed over for the Akiva Award because, she is told, she is a woman. It is 1942. Another student is selected for the award but learns the truth and refuses it. He is Reuvan Malter, first introduced in *The Chosen*.

Ilana Davita had wanted the prize because it would have given her the opportunity to tell her Jewish community a few words of farewell. "I had made this community my home, and now I felt betrayed by it. . . . I felt suddenly alone. And for the first time I began to understand how a single event could change a person's life." Later, in a vision, Jakob Daw and Davita's father appear, as well as Aunt Sarah. They want to hear her words, and so Davita speaks. She does not understand a world that kills its very best. She had wanted to speak public words of good-bye to her father and Jakob Daw the storyteller. The harp appears in her vision as well, singing in memorial to all the Davitas who would never have an opportunity to "speak their few words to this century."

In the end, Davita will go on to public school, angry with "sacred discontent." In an interview, Potok explained that Davita's experience was based on that of his wife, who was passed over as valedictory speaker because of her sex. *Davita's Harp* is a new exploration for Potok, that of Orthodoxy and feminism. Yet the novel also draws from Gershon Loran, David Lurie, and Asher Lev in recognizing the power of the artist's imagination to transform pain and ambiguity into some kind of meaning. A writer is a kind of harp, playing new music that mends the world.

THE GIFT OF ASHER LEV

The Gift of Asher Lev is framed by death. It begins with the funeral of Yitzchok Lev, Asher's uncle, and the ending of Asher's exile in France to attend the services in Brooklyn. Asher Lev is forty-five; he is joined by his wife Devorah, their daughter Rocheleh, eleven, and five-year-old son Avrumel. Though his family adapts well to the life of the Brooklyn Hasidim, Asher is haunted by the memory of a strange telephone call he received eighteen years earlier, the last time he had visited his parents in New York. It was a voice from the "Other Side," threatening death.

Asher is unable to paint (though he is given to sketching) and he seems to wander aimlessly through the local shops and galleries, as if waiting for a renewal of his gift. In the last year, critics had detected Asher's repetition of old themes, and he feels in danger of losing his gift should he become acclimated to his parents' community. Morose and determined to flee to France again, Asher is asked by the Rebbe to stay, at least for a while. Eventually it becomes clear to Asher that he and the aging Rebbe are woven inextricably together, as darkness and light. The Rebbe has no heir, and it is apparent that the leadership of the Ladover must pass soon to Asher's father; but there can be stability in the community only if there is assurance of the line of succession. If not Asher, then the next heir must be Avrumel, Asher's only son.

By the end of the novel, which takes Asher's story to the late 1980's, the artist has exiled himself again to France, but not without sacrifice. He has left his wife and children in New York, promising to return to them several months hence; yet in his isolation he has begun to paint again. "What kind of God creates such situations?" Asher asks himself as he walks with Devorah. "He gives me a gift and a son, and forces me to choose between them." Later, in France, Asher is visited by the image of the far-away Rebbe: "Slowly you begin to unravel the riddle," the vision says. "Your answer may save us and return you to your work. . . . It is sometimes possible for a man to acquire all of the world to come by means of a single act in this world. . . . You will redeem all that you have done and all that you are yet to do." Paradoxically, the sacrifice of Avrumel for the good of the community is a kind of death that redeems that artist himself; a gift on behalf of the world to come in exchange for the gift of the world as it is, in all its ambiguity and horror, and the ability to capture it on canvas.

I AM THE CLAY

Like *The Book of Lights*, *I Am the Clay* is a third-person narrative that grew in part from Potok's experiences in Korea. As they flee the North Korean and Chinese armies, a nameless old man and a woman named Gyu find a boy, Kim Sin, who is terribly wounded. The man wants to leave the boy, but the woman insists on taking him with them and heals him of his wounds. Eventually, they return to the village of the old couple to discover that it has not been destroyed. The boy then travels to his village, discovers that it has been razed, and returns to the village of the man and woman. Nearby is an American military installation where the boy gets a job, eventually working for a Jewish chaplain. After the boy reluctantly gets involved with a thief, the chaplain helps him escape by finding him a job in Seoul. By this time, the woman is dead, and the man has learned to love the boy.

The book treats the conflicts between the old, rural way of life and the new, technological way of life as well as between the old religious ideas and the reality of war. When the old man and woman return to their village, they think things will be the same because it has been spared, but they are wrong.

Like the biblical Job, to whom the novel's title alludes, the man, woman, and boy do not understand why they suffer. The woman has learned the words "I am the clay" from a missionary, from whom she has also learned to make the sign of the cross. Blending the sign of the cross into her own ideas about magic, she illustrates Potok's idea of the unity of all people. Although the novel has little to do with Jews, *I Am the Clay* treats one of Potok's central problems: testing one's beliefs in the face of an ambiguous, often harsh, and rapidly changing reality.

Dan Barnett, updated by Richard Tuerk

OTHER MAJOR WORKS

SHORT FICTION: *Zebra and Other Stories*, 1998.

NONFICTION: *Wanderings: Chaim Potok's History of the Jews*, 1978; *Tobiasse: Artist in Exile*, 1986; *The Gates of November: Chronicles of the Slepak Family*, 1996.

CHILDREN'S LITERATURE: *The Tree of Here*, 1993; *The Sky of Now*, 1995.

BIBLIOGRAPHY

Abramson, Edward A. *Chaim Potok*. Boston: Twayne, 1986. The first book-length study of Potok, this volume is the fullest available introduction to his life and works. After a biographical sketch, Abramson discusses each of Potok's novels through *Davita's Harp* and also devotes a chapter to *Wanderings*. Supplemented by a chronology, notes, a good selected bibliography (including a list of secondary sources with brief annotations), and an index.

Potok, Chaim. "An Interview with Chaim Potok." Interview by Elaine M. Kauvar. *Contemporary Literature* 27 (Fall, 1986): 290-317. In this lengthy and wide-ranging interview, Potok discusses his work through *Davita's Harp*. He is revealed as a novelist who, more than most, writes with a clearly formed plan in mind. Of particular interest is his intention to take up the stories of the protagonists of his first six novels and interweave them in subsequent works.

_____. "Judaism Under the Secular Umbrella." Interview by Cheryl Forbes. *Christianity Today* 22 (September 8, 1978): 14-21. In this excellent interview, Potok defines his concept of "core to core culture confrontation" and explains how each of his novels through *In the Beginning* deals with such a confrontation. In *The Chosen*, for example, the confrontation is between Orthodox Judaism and Freudian psychoanalysis (which Potok identifies with "the core of Western secular humanism"); in *My Name Is Asher Lev*, there is a conflict between Judaism and art's claim to autonomy.

Shaked, Gershon. "Shadows of Identity: A Comparative Study of German Jewish and American Jewish Literature." In *What Is Jewish Literature?*, edited by Hana Wirth-Nesher. Philadelphia: Jewish Publication Society, 1994. Briefly places *The Chosen* in the context of literature in which Jewish authors and their characters have a dual identity: Jewish as well as that of the country in which they live.

Studies in American Jewish Literature 4 (1985). This special issue devoted to Potok includes several valuable critical essays, an interview with Potok conducted in 1981 by S. Lillian Kremer, and an autobiographical essay by Potok, "The First Eighteen Years." An indispensable source.

ANTHONY POWELL

Born: London, England; December 21, 1905

PRINCIPAL LONG FICTION

Afternoon Men, 1931
Venusberg, 1932
From a View to a Death, 1933
Agents and Patients, 1936
What's Become of Waring, 1939
A Question of Upbringing, 1951
A Buyer's Market, 1952
The Acceptance World, 1955
At Lady Molly's, 1957
Casanova's Chinese Restaurant, 1960
The Kindly Ones, 1962
The Valley of Bones, 1964
The Soldier's Art, 1966
The Military Philosophers, 1968
Books Do Furnish a Room, 1971
Temporary Kings, 1973
Hearing Secret Harmonies, 1975 (previous 12 titles known as *A Dance to the Music of Time*)
O, How the Wheel Becomes It!, 1983
The Fisher King, 1986

OTHER LITERARY FORMS

Although Anthony Powell has produced much writing other than his long fiction, he remains primarily a novelist. Powell has been an editor, an author of prefaces, a prolific book reviewer, and a screenwriter. While his miscellaneous writing includes light verse and fictional sketches, the stories, such as the ironic sequels to Charles Dickens's *A Christmas Carol* (1843) and D. H. Lawrence's *Lady Chatterley's Lover* (1928), are facile parodies, amusing but of limited interest. His skill in characterization and the fine art of gossip, basic to his major work, *A Dance to the Music of Time*, helps explain Powell's empathy with a seventeenth century expert in these matters, John Aubrey, author of *Brief Lives* (1813). Powell edited Aubrey's works and wrote a biographical study, *John Aubrey and His Friends* (1948, 1963). Powell also wrote two plays, *The Garden God* and

The Rest I'll Whistle (published together in 1971). These comedies of manners, while containing crisp dialogue and entertaining dramatic scenes, do not suggest that Powell is a dramatist *manqué*. Finally, he has written his memoirs, in four volumes under the general title *To Keep the Ball Rolling* (1976, 1978, 1980, 1982). These books provide a valuable account of experiences that Powell transmuted into fiction; they also present vivid characterizations of many of Powell's contemporaries, including Constant Lambert, the Sitwells, Evelyn Waugh, Cyril Connolly, and George Orwell. In 1990, Powell published a substantial selection of his essays and reviews, *Miscellaneous Verdicts: Writings on Writers, 1946-1989*, followed in 1991 by a second collection, *Under Review: Further Writings on Writers 1946-1989*. Three volumes of Powell's journals were also published between 1995 and 1997.

ACHIEVEMENTS

Powell's career as a novelist started with five novels published in the 1930's. These books had generally favorable reviews and reasonable sales; they established Powell's reputation as a skilled and successful, if perhaps minor, novelist. His reputation grew steadily with his twelve-volume sequence *A Dance to the Music of Time*, begun after World War II and completed in 1975, and by the 1980's he was generally recognized as one of the major English writers of the century. He is frequently compared to Marcel Proust, although, as Evelyn Waugh pointed out, Powell's *roman-fleuve* is more realistic and much funnier.

A Dance to the Music of Time is indeed funny. Becoming more somber in tone as it proceeds, incorporating numerous tragic events, never lacking a certain fundamental seriousness, the series nevertheless re-

(Express Newspapers/Archive Photos)

mains comic, a comedy in more aspects than Honoré de Balzac's meaning of a broad social portrait. The series does present a picture of various segments of English society—essentially the privileged segments—during the empire's decline since World War I. It has, thus, a certain limited value as sociological documentation—as what W. D. Quesenbery termed an "anatomy of decay"—but this is at best a secondary aspect. Primarily as excellent entertainment, the novels are appreciated by a wide range of readers. One may enjoy, in each of the individual novels, the wit, especially in dialogue, the characterization, and incident. In the series as a whole, there is the additional pleasure of observing the complex interactions of the characters as they appear, disappear, and reappear, forming unexpected patterns in the "dance," the whole bound together, if somewhat loosely, by theme.

From the first volume of the sequence, *A Question of Upbringing*, the work was well-received, although it was, of course, only as subsequent volumes appeared that readers, in increasing numbers, came to appreciate the complex interconnections of the separate books. Powell's wit and style were commended, as was his characterization, expecially the creation, in Kenneth Widmerpool, of one of the great comic villains in all of English literature. It was the narrative structure, however, that eventually produced the most critical interest.

Although the series moves chronologically forward, through the half century from 1921 to 1971, it is presented through the memory of the narrator, Nicholas Jenkins, who employs flashback and foreshadowing in a complex manner, recalling, for example, in the sixth book, his childhood in 1914. Such a structure suggests Proust's *À la recherche du temps perdu* (1913-1927; *Remembrance of Things Past*, 1922-1931). The comparison is relevant, and both Powell and his protagonist Nick Jenkins admire the French writer. Powell's narrator is not similar to Proust's however; Nick's mind operates differently. In addition, Henri Bergson's theory of time, so important to Proust, has limited relevance to Powell's work.

If Powell is not an English Proust, comparisons with other novel-sequences make even clearer the unique quality of *A Dance to the Music of Time*. In its focus upon the individuality of character, it is diametrically opposed, for example, to "unanimism," the ideology of collective experience which informs Jules Romains's *roman-fleuve Les Hommes de bonne volonté* (1932-1947). One of the few English novel-sequences of comparable length, C. P. Snow's *Strangers and Brothers* (1940-1970), employs a structure quite different from Powell's. The eleven volumes of Snow's work shift between those that focus on the life of the central figure, Lewis Eliot, and those that do not, whereas Nick Jenkins remains in each book simultaneously a participant in, and an observer of, the "dance" that the series chronicles.

Powell's achievement, springing from an interest in character, expressed through matchless style, and distinctly structured, has then, as does any great work of art, a *sui generis* excellence. It has won Powell a devoted and varied audience; the British Broadcasting Corporation has produced the series; *A Dance to the Music of Time*'s translations include a Bulgarian version. A share of worldly honors, such as an honorary fellowship in the Modern Language Association of America and an honorary D.Litt. from Oxford, have come to Powell. Perhaps more significantly, he has earned the respect of fellow writers, those his own age and those younger, those who share his conservative beliefs and those who do not. In sincere flattery, at least one other writer, the major Canadian novelist Hugh Hood, is writing his own series of novels in admiring emulation of Powell's work.

BIOGRAPHY

Anthony Dymoke Powell (pronounced "Antony Diemoke Pole") was born December 21, 1905, in London, England. His mother was the daughter of a barrister; his father, himself the son of a colonel, was a lieutenant in the army who was to win decoration in World War I and retire as a lieutenant colonel. Powell, his parents' only child, spent his early years in a military environment. He was to have a continuing respect for the service; General Conyers, in *A Dance to the Music of Time*, is only one of a number of sympathetically portrayed army officers in Powell's fiction.

As a member of a well-to-do family, Powell had an upper-class education and acquired the values of his class. He entered Eton in 1918, where he made friends, such as Hubert Duggan, a source for Stringham, who were to contribute to his subsequent characterizations. When, in 1923, Powell matriculated at Balliol College, Oxford, he continued to collect the friends and the personal impressions that were to serve him well when he later described Nick Jenkins's experiences. Powell's memoirs, *To Keep the Ball Rolling*, written after *A Dance to the Music of Time*, are invaluable in dealing with the complex issue of the relation between fiction and "real life," but it may be said that Powell is not always entirely forthcoming, and that many of his fictional characters are based, often rather closely, upon particular prototypes.

While at Oxford, Powell made various vacation trips to the Continent; in 1924, he traveled to Finland, where his father was stationed. Later, he drew upon this travel in his early novel *Venusberg*.

Powell was graduated from Oxford in 1926, and went to work for the publishing firm of Duckworth, in London. There, Powell lived the quasibohemian life that is described in *A Buyer's Market* and subsequent volumes in *A Dance to the Music of Time*, and which is also reflected in his five prewar novels. He spent much time in the company of painters and musicians, meeting, among them, the composer Constant Lambert, who was to become a lifelong friend and the prototype for Hugh Moreland in Powell's series.

On December 3, 1934, Powell married Lady Violet Packenham; they were to have two sons, Tristam and John. With his marriage, Powell acquired a large set of interesting in-laws; collectively, they were to contribute something to his fictional portrait of the Tollands; his brother-in-law Frank Pakenham, the seventh Earl of Longford, was to serve as a major source for the character Kenneth Widmerpool.

After his wedding, Powell left Duckworth's, and, in 1936, worked as a scriptwriter for Warner Bros. in London. There he met Thomas Phipps, the original of Chips Lovell. In 1937, he went, via the Panama Canal to Hollywood, California, in search of a script-

writing job. Although the job did not work out, before returning, the Powells enjoyed an interesting interlude that included a meeting with F. Scott Fitzgerald. Upon his return to London, Powell engaged in journalism and wrote his fifth novel, *What's Become of Waring*. As World War II began, Powell, in 1939, was commissioned a lieutenant in the Welsh Regiment.

His war experiences are fairly accurately portrayed in the military trilogy, the third "movement" of the four in *A Dance to the Music of Time*. Powell, like Nick Jenkins, served first in a line regiment in Northern Ireland; he was transferred, in 1941, to Army Intelligence, worked as a liaison officer with Allied forces, served in France and Belgium, and gained the rank of major.

Just as Nick, after leaving the army at the end of the war, worked on a study of Robert Burton, so did Powell engage in historical research on John Aubrey, publishing his study in 1948, and an edited collection of Aubrey's work the next year. With Aubrey "finally out of the way," as Powell writes, he turned again to novel-writing, and began with *A Question of Upbringing*, his *roman-fleuve*. The novels in the series appeared at fairly regular intervals, averaging one every two years from 1951 until 1975. During these years, Powell continued his career in journalism, contributing sketches, articles, and reviews to *Punch*, the London *Daily Telegraph*, and other periodicals. In 1956, he was made a C.B.E; in 1961 he lectured in America at Dartmouth College, Amherst College, and Cornell University. He was appointed a trustee of the National Portrait Gallery in 1962. His plays, *The Garden God* and *The Rest I'll Whistle*, were published together in 1971, the same year in which the University of Sussex awarded him the D.Litt.

During his outwardly quiet postwar years, Powell continued to enjoy and expand his circle of friends, thereby finding some additional prototypes for the characters introduced in the later volumes of his series. The writer Julian Maclaren-Ross, the prototype of X. Trapnel, is a notable example.

Upon completing *A Dance to the Music of Time*, Powell began his memoirs, publishing *Infants of the Spring* in 1976, followed, at two-year intervals, by *Messengers of Day, Faces in My Time*, and *The Strangers All Are Gone*. In 1983, a year after the appearance of the final volume of his memoirs, Powell published a short novel or novella, *O, How the Wheel Becomes It!*, a satirical *jeu d' esprit*, his first work of fiction since the completion of *A Dance to the Music of Time*. This was followed in 1986 by *The Fisher King*, a full-length novel published to excellent reviews. During most of the period of his major work, Powell and his wife lived at Somerset. In the 1980's Powell continued to receive honors for writing, including a D.Litt. from Oxford in 1980.

Anthony Powell has been one of the major figures of British letters since the 1920's and 1930's, and by the late 1990's he was the last surviving member of the so-called Brideshead generation, as described by Waugh. While he was a student at Eton, perhaps England's most prestigious public school, Powell's contemporaries included Harold Acton, Cyril Connolly, and George Orwell. At Oxford University he was a colleague of Waugh, Peter Quennell, and Maurice Bowra.

ANALYSIS

Of the many pleasures and rewards offered by Anthony Powell's novels, none surpasses that to be found in coming to know, and continually being surprised by what happens to, a variety of fascinating characters. For Powell, an interest in character is primary. This can be seen in his absorption in the biographies sketched by John Aubrey, in the series of verbal portraits which dominate *To Keep the Ball Rolling*, and in his statement that a concern for character was central in his beginning *A Dance to the Music of Time*.

A DANCE TO THE MUSIC OF TIME

Successful fiction, though, involves more than the presentation of a series of characters, however intriguing. When characterization is conveyed with wit, both in dialogue and description, when the style becomes a pleasure in itself, as it does in Powell's work, one has enough ingredients to produce writing worth reading, but not enough for a novel, certainly not for a novel of the scope and stature of *A Dance to the Music of Time*. Such a novel, like any successful

work of art, must satisfy the aesthetic requirement of unity—a sense of structure and order must be conveyed.

Although not the sole ingredient upon which a unified structure depends, character does help provide this sense of balance. For example, a degree of unity is achieved by having a single narrator, Nicholas Jenkins. Yet, *A Dance to the Music of Time* is not really the story of Nick Jenkins, just as it is not essentially the story of Kenneth Widmerpool, important as both these characters are. Although himself a participant in the "dance," Nick basically observes and reports; he does not give structure to the events that he relates: No persona, only Powell himself, can do this.

Many writers, certainly, achieve structure through plot, which may be the soul of fiction as Aristotle thought it was of drama. For Powell, however, the demands normally implied by "plot" run counter to his fundamental sense of time's complex mutability; to give his work a definite beginning, middle, and end, with action rising to and falling from a specific climax, would be justified neither by his sense of reality nor his artistic intentions.

This is not to say that conscious arrangement of incident is not present in *A Dance to the Music of Time*. On the contrary, because the author has exercised intelligent concern for such arrangement, continual surprises are enjoyed in a first reading, and anticipation of the irony of coming events gives a special pleasure to rereading the series. It would be yielding too readily to the seductive appeal of paradox, however, to claim that it is a crafted sense of the random which gives basic structure to *A Dance to the Music of Time*—that its order lies in its apparent lack of order.

If not to be found primarily in character or plot, what is the key to the structure of the dance? Unwilling, with reason, to accept the idea that it *has* no clear structure, that it is, even if cut from a loaf made of remarkably milled flour, essentially "a slice of life," critics have proposed a variety of answers.

The title of the series, as Powell has explained, derives from an allegorical painting in the Wallace Collection in London, Nicholas Poussin's *A Dance to the Music of Time*. Comparisons between the painting and the novel may be ingeniously extended, but it seems improbable that they were extensively worked out by Powell as he began a series which, he writes in *Faces in My Time*, would consist of a number of volumes, "just how many could not be decided at the outset." It would appear more probable that the Poussin painting, expressing the French artist's sense of the permutations time produces in human life, while an important analogue to Powell's intention in the series, was only one of a number of sources of the work's pattern. Another source might have been Thomas Nashe's *Summer's Last Will and Testament* (1592), a masque organized around the four seasons, contrasting the arts and the utilitarian spirit, and involving a sophisticated, semidetached "presenter"; it was the basis of a musical composition by Powell's close friend Constant Lambert.

Other structural keys have been proposed, including the importance of mysticism (the Dr. Trelawney, Mrs. Erdleigh aspect) and the signs of the zodiac. There would seem to be some validity in most of these interpretations, but the attempt to see any one as a single key to the series appears reductionist, in the sense that a strict Freudian or Marxist reading of William Shakespeare is too limiting. Insofar as the pattern of the dance can be extrapolated from the work itself, most critics have agreed that it must be seen as a reflection of theme.

Of the many thematic strands, that which is central appears to be the conflict between power and art, or imagination and will. Jenkins himself suggests this at more than one point in the series. From the perspective of this conflict, in which Widmerpool, the extreme example of the self-centered power seeker, is thematically contrasted to Hugh Moreland the musician, and later to X. Trapnel the writer, the characters and their actions fall into a meaningful, if somewhat shadowy, pattern. The pattern is hardly simple, though; few characters are purely villainous or heroic; some artists seek power; some professional soldiers and businessmen are artistic and imaginative; both victories and defeats tend to be temporary.

Furthermore, the sexual designs woven in the "dance" complicate a bipolar view of theme. Sexual attraction, or love, in the novel usually involves both

an imaginative appreciation of a perceived beauty in the desired partner, and some attempt to impose one's will upon another. Thus, with vagaries of desire, thematic antitheses and syntheses may fluctuate within individual characters. It is clear, however, that when Matilda Wilson goes from the artist Moreland to the industrialist Sir Magnus Donners, or Pamela Flitton leaves Widmerpool for the novelist X. Trapnel, a thematic point is made. (Indeed, the women in the series, generally less convincingly presented than the men, often seem to serve as scoring markers in the thematic game.)

That this thematic conflict, while it should not be simplistically defined, was essential to Powell's concept of the work's structure is shown additionally by the way prototypes were transmuted into fictional characters. Frank Pakenham, for example, unlike his fictional "counterpart" Widmerpool, not only would seem to have a number of virtues, but also has enjoyed a long and happy marriage, blessed by eight children. Clearly, the structure of the series requires that such satisfaction be denied its thematic villain.

A suggestion, then, may be made as to the probable way Powell proceeded in constructing his series. He apparently started with a novelist's interest in certain people that he knew, those he felt would be worth portraying. Then, to create order in his work, he fitted these people's fictional representatives into thematic patterns, changing reality as needed to accomplish this patterning. Using the thematically identified characters, he then, at a lower order of priority, considered and manipulated the plot, using plot itself to demonstrate another major theme, that of "mutability." The result was a uniquely constructed work of art.

AFTERNOON MEN

Before beginning his major work, Powell wrote five novels; a case can be made for their being excellent works in their own right. Had Powell not gone on to write his *roman-fleuve*, they may have gained him a certain lasting recognition. As it is, inevitably they are regarded primarily as preparation for his masterpiece. The use of the "detached" narrator, coincidence in plot, ironic style, clipped dialogue, the theme of power, art, and love—all these attributes of

A Dance to the Music of Time are anticipated in the early novels. *Afternoon Men*, picturing a London social scene the young Powell knew well, is the first of the five early novels. Powell has described it as "something of an urban pastoral . . . depicting the theme of unavailing love," with not much plot in the conventional sense. He sees the design of this first novel to be "not without resemblance to the initial framework" of the sequence. Although the protagonist, William Atwater, is not the narrator—the story is told mainly from his point of view, with the author occasionally intruding in his own voice—he may be compared, in his wit and detached forbearance, to Nicholas Jenkins. It is essentially in its ironic style, however, especially in the dialogue, that *Afternoon Men* anticipates the later series.

VENUSBERG and FROM A VIEW TO A DEATH

Venusberg, Powell's second novel, also has a protagonist, Lushington, who is comparable to Nick Jenkins. Flashback, a technique later significant to the series, is employed in this novel's construction, and the theme of love is extended to include adultery, while power and clairvoyance, topics prominent in *A Dance to the Music of Time*, are introduced. Powell's next novel, *From a View to a Death*, dealing with the interrelated themes of art, love, and power, emphasizes the latter. Arthur Zouch, a painter and womanizer, uses art and love in his search for the power he believes is his by right of his being an *Übermensch*. Fittingly, for one who not only debases the gift of imagination but is also a would-be social climber, he is defeated by a member of the country gentry. Technically, the book is interesting in that Powell experiments with a shifting point of view.

AGENTS AND PATIENTS

Art, sex, and power—specifically power derived from money—are the subjects that provide structure in *Agents and Patients*. In this novel, each of two confidence men, Maltravers and Chipchase, attempts to fleece a naïve young man, Blore Smith, Maltravers by playing upon Smith's sexual innocence, Chipchase by playing upon his artistic innocence. As the title, drawn from John Wesley, suggests, the issue of free will and determinism, significant in a less direct way in *A Dance to the Music of Time*, is an underlying theme. Excellent as it is as satiric comedy, *Agents and Patients* puts such an emphasis upon plot and theme that the characterization, usually Powell's strongest suit, tends somewhat toward caricature.

WHAT'S BECOME OF WARING

What's Become of Waring, Powell's last novel before the war, is perhaps a less impressive achievement than the four that preceded it. It is, however, close to *A Dance to the Music of Time* in more than chronology. Although it has a carefully worked out, conventional plot, Powell still manages, as James Tucker observes, to "slip out of it and pursue his concern for people." In this work, a first-person narrator is employed. He is a publisher's reader; the work draws upon Powell's experience at Duckworth's. Never named, the narrator, in his overall attitude and as a partial alter ego for Powell, resembles Nicholas Jenkins. Again, the mystical element, later present in the series, is introduced through seances. Significantly, given the thematic center of *A Dance to the Music of Time*, *What's Become of Waring* ends with the narrator, as he drifts off to sleep, free-associating on the idea of power.

A QUESTION OF UPBRINGING

That Powell, after his lengthy hiatus from novel writing, returned to the idea of the quest for power is clear even from the first of the three volumes that constitute "Spring," the initial movement of his sequence. *A Question of Upbringing* introduces, at the very start, the series' most important character, Widmerpool, and it is clear that even as a schoolboy he is determined to dominate.

The early introduction of the major themes is an important aid to unity, for the start of a long series poses particular problems for its author. As Powell suggests in *Faces in My Time*, early volumes, in preparation for future ones, must introduce undeveloped characters and potential situations; additionally, some characters and situations, in view of their subsequent importance, must be overemphasized. These requirements may tend to confuse the reader, unless patterns are perceived.

A Question of Upbringing, which covers Nick's youth at public school and university, introduces an important pattern of repetition of related incidents by having Nick meet his Uncle Giles at both the beginning and the end of the volume. Another recurring structural device, the alternation of scenes described in dramatic detail with linking sections provided by Nick's subjective impressions, is present, as are the patterning devices of allusion and symbolism. The series begins with a scene of workmen gathered around a fire, repeated at the conclusion of the sequence, twelve volumes later, and mentions the Poussin painting which provides the title for the whole sequence. References to paintings are important throughout the series, including the Tiepolo ceiling in *Temporary Kings* and the oft-mentioned Modigliani drawing which is rescued in the final volume.

A BUYER'S MARKET

Although the themes of love and art (which, along with the interrelated theme of power dominate the series) are present in the first volume, they are more prominent in the second, *A Buyer's Market*. In this book, dominated by the social life of parties and dances which Nick, down from the university, enjoys, not only do sexual activities become important to Nick (a late bloomer as compared to his friends Templer and Stringham), but also the theme of the quest for power is extended to include politics. The radical young woman, Gypsy Jones (with whom Nick apparently loses his virginity), is utilized in one of Powell's recurring attacks upon the political Left, as well as to serve as an object of frustrated lust for Widmerpool, whose sex life is to be, throughout the series, eccentric and unsatisfactory.

THE ACCEPTANCE WORLD

The Acceptance World, the third volume in this movement, begins with another meeting between Nick and his Uncle Giles, who is now associated with Mrs. Erdleigh, a clairvoyant. She plays a major role in the dramatization of the subtheme of mysticism. Mysticism in the series, as seen later in Dr. Trelawney, and finally in Scorpio Murtlock, is related to an attempt to escape from what Mrs. Erdleigh calls the "puny fingers of Time," and gain power. Power in *The Acceptance World*, though, is considered more in political terms; there is an extension of the political satire against the Left, especially through Quiggin (whose character owes something to Cyril Connolly's), a uni-

versity friend of Jenkins who moves in left-wing intellectual circles.

The volume's love interest involves Nick in a serious affair with Jean Templer, a school friend's sister. Much later in the series, in *The Military Philosophers*, Nick realizes that Jean, who breaks off the affair, really is attracted to money and power; she ultimately marries a Colonel Flores, who becomes a Latin American dictator. As Nick reflects in the first volume, "being in love is a complicated matter"; staying in love is even more so. The balance of thematic opposites, necessary to love, is seldom maintained. Nick is to be virtually unique in the series by virtue of his lasting, successful marriage, but the reader is given little direct insight into the secret of his success.

AT LADY MOLLY'S

Nick's courtship and engagement are described in the first volume of the second movement, "Summer." This volume is entitled *At Lady Molly's*; Lady Molly Jeavons is a fictional amalgam of actual people including Rosa Lewis, the famous proprietor of the Cavendish Hotel, and Lady Astor, celebrated mistress of the magnificent country mansion, Cliveden, the prototype of the novel's Dogdene. Lady Molly, whose easygoing hospitality attracts a variety of guests, is the aunt of Chips Lovell (a character based on Thomas Phipps), who works with Nick as a scriptwriter for films. Powell here, as throughout the series, introduces new characters, thereby continually revivifying his novel, personifying its themes with variety, and causing the reader to wonder who, as well as what, is coming next. The actions of the two most permanent characters, Nick and Widmerpool, form the core of the volume; Nick's developing and successful love for Isobel Tolland is contrasted with the debacle that occurs when Widmerpool attempts a premarital seduction of his fiancée, Mildred Haycock.

CASANOVA'S CHINESE RESTAURANT

Love and marriage are even more central to the next book, *Casanova's Chinese Restaurant*, which introduces and focuses upon one of the series' most important and attractively realized characters, the composer Hugh Moreland, who becomes one of Nick's closest friends, just as Moreland's real-life prototype, Constant Lambert, became very important to Powell. Moreland is, thematically, *the* artist. As such, he is Widmerpool's antithesis, even though the two have too little in common to be antagonists other than thematically—the few occasions when they encounter each other are singularly, but not surprisingly, undramatic. One critic has suggested that even their names, Widmerpool's suggesting wetness, and Moreland's the opposite, indicate their antithesis. (Powell's names, as most readers will have noticed, are frequently suggestive and apt, as well as sometimes amusing—consider, for example, the name of the sexually experienced woman whom Widmerpool so decidedly fails to satisfy, Mrs. Haycock.)

A more significant difference between Moreland and Widmerpool is in their way of talking. Moreland produces very witty and pleasurable conversation; Widmerpool is given to pompous pronouncements that often entertain the reader by their unconscious self-satire. Like Widmerpool, however, although quite differently and for different reasons, Moreland has trouble with his love life; interconnections of art and love form much of the subject matter of the volumes in this movement.

THE KINDLY ONES

Other perspectives on love are introduced in *The Kindly Ones*, the last volume of "Summer," in which Widmerpool temporarily fades into the background, until the last chapter. The work begins with a flashback to Nick's childhood in 1914, thereby relating World War I to the approach of World War II in 1938, the time to which the book returns. The chronology is particularly complicated in this volume, and coincidence, always a feature of the series' plotting, is pushed to its limits when Nick, having gone to the seaside hotel where his Uncle Giles has died, meets, along with others from his past, Bob Duport, the former husband of Nick's past lover, Jean. The fact that for many readers, the complex structure of *The Kindly Ones* is unobtrusively successful, provides some measure of Powell's legerdemain.

At the end of *The Kindly Ones*, Nick has arranged for his commission in the army; the third movement, "Autumn," carries him though World War II. The

reader learns from the autobiographical *Faces in My Time* that Nick's army experiences closely parallel Powell's own. Nick's service is distinguished, but the focus is more upon the tedium of war than its heroism.

In treating this often tedious, but different world of the service, Powell faced technical problems. He had to maintain the structure of his series within an entirely new environment. New characters, some from a social background that the novel had previously ignored, had to be used in a manner in accordance with the controlling themes. Furthermore, the style had to make some adaptation to the grim subject matter. Powell was not going to emphasize the comic elements of war, even though they are not ignored. The basic solution to these problems was to alternate the army scenes with those occurring when Nick is on leave. Thereby, the reader is able to experience the new, while still maintaining an interest in the old characters and themes.

THE VALLEY OF BONES

The first volume of the movement, *The Valley of Bones*, introduces, among many new characters, a particularly significant one, Captain Gwatkin. Gwatkin, while no artist—he had worked in a local Welsh bank—is a man of imagination, a sort of Miniver Cheevy actually in armor. He has romantic ambitions to be a perfect soldier, ambitions doomed to failure in his encounters with the men of power who are his superiors. Although he is eventually relieved of his command, Gwatkin finds some consolation in love, only to lose it when he learns of the infidelity of his beloved barmaid Maureen. Between these army scenes, Nick, while on leave, observes the continued amatory maneuvers of his friends and relations. The book ends with the dramatic appearance of Widmerpool as an influential major.

THE SOLDIER'S ART

In the next volume, *The Soldier's Art*, Nick is working as Widmerpool's junior assistant, in a position to observe his superior's continuing struggle for power, transferred from civilian to military life. Widmerpool hovers upon the verge of disaster, but at the end of the book his career is saved. Previously, he had failed to assist an old school fellow of his and

Nick's, Stringham, now reduced to being an enlisted man working in the officers' mess, subsequently to die in a Japanese prisoner-of-war camp. Meanwhile, personal entanglements continue to form new patterns, while some of the characters, including Chips Lovell and Lady Molly, are killed in a bombing raid.

THE MILITARY PHILOSOPHERS

The final volume of the movement, *The Military Philosophers*, finds Nick in the war office, working on liaison with Allied troops. This book, stylistically notable for its increased use of allusion, presents a number of the real personnel with whom Powell worked, little changed in their fictional guises. It is, however, an imagined character, or at least one for whom no prototype has been established, who reappears at this point, having been briefly introduced earlier as a young girl, subsequently to be a major figure. Pamela Flitton is, like Widmerpool, Stringham, Moreland, and Trapnel, one of the series' most memorable creations. She is a kind of ubiquitous nemesis, capable of bringing down the men of both art and power. Outstanding even in a cast of remarkably unusual and individual characters, she is made by Powell larger than life and yet believable, beautiful and yet repulsive, contemptible and yet capable of arousing the reader's sympathies. Although not all readers find her entirely convincing, she is certainly one of Powell's most fascinating characters. As the war ends, she is engaged to Widmerpool. No one could deserve her less, or more. With Pamela's entrance into the series, the tone, previously not essentially grim, even with the many deaths occurring during the war, changes.

BOOKS DO FURNISH A ROOM

In the final movement of the series, "Winter," the style also changes as Powell moves toward a concluding "wintery silence." While a sense of the comic is never abandoned, the mood becomes more somber, the action more direct. The first novel in this movement, *Books Do Furnish a Room*, is primarily the story of X. Trapnel, a novelist heavily based on Powell's friend, Julian Maclaren Ross. Trapnel, the artist, is juxtaposed with Widmerpool, the man of power, through the agency of Pamela Flitton, who leaves Widmerpool to live with Trapnel. The triumph of the artist is temporary, however, for not only is Pamela discovered to be both sexually insatiable and frigid, but she also destroys a manuscript of Trapnel's most recent novel by dumping it in the Maida Vale Canal, and returns to Widmerpool.

TEMPORARY KINGS

In the next volume, *Temporary Kings*, which begins at an international literary conference in Venice, where the first half of the novel is set, Pamela is a dominant character. Her sexual debauchery continues, unsettling Widmerpool, but she encounters a man upon whom her charms fail, Professor Russell Gwinnett. Continuing his ability to rejuvenate the series by introducing new characters, Powell brings in this American scholar with necrophilic tastes, who is writing a book on Trapnel. Nick finds him "an altogether unfamiliar type," with "nothing simple" about his personality.

Thematically, Gwinnett, a curious variant of the *deus ex machina*, may embody a kind of resolution of the conflict between art and power. Having both an involvement with art and an exceptionally strong will, Gwinnett, whose superior psychic strength provokes Pamela's suicide, perhaps in a necrophilic ritual, may be thought to have avenged Trapnel, if not Widmerpool. Any resolution with Gwinnett is, however, a dark one, incorporating the cult rites with which he becomes involved before returning to America, and necessarily suggesting that to which he is most strongly related, death.

HEARING SECRET HARMONIES

The final volume of the sequence, *Hearing Secret Harmonies*, is focused on Widmerpool, who, with the exception of Nick himself, is the series' most enduring character. After becoming a kind of hero to rebellious youth, he joins a pagan religious cult and struggles with its leader, Scorpio Murtlock, for dominance. Finally, running at the end, just as he was in his first appearance in the sequence, he falls dead, exhausted by his effort to take the lead in a ritual run.

The ending of such a long work poses a particular problem. After twelve books, certainly some feeling of conclusion must be produced, yet the whole structure, the whole sense of the continually evolving dance of time, renders any strong sense of climax inappropriate. Powell, by having Nick learn at secondhand of Widmerpool's death, and then returning to the initial image of the workmen's fire, quoting Robert Burton, and providing a carefully worded final image, skillfully solves this problem. The ending is a final reminder of the quality of literary skill and talent that is sustained through all the volumes of singularly satisfactory achievement.

THE FISHER KING

The Fisher King was Powell's second novel to be published after the completion of *A Dance to the Music of Time*. Most of the action involves a group of characters taking a summer cruise around the British Isles. Aboard the cruise ship *Alecto* is Saul Henchman, a famous photographer who received disabling and disfiguring injuries in World War II. He is traveling with his assistant and companion, a beautiful woman named Barberina Rookwood. Much of the story is narrated by another passenger, Valentine Beals, a writer of historical novels. As the cruise progresses, Henchman reveals himself as a thoroughly unpleasant individual, Beals is seen to be gossipy and pretentious, and Rookwood inspires the admiration of men and women alike. Three men on the cruise— Henchman, Gary Lamont, and Robin Jilson—vie for her attention.

The Fisher King provides numerous connections between its characters and mythological figures, generally commented on by Beals. Beals's interpretations and speculations are flawed in a number of ways, however, and Powell is perhaps suggesting that myth can still illuminate intriguing aspects of human behavior but cannot truly predict how humans will act. Throughout, Powell is less concerned with drawing precise mythological parallels than with providing an amusing and intellectually entertaining story of people and their foibles.

William B. Stone, updated by Eugene Larson and
McCrea Adams

OTHER MAJOR WORKS

PLAYS: *"The Garden God" and "The Rest I'll Whistle": The Text of Two Plays*, pb. 1971.
POETRY: *Caledonia: A Fragment*, 1934.

NONFICTION: *John Aubrey and His Friends*, 1948, 1963; *To Keep the Ball Rolling*, 1976-1982 (includes *Infants of the Spring*, 1976; *Messengers of Day*, 1978; *Faces in My Time*, 1980; *The Strangers All Are Gone*, 1982); *Miscellaneous Verdicts: Writings on Writers, 1946-1989*, 1990; *Under Review: Further Writings on Writers 1946-1989*, 1991; *Journals 1982-1986*, 1995; *Journals 1987-1989*, 1996; *Journals 1990-1992*, 1997.

BIBLIOGRAPHY

Brennan, Neil. *Anthony Powell*. Boston: Twayne, 1974. Covers Powell's work up to 1973, when the eleventh volume of *A Dance to the Music of Time* was published. One-third of this study is devoted to *A Dance to the Music of Time*, Powell's tour de force; the rest is an analysis of his other works, including early novels such as *Afternoon Men* and *From a View to a Death*. Contains a chronology of Powell which includes his family ancestry.

Joyau, Isabelle. *Investigating Powell's "A Dance to the Music of Time."* New York: St. Martin's Press, 1994. An academic, Joyau writes an insightful and appreciative analysis of Powell's *A Dance to the Music of Time*, discussing structure, literary techniques, and characters.

Morris, Robert K. *The Novels of Anthony Powell*. Pittsburgh: University of Pittsburgh Press, 1968. The first book-length study of Powell's writing. Morris discusses all Powell's novels up to 1968 and focuses on what he discerns as Powell's central theme: the struggle between the power hungry and the sensualists. The second part of this study analyzes the first eight volumes of *A Dance to the Music of Time*.

Selig, Robert L. *Time and Anthony Powell*, Cranbury, N.J.: Associated University Presses, 1991. An analysis of Powell's use of time in *A Dance to the Music of Time*, both within the series and as the reader's sense of time is affected.

Spurling, Hilary. *Invitation to the Dance: A Guide to Anthony Powell's "Dance to the Music of Time."* Boston: Little, Brown, 1977. Spurling intends this as a reference cum "bedside companion for readers who want to refresh their memories." Whether or not it makes for bedside reading, this volume certainly is a useful guide to the complexities of Powell's opus. Contains a synopsis of each volume, by chapter and time sequence, and includes an extensive character index.

Taylor, D. J. "A Question of Upbringing." *The* [London] *Sunday Times Books*, January 29, 1995, 8. Taylor, a journalist and novelist, interviewed Powell about his career and recent life at the Powell country house in western England.

Tucker, James. *The Novels of Anthony Powell.* New York: Columbia University Press, 1976. An extensive appraisal of the twelve volumes of *A Dance to the Music of Time.* Includes a "who's who" of characters, themes, style, narrative, and method. A scholarly work, but quite readable. Also contains a bibliography.

DAWN POWELL

Born: Mount Gilead, Ohio; November 28, 1897

Died: New York, New York; November 14, 1965

PRINCIPAL LONG FICTION

Whither, 1925
She Walks in Beauty, 1928
The Bride's House, 1929
Dance Night, 1930
The Tenth Moon, 1932
Jig Saw: A Comedy, 1934
The Story of a Country Boy, 1934
Turn, Magic Wheel, 1936
The Happy Island, 1938
Angels on Toast, 1940, 1989 (rev. as *A Man's Affair,* 1956)
A Time to Be Born, 1942, 1991
My Home Is Far Away, 1944, 1995

(Library of Congress)

The Locusts Have No King, 1948, 1990
The Wicked Pavilion, 1954, 1990
A Cage for Lovers, 1957
The Golden Spur, 1962

OTHER LITERARY FORMS

Though Dawn Powell is known primarily as a novelist, she had originally intended to write for the theater. Her play *Big Night* was produced by the Group Theatre in 1933, and *Jig Saw,* based on her novel *Jig Saw: A Comedy,* had a short run in 1934. Powell also wrote a musical comedy and scripts for radio, television, and film and published essays, reviews, and short stories in distinguished national magazines. A number of her short stories were collected in *Sunday, Monday and Always* (1952).

ACHIEVEMENTS

While such contemporaries as Ernest Hemingway and John Dos Passos considered Dawn Powell one of the finest writers of their time, she never attained their popularity. Shortly before her death in 1965, Powell was honored with an honorary doctorate and an award from the National Institute of Arts and Letters, but despite occasional attempts by her admirers, such as Edmund Wilson, to call attention to her achievements, she remained relatively obscure, and her sixteen novels, all out of print, were difficult to find. Fortunately, in the next two decades, there was a revolution in the American sensibility. One of the results of the feminist movement was that the critics and publishers had to admit sins of omission; they had minimized the talent of many fine women writers simply because they were women. Dawn Powell, who has been called an American equivalent to English satiric novelists such as Evelyn Waugh and Anthony Powell, is an obvious example. In 1987, author and critic Gore Vidal launched the campaign to obtain proper recognition for Powell. In a lengthy essay published in *The New York Review of Books*, he traced her life and her literary career and concluded by bemoaning the fact that the novels of the person he considered America's best comic novelist were all out of print. As a result of his article, several of her later books were reprinted, all with Vidal's essay as an introduction, and the reviews that followed suggest that Powell may at last receive the recognition denied her during her lifetime.

BIOGRAPHY

Dawn Powell was born in Mount Gilead, Ohio, on November 28, 1897, the daughter of Roy K. Powell, a traveling salesman, and Hattie B. Sherman Powell. For six years, after the death of her mother when Dawn was six, she and her two sisters lived with various relatives on farms and in small towns. After her father's remarriage, the girls went to live with him and their stepmother on a farm. Dawn was already a dedicated writer; indeed, after her stepmother punished her by burning her stories, Dawn fled to the home of an aunt. After graduating from high school, Powell went to Lake Erie College, where she re-

ceived her B.A. in 1918. That year she moved to New York to serve in the Navy auxiliary, remaining there working in public relations and in advertising. In 1920, she married Joseph Roebuck Gousha, an executive with an advertising agency, by whom she had one son, Joseph Roebuck Gousha, Jr. Failing in her attempts to break into the theatrical world as a playwright, Powell began writing novels, publishing the first, *Whither*, in 1925. Over the next four decades, fifteen more were to appear, the early ones set in her native Ohio, most of the later ones in Greenwich Village, in what became her world, the small circle of writers, publishers, actors, producers, artists, and critics who were at the intellectual center of the nation. Still without wide recognition, Dawn Powell died of cancer at St. Luke's Hospital in New York City on November 14, 1965.

ANALYSIS

The primary purpose of a Powell novel is to describe a society. To do so, Powell brings a number of characters together, perhaps in an Ohio boardinghouse, perhaps at a New York party or a bar. Then the characters seem to take over, as if they are determined to dramatize their own world. They act and interact, they talk, they boast, they scheme, they lie, and they confess to one another. To this extent, Powell's novels could be called realistic. They also, however, include an element of satire. It is primarily noticeable in the characters' inner deliberations, which Powell reveals to her readers in illuminating detail. The characters' confusion about facts, their muddled reasoning, and above all their clearly selfish motivations, reported with such painstaking care, leave the reader no doubt as to Powell's satiric intentions, which are further stressed in her occasional wry and witty comments.

Although Powell's first book, *Whither*, was set in New York City, all but one of the six novels published during the next six years were placed in the rural Midwest. These works introduce the themes that would dominate Powell's later work: the alienation of an individual from society, the frustration of the failing artist, the random nature of love, the limits of friendship, and above all the rule of money. Beginning with *Turn, Magic Wheel*, Powell wrote a series of seven novels to which Vidal refers as her "New York cycle." Most critics consider these novels to represent Powell's highest artistic achievement and, indeed, a unique contribution to American literature.

ANGELS ON TOAST

The third of these novels, *Angels on Toast*, illustrates Powell's approach. The world that she both summarizes and satirizes is defined in the first chapter of the book. The story begins with two businessmen, Jay Oliver and Lou Donovan, on the train from Chicago to New York. The self-absorption that marks most of Powell's characters is evident from the first. Their world is neither abstract nor cosmopolitan. At its simplest it is made up of their own bodies and their own clothes. Jay admires his own shoes, which he thinks reflect his polished personality, and his socks, which are so dazzling that he must mention how expensive they were. Lou contemplates and assesses his weight, his shoulders, then is delighted to tell Jay how much his shirt cost and to invite him to feel the material. For men so fascinated with the most trivial details about themselves, it is not surprising that both friendship and love are limited in depth. From the facile comment that Jay is his best friend, Lou soon has moved to the notion that Jay may know too much about him; indeed, it is Jay's company that is his best friend, not Jay himself, Lou muses. If Jay were replaced, the new man would become Lou's best friend. Lou's capacity for love is similarly limited by circumstances. For example, when he married above himself, he found it convenient to forget having been married before, and he is now worried because that ex-wife has turned up in Chicago. In a typical Powell passage, however, Lou congratulates himself because he has been faithful to his wife, except for casual encounters in places where she would never go. Jay, on the other hand, is shockingly unfaithful, picking up his regular mistress on the train and taking her to New York with him. It is not adultery, but taking such chances, that Lou considers immoral.

Thus by re-creating conversations and by reporting her characters' thoughts, Dawn Powell reveals their attitudes and their values. Her satirical intention is clear, when she lets Lou congratulate himself for

what are in fact very low moral standards; it is obvious that for him and his society, love and friendship will never stand in the way of making money.

In Powell's later novels, New York City itself might as well be listed as one of the characters. It is symbolic that the first chapter takes place on the way to New York, instead of on the way back to Chicago. In New York, the businessmen think they can get away with anything. It is, of course, ironic that the city proves to be much smaller than the out-of-town visitors think it is; unfortunately, paths do cross, and wives do find out what is occurring.

In *Angels on Toast*, the compelling attraction of New York City is also dramatized in the attitude of an eccentric old lady who lives in a seedy hotel. When her daughter suggests that they both move to Connecticut, the idea is greeted with horror. Obviously, even a dingy hotel in New York is better than a mansion anywhere else. Actually, the old lady's real home is the hotel bar; its inhabitants are the only people she needs or wishes to know.

Except for the fact that Ebie Vane is a commercial artist, the conflict between the creator and his crass, indifferent world is not as important in *Angels on Toast* as it is in Powell's last three novels, in which the alienation of the artist from society is a major theme. The cohesiveness of New York's literary and theatrical world is suggested by the title of the first of these books, *The Locusts Have No King*. The quotation, which comes from the biblical Proverbs, emphasizes the idea that although there is no single leader among locusts, they seem to have a mysterious single direction. They move in hordes, and, it should be added, destructive hordes. It is such mindless human groups which can destroy the will and the hopes of an artist or, perhaps worse, turn an artist into a commercial success at the cost of creative integrity and personal relationships.

THE LOCUSTS HAVE NO KING

At the beginning of *The Locusts Have No King*, there seems to be no possibility that the protagonist, Frederick Olliver, a writer of scholarly books, will ever become successful enough to find his soul endangered. In contrast, his mistress Lyle Gaynor, a successful playwright, is a celebrity who knows every other celebrity in the literary world. Lyle is completely devoted to Frederick. Indeed, she would marry him except for the fact that she feels a duty to remain with her ill-tempered husband because he is an invalid. In order to help Frederick, Lyle includes him in every party she gives and arranges for him to be invited to every party she attends. Nevertheless, Frederick always feels that he is an alien in Lyle's world. In response, he voices his scorn of the successful, including his generous mistress. The fact that one lover is inside the magic circle and the other is outside, clearly imperils their relationship.

Powell's theme of alienation appears in three different typical situations. The first involves characters such as Frederick, who, though they are not new to New York, have simply not had enough success to be accepted. The second involves a young person who, like Jonathan Jaimison in *The Golden Spur* and like the young Dawn Powell herself in 1918, has recently arrived in New York City, usually from the Midwest, and must be initiated into its ways. Although the misunderstandings and mistakes of the innocent can be highly comic, they do not provide the occasions of satire that Powell sees in the third kind of alienation. Like all the great satirists, she delights in exposing the pretensions of characters who attempt to be accepted in a complex, cultivated society but who are too foolish to master its mannerisms or even its idiom.

An example of this kind of alienated character, who unlike the other types has no hope of being accepted as a result of eventual success or deliberate adaptation, is Dodo Brennan in *The Locusts Have No King*. Dodo has chosen to think of herself as a Southern belle, and she has come from Baltimore to conquer New York with cuteness. Unfortunately, her poses and her baby talk make her ludicrous. Although Frederick becomes involved with Dodo and introduces her into Lyle's circle, Dodo's vulgarity, her stupidity, and her inability to realize that her idiotic speeches have no resemblance to wit ensure her status as a permanent alien in the literary world.

In *The Locusts Have No King*, however, the theme of alienation is most important as it relates to the central love story. When by chance Frederick and Lyle reverse their places in society, when Lyle's fortunes decline and Frederick becomes a commercial success, ironically the psychological barriers to their union disappear. Unlike most of Powell's lovers, whose short-term entanglements are motivated by chance, lust, and ambition, Frederick and Lyle prove to be capable of profound attachment, which only grows stronger in the face of change.

THE WICKED PAVILION

Even though sexual liaisons are important in Powell's novels, the real action takes place not in bedrooms but in the living rooms and bars where her characters gather. Although the title of her next novel, *The Wicked Pavilion*, is taken from a reference to the Brighton Pavilion in England, Powell's pavilion is simply a New York café, where many of the characters from her preceding books reappear, now older but hardly wiser. The book is carefully crafted, with two plots that are intertwined, both of which depend upon frequent appearances in the Café Julien. One of them involves an incomplete love story. Haunted by the memory of his passion for a young woman whom he met at the café during the war, Rick Prescott has returned to search for her and for the happiness he believes that he somehow lost. In developing this plot, Powell again emphasizes the transitory nature of most human relationships, especially love, which, despite lovers' illusions, depends heavily on chance and on the imagination.

The second plot exposes the phoniness of the artistic world. When a painter dies, two of his unsuccessful fellow artists discover that they can make a large amount of money by forging works supposedly painted by him; their scheme is complicated, however, when they find that he is not dead but has pretended to die and is now profiting by the greatly increased value of his old paintings, as well as of the new ones he is producing, which he can market as lost masterpieces. It is evident that Powell is in sympathy with the artists, who on at least one occasion have thus triumphed over the commerciality of art dealers and the arrogant stupidity of art critics.

THE GOLDEN SPUR

In Dawn Powell's final novel, *The Golden Spur*, it is not the artist but the innocent who triumphs over the glittering and corrupt world that Powell knew, loved, and satirized. Again, the title refers to a bar, but in this case the reference is not oblique. The Golden Spur is indeed the name of a bar that has a special significance to a young man from the Midwest, Jonathan Jaimison. In her youth, his mother, then Constance Birch, had come to New York as a real innocent, had fallen in love with the city and with one of its residents, and then, pregnant, had returned to Ohio to marry an unsuspecting flour salesman named John Jaimison. Now another innocent, Connie's son, has come to New York City. In his response to the city, he is like his mother. Within eighteen hours he is hopelessly in love with it. Unlike her, however, he is not destined to become a victim. As he seeks out the various men mentioned in his mother's diaries, any of whom might possibly be his father, he finds that instead of being horrified at the prospect of scandal, they are all pleased. Even those who cannot remember Connie would like to talk themselves into the memory of an affair with her, which could have produced this appealing son. Yet the prospective son is less than enthusiastic about the various candidates, who, though they may be rich and famous, do not live up to the dream father who has appeared in his imagination.

Certainly, Powell is pointing out that reality rarely equals illusion. In this final book, however, there is a special significance in Jonathan's disenchantment. Like Dawn Powell herself, in her sixties at the time that *The Golden Spur* appeared, the people of the magic circle have aged, and the old New York is dead. At the end of *The Wicked Pavilion*, the Café Julien was torn down; at the end of *The Golden Spur*, an artist insists that the real money of the twenty-first century will be not in creation but in demolition. His ambition does not stop with seedy hotels and run-down cafés; he yearns to take the big ball to the Metropolitan Museum of Art. Thus Powell's final book does not mark merely the end of a young man's dream; it commemorates the end of the world she knew.

In Robert van Gelder's book of interviews, *Writers and Writing* (1946), Dawn Powell answered the repeated criticism of her work—that she did not deal with significant people—by pointing out that most people have no real goals in life. The answer was that of a realist. Still, she might better have appealed to the standards of her genre. The satirist causes readers to laugh at people, not to revere them. In her last and best novels, Dawn Powell points out the follies and the vices of New Yorkers like those she knew: the vulnerable or vulgar innocence of newcomers, the desperate need of the alien to become accepted, the misuse of reason to justify lust and ambition, the betrayal of love and friendship, and above all, the enslavement to greed. It is appropriate that Dawn Powell has had a revival. Certainly she immortalized a society forever gone, but more important, she created characters whose weaknesses are all too universally human.

Rosemary M. Canfield Reisman

OTHER MAJOR WORKS

SHORT FICTION: *Sunday, Monday and Always*, 1952; *Dawn Powell at Her Best*, 1994 (Tim Page, editor).

PLAYS: *Big Night*, pr. 1933; *Jig Saw*, pr. 1934; *The Lady Comes Across*, pr. 1941.

NONFICTION: *The Diaries of Dawn Powell, 1931-1965*, 1995.

BIBLIOGRAPHY

Page, Tim. *Dawn Powell: A Biography*. New York: Holt, 1998. The first comprehensive account of Powell's life and work by one of her finest critics. Includes detailed notes and an extensive bibliography.

Trilling, Diana. "Fiction in Review." *The Nation* 166 (May 29, 1948): 611-612. Trilling expresses the standard criticism of Powell: that she dealt with less than serious themes and that her characters were too unimportant to be worthy of consideration. Her viewpoint is rebutted in Gore Vidal's essay, cited below.

Van Gelder, Robert. *Writers and Writing*. New York: Charles Scribner's Sons, 1946. This interview, dated November 3, 1940, focuses on the reason for Powell's small readership, which she believes has to do with the fact that her work is satirical in nature. Powell comments in particular on her most recent work at the time, *Angels on Toast*.

Vidal, Gore. "Dawn Powell, the American Writer." *The New York Review of Books* 34 (November 5, 1987): 52-60. This essay, which also serves as the introduction to the Vintage Press editions of *Angels on Toast*, *The Golden Spur*, and *The Wicked Pavilion*, is perhaps the most important work of Powell criticism to date. In it, Vidal summarizes her life, suggests reasons for her obscurity, presents a chronological summary of her novels, and discusses her importance in American literature.

Wilson, Edmund. "Greenwich Village in the 50's." *The New Yorker* 38 (November 17, 1962): 233-236. A review of *The Golden Spur* by one of the literary giants who shared Powell's world. Wilson compares her genius to that of Anthony Powell, Evelyn Waugh, and Muriel Spark.

_____. *The Thirties: From Notebooks and Diaries of the Period*, edited by Leon Edel. New York: Farrar, Straus & Giroux, 1980. An excellent source, not only because of the references to Dawn Powell but also because it provides a full picture of her period. Edel's introduction is also illuminating. Illustrated.

J. F. POWERS

Born: Jacksonville, Illinois; July 8, 1917
Died: Collegeville, Minnesota; June 12, 1999

PRINCIPAL LONG FICTION
Morte d'Urban, 1962
Wheat That Springeth Green, 1988

OTHER LITERARY FORMS

J. F. Powers was highly regarded for his prowess as a short-story writer. "Lions, Harts, Leaping Does" (1943), only his second story to be published, appeared in the O. Henry and Martha Foley anthologies in 1944. His first short-story collection, *Prince of Darkness and Other Stories*, was published by

Doubleday in 1947. (Random House reissued the collection in 1979.) Doubleday published his second collection of stories, *The Presence of Grace*, in 1956. In 1963, Time published *Lions, Harts, Leaping Does, and Other Stories*, a collection culled from Powers's first two books. His next collection, *Look How the Fish Live*, was published by Knopf in 1975. Powers's stories appeared first in magazines such as *Accent, Colliers, Commonweal, The Nation, Kenyon Review, Partisan Review*, and *The New Yorker*. Powers also wrote reviews of poetry and fiction, autobiographical pieces, and articles dealing with social issues. His nonfiction, like most of his fiction, is often satirical in tone.

ACHIEVEMENTS

Powers is to be numbered among those American writers—others include Katherine Anne Porter and J. D. Salinger—who produced a relatively small body of work distinguished by meticulous craftsmanship. Powers was praised by critics and fellow writers such as Alfred Kazin, William Gass, Thomas Merton, and Stanley Edgar Hyman. The Irish master of the short story, Frank O'Conner, judged Powers to be "among the greatest of living story tellers." When he drew negative critical response, it was often for what is deemed to be his overly parochial concerns and his narrow focus on the world of the Catholic Church in the United States, especially of the clergy. In fact, Powers's narrow focus can be seen as a source of strength; he wrote about what he knew best and, like excellent writers everywhere, discovered the universal in the particular. He has a permanent place in American literature as one of the most accomplished short-story writers of the twentieth century.

BIOGRAPHY

James Farl Powers was born in Jacksonville, Illinois, on July 8, 1917, to James Ansbury and Zella Routzong Powers. He is one of three children. His father was a manager for Swift and Company, and the family lived in comfortable circumstances. Jacksonville was a predominantly Protestant community, and that made the Catholic Powers family part of a minority.

In 1924, the Powerses moved to Rockford, Illinois, where they lived for seven years and where James attended public schools. After another move, to Quincy, Illinois, in 1931, Powers became a student at the Franciscan-run Quincy Academy, from which he was graduated in 1935. He then moved to Chicago, where, over the next eight years, he held various jobs: insurance salesman, clerk at Marshall Field, chauffeur, editor with the Chicago Historical Records Survey, and clerk at Brentano's bookstore. From 1938 to 1940, he took night courses at Northwestern University. While working at Brentano's, in 1942, he wrote his first story, "He Don't Plant Cotton," published the following year in *Accent* magazine. He was fired from Brentano's for refusing to buy war bonds.

In 1943, Powers experienced what critic John V. Hagopian (in *J. F. Powers*, 1968) described as a religious crisis. Since moving to Chicago, he had become increasingly sensitive to social issues; the status of African Americans and war were two issues with which he was particularly concerned. His moral revulsion at the injustices to which African Americans were subjected was tellingly expressed in such stories as "He Don't Plant Cotton" and "The Trouble." Powers became a pacifist in 1943. Arrested two weeks after he failed to report for induction, he was, after pleading not guilty and waiving trial by jury, sentenced to serve three years in Sandstone Federal Prison in Minnesota. He was paroled in late 1944 after serving thirteen months of his sentence. He then went to St. Paul and worked as a hospital orderly. In 1945, he met Elizabeth Alice Wahl at St. Benedict's College, St. Joseph's, Minnesota, and the following

(Hugh Powers)

year they were married. She, like Powers, pursued a writing career.

Powers was a resident at the Yaddo community in 1947, the year in which *Prince of Darkness and Other Stories*, his first collection of stories, was published. The book met with favorable critical response. In 1948, Powers received grants from the Guggenheim Foundation and the National Institute of Arts and Letters, and taught at St. John's University of Collegeville, Minnesota. He continued teaching for several years, this time at Marquette University, and had another residency at Yaddo. Throughout the 1950's, Powers and his growing family (he and his wife had five children—Katherine, Mary, James, Hugh, and Jane) lived in either Minnesota or Ireland. In 1956, the year in which his second collection of stories, *The Presence of Grace*, was published, he taught at the University of Michigan. Powers once said that teaching was something he turned to out of need, when he ran out of money.

Powers's first novel, *Morte d'Urban*, was published by Doubleday in 1962. It won the 1963 National Book Award and the Thermod Monsen Award, given by the Chicago critics for the best book written by a midwesterner. Powers was writer-in-residence at Smith College between 1965 and 1966. The short-story collection *Look How the Fish Live* appeared in 1975. His second novel, *Wheat That Springeth Green*, was published in 1988. Besides receiving grants from the National Institute of Arts and Letters and the Guggenheim Foundation, Powers received Rockefeller Fellowships on three occasions.

ANALYSIS

J. F. Powers is an idealist; he is also a moralist. The two attitudes need not necessarily be incorporated in a single person, but they naturally combine when, as is the case with Powers, the ideal is perceived to be something which is not only to be admired but also to be sought. The vision of the pure idealist tends to be illuminated chiefly by aesthetic considerations; a discrepancy between the ideal and the real is seen primarily as an artistic failure. For the idealist-moralist, on the other hand, the discrepancy between the ideal and the real, while it can profitably

be seen in aesthetic terms, is essentially a matter of morality. To call Powers an idealist is not to say that he is a perfectionist. Falling short of the ideal is, for fallen human beings, to be expected; but to abandon the ideal, to give up the pursuit of perfection, is to fail morally. As a moralist, Powers has quite distinct notions of what constitutes good and evil, and the difference between them is sharp. His morality is based on Catholic theology.

Powers's "world," his equivalent of William Faulkner's Yoknapatawpha County, is the American Catholic Church, more particularly that Church as it manifests itself in the Midwest, more particularly still, the clergy of that Church. Unquestionably, Powers's best fiction is that written about Catholic priests. Choosing to write about priests was in itself an ingenious artistic ploy. The priest is by vocation, if not by disposition, an idealist, and therefore presents for an idealist-moralist an excellent focal point for examining the discrepancy between the ideal and the real. His characters are not drawn from the common people but from a kind of scaled-down aristocracy, people from whom readers would be justified in expecting more because more has been given them.

MORTE D'URBAN

Some of the critical reaction that followed immediately upon the publication of *Morte d'Urban* was adverse. Perhaps because of the fact that certain chapters had previously been published individually as short stories, the judgment was made that the work lacked the unity of structure necessary for a novel and was only a gathering of loosely associated tales. Only the most superficial reading of the work could sustain a judgment of this sort, for the novel is possessed of remarkable unity of theme and structure. The chief unifying element in the novel is its main character, Father Urban Roche. Father Urban is presented as a very attractive character, but a peculiar kind of deceptive satire, at which Powers excels, is at work in the novel. So attractive is Father Urban that the unwary reader might be led erroneously to conclude that the novel demonstrates the insensitivity of the powers-that-be within the Catholic Church, treating in shabby fashion a man of Father Urban's talent and charm.

Morte d'Urban is essentially a comic novel, not only in the sense that it is funny, which it certainly is, but also, and more important, in the sense that it is the obverse of tragic. It is the story of a priest who, though by no means a bad man, is not manifesting in his life the type of goodness of which he is capable and, more pointedly, to which he is dedicated by vows. Father Urban is a Roman Catholic priest, but on the basis of the attitudes that dominate his consciousness and the behavior in which he engages, he is more appropriately identifiable as the all-American boy. He is Sinclair Lewis's George F. Babbitt with a Roman collar, always on the lookout for the ecclesiastical main chance. He is intelligent, imaginative, witty, well spoken, and possessed of a seemingly inexhaustible fund of energy. He is doubtless sincere in his conviction that the various projects to which he dedicates his talents are eminently worthwhile—that is, for the good of the Church and, ultimately, for the greater glory of God. Father Urban is an activist, and there is something almost intrinsically admirable in the activist, but he is a man for whom activity has become altogether too much. His "can do" attitude toward his vocation, which puts a premium on tangible results, has been nurtured over the years at the expense of his interior life. While ostensibly a man oriented toward the spiritual, he is in fact a materialist.

Father Urban is a member of the Order of St. Clement, the Clementines, of whom it has been said that their uniqueness consists in their being noted for nothing at all. He concurs in this cruel judgment, but if he belongs to a third-rate order, he takes consolation in the fact that he is its star, the scintillating exception in an organization composed, for the most part, of bland mediocrities. He behaves toward his confreres with *pro forma* charitableness, a disguise for condescension. He is in fact an accomplished preacher, and in much demand as a conductor of parish missions. When he is assigned to the Order's latest white elephant, then, a retreat house in rural Minnesota, his paranoid conviction that he is persecuted by his foolish superiors because they are jealous of his talents is only more firmly established. After a depressing first few months in his new assignment,

and thanks to the reinvigorating experiences associated with his filling-in as pastor at a nearby parish, he regains his old gusto. His term as acting pastor of St. Monica's allows him to display with verve all his talents as a get-up-and-go priest, a cleric with zip who knows the right people to befriend and is always building for the future—a brisk optimist and a "bricks and mortar man" *par excellence*. When the priest for whom he is substituting dies suddenly (of a heart attack while vacationing in the Bahamas), Father Urban entertains the possibility that the bishop might appoint him as the permanent pastor of St. Monica's. He cleverly attempts to further his cause with the bishop, but to no avail. The appointment is given to another priest.

Father Urban, though disappointed, is not floored by this turn of events, for by this time, he has begun to see possibilities for the retreat house, St. Clement's Hill. With the financial backing of Billy Cosgrove, a wealthy Chicago layman and friend, he secures the permission of the Clementine Provincial Superior and the local bishop to build a nine-hole golf course at St. Clement's Hill. The idea behind the venture is to make the facility more attractive for the better sort of Catholic laymen, those who will not only come there to make a retreat but also leave behind them a generous donation. It would seem that Father Urban's characteristic *modus operandi* has stood him in good stead even in the backlands of Minnesota, but his streak of successes is put in jeopardy by the rumor that the bishop may take the retreat house away from the Clementine Order and turn it into a seminary for his diocese. The bishop visits St. Clement's Hill with a young priest of the diocese who is an expert golfer. They all take to the links together, and as the game progresses, it becomes evident to Father Urban that in his match with the young priest, the bishop's man, he has symbolically entered the lists and is involved in a trial of strength. Whatever might be the eventual fate of St. Clement's Hill, it becomes a point of honor for him that he win the golf match. Having made a nice approach shot to the final green, he is apparently on the verge of doing so when events are suddenly reversed: Father Urban is struck on the head and knocked unconscious by a golf ball hit by the bishop. This seemingly absurd incident marks the turning point of the novel.

After the accident on the golf course, as a result of which the bishop drops his plans to take over the retreat house, Father Urban's attitude toward life and toward his vocation slowly changes. His being felled by a golf ball, while not comparable to St. Paul's being knocked off his horse on the road to Damascus, precipitates a period of reassessment. During this period, Father Urban undergoes three trials, which is consonant with the Arthurian theme—one of the informing elements of the novel. In one trial, he tries and fails to persuade Mrs. Thwaites, an elderly benefactress, with whom he had previously attempted to ingratiate himself, to restore to an innocent employee money which she had effectively stolen from her. His eyes are thus opened to the unpretty realities of Mrs. Thwaites's hypocrisy and stark avariciousness, which in the past he was inclined to overlook as supportable eccentricities. In the second trial, he goes on a fishing trip with his friend Billy Cosgrove, which results in the dissolution of the friendship. The experience proves to be painful but educational. He is made fully aware that Billy Cosgrove is not a noble human being. He is rich, yes, but he is also egotistical, childish, and pathologically cruel. In the third trial, Father Urban is put upon by Mrs. Thwaites's daughter, Sally Hopwood, rich, sophisticated, bored, and bereft of principles, who attempts to seduce him. She fails, but out of the ordeal, Father Urban comes to a new, and disturbing, consciousness of himself; he realizes that had he chosen to follow a vocation other than the priesthood, his outlook on life would not have been appreciably different from the one he entertains as a priest. He is brought to see that there is something fundamentally lacking in the quality of his priestly life.

The novel is brought to an abrupt and significant close after Father Urban is elected as the Provincial Superior of the Chicago Province of the Clementines. It is a position for which, when he was possessed of the consciousness of the "old man," he had often longed, as it would provide him with the power base to implement the kind of progressive reforms about which he had always dreamed. Here would be his chance to get the Clementines off dead-center, to shake them up, to move them toward becoming a first-rate order that had a reputation for gumption. Those who elect Father Urban to the post have in mind the type of man who can make the right kind of friends for the order, people such as Billy Cosgrove, people who have the money to make things happen. The Father Urban who moves back to Chicago from Minnesota to become Father Provincial, however, is a radically changed man. He has undergone a conversion.

Father Urban does not die physically, but as the title *Morte d'Urban* suggests, a death does take place. Father Urban dies to the kind of life, superficial and meretricious, to which he had devoted the better part of his days and turns to a life which, though less flamboyant, is decidedly more promising.

Wheat That Springeth Green

Powers's long-awaited second novel, *Wheat That Springeth Green*, was published in 1988. Although it was nominated for a National Book Award shortly after its publication, that honor was to elude Powers this time around. Like its predecessor, *Morte d'Urban*, this second novel is primarily the story of a priest. In this case, the protagonist is Father Joe Hackett, who is a member of the presbyterate of an unnamed diocese in Minnesota. The novel might be described as a portrait of a modern priest that is set against the background of a church, as well as a larger society, that finds itself in a state of disorientation and turmoil.

The narrative covers the whole of Father Hackett's life, but equal time is not given to every stage. Most of the action of the novel takes place in the late 1960's, when the protagonist is in his forties. The reader is introduced to Joe Hackett when he is little more than a toddler, but even at so tender an age he comes across as someone with a penchant for easy egocentrism. One's next glimpse of him is as a boy of grade-school age, revealing two incongruous personality traits that seem to be permanent by the time he reaches adulthood—a scrappy competitiveness and a tendency to run and hide when the world is not going the way he wants it to go. Next Powers provides a brief look at Joe's adolescent years, the centerpiece of which is a set of rather fantastical sexual escapades with the girls next door. One suspects that this chapter is to be read as a parody of the adolescent imagination. In the following chapter, Joe is a young man in his early twenties; he has put his sinful ways behind him and is now a seminary student, preparing for the Catholic priesthood. He is an earnest seminarian, possessed of a considerable capacity to take himself with the utmost seriousness. This displays itself in odd behavior at times. For one who is an advanced student in theology, and apparently doing quite well in his studies, he nurtures comically crude and naïve notions concerning the nature and requirements of the spiritual life.

The reader next encounters Joe as a young priest. One watches, and is not terribly surprised, as his tenuously founded idealism begins to give way to a spiritless pragmatism. Discovering that the daily life of a priest is often composed of prosaic and undramatic demands, he loses his initial fervor. He makes accommodations. Slowly and subtly, he becomes worldly, although his worldliness is not something of which he himself is fully aware. In fact, he tends to interpret this worldliness as something positive: his own peculiar, and canny, brand of antiestablishmentarianism. An ominous accompaniment of this downward slide is a steady increase in his drinking. Joe is, indeed, in the incipient stages of alcoholism, which, typically, he does not admit to himself.

The latter two-thirds of the novel takes place in the present, relative to the narrative. The year is 1968; Father Joe, now forty-four years old, is the comfortably established pastor of a well-to-do suburban parish. He fulfills his rather tightly circumscribed duties in a conscientious fashion and shows a lively alertness to the particulars of his situation. Significantly, he is guided by what has now become a conviction that his is the right way of doing things. He has developed a strong, although low-key, propensity to regard himself as somewhat the ecclesiastical "genuine article." On occasion, he seems to view himself as a lonely warrior for the right, engaged in constant battle on several fronts with several varieties of benighted bumblers and pretenders, both inside and outside the Church, by whom he is surrounded. By

this time, he has become a habitual drinker, dependent upon alcohol to see him through the day. The novel ends abruptly, as if *in medias res*, after Father Joe seemingly undergoes a sort of conversion experience, which is as sudden as it is difficult to understand. In his final state, which is simply announced to the reader, Father Joe has given up drinking, as well as his suburban pastorate; he now ministers among the poor in the inner city. Somehow, the authenticity of this latest transformation is less than fully convincing. Has Father Joe finally found himself and his proper place in the Church and in the world, or is it but the stage to a further impetuous move?

It is possible to read *Wheat That Springeth Green* as an extended exercise in irony, the kind of thing one would expect from Powers. Clues to such a reading can be found, for example, in the parallels one can make between the objects of Father Joe's constant criticism and the patterns of his own behavior. He is an acute and relentless critic, in general, of the ways of the world, and, in particular, of certain ways and personality types to be found within the Church. Specifically, he has what comes close to being an obsessive concern for what he regards as the Church's preoccupation with money. He strives to present himself as the refreshing antithesis of the type of pastor who is absorbed with money, but whether his own way of handling the finances of his parish does not in the end succeed in giving more, or at least as much, attention to money matters is debatable. Father Joe appears to have convinced himself that he is virtuously antimaterialistic because he is not concerned with "big bucks," but what the reader witnesses is a man whose daily concerns are taken up primarily with things material. Materialism is no less materialism for being low-budget. The point is that the demands of a genuine poverty of spirit do not seem to be key factors in Father Joe's life. In addition, Father Joe has a low tolerance for those among his fellow clerics whom he sees as mindless and unimaginative—not to say cowardly—functionaries, people with little or no understanding of the Church's mission and how a priest should be leading his life.

This attitude of Father Joe is in many respects commendable. Yet it loses much of its moral force when one considers that Father Joe himself scarcely comes across as a paragon of priestly virtue. He is not what would be identified as "pastoral" in his inclinations; he is anything but outgoing, and any thought to the continuing spiritual needs of his parishioners that he may have fails to manifest itself in his day-to-day activities. Moreover, he has a habit of confining himself to the immediate precincts of the rectory.

Father Joe's idea of a good pastor is all too easily reducible to the role of the faithful middle manager, someone who keeps regular office hours, makes sure the parish books are kept in the black, and maintains an eccentrically rigid control over the population of the parish school. In sum, it is difficult to see how Father Joe's interpretation of the proper duties of the conscientious priest stands as a marked improvement over the behavior he vigorously criticizes. Hence the irony.

Father Joe Hackett, then, is an intensely ordinary priest, a priest who is running on the outside of the track, and perhaps a bit behind the pack, but who has long since persuaded himself that all the while he has been sticking to the inside rail. He is certainly not a bad man. For that matter, neither is he mediocre. Nevertheless, he is possessed of a kind of ordinariness which can prove dangerous because of its penchant for mistaking moral limitations for real moral advantages. Be that as it may, Father Joe falls far short of qualifying as the great midwestern hope of a confused and blundering Church.

Dennis Q. McInerny, bibliography updated by
William Hoffman

OTHER MAJOR WORKS

SHORT FICTION: *Prince of Darkness and Other Stories*, 1947; *The Presence of Grace*, 1956; *Lions, Harts, Leaping Does, and Other Stories*, 1963; *Look How the Fish Live*, 1975; *The Old Bird: A Love Story*, 1991 (limited special edition).

BIBLIOGRAPHY

Evans, Fallon, comp. *J. F. Powers*. St. Louis: Herder, 1968. A strong collection of essays on Powers in Herder's Christian critic series; includes essays by Thomas Merton, William Gass, and Hayden Carruth as well as an interview with Powers.

Hagopian, John V. *J. F. Powers*. New York: Twayne, 1968. Following the general plan of Twayne's American Authors series, the volume provides a useful and comprehensive account of Powers and his work to 1968. The critical analysis is thoughtful and reliable.

Long, J. V. "Clerical Character(s)." *Commonweal*, May 8, 1998, 11-14. Long offers a retrospective analysis of the leading characters in *Morte d'Urban* and *Wheat That Springeth Green* and the sacred-versus-secular issues confronting them. It is an interesting look back in the light of changes in American Catholicism since the 1950's.

McInerny, Ralph. "The Darkness of J. F. Powers." *Crisis*, March, 1989, 44-46. Novelist Ralph McInerny first discusses Powers's place and importance in modern fiction. He then provides a careful critique of *Wheat That Springeth Green*. He finds that though the novel is structurally weak, it nevertheless carries considerable force because of Powers's sheer verve as a writer.

Merton, Thomas. "*Morte D'Urban:* Two Celebrations." *Worship* 36 (November, 1962): 645-650. This article contains some astute insights into Powers's first novel, especially with respect to how it makes use of satire. Merton, himself a Catholic priest, has some particularly pertinent things to say about the protagonist of the novel, Father Urban. In all, Merton regards Powers's character as artistically successful.

Schmitz, Anthony. "The Alphabet God Uses." *Minnesota Monthly*, December, 1988, 35-39. In this lively and informative interview, Powers talks about his writing as well as larger philosophical and religious issues. Especially revealing are his attitudes toward the Catholic Church. The article offers some interesting details concerning Powers's biography.

Votteler, Thomas, ed. *Short Story Criticism: Excerpts from Criticism of the Works of Short Fiction Writers*. Vol. 4. Detroit: Gale Research, 1990. Contains a chapter on Powers with a good selection of criticism on his short fiction.

REYNOLDS PRICE

Born: Macon, North Carolina; February 1, 1933

PRINCIPAL LONG FICTION

A Long and Happy Life, 1962
A Generous Man, 1966
Love and Work, 1968
The Surface of Earth, 1975
The Source of Light, 1981
*Mustian: Two Novels and a Story, Complete and
    Unabridged*, 1983
Kate Vaiden, 1986
Good Hearts, 1988
The Tongues of Angels, 1990
*The Foreseeable Future: Three Long
    Stories*, 1991
Blue Calhoun, 1992
*The Honest Account of a Memorable Life:
    An Apocryphal Gospel*, 1994
The Promise of Rest, 1995

OTHER LITERARY FORMS

Although he is best known as a novelist, Price's short fiction is sensitively written and helps to give readers a balanced picture of his writing. His poetry, his retelling of biblical stories, and his dramas, while they are not consistently of the quality of his best novels, are all clearly the work of an author with a strong sense of what he is doing. His collections of essays include some extremely interesting insights into what Price is trying to accomplish philosophically and stylistically in his long fiction. *Late Warning: Four Poems* (1968), *Lessons Learned: Seven Poems* (1977), *Vital Provisions* (1982), and *The Laws of Ice* (1986) are collections of Reynolds Price's poetry. *The Names and Faces of Heroes* (1963) is an early collection of his short stories; it was followed by *Permanent Errors* (1970). *Things Themselves: Essays and Scenes* (1972) and *A Common Room: Essays 1954-1987* (1987) contain his most salient essays on writing.

Among Price's retellings of biblical stories are *Presence and Absence: Versions from the Bible* (1973), *Oracles: Six Versions from the Bible* (1977), and *A Palpable God: Thirty Stories Translated from the Bible with an Essay on the Origins and Life of Narrative* (1978). His dramas include *Early Dark* (1977), *Private Contentment* (1984), and the teleplay *House Snake* (1986). Price's autobiography is *Clear Pictures: First Loves, First Guides* (1989).

ACHIEVEMENTS

Early in his career Price won the literature award from the National Institute of Arts and Letters, and he has received the Sir Walter Raleigh Award five times. In 1986 *Kate Vaiden* won the National Book Critics Circle Award, and in 1994 Price's *The Col-

(Margaret Sartor)

lected Stories (1993) was a finalist for the Pulitzer Prize in fiction. In 1988, in recognition of his achievements, Price was elected to the American Academy of Arts and Letters.

BIOGRAPHY

Born on February 1, 1933, in the rural North Carolina town of Macon, the son of William Solomon and Elizabeth Rodwell Price, Edward Reynolds Price was a child of the Depression. Although because of the closeness of his family structure his welfare was not seriously threatened by it, the boy was aware of the social dislocations around him and had what his biographer, Constance Rooke, calls Dickensian terrors of abandonment and destitution. His parents, hard pressed economically, lost their house when the father could not raise a fifty-dollar mortgage payment.

Upon graduation from Needham-Broughten High School in Raleigh, Price became an English major at Duke University in 1951, where he came under the influence of William Blackburn, who taught creative writing. Through Blackburn, he met Eudora Welty, who respected his work and ten years later was instrumental in helping to get Price's first book, *A Long and Happy Life*, published.

Upon receiving the bachelor's degree from Duke, Price attended Merton College, University of Oxford, as a Rhodes Scholar; there he received the bachelor of letters degree in 1958. He returned to Duke University in that year as an assistant professor of English and, except for brief intervals, continued to teach there. Beginning in 1977, he served as James B. Duke Professor of English at that institution, where he regularly taught courses in creative writing and on the poetry of John Milton.

Price, who has never been married, burst on the literary scene auspiciously when *Harper's* magazine devoted the whole of its April, 1962, issue to printing *A Long and Happy Life*, which was being released in hardcover at about the same time. The critical reception of this first novel was enthusiastic and brought Price the prestigious Faulkner Foundation Award for a first novel.

In 1963, he visited England, and in the same year a collection of his short stories, *The Names and Faces of Heroes*, was released. This collection included "Michael Egerton," the short story that had first impressed Eudora Welty when she gave a reading at Duke in the early 1950's. The title story, told from the perspective of a young boy, is an especially sensitive study in point of view.

Price's second novel, *A Generous Man*, appeared in 1966 and focused on the Mustian family, as had his first book. The second book is a warm, rollicking story based on a hunt for a python named Death that has escaped from a snake show after being bitten by a dog diagnosed as rabid. The concept is openly allegorical, and Price drives home the allegory well while also presenting an extremely amusing story, with the hydrophobic python constituting the most outrageous phallic symbol in American literature. In 1977, Price produced a play, *Early Dark*, based on the Mustian cycle, and, in 1983, *Mustian: Two Novels and a Story, Complete and Unabridged* was issued, consisting of the first two novels and "The Chain of Love," a short story.

Love and Work and the loosely woven collection *Permanent Errors* both explore matters of heredity and its effect upon people. Neither received overwhelming praise, although they had support among some critics. Price, however, was busy with a much larger project, an ambitious saga of the Kendal-Mayfield family through four generations. The first novel of this story, *The Surface of Earth*, was received with skepticism by some critics when it appeared in 1975, but few could deny the creative zeal it reflected. The second volume of the Kendal-Mayfield story was published in 1981 under the title *The Source of Light*, and it, too, received mixed reviews.

A turning point in Price's life came in 1984, when he was in the middle of writing *Kate Vaiden*. He was stricken with spinal cancer, and the surgery that saved his life also left him a paraplegic. Pain drove Price to seek the help of a psychiatrist, who used hypnosis to control Price's pain. Little did he suspect that through hypnosis he would be put in touch with a distant past that he had not realized existed. Suddenly details of his earliest childhood and of his family surfaced.

When *Kate Vaiden* was published in 1986, it was, because of these unexpected insights, a quite different novel from the one Price had originally projected. Price's hypnosis unlocked the memories from which his autobiography, *Clear Pictures: First Loves, First Guides*, published in 1989, evolved. *The Tongues of Angels*, a novel published in 1990, is also a product of Price's hypnotic communication with his past.

A further literary product of Price's painful illness is his personal narrative *A Whole New Life* (1994). The book not only offers a detailed account of his "mid-life collision with cancer and paralysis" but also celebrates his emergence from that trial into a new and, he affirms, better life. Price's own confrontation with mortality no doubt adds resonance to all his subsequent writings, such as the poignant description of Wade's suffering and death in *The Promise of Rest*. Furthermore, as an affirmation of God's strange grace, *A Whole New Life* displays kinship with Price's numerous retellings of stories from the Bible.

While focusing on long fiction, Price continued to produce notable works in other genres. The plays in his trilogy *New Music* premiered in 1989 and have subsequently been produced throughout the country. Price also wrote a television play, *Private Contentment* (1983), for the American Playhouse series aired by the Public Broadcasting Service (PBS). Along with his lyric poems, Price wrote the texts of songs ("Copperline" and "New Hymn") for his fellow North Carolinian, James Taylor.

ANALYSIS

Any reading of all Reynolds Price's novels quickly demonstrates that Price's work, throughout his career, grapples with puzzling questions. Preeminent among these questions is the effect that families have on communities and on the broader societies outside the isolated communities that provide Price with his microcosms.

Focusing on a single region of North Carolina just south of the Virginia border, Price moved beyond the limitations one sometimes finds in regional writers and in his work deals with universal themes, particularly with those that concern original sin and free choice; biological determinism, particularly as it is reflected in heredity; and the meanings of and relationships between life and death. In Price's novels, children inherit the burden of sin passed on by their parents, and, try as they will, they cannot escape this burden. They have free will, they can make choices, but the choices they make are almost identical to the choices their progenitors have made before them, so they grow up to be like those who have spawned them, no matter how much they struggle to avoid such a resemblance.

KATE VAIDEN

Price harbored from his earliest memories questions about his mother and about his parents' relationship to each other. He seldom forgot that his mother almost died in bearing him and that she was left mutilated by his difficult birth. His later relationships with her were always colored by that recollection and by the feeling of guilt it caused him. The guilt of the child is reflected most clearly in *Kate Vaiden*, where Kate blames herself for an act that was as much out of her control as was Elizabeth's difficult confinement out of Reynolds's control.

Despite Kate's innocence of any blame, she continues to blame herself after her father murders her mother and then turns the gun on himself, and her entire adult life—indeed, her life from age eleven onward—is so profoundly affected by that single event, which brought an end to her childhood innocence, that it takes her forty-five years to begin to come to grips with her problems in any effective way. *Kate Vaiden* does not end on any realistic note of hope or promise; rather, it ends with a large question mark. Through writing the novel, however, Price presumably enhanced his understanding of his mother, who, like Kate, was orphaned at an early age.

LOVE AND WORK

Price was working toward the solution of problems like those that *Kate Vaiden* poses in his earlier *Love and Work*, in which Thomas Eborn, like Price himself a novelist and a professor, is forced to examine his relationship to his mother and his parents' relationship to each other and to society when his mother dies unexpectedly. Tom has been a dutiful son; he has helped provide for his mother financially.

Yet he is also a compulsive writer who husbands his time and guards it jealously, organizing his life in such a way that he will always be able to write.

Because of this dedication, he misses his mother's last telephone call; he is busy writing and will not talk with her. Shortly thereafter, she is dead. Price creates in this novel a story that uses place most effectively. Tom Eborn teaches in a southern town not unlike Durham, North Carolina, where Price spent his professional career. Tom has arranged his life to eliminate from it any unnecessary distractions, and in doing this he has excluded from it as well much human contact. Tom's turf—completely his own—is his study, his inviolable space where he can be alone, where he can create. No one dare intrude upon it. His mother's unanticipated death, however, makes Tom realize the wrongness of isolating himself as fully as he has from humankind.

It is clear that one can find much of Reynolds Price in Tom Eborn. To make a simple equation between the two, however, would be fatuous and misleading. *Love and Work* is a novel, and although Price once said that a writer's experience and background have as much to do with writing fiction as has imagination, he also warned that writers slip in and out of autobiography, so that their novels cannot be read as accurate autobiographical statements.

One can profitably read *Love and Work* against Price's consciously constructed autobiography, *Clear Pictures: First Loves, First Guides*, and can find the correspondence between his life and Tom Eborn's. Such a comparison will show Price's departures from autobiographical revelation in this novel. The same caveat must be made for *Kate Vaiden*, which strongly reflects Price's background but which is far from an authentic autobiographical representation.

A LONG AND HAPPY LIFE

Price's consuming interest in the family as the fundamental unit of society is found in his first novel, *A Long and Happy Life*, and pervades his future writing. *A Long and Happy Life* and *A Generous Man*, along with several of Price's short stories and his novel, *Good Hearts*, have to do with the Mustian family, who live in Macon, North Carolina, the town on the Virginia border in which Price was born and

reared. *A Long and Happy Life* revolves around the romance between twenty-year-old Rosacoke Mustian and her boyfriend of six years, Wesley Beavers, two years her senior.

Wesley motorcycles to his native Macon to visit Rosacoke whenever he can take a weekend away from the naval base in Norfolk, 130 miles to the northeast. Wesley is sexually experienced, but Rosacoke is a virgin when the story opens in July. On a scorching day, Rosacoke rides on the back of Wesley's motorcycle to the black church from which her friend Mildred Sutton is to be buried. Mildred has died while giving birth to her child Sledge.

Wesley roars up to the church, deposits Rosacoke, and stays outside polishing his bike. The church moans in ecstasies of religious transport. One woman cries, "Sweet Jesus," and Wesley, hearing her cry, is transported to a sweaty bed in Norfolk, where one of his many women uttered an identical cry at a crucial point in their lovemaking.

Reminded of this, Wesley zooms off in a cloud of red dust so dry and thick that reading about it almost makes one want to wash it off. Wesley has to get ready for the afternoon, for the church picnic that he and Rosacoke will attend. Price's descriptions in this portion of the book are masterful and memorably comic, although the import of what is being communicated is deadly serious and universally significant.

At the church picnic, Wesley tries to seduce Rosacoke, but she resists him, as she always has in the past. The picnic itself is a jolly affair. As the picnickers are about to sit down to their meals, Uncle Simon discovers that his false teeth are missing. Those who have not already begun to consume their barbecued pork and Brunswick stew help Simon look for his teeth. Someone asks him when he last remembers having them.

Simon, after due deliberation, proclaims that he took them out while he was stirring the large kettle of Brunswick stew. With this revelation, all eating comes to an abrupt halt. Simon eventually finds his teeth—they were in his back pocket all along. Still, the eating never quite gets back to normal, because of the general uncertainty about where the lost dentures were. Vignettes like this help Price to convey a deeply philosophical message to readers without immersing them in specialized terminology or in abstruse and abstract thinking.

A GENEROUS MAN

In *A Generous Man*, published four years after *A Long and Happy Life*, Price goes back several years in time and writes about the Mustian family before Wesley Beavers was known to them. Rosacoke is only eleven years old during the action of the later novel. The basic concept of the book is so outrageous that it would have seemed completely ridiculous if not handled delicately and well.

This novel essentially takes up a young boy's coming-of-age. Milo, Rosacoke's fifteen-year-old brother, has just lost his virginity to Lois Provo, the girl who runs the snake show at the Warren County Fair. Years ago, Lois's mother was impregnated by a bounder, who proves to be Milo's cousin. Once the truth was known, he abandoned the woman, leaving her only her memories and his eighteen-foot python, Death, which still thrives.

Milo, the morning after his maiden voyage with Lois, wakens to find that his dog, Phillip, is ill. The family gathers for a trip to the alcoholic veterinarian, who promptly diagnoses the dog's illness as rabies. For reasons unrevealed, he neither confines the dog nor destroys it. Instead, he provides a muzzle, and the Mustians leave with their muzzled mutt to go to the fair.

Rato, the retarded son, takes the dog's muzzle off. Despite his retardation, Rato has known all along that the dog does not have rabies but is merely suffering from worms, a bit of information he keeps to himself, not wanting to put his knowledge of dogs and their maladies up against the vet's.

As it turns out, Phillip has a prejudice against snakes, and when he encounters Death, he attacks it. By the time the dust has settled, the dog, the snake, and the retarded Rato have disappeared into the woods. Sheriff Rooster Pomeroy, citing the dangers of having a hydrophobic snake abroad among the loblolly and kudzu, collects a posse, a group of men keen for excitement and camaraderie, to hunt down the missing boy, the dog, and, most urgently, the snake. Spirits are high, and liquor flows freely.

In the course of the hunt, Milo, unaccustomed to alcohol, gets drunk enough to wander out of the woods, straight to Pomeroy's house, where Mrs. Pomeroy has been left alone. Because the sheriff is impotent, Mrs. Pomeroy finds her sexual satisfaction wherever she can, and Milo looks very good to her. They end up in her bed, where, during their pillow talk, Milo learns that Mrs. Pomeroy's first sexual encounter was with his cousin, the same bounder who sired Lois and gave Death to her mother.

Despite his prurient intentions, Milo cannot complete his act because the doorbell rings, prompting him to bolt through the open window, carrying his clothing with him. He rejoins the unlikely search, and it is he who finds Death. The snake wraps itself around Milo, almost choking the life out of him, but ironically Sheriff Pomeroy comes to the rescue and defeats Death with a well-placed gunshot.

Soon Milo wants to resume his lovemaking with Lois, but she is unwilling, because their first encounter left her quite unsatisfied. She classifies Milo among those men who are takers rather than givers in love encounters, and she lets him know it. He promises to reform; in his second encounter with her, his performance is indeed altered. Thus the book's title: Milo has become a man, but, having learned that he must give as well as take, he must mature further to become a generous man.

THE KENDAL-MAYFIELD SAGA

Price's difficulties with the critics when he produced the first volume of the Kendal-Mayfield saga, *The Surface of Earth*, stemmed largely from an inability of many northeastern critics to respond with understanding to a convoluted familial saga that had heavy biblical overtones, that had to do fundamentally with original sin, guilt, conflicted race relations, incestuous feelings, incredibly frequent suicides, and much that is a more common part of rural Southern experience than of urban Northern experience. Southern families like the two Price writes about in the Kendal-Mayfield novels are smothering families. Their members sometimes try to escape, but the magnetic pull back into the decaying bosom of the family is too strong for them to resist. In that respect, this saga is not unlike William Faulkner's *The*

Sound and the Fury (1929), in which the Compsons can never escape their heredity and all that it has predestined for them.

It is significant that the family members in the Kendal-Mayfield saga (including those in *The Source of Light* and *The Promise of Rest*, sequels to *The Surface of Earth*) resemble one another so closely. Not only do they sound alike but, more tellingly, they also think alike and act alike from generation to generation. Readers become particularly aware of this because of the compression of the novels: a large time span is telescoped into a few hundred pages.

On a literal level, the events of the saga might seem unlikely; taken symbolically, they assume a broader and deeper meaning and a greater artistic plausibility. Perhaps reflection on the outrageous unreality of parts of *A Generous Man* can help readers to understand some of the quintessential symbolic elements of the Kendal-Mayfield saga. Such comparable sagas as the five novels that make up John Galsworthy's *The Forsyte Saga* (1922) or the three novels of Sigrid Undset's *Kristin Lavransdatter* (1920-1922) suffer from a similar sense of unreality if they are read without conscious consideration of their symbolic contexts.

A considerable amount of the symbolic content of Price's Kendal-Mayfield novels can be found in the dream sequences that are integral to the books. There are more than twenty of them in the first novel, and these sequences serve many purposes beyond suggesting the subconscious state of the characters who have the dreams.

THE SURFACE OF EARTH

The beginning of the Kendal family history as Price reveals it in *The Surface of Earth* is Bedford Kendal's rendition to his children of their grandparents' tragedy. Their grandmother died while giving birth to their mother. Their grandfather, considering himself responsible for his wife's death, killed himself, leaving his newborn daughter (like Price's own mother) an orphan. Bedford, having married this orphan when she grew to adulthood, soon realized that she was consumed by guilt and that she had a strong aversion to sex, all tied up with the guilt she suffered at the thought of having, through her birth, killed

her own mother and driven her father to suicide.

Bedford's children, hearing this story, build up their own guilt feelings and their own aversions to sex. His daughter Eva, the strongest student of thirty-two-year-old Latin teacher Forrest Mayfield, elopes with him. Forrest is looking for family ties and thinks that he has found them among the Kendals, who, on the surface, seem to be an enviable family. Yet his marrying Eva disrupts the family's delicate balance, so all that Forrest hopes for in the marriage is not available to him.

The title of book 1 in the novel, "Absolute Pleasures," seems to be both an irony and a warning. Eva has her absolute pleasure, her unremitting sexual release on her wedding night, but then guilt possesses her. She dreams an Electra dream of her father stretched out over her body, and she is never able to enjoy sex again. She passes on her sexual aversion to her children, suggesting to her son Rob that he masturbate rather than become ensnared in love relationships with women.

Forrest, meanwhile, has his own hereditary baggage to carry. Forrest and Eva, whose names, as Rooke notes, suggest something primal and essentially sexual, ironically are trapped by their pasts. Price emphasizes another theme on which he has dwelt before: marriage disrupts the family balance, but guilt over that disruption—at least among the Kendals and the Mayfields—in turn disrupts the marriage. The family and heredity are exacting taskmasters, and they are inescapable.

Eva, like many of Price's women, barely survives the birth of her son Rob, and in this difficult birth, which also severely threatens the life of the infant, one sees an entire cycle recurring. The mother, with her cargo of guilt about sex and about her mother's death in childbirth, has a difficult delivery that will increase her aversion to sex and that will impose upon her newborn child the same guilt with which she has lived. So has it always been with the Kendals; so presumably will it always be.

Eva and Forrest both settle for lives of frequent masturbation, and their masturbation fantasies are tied to their respective father and mother. Forrest, having abjured further sexual encounters with Eva, meditates on a poem by Gaius Valerius Catullus that has to do with ritual castration. He ultimately leaves Eva and makes a ritualized journey back to Bracey, his hometown, to live with his sister Hatt, a widow.

Book 2 of *The Surface of Earth*, the real heart of the novel, is the story of Eva and Forrest's son, Rob Mayfield, named for his paternal grandfather. Rob, now seventeen, is leaving the family nest, but the family surges within him. He has no more hope of leaving it than did any of the Kendals before him. There is no escape from either the biological heredity or the strong pull of memory and custom that families impose.

Rob, obsessed with Oedipal feelings since the onset of puberty, hopes that contact with other women will help him to overcome the shameful feelings that disturb his equilibrium. He tries to seduce his date for the senior prom, but she denies him, whereupon he sheds her. Like Milo in *A Generous Man*, his sexual thoughts are only of his own gratification, and his masturbation gives him an independence when he is rebuffed.

Rob contemplates suicide several times in his period of flight from the nest. He comes closest to it when he sees a clutch of boys shooting at a turtle, trying to kill it. The turtle comes to represent for Rob all the isolation and insensitivity that have plagued his recent life, that have brought him closer to suicide than ever in the past.

Rob seeks to overcome his problems by marrying Rachel, whose father manages a hotel, Panacea Springs, in Goshen. Not in love with Rachel, Rob wavers in his commitment to marry her, and he goes— as his father before him had gone to the first Rob— to his father for counsel. Forrest is now living in a heterodox arrangement with Polly, a woman with whom he makes love only ten times a year, fearing that more frequent contact would jeopardize what they have struggled to achieve. Having seen his father's relationship, Rob can now return to Rachel and marry her.

The dinner on the night before the wedding brings together all the elements of the family that Price needs to show to make his story work. In this evening of premarital celebration, the family history and all

that it implies is made clear. That being done, the only task remaining to Price artistically is to kill Rachel off in childbirth, which he promptly does. Rachel dies giving birth to Hutch, whose story becomes the next portion of the saga.

THE SOURCE OF LIGHT

The Source of Light is a more optimistic book than its predecessor. It focuses on Hutch and on the aging and death of his father. In *The Source of Light*, both Hutch and Rob seem to have reached an accord in their lives, to have matured into acceptance of what seems for them inevitable. The pull of the family and the inevitability of their heredity are both still operative, but they are less oppressive than they were in the earlier book.

THE TONGUES OF ANGELS

Set primarily at a summer camp for boys in western North Carolina, *The Tongues of Angels* is the story of a young man's rite of passage and a commentary on his continuing source of inspiration as a mature artist. Bridge Boatner is now a successful painter, but when his sons ask about the inscription on the back of his first significant landscape, he recounts the circumstances under which he produced it. At the age of twenty-one, Bridge recoiled from the recent death of his father by becoming a counselor at Camp Juniper. There he formed a brief but intense friendship with a troubled but immensely gifted camper, Raphael (Rafe) Noren, for whom the painting was intended as a gift.

Rafe's angelic name suggests the mysterious nature of his great talents (especially in Native American dancing), but he also exhibits a profound need for love. Having seen his own mother murdered, Rafe is drawn toward Bridge even though he confides little. Bridge enlists Rafe as a model for sketches of angels, and in so doing he, perhaps inadvertently, contributes to the camper's death. In recalling that traumatic event, however, Bridge observes that even now he creates as an artist not merely because of his past errors but by actually using those errors as instruments.

THE PROMISE OF REST

With *The Promise of Rest* Price returns to the Mayfield family saga and completes the trilogy collectively titled A Great Circle. This final novel in the series boldly confronts the twin furies of sexuality and race that have tormented the Mayfields for nine decades.

After more than thirty years of marriage, Ann has left Hutch. Although Hutch has been faithful to her, she feels isolated because of his close friendship with Strawson Stewart, who was once Hutch's student and lover and is still the tenant on the Mayfield homeplace.

Hutch remains a successful poet and teacher at Duke University, but he is devastated by news that his only son, Wade, is suffering from acquired immunodeficiency syndrome (AIDS) in New York City. Wade was estranged from his family, not because of his homosexuality but because his black lover, Wyatt, condemned Hutch and Ann as racists. After Wyatt commits suicide, Hutch brings Wade home to die. At first Hutch tries to exclude Ann from the deathbed watch, but their mutual pain eventually pulls them back together. After Wade's death they learn that he loved not only Wyatt but also Wyatt's sister, Ivory, and with her he fathered a child.

This child, Raven, bears the given name of both Hutch and Wade, and he is proof that the Mayfield clan will not soon become extinct. Raven's link with his grandparents remains tenuous, but in the final scene of the novel he goes with Hutch to visit an aging black cousin and to spread Wade's ashes on the Mayfield farm. Thus, the book affirms racial unity and solace after the pain of death. With a long heritage of sexual confusion and miscegenation, the Mayfields may not readily achieve peaceful rest, but its promise is surely genuine.

Throughout his writing, Price is concerned with showing that people cannot outrun their past. Price's characters are dots on a long, seemingly infinite continuum, and the continuum assumes a life of its own. It is like a steadily flowing river that moves unrelentingly toward the sea. Anything in it that tries to swim upstream is destined to be defeated. Even the strongest of swimmers, the ones who make a little progress against the inevitable flow, will be caught ultimately by the flow and swept along with it.

Underlying this theme of the strength of the family and the inability of people to resist their heredities

is a pervasive theme of guilt, all of it tied up with pleasure, as manifested by sex, versus death or mutilation, as represented by the childbirth catastrophes of many of Price's characters.

Price's intimate and sensitive knowledge of southern rural life enables him to write some of the most accurate and memorable descriptions in print of the locale in which most of his stories are set. He has grasped the speech rhythms, vocabulary, and syntax of northern North Carolina with an authenticity that remains consistent throughout his novels and stories, as do the unshakably consistent points of view of his characters.

R. Baird Shuman, updated by Albert Wilhelm

OTHER MAJOR WORKS

SHORT FICTION: *The Names and Faces of Heroes*, 1963; *Permanent Errors*, 1970; *The Collected Stories*, 1993.

PLAYS: *Early Dark*, pb. 1977; *Private Contentment*, pb. 1984; *New Music: A Trilogy*, pr. 1989; *Full Moon and Other Plays*, pb. 1993.

TELEPLAY: *House Snake*, 1986.

POETRY: *Late Warning: Four Poems*, 1968; *Lessons Learned: Seven Poems*, 1977; *Nine Mysteries (Four Joyful, Four Sorrowful, One Glorious)*, 1979; *Vital Provisions*, 1982; *The Laws of Ice*, 1986; *The Use of Fire*, 1990.

NONFICTION: *Things Themselves: Essays and Scenes*, 1972; *A Common Room: Essays 1954-1987*, 1987; *Clear Pictures: First Loves, First Guides*, 1989; *A Whole New Life*, 1994; *Three Gospels*, 1996.

TRANSLATIONS: *Presence and Absence: Versions from the Bible*, 1973; *Oracles: Six Versions from the Bible*, 1977; *A Palpable God: Thirty Stories Translated from the Bible with an Essay on the Origins and Life of Narrative*, 1978.

BIBLIOGRAPHY

Kreyling, Michael. "Reynolds Price." In *The History of Southern Literature*, edited by Louis D. Rubin et al. Baton Rouge: Louisiana State University Press, 1985. Although this article is brief, it is easily accessible and does much to update the earlier sources about Price. It appeared too early to deal with his post-hypnotic years and with such books as *Kate Vaiden* and *Good Hearts*, but it is a fresh point of view clearly expressed.

Price, Reynolds. "A Conversation with Reynolds Price." Interview by Wallace Kaufman. *Shenandoah* 17 (Summer, 1966): 3-25. The most important early interview with Price, and one of the most extensive. It is reproduced in its entirety under the title "Notice, I'm Still Smiling," in *Kite Flying and Other Irrational Acts*, edited by John Carr (Baton Rouge: Louisiana State University Press, 1972). Kaufman has excellent insights into Price's southernness but realizes that his writing goes far beyond regionalism.

_____. "Reynolds Price on Writing." Interview by Ashby Bland Crowder. *Southern Review* 22 (Spring, 1986): 329-341. Anyone interested in Price as a stylist must read this interview, for it is the best brief treatment in print of how Price approaches his writing, both physically and philosophically. Crowder is an excellent interviewer. The piece is easily accessible to the reader not overly familiar with Price's work.

Rooke, Constance. *Reynolds Price*. Boston: Twayne, 1983. An early full-length treatment of Price. Despite its excellent coverage and intelligent analysis, it is badly dated because some of Price's most interesting work came after his hypnosis in 1984. One hopes that Rooke will bring out a revised edition or that some other scholar will do a solid analytical study of this author, whose versatility continues to amaze and whose command of his major medium has not waned.

Sadler, Lynn Veach. "Reynolds Price and Religion: The 'Almost Blindingly Lucid' Palpable World." *Southern Quarterly* 26 (Winter, 1988): 1-11. Religion, both traditional and nontraditional, plays a fundamental part in Price's novels, and this article intelligently assesses some of his central religious beliefs, partly as shown through his translated biblical stories but also as they are revealed in some of his other work.

Schiff, James, ed. *Critical Essays on Reynolds Price*. New York: G. K. Hall, 1998. After a section of personal tributes and reminiscences, this volume provides twenty-three reviews and twelve critical essays (three of which are not available elsewhere). One essay deals with the play trilogy *New Music*, but most focus on Price's fiction, especially *A Long and Happy Life*.

_____. *Understanding Reynolds Price*. Columbia: University of South Carolina Press, 1996. While devoting brief attention to Price's essays, memoirs, plays, poems, and short stories, Schiff focuses mainly on the long fiction. Intended as an introductory work, this volume provides concise but perceptive commentary on the major novels.

J. B. PRIESTLEY

Born: Bradford, England; September 13, 1894
Died: Stratford-upon-Avon, England; August 14, 1984

PRINCIPAL LONG FICTION
Adam in Moonshine, 1927
Benighted, 1927
Farthing Hall, 1929 (with Hugh Walpole)
The Good Companions, 1929
Angel Pavement, 1930
Faraway, 1932
I'll Tell You Everything, 1933 (with George Bullett)
Wonder Hero, 1933
They Walk in the City: The Lovers in the Stone Forest, 1936
The Doomsday Men: An Adventure, 1938
Let the People Sing, 1939
Blackout in Gretley: A Story of—and for—Wartime, 1942
Daylight on Saturday: A Novel About an Aircraft Factory, 1943
Three Men in New Suits, 1945
Bright Day, 1946
Jenny Villiers: A Story of the Theatre, 1947
Festival at Farbridge, 1951 (pb. in U.S. as *Festival*)

Low Notes on a High Level: A Frolic,
  1954

The Magicians, 1954

*Saturn over the Water: An Account of His
  Adventures in London, South America,
  and Australia by Tim Bedford, Painter,
  Edited with Some Preliminary and
  Concluding Remarks by Henry
  Sulgrave and Here Presented to the
  Reading Public*, 1961

*The Thirty-first of June: A Tale of True
  Love, Enterprise, and Progress in the
  Arthurian and ad-Atomic Ages*, 1961

The Shape of Sleep: A Topical Tale, 1962

*Sir Michael and Sir George: A Tale of
  COMSA and DISCUS and the New
  Elizabethans*, 1964 (also known as *Sir
  Michael and Sir George: A Comedy of
  New Elizabethans*)

*Lost Empires: Being Richard Herncastle's
  Account of His Life on the Variety
  Stage from November, 1913, to August,
  1914, Together with a Prologue and
  Epilogue*, 1965

Salt Is Leaving, 1966

It's an Old Country, 1967

*The Image Men: Out of Town and London
  End*, 1968

The Carfitt Crisis, 1975

*Found, Lost, Found: Or, The English Way
  of Life*, 1976

My Three Favorite Novels, 1978

(CORBIS/Hulton-Deutsch Collection)

OTHER LITERARY FORMS

In addition to the nearly thirty novels that he published after *Adam in Moonshine* in 1927, J. B. Priestley wrote approximately fifty plays, upon which his future reputation will largely depend. These include such memorable works as *Dangerous Corner* (1932), *Eden End* (1934), *Time and the Conways* (1937), *An Inspector Calls* (1946), *The Linden Tree* (1947), and *The Scandalous Affair of Mr. Kettle and Mrs. Moon* (1955). He also collaborated with Iris Murdoch on the successful stage adaptation of her novel *A Severed Head* (1963).

There is, besides, a long list of impressive works which characterize Priestley as the twentieth century equivalent of an eighteenth century man of letters, a term he professed to despise. This list includes accounts of his travels both in England and abroad, the best of these being *English Journey* (1934), an account of English life during the Depression; *Russian Journey* (1946); and *Journey down a Rainbow* (1955), written in collaboration with Jacquetta Hawkes. Priestley produced several books of reminiscence and recollection, which include *Rain upon Godshill* (1939), *Margin Released* (1962), and *Instead of the Trees* (1977). His literary criticism includes studies of George Meredith, Charles Dickens, and Anton Chekhov; and his familiar essays, thought by many to be among his finest works, are represented in the volume entitled *Essays of Five Decades* (1968), and by *Postscripts* (1940), his broadcasts in support of England at war. Priestley created several picture books of social criticism such as *The Prince of Pleasure and His Regency, 1811-1820* (1969), *The Edwardians* (1970), and *Victoria's Heyday* (1972), and his far-reaching historical surveys detail an idiosyncratic view of people in time: *Literature and Western Man* (1960) and *Man and Time* (1964). Priestley's short-story collections include *Going Up* (1950) and *The Other Place and Other Stories of the Same Sort* (1953).

As this list indicates, no aspect of modern life escaped Priestley's scrutiny, and no genre was left untried. In a long and prestigious career, he earned for himself a secure place in the annals of literature.

ACHIEVEMENTS

Although Priestley's accomplishments in the theater may prove more significant than his work in the novel, perhaps because of his experimentation within the dramatic genre, his fiction has nevertheless secured for him a high place in contemporary literature; it has been read and cherished by a large and very appreciative audience. *The Good Companions*, a runaway best-seller in 1929, allowed Priestley to turn his attention from journalism and the novel to the theater in the 1930's, but he kept returning to the novel form throughout his career.

Priestley produced no novel that equals James Joyce's *Ulysses* (1922) in scope or intellectual subtlety, no novel as prophetic as D. H. Lawrence's *The Rainbow* (1915), no novel illustrative of the intuitive faculty equal to Virginia Woolf's *To the Lighthouse* (1927), or of ethical concern equal to Joseph Conrad's *The Secret Agent* (1907) or William Faulkner's *Light in August* (1932). His place on the scale of literary achievement may be lower than theirs, but his audience has been, by and large, greater. Priestley aimed for and caught a popular audience that remained loyal to him through five decades of writing. His novels and plays have been widely translated and acted, most notably in the Soviet Union. His craft in the novel genre shows the influence of Charles Dickens, of the English Romantics, especially of

William Wordsworth and William Hazlitt, and of the English music hall and its traditions. Priestley himself made no great claims for his fiction, beyond good-naturedly protesting once or twice that there is more to it than meets the top-speed reviewer's eye. His finest novel, *Bright Day*, however, earned general critical approval when it was published in 1946, and merited the praise of Carl Jung, who found its theme consonant with his notion of the oneness of all people.

BIOGRAPHY

John Boynton Priestley was born in Bradford, Yorkshire, on September 13, 1894. His mother died soon after his birth, and he was reared by a kind and loving stepmother. His father Jonathan was a schoolmaster whom Priestley has characterized in the autobiographical *Margin Released* as the man Socialists have in mind when they write about Socialists.

Bradford, in Priestley's early years, offered much to feed a romantic boy's imagination: theater, the music halls, a playgoer's society, an arts club, the concert stage, a busy market street, and a grand-scale arcade called the Swan. A tram ride away were the Yorkshire Dales and moors. As a young man, Priestley worked in a wool office, writing poetry and short stories into handmade notebooks in his spare time. An important early influence was Richard Pendlebury, his English master. Priestley later observed that Bradford and its environs did more for his education than did Cambridge University, which he attended years later.

In 1915, Priestley enlisted in the army. He was sent to France, invalided back to England after being wounded, and then sent back to France. Significantly, his experience of war does not figure explicitly in any fictional piece, with the single exception of a haunting short story entitled *The Town Major of Miraucourt* (1930). Priestley's entire creative output may, however, have been an attempt to put war and its ravages into a long-range context, a notion that pervades his *Postscripts* broadcasts for the British Broadcasting Corporation (BBC) during World War II. At the end of his army service, Priestley went to Cambridge, where he studied, between 1919 and 1922, literature, history, and political theory. His first book, *Brief Diversions* (1922), received good reviews but did not sell.

Leaving Cambridge for London and the precarious life of a journalist, Priestley worked for J. C. Squire and the *London Mercury*, for the *Daily News*, and for the Bodley Head Press. Meanwhile, he published critical books on George Meredith, Thomas Love Peacock, and modern literature. His first novel, *Adam in Moonshine*, appeared in 1927. Shortly thereafter, Hugh Walpole offered to collaborate with Priestley on a novel called *Farthing Hall* in order to give the younger writer a much-needed publisher's advance so that he could continue his work. In 1929, *The Good Companions* appeared, and Priestley was fully embarked on a long and distinguished career.

Priestley was married three times; his first marriage, to Pat Tempest, came in 1919. A year after her death, in 1925, he married Mary Holland Wyndham Lewis, from whom he was divorced in 1952. The two marriages produced four daughters and a son. In 1953, he married the distinguished anthropologist Jacquetta Hawkes. During his adult life, Priestley resided in London, on the Isle of Wight, and in Alveston, just outside Stratford-upon-Avon. He traveled widely, frequently using his journeys as background for his novels and plays. During World War II, he and his wife ran a hostel for evacuated children; after the war he campaigned vigorously for nuclear disarmament. He served as a UNESCO delegate and on the board of the National Theatre. He refused a knighthood and a life-peerage but did, in 1977, accept membership in the Order of Merit. In 1973, he happily accepted conferment of the Freedom of the City from his native Bradford.

Priestley did not retire from his writing work until well after he turned eighty. He died in 1984, one month shy of his ninetieth birthday.

ANALYSIS

In his novels J. B. Priestley largely portrays a Romantic view of life. His focus is primarily England and the English national character, and on those aspects of people that ennoble and spiritualize them. Yet, there is a no-nonsense view of life portrayed in his fiction; hard work, dedication to ideals, willingness to risk all in a good cause are themes which figure prominently. At times, the darker aspects of humanity becloud this gruff but kindly Yorkshireman's generally sunny attitudes. Ultimately, life in Priestley's fictional universe is good, provided the individual is permitted to discover his potential. In politics, this attitude reduces to what Priestley has called "Liberal Socialism." For Priestley, too much government is not good for the individual.

Romanticism largely dictated characterization in Priestley's novels, and his most valid psychological portraits are of individuals who are aware of themselves as enchanted and enchanting. These characters are usually portrayed as questers. It is Priestley's symbolic characters, however, who are the most forcefully portrayed, occasionally as god-figures, occasionally as devil-figures, but mostly as organizers—as stage-managers, impresarios, factory owners, butlers. Priestley's female characters fall generally into roles as ingenues or anima-figures. There are, however, noteworthy exceptions, specifically Freda Pinnel in *Daylight on Saturday*.

It is primarily through the presentation of his organizers that Priestley's chief plot device emerges: the common cause. A group of disparate characters is assembled and organized into a common endeavor; democratic action follows as a consequence. "Liberal democracy. Expensive and elaborate, but best in the end," says a choric figure in *Festival at Farbridge*, echoing one of his author's deepest convictions.

A Romantic view of people in space and time also dictated the kind of novels that Priestley wrote. His fiction falls easily into three main categories. The first is the seriously conceived and carefully structured novel, in which symbolism and consistent imagery figure as aspects of craft. The best of this group are *Angel Pavement*, *Bright Day*, and *It's an Old Country*. The second category can be termed the frolic or escapade. This group includes *The Good Companions*, *Festival at Farbridge*, and the delightful *Sir Michael and Sir George*. The third category is the thriller or entertainment, which includes such science-fiction works as *The Doomsday Men* and *Saturn over the Water* as well as the detective story

Salt Is Leaving. Priestley's favorite novel, and his longest, *The Image Men*, published in two volumes in 1968 and as one in 1969, incorporates these three categories within a controlled and incisive satirical mode.

In many of his works, but more so in his plays than in his fiction, Priestley dramatized a theory concerning the nature of time and experience which derived from his understanding of John William Dunne's *An Experiment with Time* (1927) and *The Serial Universe* (1934) and P. D. Ouspensky's *A New Model of the Universe* (1931). Briefly stated, this time theory, most explicit in *The Magicians*, a gothic tale which presents Priestley's characterizations of the Wandering Jew, and *Jenny Villiers*, originally written as a play for the Bristol Old Vic, proposes a means of transcendence. Priestley believed that Dunne's Serialism— "we observe something, and we are conscious of our observation . . . and we are conscious of the observation of the observation, and so forth"—permitted him to deal with character "creatively." For the ordinary individual, to "Observer One," the fourth dimension appears as time. The self within dreams becomes "Observer Two," to whom the fifth dimension appears as time. Unlike the three-dimensional outlook of Observer One, Observer Two's four-dimensional outlook enables him to receive images from coexisting past and future times. From Ouspensky, Priestley refined the notion that time, like space, has three dimensions; these three dimensions, however, can be regarded as a continuation of the dimensions of space. Wavelike and spiral, time provides for eternal recurrence, but a recurrence not to be confused with Friedrich Nietzsche's "eternal retour," with reincarnation, or with the Bergsonian *durée*. Ouspensky provided Priestley with the possibility of re-creation—that is, of intervention in space and time through an inner development of self. In other words, self-conscious awareness of self in past time can re-create the past in the present; sympathetic re-creation of self and others in what Priestley terms "time alive" can give new meaning to the present and shape the future. For Priestley, the seer— whether he be a painter or a musician, or the organizer of a festival or of a traveling group of entertain-

ers, or even a butler in a country house—by looking creatively into the past, ameliorates the present and shapes a brighter future. Consequently, the organizer is Priestley's most forceful and symbolic character, and the thematic purpose of his novels depends upon an understanding of this character's motives.

THE GOOD COMPANIONS

Priestley's first successful novel, *The Good Companions*, presents a cozy fairy tale against an essentially realistic background, the English music halls of the 1920's. A determined spinster, Elizabeth Trant, organizes a down-and-out group of entertainers who have called themselves the Dinky Doos into a successful group renamed the Good Companions. The adventures of these troupers on the road and on the boards provide the novel with its zest and comedy.

ANGEL PAVEMENT

Angel Pavement is in some ways a departure from this earlier work inasmuch as its tone appears dark and ominous. In *Angel Pavement*, the organizer is not a cheerful woman of thirty-seven giving herself a holiday on the roads as an impresario, but a balding, middle-aged adventurer named Golspie. "A thick figure of a man but now slow and heavy," Golspie enters the London firm of Twigg and Dersingham, dealers in wood veneers, and breathes new life into the business in a period of economic depression. With his only commitment being his daughter Lena, Golspie seems at first the firm's savior, for he provides a supply of veneer from the Baltic at half the domestic price. Perhaps because he and his daughter are rejected by the more polite segments of London society, Golspie feels it unnecessary to play fair with his employers. Eventually, he ruins Twigg and Dersingham, putting the employees out of work. At the novel's end, he and Lena leave London for South America and new adventure.

What most distinguishes *Angel Pavement* is its portrayal of the city, London, in the midst of the Depression, and of those who people it. Lilian Matfield, the head secretary, is fascinated by Golspie but refuses to accept the life of adventure he offers her, and Henry Smeeth, the bookkeeper, accepts a raise in salary, only to discover that once Golspie has abandoned Twigg and Dersingham, the company is bankrupt and he is out of work. The streets, the offices, the pubs, the tobacco stands, the amusements, all combine to present a view of human enervation and despair. A confidence man but not exactly a charlatan, Golspie locks the novel to a seemingly pessimistic view. Despite the enervation and apathy portrayed, Golspie offers freedom. Through his sinister organizer, Priestley portrays the life of romance that lies beneath the ordinary. What *Angel Pavement* finally achieves is a startling view of the modern metropolis as a prison from which only the romantic can escape.

BRIGHT DAY

One of his own favorite works, Priestley's *Bright Day* has been justly admired by critics and readers alike. Its uniqueness lies not so much in its dexterous use of such novelistic techniques as the time-shift and memory digression as in the way it looks behind and beyond its immediate focus into that sense of race and identity all people share. Although the novel deals with time, Priestley here shows a greater indebtedness to Henri Bergson and Marcel Proust than he does to Ouspensky and Dunne.

Music, specifically a Franz Schubert trio, returns a middle-aged screen-writer, Gregory Dawson, the narrator, who has taken refuge from his unhappy life in a genteel hotel in Cornwall, to a memory of youth and joy. An old couple reminds him of the boy of eighteen he was when he fell in love with a family called Alington in Bruddersford, a wool-producing northern town. The Alingtons, charming and gracious, had sentimentally attached the young Gregory to themselves and had introduced the would-be writer to their world, which he had seen as one of grace and beauty. Ironically, the old couple who trigger the middle-aged Dawson's memories are in fact the Eleanor and Malcolm Nixey who had opportunistically intruded on his youthful idyll and brought an end to the prosperous wool business on which the Alingtons and their gracious world depended, and to Gregory's idealism as well.

In *Bright Day*, Priestley, concerned with a rite of passage, presents Gregory's initiation into a world of greed and suspicion, of appearance and falsehood; his is in fact an initiation into the modern world, and

the novel symbolically spans the period of the two world wars. In the course of reconstructing the past, Gregory comes to terms with himself in the present, and it is his recognition of self in time that makes a commitment to the future possible for him. This liberation is confirmed by the stunning revelation made to him by Laura Bradshaw, who had also known the Alingtons, that Joan Alington in a jealous rage had pushed her sister Eva to her death from a cliff. The cancer of destruction had been in the Alingtons themselves; the Nixeys had merely served as catalysts.

Although Gregory Dawson is a quester for truth through self-knowledge, he is much more than a symbolic character. His psychological validity makes his growth in the course of the novel persuasive and compelling. The rediscovery of his romantic self in the present time of the novel is the rediscovery of a moment of beauty that had lain dormant in the rich soil of his memory. Many of Priestley's novels largely describe romance; *Bright Day* recreates its essence, as does Evelyn Waugh's *Brideshead Revisited* (1945, 1959), with which it has much in common.

LOST EMPIRES

Published in 1965 and representative of the novels Priestley produced in the later stages of his career, *Lost Empires* is in some ways a return to the world of *The Good Companions*, employing as it does the music hall as background. Unlike *The Good Companions*, however, whose chief interest was the high jinks of the troupers on the road, the theater serves here as a metaphor for the theme of appearance and reality and allows Priestley to allegorize loosely the politics of a world destined for war.

The protagonist, Dick Herncastle, one of Priestley's romantic questers here presented as an artist, is contrasted to his uncle, Nick Ollanton, the organizer, who is portrayed as a magician or mesmerizer. Ollanton and his "turn" allegorize the political activist and his propaganda techniques as he bends people to his will, much as does Thomas Mann's Cipolla in "Mario and the Magician." A time-perspective on Ollanton's influence on young Dick, who works as his assistant, is presented by means of a deftly presented prologue and epilogue, which encompass the action proper of the novel, set in the period of World War I. The main action ends with Dick succumbing to the illusion of a better world after the end of the war, and with Ollanton himself leaving the Old World for the United States, revealing his bag of tricks as a private escape from the "bloody mincing machine" of global war. There, he will manufacture machine-gun sights for warplanes. The novel proper, however, ends with the account in the prologue of Dick's return from the war and his successful career as a watercolorist, an illusionist of another sort.

The charm of *Lost Empires* goes well beyond its symbolic dimension; it lies chiefly in the presentations of the performers and the turns they perform on the boards. The juggler Ricardo, the comedian Beamish, the ballad singer Lily Farrish, and many others add to the plot and charm of the novel. That they are logically placed within the melodramatic and symbolic structure of the novel is simply another testimony to the skill of their author.

A. A. DeVitis

OTHER MAJOR WORKS

SHORT FICTION: *The Town Major of Miraucourt*, 1930; *Going Up: Stories and Sketches*, 1950; *The Other Place and Other Stories of the Same Sort*, 1953; *The Carfitt Crisis and Two Other Stories*, 1975.

PLAYS: *The Good Companions*, pr. 1931 (adaptation of his novel; with Edward Knoblock); *Dangerous Corner*, pr., pb. 1932; *The Roundabout*, pr. 1932; *Laburnum Grove*, pr. 1933; *Eden End*, pr., pb. 1934; *Cornelius*, pr., pb. 1935; *Duet in Floodlight*, pr., pb. 1935; *Bees on the Boat Deck*, pr., pb. 1936; *Spring Tide*, pr., pb. 1936 (with George Billam); *People at Sea*, pr., pb. 1937; *Time and the Conways*, pr., pb. 1937; *I Have Been Here Before*, pr., pb. 1937; *Music at Night*, pr. 1938; *Mystery at Greenfingers*, pr., pb. 1938; *When We Are Married*, pr., pb. 1938; *Johnson over Jordan*, pr., pb. 1939; *The Long Mirror*, pr., pb. 1940; *Goodnight, Children*, pr., pb. 1942; *They Came to a City*, pr. 1943, pb. 1944; *Desert Highway*, pr., pb. 1944; *The Golden Fleece*, pr. 1944; *How Are They at Home?*, pr., pb. 1944; *An Inspector Calls*, pr. 1946;

Ever Since Paradise, pr. 1946; *The Linden Tree*, pr. 1947; *The Rose and Crown*, pb. 1947 (one act); *The High Toby*, pb. 1948 (for puppet theater); *Home Is Tomorrow*, pr. 1948; *The Plays of J. B. Priestley*, pb. 1948-1950 (3 volumes); *Summer Day's Dream*, pr. 1949; *Bright Shadow*, pr., pb. 1950; *Seven Plays of J. B. Priestley*, pb. 1950; *Dragon's Mouth*, pr., pb. 1952 (with Jacquetta Hawkes); *Treasure on Pelican*, pr. 1952; *Mother's Day*, pb. 1953 (one act); *Private Rooms*, pb. 1953 (one act); *Try It Again*, pb. 1953 (one act); *A Glass of Bitter*, pb. 1954 (one act); *The White Countess*, pr. 1954 (with Hawkes); *The Scandalous Affair of Mr. Kettle and Mrs. Moon*, pr., pb. 1955; *These Our Actors*, pr. 1956; *The Glass Cage*, pr. 1957; *The Pavilion of Masks*, pr. 1963; *A Severed Head*, pr. 1963 (with Iris Murdoch; adaptation of Murdoch's novel).

SCREENPLAY: *Last Holiday*, 1950.

POETRY: *The Chapman of Rhymes*, 1918.

NONFICTION: *Brief Diversions: Being Tales, Travesties, and Epigrams*, 1922; *Papers from Lilliput*, 1922; *I for One*, 1923; *Figures in Modern Literature*, 1924; *Fools and Philosophers: A Gallery of Comic Figures from English Literature*, 1925 (pb. in U.S. as *The English Comic Characters*); *George Meredith*, 1926; *Talking: An Essay*, 1926; *The English Novel*, 1927, 1935, 1974; *Open House: A Book of Essays*, 1927; *Thomas Love Peacock*, 1927; *Too Many People and Other Reflections*, 1928; *Apes and Angels: A Book of Essays*, 1928; *The Balconinny and Other Essays*, 1929 (pb. in U.S. as *The Balconinny*, 1931); *English Humour*, 1929, 1976; *The Lost Generation: An Armistice Day Article*, 1932; *Self-Selected Essays*, 1932; *Albert Goes Through*, 1933; *English Journey: Being a Rambling but Truthful Account of What One Man Saw and Heard and Felt and Thought During a Journey Through England During the Autumn of the Year 1933*, 1934; *Four-in-Hand*, 1934; *Midnight on the Desert: A Chapter of Autobiography*, 1937 (pb. in U.S. as *Midnight on the Desert: Being an Excursion into Autobiography During a Winter in America, 1935-1936*, 1937); *Rain upon Godshill: A Further Chapter of Autobiography*, 1939; *Britain Speaks*, 1940; *Postscripts*, 1940 (radio talks); *Out of the People*, 1941; *Britain at War*, 1942; *British Women Go to*

War, 1943; *The Man-Power Story*, 1943; *Here Are Your Answers*, 1944; *The New Citizen*, 1944; *Letter to a Returning Serviceman*, 1945; *Russian Journey*, 1946; *The Secret Dream: An Essay on Britain, America, and Russia*, 1946; *The Arts Under Socialism: Being a Lecture Given to the Fabian Society, with a Postscript on What Government Should Do for the Arts Here and Now*, 1947; *Theatre Outlook*, 1947; *Delight*, 1949; *Journey Down a Rainbow*, 1955 (with Jacquetta Hawkes); *All About Ourselves and Other Essays*, 1956; *The Writer in a Changing Society*, 1956; *The Art of the Dramatist: A Lecture Together with Appendices and Discursive Notes*, 1957; *The Bodley Head Leacock*, 1957; *Thoughts in the Wilderness*, 1957; *Topside: Or, The Future of England, a Dialogue*, 1958; *The Story of Theatre*, 1959; *Literature and Western Man*, 1960; *William Hazlitt*, 1960; *Charles Dickens: A Pictorial Biography*, 1962; *Margin Released: A Writer's Reminiscences and Reflections*, 1962; *The English Comic Characters*, 1963; *Man and Time*, 1964; *The Moments and Other Pieces*, 1966; *All England Listened: J. B. Priestley's Wartime Broadcasts*, 1968; *Essays of Five Decades*, 1968 (Susan Cooper, editor); *Trumpets over the Sea: Being a Rambling and Egotistical Account of the London Symphony Orchestra's Engagement at Daytona Beach, Florida, in July-August, 1967*, 1968; *The Prince of Pleasure and His Regency, 1811-1820*, 1969; *Anton Chekhov*, 1970; *The Edwardians*, 1970; *Over the Long High Wall: Some Reflections and Speculations on Life, Death, and Time*, 1972; *Victoria's Heyday*, 1972; *The English*, 1973; *Outcries and Asides*, 1974; *A Visit to New Zealand, Particular Pleasures: Being a Personal Record of Some Varied Arts and Many Different Artists*, 1974; *The Happy Dream: An Essay*, 1976; *Instead of the Trees*, 1977 (autobiography).

CHILDREN'S LITERATURE: *Snoggle*, 1972.

EDITED TEXTS: *Essayist Past and Present: A Selection of English Essays*, 1925; *Tom Moore's Diary: A Selection*, 1925; *The Book of Bodley Head Verse*, 1926; *The Female Spectator: Selections from Mrs. Eliza Heywood's Periodical, 1744-1746*, 1929; *Our Nation's Heritage*, 1939; *Scenes of London Life, from "Sketches by Boz" by Charles Dickens*, 1947; *The Best of Leacock*, 1957; *Four English Novels*, 1960; *Four English Biographies*, 1961; *Adventures in English Literature*, 1963; *An Everyman Anthology*, 1966.

BIBLIOGRAPHY

Atkins, John. *J. B. Priestley: The Last of the Sages*. London: John Calder, 1981. Cites Priestley as a major but neglected writer. A comprehensive look at his novels and plays as well as his career as a critic. Contains much valuable information.

Braine, John. *J. B. Priestley*. London: Weidenfeld & Nicolson, 1978. Not a critical analysis of Priestley's work, by Braine's admission, but a look at a selection of his writings. Braine, a fellow Bradfordian, offers a knowledgeable view of Priestley.

Brome, Vincent. *J. B. Priestley*. London: Hamish Hamilton, 1988. The first biography of Priestley. Brome, a seasoned biographer and prolific author, renders a lively portrait, doing justice to Priestley's many different careers as novelist, playwright, essayist, and public intellectual.

Cook, Judith. *Priestley*. London: Bloomsbury, 1997. An excellent biography of Priestley. Includes bibliographical references and an index.

Cooper, Susan. *J. B. Priestley: Portrait of an Author*. London: Redwood Press, 1970. A sympathetic account of Priestley written in an informal style. Cooper gives both criticism of his work and a look at the man himself: "warm hearted, generous."

DeVitis, A. A., and Albert E. Kalson. *J. B. Priestley*. Boston: Twayne, 1980. A good introduction to Priestley, which focuses on some eighty novels and plays, from the late 1920's to the 1960's. The authors note that Priestley's work has an "unerring ability to deal incisively with the idiosyncrasies of the English national character."

Evans, Gareth Lloyd. *J. B. Priestley: The Dramatist*. London: Heinemann, 1964. Analyzes the three collected volumes of Priestley's plays, which Evans has divided into "Time-plays," "Comedies," and "Sociological plays." An authoritative study that is primarily concerned with the dominant themes in Priestley's plays.